THE URANTIA BOOK WORKBOOKS

URANTIA®

URANTIA FOUNDATION
533 WEST DIVERSEY PARKWAY
CHICAGO, ILLINOIS 60614
U.S.A.

URANTIA®

®: Registered Mark of URANTIA Foundation

THE URANTIA BOOK WORKBOOKS

VOLUME V

Theology

This series of workbooks originally was published in the 1950s and 1960s to assist those early students who wanted to pursue an in-depth study of *The Urantia Book*. The workbook creators recognized that the materials were imperfect and were far from being definitive works on these subjects. Current students may be able to make more exhaustive analyses due to advances in knowledge and computerization of the text that are available today. Nevertheless, we recognize the enormous effort that went into this attempt to enhance understanding of *The Urantia Book* by some of its earliest students. We think these materials will be of interest to many and are therefore republishing them for their historic and educational value.

FIRST PRINTING 2003

THE URANTIA BOOK WORKBOOKS
VOLUME V
THEOLOGY

The Urantia Book Workbooks

Volume I: Transcripts of Lecture and Discussion of the Foreword and An Analytic Study of Part One of *The Urantia Book*
Volume II: Science in *The Urantia Book*
Volume III: Topical Studies in *The Urantia Book* and A Short Course in Doctrine
Volume IV: The Teachings of Jesus in *The Urantia Book*, The Life of Jesus Compared to the Four Gospels
Volume V: Urantia Doctrine: The Theology of *The Urantia Book*
Volume VI: History of The Bible and A Detailed Study of the Books of The Bible.
Volume VII: Quick Reference Dictionary, Terms and Defined in *The Urantia Book*, and A Keyword Index to the Table of Contetnts
Volume VIII: Worship and Wisdom: Gems from *The Urantia Book*

"URANTIA", "URANTIAN", "THE URANTIA BOOK", and ⓘ are the trademarks, service marks, and collective membership marks of URANTIA Foundation.

© 1956, 1957, 1959, 2003 URANTIA Foundation

All rights reserved, including translation, under the Berne Convention, Universal Copyright Convention, and other international copyright conventions.

To request permission to translate or to reproduce material contained in *The Urantia Book Workbooks* or the *The Urantia Book* by any means (including electronic, mechanical, or other—such as photocopying, recording, or any information storage and retrieval system), please contact Urantia Foundation. Copies of Urantia Foundation's current Copyright and Trademark Policies are available upon request.

ISBN:
0-942430-95-6

PUBLISHED BY **URANTIA FOUNDATION**
Original Publisher since 1955
533 Diversey Parkway
Chicago, Illinois 60614 U.S.A.
Telephone: +1 (773) 525-3319
Fax: +1 (773) 525-7739
Website: http://www.urantia.org
E-mail: urantia@urantia.org

Information

URANTIA Foundation has Representatives in Argentina, Belgium, Brazil, Bulgaria, Colombia, Ecuador, Estonia, Greece, Indonesia, Korea, Lithuania, México, Norway, Perú, Senegal, Spain, Uruguay, and Venezuela. If you require information on study groups, where you can obtain *The URANTIA Book*, or a Representative's telephone number, please contact the office nearest you or the head office in Chicago, Illinois.

International Offices:

Head Office
533 West Diversey Parkway
Chicago, Illinois 60614 U.S.A.
Tel.: +(773) 525-3319
Fax: +(773) 525-7739
Website: www.urantia.org
E-mail: urantia@urantia.org

Canada—English
PO Box 92006
West Vancouver, BC Canada V7V 4X4
Tel: +(604) 926-5836
Fax: +(604) 926-5899
E-mail: urantia@telus.net

Finland/Estonia/Sweden
PL 18,
15101 Lahti Finland
Tel./Fax: +(358) 3 777 8191
E-mail: urantia-saatio@urantia.fi

Great Britain/Ireland
Tel./Fax: +(44) 1491 641-922
E-Mail: urantia@easynet.co.uk

Australia/New Zealand/Asia
Tel./Fax: +(61) 2 9970-6200
E-mail: urantia@urantia.org.au

Canada—French
C. P. 233
Cap-Santé (Québec) Canada G0A 1L0
Tel.: +(418) 285-3333
Fax: +(418) 285-0226
E-mail: fondation@urantia-quebec.org

St. Petersburg, Russia
Tel./Fax: +(7) 812-580-3018
E-mail: vitgen@peterlink.ru

Other books available from URANTIA Foundation:

The URANTIA Book	hard cover			ISBN 0-911560-02-5
The URANTIA Book	leather collector		($7^5/_8$" x $5^3/_4$")	ISBN 0-911560-75-0
The URANTIA Book	small hard cover		($8^7/_{16}$" x $5^1/_2$")	ISBN 0-911560-07-6
The URANTIA Book	paperback		($8^7/_{16}$" x $5^1/_2$")	ISBN 0-911560-51-3
The URANTIA Book	gift-box leather		($8^7/_{16}$" x $5^1/_2$")	ISBN 0-911560-08-4
The URANTIA Book	softcover		($8^7/_{16}$" x $5^1/_2$")	ISBN 0-911560-50-5
Le Livre d'URANTIA	hard cover	French		ISBN 0-911560-05-X
Le Livre d'URANTIA	soft cover	French		ISBN 0-911560-53-X
El libro de URANTIA	paperback	Spanish	($8^7/_{16}$" x $5^1/_2$")	ISBN 1-883395-02-X
El libro de URANTIA	hard cover	Spanish	($8^7/_{16}$" x $5^1/_2$")	ISBN 1-883395-03-8
URANTIA-kirja	hard cover	Finnish		ISBN 0-911560-03-3
URANTIA-kirja	soft cover	Finnish		ISBN 0-911560-52-1
The URANTIA Book Concordance		English Index		ISBN 0-911560-00-9
The URANTIA Book	Audio	English		ISBN 0-911560-30-0
The URANTIA Book	CD ROM	English, Finnish, French		ISBN 0-911560-63-7

The URANTIA Book Workbooks

Title	Format	Language	ISBN
Forward and Part I	Paperback	English	ISBN 0-942430-99-9
Science	Paperback	English	ISBN 0-942430-98-0
Topical and Doctrinal Study	Paperback	English	ISBN 0-942430-97-2
Jesus	Paperback	English	ISBN 0-942430-96-4
Theology	Paperback	English	ISBN 0-942430-95-6
Bible Study	Paperback	English	ISBN 0-942430-94-8
Terminology	Paperback	English	ISBN 0-942430-93-X
Worship and Wisdom	Paperback	English	ISBN 0-942430-92-1

Dutch, Korean, Portuguese, and Russian translations also available from Urantia Foundation.

INTRODUCTION

Much has already been written regarding the study groups called "The Forum" and "The Seventy". Therefore I will try to confine my remarks more closely to the compiling and printing of several workbooks by Dr. William Sadler to be used in conjunction with *The Urantia Book*.

"The Forum" was the larger of the two groups and met on Sunday afternoons. The Wednesday night group was much smaller, studied in more depth, and was called "The Seventy" as that was the number of its members. Both met at the home of Dr. Sadler at 533 Diversey Parkway in Chicago. Doctor and some others in the group felt that something concrete was needed to train teachers for the future. Workbooks would help the teachers to form classes in the state or country in which they lived and use them to understand and present the concepts and new ideas from the Book in a uniform manner.

For several years members of the Wednesday night group were asked to prepare topical papers and teach the contents to the others in the group thus giving them experience in teaching. Dr. Sadler and his son, Bill, also taught the members of the group the information contained in the Papers of *The Urantia Book*. From the information Dr. Sadler taught at these classes the workbooks were developed for use by the group and for future teachers of the revelation.

The titles of the workbooks were:
Urantia Doctrine;
The Theology of *The Urantia Book*, Part I, Part II, and Part III;
Worship and Wisdom;
The Short Course in Doctrine,
 Summary of The Theology of *The Urantia Book*;
Science in *The Urantia Book* Volume I (with the collaboration of Alvin Kulieke);
    and
The Teachings Of Jesus.

Dr. Sadler possessed a great intellect, which may be one of the reasons he was selected by the Contact Commission to be the recipient of the *Urantia Papers*. He was able to understand and present, in a form that is understandable for others, many of the more difficult concepts and information in *The Urantia Book*. This is a great advantage for students who may be teaching these concepts in the future. The reprinting of these study aids will help many students of *The Urantia Book* gain a more comfortable understanding of the more difficult teachings in the book and an insight into Dr. Sadler's plan for instructing the future teachers of the revelation.

What a legacy has been left to us!

Katharine

Katharine Lea Jones Harries

THE THEOLOGY OF *THE URANTIA BOOK*

TABLE OF CONTENTS

	PAGE

PART I — THE DOCTRINE OF GOD 25
   I.   The First Source and Center 26
   II. The I AM 28
   III. God the Father 32
       1. Introduction 33
       2. God Is Spirit 34
       3. The Mystery of God 34
       4. The Personality of God 35
       5. The Nature of God 39
       6. The Attributes of God 44
       7. God's Relation to the Universe 49
       8. God's Relation to the Individual 53
   IV. God the Son 59
       1. Introduction 60
       2. Identity of the Son 60
       3. Nature of the Eternal Son 61
       4. Minister of the Father's Love 61
       5. Attributes of the Eternal Son 62
       6. Limitations of the Eternal Son 63
       7. Personality of the Eternal Son 64
       8. Spirit Gravity 64
       9. The Son's Relation to the Individual 67
      10. The Divine Perfection Plan 67
      11. The Spirit of Bestowal 68
      12. The Supreme Revelation of the Father 69
   V. God the Spirit 70
       1. Introduction 71
       2. The God of Action 71
       3. Nature of the Infinite Spirit 72
       4. Relation to the Father and Son 73
       5. The Spirit of Divine Ministry 75
       6. Personality of the Infinite Spirit 76

	7.	Attributes of the Infinite Spirit 77
	8.	The Universal Manipulator 78
	9.	The Ministry of Mind 78
	10.	Universe Reflectivity 81
	11.	Personalities of the Infinite Spirit 81
VI.		**God the Sevenfold** 82
VII.		**God the Supreme** 84
	1.	Introduction 85
	2.	Relation of the Supreme to the Paradise Trinity 85
	3.	Nature of the Supreme 87
	4.	The Supreme Mind 89
	5.	The Almighty and God the Sevenfold 90
	6.	The Almighty and Paradise Deity 90
	7.	The Almighty and the Supreme Creators .. 91
	8.	Source of Evolutionary Growth 93
	9.	Relation of the Supreme to Universe Creatures 95
	10.	The Finite God 99
	11.	The Oversoul of Creation 101
	12.	The Future of the Supreme 102
	13.	Omnipresence and Ubiquity 104
	14.	Universe Mechanisms 105
VIII.		**God the Ultimate** 107
	1.	God the Ultimate 107
	2.	The Transcendental Level 109
IX.		**God the Absolute** 113
X.		**Deity** 114

PART II – THE PARADISE TRINITY 119	
I.	Introduction 120
II.	The Trinity Union of Deity 121
III.	Functions of the Trinity 123
IV.	Stationary Sons of the Trinity 124
V.	Trinity Attitude Toward Reality 128
VI.	Co-ordinate Trinity Origin Beings 129
VII.	Urantian Trinity Concepts 131
VIII.	The Seven Triunities. 132

IX.	Triunities and Triodities 136
X.	The Trinity of Trinities 137
XI.	Ultimate and Absolute Trinities 138

Part III – The Absolutes 141
I.	Concept of the Absolutes 142
II.	The Seven Absolutes 143
III.	The Deity Absolute 143
IV.	The Unqualified Absolute 144
V.	The Universal Absolute 144
VI.	Absolute Levels and Responses 146

Part IV – Paradise 149
I.	Introduction 150
II.	Center and Source of All Things 151
III.	The Divine Residence 152
IV.	Nature of Paradise 152
V.	Upper Paradise 154
VI.	Peripheral Paradise 156
VII.	Nether Paradise 156
VIII.	Space Functions of Paradise 158
IX.	Destiny of Ascendant Creatures 159

Part V – The Paradise-Havona System 161
I.	Introduction 162
II.	Geography 162
III.	Constitution of Havona 165
IV.	The Havona Worlds 165
V.	Worlds of the Father 166
VI.	Worlds of the Son 170
VII.	Worlds of the Spirit 170
VIII.	Purpose of the Central Universe 171
IX.	Life in Havona 174

Part VI – Cosmology 177
I.	Introduction 178
II.	Paradise Gravity 179
III.	Domains of the Unqualified Absolute ... 182
IV.	Space Respiration 184
V.	Space and Motion 185

VI.	Space and Time 187
VII.	Universe Overcontrol 189
VIII.	The Seven Superuniverses 190
IX.	Orvonton 192
X.	The Spheres of Space 198
XI.	Energy Control and Regulation 199
XII.	Astronomy 201
XIII.	Sun Stability 206
XIV.	Universe Levels of Reality 207

Part VII – The Local Universe 211

Part VIII – Evolution 221
- I. Introduction 222
- II. Material Mind Systems 223
- III. Universe Mechanisms 223
- IV. Pattern and Form — Mind Systems 225
- V. Evolution of Human Mind 226
- VI. Life Carrier Functions 227
- VII. Fostering Evolution 229
- VIII. The Urantia Adventure 231
- IX. Evolutionary Vicissitudes 239
- X. Evolution in Time and Space 241
- XI. Factors in Social Progress 243
- XII. Land Techniques 244
- XIII. Cultural Evolution 245
- XIV. Dawn of Industry 247
- XV. Fire and Animals 249
- XVI. Maintenance of Civilization 250
- XVII. Control and Overcontrol 252
- XVIII. The Universal Rule of Evolution 253

Part IX – The Supreme Spirits 257
- I. Introduction 258
- II. Relation to Triune Deity 259
- III. Attributes and Functions 262
- IV. Relation to Creatures 264
- V. The Cosmic Mind 265
- VI. The Seven Supreme Executives 267

Table of Contents

- VII. Majeston—Chief of Reflectivity 267
- VIII. The Reflective Spirits 268
- IX. The Solitary Messengers 270
- X. Service of Solitary Messengers 272
- XI. Higher Personalities of the Infinite Spirit 274
- XII. Messenger Hosts of Space 278

Part X – The Paradise Sons 287
- I. Introduction 288
- II. Magisterial Sons 288
- III. Bestowal of the Sons 291
- IV. Trinity Teacher Sons 294
- V. Trinity-Embraced Sons 296
- VI. Mighty Messengers 299
- VII. Those High in Authority 300
- VIII. Those without Name and Number 301
- IX. Trinitized Custodians 301
- X. Trinitized Ambassadors 301
- XI. High Son Assistants 302
- XII. Technique of Trinitization 302

Part XI – Angels 307
- I. Ministering Spirits 308
- II. Primary Supernaphim 309
- III. Secondary Supernaphim 310
- IV. Tertiary Supernaphim 311
- V. Primary Seconaphim 312
- VI. Secondary Seconaphim 313
- VII. Tertiary Seconaphim 314
- VIII. Ministering Spirits of the Local Universe 314
- IX. Seraphim 315
- X. Cherubim and Sanobim 319
- XI. Supreme Seraphim 320
- XII. Superior Seraphim 320
- XIII. Supervisor Seraphim 321
- XIV. Administrator Seraphim 321
- XV. Planetary Helpers 321

Table of Contents

- XVI. Transition Ministers 321
- XVII. Guardian Angels 322
- XVIII. Seraphic Destiny 327
- XIX. Seraphim of Planetary Supervision 329

PART XII – THE CREATOR SONS 333
- I. Introduction 334
- II. Origin and Nature of Creator Sons 335
- III. Creators of Local Universes 337
- IV. Local Universe Sovereignty 339
- V. The Michael Bestowals 343
- VI. Destiny of Master Michaels 345
- VII. Local Universe Organization 346
- VIII. Michael of Nebadon 347
- IX. The Seven Bestowals of Michael 348

PART XIII – LOCAL UNIVERSE CREATIVE SPIRIT 351
- I. Personalization of the Creative Spirit ... 352
- II. Nature of the Divine Minister 353
- III. Universe Son and Creative Spirit 353
- IV. The Ministry of the Spirit 354
- V. The Spirit as Related to Man 356
- VI. Seven Stages of Development 358
- VII. Seven Adjutant Mind-spirits 359

PART XIV – THE POWER DIRECTORS 363
- I. Introduction 364
- II. Seven Supreme Power Directors 365
- III. Supreme Power Centers 367
- IV. Master Physical Controllers 369
- V. Master Force Organizers 370
- VI. Paradise Forces and Energies 371
- VII. Universal Nonspiritual Energy Systems 372
- VIII. Classification of Matter 372
- IX. Energy and Matter Transmutations 373
- X. Wave Energy Manifestations 376
- XI. Ultimatons and Electrons 376
- XII. Atomic Matter 377

Table of Contents

Part XV – Local Universe Sons 383
    I.   Introduction 384
    II.   Gabriel 385
    III. The Melchizedeks 385
    IV. The Vorondadeks 388
    V.   The Lanonandeks 389
    VI. The Life Carriers 391
    VII. Brilliant Evening Stars 394
    VIII. Archangels 394
    IX. Other Groups of Sons 395
    X.   Material Sons 396

Part XVI – Permanent Citizens 399
    I.   The Planets—Midwayers 400
    II.   The Local Systems—Material Sons 404
    III. The Constellations—Univitatia 405
    IV. The Local Universe—Susatia and
           Spirit-Fused Mortals 406
    V.   The Superuniverse—Abandonters
           and Son-Fused Mortals 406
    VI. Havona—Havona Natives 407
    VII. Paradise—Paradise Citizens
           (Probationary Nursery Children) 407

Part XVII – Man 411
    I.   Introduction 412
    II.   Andon and Fonta 413
    III. The Prince's Corporeal Staff 415
    IV. The Colored Races 416
    V.   Adam and Eve 417
    VI. The Violet Race 418
    VII. The Sumerians and Aryans 421
    VIII. Racial Types 422
    IX. The Blue Man 424
    X.   The Red and Yellow Races 426
    XI. Civilization 428
    XII. Human Free Will 431
    XIII. The Divine Monitor 431

XIV.	God-Consciousness	433
XV.	Urantia Personality	434
XVI.	Faith Sons of God	440
XVII.	The Seven Stages of Light and Life	440
XVIII.	Personality Survival	444

PART XVIII – EDUCATION 451

PART XIX – MARRIAGE AND THE HOME 457
I.	Introduction	458
II.	The Mating Instinct	458
III.	Early Marriage Mores	459
IV.	Racial Mixtures	460
V.	Marriage as a Social Institution	461
VI.	Plural Marriages	464
VII.	True Monogamy	465
VIII.	Woman's Early Status	466
IX.	Ideals of Family Life	467
X.	Dangers of Self-Gratification	469
XI.	Child Culture	470

PART XX – THE STATE 473
I.	War	474
II.	Early Human Associations	476
III.	Clubs and Secret Societies	476
IV.	Monarchial Government	477
V.	Human Rights	478
VI.	Evolution of Justice	479
VII.	Representative Government	481
VIII.	Ideals of Statehood	482
IX.	Progressive Civilization	483
X.	Private Property and Slavery	485
XI.	Superhuman Government	486

PART XXI – ASCENDING SONS OF GOD 491
I.	Introduction	492
II.	Ascending Mortals—Father-Fused	492
III.	Son-Fused Mortals	496
IV.	Spirit-Fused Mortals	497
V.	Evolutionary Seraphim	499

VI.	Material Sons	499
VII.	Translated Midwayers	499
VIII.	Personalized Adjusters	500
IX.	Midsoniters	500
X.	The Mansion Worlds	501
XI.	The System Sojourn	505
XII.	In Havona	506
XIII.	On Paradise	508

PART XXII – THE MORONTIA LIFE 511
I.	Introduction	512
II.	Morontia Companions	513
III.	Reversion Directors	514
IV.	Mansion World Teachers	516
V.	Morontia World Seraphim	516
VI.	Morontia Mota	517
VII.	Morontia Progressors	518
VIII.	Celestial Artisans	519
IX.	The Probation Nursery	520
X.	The Morontia Self	520
XI.	The Morontia Worlds	522
XII.	The Spornagia	523
XIII.	Morontia Power Supervisors	525

PART XXIII – THE CORPS OF THE FINALITY 527
I.	Introduction	528
II.	Havona Natives	529
III.	Gravity Messengers	530
IV.	Glorified Mortals	531
V.	Adopted Seraphim	533
VI.	Glorified Material Sons	533
VII.	Glorified Midwayers	534
VIII.	Evangels of Light	534

PART XXIV – YAHWEH 537
I.	Introduction	538
II.	Deity Among the Semites	538
III.	Moses	540
IV.	Yahweh After Moses	541

V.	Samuel	542
VI.	Elijah	543
VII.	Amos and Hosea	544
VIII.	The First Isaiah	545
IX.	Jeremiah	546
X.	The Second Isaiah	546

PART XXV – SIN 549

I.	The Concept of Sin	550
II.	The Lucifer Rebellion	555
III.	Repercussions of Sin	570
IV.	Sacrifices—Atonement	571
V.	Forgiveness of Sin	572
VI.	Natural Urges	574
VII.	Penalty for Sin	575
VIII.	The Devil	575

PART XXVI – THE PLAN OF SALVATION 577

I.	Introduction	578
II.	The Love of God	578
III.	The Eternal and Divine Purpose	579
IV.	The Plan of Perfection Attainment	580
V.	The Bestowal Plan	582
VI.	The Plan of Mercy Ministry	582
VII.	The Salvage Plan	583
VIII.	The Faith Sons of God	584
IX.	Providence	585
X.	Jesus' Life on Earth	588
XI.	The Atonement Idea	589
XII.	The Religion of Survival	592
XIII.	Progress Through Havona	594

PART XXVII – ADAM AND EVE 597

I.	Introduction	598
II.	The Edenic Regime	600
III.	The Garden of Eden	601
IV.	The Tree of Life	603
V.	Arrival of Adam and Eve	604
VI.	Temptation of Eve	608

VII.	Realization of Default	611
VIII.	Leaving the Garden	612
IX.	The Second Garden	614
X.	Cain and Abel	615
XI.	The Violet Race	616
XII.	Death of Adam and Eve	618
XIII.	Survival of Adam and Eve	618

PART XXVIII — MACHIVENTA MELCHIZEDEK 623

I.	Introduction	624
II.	The Machiventa Incarnation	624
III.	Melchizedek's Teachings	626
IV.	The Selection of Abraham	628
V.	The Covenant with Abraham	630
VI.	Melchizedek Missionaries	632
VII.	Departure of Melchizedek	632
VIII.	Present Status of Melchizedek	633
IX.	Teachings of Melchizedek in the Orient	634
X.	Teachings in the Levant	635
XI.	Teachings in the Occident	636

NOTE: All Bible references are from the *Revised Standard Version* (1952). All other quotations are from *The Urantia Book* unless otherwise noted.

THE THEOLOGY OF
THE URANTIA BOOK

BIBLICAL ABBREVIATIONS USED IN THIS SECTION

The Old Testament

Gen .... The Book of Genesis	Job .... The Book of Job
Ex .... The Book of Exodus	Ps .... The Book of Psalms
Lev .... The Book of Leviticus	Prov ...... The Book of Proverbs
Num ...... The Book of Numbers	Eccl .... Ecclesiastes
Deut ...... The Book of Deuteronomy	Song ...... The Song of Songs
	Isa .... The Book of Isaiah
Josh .... The Book of Joshua	Jer .... The Book of Jeremiah
Judges .... The Book of Judges	Lam .... Lamentations
Ruth ...... The Book of Ruth	Eze .... The Book of Ezekiel
1 Sam ..... The First Book of Samuel	Dan .... The Book of Daniel
2 Sam ..... The Second Book of Samuel	Hos .... The Book of Hosea
	Joel .... The Book of Joel
1 Kings ... The First Book of Kings	Amos ..... The Book of Amos
2 Kings ... The Second Book of Kings	Obad ..... The Book of Obadiah
1 Chron .. The First Book of Chronicles	Jon .... The Book of Jonah
	Nah .... The Book of Nahum
2 Chron .. The Second Book of Chronicles	Hab .... The Book of Habakkuk
	Zeph ...... The Book of Zephaniah
Ezra .... The Book of Ezra	Hag .... The Book of Haggai
Neh .... The Book of Nehemiah	Zec .... The Book of Zechariah
Esther .... The Book of Esther	Mal .... The Book of Malachi

The New Testament

Matt ...... The Gospel According to Matthew	1 Thess ... The First Epistle to the Thessalonians
Mark ...... The Gospel According to Mark	2 Thess ... The Second Epistle to the Thessalonians
Luke ...... The Gospel According to Luke	1 Tim ..... The First Epistle to Timothy
	2 Tim ..... The Second Epistle to Timothy
John ...... The Gospel According to John	Tit .... The Epistle to Titus
	Phmon ... The Epistle to Philemon
Acts .... The Acts of the Apostles	Heb .... The Epistle to the Hebrews
Rom ...... The Epistle to the Romans	
1 Cor ..... The First Epistle to the Corinthians	Jas .... The Epistle of James
	1 Peter ... The First Epistle of Peter
2 Cor ..... The Second Epistle to the Corinthians	2 Peter ... The Second Epistle of Peter
Gal .... The Epistle to the Galatians	1 John .... The First Epistle of John
	2 John .... The Second Epistle of John
Eph .... The Epistle to the Ephesians	3 John .... The Third Epistle of John
Phil .... The Epistle to the Philippians	Jude ...... Jude
	Rev .... Revelation
Col .... The Epistle to the Colossians	

PART I
THE DOCTRINE OF GOD

Part One
THE DOCTRINE OF GOD

I. THE FIRST SOURCE AND CENTER

1. **Proposition.** The God of the First Source and Center is primal, infinite, and eternal — limited only by volition.

    "God, as the First Source and Center, is primal in relation to total reality — unqualifiedly. The First Source and Center is infinite as well as eternal and is therefore limited or conditioned only by volition." (p. 5)

2. **Proposition.** The Universal Father is the infinite personality of the First Source and Center.

    "God — the Universal Father — is the personality of the First Source and Center and as such maintains personal relations of infinite control over all co-ordinate and subordinate sources and centers. Such control is personal and infinite in *potential*, even though it may never actually function owing to the perfection of the function of such co-ordinate and subordinate sources and centers and personalities." (p. 5)

3. **Proposition.** The God of the First Source and Center exercises cosmic overcontrol by absolute Paradise gravity.

    "As a physical controller in the material universe of universes, the First Source and Center functions in the patterns of the eternal Isle of Paradise, and through this absolute gravity center the eternal God exercises cosmic overcontrol of the physical level equally in the central universe and throughout the universe of universes." (p. 24)

4. **Proposition.** The multiform inter-relations of God do not preclude direct Thought Adjuster relations with his creatures.

    "As mind, God functions in the Deity of the Infinite Spirit; as spirit, God is manifest in the person of the Eternal Son and in the persons of the divine children of the Eternal Son. This interrelation of the First Source and Center with the co-ordinate Persons and Absolutes of Paradise does not in the least preclude the *direct* personal action of the Universal Father throughout all creation and on all levels thereof. Through the presence of his fragmentized spirit the Creator Father maintains immediate contact with his creature children and his created universes." (p. 24)

5. **Proposition.** The First Source and Center transcends all matter, mind, and spirit.

> "This concept of indivisibility in association with the concept of unity implies transcendence of both time and space by the Ultimacy of Deity; therefore neither space nor time can be absolute or infinite. The First Source and Center is that infinity who unqualifiedly transcends all mind, all matter, and all spirit." (p. 31)

6. **Proposition.** The divine potential is never diminished by the limitless endowment of the universe of universes.

> "And subsequent to this bestowal of limitless force and power upon a boundless universe, the Infinite would still be surcharged with the same degree of force and energy; the Unqualified Absolute would still be undiminished; God would still possess the same infinite potential, just as if force, energy, and power had never been poured forth for the endowment of universe upon universe." (p. 49)

7. **Proposition.** Finite actualities are derived from the First Source and Center by means of self-existent free will.

> "Finite possibility is inherent in the Infinite, but the transmutation of possibility to probability and inevitability must be attributed to the self-existent free will of the First Source and Center, activating all triunity associations. Only the infinity of the Father's will could ever have so qualified the absolute level of existence as to eventuate an ultimate or to create a finite." (p. 1158)

8. **Proposition.** Creative actuality begins with the finite and consists of Havona primary maximums and superuniverse secondary maximums.

> "These inconceivable transactions mark the beginning of universe history, mark the coming into existence of time itself. To a creature, the beginning of the finite *is* the genesis of reality; as viewed by creature mind, there is no actuality conceivable prior to the finite. This newly appearing finite reality exists in two original phases:
> "1. *Primary maximums*, the supremely perfect reality, the Havona type of universe and creature.
> "2. *Secondary maximums*, the supremely perfected reality, the superuniverse type of creature and creation." (p. 1158)

II. THE I AM

1. **PROPOSITION.** The I AM achieved Deity liberation from the fetters of unqualified infinity by that free will which produced the first absolute divinity tension.

    "As a time-space creature would view the origin and differentiation of Reality, the eternal and infinite I AM achieved Deity liberation from the fetters of unqualified infinity through the exercise of inherent and eternal free will, and this divorcement from unqualified infinity produced the first *absolute divinity-tension*. This tension of infinity differential is resolved by the Universal Absolute, which functions to unify and co-ordinate the dynamic infinity of Total Deity and the static infinity of the Unqualified Absolute." (p. 6)

2. **PROPOSITION.** The I AM achieves personality by becoming the Eternal Father of the Original Son and the Eternal Source of Paradise.

    "In this original transaction the theoretical I AM achieved the realization of personality by becoming the Eternal Father of the Original Son simultaneously with becoming the Eternal Source of the Isle of Paradise." (p. 6)

3. **PROPOSITION.** The I AM concept is a philosophic concession to the time-bound space-fettered finite mind of man.

    "*The concept of the I AM* is a philosophic concession which we make to the time-bound, space-fettered, finite mind of man, to the impossibility of creature comprehension of eternity existences — non-beginning, nonending realities and relationships. To the time-space creature, all things must have a beginning save only the ONE UNCAUSED—the primeval cause of causes. Therefore do we conceptualize this philosophic value-level as the I AM, at the same time instructing all creatures that the Eternal Son and the Infinite Spirit are coeternal with the I AM; in other words, that there never was a time when the I AM was not the *Father* of the Son and, with him, of the Spirit." (p. 6)

4. **PROPOSITION.** Absolute causation resides in the Universal Father functioning as the I AM.

    "Absolute primal causation in infinity the philosophers of the universes attribute to the Universal Father functioning as the infinite, the eternal, and the absolute I AM." (p. 1152)

5. **Proposition.** The concept of the I AM connotes unqualified infinity — the source of all reality.

> "*The I AM is the Infinite; the I AM is also infinity.* From the sequential, time viewpoint, all reality has its origin in the infinite I AM, whose solitary existence in past infinite eternity must be a finite creature's premier philosophic postulate. The concept of the I AM connotes *unqualified infinity*, the undifferentiated reality of all that could ever be in all of an infinite eternity." (p. 1152)

6. **Proposition.** The existential concept of the I AM is without qualification — except to state that the I AM is.

> "As an existential concept the I AM is neither deified nor undeified, neither actual nor potential, neither personal nor impersonal, neither static nor dynamic. No qualification can be applied to the Infinite except to state that the I AM *is*. (p. 1153)

7. **Proposition.** The I AM concept functions at the past-eternity moment prior to the differentiation of all reality.

> "At some infinitely distant, hypothetical, past-eternity moment, the I AM may be conceived as both thing and no thing, as both cause and effect, as both volition and response. At this hypothetical eternity moment there is no differentiation throughout all infinity. Infinity is filled by the Infinite; the Infinite encompasses infinity. This is the hypothetical static moment of eternity; actuals are still contained within their potentials, and potentials have not yet appeared within the infinity of the I AM. But even in this conjectured situation we must assume the existence of the possibility of self-will." (p. 1153)

8. **Proposition.** The portrayal of the origins of reality demands a moment of first volitional expression — the differentiation of the Infinite One from Infinitude.

> "In following the chronological portrayal of the origins of reality, there must be a postulated theoretical moment of 'first' volitional expression and 'first' repercussional reaction within the I AM. In our attempts to portray the genesis and generation of reality, this stage may be conceived as the self-differentiation of *The Infinite One* from *The Infinitude,*..." (p. 1154)

9. **PROPOSITION.** The solitary I AM metamorphoses into the time concept of the triune and later on as sevenfold.

> "By these internal metamorphoses the I AM is establishing the basis for a sevenfold self-relationship. The philosophic (time) concept of the solitary I AM and the transitional (time) concept of the I AM as triune can now be enlarged to encompass the I AM as sevenfold." (p. 1154)

10. **PROPOSITION.** The sevenfold nature of the I AM is suggested by the Seven Absolutes of Infinity.

    1. The Universal Father
    2. The Universal Controller
    3. The Universal Creator
    4. The Infinite Upholder
    5. The Infinite Potential
    6. The Infinite Capacity
    7. The Universal One of Infinity

    > "This sevenfold — or seven phase — nature may be best suggested in relation to the Seven Absolutes of Infinity:
    >
    > "1. *The Universal Father.* I AM father of the Eternal Son. This is the primal personality relationship of actualities. The absolute personality of the Son makes absolute the fact of God's fatherhood and establishes the potential sonship of all personalities."
    >
    > 2. *The Universal Controller.* I AM cause of eternal Paradise. This is the primal impersonal relationship of actualities, the original nonspiritual association.
    >
    > "3. *The Universal Creator.* I AM one with the Eternal Son. This union of the Father and the Son (in the presence of Paradise) initiates the creative cycle, which is consummated in the appearance of conjoint personality and the eternal universe.
    >
    > "4. *The Infinite Upholder.* I AM self-associative. This is the primordial association of the statics and potentials of reality. In this relationship, all qualifieds and unqualifieds are compensated. This phase of the I AM is best understood as the Universal Absolute — the unifier of the Deity and the Unqualified Absolutes.

> "5. *The Infinite Potential*. I AM self-qualified. This is the infinity bench mark bearing eternal witness to the volitional self-limitation of the I AM by virtue of which there was achieved threefold self-expression and self-revelation. This phase of the I AM is usually understood as the Deity Absolute.
>
> "6. *The Infinite Capacity*. I AM static-reactive. This is the endless matrix, the possibility for all future cosmic expansion. This phase of the I AM is perhaps best conceived as the supergravity presence of the Unqualified Absolute.
>
> "7. *The Universal One of Infinity*. I AM as I AM. This is the stasis or self-relationship of Infinity, the eternal fact of infinity-reality and the universal truth of reality-infinity. In so far as this relationship is discernible as personality, it is revealed to the universes in the divine Father of all personality — even of absolute personality." (pp. 1154-55)

11. **PROPOSITION.** The I AM postulate of the Infinite and the Absolute transcends all time — past, present, and future.

    > "On the levels of the infinite and the absolute the moment of the present contains all of the past as well as all of the future. I AM signifies also I WAS and I WILL BE." (p. 1296)

12. **PROPOSITION.** The I AM must exist before all existentials and after all experientials.

    > "The I AM, in the final analysis, must exist *before* all existentials and *after all* experientials. "While these ideas may not clarify the paradoxes of eternity and infinity in the human mind, they should at least stimulate such finite intellects to grapple anew with these never-ending problems, problems which will continue to intrigue you on Salvington and later as finaliters and on throughout the unending future of your eternal careers in the wide-spreading universes." (p. 1174)

BIBLE

God said to Moses, "I AM who I AM," and he said, "Say this to the people of Israel, 'I AM has sent me to you.'" **Ex. 3:4.**

III. GOD THE FATHER

1. Introduction
2. God Is Spirit
3. The Mystery of God
4. The Personality of God
5. The Nature of God
   - A. The Infinity of God
   - B. The Justice of God — Righteousness
   - C. The Mercy of God
   - D. The Love of God
   - E. The Goodness of God — Holiness
6. The Attributes of God
   - A. God's Omnipresence — Everywhereness
   - B. God's Omnipotence — Infinite Power
   - C. God's Omniscience — Universal Knowledge
   - D. The Primacy of God
7. God's Relation to the Universe
   - A. God and Nature
   - B. God's Faithfulness — Changelessness
   - C. Delegation of Power
   - D. God's Eternal Purpose
   - E. Erroneous Ideas of God
8. God's Relation to the Individual
   - A. The Approach to God
   - B. The Presence of God
   - C. God in Religion
   - D. The God of Personality

III. GOD THE FATHER

1. INTRODUCTION

1. **PROPOSITION.** The Universal Father is a Creator, Controller, and Upholder.

    "The Universal Father is the God of all creation, the First Source and Center of all things and beings. First think of God as a creator, then as a controller, and lastly as an infinite upholder." (p. 21)

2. **PROPOSITION.** Creatorship is the aggregate acting nature of God.

    "Creatorship is hardly an attribute of God; it is rather the aggregate of his acting nature. And this universal function of creatorship is eternally manifested as it is conditioned and controlled by all the co-ordinated attributes of the infinite and divine reality of the First Source and Center." (p. 44)

3. **PROPOSITION.** In science, God is a cause; in philosophy, a reality; in religion, a loving Father.

    "In science, God is the First Cause; in religion, the universal and loving Father; in philosophy, the one being who exists by himself, not dependent on any other being for existence but beneficently conferring reality of existence on all things and upon all other beings." (p. 59)

4. **PROPOSITION.** God is known by many names — on bestowal worlds, he is called "Our Father."

    "In one near-by constellation God is called the Father of Universes. In another, the Infinite Upholder, and to the east, the Divine Controller. He has also been designated the Father of Lights, the Gift of Life, and the All-powerful One.
    "On those worlds where a Paradise Son has lived a bestowal life, God is generally known by some name indicative of personal relationship, tender affection, and fatherly devotion. On your constellation headquarters God is referred to as the Universal Father, and on different planets in your local system of inhabited worlds he is variously known as the Father of Fathers, the Paradise Father, the Havona Father, and the Spirit Father. Those who know God through the revelations of the bestowals of the Paradise Sons, eventually yield to the sentimental appeal of the touching relationship of the creature-Creator association and refer to God as "our Father." (p. 23)

BIBLE TEXTS

"And Ezra said: Thou art the Lord, thou alone; thou has made heaven, the heaven of heavens, with all their host, the earth and all that is on it, the seas and all that is in them; and thou preservest all of them; and the host of heaven worship thee." **Neh. 9:6**

"By the word of the Lord the heavens were made, and all their host by the breath of his mouth." **Ps. 33:6**

"Who has measured the waters in the hollow of his hand and marked off the heavens with a span" enclosed the dust of the earth in a measure and weighed the mountains in scales and the hills in a balance." **Isa. 40:12**

"Lift up your eyes and see: who created these? "Who brings out their host by number, calling them all by name; by the greatness of his might, and because he is strong in power not one is missing." **Isa. 40:26**

2. GOD IS SPIRIT

1. **PROPOSITION.** God is spirit — an infinite spirit person.

    "'God is spirit.' He is a universal spiritual presence. The Universal Father is an infinite spiritual reality; he is 'the sovereign, eternal, immortal, invisible, and only true God.'" (p. 25)

2. **PROPOSITION.** God is a universal spirit.

    "God is a universal spirit; God is the universal person. The supreme personal reality of the finite creation is spirit; the ultimate reality of the personal cosmos is absonite spirit." (p. 25)

BIBLE TEXTS

"God is spirit, and those who worship him must worship in spirit and truth." **John 4:24.**

"To the king of the ages, immortal, invisible, the only God." **I Tim. 1:17**

3. THE MYSTERY OF GOD

1. **PROPOSITION.** Only by faith can the infinite mystery of God be experienced by the finite mind.

    "As a reality in human spiritual experience God is not a mystery. But when an attempt is made to make plain the realities of the spirit world to the physical minds of the material order, mystery appears: mysteries so subtle and so profound that only the faith- grasp of the God-knowing mortal can achieve the philosophic miracle of the recognition of the

Infinite by the finite, the discernment of the eternal God by the evolving mortals of the material worlds of time and space." (p. 27)

2. **PROPOSITION.** God is invisible to material creatures because the eye cannot see him — but faith can.

"The Universal Father is not invisible because he is hiding himself away from the lowly creatures of materialistic handicaps and limited spiritual endowments. The situation rather is: 'You cannot see my face, for no mortal can see me and live.' No material man could behold the spirit God and preserve his mortal existence. The glory and the spiritual brilliance of the divine personality presence is impossible of approach by the lower groups of spirit beings or by any order of material personalities. The spiritual luminosity of the Father's personal presence is a 'light which no mortal man can approach; which no material creature has seen or can see.' But it is not necessary to see God with the eyes of the flesh in order to discern him by the faith-vision of the spiritualized mind." (p. 25)

3. **PROPOSITION.** To every creature God reveals as much of himself as he can comprehend.

"To every spirit being and to every mortal creature in every sphere and on every world of the universe of universes, the Universal Father reveals all of his gracious and divine self that can be discerned or comprehended by such spirit beings and by such mortal creatures. God is no respecter of persons, either spiritual or material. The divine presence which any child of the universe enjoys at any given moment is limited only by the capacity of such a creature to receive and to discern the spirit actualities of the supermaterial world." (p. 27)

BIBLE TEXTS

"But, he said, you cannot see my face; for man shall not see me and live."
Ex. 33:20

"Who alone has immortality and dwells in unapproachable light, whom no man has ever seen or can see." **I Tim. 6:16**

4. THE PERSONALITY OF GOD

1. **PROPOSITION.** God functions on three subinfinite personality levels.

"God, the Universal Father, functions on three Deity-personality levels of subinfinite value and relative divinity expression:

> "1. *Prepersonal* — as in the ministry of the Father fragments, such as the Thought Adjusters.
> "2. *Personal* — as in the evolutionary experience of created and procreated beings.
> "3. *Superpersonal* — as in the eventuated existences of certain absonite and associated beings." (p. 3)

2. **PROPOSITION.** God is a term which always denotes personality.

   > "The term God always denotes *personality*. Deity may, or may not, refer to divinity personalities." (p. 4)

3. **PROPOSITION.** God is a word designating all personal relations of Deity.

   > "GOD is a word symbol designating all personalizations of Deity. The term requires a different definition on each personal level of Deity function and must be still further redefined within each of these levels." (p. 3)

4. **PROPOSITION.** God is personality.

   > "Without God and except for his great and central person, there would be no personality throughout all the vast universe of universes. *God is personality*." (p. 28)

5. **PROPOSITION.** Religious experience implies the personality of God—but only revelation validates it.

   > "The idea of the personality of the Universal Father is an enlarged and truer concept of God which has come to mankind chiefly through revelation. Reason, wisdom, and religious experience all infer and imply the personality of God, but they do not altogether validate it. Even the indwelling Thought Adjuster is prepersonal." (p. 28)

6. **PROPOSITION.** The concept of the personality of God is the measure of religious maturity.

   > "The truth and maturity of any religion is directly proportional to its concept of the infinite personality of God and to its grasp of the absolute unity of Deity. The idea of a personal Deity becomes, then, the measure of religious maturity after religion has first formulated the concept of the unity of God." (p. 28)

7. **PROPOSITION.** God's infinity should not eclipse his personality.

   > "Do not permit the magnitude of God, his infinity, either to obscure or eclipse his personality. 'He who planned the ear, shall he not hear? He who formed the eye, shall he not see?'

The Universal Father is the acme of divine personality; he is the origin and destiny of personality throughout all creation. God is both infinite and personal; he is an infinite personality. The Father is truly a personality, notwithstanding that the infinity of his person places him forever beyond the full comprehension of material and finite beings." (p. 27)

8. **PROPOSITION.** While God must be much more than personality, he cannot be anything less.

   "Therefore, although you may know that God must be much more than the human conception of personality, you equally well know that the Universal Father cannot possibly be anything less than an eternal, infinite, true, good, and beautiful personality." (p. 27)

9. **PROPOSITION.** To science God is a cause; to philosophy an idea; to religion a person.

   "God is to science a cause, to philosophy an idea, to religion a person, even the loving heavenly Father." (p. 30)

10. **PROPOSITION.** The personality concept of God favors fellowship which cannot exist between nonpersonal things.

    "When Jesus talked about 'the living God,' he referred to a personal Deity — the Father in heaven. The concept of the personality of Deity facilitates fellowship; it favors intelligent worship; it promotes refreshing trustfulness. Interactions can be had between nonpersonal things, but not fellowship." (p. 31)

11. **PROPOSITION.** Truth and beauty may exist without personality, but goodness and love are associated only with persons.

    "The concept of truth might possibly be entertained apart from personality, the concept of beauty may exist without personality, but the concept of divine goodness is understandable only in relation to personality. Only a *person* can love and be loved." (p. 31)

12. **PROPOSITION.** God's conduct is personal — conscious and volitional. He is not a slave to his own perfection and infinity.

    "And all this steadfastness of conduct and uniformity of action is personal, conscious, and highly volitional, for the great God is not a helpless slave to his own perfection and infinity. God is not a self-acting automatic force; he is not a slavish law-bound power. God is neither a mathematical equation nor a chemical formula. He is a freewill and primal personality. He is the Universal Father, a being surcharged with personality and the universal fount of all creature personality." (p. 138)

13. **Proposition.** God is a perfect person who can know and be known — who can love and be loved.

"Notwithstanding that God is an eternal power, a majestic presence, a transcendent ideal, and a glorious spirit, though he is all these and infinitely more, nonetheless, he is truly and everlastingly a perfect Creator personality, a person who can 'know and be known,' who can 'love and be loved,' and one who can befriend us; while you can be known, as other humans have been known, as the friend of God. He is a real spirit and a spiritual reality." (p. 28)

14. **Proposition.** By trinitization the Father divests himself of unqualified personality, thus becoming the loving father of all his universe children.

"By the technique of trinitization the Father divests himself of that unqualified spirit personality which is the Son, but in so doing he constitutes himself the Father of this very Son and thereby possesses himself of unlimited capacity to become the divine Father of all subsequently created, eventuated, or other personalized types of intelligent will creatures. As the *absolute and unqualified personality* the Father can function only as and with the Son, but as a *personal Father* he continues to bestow personality upon the diverse hosts of the differing levels of intelligent will creatures, and he forever maintains personal relations of loving association with this vast family of universe children." (p. 109)

15. **Proposition.** Five arguments to prove the personality of God. Presented by Nathaniel to Rodan.

See (p. 1784)

BIBLE TEXTS

"He who planted the ear, does he not hear? He who formed the eye, does he not see?" **Ps. 94:9**

"Abraham believed God, and it was reckoned to him as righteousness; and he was called the friend of God." **Jas. 2:23**

PART I — THE DOCTRINE OF GOD

5. THE NATURE OF GOD

1. **PROPOSITION.** Of all the things God might be, he is more — a loving Father.

    "The eternal God is infinitely more than reality idealized or the universe personalized. God is not simply the supreme desire of man, the mortal quest objectified. Neither is God merely a concept, the power-potential of righteousness. The Universal Father is not a synonym for nature, neither is he natural law personified. God is a transcendent reality, not merely man's traditional concept of supreme values. God is not a psychological focalization of spiritual meanings, neither is he 'the noblest work of man.' God may be any or all of these concepts in the minds of men, but he is more. He is a saving person and a loving Father to all who enjoy spiritual peace on earth, and who crave to experience personality survival in death." (p. 23)

2. **PROPOSITION.** God is neither manlike nor machinelike.

    "God is neither manlike nor machinelike. The First Father is universal spirit, eternal truth, infinite reality, and father personality." (p. 23)

3. **PROPOSITION.** The nature of God is best understood by the life and teachings of Jesus.

    "The nature of God can best be understood by the revelation of the Father which Michael of Nebadon unfolded in his manifold teachings and in his superb mortal life in the flesh. The divine nature can also be better understood by man if he regards himself as a child of God and looks up to the Paradise Creator as a true spiritual Father." (p. 33)

A. *The Infinity of God*

    1. **PROPOSITION.** Notwithstanding God's eternity and infinity, he is absolute in volition.

        "The Father is infinite and eternal, but to deny the possibility of his volitional self-limitation amounts to a denial of this very concept of his volitional absoluteness." (p. 59)

    2. **PROPOSITION.** There is no limit to the number of spirit monitors which God can bestow.

        "The fact that he sends forth spirit messengers from himself to indwell the men and women of your world and other worlds in no wise lessens his ability to function as a divine and all-powerful spirit personality; and there is absolutely no limit to the extent or number of such spirit Monitors which he can and may send out." (p. 50)

3. **PROPOSITION.** The unstinted bestowal of himself upon his universes does not diminish his potential of power, wisdom, and love.

   "The successive bestowal of himself upon the universes as they are brought into being in no wise lessens the potential of power or the store of wisdom as they continue to reside and repose in the central personality of Deity. In potential of force, wisdom, and love, the Father has never lessened aught of his possession nor become divested of any attribute of his glorious personality as the result of the unstinted bestowal of himself upon the Paradise Sons, upon his subordinate creations, and upon the manifold creatures thereof." (p. 49)

4. **PROPOSITION.** Regardless of how much you comprehend God the Father, you will always be staggered by the concept of the Father-I AM.

   "No matter how much you may grow in Father comprehension, your mind will always be staggered by the unrevealed infinity of the Father-I AM, the unexplored vastness of which will always remain unfathomable and incomprehensible throughout all the cycles of eternity. No matter how much of God you may attain, there will always remain much more of him, the existence of which you will not even suspect. And we believe that this is just as true on transcendental levels as it is in the domains of finite existence. The quest for God is endless!" (p. 1169)

5. **PROPOSITION.** Inability to attain the infinity of God should not prevent our enjoying him on finite levels.

   "Such inability to attain God in a final sense should in no manner discourage universe creatures; indeed, you can and do attain Deity levels of the Sevenfold, the Supreme, and the Ultimate, which mean to you what the infinite realization of God the Father means to the Eternal Son and to the Conjoint Actor in their absolute status of eternity existence. Far from harassing the creature, the infinity of God should be the supreme assurance that throughout all endless futurity an ascending personality will have before him the possibilities of personality development and Deity association which even eternity will neither exhaust nor terminate." (p. 1169)

BIBLE TEXTS

"*Who does great things and unsearchable, marvelous things without number.*" **Job 5:9**

PART I — *The Doctrine of God*

"Behold, God is great, and we know him not; the number of his years is unsearchable." **Job. 36:26**

"Declaring the end from the beginning and from ancient times things not yet done, saying, my counsel shall stand, and I will accomplish all my purpose." **Isa. 46:10**

B. *The Justice of God — Righteousness*

1. **PROPOSITION.** Willful sin and iniquity are automatically suicidal. "Undiluted evil, complete error, willful sin, and unmitigated iniquity are inherently and automatically suicidal." (p. 37)
2. **PROPOSITION.** The final result of wholehearted sin is annihilation. "The final result of wholehearted sin is annihilation. In the last analysis, such sin-identified individuals have destroyed themselves by becoming wholly unreal through their embrace of iniquity." (p. 37)

BIBLE TEXTS

"The Lord is just in all his ways, and kind in all his doings." **Ps. 145:17**

"The Lord works vindication and justice for all who are oppressed." **Ps. 103:6**

"God is a righteous judge." **Ps. 7:9**

"Take heed what you do, for there is no perversion of justice with the Lord our God, or partiality, or taking of bribes." **II Chron. 19:7**

C. *The Mercy of God*

1. **PROPOSITION.** The creature's need is sufficient to insure the full flow of the Father's mercy.
"The creature's need is wholly sufficient to insure the full flow of the Father's tender mercies and his saving grace. Since God knows all about his children, it is easy for him to forgive. The better man understands his neighbor, the easier it will be to forgive him, even to love him." (p. 38)
2. **PROPOSITION.** Mercy is a wise and understanding application of justice — not a contravention.
"Mercy is not a contravention of justice but rather an understanding interpretation of the demands of supreme justice as it is fairly applied to the subordinate spiritual beings and to the material creatures of the evolving universes. Mercy is the justice of the Paradise Trinity wisely and lovingly visited upon

the manifold intelligences of the creations of time and space as it is formulated by divine wisdom and determined by the all-knowing mind and the sovereign free will of the Universal Father and all his associated Creators." (p. 38)

BIBLE TEXTS

"Blessed be the Lord God and Father of our Lord Jesus Christ, the Father of mercies and God of all comfort." **II Cor. 1:3**

D. The Love of God

1. **PROPOSITION.** God is love.
   "'God is love; therefore his only personal attitude towards the affairs of the universe is always a reaction of divine affection. The Father loves us sufficiently to bestow his life upon us. 'He makes his sun to rise on the evil and on the good and sends rain on the just and on the unjust.'" (p. 38)

2. **PROPOSITION.** The Father's love follows us throughout the endless circle of the eternal ages.
   "The Father's love follows us now and throughout the endless circle of the eternal ages. As you ponder the loving nature of God, there is only one reasonable and natural personality reaction thereto: You will increasingly love your Maker." (p. 40)

3. **PROPOSITION.** The love of God is intelligent, wise, and farseeing. God is love, but love is not God.
   "But the love of God is an intelligent and farseeing parental affection. The divine love functions in unified association with divine wisdom and all other infinite characteristics of the perfect nature of the Universal Father. God is love, but love is not God." (p. 40)

4. **PROPOSITION.** Love is the dominant characteristic of all God's personal dealings with his children.
   "When man loses sight of the love of a personal God, the kingdom of God becomes merely the kingdom of good. Notwithstanding the infinite unity of the divine nature, love is the dominant characteristic of all God's personal dealings with his creatures." (p. 40)

5. **PROPOSITION.** Love identifies the volitional will of God.
   "Love identifies the volitional will of God. The goodness of God rests at the bottom of the divine free-willness — the universal tendency to love, show mercy, manifest patience, and minister forgiveness." (p. 42)

6. **PROPOSITION.** It is wrong to think that God only loves us because of the sacrifices of his Sons.

    "It is wrong to think of God as being coaxed into loving his children because of the sacrifices of his Sons or the intercession of his subordinate creatures, 'for the Father himself loves you.'" (p. 39)

7. **PROPOSITION.** The face which God turns toward all persons is the face of a loving Father.

    "And the face which the Infinite turns toward all universe personalities is the face of a Father, the Universal Father of love." (p. 1153)

BIBLE TEXTS

"He who does not love does not know God; for God is love." **I John 4:8**

"See what love the Father has given us, that we should be called the children of God." **I John 3:1**

"But the steadfast love of the Lord is from everlasting to everlasting upon those who fear him, and his righteousness to children's children." **Ps. 103:17**

"For the Father himself loves you." **John 16:27**

E. The Goodness of God — Holiness

1. **PROPOSITION.** God is final goodness plus a free will of creative infinity.

    "God is the being of absolute self-determination; there are no limits to his universe reactions save those which are self-imposed, and his freewill acts are conditioned only by those divine qualities and perfect attributes which inherently characterize his eternal nature. Therefore is God related to the universe as the being of final goodness plus a free will of creative infinity." (p. 58)

2. **PROPOSITION.** In bestowing himself upon the universes, God reserves only that which is required to insure the bestowal.

    "The Universal Father has poured out himself, as it were, to make all creation rich in personality possession and potential spiritual attainment. God has given us himself that we may be like him, and he has reserved for himself of power and glory only that which is necessary for the maintenance of those things for the love of which he has thus divested himself of all things else." (p. 364)

BIBLE TEXTS

"Do you not know that God's kindness is meant to lead you to repentance?" **Rom. 2:4**

"Our God is a God of salvation." **Ps. 68:20**

"The Lord is gracious and merciful." **Ps. 111:4**

"Taste and see that the Lord is good." **Ps. 34:8**

"But as he who called you is holy, be holy yourselves in all your conduct." **I Pet. 1:15**

6. THE ATTRIBUTES OF GOD

A. *God's Omnipresence — Everywhereness*

1. **PROPOSITION.** Omnipresence is a part of God's infinite nature.
   "The omnipresence of God is in reality a part of his infinite nature; space constitutes no barrier to Deity. God is, in perfection and without limitation, discernibly present only on Paradise and in the central universe. (p. 45)

2. **PROPOSITION.** The Universal Father is everywhere present.
   "The ability of the Universal Father to be everywhere present, and at the same time, constitutes his omnipresence. God alone can be in two places, in numberless places, at the same time. God is simultaneously present 'in heaven above and on the earth beneath'; as the Psalmist exclaimed: 'Whither shall I go from your spirit? or whither shall I flee from your presence?'" (p. 44)

3. **PROPOSITION.** The Universal Controller is present in the gravity circuits of the universes.
   "The Universal Controller is potentially present in the gravity circuits of the Isle of Paradise in all parts of the universe at all times and in the same degree, in accordance with the mass, in response to the physical demands for this presence, and because of the inherent nature of all creation which causes all things to adhere and consist in him." (p. 45)

4. **PROPOSITION.** The everywhere spirit presence of the Father is coordinated with the spirit presence of the Son.
   "The everywhere-present spirit of the Universal Father is coordinated with the function of the universal spirit presence of the Eternal Son and the everlasting divine potential of the Deity Absolute." (p. 46)

PART I — THE DOCTRINE OF GOD

BIBLE TEXTS

"Whither shall I go from thy spirit? or whither shall I flee from thy presence?" **Ps. 139:7**

B. *God's Omnipotence — Infinite Power*

1. **PROPOSITION.** God is omnipotent.
   "Of all the divine attributes, his omnipotence, especially as it prevails in the material universe, is the best understood. Viewed as an unspiritual phenomenon. God is energy." (p. 47)
2. **PROPOSITION.** God upholds the worlds in space.
   "He upholds the worlds in space and swings the universes around the endless circle of the eternal circuit." (p. 46)
3. **PROPOSITION.** The omnipotent Father dominates the absolute levels of material, mindal, and spiritual energies.
   "The omnipotence of the Father pertains to the everywhere dominance of the absolute level, whereon the three energies, material, mindal, and spiritual, are indistinguishable in close proximity to him — the Source of all things." (p. 47)
4. **PROPOSITION.** The divine omnipotence is only limited by:
   a. The Love of God
   b. The Will of God
   c. The Law of God
   "The divine omnipotence is perfectly co-ordinated with the other attributes of the personality of God. The power of God is, ordinarily, only limited in its universe spiritual manifestation by three conditions or situations:
   "1. By the nature of God, especially by his infinite love, by truth, beauty, and goodness.
   "2. By the will of God, by his mercy ministry and fatherly relationship with the personalities of the universe.
   "3. By the law of God, by the righteousness and justice of the eternal Paradise Trinity." (p. 48)
5. **PROPOSITION.** God's power and presence are only limited by the will of God.
   "God is unlimited in power, divine in nature, final in will, infinite in attributes, eternal in wisdom, and absolute in reality. But all these characteristics of the Universal Father are unified in Deity and universally expressed in the Paradise Trinity and in the divine Sons of the Trinity. Otherwise, outside of Paradise and the central universe of Havona, everything pertaining to God is limited by the evolutionary presence of the Supreme,

conditioned by the eventuating presence of the Ultimate, and co-ordinated by the three existential Absolutes — Deity, Universal, and Unqualified. And God's presence is thus limited because such is the will of God." (p. 48)

6. **PROPOSITION.** The universal lines of gravity converge in the Paradise presence of God.
"The Father is always to be found at this central location. Did he move, universal pandemonium would be precipitated, for there converge in him at this residential center the universal lines of gravity from the ends of creation." (p. 119)

BIBLE TEXTS

"But with God all things are possible." **Matt. 19:26**

"And he does according to his will in the host of heaven and among the inhabitants of the earth." **Dan. 4:35**

"I know that thou canst do all things, and that no purpose of thine can be thwarted." **Job 42:2**

C. *God's Omniscience — Universal Knowledge*

1. **PROPOSITION.** God knows all things.
"'God knows all things.' The divine mind is conscious of, and conversant with, the thought of all creation. His knowledge of events is universal and perfect. The divine entities going out from him are a part of him; he who 'balances the clouds' is also 'perfect in knowledge.' 'The eyes of the Lord are in every place.'" (p. 48)

2. **PROPOSITION.** God sees the end from the beginning — his plan embraces all creation.
"The Universal Father sees the end from the beginning, and his divine plan and eternal purpose actually embrace and comprehend all the experiments and all the adventures of all his subordinates in every world, system, and constellation in every universe of his vast domains." (p. 34)

3. **PROPOSITION.** God is free from conflicting attitudes — antagonisms. His free will is the satisfaction of the eternal nature.
"The heavenly Father is never torn by conflicting attitudes towards his universe children; God is never a victim of attitudinal antagonisms. God's all-knowingness unfailingly directs his free will in the choosing of that universe conduct which perfectly, simultaneously, and equally satisfies the demands of all his divine attributes and the infinite qualities of his eternal nature." (p. 38)

PART I — THE DOCTRINE OF GOD

4. **PROPOSITION.** Only God knows the number of stars. And he knows our ups and downs.

   "The Universal Father is the only personality in all the universe who does actually know the number of the stars and planets of space. All the worlds of every universe are constantly within the consciousness of God. He also says: 'I have surely seen the affliction of my people, I have heard their cry, and I know their sorrows.'" (p. 49)

5. **PROPOSITION.** God's foreknowledge does not in any way abrogate the freedom of his children.

   "We are not wholly certain as to whether or not God chooses to foreknow events of sin. But even if God should foreknow the freewill acts of his children, such foreknowledge does not in the least abrogate their freedom. One thing is certain; God is never subjected to surprise." (p. 49)

6. **PROPOSITION.** Omniscience does not imply the knowing of the unknowable.

   "Omnipotence does not imply the power to do the nondoable, the ungodlike act. Neither does omniscience imply the knowing of the unknowable. But such statements can hardly be made comprehensible to the finite mind. The creature can hardly understand the range and limitations of the will of the Creator." (p. 49)

BIBLE TEXTS

"For God is greater than our hearts, and he knows everything." **I John 3:20**

"And before him no creature is hidden, but all are open and laid bare to the eyes of him with whom we have to do." **Heb. 4:13**

"The wondrous works of him who is perfect in knowledge." **Job 37:16**

"The Lord looks down from heaven, he sees all the sons of men." **Ps. 33:13**

"He determines the number of the stars, he gives to all of them their names." **Ps. 147:4**

"The eyes of the Lord are in every place." **Prov. 15:3**

"For your Father knows that you need before you ask him." **Matt. 6:8**

D. The Primacy of God

1. **PROPOSITION.** God is the universal unity of unqualified reality.

   "The Universal Father is the explanation of universal unity as it must be supremely, even ultimately, realized in the postultimate unity of absolute values and meanings — unqualified Reality." (p. 645)

2. **PROPOSITION.** The Father's wisdom and power are adequate for all universe exigencies.

   "The Universal Father is not a transient force, a shifting power, or a fluctuating energy. The power and wisdom of the Father are wholly adequate to cope with any and all universe exigencies." (p. 47)

3. **PROPOSITION.** God is still primal. His hand is ever on the mighty lever of universe circumstances.

   "With divine selflessness, consummate generosity, the Universal Father relinquishes authority and delegates power, but he is still primal; his hand is on the mighty lever of the circumstances of the universal realms; he has reserved all final decisions and unerringly wields the all-powerful veto scepter of his eternal purpose with unchallengeable authority over the welfare and destiny of the outstretched, whirling, and ever-circling creation." (p. 52)

4. **PROPOSITION.** God's upholding reach extends around the circle of eternity.

   "At this very moment, as during the remote ages of the past and in the eternal future, God continues to uphold. The divine reach extends around the circle of eternity. The universe is not wound up like a clock to run just so long and then cease to function; all things are constantly being renewed." (p. 55)

5. **PROPOSITION.** In time and space God is revealed as pure energy and pure spirit.

   "As the universal mind gravity is centered in the Paradise personal presence of the Infinite Spirit, so does the universal spirit gravity center in the Paradise personal presence of the Eternal Son. The Universal Father is one, but to time-space he is revealed in the dual phenomena of pure energy and pure spirit." (p. 639)

6. **PROPOSITION.** Only on absolute levels of infinity is there oneness of mind, matter, and spirit.

   "Only the levels of infinity are absolute, and only on such levels is there finality of oneness between matter, mind, and spirit." (p. 25)

BIBLETEXTS

"The earth is the Lord's and the fullness thereof." **Ps. 24:1**.

"He is before al things, and in him all things hold together." **Col. 1:17**.

7. GOD'S RELATION TO THE UNIVERSE

A. God and Nature

1. **Proposition.** Only in a limited sense is nature the habit of God—nature is modified by finite evolution.

   "Nature is in a limited sense the physical habit of God. The conduct, or action, of God is qualified and provisionally modified by the experimental plans and the evolutionary patterns of a local universe, a constellation, a system, or a planet."(p. 56)

2. **Proposition.** Nature is a combination of Paradise perfection and evolutionary imperfection.

   "Nature is a time-space resultant of two cosmic factors: first, the immutability, perfection, and rectitude of Paradise Deity, and second, the experimental plans, executive blunders, insurrectionary errors, incompleteness of development, and imperfection of wisdom of the extra-Paradise creatures, from the highest to the lowest. Nature therefore carries a uniform, unchanging, majestic, and marvelous thread of perfection from the circle of eternity; but in each universe, on each planet, and in each individual life, this nature is modified, qualified, and perchance marred by the acts, the mistakes, and the disloyalties of the creatures of the evolutionary systems and universes; and therefore must nature ever be of a changing mood, whimsical withal, though stable underneath, and varied in accordance with the operating procedures of a local universe." (p. 56)

3. **Proposition.** Nature is marred by misthinking and scarred by rebellion. Nature is not God.

   "And nature is marred, her beautiful face is scarred, her features are seared, by the rebellion, the misconduct, the misthinking of the myriads of creatures who are a part of nature, but who have contributed to her disfigurement in time. No, nature is not God. Nature is not an object of worship." (p. 57)

BIBLE TEXTS

"Forever, O Lord, thy word is firmly fixed in the heavens."**Ps. 119:89**

"When thou sendest forth thy spirit, they are created, and thou renewest the face of the ground." **Ps. 104:30**

"He reflects the glory of God and bears the very stamp of his nature, upholding the universe by his word of power." **Heb. 1:3**

B. *God's Faithfulness — Changelessness*

1. **PROPOSITION.** God is stationary, self-contained, and changeless.
   "God is the only stationary, self-contained, and changeless being in the whole universe of universes, having no outside, no beyond, no past, and no future. God is purposive energy (creative spirit) and absolute will, and these are self-existent and universal." (p. 58)

2. **PROPOSITION.** The laws of an unchanging God stabilize the everywhere changing universe.
   "God is the one and only self-caused fact in the universe. He is the secret of the order, plan, and purpose of the whole creation of things and beings. The everywhere-changing universe is regulated and stabilized by absolutely unchanging laws, the habits of an unchanging God. The fact of God, the divine law, is changeless; the truth of God, his relation to the universe, is a relative revelation which is ever adaptable to the constantly evolving universe." (p. 1126)

3. **PROPOSITION.** God and the universe are not identical — one is cause, the other effect.
   "The universe and God are not identical; one is cause, the other effect. The cause is absolute, infinite, eternal, and changeless; the effect, time-space and transcendental but ever changing, always growing." (p. 1126)

4. **PROPOSITION.** God's perfection is complete, his counsel inimitable, his acts infallible.
   "There is finality of completeness and perfection of repleteness in the mandates of the Father. 'Whatsoever God does, it shall be forever; nothing can be added to it nor anything taken from it.' The Universal Father does not repent of his original purposes of wisdom and perfection. His plans are steadfast, his counsel immutable, while his acts are divine and infallible. 'A thousand years in his sight are but as yesterday when it is past and as a watch in the night.' The perfection of divinity and the magnitude of eternity are forever beyond the full grasp of the circumscribed mind of mortal man." (p. 35)

BIBLE TEXTS

"For I the Lord do not change." **Mal. 3:6**

"Every good endowment and every perfect gift is from above, coming down from the Father of Lights with whom there is no variation or shadow due to change." **Jas. 1:17**

PART I — THE DOCTRINE OF GOD

"Therefore let those who suffer according to God's will do right and entrust their souls to a faithful Creator." **I Pet. 4:19**

"A God of faithfulness."**Deut. 32:4**

"For the word of the Lord is upright; and all his work is done in faithfulness." **Ps. 33:4**

"He is faithful and just, and will forgive our sins." **John 1:9**

"God is faithful." **I Cor. 1:9**

"If we confess our sins, he is faithful and just, and will forgive our sins." **I John 1:9**

"Great is thy faithfulness." **Lam. 3:21**

"All his work is done in faithfulness." **Ps. 33:4**

"Thy faithfulness endures to all generations." **Ps. 119:90**

C. Delegation of Power

1. **PROPOSITION.** In divesting himself of absoluteness, God retained absolute volition and fatherhood.
   "We observe that the Father has divested himself of all direct manifestations of absoluteness except absolute fatherhood and absolute volition. We do not know whether volition is an inalienable attribute of the Father; we can only observe that he did *not* divest himself of volition. Such infinity of will must have been eternally inherent in the First Source and Center." (p. 111)

2. **PROPOSITION.** All of God's delegations of power and authority are self-imposed.
   "All these relinquishments and delegations of jurisdiction by the Universal Father are wholly voluntary and self-imposed. The all-powerful Father purposefully assumes these limitations of universe authority." (p. 112)

3. **PROPOSITION.** The Father rules through his sons — and on down through the subordinates of these sons.
   "The Father rules through his Sons; on down through the universe organization there is an unbroken chain of rulers ending with the Planetary Princes, who direct the destinies of the evolutionary spheres of the Father's vast domains. It is no mere poetic expression that exclaims: 'The earth is the Lord's and the fullness thereof.' 'He removes kings and sets up kings.' 'The Most Highs rule in the kingdoms of men.'" (p. 51)

4. **Proposition.** God is a silent partner in Deity only in that he never does that which others can do.

   "Do not entertain the idea that, since the Universal Father has delegated so much of himself and his power to others, he is a silent or inactive member of the Deity partnership. Aside from personality domains and Adjuster bestowal, he is apparently the least active of the Paradise Deities in that he allows his Deity co-ordinates, his Sons, and numerous created intelligences to perform so much in the carrying out of his eternal purpose. He is the silent member of the creative trio only in that he never does aught which any of his co-ordinate or subordinate associates can do." (p. 362)

D. *God's Eternal Purpose*

   1. **Proposition.** God is executing an eternal purpose throughout the universe of universes.

      "The Universal Father has an eternal purpose pertaining to the material, intellectual, and spiritual phenomena of the universe of universes, which he is executing throughout all time." (p. 54)
      (See Eph. 3:11)

E. *Erroneous Ideas of God*

   1. **Proposition.** Being created in the "image of God" refers to the indwelling Mystery Monitors.

      "Even though you are 'the offspring of God,' you ought not to think that the Father is like yourselves in form and physique because you are said to be created 'in his image' — indwelt by Mystery Monitors dispatched from the central abode of his eternal presence." (p. 25)

   2. **Proposition.** God is not jealous of his creatures — he might be jealous *for* them.

      "All too long has man thought of God as one like himself. God is not, never was, and never will be jealous of man or any other being in the universe of universes. Knowing that the Creator Son intended man to be the masterpiece of the planetary creation, to be the ruler of all the earth, the sight of his being dominated by his own baser passions, the spectacle of his bowing down before idols of wood, stone, gold, and selfish ambition — these sordid scenes stir God and his Sons to be jealous *for* man, but never of him." (p. 57)

3. **Proposition.** God makes no mistakes and harbors no regrets. He does grieve over the spiritual poverty of his children.
"But though the Father neither makes mistakes, harbors regrets, nor experiences sorrows, he is a being with a father's affection, and his heart is undoubtedly grieved when his children fail to attain the spiritual levels they are capable of reaching with the assistance which has been so freely provided by the spiritual-attainment plans and the mortal-ascension policies of the universes." (p. 58)

4. **Proposition.** God repents of nothing — his wisdom and insight are unqualifiedly perfect.
"God repents of nothing he has ever done, now does, or ever will do. He is all-wise as well as all-powerful. Man's wisdom grows out of the trials and errors of human experience; God's wisdom consists in the unqualified perfection of his infinite universe insight, and this divine foreknowledge effectively directs the creative free will." (p. 58)

5. **Proposition.** God is incapable of wrath and anger — such reactions are foreign to his gracious nature.
"The eternal God is incapable of wrath and anger in the sense of these human emotions and as man understands such reactions. These sentiments are mean and despicable; they are hardly worthy of being called human, much less divine; and such attitudes are utterly foreign to the perfect nature and gracious character of the Universal Father." (p. 57)

8. GOD'S RELATION TO THE INDIVIDUAL

A. *The Approach to God*

1. **Proposition.** God is not in hiding — he craves to reveal himself. It is our finitude that separates us from the Father.
"Our Father is not in hiding; he is not in arbitrary seclusion. He has mobilized the resources of divine wisdom in a never-ending effort to reveal himself to the children of his universal domains. There is an infinite grandeur and an inexpressible generosity connected with the majesty of his love which causes him to yearn for the association of every created being who can comprehend, love, or approach him; and it is, therefore, the limitations inherent in you, inseparable from your finite personality and material existence, that determine the time and place and circumstances in which you may achieve the goal of the journey of mortal ascension and stand in the presence of the Father at the center of all things." (p. 62)

THE THEOLOGY OF THE URANTIA BOOK

    2. **PROPOSITION.** God is approachable — the Father is attainable. Divine love opens the way for our Paradise ascent.

    "To each of you and to all of us, God is approachable, the Father is attainable, the way is open; the forces of divine love and the ways and means of divine administration are all interlocked in an effort to facilitate the advancement of every worthy intelligence of every universe to the Paradise presence of the Universal Father." (p. 63)

B.   The Presence of God

    1. **PROPOSITION.** The magnitude and grandeur of God should not overawe us — the Father dwells with us.

    "Do not allow the magnitude of the infinity, the immensity of the eternity, and the grandeur and glory of the matchless character of God to overawe, stagger, or discourage you; for the Father is not very far from any one of you; he dwells within you, and in him do we all literally move, actually live, and veritably have our being." (p. 139)

    2. **PROPOSITION.** The positive proof of God is found in the personal religious experience of God-knowing mortals.

    "Those who know God have experienced the fact of his presence; such God-knowing mortals hold in their personal experience the only positive proof of the existence of the living God which one human being can offer to another. The existence of God is utterly beyond all possibility of demonstration except for the contact between the Godconsciousness of the human mind and the God-presence of the Thought Adjuster that indwells the mortal intellect and is bestowed upon man as the free gift of the Universal Father." (p. 24)

    3. **PROPOSITION.** Wrongdoing does not alienate God, but our choice can influence the Divine Presence.

    "The fluctuations of the Father's presence are not due to the changeableness of God. The Father does not retire in seclusion because he has been slighted; his affections are not alienated because of the creature's wrongdoing. Rather, having been endowed with the power of choice (concerning Himself), his children, in the exercise of that choice, directly determine the degree and limitations of the Father's divine influence in their own hearts and souls." (p. 46)

    4. **PROPOSITION.** Though God functions through myriads of divine associates — even though he abides on Paradise, the divine presence also dwells in the minds of men.

    "Even though the Paradise Father functions through his divine creators and his creature children, he also enjoys the most intimate inner contact with you, so sublime, so highly personal, that it is even beyond my comprehension — that mysterious communion of the Father fragment with the human soul and with the mortal mind of its actual indwelling. Knowing what you do of these gifts of God, you therefore know that the Father is in intimate touch, not only with his divine associates, but also with his evolutionary mortal children of time. The Father indeed abides on Paradise, but his divine presence also dwells in the minds of men." (p. 139)

BIBLE TEXTS

"The Eternal God is your dwelling place, and underneath are the everlasting arms." **Deut. 33:27**

C. God in Religion

   1. **PROPOSITION.** God's reality is demonstrated by the Mystery Monitor whose presence is disclosed by:
      a. Intellectual capacity for knowing God.
      b. Spiritual urge to find God.
      c. Craving to be like God.

      "The actuality of the existence of God is demonstrated in human experience by the indwelling of the divine presence, the spirit Monitor sent from Paradise to live in the mortal mind of man and there to assist in evolving the immortal soul of eternal survival. The presence of this divine Adjuster in the human mind is disclosed by three experiential phenomena:

      "1. The intellectual capacity for knowing God — God-consciousness.

      "2. The spiritual urge to find God — God-seeking.

      "3. The personality craving to be like God — the wholehearted desire to do the Father's will." (p. 24)

   2. **PROPOSITION.** Neither science nor logic can prove God's existence; only human experience can validate his reality.

      "The existence of God can never be proved by scientific experiment or by the pure reason of logical deduction. God can be realized only in the realms of human experience; nevertheless, the true concept of the reality of God is reasonable to logic, plausible to philosophy, essential to religion, and indispensable to any hope of personality survival." (p. 24)

   3. **PROPOSITION.** God is cognizant of the progressive struggles of every being in the evolutionary cosmos.

      "The Universal Father realizes in the fullness of the divine consciousness all the individual experience of the progressive struggles of the expanding minds and the ascending spirits of every entity, being, and personality of the whole evolutionary creation of time and space. And all this is literally true, for 'in Him we all live and move and have our being.'" (p. 29)

4. **Proposition.** What unintended homage the mechanist pays God when he conceives universe laws to be self-acting and self-explanatory.

   "The mechanistic philosopher professes to reject the idea of a universal and sovereign will, the very sovereign will whose activity in the elaboration of universe laws he so deeply reveres. What unintended homage the mechanist pays the law-Creator when he conceives such laws to be self-acting and self-explanatory!" (p. 53)

5. **Proposition.** While it is a blunder to humanize God, that is not so stupid as to mechanize him.

   "It is a great blunder to humanize God, except in the concept of the indwelling Thought Adjuster, but even that is not so stupid as completely to *mechanize* the idea of the First Great Source and Center." (p. 53)

6. **Proposition.** Does God suffer? Some think he does, but we do not understand how; perhaps through the Thought Adjuster.

   "Does the Paradise Father suffer? I do not know. The Creator Sons most certainly can and sometimes do, even as do mortals. The Eternal Son and the Infinite Spirit suffer in a modified sense. I think the Universal Father does, but I cannot understand *how*; perhaps through the personality circuit or through the individuality of the Thought Adjusters and other bestowals of his eternal nature. He has said of the mortal races, 'In all your afflictions I am afflicted.' He unquestionably experiences a fatherly and sympathetic understanding, he may truly suffer, but I do not comprehend the nature thereof." (p. 53)

7. **Proposition.** In addition to infinity of attributes, God:
   Exercises sovereign will.
   Is self-conscious of divinity.
   Pursues an eternal purpose.
   Manifests a Father's love.

   "The infinite and eternal Ruler of the universe of universes is power, form, energy, process, pattern, principle, presence, and idealized reality. But he is more; he is personal; he exercises a sovereign will, experiences self-consciousness of divinity, executes the mandates of a creative mind, pursues the satisfaction of the realization of an eternal purpose, and manifests a Father's love and affection for his universe children. And all these more personal traits of the Father can be better understood by observing them as they were revealed in the bestowal life of Michael, your Creator Son, while he was incarnated on Urantia." (p. 53)

8. **Proposition.** The Urantia benediction.
"God the Father loves men; God the Son serves men; God the Spirit inspires the children of the universe to the ever-ascending adventure of finding God the Father by the ways ordained by God the Sons through the ministry of the grace of God the Spirit." (p. 53)

D. *The God of Personality*

1. **Proposition.** God is the bestower, conservator, and destiny of personality.
"God the Father is the bestower and the conservator of every personality. And the Paradise Father is likewise the destiny of all those finite personalities who wholeheartedly choose to do the divine will, those who love God and long to be like him." (p. 70)

2. **Proposition.** God bestows personality, endowing it with creative consciousness and free will.
"The bestowal of personality is the exclusive function of the Universal Father, the personalization of the living energy systems which he endows with the attributes of relative creative consciousness and the freewill control thereof. There is no personality apart from God the Father, and no personality exists except for God the Father." (p. 70)

3. **Proposition.** Personality is an unsolved mystery.
"Personality is one of the unsolved mysteries of the universes. We are able to form adequate concepts of the factors entering into the make-up of various orders and levels of personality, but we do not fully comprehend the real nature of the personality itself." (p. 70)

4. **Proposition.** The personality circuit of all creation centers in the person of the Universal Father.
"The personality circuit of the universe of universes is centered in the person of the Universal Father, and the Paradise Father is personally conscious of, and in personal touch with, all personalities of all levels of self-conscious existence. And this personality consciousness of all creation exists independently of the mission of the Thought Adjusters." (p. 71)

5. **Proposition.** God bestows himself upon his spirit children and makes personal contact with mortals by means of his prepersonal fragments.
"God has distributed the infinity of his eternal nature throughout the existential realities of his six absolute co-ordinates, but he may, at any time, make direct personal contact with any part or phase or kind of creation through the agency of his prepersonal fragments. And the eternal God has also reserved to himself the prerogative of bestowing personality upon the divine Creators and the living creatures of the universe of universes, while he has further reserved the prerogative of maintaining direct and parental contact with all these personal beings through the personality circuit." (p. 62)
6. **Proposition.** When all is said and done — God is our Father.
"And this represents my efforts to present the relation of the living God to the children of time. And when all is said and done, I can do nothing more helpful than to reiterate that God is your universe Father, and that you are all his planetary children." (p. 72)

IV. GOD THE SON

1. Introduction
2. Identity of the Son
3. Nature of the Eternal Son
4. Minister of the Father's Love
5. Attributes of the Eternal Son
6. Limitations of the Eternal Son
7. Personality of the Eternal Son
8. Spirit Gravity
9. The Son's Relation to the Individual
10. The Divine Perfection Plan
11. The Spirit of Bestowal
12. The Supreme Revelation of the Father

IV. GOD THE SON

1. INTRODUCTION

1. **PROPOSITION.** The Eternal Son experiences sonship with the Father and co-paternity to the Infinite Spirit.

    "The Eternal Son alone experiences the fullness of divine personality relationship, consciousness of both sonship with the Father and paternity to the Spirit and of divine equality with both Father-ancestor and Spirit-associate." (p. 110)

2. **PROPOSITION.** The Son gives origin to a vast spirit host — not personalities.

    "The Son gives origin to a vast spirit host, but such derivations are not personalities. When the Son creates personality, he does so in conjunction with the Father or with the Conjoint Creator, who may act for the Father in such relationships." (p. 77)

3. **PROPOSITION.** The Son is the upholder of spirit realities — the counterpart of Paradise.

    "As the upholder of spirit realities, the Second Source and Center is the eternal counterpoise of the Isle of Paradise, which so magnificently upholds all things material." (p. 81)

2. IDENTITY OF THE SON

1. **PROPOSITION.** The Eternal Son is the perfect and final expression of the Father's first absolute personal concept.

    "The Eternal Son is the perfect and final expression of the 'first' personal and absolute concept of the Universal Father. Accordingly, whenever and however the Father personally and absolutely expresses himself, he does so through his Eternal Son, who ever has been, now is, and ever will be, the living and divine Word." (p. 73)

2. **PROPOSITION.** The Eternal Son is the second person of Deity, the associate creator, and the Second Source and Center.

    "The Eternal Son is the original and only-begotten Son of God. He is God the Son, the Second Person of Deity and the associate creator of all things. As the Father is the First Great Source and Center, so the Eternal Son is the Second Great Source and Center." (p. 73)

3. **PROPOSITION.** The Eternal and Original Son has been confused with your Creator Son — Michael of Nebadon.

    "On your world, but not in your system of inhabited spheres, this Original Son has been confused with a co-ordinate Creator

Son, Michael of Nebadon, who bestowed himself upon the mortal races of Urantia." (p. 74)

3. NATURE OF THE ETERNAL SON

1. **PROPOSITION.** The Eternal Son is the Eternal Word. He is God the Father personally manifest to the universes.

    "The Eternal Son is the eternal Word of God. He is wholly like the Father; in fact, the Eternal Son is God the Father personally manifest to the universe of universes. And thus it was and is and forever will be true of the Eternal Son and of all the co-ordinate Creator Sons: 'He who has seen the Son has seen the Father.'" (p. 74)

2. **PROPOSITION.** The Son is the personal and spiritual nature of God the Father revealed to the universes.

    "The Son is the spiritual and personal nature of God made manifest to the universes — the sum and substance of the First Source and Center, divested of all that which is nonpersonal, extradivine, nonspiritual, and pure potential." (p. 79)

3. **PROPOSITION.** The spirit and mind of the Eternal Son are beyond the comprehension of mortal man.

    "The Eternal Son is spirit and has mind, but not a mind or a spirit which mortal mind can comprehend. Mortal man perceives mind on the finite, cosmic, material, and personal levels." (p. 78)

4. **PROPOSITION.** The Eternal Son dominates all actual spirit values.

    "Viewed from the personality standpoint and by persons, the Eternal Son and the Deity Absolute appear to be related in the following way: The Eternal Son dominates the realm of actual spiritual values, whereas the Deity Absolute seems to pervade the vast domain of potential spirit values." (p. 83)

4. MINISTER OF THE FATHER'S LOVE

1. **PROPOSITION.** The Eternal Son is the mercy minister; all his mandates are keyed in tones of mercy.

    "The Eternal Son is the great mercy minister to all creation. Mercy is the essence of the Son's spiritual character. The mandates of the Eternal Son, as they go forth over the spirit circuits of the Second Source and Center, are keyed in tones of mercy." (p. 75)

2. Proposition. With mercy, the Son overshadows the justice of the Trinity. As God is love, the Son is mercy.

> "The Son shares the justice and righteousness of the Trinity but overshadows these divinity traits by the infinite personalization of the Father's love and mercy; the Son is the revelation of divine love to the universes. As God is love, so the Son is mercy." (p. 75)

5. ATTRIBUTES OF THE ETERNAL SON

1. Proposition. The Eternal Son is the fullness of God's absoluteness in spirit and personality.

> "The Eternal Son possesses all the Father's character of divinity and attributes of spirituality. The Son is the fullness of God's absoluteness in personality and spirit, and these qualities the Son reveals in his personal management of the spiritual government of the universe of universes." (p. 75)

2. Proposition. The Father and Son are alike in divine goodness. The Son looks upon all creatures both as father and as brother.

> "In divine goodness I discern no difference between the Father and the Son. The Father loves his universe children as a father; the Eternal Son looks upon all creatures both as father and as brother." (p. 75)

3. Proposition. The omnipresent spirit of the Son is with you — but not a part of you.

> "Spiritually the Eternal Son is omnipresent. The spirit of the Eternal Son is most certainly with you and around you, but not within you and a part of you like the Mystery Monitor." (p. 76)

4. Proposition. The Son is universally and spiritually self-conscious. Like the Father, he knows all things.

> "The Original Son is universally and spiritually self-conscious. In wisdom the Son is the full equal of the Father. In the realms of knowledge, omniscience, we cannot distinguish between the First and Second Sources; like the Father, the Son knows all; he is never surprised by any universe event; he comprehends the end from the beginning." (p. 76)

5. Proposition. The Son does not function in the physical domains. He functions on mind levels through the Conjoint Actor.

> "The Eternal Son does not personally function in the physical domains, nor does he function, except through the Conjoint Actor, in the levels of mind ministry to creature beings. But these qualifications do not in any manner otherwise limit the

Eternal Son in the full and free exercise of all the divine attributes of *spiritual* omniscience, omnipresence, and omnipotence." (p. 77)

6. LIMITATIONS OF THE ETERNAL SON

1. **PROPOSITION.** The Eternal Son is omnipotent only in the spiritual realm.

    "The Son is omnipotent only in the spiritual realm. In the eternal economy of universe administration, wasteful and needless repetition of function is never encountered; the Deities are not given to useless duplication of universe ministry." (p. 76)

2. **PROPOSITION.** The Eternal Son is an infinite and exclusively personal being who cannot fragmentize his nature.

    "The Eternal Son, as an infinite and exclusively personal being, cannot fragmentize his nature, cannot distribute and bestow individualized portions of his selfhood upon other entities or persons as do the Universal Father and the Infinite Spirit." (p. 78)

3. **PROPOSITION.** The Eternal Son transmits creatorship powers only to the first and direct personalization.

    "The Eternal Son transmits creatorship powers only to the first or direct personalization. Therefore, when the Father and the Son unite to personalize a Creator Son, they achieve their purpose; but the Creator Son thus brought into existence is never able to transmit or delegate the prerogatives of creatorship to the various orders of Sons which he may subsequently create, notwithstanding that, in the highest local universe Sons, there does appear a very limited reflection of the creative attributes of a Creator Son." (p. 77)

4. **PROPOSITION.** The Son maintains a superpersonal representation in the superuniverses. They are finite — neither absonite nor absolute.

    "In the superuniverses the Son is not personally present or resident; in these creations he maintains only a superpersonal representation. These spirit manifestations of the Son are not personal; they are not in the personality circuit of the Universal Father. We know of no better term to use than to designate them *superpersonalities*; and they are finite beings; they are neither absonite nor absolute." (p. 83)

7. PERSONALITY OF THE ETERNAL SON

1. PROPOSITION. The Eternal Son is absolute personality — that personality from which the Father escaped by trinitization.

   "The Eternal Son is that infinite personality from whose unqualified personality fetters the Universal Father escaped by the technique of trinitization, and by virtue of which he has ever since continued to bestow himself in endless profusion upon his ever-expanding universe of Creators and creatures. The Son is *absolute personality*." (p. 79)

2. PROPOSITION. Concerning nature and attributes, the Son is the equal, complement, and counterpart of the Father.

   "Concerning identity, nature, and other attributes of personality, the Eternal Son is the full equal, the perfect complement, and the eternal counterpart of the Universal Father. In the same sense that God is the Universal Father, the Son is the Universal Mother. And all of us, high and low, constitute their universal family." (p. 79)

8. SPIRIT GRAVITY

1. PROPOSITION. Spirit gravity is just as real as physical gravity.

   "The bestowal of spirit and the spiritualization of personalities, the domain of spiritual gravity, is the realm of the Eternal Son. And this spirit gravity of the Son, ever drawing all spiritual realities to himself, is just as real and absolute as is the all-powerful material grasp of the Isle of Paradise." (p. 139)

2. PROPOSITION. The Son motivates the spirit level of cosmic reality — all actualized spiritual values.

   "The Eternal Son motivates the spirit level of cosmic reality; the spiritual power of the Son is absolute in relation to all universe actualities. He exercises perfect control over the interassociation of all undifferentiated spirit energy and over all actualized spirit reality through his absolute grasp of spirit gravity." (p. 76)

3. PROPOSITION. The spirit gravity circuit centers in the Eternal Son. All true spirit values are held in his grasp.

   "The pure and universal spirit gravity of all creation, this exclusively spiritual circuit, leads directly back to the person of the Second Source and Center on Paradise. He presides over the control and operation of that ever-present and unerring spiritual grasp of all true spirit values. Thus does the Eternal Son exercise absolute spiritual sovereignty." (p. 81)

4. **PROPOSITION.** Spirit gravity acts independently of time and space.

    "This gravity control of spiritual things operates independently of time and space; therefore is spirit energy undiminished in transmission. Spirit gravity never suffers time delays, nor does it undergo space diminution. It does not decrease in accordance with the square of the distance of its transmission; the circuits of pure spirit power are not retarded by the mass of the material creation. And this transcendence of time and space by pure spirit energies is inherent in the absoluteness of the Son; it is not due to the interposition of the antigravity forces of the Third Source and Center." (p. 82)

5. **PROPOSITION.** Every new spirit reality necessitates the instantaneous readjustment of universal spirit gravity.

    "Every time a spiritual reality actualizes in the universes, this change necessitates the immediate and instantaneous readjustment of spirit gravity." (p. 82)

6. **PROPOSITION.** This same spirit drawing power is inherent in many Paradise sons.

    "The Son's spiritual drawing power is inherent to a lesser degree in many Paradise orders of sonship. For there do exist within the absolute spirit-gravity circuit those local systems of spiritual attraction that function in the lesser units of creation." (p. 82)

7. **PROPOSITION.** Spirit gravity also operates as between individuals and groups — "kindred spirits."

    "Spirit-gravity pull and response thereto operate not only on the universe as a whole but also even between individuals and groups of individuals. There is a spiritual cohesiveness among the spiritual and spiritized personalities of any world, race, nation, or believing group of individuals. There is a direct attractiveness of a spirit nature between spiritually minded persons of like tastes and longings. The term *kindred spirits* is not wholly a figure of speech." (p. 82)

8. **PROPOSITION.** We measure spirit gravity just as you attempt to compute physical gravity.

    "In accordance with well-known laws, we can and do measure spiritual gravity just as man attempts to compute the workings of finite physical gravity." (p. 82)

9. **Proposition.** In dealing with spirit gravity we often encounter the unpredictable reactions of the Deity Absolute.

> "But alongside this very dependable and predictable function of the spiritual presence of the Eternal Son, there are encountered phenomena which are not so predictable in their reactions. Such phenomena probably indicate the co-ordinate action of the Deity Absolute in the realms of emerging spiritual potentials." (p. 83)

10. **Proposition.** While the Son does not indwell man, he ever fosters our spiritual security.

> "At no stage of the entire mortal ascension does the spirit of the Eternal Son indwell the mind or soul of the pilgrim of time, but his beneficence is ever near and always concerned with the welfare and spiritual security of the advancing children of time." (p. 84)

11. **Proposition.** The spirit gravity circuit transmits our prayers to Deity.

> "The spirit-gravity circuit is the basic channel for transmitting the genuine prayers of the believing human heart from the level of human consciousness to the actual consciousness of Deity." (p. 84)

12. **Proposition.** The discriminative operation of spirit gravity may be compared to the differential neural circuits of the human body.

> "The discriminative operation of the spirit-gravity circuit might possibly be compared to the functions of the neural circuits in the material human body: Sensations travel inward over the neural paths; some are detained and responded to by the lower automatic spinal centers; others pass on to the less automatic but habit-trained centers of the lower brain, while the most important and vital incoming messages flash by these subordinate centers and are immediately registered in the highest levels of human consciousness." (p. 84)

13. **Proposition.** Spirit realities respond to spirit gravity in accordance with their spiritual qualities — values. Spirit gravity deals only with quality.

> "Spirit realities respond to the drawing power of the center of spiritual gravity in accordance with their qualitative value, their actual degree of spirit nature. Spirit substance (quality) is just as responsive to spirit gravity as the organized energy of physical matter (quantity) is responsive to physical gravity." (p. 82)

14. **Proposition.** Spirit gravity is absolute. Rebellion may nullify local circuits — but not spirit gravity.

> "Like the material gravity of Paradise, the spiritual gravity of the Eternal Son is absolute. Sin and rebellion may interfere with the operation of local universe circuits, but nothing can suspend the spirit gravity of the Eternal Son." (p. 82)

15. **Proposition.** The secret of the Paradise ascension is this spiritual gravity pull of the Eternal Son.

> "The spiritual-gravity pull of the Eternal Son constitutes the inherent secret of the Paradise ascension of surviving human souls. All genuine spirit values and all bona fide spiritualized individuals are held within the unfailing grasp of the spiritual gravity of the Eternal Son." (p. 84)

9. THE SON'S RELATION TO THE INDIVIDUAL

1. Proposition. The Eternal Son is incapable of fragmentation. He ministers as a person and as a spiritual influence.

> "The purely personal nature of the Eternal Son is incapable of fragmentation. The Eternal Son ministers as a spiritual influence or as a person, never otherwise." (p. 86)

2. **Proposition.** While the Eternal Son cannot contact man as does the Father, his sons can bestow themselves upon the mortal races.

> "The Eternal Son cannot contact directly with human beings as does the Father through the gift of the prepersonal Thought Adjusters, but the Eternal Son does draw near to created personalities by a series of downstepping gradations of divine sonship until he is enabled to stand in man's presence and, at times, as man himself." (p. 86)

10. THE DIVINE PERFECTION PLAN

1. **Proposition.** The Eternal Son is the divine trustee of the Father's plan of creature ascension to Paradise.

> "The Eternal Son is the personal trustee, the divine custodian, of the Father's universal plan of creature ascension. Having promulgated the universal mandate, 'Be you perfect, even as I am perfect,' the Father intrusted the execution of this tremendous undertaking to the Eternal Son; and the Eternal Son shares the fostering of this supernal enterprise with his divine co-ordinate, the Infinite Spirit." (p. 86)

11. THE SPIRIT OF BESTOWAL

1. **PROPOSITION.** The sons of the Eternal Son can incarnate in the likeness of mortal flesh.

   "To share the experience of created personalities, the Paradise Sons of God must assume the very natures of such creatures and incarnate their divine personalities as the actual creatures themselves. Incarnation, the secret of Sonarington, is the technique of the Son's escape from the otherwise all-encompassing fetters of personality absolutism." (p. 86)

2. **PROPOSITION.** Long ago the Eternal Son bestowed himself upon each of the circuits of Havona.

   "Long, long ago the Eternal Son bestowed himself upon each of the circuits of the central creation for the enlightenment and advancement of all the inhabitants and pilgrims of Havona, including the ascending pilgrims of time. On none of these seven bestowals did he function as either an ascender or a Havoner. He existed as himself." (p. 86)

3. **PROPOSITION.** The original Michael bestowed himself on Havona — sharing the experience of ascending pilgrims.

   "Whatever our difficulty in comprehending the bestowals of the Second Person of Deity, we do comprehend the Havona bestowal of a Son of the Eternal Son, who literally passed through the circuits of the central universe and actually shared those experiences which constitute an ascender's preparation for Deity attainment. This was the original Michael, the first-born Creator Son, and he passed through the life experiences of the ascending pilgrims from circuit to circuit, personally journeying a stage of each circle with them in the days of Grandfanda, the first of all mortals to attain Havona." (p. 87)

4. **PROPOSITION.** The best comprehension of the Eternal Son is gained by meditating on the earth life of Jesus.

   "More of the character and merciful nature of the Eternal Son of mercy you should comprehend as you meditate on the revelation of these divine attributes which was made in loving service by your own Creator Son, onetime Son of Man on earth, now the exalted sovereign of your local universe — the Son of Man and the Son of God." (p. 89)

12. THE SUPREME REVELATION OF THE FATHER

1. **PROPOSITION.** The Eternal Son is a complete and final revelation of the Father — he is one with the Father.

   "The Eternal Son is a complete, exclusive, universal, and final revelation of the spirit and the personality of the Universal Father. All knowledge of, and information concerning, the Father must come from the Eternal Son and his Paradise Sons. The Eternal Son is from eternity and is wholly and without spiritual qualification one with the Father. In divine personality they are co-ordinate; in spiritual nature they are equal; in divinity they are identical." (p. 88)

2. **PROPOSITION.** The Eternal Son and his Sons are making a universal revelation of the Father to men and angels.

   "The primal Son and his Sons are engaged in making a universal revelation of the spiritual and personal nature of the Father to all creation. In the central universe, the superuniverses, the local universes, or on the inhabited planets, it is a Paradise Son who reveals the Universal Father to men and angels. The Eternal Son and his Sons reveal the avenue of creature approach to the Universal Father." (p. 89)

3. **PROPOSITION.** The Eternal Son is the spiritual personalization of the Father's concept of divine reality, unqualified spirit, and absolute personality.

   "The Eternal Son is the spiritual personalization of the Paradise Father's universal and infinite concept of divine reality, unqualified spirit, and absolute personality. And thereby does the Son constitute the divine revelation of the creator identity of the Universal Father." (p. 73)

4. **PROPOSITION.** The Son is the executive of the spiritual aspects of the Father's eternal purpose now unfolding in the evolving universes.

   "The Original Son is ever concerned with the execution of the spiritual aspects of the Father's eternal purpose as it progressively unfolds in the phenomena of the evolving universes with their manifold groups of living beings. We do not fully comprehend this eternal plan, but the Paradise Son undoubtedly does." (p. 81)

V. GOD THE SPIRIT

1. Introduction
2. The God of Action
3. Nature of the Infinite Spirit
4. Relation to the Father and Son
5. The Spirit of Divine Ministry
6. Personality of the Infinite Spirit
7. Attributes of the Infinite Spirit
8. The Universal Manipulator
9. The Ministry of Mind
10. Universe Reflectivity
11. Personalities of the Infinite Spirit

V. GOD THE SPIRIT

1. INTRODUCTION

1. **Proposition.** The conjoint conception of an identical and infinite action by the Father-Son union gave eternity origin to the Infinite Spirit.

   "In the dawn of eternity both the Father and the Son become infinitely cognizant of their mutual interdependence, their eternal and absolute oneness; and therefore do they enter into an infinite and everlasting covenant of divine partnership. This never-ending compact is made for the execution of their united concepts throughout all of the circle of eternity; and ever since this eternity event the Father and the Son continue in this divine union.

   "We are now face to face with the eternity origin of the Infinite Spirit, the Third Person of Deity. The very instant that God the Father and God the Son conjointly conceive an identical and infinite action — the execution of an absolute thought-plan — that very moment, the Infinite Spirit springs full-fledgedly into existence." (p. 90)

2. THE GOD OF ACTION

1. **Proposition.** Personalization of the Infinite Spirit sets the stage for the creative panorama of the eternal ages.

   "In the eternity of the past, upon the personalization of the Infinite Spirit the divine personality cycle becomes perfect and complete. The God of Action is existent, and the vast stage of space is set for the stupendous drama of creation — the universal adventure — the divine panorama of the eternal ages." (p. 90)

2. **Proposition.** The God of Action functions and the dead vaults of space are astir.

   "The God of Action functions and the dead vaults of space are astir. One billion perfect spheres flash into existence. Prior to this hypothetical eternity moment the space-energies inherent in Paradise are existent and potentially operative, but they have no actuality of being; neither can physical gravity be measured except by the reaction of material realities to its incessant pull." (p. 91)

3. **PROPOSITION.** He is the manipulator of energy — action, motion, co-ordination, and stabilization.

> "The Conjoint Creator is not energy nor the source of energy nor the destiny of energy; he is the *manipulator* of energy. The Conjoint Creator is action — motion, change, modification, co-ordination, stabilization, and equilibrium." (p. 101)

4. **PROPOSITION.** As the divine Sons are the "Word of God," the children of the Infinite Spirit are the "Act of God."

> "The divine Sons are indeed the 'Word of God,' but the children of the Spirit are truly the 'Act of God.' God speaks through the Son and, with the Son, acts through the Infinite Spirit..." (p. 111)

3. NATURE OF THE INFINITE SPIRIT

1. **PROPOSITION.** The Conjoint Actor is the execution of the first Father-Son absolute plan for action.

> "...the Conjoint Actor is the perfect execution of the 'first' completed creative concept or plan for combined action by the Father-Son personality partnership of absolute thought-word union." (p. 93)

2. **PROPOSITION.** Of all aspects of the Father's nature, the Conjoint Creator most strikingly reveals his infinity.

> "There is mystery indeed in the person of the Infinite Spirit but not so much as in the Father and the Son. Of all aspects of the Father's nature, the Conjoint Creator most strikingly discloses his infinity. Even if the master universe eventually expands to infinity, the spirit presence, energy control, and mind potential of the Conjoint Actor will be found adequate to meet the demands of such a limitless creation." (p. 92)

3. **PROPOSITION.** The Spirit is ministry — the personification of the Father's love and the Son's mercy.

> "God is love, the Son is mercy, the Spirit is ministry — the ministry of divine love and endless mercy to all intelligent creation. The Spirit is the personification of the Father's love and the Son's mercy; in him are they eternally united for universal service. The Spirit is *love applied* to the creature creation, the combined love of the Father and the Son." (p. 94)

4. **Proposition.** The Conjoint Actor possesses unique prerogatives of synthesis for energies, intellects, and spirits.

> "The Conjoint Actor possesses unique prerogatives of synthesis, infinite capacity to co-ordinate all existing universe energies, all actual universe spirits, and all real universe intellects; the Third Source and Center is the universal unifier of the manifold energies and diverse creations which have appeared in consequence of the divine plan and the eternal purpose of the Universal Father." (p. 98)

5. **Proposition.** The perfect, changeless, and absolute Spirit pervades all space.

> "The Infinite Spirit pervades all space; he indwells the circle of eternity; and the Spirit, like the Father and the Son, is perfect and changeless — absolute." (p. 98)

6. **Proposition.** The Third Person of Deity is:
   a. *Omnipresent spiritual influence*
   b. *Universal Manipulator of energy*
   c. *Conjoint Actor for the Father-Son*
   d. *Absolute Mind*
   e. *God of Action*

> "As the Infinite Spirit, he is an omnipresent spiritual influence. As the Universal Manipulator, he is the ancestor of the power-control creatures and the activator of the cosmic forces of space. As the Conjoint Actor, he is the joint representative and partnership executive of the Father-Son. As the Absolute Mind, he is the source of the endowment of intellect throughout the universes. As the God of Action, he is the apparent ancestor of motion, change, and relationship." (p. 99)

4. RELATION TO THE FATHER AND SON

1. **Proposition.** The Infinite Spirit eternalizes concurrently with the birth of Havona and deitizes by this very act of conjoint creation.

> "The Infinite Spirit eternalizes concurrently with the birth of the Havona worlds, this central universe being created by him and with him and in him in obedience to the combined concepts and united wills of the Father and the Son. The Third Person deitizes by this very act of conjoint creation, and he thus forever becomes the Conjoint Creator." (p. 91)

2. **PROPOSITION.** The Conjoint Creator is from eternity and is without qualification one with the Father and the Son.

   "The Conjoint Creator is from eternity and is wholly and without qualification one with the Universal Father and the Eternal Son. The Infinite Spirit reflects in perfection not only the nature of the Paradise Father but also the nature of the Original Son." (p. 92)

3. **PROPOSITION.** The Infinite Spirit is the effective agent for the execution of the Father-Son plan of perfection attainment for evolutionary creatures.

   "The Infinite Spirit is the effective agent of the all-loving Father and the all-merciful Son for the execution of their conjoint project of drawing to themselves all truth-loving souls on all the worlds of time and space. The very instant the Eternal Son accepted his Father's plan of perfection attainment for the creatures of the universes, the moment the ascension project became a Father-Son plan, that instant the Infinite Spirit became the conjoint administrator of the Father and the Son for the execution of their united and eternal purpose." (p. 93)

4. **PROPOSITION.** The Conjoint Actor is the correlator of all actual reality; repository of the Father's thought and the Son's word.

   "The Conjoint Actor is the correlator of all actual reality; he is the Deity repository of the Father's thought and the Son's word and in action is eternally regardful of the material absoluteness of the central Isle." (p. 99)

5. **PROPOSITION.** The Spirit is absolute in the administration of the mind realms.

   "The Third Person of Deity is the intellectual center and the universal administrator of the mind realms; herein is he absolute — his sovereignty is unqualified." (p. 99)

6. **PROPOSITION.** The Spirit compensates for the incompleteness of experiential Deity — the Supreme and the Ultimate.

   "The Conjoint Actor seems to be motivated by the Father-Son partnership, but all his actions appear to recognize the Father-Paradise relationship. At times and in certain functions he seems to compensate for the incompleteness of the development of the experiential Deities — God the Supreme and God the Ultimate." (p. 99)

7. **Proposition.** The Eternal Son is a spiritualized personalization of the Father; the Infinite Spirit is a personalized spiritualization of the Eternal Son and the Universal Father.

> "The Infinite Spirit is just as much a complement of the Eternal Son as the Son is a complement of the Universal Father. The Eternal Son is a spiritualized personalization of the Father; the Infinite Spirit is a personalized spiritualization of the Eternal Son and the Universal Father." (p. 100)

5. THE SPIRIT OF DIVINE MINISTRY

1. **Proposition.** The Conjoint Creator is the combined portrayal of the Father's unending love and the Son's eternal mercy.

> "The Conjoint Creator is truly and forever the great ministering personality, the universal mercy minister. To comprehend the ministry of the Spirit, ponder the truth that he is the combined portrayal of the Father's unending love and of the Son's eternal mercy." (p. 95)

2. **Proposition.** Superbly endowed with patience and love — he overshadows justice with mercy.

> "…[T]he Infinite Spirit is superbly endowed with those attributes of patience, mercy, and love which are so exquisitely revealed in his spiritual ministry. The Spirit is supremely competent to minister love and to overshadow justice with mercy. God the Spirit possesses all the supernal kindness and merciful affection of the Original and Eternal Son." (p. 100)

3. **Proposition.** On the anvils of justice the hammers of suffering are wielded by the children of mercy.

> "The universe of your origin is being forged out between the anvil of justice and the hammer of suffering; but those who wield the hammer are the children of mercy, the spirit offspring of the Infinite Spirit." (p. 100)

4. **Proposition.** The Spirit ministers the Son's mercy and the Father's love in harmony with the justice of the Paradise Trinity.

> "The Infinite Spirit, the Conjoint Creator, is a universal and divine minister. The Spirit unceasingly ministers the Son's mercy and the Father's love, even in harmony with the stable, unvarying, and righteous justice, of the Paradise Trinity." (p. 98)

5. **Proposition.** On Urantia, the omnipresent Infinite Spirit has been confused with the Holy Spirit of the local universe.

> "In your sacred writings the term *Spirit of God* seems to be used interchangeably to designate both the Infinite Spirit on Paradise and the Creative Spirit of your local universe. The Holy Spirit is the spiritual circuit of this Creative Daughter of the Paradise Infinite Spirit. The Holy Spirit is a circuit indigenous to each local universe and is confined to the spiritual realm of that creation; but the Infinite Spirit is omnipresent." (p. 95)

6. PERSONALITY OF THE INFINITE SPIRIT

1. **Proposition.** The Infinite Spirit is a true and divine personality.

> "Do not allow the widespread bestowal and the far-flung distribution of the Third Source and Center to obscure or otherwise detract from the fact of his personality. The Infinite Spirit is a universe presence, an eternal action, a cosmic power, a holy influence, and a universal mind; he is all of these and infinitely more, but he is also a true and divine personality. "The Infinite Spirit is a complete and perfect personality, the divine equal and co-ordinate of the Universal Father and the Eternal Son." (p. 96)

2. **Proposition.** The Father and the Son bestow the "conjoint personality" of their eternal union upon the Infinite Spirit.

> "With the coming into being of the Conjoint Actor and the materialization of the central core of creation, certain eternal changes took place. God gave himself as an absolute personality to his Eternal Son. Thus does the Father bestow the 'personality of infinity' upon his only-begotten Son, while they both bestow the 'conjoint personality' of their eternal union upon the Infinite Spirit." (p. 109)

3. **Proposition.** Notwithstanding the far-flung universe activities of the Conjoint Creator — he is a person.

> " 'The love of the Spirit' is real, as also are his sorrows; therefore 'Grieve not the Spirit of God.' Whether we observe the Infinite Spirit as Paradise Deity or as a local universe Creative Spirit, we find that the Conjoint Creator is not only the Third Source and Center but also a divine person. This divine personality also reacts to the universe as a person. The Spirit

speaks to you, 'He who has an ear, let him hear what the Spirit says.' 'The Spirit himself makes intercession for you.' The Spirit exerts a direct and personal influence upon created beings, 'For as many as are led by the Spirit of God, they are the sons of God.'" (p. 96)

4. **PROPOSITION.** All of the personal and nonpersonal doings of the Infinite Spirit are volitional acts.

"The nonpersonal, impersonal, and otherwise not personal doings of the Third Source and Center are all volitional acts of the Conjoint Actor himself; they are not reflections, derivations, or repercussions of anything or anybody." (p. 101)

7. ATTRIBUTES OF THE INFINITE SPIRIT

1. **PROPOSITION.** Omnipresence is the outstanding attribute of the Infinite Spirit.

"The outstanding attribute of the Infinite Spirit is omnipresence. Throughout all the universe of universes there is everywhere present this all-pervading spirit, which is so akin to the presence of a universal and divine mind. Both the Second Person and the Third Person of Deity are represented on all worlds by their ever-present Spirits." (p. 95)

2. **PROPOSITION.** While sharing the attributes of the Father — the Spirit is inclined towards the mercy of the Son.

"Though in every way sharing the perfection, the righteousness, and the love of the Universal Father, the Infinite Spirit inclines towards the mercy attributes of the Eternal Son, thus becoming the mercy minister of the Paradise Deities to the grand universe." (p. 92)

3. **PROPOSITION.** The Infinite Spirit possesses the unique power of antigravity.

"The Infinite Spirit possesses a unique and amazing power — *antigravity*. This power is not functionally (observably) present in either the Father or the Son. This ability to withstand the pull of material gravity, inherent in the Third Source, is revealed in the personal reactions of the Conjoint Actor to certain phases of universe relationships. And this unique attribute is transmissible to certain of the higher personalities of the Infinite Spirit." (p. 101)

4. **Proposition.** Antigravity acts within a local frame and only with reference to material gravity.

> "Antigravity can annul gravity within a local frame; it does so by the exercise of equal force presence. It operates only with reference to material gravity, and it is not the action of mind. The gravity-resistant phenomenon of a gyroscope is a fair illustration of the *effect* of antigravity but of no value to illustrate the *cause* of antigravity." (p. 101)

8. THE UNIVERSAL MANIPULATOR

1. **Proposition.** Nothing foreshadowed that the Infinite Spirit would personalize with prerogatives of energy manipulation.

> "A strange thing occurred when, in the presence of Paradise, the Universal Father and the Eternal Son unite to personalize themselves. Nothing in this eternity situation foreshadows that the Conjoint Actor would personalize as an unlimited spirituality co-ordinated with absolute mind and endowed with unique prerogatives of energy manipulation. His coming into being completes the Father's liberation from the bonds of centralized perfection and from the fetters of personality absolutism." (p. 98)

2. **Proposition.** The God of Action is the activator of the Paradise pattern of infinity. He injects spontaneity into the physical creation.

> "Paradise is the pattern of infinity; the God of Action is the activator of that pattern. Paradise is the material fulcrum of infinity; the agencies of the Third Source and Center are the levers of intelligence which motivate the material level and inject spontaneity into the mechanism of the physical creation." (p. 101)

9. THE MINISTRY OF MIND

1. **Proposition.** Absolute mind is the mind of the Infinite Spirit. Spirit is innately minded.

> "The absolute mind is the mind of the Third Person; it is inseparable from the personality of God the Spirit. Mind, in functioning beings, is not separated from energy or spirit, or both. Mind is not inherent in energy; energy is receptive and responsive to mind; mind can be superimposed upon energy, but consciousness is not inherent in the purely material level. Mind does not have to be added to pure spirit, for spirit is innately conscious and identifying. Spirit is always intelligent, *minded* in some way." (p. 102)

2. **Proposition.** The Conjoint Actor is absolute only in the domain of mind — his mind is infinite.

> "The Conjoint Creator is absolute only in the domain of mind, in the realms of universal intelligence. The mind of the Third Source and Center is infinite; it utterly transcends the active and functioning mind circuits of the universe of universes." (p. 102)

3. **Proposition.** The divine mind is better discerned in finite beings as the cosmic mind of the Paradise Master Spirits.

> "The mind presence of God is correlated with the absolute mind of the Conjoint Actor, the Infinite Spirit, but in the finite creations it is better discerned in the everywhere functioning of the cosmic mind of the Paradise Master Spirits." (p. 45)

4. **Proposition.** The Infinite Mind is independent of space and ignores time.

> "Infinite mind ignores time, ultimate mind transcends time, cosmic mind is conditioned by time. And so with space: The Infinite Mind is independent of space, but as descent is made from the infinite to the adjutant levels of mind, intellect must increasingly reckon with the fact and limitations of space." (p. 102)

5. **Proposition.** The Conjoint Actor is the creator of cosmic mind which is the source of the mind of man.

> "The Conjoint Creator is the ancestor of the cosmic mind, and the mind of man is an individualized circuit, an impersonal portion, of that cosmic mind as it is bestowed in a local universe by a Creative Daughter of the Third Source and Center." (p. 103)

6. **Proposition.** Every universe mind is grasped by the absolute mind-circuit of the Infinite Spirit.

> "The Third Source and Center, the universal intelligence, is personally conscious of every *mind*, every intellect, in all creation, and he maintains a personal and perfect contact with all these physical, morontial, and spiritual creatures of mind endowment in the farflung universes. All these activities of mind are grasped in the absolute mind-gravity circuit which focalizes in the Third Source and Center and is a part of the personal consciousness of the Infinite Spirit." (p. 103)

7. **PROPOSITION.** The unpredictability of the finite mind may be due to the incompleteness of the Supreme Being.

> "Certain phases of the unpredictability of finite mind may be due to the incompleteness of the Supreme Being, and there is a vast zone of activities wherein the Conjoint Actor and the Universal Absolute may possibly be tangent. There is much about mind that is unknown, but of this we are sure: The Infinite Spirit is the perfect expression of the mind of the Creator to all creatures; the Supreme Being is the evolving expression of the minds of all creatures to their Creator." (p. 104)

8. **PROPOSITION.** Every liaison between the material and the spiritual is the act of the Infinite Spirit.

> "Whenever and wherever there occurs a liaison between the material and the spiritual, such a mind phenomenon is an act of the Infinite spirit. Mind alone can interassociate the physical forces and energies of the material level with the spiritual powers and beings of the spirit level." (p. 136)

9. **PROPOSITION.** The dual universe of matter and spirit renders the mind God inevitable. His mind is infinite in potential and universal in bestowal.

> "Mind is the functional endowment of the Infinite Spirit, therefore infinite in potential and universal in bestowal. The primal thought of the Universal Father eternalizes in dual expression: the Isle of Paradise and his Deity equal, the spiritual and Eternal Son. Such duality of eternal reality renders the mind God, the Infinite Spirit, inevitable. Mind is the indispensable channel of communication between spiritual and material realities. The material evolutionary creature can conceive and comprehend the indwelling spirit only by the ministry of mind." (p. 638)

10. **PROPOSITION.** The predictability of the mind-gravity circuit is somewhat modified by the function of the Universal Absolute.

> "The mind-gravity circuit is dependable; it emanates from the Third Person of Deity on Paradise, but not all the observable function of mind is predictable. Throughout all known creation there parallels this circuit of mind some little-understood presence whose function is not predictable. We believe that this unpredictability is partly attributable to the function of the Universal Absolute. What this function is, we do not know; what actuates it, we can only conjecture; concerning its relation to creatures, we can only speculate." (p. 104)

10. UNIVERSE REFLECTIVITY

1. **Proposition.** The Conjoint Actor can co-ordinate all levels of universe actuality simultaneously at any given point — universal reflectivity.

   "The Conjoint Actor is able to co-ordinate all levels of universe actuality in such manner as to make possible the simultaneous recognition of the mental, the material, and the spiritual. This is the phenomenon of *universe reflectivity*, that unique and inexplicable power to see, hear, sense, and know all things as they transpire throughout a superuniverse, and to focalize, by reflectivity, all this information and knowledge at any desired point." (p. 105)

11. PERSONALITIES OF THE INFINITE SPIRIT

1. **Proposition.** There are three grand divisions of the family of the Infinite Spirit.

   "*The functional family of the Third Source and Center...* falls into three great groups:
   "I. *The Supreme Spirits.* A group of composite origin that embraces, among others, the following orders:
       1. The Seven Master Spirits of Paradise.
       2. The Reflective Spirits of the Superuniverses.
       3. The Creative Spirits of the Local Universes.
   "II. *The Power Directors.* A group of control creatures and agencies that function throughout all organized space.
   "III. *The Personalities of the Infinite Spirit.* This designation does not necessarily imply that these beings are Third Source personalities though some of them are unique as will creatures. They are usually grouped in three major classifications:
       1. The Higher Personalities of the Infinite Spirit.
       2. The Messenger Hosts of Space.
       3. The Ministering Spirits of Time." (p. 107)

2. **Proposition.** Every time the Father and Son produce a Creator Son, the Infinite Spirit becomes ancestor to a local universe Creative Spirit.

   "The next and continuing creative act of the Infinite Spirit is disclosed, from time to time, in the production of the Creative Spirits. Every time the Universal Father and the Eternal Son become parent to a Creator Son, the Infinite Spirit becomes ancestor to a local universe Creative Spirit who becomes the close associate of that Creator Son in all subsequent universe experience." (p. 106)

3. PROPOSITION. The Third Source and Center bestows non-Father personality in creative association with the Eternal Son.

> "The Father bestows personality by his personal free will. Why he does so we can only conjecture; how he does so we do not know. Neither do we know why the Third Source bestows non-Father personality, but this the Infinite Spirit does in his own behalf, in creative conjunction with the Eternal Son and in numerous ways unknown to you. The Infinite Spirit can also act for the Father in the bestowal of First Source personality." (p. 106)

VI. GOD THE SEVENFOLD

1. PROPOSITION. To compensate for creature limitations and finity of status, the Father established the sevenfold approach to Deity.

   > "To atone for finity of status and to compensate for creature limitations of concept, the Universal Father has established the evolutionary creature's sevenfold approach to Deity:
   > "1. The Paradise Creator Sons.
   > "2. The Ancients of Days.
   > "3. The Seven Master Spirits.
   > "4. The Supreme Being.
   > "5. God the Spirit.
   > "6. God the Son.
   > "7. God the Father." (p. 11)

2. PROPOSITION. God the Sevenfold embraces Deity personalities functioning in time and space and beyond the borders of the central universe.

   > "*God the Sevenfold* — Deity personality anywhere actually functioning in time and space. The personal Paradise Deities and their creative associates functioning in and beyond the borders of the central universe and power-personalizing as the Supreme Being on the first creature level of unifying Deity revelation in time and space. This level, the grand universe, is the sphere of the time-space descension of Paradise personalities in reciprocal association with the time-space ascension of evolutionary creatures." (p. 4)

3. PROPOSITION. God the Sevenfold functionally co-ordinates finite evolution.

   > "As God the Sevenfold functionally co-ordinates finite evolution, so does the Supreme Being eventually synthesize destiny attainment. The Supreme Being is the deity culmination

of grand universe evolution — physical evolution around a spirit nucleus and eventual dominance of the spirit nucleus over the encircling and whirling domains of physical evolution. And all of this takes place in accordance with the mandates of personality: Paradise personality in the highest sense, Creator personality in the universe sense, mortal personality in the human sense, Supreme personality in the culminating or experiential totaling sense." (p. 1164)

4. **Proposition**. God the Sevenfold is deeply concerned with mortal man and culminates in the actualizing Supreme Being.

"Mortal man appears to be necessary to the full function of God the Sevenfold as this divinity grouping culminates in the actualizing Supreme. There are many other orders of universe personalities who are equally necessary to the evolution of the almighty power of the Supreme, but this portrayal is presented for the edification of human beings, hence is largely limited to those factors operating in the evolution of God the Sevenfold which are related to mortal man." (p. 1273)

VII. GOD THE SUPREME

1. Introduction
2. Relation of the Supreme to the Paradise Trinity
3. Nature of the Supreme
4. The Supreme Mind
5. The Almighty and God the Sevenfold
6. The Almighty and Paradise Deity
7. The Almighty and the Supreme Creators
8. Source of Evolutionary Growth
9. Relation of the Supreme to Universe Creatures
10. The Finite God
11. The Oversoul of Creation
12. The Future of the Supreme
13. Omnipresence and Ubiquity
14. Universe Mechanisms

VII. GOD THE SUPREME

1. INTRODUCTION

1. **PROPOSITION.** God the Supreme evolves in association with the Supreme Power Directors, the Supreme Spirits, and God the Sevenfold.

   "Throughout the evolutionary ages the physical power potential of the Supreme is vested in the Seven Supreme Power Directors, and the mind potential reposes in the Seven Master Spirits. The Infinite Mind is the function of the Infinite Spirit; the cosmic mind, the ministry of the Seven Master Spirits; the Supreme Mind is in process of actualizing in the co-ordination of the grand universe and in functional association with the revelation and attainment of God the Sevenfold." (p. 1269)

2. **PROPOSITION.** The evolving mind of the Supreme Being is a relationship between finite and absolute mind.

   "The relationship between the finite cosmic mind and the divine absolute mind appears to be evolving in the experiential mind of the Supreme. We are taught that, in the dawn of time, this experiential mind was bestowed upon the Supreme by the Infinite Spirit, and we conjecture that certain features of the phenomenon of reflectivity can be accounted for only by postulating the activity of the Supreme Mind." (p. 105)

2. RELATION OF THE SUPREME TO THE PARADISE TRINITY

1. **PROPOSITION.** The Supreme Being is not the Paradise Trinity functioning on finite levels.

   "The Supreme Being is something less and something other than the Trinity functioning in the finite universes; but within certain limits and during the present era of incomplete power-personalization, this evolutionary Deity does appear to reflect the attitude of the Trinity of Supremacy. The Father, Son, and Spirit do not personally function with the Supreme Being, but during the present universe age they collaborate with him as the Trinity. We understand that they sustain a similar relationship to the Ultimate. We often conjecture as to what will be the personal relationship between the Paradise Deities and God the Supreme when he has finally evolved, but we do not really know." (p. 115)

2. **Proposition.** The Supreme Being is wholly dependent on the Trinity for personal and spirit nature.

   "The Supreme Being is absolutely dependent on the existence and action of the Paradise Trinity for the reality of his personal and spirit nature. While the growth of the Supreme is a matter of triodity relationship, the spirit personality of God the Supreme is dependent upon, and is derived from, the Paradise Trinity, which ever remains as the absolute center-source of perfect and infinite stability around which the evolutionary growth of the Supreme progressively unfolds." (p. 1264)

3. **Proposition.** God the Supreme is the personalization of the totality of evolutionary universe experience.

   "God the Supreme is the personalization of all universe experience, the focalization of all finite evolution, the maximation of all creature reality, the consummation of cosmic wisdom, the embodiment of the harmonious beauties of the galaxies of time, the truth of cosmic mind meanings, and the goodness of supreme spirit values." (p. 1304)

4. **Proposition.** God the Supreme synthesizes finite diversities into an experiential whole.

   "And God the Supreme will, in the eternal future, synthesize these manifold finite diversities into one experientially meaningful whole, even as they are now existentially united on absolute levels in the Paradise Trinity." (p. 1304)

5. **Proposition.** Actual sovereignty of the Supreme in the grand universe implies the vicegerency of the present Trinity administrators.

   "This concept implies the actual sovereignty of the Supreme in the grand universe. It is altogether likely that the present Trinity administrators will continue as his vicegerents, but we believe that the present demarcations between the seven superuniverses will gradually disappear, and that the entire grand universe will function as a perfected whole." (p. 1292)

6. **Proposition.** The functions of the Almighty Supreme are related to Trinity functions.

   "The Father, Son, and Spirit — as the Trinity — are not the Almighty Supreme, but the supremacy of the Almighty can never be manifest without them. The *growth* of the Almighty is centered on the Absolutes of actuality and predicated on the Absolutes of potentiality. But the *functions* of the Almighty Supreme are related to the functions of the Paradise Trinity." (p. 1304)

7. **Proposition.** In this universe age, we can view the evolving Supreme as a partial portraiture of the Paradise Trinity.

   "It would appear that, in the Supreme Being, all phases of universe activity are being partially reunited by the personality of this experiential Deity. When, therefore, we desire to view the Trinity as one God, and if we limit this concept to the present known and organized grand universe, we discover that the evolving Supreme Being is the partial portraiture of the Paradise Trinity." (p. 1304)

8. **Proposition.** The Supreme evolves as the personality synthesis of finite mind, matter, and spirit.

   "And we further find that this Supreme Deity is evolving as the personality synthesis of finite matter, mind, and spirit in the grand universe." (p. 1304)

3. NATURE OF THE SUPREME

1. **Proposition.** The Supreme Being is the co-ordinator of all creature-Creator activities — the correlator of time-space divinity.

   "*The Supreme Being* is not a direct creator, except that he is the father of Majeston, but he is a synthetic co-ordinator of all creature-Creator universe activities. The Supreme Being, now actualizing in the evolutionary universes, is the Deity correlator and synthesizer of time-space divinity, of triune Paradise Deity in experiential association with the Supreme Creators of time and space. When finally actualized, this evolutionary Deity will constitute the eternal fusion of the finite and the infinite — the everlasting and indissoluble union of experiential power and spirit personality." (p. 11)

2. **Proposition.** God the Supreme was a spiritual person in Havona before the creation of the grand universe.

   "God the Supreme as a person existed in Havona before the creation of the seven superuniverses, but he functioned only on spiritual levels. The evolution of the Almighty power of Supremacy by diverse divinity synthesis in the evolving universes eventuated in a new power presence of Deity which co-ordinated with the spiritual person of the Supreme in Havona by means of the Supreme Mind, which concomitantly translated from the potential resident in the infinite mind of the Infinite Spirit to the active functional mind of the Supreme Being." (p. 641)

3. PROPOSITION. In the Deity of the Supreme, the Father-I AM has achieved relative liberation from the limitations of infinity, eternity, and absoluteness.

> "In the Deity of the Supreme the Father-I AM has achieved relatively complete liberation from the limitations inherent in infinity of status, eternity of being, and absoluteness of nature. But God the Supreme has been freed from all existential limitations only by having become subject to experiential qualifications of universal function. In attaining capacity for experience, the finite God also becomes subject to the necessity therefor; in achieving liberation from eternity, the Almighty encounters the barriers of time; and the Supreme could only know growth and development as a consequence of partiality of existence and incompleteness of nature, nonabsoluteness of being." (p. 1266)

4. PROPOSITION. The Almighty Supreme is an evolving Deity of incomplete power and personality.

> "The Almighty Supreme is a living and evolving Deity of power and personality. His present domain, the grand universe, is also a growing realm of power and personality. His destiny is perfection, but his present experience encompasses the elements of growth and incomplete status." (p. 1268)

5. PROPOSITION. Throughout eternity God the Supreme will voice the reality of volitional experience in the Trinity relationships of Deity.

> "The Supreme is the beauty of physical harmony, the truth of intellectual meaning, and the goodness of spiritual value. He is the sweetness of true success and the joy of everlasting achievement. He is the oversoul of the grand universe, the consciousness of the finite cosmos, the completion of finite reality, and the personification of Creator-creature experience. Throughout all future eternity God the Supreme will voice the reality of volitional experience in the trinity relationships of Deity." (p. 1278)

6. PROPOSITION. The Supreme is the channel of creative infinity for the galactic panoramas of space and the personality dramas of time.

> "The Supreme is the divine channel through which flows the creative infinity of the triodities that crystallizes into the galactic panorama of space, against which takes place the magnificent personality drama of time: the spirit conquest of energy-matter through the mediation of mind ." (p. 1281)

7. **PROPOSITION.** The Supreme is creatorlike as well as creaturelike — the within and the without of all things and beings.

> "We seek the Supreme in the universes, but we find him not. 'He is the within and the without of all things and beings, moving and quiescent. Unrecognizable in his mystery, though distant, yet is he near.' The Almighty Supreme is 'the form of the yet unformed, the pattern of the yet uncreated.' The Supreme is your universe home, and when you find him, it will be like returning home. He is your experiential parent, and even as in the experience of human beings, so has he grown in the experience of divine parenthood. He knows you because he is creaturelike as well as creatorlike ." (p. 1287)

8. **PROPOSITION.** The Supreme embraces all of infinity that a finite creature can ever really comprehend.

> "The Supreme is not infinite, but he probably embraces all of infinity that a finite creature can ever really comprehend. To understand more than the Supreme is to be more than finite!" (p. 1290)

4. THE SUPREME MIND

1. **PROPOSITION.** The material and spiritual may achieve completion of development — but mind never ceases to progress.

> "We really know less about the mind of Supremacy than about any other aspect of this evolving Deity. It is unquestionably active throughout the grand universe and is believed to have a potential destiny of master universe function which is of vast extent. But this we do know: Whereas physique may attain completed growth, and whereas spirit may achieve perfection of development, mind never ceases to progress — it is the experiential technique of endless progress. The Supreme is an experiential Deity and therefore never achieves completion of mind attainment." (p. 1269)

2. **PROPOSITION.** Supreme power and supreme spirit are unified by Supreme Mind — factualizing as the Supreme Being.

> "It is conjectured that at this far-distant time the spirit person of the Supreme and attained power of the Almighty will have achieved co-ordinate development, and that both, as unified in and by the Supreme Mind, will factualize as the Supreme Being, a completed actuality in the universes — an actuality which will be observable by all creature intelligences, reacted to by all created energies, co-ordinated in all spiritual entities, and experienced by all universe personalities." (p. 1292)

5. THE ALMIGHTY AMD GOD THE SEVENFOLD

1. **PROPOSITION.** In Havona, the Supreme reflects Paradise Deity and expands outward in God the Sevenfold.

   "*God the Supreme* in Havona is the personal spirit reflection of the triune Paradise Deity. This associative Deity relationship is now creatively expanding outward in God the Sevenfold and is synthesizing in the experiential power of the Almighty Supreme in the grand universe." (p. 11)

2. **PROPOSITION.** When God the Supreme rules evolutionary creation, will God the Sevenfold function in outer space?

   "It is a fact that, as the creations of time and space are progressively settled in evolutionary status, there is observed a new and fuller functioning of God the Supreme concomitant with a corresponding withdrawing of the first three manifestations of God the Sevenfold. If and when the grand universe becomes settled in light and life, what then will be the future function of the Creator-Creative manifestions of God the Sevenfold if God the Supreme assumes direct control of these creations of time and space? Are these organizers and pioneers of the time-space universes to be liberated for similar activities in outer space? We do not know, but we speculate much concerning these and related matters." (p. 642)

3. **PROPOSITION.** Finaliters embrace the full potential of comprehending God the Sevenfold unifying in the Supreme.

   "Ascendant finaliters, having been born in the local universes, nurtured in the superuniverses, and trained in the central universe, embrace in their personal experiences the full potential of the comprehension of the time-space divinity of God the Sevenfold unifying in the Supreme. Finaliters serve successively in superuniverses other than those of nativity, thereby superimposing experience upon experience until the fullness of the sevenfold diversity of possible creature experience has been encompassed." (p. 643)

6. THE AIMIGHTY AND PARADISE DEITY

1. **PROPOSITION.** God the Supreme derives his spirit and personality attributes from the Paradise Trinity.

   "God the Supreme derives his spirit and personality attributes from the Paradise Trinity, but he is power-actualizing in the doings of the Creator Sons, the Ancients of Days, and the

Master Spirits, whose collective acts are the source of his growing power as almighty sovereign to and in the seven superuniverses." (p. 1269)

2. **Proposition.** The growth of the Supreme Being is predicated on both the Paradise Deities and the Absolutes.

"The Supreme Being embraces possibilities for cosmic ministry that are not apparently manifested in the Eternal Son, the Infinite Spirit, or the nonpersonal realities of the Isle of Paradise. This statement is made with due regard for the absoluteness of these three basic actualities, but the growth of the Supreme is not only predicated on these actualities of Deity and Paradise but is also involved in developments within the Deity, Universal, and Unqualified Absolutes." (p. 1265)

7. THE AlMIGHTY AND THE SUPREME CREATORS

1. **Proposition.** During evolution, the power of the Supreme depends much on God the Sevenfold, the Conjoint Actor, and the Seven Master Spirits.

"During those ages in which the sovereignty of Supremacy is undergoing its time development, the almighty power of the Supreme is dependent on the divinity acts of God the Sevenfold, while there seems to be a particularly close relationship between the Supreme Being and the Conjoint Actor together with his primary personalities, the Seven Master Spirits." (p. 1272)

2. **Proposition.** The Infinite Spirit compensates for the incompleteness of the evolving Supreme.

"The Infinite Spirit as the Conjoint Actor functions in many ways which compensate the incompletion of evolutionary Deity and sustains very close relations to the Supreme. This closeness of relationship is shared in measure by all of the Master Spirits but especially by Master Spirit Number Seven, who speaks for the Supreme. This Master Spirit knows — is in personal contact with — the Supreme." (p. 1272)

3. **Proposition.** The Master Spirits create the Spirits of the Circuits in response to the will of the Supreme Being.

"These Master Spirits are not only the supporters and augmenters of the sovereignty of Supremacy, but they are in turn affected by the creative purposes of the Supreme. Ordinarily, the collective creations of the Master Spirits are of the quasi-material order (power directors, etc.), while their individual creations are of the spiritual order (supernaphim, etc.). But when the Master Spirits *collectively* produced the Seven Circuit Spirits in response to the will and purpose of the Supreme Being, it is to be noted that the offspring of this creative act are spiritual, not material or quasimaterial." (p. 1272)

4. **PROPOSITION.** The Supreme Being is concerned with the creators and controllers of God the Sevenfold.

"You have been instructed in the relationship of God the Sevenfold to the Supreme Being, and you should now recognize that the Sevenfold encompasses the controllers as well as the creators of the grand universe. These sevenfold controllers of the grand universe embrace the following:
   1. The Master Physical Controllers.
   2. The Supreme Power Centers.
   3. The Supreme Power Directors.
   4. The Almighty Supreme.
   5. The God of Action — the Infinite Spirit.
   6. The Isle of Paradise.
   7. The Source of Paradise — the Universal Father.

"These seven groups are functionally inseparable from God the Sevenfold and constitute the physical-control level of this Deity association." (p. 1273)

5. **PROPOSITION.** The evolving Almighty Supreme is the physical overcontroller of the grand universe.

"The Almighty Supreme is evolving as the overcontroller of the physical power of the grand universe. In the present universe age this potential of physical power appears to be centered in the Seven Supreme Power Directors, who operate through the fixed locations of the power centers and through the mobile presences of the physical controllers." (p. 1274)

6. **PROPOSITION.** Michael's seven bestowals contributed a new revelation of the Supreme to Nebadon and enhanced the sovereignty of both.

"The completion of these seven bestowals resulted in the liberation of Michael's supreme sovereignty and also in the creation of the possibility for the sovereignty of the Supreme in Nebadon. On none of Michael's bestowals did he reveal God the Supreme, but the sum total of all seven bestowals is a new Nebadon revelation of the Supreme Being." (p. 1318)

PART I — *The Doctrine of God*

8. SOURCE OF EVOLUTIONATARY GROWTH

1. **Proposition.** The Supreme grows as a result of the evolutionary mastery of the finite possibilities of the grand universe.

    "The Supreme not only grows as the Creators and creatures of the evolving universes attain to Godlikeness, but this finite Deity also experiences growth as a result of the creature and Creator mastery of the finite possibilities of the grand universe. The motion of the Supreme is twofold: intensively toward Paradise and Deity and extensively toward the limitlessness of the Absolutes of potential." (p. 1265)

2. **Proposition.** The experience of every evolving mortal is a part of the experience of the Almighty Supreme.

    "The experience of every evolving creature personality is a phase of the experience of the Almighty Supreme. The intelligent subjugation of every physical segment of the superuniverses is a part of the growing control of the Almight Supreme. The creative synthesis of power and personality is a part of the creative urge of the Supreme Mind and is the very essence of the evolutionary growth of unity in the Supreme Being." (p. 1268)

3. **Proposition.** Universe experience is the foundation upon which the Supreme achieves deity evolution.

    "But the local universes are the real laboratories in which are worked put the mind experiments, galactic adventures, divinity unfoldings, and personality progressions which, when cosmically totaled, constitute the actual foundation upon which the Supreme is achieving deity evolution in and by experience." (p. 1272)

4. **Proposition.** Does the Supreme actualize in response to universal evolution, or does the universe evolve in response to the actualization of the Supreme?

    "One of the most intriguing questions in finite philosophy is this: Does the Supreme Being actualize in response to the evolution of the grand universe, or does this finite cosmos progressively evolve in response to the gradual actualization of the Supreme? Or is it possible that they are mutually interdependent for their development? that they are evolutionary reciprocals, each initiating the growth of the other? Of this we are certain: Creatures and universes, high and low, are evolving within the Supreme, and as they evolve, there is appearing the unified summation of the entire finite activity of this universe age. And this is the appearance of the Supreme Being, to all personalities the evolution of the almighty power of God the Supreme."(p. 1281)

5. **PROPOSITION.** The Supreme is the sum total of all finite growth, self-realized on deity levels of maximum finite completion.

    "The cosmic reality variously designated as the Supreme Being, God the Supreme, and the Almighty Supreme, is the complex and universal synthesis of the emerging phases of all finite realities. The far-flung diversification of eternal energy, divine spirit, and universal mind attains finite culmination in the evolution of the Supreme, who is the sum total of all finite growth, self-realized on deity levels of finite maximum completion." (p. 1281)

6. **PROPOSITION.** As we strive for self-realization, the God of experience achieves almighty supremacy.

    "And so, as we strive for self-expression, the Supreme is striving in us, and with us, for deity expression. As we find the Father, so has the Supreme again found the Paradise Creator of all things. As we master the problems of self-realization, so is the God of experience achieving almighty supremacy in the universes of time and space." (p. 1284)

7. **PROPOSITION.** As God is our Father, the Supreme Being is our universe Mother. From the cocoon of human experience they evolve the finaliter of eternal destiny and service.

    "All soul-evolving humans are literally the evolutionary sons of God the Father and God the Mother, the Supreme Being. But until such time as mortal man becomes soul-conscious of his divine heritage, this assurance of Deity kinship must be faith realized. Human life experience is the cosmic cocoon in which the universe endowments of the Supreme Being and the universe presence of the Universal Father (none of which are personalities) are evolving the morontia soul of time and the human-divine finaliter character of universe destiny and eternal service." (p. 1289)

PART I — THE DOCTRINE OF GOD

9. RELATION OF THE SUPREME TO UNIVERSE CREATURES

1. **PROPOSITION.** Ascenders gain some comprehension of the Supreme in Havona, but not even the finaliters find him.

    "While ascending mortals achieve power comprehension of the Almighty on the capitals of the superuniverses and personality comprehension of the Supreme on the outer circuits of Havona, they do not actually find the Supreme Being as they are destined to find the Paradise Deities. Even the finaliters, sixth-stage spirits, have not found the Supreme Being, nor are they likely to until they have achieved seventh-stage-spirit status, and until the Supreme has become actually functional in the activities of the future outer universes." (p. 641)

2. **PROPOSITION.** The Supreme Being performs a threefold function in human experience.

    "The Supreme Being has a threefold function in the experience of mortal man: First, he is the unifier of time-space divinity, God the Sevenfold; second, he is the maximum of Deity which finite creatures can actually comprehend; third, he is mortal man's only avenue of approach to the transcendental experience of consorting with absonite mind, eternal spirit, and Paradise personality." (p. 643)

3. **PROPOSITION.** The Adjuster, Holy Spirit, and Spirit of Truth are unified in human experience by the ministry of the Supreme.

    "Revelation as an epochal phenomenon is periodic; as a personal human experience it is continuous. Divinity functions in mortal personality as the Adjuster gift of the Father, as the Spirit of Truth of the Son, and as the Holy Spirit of the Universe Spirit, while these three supermortal endowments are unified in human experiential evolution as the ministry of the Supreme." (p. 1107)

4. **PROPOSITION.** As the Supreme attains all evolutionary qualities, mortals are participants, hence the capacity to know the Supreme.

    "Thus does the Supreme Being eventually attain to the embrace of all of everything evolving in time and space while investing these qualities with spirit personality. Since creatures, even mortals, are personality participants in this majestic transaction, so do they certainly attain the capacity to know the Supreme and to perceive the Supreme as true children of such an evolutionary Deity." (p. 1165)

5. **Proposition.** The realities of the Absolutes are not perceivable, but the Supreme is experiencible.

> "God the Supreme is experiential; therefore is he completely experiencible. The existential realities of the seven Absolutes are not perceivable by the technique of experience; only the *personality realities* of the Father, Son, and Spirit can be grasped by the personality of the finite creature in the prayer-worship attitude." (p. 1165)

6. **Proposition.** The cosmic tension of God-striving finds resolution in the union of almighty power and the spirit person of the Supreme Being.

> "Man's urge for Paradise perfection, his striving for God-attainment, creates a genuine divinity tension in the living cosmos which can only be resolved by the evolution of an immortal soul; this is what happens in the experience of a single mortal creature. But when all creatures and all Creators in the grand universe likewise strive for God-attainment and divine perfection, there is built up a profound cosmic tension which can only find resolution in the sublime synthesis of almighty power with the spirit person of the evolving God of all creatures, the Supreme Being." (p. 1276)

7. **Proposition.** The scheme of descending God-revealing Creators and ascending God-seeking creatures is revelatory of the Deity evolution of the Supreme.

> "In the persons of the Supreme Creators the Gods have descended from Paradise to the domains of time and space, there to create and to evolve creatures with Paradise-attainment capacity who can ascend thereto in quest of the Father. This universe procession of descending God-revealing Creators and ascending God-seeking creatures is revelatory of the Deity evolution of the Supreme, in whom both descenders and ascenders achieve mutuality of understanding, the discovery of eternal and universal brotherhood. The Supreme Being thus becomes the finite synthesis of the experience of the perfect-Creator cause and the perfecting-creature response." (p. 1278)

8. **Proposition.** The evolving Supreme portrays the combined experiences of Creators and creatures with the vicissitudes of the finite cosmos.

> "The evolving divine nature of the Supreme is becoming a faithful portrayal of the matchless experience of all creatures and of all Creators in the grand universe. In the Supreme, creatorship and creaturehood are at one; they are forever

united by that experience which was born of the vicissitudes attendant upon the solution of the manifold problems which beset all finite creation as it pursues the eternal path in quest of perfection and liberation from the fetters of incompleteness." (p. 1279)

9. **Proposition.** God the Supreme is truth, beauty, and goodness — the finite maximum of ideational experience.

> "Truth, beauty, and goodness are correlated in the ministry of the Spirit, the grandeur of Paradise, the mercy of the Son, and the experience of the Supreme. God the Supreme *is* truth, beauty, and goodness, for these concepts of divinity represent finite maximums of ideational experience. The eternal sources of these triune qualities of divinity are on superfinite levels, but a creature could only conceive of such sources as supertruth, superbeauty, and supergoodness." (p. 1279)

10. **Proposition.** Cosmic morality is predicated on the creature's appreciation of experiential obligation to experiential Deity.

> "The temperal relation of man to the Supreme is the foundation for cosmic morality, the universal sensitivity to, and acceptance of, *duty*. This is a morality which transcends the temporal sense of relative right and wrong; it is a morality directly predicated on the self-conscious creature's appreciation of experiential obligation to experiential Deity." (p. 1284)

11. **Proposition.** Man's refusal of the Paradise ascent delays divinity expression in the grand universe.

> "To the extent that the human self thus refuses to take part in the Paradise ascent, to just that extent is the Supreme delayed in achieving divinity expression in the grand universe.
>
> "Into the keeping of mortal man has been given not only the Adjuster presence of the Paradise Father but also control over the destiny of an infinitesimal fraction of the future of the Supreme. For as man attains human destiny, so does the Supreme achieve destiny on deity levels." (p. 1285)

12. **Proposition.** Rejection of ascension is cosmic suicide. Personality of a nonascender returns to the Supreme as a drop of water returns to the sea.

> "The human personality can truly destroy individuality of creaturehood, and though all that was worth while in the life of such a cosmic suicide will persist, *these qualities will not*

persist as an individual creature. The Supreme will again find expression in the creatures of the universes but never again as that particular person; the unique personality of a nonascender returns to the Supreme as a drop of water returns to the sea." (p. 1283)

13. **Proposition.** Uncertainty characterizes the relation of the Supreme to catastrophic events.

> "The mortal mind can immediately think of a thousand and one things — catastrophic physical events, appalling accidents, horrific disasters, painful illnesses, and world-wide scourges — and ask whether such visitations are correlated in the unknown maneuvering of this probable functioning of the Supreme Being. Frankly, we do not know; we are not really sure." (p. 115)

14. **Proposition.** The experiential approach to the Supreme is differential for mortals and central universe natives.

> "There is no approach to the Supreme except through experience, and in the current epochs of creation there are only three avenues of creature approach to Supremacy;
> "1. The Paradise Citizens descend from the eternal Isle through Havona, where they acquire capacity for Supremacy comprehension through observation of the Paradise-Havona reality differential and by exploratory discovery of the manifold activities of the Supreme Creator Personalities, ranging from the Master Spirits to the Creator Sons.
> "2. The time-space ascenders coming up from the evolutionary universes of the Supreme Creators make close approach to the Supreme in the traversal of Havona as a preliminary to the augmenting appreciation of the unity of the Paradise Trinity.
> "3. The Havona natives acquire a comprehension of the Supreme through contacts with descending pilgrims from Paradise and ascending pilgrims from the seven superuniverses. Havona natives are inherently in position to harmonize the essentially different viewpoints of the citizens of the eternal Isle and the citizens of the evolutionary universes." (p. 1289)

15. **Proposition.** We find the Father in our hearts, but we discover the Supreme in the hearts of other mortals.

> "Man can discover the Father in his heart, but he will have to search for the Supreme in the hearts of all other men; and

when all creatures perfectly reveal the love of the Supreme, then will he become a universe actuality to all creatures. And that is just another way of saying that the universes will be settled in light and life." (p. 1290)

16. **Proposition.** Through the Adjuster, man's soul gains experience from the pre-existent potential within the Supreme.

   "Even the experience of man and Adjuster must find echo in the divinity of God the Supreme, for, as the Adjusters experience, they are like the Supreme, and the evolving soul of mortal man is created out of the pre-existent possibility for such experience within the Supreme." (p. 1287)

17. **Proposition.** As God the Father journeys through the cosmos with man, the very way traversed is the presence of the Supreme.

   "But no God-knowing mortal can ever be lonely in his journey through the cosmos, for he knows that the Father walks beside him each step of the way, while the very way that he is traversing is the presence of the Supreme." (p. 1291)

10. THE FINITE GOD

1. **Proposition.** God the Supreme is the evolving and actualizing God of time and space — realizing creature-Creator identity.

   "*God the Supreme* — the actualizing or evolving God of time and space. Personal Deity associatively realizing the time-space experiential achievement of creature-Creator identity. The Supreme Being is personally experiencing the achievement of Deity unity as the evolving and experiential God of the evolutionary creatures of time and space." (p. 4)

2. **Proposition.** The Supreme is a derived Deity — the transformation of potentials into actuals on the finite level.

   "Any consideration of the *origins* of God the Supreme must begin with the Paradise Trinity, for the Trinity is original Deity while the Supreme is derived Deity. Any consideration of the growth of the Supreme must give consideration to the existential triodities, for they encompass all absolute actuality and all infinite potentiality (in conjunction with the First Source and Center). And the evolutionary Supreme is the culminating and personally volitional focus of the transmutation — the transformation — of potentials to actuals in and on the finite level of existence. The two triodities, actual and potential, encompass the totality of the interrelationships of growth in the universes." (p. 1263)

3. **PROPOSITION.** The power-mind-spirit personality actualization of the Supreme is an evolutionary inevitability.

    "The Paradise Trinity is considered to be the absolute inevitability; the Seven Master Spirits are apparently Trinity inevitabilities; the power-mind-spirit-personality actualization of the Supreme must be the evolutionary inevitability." (p. 1266)

4. **PROPOSITION.** When the grand universe achieves the will of God, the Almighty Deity potential factualizes as the Supreme Being.

    "If all grand universers should ever relatively achieve the full living of the will of God, then would the time-space creations be settled in light and life, and then would the Almighty, the deity potential of Supremacy, become factual in the emergence of the divine personality of God the Supreme." (p. 1278)

5. **PROPOSITION.** The finite God cannot be discovered by any one creature until the day of attained perfection when all creatures simultaneously find him.

    "It is not only man's own limitations which prevent him from finding the finite God; it is also the incompletion of the universe; even the incompletion of all creatures — past, present, and future — makes the Supreme inaccessible. God the Father can be found by any individual who has attained the divine level of Godlikeness, but God the Supreme will never be personally discovered by any one creature until that far-distant time when, through the universal attainment of perfection, *all* creatures will simultaneously find him." (p. 1290)

6. **PROPOSITION.** The concept of the Supreme is essential to the co-ordination of the divine and unchanging overworld with the finite and ever-changing underworld.

    "The linking of the absolute and eternal truth of the Creator with the factual experience of the finite and temporal creature eventuates a new and emerging value of the Supreme. The concept of the Supreme is essential to the co-ordination of the divine and unchanging overworld with the finite and ever-changing underworld." (p. 1297)

7. **PROPOSITION.** When the kingdom of God becomes actual in the heart of every individual on a world, the sovereignty of the Supreme Being has been there attained.

    "The kingdom of God is in the hearts of men, and when this kingdom becomes actual in the heart of every individual on a world, then God's rule has become actual on that planet; and this is the attained sovereignty of the Supreme Being." (p. 1306)

8. **PROPOSITION.** With God the Supreme, achievement is the prerequisite — you must do something.

   "With God the Father, sonship is the great relationship. With God the Supreme, achievement is the prerequisite to status — one must do something as well as be something." (p. 1260)

11. THE OVERSOUL OF CREATION

1. **PROPOSITION.** Providence is the realm of the Supreme and the Conjoint Actor — the Immanence of the Projected Incomplete.

   "There is also an organic unity in the universes of time and space which seems to underlie the whole fabric of cosmic events. This living presence of the evolving Supreme Being, this Immanence of the Projected Incomplete, is inexplicably manifested ever and anon by what appears to be an amazingly fortuitous co-ordination of apparently unrelated universe happenings. This must be the function of Providence — the realm of the Supreme Being and the Conjoint Actor." (p. 56)

2. **PROPOSITION.** Mortal survival enlarges the experiential sovereignty of the Supreme.

   "Throughout the grand universe the Supreme struggles for expression. His divine evolution is in measure predicated on the wisdom-action of every personality in existence. When a human being chooses eternal survival, he is co-creating destiny; and in the life of this ascending mortal the finite God finds an increased measure of personality self-realization and an enlargement of experiential sovereignty." (p. 1283)

3. **PROPOSITION.** The personality of non-survivors is absorbed into the oversoul of creation — the Deity of the Supreme.

   "But if a creature rejects the eternal career, that part of the Supreme which was dependent on this creature's choice experiences inescapable delay, a deprivation which must be compensated by substitutional or collateral experience; as for the personality of the nonsurvivor, it is absorbed into the oversoul of creation, becoming a part of the Deity of the Supreme." (p. 1283)

4. **Proposition.** The Supreme is the cosmic oversoul of the Grand Universe. In him the realities of the cosmos find a Deity reflection.

> "The great Supreme is the cosmic oversoul of the grand universe. In him the qualities and quantities of the cosmos do find their deity reflection; his deity nature is the mosaic composite of the total vastness of all creature-Creator nature throughout the evolving universes. And the Supreme is also an actualizing Deity embodying a creative will which embraces an evolving universe purpose." (p. 1285)

12. THE FUTURE OF THE SUPREME

1. **Proposition.** In Havona, the Supreme is a spirit person; in the grand universe, a power-personality; in the master universe, an unknown mind potential.

> "The Supreme Being functions primarily in the central universe as a spirit personality; secondarily in the grand universe as God the Almighty, a personality of power. The tertiary function of the Supreme in the master universe is now latent, existing only as an unknown mind potential. No one knows just what this third development of the Supreme Being will disclose. Some believe that, when the superuniverses are settled in light and life, the Supreme will become functional from Uversa as the almighty and experiential sovereign of the grand universe while expanding in power as the superalmighty of the outer universes. Others speculate that the third stage of Supremacy will involve the third level of Deity manifestation. But none of us really know." (p. 1268)

2. **Proposition.** The Father conceives the finite, the Creator Sons factualize it, the Supreme insures its culminating destiny with the absonite.

> "The Supreme apparently cannot initiate original causation but appears to be the catalyzer of all universe growth and is seemingly destined to provide totality culmination as regards the destiny of all experiential-evolutionary beings. The Father originates the concept of a finite cosmos; the Creator Sons factualize this idea in time and space with the consent and cooperation of the Creative Spirits; the Supreme culminates the total finite and establishes its relationship with the destiny of the absonite." (p. 1283)

3. **Proposition.** In the next universe age, outer-spacers will pass through the Supreme rule of the grand universe.

> "As existent upon the consummation of the present universe age, the Supreme Being will function as an experiential sovereign in the grand universe. Outer-spacers — citizens of the next universe age — will have a postsuperuniverse growth potential, a capacity for evolutionary attainment presupposing the sovereignty of the Almighty Supreme, hence excluding creature participation in the power-personality synthesis of the present universe age." (p. 1280)

4. **Proposition.** When God the Supreme rules the time-space universes, it will be under the overcontrol of God the Ultimate — the transcendental Almighty.

> "If God the Supreme ever assumes direct control of the universes of time and space, we are confident such a Deity administration will function under the overcontrol of the Ultimate. In such an event God the Ultimate would begin to become manifest to the universes of time as the transcendental Almighty (the Omnipotent) exercising the overcontrol of supertime and transcended space concerning the administrative functions of the Almighty Supreme." (p. 1296)

5. **Proposition.** The concept of the completed evolution of the Supreme is now complicated by three inherent problems.

> "While this is an entirely proper concept of the future of the Supreme, we would call attention to certain problems inherent in this concept:
>
> "1. The Unqualified Supervisors of the Supreme could hardly be deitized at any stage prior to his completed evolution, and yet these same supervisors even now qualifiedly exercise the sovereignty of supremacy concerning the universes settled in light and life.
>
> "2. The Supreme could hardly function in the Trinity Ultimate until he had attained complete actuality of universe status, and yet the Trinity Ultimate is even now a qualified reality, and you have been informed of the existence of the Qualified Vicegerents of the Ultimate.
>
> "3. The Supreme is not completely real to universe creatures, but there are many reasons for deducing that he is quite real to the Sevenfold Deity, extending from the Universal Father on Paradise to the Creator Sons and the Creative Spirits of the local universes." (p. 1291)

6. **PROPOSITION.** At the end of the variegated and long evolutionary struggle, the brief relaxation will be followed by the challenge for the attainment of God the Ultimate.

> "The perfected grand universe of those future days will be vastly different from what it is at present. Gone will be the thrilling adventures of the organization of the galaxies of space, the planting of life on the uncertain worlds of time, and the evolving of harmony out of chaos, beauty out of potentials, truth out of meanings, and goodness out of values. The time universes will have achieved the fulfillment of finite destiny! And perhaps for a space there will be rest, relaxation from the agelong struggle for evolutionary perfection. But not for long! Certainly, surely, and inexorably the enigma of the emerging Deity of God the Ultimate will challenge these perfected citizens of the settled universes just as their struggling evolutionary forebears were once challenged by the quest for God the Supreme. The curtain of cosmic destiny will draw back to reveal the transcendent grandeur of the alluring absonite quest for the attainment of the Universal Father on those new and higher levels revealed in the ultimate of creature experience." (p. 1293)

7. **PROPOSITION.** The eternal future will reveal God the Supreme in the mind and soul of ascenders, even as the Father was revealed in the earth life of Jesus.

> "In the eternal future, God the Supreme will be actualized — creatively expressed and spiritually portrayed — in the spiritualized mind, the immortal soul, of ascendant man, even as the Universal Father was so revealed in the earth life of Jesus." (p. 1286)

13. OMNIPRESENCE AND UBIQUITY

1. **PROPOSITION.** Choosing to do the will of God is a cosmic value reacted to by the ubiquitous force of the Supreme Being.

> "The act of the creature's choosing to do the will of the Creator is a cosmic value and has a universe meaning which is immediately reacted to by some unrevealed but ubiquitous force of co-ordination, probably the functioning of the ever-enlarging action of the Supreme Being." (p. 1288)

2. **PROPOSITION.** God the Supreme may not be time-space omnipresent, but he is the divine ubiquitous *becoming*.

> "God the Supreme may not be a demonstration of the time-space omnipresence of Deity, but he is literally a manifestation of

divine ubiquity. Between the spiritual presence of the Creator and the material manifestations of creation there exists a vast domain of the ubiquitous *becoming* — the universe emergence of evolutionary Deity." (p. 1296)

3. **PROPOSITION.** The factualized Supreme may be resident on Uversa, but his ubiquity will penetrate the universe of universes.

"It is possible that the Supreme may then be personally resident on Uversa, the headquarters of Orvonton, from which he will direct the administration of the time creations, but this is really only a conjecture. Certainly, though, the personality of the Supreme Being will be definitely contactable at some specific locality, although the ubiquity of his Deity presence will probably continue to permeate the universe of universes. What the relation of the superuniverse citizens of that age will be to the Supreme we do not know, but it may be something like the present relationship between the Havona natives and the Paradise Trinity." (p. 1292)

14. UNIVERSE MECHANISMS

1. **PROPOSITION.** In the Supreme and the Ultimate impersonal realities with their volitional counterparts — a new relationship between pattern and person.

"We understand something of how the mechanism of Paradise is correlated with the personality of the Eternal Son; this is the function of the Conjoint Actor. And we have theories regarding the operations of the Universal Absolute with respect to the theoretical mechanisms of the Unqualified and the potential person of the Deity Absolute. But in the evolving Deities of Supreme and Ultimate we observe that certain impersonal phases are being actually united with their volitional counterparts, and thus there is evolving a new relationship between pattern and person." (p. 1303)

2. **PROPOSITION.** Providence does not imply God's predecision — cosmic tyranny. Man has relative powers of choice.

"Providence does not mean that God has decided all things for us and in advance. God loves us too much to do that, for that would be nothing short of cosmic tyranny. Man does have relative powers of choice. Neither is the divine love that shortsighted affection which would pamper and spoil the children of men." (p. 1304)

3. **Proposition.** Reflectivity is an association of energy, mind, and spirit under the overcontrol of the Supreme.

> "The phenomenon of reflectivity, as it is disclosed on the superuniverse headquarters worlds in the amazing performances of the reflective personalities there stationed, represents the most complex interassociation of all phases of existence to be found in all creation. Lines of spirit can be traced back to the Son, physical energy to Paradise, and mind to the Third Source; but in the extraordinary phenomenon of universe reflectivity there is a unique and exceptional unification of all three, so associated as to enable the universe rulers to know about remote conditions instantaneously, simultaneously with their occurrence." (p. 105)

4. **Proposition.** The reflectivity of the Supreme explains the consciousness of the cosmos.

> "If the Supreme is not concerned in reflectivity, we are at a loss to explain the intricate transactions and unerring operations of this consciousness of the cosmos." (p. 105)

VIII. GOD THE ULTIMATE

1.   **God the Ultimate**
2.   **The Transcendental Level**

1. GOD THE ULTIMATE

1. **Proposition.** God the Ultimate is the eventuated and evolving God of the absonite level of supertime and transcended space.

   "*God the Ultimate* — the eventuating God of supertime and transcended space. The second experiential level of unifying Deity manifestation. God the Ultimate implies the attained realization of the synthesized absonite-superpersonal, time-space-transcended, and eventuated-experiential values, co-ordinated on final creative levels of Deity reality." (p. 4)

2. **Proposition.** The Ultimate functions on the second level of unifying deity expression as absonite overcontroller and upholder.

   "*Ultimate* — self-projected and time-space-transcending Deity. Deity omnipotent, omniscient, and omnipresent. Deity functioning on the second level of unifying divinity expression as effective over-controllers and absonite upholders of the master universe. As compared with the ministry of the Deities to the grand universe, this absonite function in the master universe is tantamount to universal overcontrol and supersustenance, sometimes called the Ultimacy of Deity." (p. 2)

3. **Proposition.** Actualization of Ultimate Deity signalizes absonite unification of the first experiential Trinity.

   "The actualization of Ultimate Deity signalizes absonite unification of the first experiential Trinity and signifies unifying Deity expansion on the second level of creative self-realization. This constitutes the personality-power equivalent of the universe experiential-Deity actualization of Paradise absonite realities on the eventuating levels of transcended time-space values. The completion of such an experiential unfoldment is designed to afford ultimate service-destiny for all time-space creatures who have attained absonite levels through the completed realization of the Supreme Being and by the ministry of God the Sevenfold." (p. 12)

4. **Proposition.** God the Ultimate is personal Deity functioning on absonite levels of supertime and transcended space.

> "*God the Ultimate* is designative of personal Deity functioning on the divinity levels of the absonite and on the universe spheres of supertime and transcended space. The Ultimate is a super-supreme eventuation of Deity. The Supreme is the Trinity unification comprehended by finite beings; the Ultimate is the unification of the Paradise Trinity comprehended by absonite beings." (p. 12)

5. **Proposition.** The Ultimate will eventually extend to the outer margins of the fourth space level — periphery of the master universe.

> "The Ultimate is, or sometime will be, space present to the outer margins of the fourth space level. We doubt that the Ultimate will ever have a space presence beyond the periphery of the master universe, but within this limit the Ultimate is progressively integrating the creative organization of the potentials of the three Absolutes." (p. 137)

6. **Proposition.** The emergence of the Ultimate will be shared by all personalities who participated in his actualization.

> "But irrespective of the administrative repercussions attendant upon the emergence of Ultimate Deity, the personal values of his transcendental divinity will be experiencible by all personalities who have been participants in the actualization of this Deity level. Transcendence of the finite can lead only to ultimate attainment. God the Ultimate exists in transcendence of time and space but is nonetheless subabsolute notwithstanding inherent capacity for functional association with absolutes." (p. 1167)

7. **Proposition.** The Ultimate is spiritually present in Havona — and we know of the Qualified Vicegerents of the Ultimate.

> "What changes will be inaugurated by the full emergence of the Ultimate we do not know. But as the Supreme is now spiritually and personally present in Havona, so also is the Ultimate there present but in the absonite and superpersonal sense. And you have been informed of the existence of the Qualified Vicegerents of the Ultimate, though you have not been informed of their present whereabouts or function." (p. 1166)

8. **PROPOSITION.** As the Supreme is associated with finites, the Ultimate is identified with transcendentals — but the Ultimate is something more than a super-Supreme.

> "As the Supreme is associated with finites, so the Ultimate is identified with transcendentals. But though we thus compare Supreme and Ultimate, they differ by something more than degree; the difference is also a matter of quality. The Ultimate is something more than a super-Supreme projected on the transcendental level. The Ultimate is all of that, but more: The Ultimate is an eventuation of new Deity realities, the qualification of new phases of the theretofore unqualified." (p. 1160)

2. THE TRANSCENDENTAL LEVEL

1. **PROPOSITION.** On absonite levels, things and beings are without beginnings and endings. Absonites are not created — they are eventuated.

> "*The absonite level* of reality is characterized by things and beings without beginnings or endings and by the transcendence of time and space. Absoniters are not created; they are eventuated — they simply are. The Deity level of Ultimacy connotes a function in relation to absonite realities. No matter in what part of the master universe, whenever time and space are transcended, such an absonite phenomenon is an act of the Ultimacy of Deity." (p. 2)

2. **PROPOSITION.** The Architects of the Master Universe are the governors of Paradise Transcendentalers. They number 28,011 persons of master minds, superb spirits, and supernal absonites.

> "The Architects of the Master Universe are the governing corps of the Paradise Transcendentalers. This governing corps numbers 28,011 personalities possessing master minds, superb spirits, and supernal absonites. The presiding officer of this magnificent group, the senior Master Architect, is the co-ordinating head of all Paradise intelligences below the level of Deity.
> "The sixteenth proscription of the mandate authorizing these narratives says: 'If deemed wise, the existence of the Architects of the Master Universe and their associates may be disclosed, but their origin, nature, and destiny may not be fully revealed.' We may, however, inform you that these Master Architects exist in seven levels of the absonite." (p. 351)

3. **Proposition.** The seven levels of the function of the Master Architects are:
   a. The Paradise level — 1 Architect
   b. The Havona level — 3 Architects
   c. The superuniverse level - 7 Architects
   d. Primary space level — 70 Architects
   e. Secondary space level — 490 Architects
   f. Tertiary space level — 3,430 Architects
   g. Quartan space level — 24,010 Architects

   See pages 351 and 352.

4. **Proposition.** All trinitized sons of time creatures and Paradise Citizens are wards of the Master Architects.

   > "All beings produced by the union of the children of time and eternity, such as the trinitized offspring of the finaliters and the Paradise Citizens, become wards of the Master Architects. But of all other creatures or entities revealed as functioning in the present organized universes, only Solitary Messengers and Inspired Trinity Spirits maintain any organic association with the Transcendentalers and the Architects of the Master Universe." (p. 352)

5. **Proposition.** The unique beings of the outer space universes, while sublime in ultimacy, will be deficient in finite experience.

   > "We venture the forecast of future and greater outer universes of inhabited worlds, new spheres peopled with new orders of exquisite and unique beings, a material universe sublime in its ultimacy, a vast creation lacking in only one important detail — the presence of actual *finite experience* in the universal life of ascendant existence. Such a universe will come into being under a tremendous experiential handicap: the deprivation of participation in the evolution of the Almighty Supreme. These outer universes will all enjoy the matchless ministry and supernal overcontrol of the Supreme Being, but the very fact of his active presence precludes their participation in the actualization of the Supreme Deity." (p. 353)

6. **Proposition.** Though ignorant of the plans of the Master Architects, we do know three things:
   a. Outer space swarms with new and uninhabited universes.
   b. The finality corps continues to mobilize on Paradise.
   c. The Supreme Person of Deity continues to evolve.

"But though we really know nothing about the plans of the Architects of the Master Universe respecting these outer creations, nevertheless, of three things we are certain:

"1. There actually is a vast and new system of universes gradually organizing in the domains of outer space. New orders of physical creations, enormous and gigantic circles of swarming universes upon universes far out beyond the present bounds of the peopled and organized creations, are actually visible through your telescopes. At present, these outer creations are wholly physical; they are apparently uninhabited and seem to be devoid of creature administration.

"2. For ages upon ages there continues the unexplained and wholly mysterious Paradise mobilization of the perfected and ascendant beings of time and space, in association with the six other finaliter corps.

"3. Concomitantly with these transactions the Supreme Person of Deity is powerizing as the almighty sovereign of the supercreations." (p. 354)

7. **Proposition.** The transcendental level embraces ten meanings and values.

"Among those realities which are associated with the transcendental level are the following:
   "1. The Deity presence of the Ultimate.
   "2. The concept of the master universe.
   "3. The Architects of the Master Universe.
   "4. The two orders of Paradise force organizers.
   "5. Certain modifications in space potency.
   "6. Certain values of spirit.
   "7. Certain meanings of mind.
   "8. Absonite qualities and realities.
   "9. Omnipotence, omniscience, and omnipresence.
   "10. Space." (p. 1160)

8. **Proposition.** The universes exist on three levels: finite, transcendental, and absolute.

"The universe in which we now live may be thought of as existing on finite, transcendental, and absolute levels. This is the cosmic stage on which is enacted the endless drama of personality performance and energy metamorphosis." (p. 1160)

9. **Proposition.** All universe realities are unified:
   a. Absolutely — by the triunities.
   b. Functionally — by the Master Architects.
   c. Relatively — by the Seven Master Spirits.

   "And all of these manifold realities are unified *absolutely* by the several triunities, *functionally* by the Architects of the Master Universe, and *relatively* by the Seven Master Spirits, the subsupreme co-ordinators of the divinity of God the Sevenfold." (p. 1160)

IX. GOD THE ABSOLUTE

1. **Proposition.** God the Absolute would be the experientialization of divinity realities now existential as the Deity Absolute.

   "God the Absolute — the experientializing God of transcended superpersonal values and divinity meanings, now existential as the *Deity Absolute*. This is the third level of unifying Deity expression and expansion." (p. 4)

2. **Proposition.** On this level. Deity experiences exhaustion of personalizable potentials, encounters completion of divinity, and undergoes depletion of capacity for self-revelation.

   "On this supercreative level, Deity experiences exhaustion of personalizable potential, encounters completion of divinity, and undergoes depletion of capacity for self-revelation to successive and progressive levels of other-personalization. Deity now encounters, impinges upon, and experiences identity with, the *Unqualified Absolute*." (p. 4)

3. **Proposition.** God the Absolute is the attainment goal of all superabsonite beings, but the potential of the Deity Absolute transcends finite concepts.

   "God the Absolute is the realization-attainment goal of all superabsonite beings, but the power and personality potential of the Deity Absolute transcends our concept, and we hesitate to discuss those realities which are so far removed from experiential actualization." (p. 13)

X. DEITY

1. **Proposition.** Deity functions on seven levels.

    "Deity functions on personal, prepersonal, and superpersonal levels. Total Deity is functional on the following seven levels:
    "1. *Static* — self-contained and self-existent Deity.
    "2. *Potential* — self-willed and self-purposive Deity.
    "3. *Associative* — self-personalized and divinely fraternal Deity.
    "4. *Creative* — self-distributive and divinely revealed Deity.
    "5. *Evolutional* — self-expansive and creature-identified Deity.
    "6. *Supreme* — self-experiential and creature-Creator-unifying Deity. Deity functioning on the first creature-identificational level as time-space overcontrollers of the grand universe, sometimes designated the Supremacy of Deity.
    "7. *Ultimate* — self-projected and time-space-transcending Deity. Deity omnipotent, omniscient, and omnipresent. Deity functioning on the second level of unifying divinity expression as effective overcontrollers and absonite upholders of the master universe. As compared with the ministry of the Deities to the grand universe, this absonite function in the master universe is tantamount to universal overcontrol and supersustenance, sometimes called the Ultimacy of Deity." (p. 2)

2. **Proposition.** Deity is personalizable as God and is characterized by unity — actual and potential.

    "Deity is personalizable as God, is prepersonal and superpersonal in ways not altogether comprehensible by man. Deity is characterized by the quality of unity — actual or potential — on all supermaterial levels of reality; and this unifying quality is best comprehended by creatures as divinity." (p. 2)

3. **Proposition.** Deity may be:
    a. Existential — the Eternal Son.
    b. Experiential — the Supreme Being.
    c. Associative — God the Sevenfold.
    d. Undivided — the Paradise Trinity.

    "Deity may be existential, as in the Eternal Son; experiential, as in the Supreme Being; associative, as in God the Sevenfold; undivided, as in the Paradise Trinity." (p. 3)

4. **Proposition.** While Deity is divine, all that which is divine is not Deity. Divinity is the characteristic unifying quality of Deity.

> "Deity is the source of all that which is divine. Deity is characteristically and invariably divine, but all that which is divine is not necessarily Deity, though it will be co-ordinated with Deity and will tend towards some phase of unity with Deity — spiritual, mindal, or personal.
>
> "Divinity is the characteristic, unifying, and co-ordinating quality of Deity." (p. 3)

5. **Proposition.** Divinity is creature comprehensible as truth, beauty, and goodness; correlated in personality as love, mercy, and ministry; on impersonal levels disclosed as power, justice, and sovereignty.

> "Divinity is creature comprehensible as truth, beauty, and goodness; correlated in personality as love, mercy, and ministry; disclosed on impersonal levels as justice, power, and sovereignty." (p. 3)

6. **Proposition.** In contemplating Deity, the concept of personality must be divested of the idea of corporeality.

> "In the contemplation of Deity, the concept of personality must be divested of the idea of corporeality. A material body is not indispensable to personality in either man or God. The corporeality error is shown in both extremes of human philosophy. In materialism, since man loses his body at death, he ceases to exist as a personality; in pantheism, since God has no body, he is not, therefore, a person. The superhuman type of progressing personality functions in a union of mind and spirit." (p. 29)

7. **Proposition.** The presence of God is variously determined on differential levels of human experience.

> "The physical presence of the Infinite is the reality of the material universe. The mind presence of Deity must be determined by the depth of individual intellectual experience and by the evolutionary personality level. The spiritual presence of Divinity must of necessity be differential in the universe. It is determined by the spiritual capacity of receptivity and by the degree of the consecration of the creature's will to the doing of the divine will." (p. 64)

8. **Proposition.** Mind equivalent — to know and be known — is indigenous to Deity.

> "The equivalent of mind, the ability to know and be known, is indigenous to Deity. Deity may be personal, prepersonal, superpersonal, or impersonal, but Deity is never mindless, that is, never without the ability at least to communicate with similar entities, beings, or personalities." (p. 78)

9. **Proposition.** Deity is manifested in seven phases.

> "Concerning the several natures of Deity, it may be said:
> "1. The Father is self-existent self.
> "2. The Son is coexistent self.
> "3. The Spirit is conjoint-existent self.
> "4. The Supreme is evolutionary-experiential self.
> "5. The Sevenfold is self-distributive divinity.
> "6. The Ultimate is transcendental-experiential self.
> "7. The Absolute is existential-experiential self." (p. 1294)

10. **Proposition.** Evolutionary Deity is essential to the attainment of destiny — linking the beginnings and the completion of all creative growth.

> "While God the Sevenfold is indispensable to the evolutionary attainment of the Supreme, the Supreme is also indispensable to the eventual emergence of the Ultimate. And the dual presence of the Supreme and the Ultimate constitutes the basic association of subabsolute and derived Deity, for they are interdependently complemental in the attainment of destiny. Together they constitute the experiential bridge linking the beginnings and the completions of all creative growth in the master universe." (p. 1294)

11. **Proposition.** Ubiquity must not be confused with omnipresence. God wills that the Supreme, Ultimate, and Absolute should unify his time-space ubiquity with his timeless and spaceless absolute presence.

> "The ubiquity of Deity must not be confused with the ultimacy of the divine omnipresence. It is volitional with the Universal Father that the Supreme, the Ultimate, and the Absolute should compensate, coordinate, and unify his time-space ubiquity and his time-space-transcended omnipresence with his timeless and spaceless universal and absolute presence. And you should remember that, while Deity ubiquity may be so often space associated, it is not necessarily time conditioned." (p. 1296)

12. **PROPOSITION.** Omnipotence does not imply the power to do the nondoable. God cannot create a square circle.

> "The omnipotence of Deity does not imply the power to do the nondoable. Within the time-space frame and from the intellectual reference point of mortal comprehension, even the infinite God cannot create square circles or produce evil that is inherently good. God cannot do the ungodlike thing. Such a contradiction of philosophic terms is the equivalent of nonentity and implies that nothing is thus created. A personality trait cannot at the same time be Godlike and ungodlike. Compossibility is innate in divine power. And all of this is derived from the fact that omnipotence not only creates things with a nature but also gives origin to the nature of all things and beings." (p. 1299)

13. **PROPOSITION.** God is omnipotent, but not omnificent — he does not do all that is done.

> "God is truly omnipotent, but he is not omnificent — he does not personally do all that is done. Omnipotence embraces the power-potential of the Almighty Supreme and the Supreme Being, but the volitional acts of God the Supreme are not the personal doings of God the Infinite." (p. 1299)

14. **PROPOSITION.** Omnificence of primal Deity would disenfranchise millions of God's concurring creative assistants and associates.

> "To advocate the omnificence of primal Deity would be equal to disenfranchising well-nigh a million Creator Sons of Paradise, not to mention the innumerable hosts of various other orders of concurring creative assistants. There is but one uncaused Cause in the whole universe. All other causes are derivatives of this one First Great Source and Center. And none of this philosophy does any violence to the free-willness of the myriads of the children of Deity scattered through a vast universe." (p. 1299)

15. **PROPOSITION.** Deity omnipotence affords security of cosmic citizenship, but the error of omnificence entails the fallacy of Pantheism.

> "To recognize Deity omnipotence is to enjoy security in your experience of cosmic citizenship, to possess assurance of safety in the long journey to Paradise. But to accept the fallacy of omnificence is to embrace the colossal error of Pantheism." (p. 1300)

PART II
THE PARADISE TRINITY

Part Two
THE PARADISE TRINITY

I. INTRODUCTION

1. **Proposition.** Revelations about the Trinity on Urantia:

   First—Staff of Caligastia
   Second—Adam and Eve
   Third—Machiventa Melchizedek

   > "The first Urantian revelation leading to the comprehension of the Paradise Trinity was made by the staff of Prince Caligastia about one-half million years ago. This earliest Trinity concept was lost to the world in the unsettled times following the planetary rebellion.
   > "The second presentation of the Trinity was made by Adam and Eve in the first and second gardens. These teachings had not been wholly obliterated even in the times of Machiventa Melchizedek about thirty-five thousand years later, for the Trinity concept of the Sethites persisted in both Mesopotamia and Egypt but more especially in India, where it was long perpetuated in Agni, the Vedic three-headed fire god.
   > "The third presentation of the Trinity was made by Machiventa Melchizedek, and this doctrine was symbolized by the three concentric circles which the sage of Salem wore on his breast plate. But Machiventa found it very difficult to teach the Palestinian Bedouins about the Universal Father, the Eternal Son, and the Infinite Spirit." (p. 1143)

2. **Proposition.** The Trinity was essential to the Father's plan of self-distribution.

   > "It would seem that the Father, back in eternity, inaugurated a policy of profound self-distribution. There is inherent in the selfless, loving, and lovable nature of the Universal Father something which causes him to reserve to himself the exercise of only those powers and that authority which he apparently finds it impossible to delegate or to bestow." (p. 108)

3. **Proposition.** As absolute Deity, God functions only in the Trinity and in relation to universe totality.

   > "Of all absolute associations, the Paradise Trinity (the first triunity) is unique as an exclusive association of personal Deity. God functions as God only in relation to God and to those who can know God, but as absolute Deity only in the Paradise Trinity and in relation to universe totality." (p. 112) [Note: The word **trinity** is not found in the Bible.]

II. THE TRINITY UNION OF DEITY

1. **PROPOSITION.** The Paradise Trinity was inevitable. It was inherent in the differentiation of the personal and the nonpersonal.

   "The original and eternal Paradise Trinity is existential and was inevitable. This never-beginning Trinity was inherent in the fact of the differentiation of the personal and the nonpersonal by the Father's unfettered will and factualized when his personal will coordinated these dual realities by mind. The post-Havona Trinities are experiential—are inherent in the creation of two subabsolute and evolutional levels of power-personality manifestation in the master universe." (p. 15)

2. **PROPOSITION.** The Paradise Trinity is the only Deity reality embracing infinity—the actualization of God the Supreme, God the Ultimate, and God the Absolute.

   "*The Paradise Trinity*—the eternal Deity union of the Universal Father, the Eternal Son, and the Infinite Spirit—is existential in actuality, but all potentials are experiential. Therefore does this Trinity constitute the only Deity reality embracing infinity, and therefore do there occur the universe phenomena of the actualization of God the Supreme, God the Ultimate, and God the Absolute." (p. 15)

3. **PROPOSITION.** The Paradise Trinity facilitates the Father's escape from personality absolutism—primacy, perfection, eternity, universality, and infinity.

   "The Paradise Trinity of eternal Deities facilitates the Father's escape from personality absolutism. The Trinity perfectly associates the limitless expression of God's infinite personal will with the absoluteness of Deity. The Eternal Son and the various Sons of divine origin, together with the Conjoint Actor and his universe children, effectively provide for the Father's liberation from the limitations otherwise inherent in primacy, perfection, changelessness, eternity, universality, absoluteness, and infinity." (p. 108)

4. **PROPOSITION.** There is only one inescapable inevitability in universe affairs—the Paradise Trinity.

   "From the present situation on the circle of eternity, looking backward into the endless past, we can discover only one inescapable inevitability in universe affairs, and that is the Paradise Trinity. I deem the Trinity to have been inevitable. As I view the past, present, and future of time, I consider nothing else in all the universe of universes to have been inevitable." (p. 108)

5. **Proposition.** The Trinity is composed of:
   a. The infinite father-personality.
   b. The unqualified personality-absolute.
   c. The conjoint personality.

   "The First Source and Center is the infinite *father-personality*, the unlimited source personality. The Eternal Son is the unqualified *personality-absolute*, that divine being who stands throughout all time and eternity as the perfect revelation of the personal nature of God. The Infinite Spirit is the *conjoint personality*, the unique personal consequence of the everlasting Father-Son union." (p. 110)

6. **Proposition.** The Trinity may be compared to a corporation of father, son, and grandson. Such an entity could be nonpersonal and yet subject to their personal wills.

   "The Trinity is an association of infinite persons functioning in a nonpersonal capacity but not in contravention of personality. The illustration is crude, but a father, son, and grandson could form a corporate entity which would be nonpersonal but nonetheless subject to their personal wills." (p. 112)

7. **Proposition.** The Trinity gives rise to the evolution, eventuation, and deitization of new meanings, values, powers, and capacities for universe manifestation.

   "The Trinity association of the three Paradise Deities results in evolution, eventuation, and deitization of new meanings, values, powers, and capacities for universal revelation, action, and administration. Living associations, human families, social groups, or the Paradise Trinity are not augmented by mere arithmetical summation. The group potential is always far in excess of the simple sum of the attributes of the component individuals." (p. 113)

8. **Proposition.** In the Trinity, the three personalizations of Deity are actually one Deity—undivided and indivisible.

   "The oneness, the indivisibility, of Paradise Deity is existential and absolute. There are three eternal personalizations of Deity— the Universal Father, the Eternal Son, and the Infinite Spirit—but in the Paradise Trinity they are *actually* one Deity, undivided and indivisible." (p. 640)

9. **PROPOSITION.** The administration of justice is never a personal act—it is always a group function. Divine justice is a function of the Paradise Trinity.

> "The Master, when on earth, admonished his followers that justice is never a *personal* act; it is always a *group* function. Neither do the Gods, as persons, administer justice. But they perform this very function as a collective whole, as the Paradise Trinity." (p. 1146)

III. FUNCTIONS OF THE TRINITY

1. **PROPOSITION.** Personal Deities have attributes but the Trinity has functions—justice administrations, totality attitudes, co-ordinate action, and cosmic overcontrol.

> "The personal Deities have attributes, but it is hardly consistent to speak of the Trinity as having attributes. This association of divine beings may more properly be regarded as having *functions*, such as justice administration, totality attitudes, co-ordinate action, and cosmic overcontrol. These functions are actively supreme, ultimate, and (within the limits of Deity) absolute as far as all living realities of personality value are concerned." (p. 113)

2. **PROPOSITION.** Justice is not a personal attitude of the Deities—it is inherent in the sovereignty of the Trinity.

> "*Justice* is inherent in the universal sovereignty of the Paradise Trinity, but goodness, mercy, and truth are the universe ministry of the divine personalities, whose Deity union constitutes the Trinity. Justice is not the attitude of the Father, the Son, or the Spirit. Justice is the Trinity attitude of these personalities of love, mercy, and ministry. No one of the Paradise Deities fosters the administration of justice. Justice is never a personal attitude; it is always a plural function." (p. 114)

3. **PROPOSITION.** The Paradise Trinity is concerned only with totals—planets or universes. The Trinity is the totality of Deity.

> "As things appear to the mortal on the finite level, the Paradise Trinity, like the Supreme Being, is concerned only with the total—total planet, total universe, total superuniverse, total grand universe. This totality attitude exists because the Trinity is the total of Deity and for many other reasons." (p. 115)

4. **Proposition.** The acts of the Trinity may be divinely meaningful, but it might not so appear to the mortals of the evolutionary worlds.

   "As a son of God you can discern the personal attitude of love in all the acts of God the Father. But you will not always be able to understand how many of the universe acts of the Paradise Trinity redound to the good of the individual mortal on the evolutionary worlds of space. In the progress of eternity the acts of the Trinity will be revealed as altogether meaningful and considerate, but they do not always so appear to the creatures of time." (p. 116)

5. **Proposition.** Justice is the collective thought of righteousness; mercy is the personal attitude of love.

   "Justice is the collective thought of righteousness; mercy is its personal expression. Mercy is the attitude of love; precision characterizes the operation of law; divine judgment is the soul of fairness, ever conforming to the justice of the Trinity, ever fulfilling the divine love of God." (p. 115)

IV. STATIONARY SONS OF THE TRINITY

1. **Proposition.** There are seven groups of Supreme Trinity Personalities.

   "Supreme Trinity Personalities are all created for specific service. They are designed by the divine Trinity for the fulfillment of certain specific duties, and they are qualified to serve with perfection of technique and finality of devotion. There are seven orders of the Supreme Trinity Personalities:

   "1. Trinitized Secrets of Supremacy.
   "2. Eternals of Days.
   "3. Ancients of Days.
   "4. Perfections of Days.
   "5. Recents of Days.
   "6. Unions of Days.
   "7. Faithfuls of Days." (p. 207)

2. **Proposition.** *Judgment*—applied justice—is the function of the Stationary Sons of the Trinity.

   "*Judgment*, the final application of justice in accordance with the evidence submitted by the personalities of the Infinite Spirit, is the work of the Stationary Sons of the Trinity, beings partaking of the Trinity nature of the united Father, Son, and Spirit." (p. 114)

3. **Proposition.** The First Source and Center is law; The Third Source interprets law. Justice is applied by the Stationary Sons.

> "All law takes origin in the First Source and Center; *he is law*. The administration of spiritual law inheres in the Second Source and Center. The revelation of law, the promulgation and interpretation of the divine statutes, is the function of the Third Source and Center. The application of law, justice, falls within the province of the Paradise Trinity and is carried out by certain Sons of the Trinity." (p. 114)

4. **Proposition.** The Trinity provides the full revelation of Deity; the Stationary Sons provide the perfect revelation of divine justice.

> "The Paradise Trinity effectively provides for the full expression and perfect revelation of the eternal nature of Deity. The Stationary Sons of the Trinity likewise afford a full and perfect revelation of divine justice. The Trinity is Deity unity, and this unity rests eternally upon the absolute foundations of the divine oneness of the three original and co-ordinate and coexistent personalities, God the Father, God the Son, and God the Spirit." (p. 108)

A. *Trinitized Secrets of Supremacy.*

1. **Proposition.** Each of the Father's seven Paradise worlds is presided over by ten Trinitized Secrets of Supremacy.
   "There are seven worlds in the innermost circuit of the Paradise satellites, and each of these exalted worlds is presided over by a corps of ten Trinitized Secrets of Supremacy. They are not creators, but they are supreme and ultimate administrators. The conduct of the affairs of these seven fraternal spheres is wholly committed to this corps of seventy supreme directors." (p. 207)

B. *Eternals of Days.*

1. **Proposition.** Each of the billion worlds of Havona is directed by an Eternal of Days.
   "Each of the billion worlds of Havona is directed by a Supreme Trinity Personality. These rulers are known as the Eternals of Days, and they number exactly one billion, one for each of the Havona spheres. They are the offspring of the Paradise Trinity, but like the Secrets of Supremacy there are no records of their origin. Forever have these two groups of all-wise fathers ruled their exquisite worlds of the Paradise-Havona system, and they function without rotation or reassignment." (p. 208)

C. Ancients of Days.
  1. **PROPOSITION.** The identical but diverse personalities of the Ancients of Days provide the uniform direction of the seven superuniverses.
  "The Ancients of Days are all basically identical; they disclose the combined character and unified nature of the Trinity. They possess individuality and are in personality diverse, but they do not differ from each other as do the Seven Master Spirits. They provide the uniform directorship of the otherwise differing seven superuniverses, each of which is a distinct, segregated, and unique creation. The Seven Master Spirits are unlike in nature and attributes, but the Ancients of Days, the personal rulers of the superuniverses, are all uniform and superperfect offspring of the Paradise Trinity." (p. 209)
  2. **PROPOSITION.** The Trinity-origin Ancients of Days mete out justice of supreme fairness to the seven superuniverses.
  "The Ancients of Days and their Trinity-origin associates mete out the just judgment of supreme fairness to the seven superuniverses. In the central universe such functions exist in theory only; there fairness is self-evident in perfection, and Havona perfection precludes all possibility of disharmony. (p. 115)
  3. **PROPOSITION.** The Ancients of Days are the most powerful executive rulers of the time-space creations.
  "In power, scope of authority, and extent of jurisdiction the Ancients of Days are the most powerful and mighty of any of the direct rulers of the time-space creations. In all the vast universe of universes they alone are invested with the high powers of final executive judgment concerning the eternal extinction of will creatures. And all three Ancients of Days must participate in the final decrees of the supreme tribunal of a superuniverse." (p. 210)
  4. **PROPOSITION.** The incomplete factualization of the Supreme is compensated by the overcontrol of the Ancients of Days.
  "The Supreme Being is achieving the sovereignty of the seven superuniverses by experiential service just as a Creator Son experientially earns the sovereignty of his local universe. But during the present age of the unfinished evolution of the Supreme, the Ancients of Days provide the co-ordinated and perfect administrative overcontrol of the evolving universes of time and space. And the wisdom of originality and the initiative of individuality characterize all the decrees and rulings of the Ancients of Days." (p. 210)

D. *Perfections of Days.*

    1. **Proposition.** The Trinity-origin Perfections of Days preside over the major sectors of the superuniverses.

    "There are just two hundred and ten Perfections of Days, and they preside over the governments of the ten major sectors of each superuniverse. They were trinitized for the special work of assisting the superuniverse directors, and they rule as the immediate and personal vicegerents of the Ancients of Days.

    "Three Perfections of Days are assigned to each major sector capital, but unlike the Ancients of Days, it is not necessary that all three be present at all times. From time to time one of this trio may absent himself to confer in person with the Ancients of Days concerning the welfare of his realm." (p. 210)

E. *Recents of Days.*

    1. **Proposition.** The Recents of Days administer the affairs of the minor sectors of the superuniverses.

    "The Recents of Days are the youngest of the supreme directors of the superuniverses; in groups of three they preside over the affairs of the minor sectors. In nature they are co-ordinate with the Perfections of Days, but in administrative authority they are subordinate. There are just twenty-one thousand of these personally glorious and divinely efficient Trinity personalities. They were created simultaneously, and together they passed through their Havona training under the Eternals of Days." (p. 211)

F. *Unions of Days.*

    1. **Proposition.** On the capital of each local universe, a Union of Days acts as Trinity adviser.

    "The Trinity personalities of the order of "Days" do not function in an administrative capacity below the level of the superuniverse governments. In the evolving local universes they act only as counselors and advisers. The Unions of Days are a group of liaison personalities accredited by the Paradise Trinity to the dual rulers of the local universes. Each organized and inhabited local universe has assigned to it one of these Paradise counselors, who acts as the representative of the Trinity, and in some respects, of the Universal Father, to the local creation.

    "There are seven hundred thousand of these beings in existence, though they have not all been commissioned. The reserve corps of the Unions of Days functions on Paradise as the Supreme Council of Universe Adjustments." (p. 212)

G. *Faithfuls of Days*.
   1. **Proposition.** The Faithfuls of Days serve on the constellation capitals as advisers to the Most High Fathers.
   "These high Trinity-origin personalities are the Paradise advisers to the rulers of the one hundred constellations in each local universe. There are seventy million Faithfuls of Days, and like the Unions of Days, not all are in service. Their Paradise reserve corps is the Advisory Commission of Interuniverse Ethics and Self-government. Faithfuls of Days rotate in service in accordance with the rulings of the supreme council of their reserve corps." (p. 213)

V. TRINTY ATTITUDE TOWARD REALITY

1. **Proposition.** While the Supreme Being is not a personalization of the Trinity, he is the nearest approach comprehensible by finite creatures.

   "The maximum self-limitation of the Trinity is its attitude toward the finite. The Trinity is not a person, nor is the Supreme Being an exclusive personalization of the Trinity, but the Supreme is the nearest approach to a power-personality focalization of the Trinity which can be comprehended by finite creatures. Hence the Trinity in relation to the finite is sometimes spoken of as the Trinity of Supremacy." (p. 113)

2. **Proposition.** Neither the Supreme nor the Ultimate are wholly representative of the Trinity, but they do in a qualified way portray Trinity attitudes.

   "The Paradise Trinity has regard for those levels of existence which are more than finite but less than absolute, and this relationship is sometimes denominated the Trinity of Ultimacy. Neither the Ultimate nor the Supreme are wholly representative of the Paradise Trinity, but in a qualified sense and to their respective levels, each seems to represent the Trinity during the prepersonal eras of experiential-power development." (p. 113)

3. **Proposition.** The attitude of the Trinity toward the Absolutes culminates in the action of total Deity.

   "*The Absolute Attitude* of the Paradise Trinity is in relation to absolute existences and culminates in the action of total Deity." (p. 113)

VI. CO-ORDINATE TRINITY ORIGIN BEINGS

A. *Perfectors of Wisdom.*

1. **Proposition.** Perfectors of Wisdom are Trinity Sons who personify divine wisdom in the superuniverses.
"The Perfectors of Wisdom are a specialized creation of the Paradise Trinity designed to personify the wisdom of divinity in the superuniverses. There are exactly seven billion of these beings in existence, and one billion are assigned to each of the seven superuniverses." (p. 215)

B. *Divine Counselors.*

1. **Proposition.** Divine Counselors are the counsel of Deity to the superuniverses.
"These Trinity-origin beings are the counsel of Deity to the realms of the seven superuniverses. They are not *reflective* of the divine counsel of the Trinity; they *are* that counsel. There are twenty one billion Counselors in service, and three billion are assigned to each superuniverse." (p. 216)

C. *Universal Censors.*

1. **Proposition.** The Censors are the judgment of Deity—the decisions of the Paradise Trinity.
"There are exactly eight billion Universal Censors in existence. These unique beings *are* the judgment of Deity. They are not merely reflective of the decisions of perfection; they *are* the judgment of the Paradise Trinity. Even the Ancients of Days do not sit in judgment except in association with the Universal Censors." (p. 217)

2. **Proposition.** Censors are totaling personalities. They summarize diverse realities and reveal the divine conclusions.
"The Censors are universe totaling personalities. When a thousand witnesses have given testimony—or a million—when the voice of wisdom has spoken and the counsel of divinity has recorded, when the testimony of ascendant perfection has been added, then the Censor functions, and there is immediately revealed an unerring and divine totaling of all that has transpired; and such a disclosure represents the divine conclusion, the sum and substance of a final and perfect decision. Therefore, when a Censor has spoken, no one else may speak, for the Censor has depicted the true and unmistakable total of all that has gone before. When he speaks, there is no appeal." (p. 218)

D. *Inspired Trinity Spirits.*

1. **Proposition.** Inspired Trinity Spirits, serving the Trinity, are one of the secret orders of creation.

    "I will be able to tell you very little concerning the Inspired Trinity Spirits, for they are one of the few wholly secret orders of beings in existence, secret, no doubt, because it is impossible for them fully to reveal themselves even to those of us whose origin is so near the source of their creation. They come into being by the act of the Paradise Trinity and may be utilized by any one or two of the Deities as well as by all three. We do not know whether these Spirits are of completed number or are constantly increasing, but we incline to the belief that their number is not fixed." (p. 219)

2. **Proposition.** Inspired Trinity Spirits and Thought Adjusters produce identical qualitative reactions upon the detection-sensitivity of the Solitary Messengers.

    "I may relate a further interesting fact: When a Solitary Messenger is on a planet whose inhabitants are indwelt by Thought Adjusters, as on Urantia, he is aware of a qualitative excitation in his detection-sensitivity to spirit presence. In such instances there is no quantitative excitation, only a qualitative agitation. When on a planet to which Adjusters do not come, contact with the natives does not produce any such reaction. This suggests that Thought Adjusters are in some manner related to, or are connected with, the Inspired Spirits of the Paradise Trinity. In some way they may possibly be associated in certain phases of their work; but we do not really know. They both originate near the center and source of all things, but they are not the same order of being. Thought Adjusters spring from the Father alone; Inspired Spirits are the offspring of the Paradise Trinity." (p. 220)

3. **Proposition.** The Melchizedeks think the Inspired Spirits may replace the Solitary Messengers assigned to certain trinitized sons.

    "The Melchizedeks of Nebadon teach that Inspired Trinity Spirits are destined, sometime in the eternal future, to function in the places of the Solitary Messengers, whose ranks are slowly but certainly being depleted by their assignment as associates of certain types of trinitized sons." (p. 219)

VII. URANTIAN TRINITY CONCEPTS

1. **Proposition.** The Hebrews had difficulty in reconciling the trinitarian concept with monotheism.

   "The Hebrews knew about the Trinity from the Kenite traditions of the days of Melchizedek, but their monotheistic zeal for the one God, Yahweh, so eclipsed all such teachings that by the time of Jesus' appearance the Elohim doctrine had been practically eradicated from Jewish theology. The Hebrew mind could not reconcile the trinitarian concept with the monotheistic belief in the One Lord, the God of Israel." (p. 1144)

2. **Proposition.** Jesus taught the Trinity concept, but his apostles grasped but little of the truth.

   "Jesus taught his apostles the truth regarding the persons of the Paradise Trinity, but they thought he spoke figuratively and symbolically. Having been nurtured in Hebraic monotheism, they found it difficult to entertain any belief that seemed to conflict with their dominating concept of Yahweh. And the early Christians inherited the Hebraic prejudice against the Trinity concept." (p. 1144)

3. **Proposition.** Not until the Urantia revelation has the Paradise Trinity become factual as to identity.

   "Not since the times of Jesus has the factual identity of the Paradise Trinity been known on Urantia (except by a few individuals to whom it was especially revealed) until its presentation in these revelatory disclosures." (p. 1145)

4. **Proposition.** The Trinity is an absolute entity—supersummative Deity.

   "And this selfsame Paradise Trinity is a real entity—-not a personality but nonetheless a true and absolute reality; not a personality but nonetheless compatible with coexistent personalities— the personalities of the Father, the Son, and the Spirit. The Trinity is a supersummative Deity reality eventuating out of the conjoining of the three Paradise Deities. The qualities, characteristics, and functions of the Trinity are not the simple sum of the attributes of the three Paradise Deities; Trinity functions are something unique, original, and not wholly predictable from an analysis of the attributes of Father, Son, and Spirit." (p. 1145)

VIII. THE SEVEN TRIUNITIES

1. **Proposition.** When the three Paradise Deities conjoin for mutual action—as persons—they constitute a triunity—not a trinity.

   "And the association of the three Paradise personalities eternalizes the first triunity, the personality union of the Father, the Son, and the Spirit. For when these three persons, *as persons*, conjoin for united function, they thereby constitute a triunity of functional unity, not a trinity—an organic entity—but nonetheless a triunity, a threefold functional aggregate unanimity." (p. 1147)

2. **Proposition.** The undivided unity of the Trinity may sustain an external relationship to the triunity of their personal members.

   "The Paradise Trinity is not a triunity; it is not a functional unanimity; rather it is undivided and indivisible Deity. The Father, Son, and Spirit (as persons) can sustain a relationship to the Paradise Trinity, for the Trinity *is* their undivided Deity. The Father, Son, and Spirit sustain no such personal relationship to the first triunity, for that *is* their functional union as three persons. Only as the Trinity—as undivided Deity—do they collectively sustain an external relationship to the triunity of their personal aggregation." (p. 1147)

3. **Proposition.** A triunity is not an entity; it is functional rather than organic; its members are partners rather than corporative associates.

   "Thus does the Paradise Trinity stand unique among absolute relationships, there are several existential triunities but only one existential Trinity. A triunity is *not* an entity. It is functional rather than organic. Its members are partners rather than corporative. The components of the triunities may be entities, but a triunity itself is an association." (p. 1147)

4. **Proposition.** The Universal Father is the absolute of Absolutes and the primal member of each of the seven triunities.

   "In attempting the description of seven triunities, attention is directed to the fact that the Universal Father is the primal member of each. He is, was, and ever will be: the First Universal Father-Source, Absolute Center, Primal Cause, Universal Controller, Limitless Energizer, Original Unity, Unqualified Upholder, First Person of Deity, Primal Cosmic Pattern, and Essence of Infinity. The Universal Father is the personal cause of the Absolutes; he is the absolute of Absolutes." (p. 1147)

5. **Proposition.** The Triunities are the functional balance wheel of infinity— the unification of all beginnings, existences, and destinies.

> "The triunities are the functional balance wheel of infinity, the unification of the uniqueness of the Seven Infinity Absolutes. It is the existential presence of the triunities that enables the Father-I AM to experience functional infinity unity despite the diversification of infinity into seven Absolutes. The First Source and Center is the unifying member of all triunities; in him all things have their unqualified beginnings, eternal existences, and infinite destinies— 'in him all things consist.'" (p. 1150)

6. **Proposition.** The First Triunity is personal and purposive—the union of love, mercy, and ministry.

> "*The First Triunity—the personal-purposive triunity.* This is the grouping of the three Deity personalities:
> 1. The Universal Father.
> 2. The Eternal Son.
> 3. The Infinite Spirit.
>
> "This is the threefold union of love, mercy, and ministry—the purposive and personal association of the three eternal Paradise personalities. This is the divinely fraternal, creature-loving, fatherly-acting, and ascension-promoting association. The divine personalities of this first triunity are personality-bequeathing, spirit-bestowing, and mind-endowing Gods." (p. 1148)

7. **Proposition.** The Second Triunity is the power-pattern triunity.

> "*The Second Triunity—the power-pattern triunity.* Whether it be a tiny ultimaton, a blazing star, or a whirling nebula, even the central or superuniverses, from the smallest to the largest material organizations, always is the physical pattern—the cosmic configuration— derived from the function of this triunity. This association consists of:
>
> "1. The Father-Son.
> "2. The Paradise Isle.
> "3. The Conjoint Actor.
>
> "Energy is organized by the cosmic agents of the Third Source and Center; energy is fashioned after the pattern of Paradise, the absolute materialization; but behind all of this ceaseless manipulation is the presence of the Father-Son, whose union first activated the Paradise pattern in the appearance of Havona concomitant with the birth of the Infinite Spirit, the Conjoint Actor." (p. 1148)

8. **Proposition.** The Third is the spirit-evolutional triunity.

> "*The Third Triunity—the spirit-evolutional triunity.* The entirety of spiritual manifestation has its beginning and end in this association, consisting of:
> "1. The Universal Father.
> "2. The Son-Spirit.
> "3. The Deity Absolute.
> "From spirit potency to Paradise spirit, all spirit finds reality expression in this triune association of the pure spirit essence of the Father, the active spirit values of the Son-Spirit, and the unlimited spirit potentials of the Deity Absolute. The existential values of spirit have their primordial genesis, complete manifestation, and final destiny in this triunity." (p. 1149)

9. **Proposition.** The Fourth is the triunity of energy infinity.

> "*The Fourth Triunity—the triunity of energy infinity.* Within this triunity there eternalizes the beginnings and the endings of all energy reality, from space potency to monota. This grouping embraces the following:
> "1. The Father-Spirit.
> "2. The Paradise Isle.
> "3. The Unqualified Absolute.
> "Paradise is the center of the force-energy activation of the cosmos— the universe position of the First Source and Center, the cosmic focal point of the Unqualified Absolute, and the source of all energy. Existentially present within this triunity is the energy potential of the cosmos-infinite, of which the grand universe and the master universe are only partial manifestations." (p. 1149)

10. **Proposition.** The Fifth is the triunity of reactive infinity.

> "*The Fifth Triunity—the triunity of reactive infinity.* This association consists of:
> 1. The Universal Father.
> 2. The Universal Absolute.
> 3. The Unqualified Absolute.
> "This grouping yields the eternalization of the functional infinity realization of all that is actualizable within the domains of nondeity reality. This triunity manifests unlimited reactive capacity to the volitional, causative, tensional, and patternal actions and presences of the other triunities." (p. 1149)

11. **PROPOSITION.** The Sixth is the triunity of cosmic-associated Deity.

> "*The Sixth Triunity—the triunity of cosmic-associated Deity.* This grouping consists of:
> 1. The Universal Father.
> 2. The Deity Absolute.
> 3. The Universal Absolute.
>
> "This is the association of Deity-in-the-cosmos, the immanence of Deity in conjunction with the transcendence of Deity. This is the last outreach of divinity on the levels of infinity toward those realities which lie outside the domain of deified reality." (p. 1150)

12. **PROPOSITION.** The Seventh is the triunity of infinite unity.

> "*The Seventh Triunity—the triunity of infinite unity.* This is the unity of infinity functionally manifest in time and eternity, the co-ordinate unification of actuals and potentials. This group consists of:
> 1. The Universal Father.
> 2. The Conjoint Actor.
> 3. The Universal Absolute.
>
> "The Conjoint Actor universally integrates the varying functional aspects of all actualized reality on all levels of manifestation, from finites through transcendentals and on to absolutes. The Universal Absolute perfectly compensates the differentials inherent in the varying aspects of all incomplete reality, from the limitless potentialities of active-volitional and causative Deity reality to the boundless possibilities of static, reactive, nondeity reality in the incomprehensible domains of the Unqualified Absolute." (p. 1150)

13. **PROPOSITION.** There are eight unrevealed triunities having to do with actualities and potentials beyond experiential supremacy.

> "These approximations are sufficient to elucidate the concept of the triunities. Not knowing the ultimate level of the triunities, you cannot fully comprehend the first seven. While we do not deem it wise to attempt any further elaboration, we may state that there are fifteen triune associations of the First Source and Center, eight of which are unrevealed in these papers. These unrevealed associations are concerned with realities, actualities, and potentialities which are beyond the experiential level of supremacy." (p. 1150)

14. **Proposition.** The inherent infinity of the I AM is eternally present in the Absolutes, functionally associated in the triunities, and transmitively active in the triodities.

> "From the existential standpoint, nothing new can happen throughout the galaxies, for the completion of infinity inherent in the I AM is eternally present in the seven Absolutes, is functionally associated in the triunities, and is transmitively associated in the triodities. But the fact that infinity is thus existentially present in these absolute associations in no way makes it impossible to realize new cosmic experientials. From a finite creature's viewpoint, infinity contains much that is potential, much that is on the order of a future possibility rather than a present actuality." (p. 1261)

IX. TRIUNITIES AND TRIODITIES

1. **Proposition.** Non-Father triune associations are called triodities. They are consequential to the triunities.

> "There are certain other triune relationships which are non-Father in constitution, but they are not real triunities, and they are always distinguished from the Father triunities. They are called variously, associate triunities, co-ordinate triunities, and *triodities*. They are consequential to the existence of the triunities." (p. 1151)

2. **Proposition.** The Triodity of Actuality is an association of the three absolute actuals.

> "*The Triodity of Actuality*. This triodity consists in the interrelationship of the three absolute actuals:
> 1. The Eternal Son.
> 2. The Paradise Isle.
> 3. The Conjoint Actor.
>
> "The Eternal Son is the absolute of spirit reality, the absolute personality. The Paradise Isle is the absolute of cosmic reality, the absolute pattern. The Conjoint Actor is the absolute of mind reality, the co-ordinate of absolute spirit reality, and the existential Deity synthesis of personality and power. This triune association eventuates the co-ordination of the sum total of actualized reality—spirit, cosmic, or mindal. It is unqualified in actuality." (p. 1151)

3. **Proposition.** The Triodity of Potentiality is an association of the three Absolutes of potentiality:

> "*The Triodity of Potentiality.* This triodity consists in the association of the three Absolutes of potentiality:
> "1. The Deity Absolute.
> "2. The Universal Absolute.
> "3. The Unqualified Absolute.
> "Thus are interassociated the infinity reservoirs of all latent energy reality—spirit, mindal, or cosmic. This association yields the integration of all latent energy reality. It is infinite in potential." (p. 1151)

X. THE TRINITY OF TRINITIES

1. **Proposition.** The Trinity of Trinities is the summation of all experiential infinity as manifested in a theoretical infinity of eternity realization; experiential infinity attains identity with the existential infinite.

> "The nature of the Trinity of Trinities is difficult to portray to the human mind; it is the actual summation of the entirety of experiential infinity as such is manifested in a theoretical infinity of eternity realization. In the Trinity of Trinities the experiential infinite attains to identity with the existential infinite, and both are as one in the pre-experiential, pre-existential I AM. The Trinity of Trinities is the final expression of all that is implied in the fifteen triunities and associated triodities. Finalities are difficult for relative beings to comprehend, be they existential or experiential; therefore must they always be presented as relativities." (p. 1170)

2. **Proposition.** The Trinity of Trinities exists in several staggering and unimaginable phases.

> "The Trinity of Trinities exists in several phases. It contains possibilities, probabilities, and inevitabilities that stagger the imaginations of beings far above the human level. It has implications that are probably unsuspected by the celestial philosophers, for its implications are in the triunities, and the triunities are, in the last analysis, unfathomable." (p. 1170)

3. **Proposition.** There are three levels of the Trinity of Trinities.

> "There are a number of ways in which the Trinity of Trinities can be portrayed. We elect to present the three-level concept, which is as follows:
> "1. The level of the three Trinities.
> "2. The level of experiential Deity.
> "3. The level of the I AM.

> "These are levels of increasing unification. Actually the Trinity of Trinities is the first level, while the second and third levels are unifications-derivatives of the first." (p. 1170)

4. **Proposition.** The Trinity of Trinities may be presented on three levels. See pages 1171-1173.

XI. ULTIMATE AND ABSOLUTE TRINITIES

1. **Proposition.** God the Ultimate will powerize and personalize as the result of the unification of the Ultimate Trinity.

   > "*The Ultimate Trinity*, now evolving, will eventually consist of the Supreme Being, the Supreme Creator Personalities, and the absonite Architects of the Master Universe, those unique universe planners who are neither creators nor creatures. God the Ultimate will eventually and inevitably powerize and personalize as the Deity consequence of the unification of this experiential Ultimate Trinity in the expanding arena of the well-nigh limitless master universe." (p. 16)

2. **Proposition.** The Absolute Trinity is the second experiential Trinity, and its unification would experientialize Absolute Deity.

   > "*The Absolute Trinity*—the second experiential Trinity—now in process of actualization, will consist of God the Supreme, God the Ultimate, and the unrevealed Consummator of Universe Destiny. This Trinity functions on both personal and superpersonal levels, even to the borders of the nonpersonal, and its unification in universality would experientialize Absolute Deity." (p. 16)

3. **Proposition.** The Trinity Absolute has the theoretical capacity to activate the Absolutes of potentiality—Deity, Universal, and Unqualified.

   > "The Ultimate is the apex of transcendental reality even as the Supreme is the capstone of evolutionary-experiential reality. And the actual emergence of these two experiential Deities lays the foundation for the second experiential Trinity. This is the Trinity Absolute, the union of God the Supreme, God the Ultimate, and the unrevealed Consummator of Universe Destiny. And this Trinity has theoretical capacity to activate the Absolutes of potentiality—Deity, Universal, and Unqualified. But the completed formation of this Trinity Absolute could take place only after the completed evolution of the entire master universe, from Havona to the fourth and outermost space level." (p. 1167)

4. **Proposition.** The Trinity Absolute is absolute in total function—qualitatively unlimited and unconditioned in potential.

> "Stated otherwise: The Trinity Absolute, as its name implies, is really absolute in total function. We do not know how an absolute function can achieve total expression on a qualified, limited, or otherwise restricted basis. Hence we must assume that any such totality function will be unconditioned (in potential). And it would also appear that the unconditioned would also be unlimited, at least from a qualitative standpoint, though we are not so sure regarding quantitative relationships." (p. 1168)

5. **Proposition.** The Paradise Trinity is infinite; the Trinity Ultimate subinfinite; the Trinity Absolute impinges upon the existential Absolutes of potentiality.

> "Of this, however, we are certain: While the existential Paradise Trinity is infinite, and while the experiential Trinity Ultimate is subinfinite, the Trinity Absolute is not so easy to classify. Though experiential in genesis and constitution, it definitely impinges upon the existential Absolutes of potentiality." (p. 1168)

PART III
THE ABSOLUTES

PART THREE
THE ABSOLUTES

I. CONCEPT OF THE ABSOLUTES

1. PROPOSITION. Total infinity resides in the seven Absolutes.

   "In these papers total reality (infinity) has been presented as it exists in the seven Absolutes:
   1. The Universal Father.
   2. The Eternal Son.
   3. The Infinite Spirit.
   4. The Isle of Paradise.
   5. The Deity Absolute.
   6. The Universal Absolute.
   7. The Unqualified Absolute." (p. 1146)

2. PROPOSITION. The Absolutes seem to supersede matter, transcend mind, and supervene spirit.

   "These absolutes seem to supersede matter, to transcend mind, and to supervene spirit. I am constantly confused and often perplexed by my inability to comprehend these complex transactions which I attribute to the presences and performances of the Unqualified Absolute, the Deity Absolute, and the Universal Absolute." (p. 55)

3. PROPOSITION. The Trinity is antecedent to the Absolutes. The Absolute is the impersonal and co-ordinate reaction of the Trinity of Trinities to all primary space situations.

   "On first thought, a concept of the Absolute as ancestor to all things—even the Trinity—seems to afford transitory satisfaction of consistency gratification and philosophic unification, but any such conclusion is invalidated by the actuality of the eternity of the Paradise Trinity. We are taught, and we believe, that the Universal Father and his Trinity associates are eternal in nature and existence. There is, then, but one consistent philosophic conclusion, and that is: The Absolute is, to all universe intelligences, the impersonal and the co-ordinate reaction of the Trinity (of Trinities) to all basic and primary space situations, intrauniversal and extrauniversal." (p. 644)

4. **Proposition.** The Paradise Trinity stands in finality, eternity, supremacy, and ultimacy as absolute.

> "To all personality intelligences of the grand universe the Paradise Trinity forever stands in finality, eternity, supremacy, and ultimacy and, for all practical purposes of personal comprehension and creature realization, as absolute. (p. 644)

5. **Proposition.** Mind cannot grasp the concept of an Absolute without breaking up the unity of such a reality.

> "Mind can never hope to grasp the concept of an Absolute without attempting first to break the unity of such a reality. Mind is unifying of all divergencies, but in the very absence of such divergencies, mind finds no basis upon which to attempt to formulate understanding concepts. (p. 1261)

II. THE SEVEN ABSOLUTES

1. **Proposition.** The seven prime relationships within the I AM eternalize as the seven Absolutes of Infinity. The Absolutes had no beginning and they are:

    1. The First Source and Center.
    2. The Second Source and Center.
    3. The Paradise Source and Center.
    4. The Third Source and Center.
    5. The Deity Absolute.
    6. The Unqualified Absolute.
    7. The Universal Absolute.

See pages 1155-56.

III. THE DEITY ABSOLUTE

1. **Proposition.** The Deity Absolute is the all-powerful activator, while the Unqualified Absolute is the all-efficient mechanizer of the universe of universes.

> "*The Deity Absolute* seems to be the all-powerful activator, while the Unqualified Absolute appears to be the all-efficient mechanizer of the supremely unified and ultimately co-ordinated universe of universes, even universes upon universes, made, making, and yet to be made." (p. 14)

IV. THE UNQUALIFIED ABSOLUTE

1. **Proposition.** The Unqualified Absolute is nonpersonal and undeified. He cannot be penetrated by fact, truth, experience, philosophy, or revelation.

   "*The Unqualified Absolute* is nonpersonal, extradivine, and undeified. The Unqualified Absolute is therefore devoid of personality, divinity, and all creator prerogatives. Neither fact nor truth, experience nor revelation, philosophy nor absonity are able to penetrate the nature and character of this Absolute without universe qualification." (p. 14)

2. **Proposition.** The Unqualified Absolute seems to dominate the nether plane of Paradise.

   "The Trinity seems to dominate the personal or upper plane, the Unqualified Absolute the nether or impersonal plane. We hardly conceive of the Unqualified Absolute as a person, but we do think of the functional space presence of this Absolute as focalized on nether Paradise." (p. 120)

3. **Proposition.** The Unqualified Absolute upholds the physical universe; the Deity Absolute motivates the overcontrol of all material reality.

   "The Unqualified Absolute upholds the physical universe, while the Deity Absolute motivates the exquisite overcontrol of all material reality; and both Absolutes are functionally unified by the Universal Absolute. This cohesive correlation of the material universe is best understood by all personalities—material, morontia, absonite, or spiritual—by the observation of the gravity response of all bona fide material reality to the gravity centering on nether Paradise." (p. 637)

V. THE UNIVERSAL ABSOLUTE

1. **Proposition.** The Universal Absolute resolves the tension created by the differentiation of reality into the deified and undeified—the personalizable and nonpersonalizable.

   "*The Universal Absolute*, we logically deduce, was inevitable in the Universal Father's absolute freewill act of differentiating universe realities into deified and undeified—personalizable and nonpersonalizable—values. The Universal Absolute is the Deity phenomenon indicative of the resolution of the tension created by the freewill act of thus differentiating universe reality, and functions as the associative co-ordinator of these sum totals of existential potentialities." (p. 14)

Part III — *The Absolutes*

2. **Proposition.** The Universal Absolute equalizes the tensions between:

   The finite and the Infinite.
   Reality potentials and actuals.
   Paradise and space.
   Time and eternity.
   Man and God.

   > "The finite can coexist in the cosmos along with the Infinite only because the associative presence of the Universal Absolute so perfectly equalizes the tensions between time and eternity, finity and infinity, reality potential and reality actuality, Paradise and space, man and God. Associatively the Universal Absolute constitutes the identification of the zone of progressing evolutional reality existent in the time-space, and in the transcended time-space, universes of subinfinite Deity manifestation." (p. 15)

3. **Proposition.** The Absolutes are co-ordinated in the Ultimate; conditioned in the Supreme; and time-space modified in God the Sevenfold.

   > "The Unqualified Absolute and the Deity Absolute are unified in the Universal Absolute. The Absolutes are co-ordinated in the Ultimate, conditioned in the Supreme, and time-space modified in God the Sevenfold. On subinfinite levels there are *three* Absolutes, but in infinity they appear to be *one*. On Paradise there are three personalizations of Deity, but in the Trinity they *are* one." (p. 644)

4. **Proposition.** The Absolute is unqualified only in infinity. The revelation of God must be relative until his power and personality become infinite in the Absolutes.

   > "Spiritual personality is absolute only on Paradise, and the concept of the Absolute is unqualified only in infinity. Deity presence is absolute only on Paradise, and the revelation of God must always be partial, relative, and progressive until his power becomes experientially infinite in the space potency of the Unqualified Absolute, while his personality manifestation becomes experientially infinite in the manifest presence of the Deity Absolute, and while these two potentials of infinity become reality-unified in the Universal Absolute. (p. 645)

VI. ABSOLUTE LEVELS AND RESPONSES

1. **Proposition.** Before the deitization of finite relativities, all diversification of reality occurred on absolute levels.

    "Prior to the deitization of the finite, it would appear that all reality diversification took place on absolute levels; but the volitional act promulgating finite reality connotes a qualification of absoluteness and implies the appearance of relativities." (p. 1158)

2. **Proposition.** The First Source and Center is the Volitional Absolute; the Second Source and Center is the Personality Absolute.

    "The First Source and Center is the Volitional Absolute; the Second Source and Center is the Personality Absolute." (p. 74)

3. **Proposition.** Finite existence represents transference from potentials to actuals within the Absolutes and repercussions appear as responses in Deity, creatures, and the universes.

    "The entire promulgation of finite existences represents a transference from potentials to actuals within the absolute associations of functional infinity. Of the many repercussions to creative actualization of the finite, there may be cited:
    "1. *The deity response*, the appearance of the three levels of experiential supremacy: the actuality of personal-spirit supremacy in Havona, the potential for personal-power supremacy in the grand universe to be, and the capacity for some unknown function of experiential mind acting on some level of supremacy in the future master universe.
    "2. *The universe response* involved an activation of the architectural plans for the superuniverse space level, and this evolution is still progressing throughout the physical organization of the seven superuniverses.
    "3. *The creature repercussion* to finite-reality promulgation resulted in the appearance of perfect beings on the order of the eternal inhabitants of Havona and of perfected evolutionary ascenders from the seven superuniverses. But to attain perfection as an evolutionary (time-creative) experience implies something other-than-perfection as a point of departure. Thus arises imperfection in the evolutionary creations. And this is the origin of potential evil. Misadaptation, disharmony, and conflict, all these things are inherent in evolutionary growth, from physical universes to personal creatures.

> "4. *The divinity response* to the imperfection inherent in the time lag of evolution is disclosed in the compensating presence of God the Sevenfold, by whose activities that which is perfecting is integrated with both the perfect and the perfected. This time lag is inseparable from evolution, which is creativity in time. Because of it, as well as for other reasons, the almighty power of the Supreme is predicated on the divinity successes of God the Sevenfold." (p. 1159)

4. **PROPOSITION.** The First Source and Center is the absolute reality which embraced all potentials and gave origin to all actuals.

    > "One basic conception of the absolute level involves a postulate of three phases:
    > 1. *The Original.* The unqualified concept of the First Source and Center, that source manifestation of the I AM from which all reality takes origin.
    > 2. *The Actual.* The union of the three Absolutes of actuality, the Second, Third, and Paradise Sources and Centers. This triodity of the Eternal Son, the Infinite Spirit, and the Paradise Isle constitutes the actual revelation of the originality of the First Source and Center.
    > 3. *The Potential.* The union of the three Absolutes of potentiality, the Deity, Unqualified, and Universal Absolutes. This triodity of existential potentiality constitutes the potential revelation of the originality of the First Source and Center." (p. 1262)

5. **PROPOSITION.** The Absolutes of potentiality operate upon the eternal level of the cosmos. On subabsolute levels the Supreme and the Ultimate function. Though the will of God may not always prevail in the part, it invariably does in the whole.

    > "The three Absolutes of potentiality are operative on the purely eternal level of the cosmos, hence never function as such on subabsolute levels. On the descending levels of reality the triodity of potentiality is manifest with the Ultimate and upon the Supreme. The potential may fail to time-actualize with respect to a part on some subabsolute level, but never in the aggregate. The will of God does ultimately prevail, not always concerning the individual but invariably concerning the total." (p. 1262)

PART IV
PARADISE

Part Four
PARADISE

I. INTRODUCTION

1. **Proposition.** The Father, in eternalizing the Original Son, simultaneously revealed the infinity potential of his nonpersonal self as Paradise.

    "In the eternity of the past, when the Universal Father gave infinite personality expression of his spirit self in the being of the Eternal Son, simultaneously he revealed the infinity potential of his nonpersonal self as Paradise. Nonpersonal and nonspiritual Paradise appears to have been the inevitable repercussion to the Father's will and act which eternalized the Original Son." (p. 127)

2. **Proposition.** Paradise is not spherical—it is ellipsoid—essentially flat.

    "In form Paradise differs from the inhabited space bodies: it is not spherical. It is definitely ellipsoid, being one-sixth longer in the north-south diameter than in the east-west diameter. The central Isle is essentially flat, and the distance from the upper surface to the nether surface is one tenth that of the east-west diameter." (p. 119)

3. **Proposition.** Time and space are nonexistent on Paradise—absolute.

    "*The absolute level* is beginningless, endless, timeless, and spaceless. For example: On Paradise, time and space are nonexistent; the time-space status of Paradise is absolute. This level is Trinity attained, existentially, by the Paradise Deities, but this third level of unifying Deity expression is not fully unified experientially. Whenever, wherever, and however the absolute level of Deity functions, Paradise-absolute values and meanings are manifest." (p. 2)

4. **Proposition.** The central Isle consists of three domains.

    "The central Isle is geographically divided into three domains of activity:
    1. Upper Paradise.
    2. Peripheral Paradise.
    3. Nether Paradise." (p. 119)

II. CENTER AND SOURCE OF ALL THINGS

1. **Proposition.** Paradise is the home of Deity and the eternal center of all things.

   "PARADISE is the eternal center of the universe of universes and the abiding place of the Universal Father, the Eternal Son, the Infinite Spirit, and their divine co-ordinates and associates. This central Isle is the most gigantic organized body of cosmic reality in all the master universe. Paradise is a material sphere as well as a spiritual abode." (p. 118)

2. **Proposition.** Paradise is the geographic center of infinity—an eternal and exclusive existence.

   "Paradise is the geographic center of infinity; it is not a part of universal creation, not even a real part of the eternal Havona universe. We commonly refer to the central Isle as belonging to the divine universe, but it really does not. Paradise is an eternal and exclusive existence." (p. 126)

3. **Proposition.** Paradise is headquarters for all personality activities and the source-center of all force-space manifestations.

   "Paradise is the universal headquarters of all personality activities and the source-center of all force-space and energy manifestations. Everything which has been, now is, or is yet to be, has come, now comes, or will come forth from this central abiding place of the eternal Gods. Paradise is the center of all creation, the source of all energies, and the place of primal origin of all personalities." (p. 127)

4. **Proposition.** Space does not exist on Paradise. It is the motionless nucleus of the quiescent zones existing between pervaded and unpervaded space.

   "Space does not exist on any of the surfaces of Paradise. If one 'looked' directly up from the upper surface of Paradise, one would 'see' nothing but unpervaded space going out or coming in, just now coming in. Space does not touch Paradise; only the quiescent *midspace zones* come in contact with the central Isle. "Paradise is the actually motionless nucleus of the relatively quiescent zones existing between pervaded and unpervaded space." (p. 124)

III. THE DIVINE RESIDENCE

1. **PROPOSITION.** Paradise is at the heart of the central universe—the geographic center of infinity and the dwelling place of the eternal God.

    "At the heart of this eternal and central universe is the stationary Isle of Paradise, the geographic center of infinity and the dwelling place of the eternal God." (p. 1)

2. **PROPOSITION.** Paradise serves many purposes, but is primarily the home of Deity.

    "Paradise serves many purposes in the administration of the universal realms, but to creature beings it exists primarily as the dwelling place of Deity." (p. 118)

3. **PROPOSITION.** On Paradise, God is cosmically focalized, spiritually personalized, and geographically resident.

    "God dwells, has dwelt, and everlastingly will dwell in this same central and eternal abode. We have always found him there and always will. The Universal Father is cosmically focalized, spiritually personalized, and geographically resident at this center of the universe of universes." (p. 118)

IV. NATURE OF PARADISE

1. **PROPOSITION.** Paradise is the Absolute of material gravity control. It is motionless and while having a universe location it has no position in space.

    "Paradise not otherwise qualified—is the Absolute of the material-gravity control of the First Source and Center. Paradise is motionless, being the only stationary thing in the universe of universes. The Isle of Paradise has a universe location but no position in space." (p. 7)

2. **PROPOSITION.** Paradise is not a creator—it is a unique controller. It influences the reactions of all who have to do with force, energy, and power.

    "Paradise is not a creator; it is a unique controller of many universe activities, far more of a controller than a reactor. Throughout the material universes Paradise influences the reactions and conduct of all beings having to do with force, energy, and power, but Paradise itself is unique, exclusive, and isolated in the universes. Paradise represents nothing and nothing represents Paradise. It is neither a force nor a presence; it is just *Paradise*." (p. 7)

3. **Proposition.** The magnificence of Paradise is material, mindal, and spiritual—the infinite endowment of divine personality.

> "The material beauty of Paradise consists in the magnificence of its physical perfection; the grandeur of the Isle of God is exhibited in the superb intellectual accomplishments and mind development of its inhabitants; the glory of the central Isle is shown forth in the infinite endowment of divine spirit personality—the light of life." (p. 118)

4. **Proposition.** Paradise is composed of absolution, stationary reality of space potency not found elsewhere in the universe of universes.

> "The eternal Isle is composed of a single form of materialization—stationary systems of reality. This literal substance of Paradise is a homogeneous organization of space potency not to be found elsewhere in all the wide universe of universes. It has received many names in different universes, and the Melchizedeks of Nebadon long since named it *absolutum*. This Paradise source material is neither dead nor alive; it is the original nonspiritual expression of the First Source and Center; it is *Paradise*, and Paradise is without duplicate." (p. 120)

5. **Proposition.** We cannot visualize the glories of Paradise. We must await our ascendant arrival.

> "But a further attempt to visualize to you the glories of Paradise would be futile. You must wait, and ascend while you wait, for truly, 'Eye has not seen, nor ear heard, neither has it entered into the mind of mortal man, the things which the Universal Father has prepared for those who survive the life in the flesh on the worlds of time and space.'" (p. 121)

6. **Proposition.** God is spirit, but Paradise is not. Spirit beings live on spheres of reality.

> "'God is spirit,' but Paradise is not. The material universe is always the arena wherein take place all spiritual activities; spirit beings and spirit ascenders live and work on physical spheres of material reality." (p. 139)

7. **Proposition.** Paradise is not Deity—it is not conscious.

> "Deity may cause much that is not Deity, and Paradise is not Deity; neither is it conscious as mortal man could ever possibly understand such a term." (p. 127)

8. **Proposition.** Paradise is the absolute of patterns. Mind and spirit relationships are transmissible—patterns are not.

> "Paradise is not ancestral to any being or living entity; it is not a creator. Personality and mind-spirit relationships are *transmissible*, but pattern is not. Patterns are never reflections; they are duplications—reproductions. Paradise is the absolute of patterns; Havona is an exhibit of these potentials in actuality." (p. 127)

V. UPPER PARADISE

1. **Proposition.** Of the three spheres of Paradise, the most Holy Area is reserved for worhsip, trinitization, and spiritual attainment.

> "On upper Paradise there are three grand spheres of activity, the *Deity presence*, the *Most Holy Sphere*, and the *Holy Area*. The vast region immediately surrounding the presence of the Deities is set aside as the Most Holy Sphere and is reserved for the functions of worship, trinitization, and high spiritual attainment. There are no material structures nor purely intellectual creations in this zone; they could not exist there." (p. 120)

2. **Proposition.** Paradise sectors are divided into residential units for one billion working groups.

> "Each of the seven sectors of Paradise is subdivided into residential units suitable for the lodgment headquarters of one billion glorified individual working groups. One thousand of these units constitute a division. One hundred thousand divisions equal one congregation. Ten million congregations constitute an assembly. One billion assemblies make one grand unit. And this ascending series continues through the second grand unit, the third, and so on to the seventh grand unit. And seven of the grand units make up the master units, and seven of the master units constitute a superior unit; and thus by sevens the ascending series expands through the superior, supersuperior, celestial, supercelestial, to the supreme units. But even this does not utilize all the space available." (p. 121)

3. **Proposition.** The seven residential zones of the Holy Area are occupied by numerous groups of Paradise sojourners.

> "The Holy Area, the outlying or residential region, is divided into seven concentric zones. Paradise is sometimes called 'the Father's House' since it is his eternal residence, and these seven zones are often designated 'the Father's Paradise mansions.' The inner or first zone is occupied by Paradise Citizens and the

natives of Havona who may chance to be dwelling on Paradise. The next or second zone is the residential area of the natives of the seven superuniverses of time and space. This second zone is in part subdivided into seven immense divisions, the Paradise home of the spirit beings and ascendant creatures who hail from the universes of evolutionary progression. Each of these sectors is exclusively dedicated to the welfare and advancement of the personalities of a single superuniverse, but these facilities are almost infinitely beyond the requirements of the present seven superuniverses." (p. 120)

4. **PROPOSITION.** On Paradise, there is always more of worship than has been formally provided for.

"There are appointed times and places for worship on Paradise, but these are not adequate to accommodate the ever-increasing overflow of the spiritual emotions of the growing intelligence and expanding divinity recognition of the brilliant beings of experiential ascension to the eternal Isle. Never since the times of Grandfanda have the supernaphim been able fully to accommodate the spirit of worship on Paradise. Always is there an excess of worshipfulness as gauged by the preparation therefor. And this is because personalities of inherent perfection never can fully appreciate the tremendous reactions of the spiritual emotions of beings who have slowly and laboriously made their way upward to Paradise glory from the depths of the spiritual darkness of the lower worlds of time and space. When such angels and mortals of time attain the presence of the Powers of Paradise, there occurs the expression of the accumulated emotions of the ages, a spectacle astounding to the angels of Paradise and productive of the supreme joy of divine satisfaction in the Paradise Deities." (p. 304)

5. **PROPOSITION.** Paradise is subject to seasons of dominating worship.

"Sometimes all Paradise becomes engulfed in a dominating tide of spiritual and worshipful expression. Often the conductors of worship cannot control such phenomena until the appearance of the threefold fluctuation of the light of the Deity abode, signifying that the divine heart of the Gods has been fully and completely satisfied by the sincere worship of the residents of Paradise, the perfect citizens of glory and the ascendant creatures of time. What a triumph of technique! What a fruition of the eternal plan and purpose of the Gods that the intelligent love of the creature child should give full satisfaction to the infinite love of the Creator Father!" (p. 304)

VI. PERIPHERAL PARADISE

1. PROPOSITION. The periphery of Paradise is partly occupied by the landing and dispatching fields—the impinging nonpervaded space zones.

   "The peripheral surface of Paradise is occupied, in part, by the landing and dispatching fields for various groups of spirit personalities. Since the nonpervaded-space zones nearly impinge upon the periphery, all personality transports destined to Paradise land in these regions. Neither upper nor nether Paradise is approachable by transport supernaphim or other types of space traversers." (p. 121)

2. PROPOSITION. While the Seven Master Spirits have their seats of authority on the seven worlds of the Infinite Spirit, they maintain force-focal centers on the periphery of Paradise.

   "The Seven Master Spirits have their personal seats of power and authority on the seven spheres of the Spirit, which circle about Paradise in the space between the shining orbs of the Son and the inner circuit of the Havona worlds, but they maintain force-focal headquarters on the Paradise periphery." (p. 121)

3. PROPOSITION. On peripheral Paradise are found seven trillion historic and prophetic exhibits of the Creator Sons.

   "Here on peripheral Paradise are the enormous historic and prophetic exhibit areas assigned to the Creator Sons, dedicated to the local universes of time and space. There are just seven trillion of these historic reservations now set up or in reserve, but these arrangements all together occupy only about four per cent of that portion of the peripheral area thus assigned." (p. 121)

VII. NETHER PARADISE

1. PROPOSITION. On nether Paradise is found the Zone of Infinity and all physical-energy and cosmic-force originate there.

   "We are informed that all physical-energy and cosmic-force circuits have their origin on nether Paradise, and that it is constituted as follows:

   "1. Directly underneath the location of the Trinity, in the central portion of nether Paradise, is the unknown and unrevealed Zone of Infinity.

   "2. This Zone is immediately surrounded by an unnamed area.

   "3. Occupying the outer margins of the under surface is a region having mainly to do with space potency and force-energy." (p. 122)

2. **Proposition.** Energies circulating through the universes pass in and out of this nether zone of the Unqualified Absolute.

   "All forms of force and all phases of energy seem to be encircuited; they circulate throughout the universes and return by definite routes. But with the emanations of the activated zone of the Unqualified Absolute there appears to be either an outgoing or an incoming—never both simultaneously. This outer zone pulsates in agelong cycles of gigantic proportions. For a little more than one billion Urantia years the space-force of this center is outgoing; then for a similar length of time it will be incoming. And the space-force manifestations of this center are universal; they extend throughout all pervadable space." (p. 123)

3. **Proposition.** The inner zone of the force center acts as a gigantic heart whose pulsations direct currents to the outermost borders of space.

   "*The inner zone* of this force center seems to act as a gigantic heart whose pulsations direct currents to the outermost borders of physical space. It directs and modifies force-energies but hardly drives them." (p. 122)

4. **Proposition.** The outer zone is the largest and most active of the three concentric belts of unidentified space potential. This space presence is responsive to the Trinity.

   "*The outer zone* is the largest and most active of the three concentric and elliptical belts of unidentified space potential. This area is the site of unimagined activities, the central circuit point of emanations which proceed spaceward in every direction to the outermost borders of the seven superuniverses and on beyond to overspread the enormous and incomprehensible domains of all outer space. This space presence is entirely impersonal notwithstanding that in some undisclosed manner it seems to be indirectly responsive to the will and mandates of the infinite Deities when acting as the Trinity. This is believed to be the central focalization, the Paradise center, of the space presence of the Unqualified Absolute." (p. 122)

VIII. SPACE FUNCTIONS OF PARADISE

1. **PROPOSITION.** All absolute potential for cosmic reality is concentrated in Paradise. Paradise exists without time and has no location in space.

    "It appears to us that the First Source and Center has concentrated all absolute potential for cosmic reality in Paradise as a part of his technique of self-liberation from infinity limitations, as a means of making possible subinfinite, even time-space, creation. But it does not follow that Paradise is time-space limited just because the universe of universes discloses these qualities. Paradise exists without time and has no location in space." (p. 120)

2. **PROPOSITION.** Space seemingly originates just below Paradise—time just above. Motion is not inherent on Paradise—it is volitional.

    "Roughly: space seemingly originates just below nether Paradise; time just above upper Paradise. Time, as you understand it, is not a feature of Paradise existence, though the citizens of the central Isle are fully conscious of nontime sequence of events. Motion is not inherent on Paradise; it is volitional." (p. 120)

3. **PROPOSITION.** Space is not a condition within, nor is it the presence of, the Unqualified Absolute. Space is a bestowal of Paradise.

    "Space is neither a subabsolute condition within, nor the presence of, the Unqualified Absolute, neither is it a function of the Ultimate. It is a bestowal of Paradise, and the space of the grand universe and that of all outer regions is believed to be actually pervaded by the ancestral space potency of the Unqualified Absolute." (p. 124)

4. **PROPOSITION.** There are upper and lower limits to horizontal space. These limits draw farther apart at greater distances from Paradise.

    "There is an upper and lower limit to horizontal space with reference to any given location in the universes. If one could move far enough at right angles to the plane of Orvonton, either up or down, eventually the upper or lower limit of pervaded space would be encountered. Within the known dimensions of the master universe these limits draw farther and farther apart at greater and greater distances from Paradise; space thickens, and it thickens somewhat faster than does the plane of creation, the universes." (p. 124)

IX. DESTINY OF ASCENDANT CREATURES

1. **Proposition.** Paradise is the goal of desire for all supermaterial personalities.

   "Although it is true that not all of the lower spirit beings of the local universes are immediately destined to Paradise, Paradise still remains the goal of desire for all supermaterial personalities." (p. 126)

2. **Proposition.** God-knowing mortals who espouse the Father's will are embarked on the long Paradise trail of the pursuit of perfection attainment.

   "Every God-knowing mortal who has espoused the career of doing the Father's will has already embarked upon the long, long Paradise trail of divinity pursuit and perfection attainment. And when such an animal-origin being does stand, as countless numbers now do, before the Gods on Paradise, having ascended from the lowly spheres of space, such an achievement represents the reality of a spiritual transformation bordering on the limits of supremacy." (p. 127)

Note: Paradise finds frequent mention in the Koran—but is only found three times in the Bible.

1. **Luke 23:43.** Jesus promises the thief on the cross that they shall meet on Paradise.
2. **2 Cor. 12:3.** Paul tells about being caught up in Paradise for a revelation.
3. **Rev. 2:7.** John tells about the tree of life being in the Paradise of God.

PART V
THE PARADISE-HAVONA SYSTEM

Part Five
THE PARADISE HAVONA SYSTEM

I. INTRODUCTION

1. **Proposition.** The Paradise-Havona System constitutes the perfect and eternal nucleus of the master universe.

   "*The Paradise-Havona System*, the eternal universe encircling the eternal Isle, constitutes the perfect and eternal nucleus of the master universe; all seven of the superuniverses and all regions of outer space revolve in established orbits around the gigantic central aggregation of the Paradise satellites and the Havona spheres." (p. 129)

2. **PROPOSITION.** Time is not reckoned on Paradise—sequence of successive events is inherent in its citizens.

   "Time is not reckoned on Paradise; the sequence of successive events is inherent in the concept of those who are indigenous to the central Isle. But time is germane to the Havona circuits and to numerous beings of both celestial and terrestrial origin sojourning thereon. Each Havona world has its own local time, determined by its circuit." (p. 153)

3. **Proposition.** The Paradise-Havona system is a unit of creative perfection.

   "On Paradise nothing is experimental, and the Paradise-Havona system is a unit of creative perfection." (p. 155)

II. GEOGRAPHY

1. **Proposition.** Havona is far distant from us and its dimensions are unbelievable. It contains one billion worlds.

   "The perfect and divine universe occupies the center of all creation; it is the eternal core around which the vast creations of time and space revolve. Paradise is the gigantic nuclear Isle of absolute stability which rests motionless at the very heart of the magnificent eternal universe. This central planetary family is called Havona and is far-distant from the local universe of Nebadon. It is of enormous dimensions and almost unbelievable mass and consists of one billion spheres of unimagined beauty and superb grandeur, but the true magnitude of this vast creation is really beyond the understanding grasp of the human mind." (p. 152)

2. **PROPOSITION.** Between Paradise and Havona there are three special circuits of seven spheres each.

> "Between the central Isle of Paradise and the innermost of the Havona planetary circuits there are situated in space three lesser circuits of special spheres. The innermost circuit consists of the seven secret spheres of the Universal Father; the second group is composed of the seven luminous worlds of the Eternal Son; in the outermost are the seven immense spheres of the Infinite Spirit, the executive-headquarters worlds of the Seven Master Spirits." (p. 143)

3. **PROPOSITION.** These twenty-one eternalized worlds are of unexcelled grandeur, each is diverse, except that the seven worlds of the Son are alike.

> "These three seven-world circuits of the Father, the Son, and the Spirit are spheres of unexcelled grandeur and unimagined glory. Even their material or physical construction is of an order unrevealed to you. Each circuit is diverse in material, and each world of each circuit is different excepting the seven worlds of the Son, which are alike in physical constitution. All twenty-one are enormous spheres, and each group of seven is differently eternalized. As far as we know they have always been; like Paradise they are eternal. There exists neither record nor tradition of their origin." (p. 143)

4. **PROPOSITION.** There are seven differing space conditions between Paradise and the inner borders of the superuniverses.

> "From the periphery of Paradise to the inner borders of the seven superuniverses there are the following seven space conditions and motions:
>
> "1. The quiescent midspace zones impinging on Paradise.
>
> "2. The clockwise processional of the three Paradise and the seven Havona circuits.
>
> "3. The semiquiet space zone separating the Havona circuits from the dark gravity bodies of the central universe.
>
> "4. The inner, counterclockwise-moving belt of the dark gravity bodies.
>
> "5. The second unique space zone dividing the two space paths of the dark gravity bodies.
>
> "6. The outer belt of dark gravity bodies, revolving clockwise around Paradise.
>
> "7. A third space zone—a semiquiet zone—separating the outer belt of dark gravity bodies from the innermost circuits of the seven superuniverses." (p. 152)

5. **Proposition.** The billion worlds of Havona exist in seven concentric circles. Each circuit is pervaded by one of the Seven Spirits of the Circuits.

> "The billion worlds of Havona are arranged in seven concentric circuits immediately surrounding the three circuits of Paradise satellites. There are upwards of thirty-five million worlds in the innermost Havona circuit and over two hundred and forty-five million in the outermost, with proportionate numbers intervening. Each circuit differs, but all are perfectly balanced and exquisitely organized, and each is pervaded by a specialized representation of the Infinite Spirit, one of the Seven Spirits of the Circuits. In addition to other functions this impersonal Spirit co-ordinates the conduct of celestial affairs throughout each circuit."(p. 152)

6. **Proposition.** Havona is surrounded by a circuit of dark gravity bodies— in every way differing from other space bodies.

> "On the outskirts of this vast central universe, far out beyond the seventh belt of Havona worlds, there swirl an unbelievable number of enormous dark gravity bodies. These multitudinous dark masses are quite unlike other space bodies in many particulars; even in form they are very different. These dark gravity bodies neither reflect nor absorb light; they are nonreactive to physical-energy light, and they so completely encircle and enshroud Havona as to hide it from the view of even near-by inhabited universes of time and space." (p. 153)

7. **Proposition.** The dark gravity bodies revolve in two opposite directional circuits.

> "The great belt of dark gravity bodies is divided into two equal elliptical circuits by a unique space intrusion. The inner belt revolves counterclockwise; the outer revolves clockwise. These alternate directions of motion, coupled with the extraordinary mass of the dark bodies, so effectively equalize the lines of Havona gravity as to render the central universe a physically balanced and perfectly stabilized creation." (p. 153)

8. **Proposition.** The two circuits of gravity bodies are differently arranged and the intervening space is unique.

> "The inner procession of dark gravity bodies is tubular in arrangement, consisting of three circular groupings. A cross section of this circuit would exhibit three concentric circles of

about equal density. The outer circuit of dark gravity bodies is arranged perpendicularly, being ten thousand times higher than the inner circuit. The up-and-down diameter of the outer circuit is fifty thousand times that of the transverse diameter. "The intervening space which exists between these two circuits of gravity bodies is *unique* in that nothing like it is to be found elsewhere in all the wide universe. This zone is characterized by enormous wave movements of an up-and-down nature and is permeated by tremendous energy activities of an unknown order." (p. 153)

III. CONSTITUTION OF HAVONA

1. **Proposition.** Havona material consists of one thousand basic elements and seven forms of energy of seven phases each.

   "The material of Havona consists of the organization of exactly one thousand basic chemical elements and the balanced function of the seven forms of Havona energy. Each of these basic energies manifests seven phases of excitation, so that the Havona natives respond to forty-nine differing sensation stimuli." (p. 154)

2. **Proposition.** The physical energies of Havona are threefold. Superuniverse energies are twofold.

   "The physical realities of Havona represent an order of energy organization radically different from any prevailing in the evolutionary universes of space. Havona energies are threefold; superuniverse units of energy-matter contain a twofold energy charge, although one form of energy exists in negative and positive phases. The creation of the central universe is threefold (Trinity); the creation of a local universe (directly) is twofold, by a Creator Son and a Creative Spirit." (p. 154)

IV. THE HAVONA WORLDS

1. **Proposition.** There is no government on Havona.

   "Concerning the government of the central universe, there is none. Havona is so exquisitely perfect that no intellectual system of government is required." (p. 155)

2. **Proposition.** Everything about Havona is beyond human imagination, but these worlds do have rivers and lakes.

   "The architecture, lighting, and heating, as well as the biologic and artistic embellishment, of the Havona spheres, are quite beyond the greatest possible stretch of human imagination. You cannot be told much about Havona; to understand its beauty and grandeur you must see it. But there are real rivers and lakes on these perfect worlds." (p. 156)

3. **PROPOSITION.** Each Havona world is an original and unique creation, embellished in accordance with the plans of its resident Eternal of Days.

   "Every one of these planets is an original, unique, and exclusive creation; each planet is a matchless, superb, and perfect production. And this diversity of individuality extends to all features of the physical, intellectual, and spiritual aspects of planetary existence. Each of these billion perfection spheres has been developed and embellished in accordance with the plans of the resident Eternal of Days. And this is just why no two of them are alike." (p. 159)

4. **PROPOSITION.** Standard time for the grand universe is the Paradise-Havona day—a little over seven minutes less than one thousand years of Urantia time.

   "You have unwittingly read the truth when your eyes rested on the statement 'A day is as a thousand years with God, as but a watch in the night.' One Paradise-Havona day is just seven minutes, three and one-eighth seconds less than one thousand years of the present Urantia leap-year calendar.
   "This Paradise-Havona day is the standard time measurement for the seven superuniverses, although each maintains its own internal time standards." (p. 153)

V. WORLDS OF THE FATHER

1. **PROPOSITION.** The seven secret worlds of the Father reflect the spiritual luminosity of the Deities to Paradise and on to the seven circuits of Havona.

   "The seven secret spheres of the Universal Father, circulating about Paradise in close proximity to the eternal Isle, are highly reflective of the spiritual luminosity of the central shining of the eternal Deities, shedding this light of divine glory throughout Paradise and even upon the seven circuits of Havona." (p. 143)

2. **PROPOSITION.** The Father's worlds are directed by the Trinitized Secrets of Supremacy.

   "The Paradise worlds of the Father are directed by the highest order of the Stationary Sons of the Trinity, the Trinitized Secrets of Supremacy." (p. 144)

3. **Proposition.** The worlds of the Father harbor specialized representations of Deity comprehended only by those groups resident on each world.

   "One of the reasons for the secrecy of these worlds is because each of these sacred spheres enjoys a specialized representation, or manifestation, of the Deities composing the Paradise Trinity; not a personality, but a unique presence of Divinity which can only be appreciated and comprehended by those particular groups of intelligences resident on, or admissible to, that particular sphere. The Trinitized Secrets of Supremacy are the personal agents of these specialized and impersonal presences of Divinity. And the Secrets of Supremacy are highly personal beings, superbly endowed and marvelously adapted to their exalted and exacting work." (p. 144)

4. **Proposition.** Divinington is the home of Thought Adjusters and numerous other orders having origin in the Universal Father.

   "1. DIVININGTON. This world is, in a unique sense, the 'bosom of the Father,' the personal-communion sphere of the Universal Father, and thereon is a special manifestation of his divinity. Divinington is the Paradise rendezvous of the Thought Adjusters, but it is also the home of numerous other entities, personalities, and other beings taking origin in the Universal Father." (p. 144)

5. **Proposition.** The secrets of Divinington include the mystery of the bestowal of Thought Adjusters.

   "*The secrets of Divinington* include the secret of the bestowal and mission of Thought Adjusters." (p. 144)

6. **Proposition.** Divinington also harbors the secrets of other Father fragments and the Gravity Messengers.

   "This sphere also holds the secrets of the nature, purpose, and activities of all other forms of Father fragments, of the Gravity Messengers, and of hosts of other beings unrevealed to you." (p. 145)

7. **Proposition.** Sonarington is headquarters for the fully accredited ascending and descending Sons of God.

   "2. SONARINGTON. This sphere is the 'bosom of the Son,' the personal receiving world of the Eternal Son. It is the Paradise headquarters of the descending and ascending Sons of God when, and after, they are fully accredited and finally approved." (p. 145)

8. **Proposition.** Among the secrets of Sonarington is that of the incarnation of the Sons of God.

> "*The secrets of Sonarington* include the secret of the incarnation of the divine Sons. When a Son of God becomes a Son of Man, is literally born of woman, as occurred on your world nineteen hundred years ago, it is a universal mystery. (p. 145)

9. **Proposition.** Spiritington is the home of high beings of the Infinite Spirit. The Seven Master Spirits forgather here.

> 3. SPIRITINGTON. This world is the 'bosom of the Spirit,' the Paradise home of the high beings that exclusively represent the Infinite Spirit. Here forgather the Seven Master Spirits and certain of their offspring from all universes. At this celestial abode may also be found numerous unrevealed orders of spirit personalities, beings assigned to the manifold activities of the universe not associated with the plans of upstepping the mortal creatures of time to the Paradise levels of eternity." (p. 145)

10. **Proposition.** Among the secrets of Spiritington is that of universal reflectivity.

> "*The secrets of Spiritington* involve the impenetrable mysteries of reflectivity. We tell you of the vast and universal phenomenon of reflectivity, more particularly as it is operative on the headquarters worlds of the seven superuniverses, but we never fully explain this phenomenon, for we do not fully understand it." (p. 145)

11. **Proposition.** Vicegerington is the home of the unrevealed Father-Son beings.

> "4. VICEGERINGTON. This planet is the 'bosom of the Father and the Son' and is the secret sphere of certain unrevealed beings who take origin by the acts of the Father and the Son." (p. 145)

12. **Proposition.** Trinitization is among the secrets of Vicegerington.

> "*The secrets of Vicegerington* include the secrets of trinitization, and trinitization constitutes the secret of authority to represent the Trinity, to act as vicegerents of the Gods." (p. 146)

13. **Proposition.** Solitarington is the home of the unrevealed beings of the Father-Spirit.

> "5. SOLITARINGTON. This world is the 'bosom of the Father and the Spirit' and is the rendezvous of a magnificent host of unrevealed beings of origin in the conjoint acts of the Universal Father and the Infinite Spirit, beings who partake of the traits of the Father in addition to their Spirit inheritance." (p. 146)

PART V — THE PARADISE–HAVONA SYSTEM

14. **PROPOSITION.** The secrets of Solitarington embrace some of trinitization and also special relations of the Infinite Spirit with some of his high children.

> "*The secrets of Solitarington.* Besides certain secrets of trinitization, this world holds the secrets of the personal relation of the Infinite Spirit with certain of the higher offspring of the Third Source and Center." (p. 146)

15. **PROPOSITION.** Seraphington is the home of the unrevealed beings of the Son and the Spirit and of the numerous orders of angels.

> "6. SERAPHINGTON. This sphere is the 'bosom of the Son and the Spirit' and is the home world of the vast hosts of unrevealed beings created by the Son and the Spirit. This is also the destiny sphere of all ministering orders of the angelic hosts, including supernaphim, seconaphim, and seraphim. There also serve in the central and outlying universes many orders of superb spirits who are not 'ministering spirits to those who shall be heirs of salvation.' All these spirit workers in all levels and realms of universe activities look upon Seraphington as their Paradise home." (p. 146)

16. **PROPOSITION.** The secrets of Seraphington include those of seraphic transport.

> "*The secrets of Seraphington* involve a threefold mystery, only one of which I may mention—the mystery of seraphic transport." (p. 147)

17. **PROPOSITION.** Ascendington is the home of ascendant evolutionary creatures.

> "7. ASCENDINGTON. This unique world is the 'bosom of the Father, Son, and Spirit,' the rendezvous of the ascendant creatures of space, the receiving sphere of the pilgrims of time who are passing through the Havona universe on their way to Paradise." (p. 147)

18. **PROPOSITION.** The secret of Ascendington is that of the evolution of the immortal soul in material creatures.

> "*The secrets of Ascendington* include the mystery of the gradual and certain building up in the material and mortal mind of a spiritual and potentially immortal counterpart of character and identity. This phenomenon constitutes one of the most perplexing mysteries of the universes—the evolution of an immortal soul within the mind of a mortal and material creature." (p. 147)

VI. WORLDS OF THE SON

1. **Proposition.** On the sacred worlds of the Son there takes origin spiritual luminosity extending to all of Havona. No personal beings sojourn on these spheres.

   "On the seven sacred worlds of the Eternal Son there appear to take origin the impersonal energies of spirit luminosity. No personal being may sojourn on any of these seven shining realms. With spiritual glory they illuminate all Paradise and Havona, and they directionize pure spirit luminosity to the seven superuniverses. These brilliant spheres of the second circuit likewise emit their light (light without heat) to Paradise and to the billion worlds of the seven-circuited central universe." (p. 143)

2. **Proposition.** These special worlds of the Son are the home of the seven phases of pure-spirit existence.

   "The seven luminous spheres of the Eternal Son are the worlds of the seven phases of pure-spirit existence. These shining orbs are the source of the threefold light of Paradise and Havona, their influence being largely, but not wholly, confined to the central universe." (p. 149)

3. **Proposition.** These worlds of the Son teem with other-than-personal life.

   "Personality is not present on these Paradise satellites; therefore is there little concerning these pure-spirit abodes which can be presented to the mortal and material personality. We are taught that these worlds teem with the otherwise-than-personal life of the beings of the Eternal Son. We infer that these entities are being assembled for ministry in the projected new universes of outer space." (p. 149)

VII. WORLDS OF THE SPIRIT

1. **Proposition.** The worlds of the Spirit are inhabited by the children of the Infinite Spirit, trinitized Sons of glorified creatures, and other unrevealed beings.

   "Between the inner circuit of Havona and the shining spheres of the Eternal Son there circle the seven orbs of the Infinite Spirit, worlds inhabited by the offspring of the Infinite Spirit, by the trinitized sons of glorified created personalities, and by other types of unrevealed beings concerned with the effective administration of the many enterprises of the various realms of universe activities." (p. 149)

2. **Proposition.** The seven worlds of the Spirit are the headquarters of the Seven Master Spirits. Their illumination extends to Havona and the grand universe, but not to Paradise.

> "The seven worlds of the Infinite Spirit are occupied by the Seven Master Spirits, who preside over the destinies of the seven superuniverses, sending forth the spiritual illumination of the Third Person of Deity to these creations of time and space. And all Havona, but not the Isle of Paradise, is bathed in these spiritualizing influences." (p. 143)

3. **Proposition.** From these seven worlds the Master Spirits equalize and stabilize the cosmic-mind circuits to the grand universe.

> "From these seven special spheres the Master Spirits operate to equalize and stabilize the cosmic-mind circuits of the grand universe. They also have to do with the differential spiritual attitude and presence of the Deities throughout the grand universe." (p. 150)

4. **Proposition.** These executive abodes of the Seven Master Spirits are in reality the headquarters of the seven superuniverses.

> "The executive abodes of the Seven Master Spirits are, in reality, the Paradise headquarters of the seven superuniverses and their correlated segments in outer space. Each Master Spirit presides over one superuniverse, and each of these seven worlds is exclusively assigned to one of the Master Spirits. There is literally no phase of the sub-Paradise administration of the seven superuniverses which is not provided for on these executive worlds." (p. 150)

VIII. PURPOSE OF THE CENTRAL UNIVERSE

1. **Proposition.** The billion worlds of Havona constitute training spheres for descending Paradise personalities and ascending evolutionary creatures.

> "The billion spheres of the central universe constitute the training worlds of the high personalities native to Paradise and Havona and further serve as the final proving grounds for ascending creatures from the evolutionary worlds of time." (p. 156)

2. **Proposition.** Havona may be the finishing school on absonite levels when the superuniverses are functioning as the intermediate schools for the graduates of the primary schools of outer space.

   "Havona will unquestionably continue to function with absonite significance even in future universe ages which may witness space pilgrims attempting to find God on superfinite levels. Havona has capacity to serve as a training universe for absonite beings. It will probably be the finishing school when the seven superuniverses are functioning as the intermediate school for the graduates of the primary schools of outer space. And we incline to the opinion that the potentials of eternal Havona are really unlimited, that the central universe has eternal capacity to serve as an experiential training universe for all past, present, or future types of created beings." (p. 163)

3. **Proposition.** The Father derives supreme satisfaction from the perfection of Havona.

   "1. *The Universal Father*—the First Source and Center. God the Father derives supreme parental satisfaction from the perfection of the central creation. He enjoys the experience of love satiety on near-equality levels. The perfect Creator is divinely pleased with the adoration of the perfect creature." (p. 160)

4. **Proposition.** Havona affords the Eternal Son proof of the effectiveness of the divine family. Here he first demonstrated the bestowal ministry.

   "2. *The Eternal Son*—the Second Source and Center. To the Eternal Son the superb central creation affords eternal proof of the partnership effectiveness of the divine family—Father, Son, and Spirit. It is the spiritual and material basis for absolute confidence in the Universal Father.

   "Havona affords the Eternal Son an almost unlimited base for the ever-expanding realization of spirit power. The central universe afforded the Eternal Son the arena wherein he could safely and securely demonstrate the spirit and technique of the bestowal ministry for the instruction of his associate Paradise Sons." (p. 160)

5. PROPOSITION. The Havona universe affords the Infinite Spirit actual proof of being the Conjoint Actor.

> "3. *The Infinite Spirit*—the Third Source and Center. The Havona universe affords the Infinite Spirit proof of being the Conjoint Actor, the infinite representative of the unified Father-Son. In Havona the Infinite Spirit derives the combined satisfaction of functioning as a creative activity while enjoying the satisfaction of absolute coexistence with this divine achievement." (p. 161)

6. PROPOSITION. In Havona, the Infinite Spirit rehearsed for the ministry to the evolutionary universes.

> "In Havona the Infinite Spirit found an arena wherein he could demonstrate the ability and willingness to serve as a potential mercy minister. In this perfect creation the Spirit rehearsed for the adventure of ministry in the evolutionary universes." (p. 161)

7. PROPOSITION. Havona is proof of the spiritual reality of the Supreme Being. Here the power-potential of the Almighty is unified with the spiritual nature of the Supreme.

> "4. *The Supreme Being*—the evolutionary unification of experiential Deity. The Havona creation is the eternal and perfect proof of the spiritual reality of the Supreme Being. This perfect creation is a revelation of the perfect and symmetrical spirit nature of God the Supreme before the beginnings of the power-personality synthesis of the finite reflections of the Paradise Deities in the experiential universes of time and space.
>
> "In Havona the power potentials of the Almighty are unified with the spiritual nature of the Supreme. This central creation is an exemplification of the future-eternal unity of the Supreme." (p. 161)

8. PROPOSITION. Havona is the educational training ground where the Creator Sons prepare for their adventures in universe creation.

> "5. *The Co-ordinate Creator Sons*. Havona is the educational training ground where the Paradise Michaels are prepared for their subsequent adventures in universe creation. This divine and perfect creation is a pattern for every Creator Son." (p. 162)

9. **Proposition.** The prepersonal Mother Spirits, associates of the Creator Sons, secure training on the Havona worlds with the Spirits of the Circuits.

> "6. *The Co-ordinate Ministering Daughters.* The Universe Mother Spirits, cocreators of the local universes, secure their prepersonal training on the worlds of Havona in close association with the Spirits of the Circuits." (p. 162)

10. **Proposition.** Havona is the home of the pattern personalities for every mortal type and here are to be found all superhuman associates of mortal ascenders.

> "7. *The Evolutionary Mortals of the Ascending Career.* Havona is the home of the pattern personality of every mortal type and the home of all superhuman personalities of mortal association who are not native to the creations of time." (p. 162)

11. **Proposition.** In Havona, mortal ascenders attain their first contact with the Supreme Being.

> "These worlds provide the stimulus of all human impulses towards the attainment of true spirit values on the highest conceivable reality levels. Havona is the pre-Paradise training goal of every ascending mortal. Here mortals attain pre-Paradise Deity—the Supreme Being. Havona stands before every will creature as the portal to Paradise and God attainment." (p. 162)

IX. LIFE IN HAVONA

1. **Proposition.** There are seven basic forms of life in Havona.

> "There are seven basic forms of living things and beings on the Havona worlds, and each of these basic forms exists in three distinct phases. Each of these three phases is divided into seventy major divisions, and each major division is composed of one thousand minor divisions, with yet other subdivisions, and so on. These basic life groups might be classified as:
> "1. Material.
> "2. Morontial.
> "3. Spiritual.
> "4. Absonite.
> "5. Ultimate.
> "6. Coabsolute.
> "7. Absolute." (p. 156)

PART V — *The Paradise–Havona System*

2. **Proposition.** Havoners, in addition to their ministry to descenders and ascenders, live a significant life of their own.

   "There is a life that is native to Havona and possesses significance in and of itself. Havoners minister in many ways to Paradise descenders and to superuniverse ascenders, but they also live lives that are unique in the central universe and have relative meaning quite apart from either Paradise or the superuniverses." (p. 157)

3. **Proposition.** Havona natives are the children of the Paradise Trinity and are nonreproducing beings.

   "The Havona natives are all the offspring of the Paradise Trinity. They are without creature parents, and they are nonreproducing beings." (p. 157)

4. **Proposition.** On the Havona worlds are to be found numerous classes of pattern beings.

   "In addition to the Havona natives, the inhabitants of the central universe embrace numerous classes of pattern beings for various universe groups—advisers, directors, and teachers of their kind and to their kind throughout creation." (p. 157)

5. **Proposition.** Sin has never appeared in Havona. Neither the natives nor the evolutionary ascenders have ever gone astray.

   "We do infer that sin can be reckoned as impossible of occurrence, but we do this on the ground that the native freewill creatures of Havona have never been guilty of transgressing the will of Deity. Through all eternity these supernal beings have been consistently loyal to the Eternals of Days. Neither has sin appeared in any creature who has entered Havona as a pilgrim. There has never been an instance of misconduct by any creature of any group of personalities ever created in, or admitted to, the central Havona universe. So perfect and so divine are the methods and means of selection in the universes of time that never in the records of Havona has an error occurred; no mistakes have ever been made; no ascendant soul has ever been prematurely admitted to the central universe." (p. 155)

PART VI
COSMOLOGY

Part Six
COSMOLOGY

I. INTRODUCTION

1. **Proposition.** From Paradise, you look outward through six concentric circles of the cosmos.

   > "Proceeding outward from Paradise through the horizontal extension of pervaded space, the master universe is existent in six concentric ellipses, the space levels encircling the central Isle:
   > "1. The Central Universe — Havona.
   > "2. The Seven Superuniverses.
   > "3. The First Outer Space Level.
   > "4. The Second Outer Space Level.
   > "5. The Third Outer Space Level.
   > "6. The Fourth and Outermost Space Level." (p. 129)

2. **Proposition.** The cosmologies of revelation are limited by the proscription of unearned knowledge.

   > "Because your world is generally ignorant of origins, even of physical origins, it has appeared to be wise from time to time to provide instruction in cosmology. And always has this made trouble for the future. The laws of revelation hamper us greatly by their proscription of the impartation of unearned or premature knowledge. Any cosmology presented as a part of revealed religion is destined to be outgrown in a very short time. Accordingly, future students of such a revelation are tempted to discard any element of genuine religious truth it may contain because they discover errors on the face of the associated cosmologies therein presented." (p. 1109)

3. **Proposition.** Notwithstanding apparent cosmic disharmony, the diverse levels of creation are unified by a divine plan and eternal purpose.

   > "The diverse levels of creation are all unified in the plans and administration of the Architects of the Master Universe. To the circumscribed minds of time-space mortals the universe may present many problems and situations which apparently portray disharmony and indicate absence of effective co-ordination; but those of us who are able to observe wider stretches of universal phenomena, and who are more experienced in this art of detecting the basic unity which underlies creative diversity and of discovering the divine oneness which overspreads all this

functioning of plurality, better perceive the divine and single purpose exhibited in all these manifold manifestations of universal creative energy." (p. 637)

4. **PROPOSITION.** The creation is unfinished. Much of the cosmic potential is still unrevealed.

> "We are convinced, from the study of physical law and from the observation of the starry realms, that the infinite Creator is not yet manifest in finality of cosmic expression, that much of the cosmic potential of the Infinite is still self-contained and unrevealed." (p. 128)

5. **PROPOSITION.** Even upon the completion of the master universe, you will look forward to a more enthralling and eternal future of uncharted infinity.

> "At the inconceivably distant future eternity moment of the final completion of the entire master universe, no doubt we will all look back upon its entire history as only the beginning, simply the creation of certain finite and transcendental foundations for even greater and more enthralling metamorphoses in uncharted infinity. At such a future eternity moment the master universe will still seem youthful; indeed, it will be always young in the face of the limitless possibilities of never-ending eternity." (p. 1170)

II. PARADISE GRAVITY

1. **PROPOSITION.** All forms of force-energy—material, mindal, or spiritual — are subject to some form of gravity. The Father can act over all four absolute gravity circuits.

> "All forms of force-energy — material, mindal, or spiritual — are alike subject to those grasps, those universal presences, which we call gravity. Personality also is responsive to gravity — to the Father's exclusive circuit; but though this circuit is exclusive to the Father, he is not excluded from the other circuits; the Universal Father is infinite and acts over *all* four absolute-gravity circuits in the master universe:
>
> "1. The Personality Gravity of the Universal Father.
> "2. The Spirit Gravity of the Eternal Son.
> "3. The Mind Gravity of the Conjoint Actor.
> "4. The Cosmic Gravity of the Isle of Paradise." (p. 131)

2. **Proposition.** Gravity is the omnipotent strand on which are strung the gleaming stars, blazing suns, and whirling spheres.

   "The inescapable pull of gravity effectively grips all the worlds of all the universes of all space. Gravity is the all-powerful grasp of the physical presence of Paradise. Gravity is the omnipotent strand on which are strung the gleaming stars, blazing suns, and whirling spheres which constitute the universal physical adornment of the eternal God, who is all things, fills all things, and in whom all things consist." (p. 125)

3. **Proposition.** The focal point of absolute gravity is Paradise, complemented by the dark gravity bodies, and equilibrated by the upper and nether space reservoirs.

   "The center and focal point of absolute material gravity is the Isle of Paradise, complemented by the dark gravity bodies encircling Havona and equilibrated by the upper and nether space reservoirs. All known emanations of nether Paradise invariably and unerringly respond to the central gravity pull operating upon the endless circuits of the elliptical space levels of the master universe." (p. 125)

4. **Proposition.** Every form of cosmic reality has the bend of the ages, the trend of the circle, as they swing around the great ellipse.

   "Every known form of cosmic reality has the bend of the ages, the trend of the circle, the swing of the great ellipse." (p. 125)

5. **Proposition.** The Havona dark gravity bodies are reactive to both linear and absolute gravity.

   "The dark gravity bodies encircling Havona are neither triata nor gravita, and their drawing power discloses both forms of physical gravity, linear and absolute." (p. 126)

6. **Proposition.** The universe is highly predictable in the quantitative sense, less so in the qualitative. Personality decisions are all but unpredictable.

   "The universe is highly predictable only in the quantitative or gravity-measurement sense; even the primal physical forces are not responsive to linear gravity, nor are the higher mind meanings and true spirit values of ultimate universe realities. Qualitatively, the universe is not highly predictable as regards new associations of forces, either physical, mindal, or spiritual, although many such combinations of energies or forces become partially predictable when subjected to critical observation. When matter, mind, and spirit are unified by creature personality, we are unable fully to predict the decisions of such a freewill being." (p. 136)

7. **PROPOSITION.** The present grand universe is making use of only five per cent of the functioning Paradise gravity. Such calculations ignore linear gravity.

> "1. *Physical Gravity.* Having formulated an estimate of the summation of the entire physical-gravity capacity of the grand universe, they have laboriously effected a comparison of this finding with the estimated total of absolute gravity presence now operative. These calculations indicate that the total gravity action on the grand universe is a very small part of the estimated gravity pull of Paradise, computed on the basis of the gravity response of basic physical units of universe matter. These investigators reach the amazing conclusion that the central universe and the surrounding seven superuniverses are at the present time making use of only about five per cent of the active functioning of the Paradise absolute-gravity grasp. In other words: At the present moment about ninety-five per cent of the active cosmic-gravity action of the Isle of Paradise, computed on this totality theory, is engaged in controlling material systems beyond the borders of the present organized universes. These calculations all refer to absolute gravity; linear gravity is an interactive phenomenon which can be computed only by knowing the actual Paradise gravity." (p. 132)

8. **PROPOSITION.** The present grand universe reveals the functioning of practically one hundred per cent of the active spirit gravity of the Second Source and Center.

> "2. *Spiritual Gravity.* By the same technique of comparative estimation and calculation these researchers have explored the present reaction capacity of spirit gravity and, with the cooperation of Solitary Messengers and other spirit personalities, have arrived at the summation of the active spirit gravity of the Second Source and Center. And it is most instructive to note that they find about the same value for the actual and functional presence of spirit gravity in the grand universe that they postulate for the present total of active spirit gravity. In other words: At the present time practically the entire spirit gravity of the Eternal Son, computed on this theory of totality, is observable as functioning in the grand universe." (p. 132)

9. **Proposition.** When it comes to mind gravity — the computations indicate that about eighty-five per cent of the mind gravity response to the total active gravity of the Third Source and Center is occurring in the present grand universe.

> "3. *Mind Gravity.* By these same principles of comparative computation these experts have attacked the problem of mind-gravity presence and response. The mind unit of estimation was arrived at by averaging three material and three spiritual types of mentality, although the type of mind found in the power directors and their associates proved to be a disturbing factor in the effort to arrive at a basic unit for mind-gravity estimation. There was little to impede the estimation of the present capacity of the Third Source and Center for mind-gravity function in accordance with this theory of totality. Although the findings in this instance are not so conclusive as in the estimates of physical and spirit gravity, they are, comparatively considered, very instructive, even intriguing. These investigators deduce that about eight-five per cent of the mind-gravity response to the intellectual drawing of the Conjoint Actor takes origin in the existing grand universe." (p. 132)

10. **Proposition.** Personality gravity is noncomputable.

> "*Personality Gravity* is noncomputable. We recognize the circuit, but we cannot measure either qualitative or quantitative realities responsive thereto." (p. 133)

III. DOMAINS OF THE UNQUALIFIED ABSOLUTE

1. **Proposition.** The Unqualified Absolute is revealer, regulator, and repository of all that which has origin in Paradise.

> "Paradise is the absolute source and the eternal focal point of all energy-matter in the universe of universes. The Unqualified Absolute is the revealer, regulator, and repository of that which has Paradise as its source and origin." (p. 126)

2. **Proposition.** Space potency is not a level of reality and it is not subject to any form of gravity. It embraces those absolute potentials which emanate from Paradise and constitute the space presence of the Unqualified Absolute.

> "Space potency is not subject to the interactions of any form of gravitation. This primal endowment of Paradise is not an actual level of reality, but it is ancestral to all relative functional nonspirit realities — all manifestations of force-energy and the

organization of power and matter. Space potency is a term difficult to define. It does not mean that which is ancestral to space; its meaning should convey the idea of the potencies and potentials existent within space. It may be roughly conceived to include all those absolute influences and potentials which emanate from Paradise and constitute the space presence of the Unqualified Absolute." (p. 126)

3. **PROPOSITION.** The Unqualified Absolute is limited to space, but there is uncertainty about the Absolute's relation to motion — even the motions of space.

"The Unqualified Absolute is functionally limited to space, but we are not so sure about the relation of this Absolute to motion. Is motion inherent therein? We do not know. We know that motion is not inherent in space; even the motions *of* space are not innate. But we are not so sure about the relation of the Unqualified to motion. Who, or what, is really responsible for the gigantic activities of force-energy transmutations now in progress out beyond the borders of the present seven superuniverses?" (p. 133)

4. **PROPOSITION.** Concerning space, we hold three opinions.

"Concerning the origin of motion we have the following opinions:
"1. We think the Conjoint Actor initiates motion *in* space.
"2. If the Conjoint Actor produces the motions *of* space, we cannot prove it.
"3. The Universal Absolute does not originate initial motion but does equalize and control all of the tensions originated by motion." (p. 133)

5. **PROPOSITION.** The Unqualified Absolute probably modifies space so as to prepare the way for the function of force organizers.

"In outer space the force organizers are apparently responsible for the production of the gigantic universe wheels which are now in process of stellar evolution, but their ability so to function must have been made possible by some modification of the space presence of the Unqualified Absolute." (p. 133)

6. **PROPOSITION.** The Unqualified Absolute pervades all space. The exact status of the Deity Absolute is not clear.

"The Unqualified Absolute pervades all space. We are not altogether clear as to the exact status of the Deity and Universal Absolutes, but we know the latter functions wherever the Deity and Unqualified Absolutes function. The Deity Absolute may be universally present but hardly space present." (p. 137)

IV. SPACE RESPIRATION

1. **Proposition.** The actual mechanism of space respiration is unknown.

    "We do not know the actual mechanism of space respiration; we merely observe that all space alternately contracts and expands. This respiration affects both the horizontal extension of pervaded space and the vertical extensions of unpervaded space which exist in the vast space reservoirs above and below Paradise. In attempting to imagine the volume outlines of these space reservoirs, you might think of an hourglass." (p. 123)

2. **Proposition.** Unpervaded space is devoid of all those realities found in pervaded space. The space reservoirs seem to counterbalance the expansion and contraction cycles of the master cosmos.

    "'Unpervaded' space means: unpervaded by those forces, energies, powers, and presences known to exist in pervaded space. We do not know whether vertical (reservoir) space is destined always to function as the equipoise of horizontal (universe) space; we do not know whether there is a creative intent concerning unpervaded space; we really know very little about the space reservoirs, merely that they exist, and that they seem to counterbalance the space-expansion-contraction cycles of the universe of universes." (p. 123)

3. **Proposition.** Pervaded space is now nearing the mid-point of the expansion phase.

    "Pervaded space is now approaching the mid-point of the expanding phase, while unpervaded space nears the mid-point of the contracting phase, and we are informed that the outermost limits of both space extensions are, theoretically, now approximately equidistant from Paradise." (p. 124)

4. **Proposition.** Space respiration alternately moves with and against Paradise gravity. This is space work — not power-energy work.

    "When the universes expand and contract, the material masses in pervaded space alternately move against and with the pull of Paradise gravity. The work that is done in moving the material energy mass of creation is *space* work but not *power-energy* work." (p. 134)

5. **Proposition.** The apparent velocity of the supposedly "exploding universe" is not real. Our observations embrace many factors of error.

> "Many influences interpose to make it appear that the recessional velocity of the external universes increases at the rate of more than one hundred miles a second for every million light-years increase in distance. By this method of reckoning, subsequent to the perfection of more powerful telescopes, it will appear that these far-distant systems are in flight from this part of the universe at the unbelievable rate of more than thirty thousand miles a second. But this apparent speed of recession is not real; it results from numerous factors of error embracing angles of observation and other time-space distortions." (p. 134)

V. SPACE AND MOTION

1. **Proposition.** The vertical section of total space slightly resembles a maltese cross.

> "The vertical cross section of total space would slightly resemble a maltese cross, with the horizontal arms representing pervaded (universe) space and the vertical arms representing unpervaded (reservoir) space." (p. 124)

2. **Proposition.** All cosmic space levels are separated by a relatively quiescent space zone.

> "The relatively quiet zone between the space levels, such as the one separating the seven superuniverses from the first outer space level, are enormous elliptical regions of quiescent space activities. These zones separate the vast galaxies which race around Paradise in orderly procession." (p. 125)

3. **Proposition.** Space, while nonresponsive to gravity, acts as an equilibrant. Pervaded space acts as antigravity on linear attraction. Space can neutralize gravity but cannot delay it.

> "Space is nonresponsive to gravity, but it acts as an equilibrant on gravity. Without the space cushion, explosive action would jerk surrounding space bodies. Pervaded space also exerts an antigravity influence upon physical or linear gravity; space can actually neutralize such gravity action even though it cannot delay it. Absolute gravity is Paradise gravity. Local or linear gravity pertains to the electrical stage of energy or matter; it operates within the central, super-, and outer universes, wherever suitable materialization has taken place." (p. 125)

4. **Proposition.** From the human viewpoint, space is nothing — negative — existing only as related to something else. There are four motions of space.

> "Space is, from the human viewpoint, nothing — negative; it exists only as related to something positive and nonspatial. Space is, however, real. It contains and conditions motion. It even moves. Space motions may be roughly classified as follows:
> "1. Primary motion — space respiration, the motion of space itself.
> "2. Secondary motion—the alternate directional swings of the successive space levels.
> "3. Relative motions — relative in the sense that they are not evaluated with Paradise as a base point. Primary and secondary motions are absolute, motion in relation to unmoving Paradise.
> "4. Compensatory or correlating movement designed to co-ordinate all other motions." (p. 133)

5. **Proposition.** Space comes the nearest being absolute of all nonabsolute things. The difficulty in understanding space is due to the fact that while material bodies exist in space, space also exists in these material bodies.

> "Space comes the nearest of all nonabsolute things to being absolute. Space is apparently absolutely ultimate. The real difficulty we have in understanding space on the material level is due to the fact that, while material bodies exist in space, space also exists in these same material bodies. While there is much about space that is absolute, that does not mean that space is absolute." (p. 1297)

6. **Proposition.** Patterns of reality occupy space, but spirit patterns exist only in relation to space — they do not occupy space, neither do they contain it. We do not know if the reality pattern of an idea occupies space.

> "All patterns of reality occupy space on the material levels, but spirit patterns only exist in relation to space; they do not occupy or displace space, neither do they contain it. But to us the master riddle of space pertains to the pattern of an idea. When we enter the mind domain, we encounter many a puzzle. Does the pattern — the reality — of an idea occupy space? We really do not know, albeit we are sure that an idea pattern does not contain space. But it would hardly be safe to postulate that the immaterial is always nonspatial." (p. 1297)

VI. SPACE AND TIME

1. PROPOSITION. Time is an indirect bestowal of Paradise — it comes because of motion and because mind is aware of sequentiality.

   "Like space, time is a bestowal of Paradise, but not in the same sense, only indirectly. Time comes by virtue of motion and because mind is inherently aware of sequentiality. From a practical viewpoint, motion is essential to time, but there is no universal time unit based on motion except in so far as the Paradise-Havona standard day is arbitrarily so recognized. The totality of space respiration destroys its local value as a time source." (p. 134)

2. PROPOSITION. Space is not infinite — not absolute. The absolute of time is eternity.

   "Space is not infinite, even though it takes origin from Paradise; not absolute, for it is pervaded by the Unqualified Absolute. We do not know the absolute limits of space, but we do know that the absolute of time is eternity." (p. 135)

3. PROPOSITION. Time and space are inseparable only in time-space creations. The only nontemporal place is Paradise area.

   "Time and space are inseparable only in the time-space creations, the seven superuniverses. Nontemporal space (space without time) theoretically exists, but the only truly nontemporal place is Paradise *area*. Nonspatial time (time without space) exists in mind of the Paradise level of function." (p. 135)

4. PROPOSITION. Relation to time does not exist without motion in space. Man's mind is less time bound than space bound.

   "Relationships to time do not exist without motion in space, but consciousness of time does. Sequentiality can consciousize time even in the absence of motion. Man's mind is less time-bound than space-bound because of the inherent nature of mind. Even during the days of the earth life in the flesh, though man's mind is rigidly space-bound, the creative human imagination is comparatively time free. But time itself is not genetically a quality of mind." (p. 135)

5. Proposition. There are three levels of time consciousness.

   "There are three different levels of time cognizance:
   "1. Mind-perceived time — consciousness of sequence, motion, and a sense of duration.
   "2. Spirit-perceived time — insight into motion Godward and the awareness of the motion of ascent to levels of increasing divinity.

"3. Personality *creates* a unique time sense out of insight into Reality plus a consciousness of presence and an awareness of duration." (p. 135)

6. **Proposition.** Time and space are conjoined mechanisms of the master universe separating finite creatures from the absolute levels of the Infinite.

> "Time and space are a conjoined mechanism of the master universe. They are the devices whereby finite creatures are enabled to coexist in the cosmos with the Infinite. Finite creatures are effectively insulated from the absolute levels by time and space. But these insulating media, without which no mortal could exist, operate directly to limit the range of finite action. Without them no creature could act, but by them the acts of every creature are definitely limited." (p. 1303)

7. **Proposition.** By ubiquity Deity manifests time-space phenomena for finite creatures. Time is a succession of instants; space a system of associated points.

> "Only by ubiquity could Deity unify time-space manifestations to the finite conception, for time is a succession of instants while space is a system of associated points. You do, after all, perceive time by analysis and space by synthesis. You co-ordinate and associate these two dissimilar conceptions by the integrating insight of personality. Of all the animal world only man possesses this time-space perceptibility. To an animal, motion has a meaning, but motion exhibits value only to a creature of personality status." (p. 1297)

8. **Proposition.** The all but motionless midspace zones are transition zones from time to eternity — hence ascenders must become unconscious in transit.

> "The relatively motionless midspace zones impinging on Paradise and separating pervaded from unpervaded space are the transition zones from time to eternity, hence the necessity of Paradise pilgrims becoming unconscious during this transit when it is to culminate in Paradise citizenship. Time-conscious *visitors* can go to Paradise without thus sleeping, but they remain creatures of time." (p. 135)

VII. UNIVERSE OVERCONTROL

1. **PROPOSITION.** The master universe is fostered by the Paradise Trinity and Deities.

    "Individuals have their guardians of destiny; planets, systems, constellations, universes, and superuniverses each have their respective rulers who labor for the good of their domains. Havona and even the grand universe are watched over by those intrusted with such high responsibilities. But who fosters and cares for the fundamental needs of the master universe as a whole, from Paradise to the fourth and outermost space level? Existentially such overcare is probably attributable to the Paradise Trinity, but from an experiential viewpoint the appearance of the post-Havona universes is dependent on:
    "1. The Absolutes in potential.
    "2. The Ultimate in direction.
    "3. The Supreme in evolutionary co-ordination.
    "4. The Architects of the Master Universe in administration prior to the appearance of specific rulers." (p. 136)

2. **PROPOSITION.** The universe is nonstatic. Stability results not from inertia, but from balanced energies, co-operative minds, co-ordinated morontias, spirit overcontrol, and personality unification.

    "The universe is nonstatic. Stability is not the result of inertia but rather the product of balanced energies, co-operative minds, co-ordinated morontias, spirit overcontrol, and personality unification. Stability is wholly and always proportional to divinity." (p. 135)

3. **PROPOSITION.** The unpredictability of primordial force or the reaction of unidentified mind are probably due to the activities of the Ultimate and the Absolutes.

    "These unknown, unfathomable unpredictables — whether pertaining to the behavior of a primordial unit of force, the reaction of an unidentified level of mind, or the phenomenon of a vast preuniverse in the making in the domains of outer space — probably disclose the activities of the Ultimate and the presence-performances of the Absolutes, which antedate the function of all universe Creators." (p. 136)

4. **PROPOSITION.** The universe of universes is unified; God is one in power and personality. God is all and in all.

> "The universe of universes is altogether unified. God is one in power and personality. There is co-ordination of all levels of energy and all phases of personality. Philosophically and experientially, in concept and in reality, all things and beings center in the Paradise Father. God is all and in all, and no things or beings exist without him." (p. 646)

5. **PROPOSITION.** The absonite architects eventuate the plan of a universe, the Supreme Creators materialize it, the Supreme Being will consummate it.

> "The absonite architects eventuate the plan; the Supreme Creators bring it into existence; the Supreme Being will consummate its fullness as it was time created by the Supreme Creators, and as it was space forecast by the Master Architects." (p. 1165)

6. **PROPOSITION.** At present the co-ordination of the master universe is the function of the Master Architects. Factualization of the Supreme signifies first stage destiny and the completion of the first experiential Trinity.

> "During the present universe age the administrative co-ordination of the master universe is the function of the Architects of the Master Universe. But the appearance of the Almighty Supreme at the termination of the present universe age will signify that the evolutionary finite has attained the first stage of experiential destiny. This happening will certainly lead to the completed function of the first experiential Trinity — the union of the Supreme Creators, the Supreme Being, and the Architects of the Master Universe. This Trinity is destined to effect the further evolutionary integration of the master creation." (p. 1165)

VIII. THE SEVEN SUPERUNIVERSES

1. **PROPOSITION.** The grand universe consists of the central creation and the seven superuniverses with an aggregate of seven trillion worlds of mortal habitation.

> "*The Grand Universe* is the present organized and inhabited creation. It consists of the seven superuniverses, with an aggregate evolutionary potential of around seven trillion inhabited planets, not to mention the eternal spheres of the central creation. But this tentative estimate takes no account of architectural administrative spheres, neither does it include the outlying groups of unorganized universes. The present ragged

PART VI — COSMOLOGY

edge of the grand universe, its uneven and unfinished periphery, together with the tremendously unsettled condition of the whole astronomical plot, suggests to our star students that even the seven superuniverses are, as yet, uncompleted." (p. 129)

2. **PROPOSITION.** Each superuniverse is organized in five chief divisions.

"Each of the seven superuniverses is constituted, approximately, as follows:
"One system embraces, approximately......................1,000 worlds
"One constellation (100 systems)..........................100,000 worlds
"One universe (100 constellations)....................10,000,000 worlds
"One minor sector (100 universes)................1,000,000,000 worlds
"One major sector (100 minor sectors)........100,000,000,000 worlds
"One superuniverse (10 major sectors)......1,000,000,000,000 worlds"
(p. 167)

3. **PROPOSITION.** The superuniverses are not primary physical organizations. Each universe is about one seventh of the inhabitable creation.

"*The Seven Superuniverses* are not primary physical organizations; nowhere do their boundaries divide a nebular family, neither do they cross a local universe, a prime creative unit. Each superuniverse is simply a geographic space clustering of approximately one seventh of the organized and partially inhabited post-Havona creation, and each is about equal in the number of local universes embraced and in the space encompassed." (p. 129)

4. **PROPOSITION.** Headquarters worlds of a superuniverse, located near its center, are special spheres as regards construction, lighting, and heating.

"While each superuniverse government presides near the center of the evolutionary universes of its space segment, it occupies a world made to order and is peopled by accredited personalities. These headquarters worlds are architectural spheres, space bodies specifically constructed for their special purpose. While sharing the light of near-by suns, these spheres are independently lighted and heated. Each has a sun which gives forth light without heat, like the satellites of Paradise, while each is supplied with heat by the circulation of certain energy currents near the surface of the sphere. These headquarters worlds belong to one of the greater systems situated near the astronomical center of their respective superuniverses." (p. 174)

5. **Proposition.** Headquarters worlds increase in size, morontial beauty, and spirit glory from the local system to Paradise.

   "The headquarters worlds of the seven superuniverses partake of the nature and grandeur of Paradise, their central pattern of perfection. In reality, all headquarters worlds are paradisiacal. They are indeed heavenly abodes, and they increase in material size, morontia beauty, and spirit glory from Jerusem to the central Isle. And all the satellites of these headquarters worlds are also architectural spheres." (p. 174)

6. **Proposition.** In a future age, we will witness outer-spacers approaching Havona through the seven superuniverses as they will be administered by God the Supreme.

   "Nevertheless, we deem that the perfected superuniverses will in some way become a part of the Paradise-ascension careers of those beings who may inhabit these outer creations. It is quite possible that in that future age we may witness outer-spacers approaching Havona through the seven superuniverses, administered by God the Supreme with or without the collaboration of the Seven Master Spirits." (p. 643)

IX. ORVONTON

1. **Proposition.** The Milky Way represents the central nucleus of Orvonton. This aggregation of space bodies represents a watchlike, elongated-circular grouping of one seventh of the inhabited evolutionary universes.

   "Practically all of the starry realms visible to the naked eye on Urantia belong to the seventh section of the grand universe, the superuniverse of Orvonton. The vast Milky Way starry system represents the central nucleus of Orvonton, being largely beyond the borders of your local universe. This great aggregation of suns, dark islands of space, double stars, globular clusters, star clouds, spiral and other nebulae, together with myriads of individual planets, forms a watchlike, elongated-circular grouping of about one seventh of the inhabited evolutionary universes." (p. 167)

2. **Proposition.** Of the ten major divisions of Orvonton, eight are identified by Urantia astronomers.

   "Of the ten major divisions of Orvonton, eight have been roughly identified by Urantcian astronomers. The other two are difficult of separate recognition because you are obliged to view these phenomena from the inside. If you could look upon the superuniverse of Orvonton from a position far-distant in space, you would immediately recognize the ten major sectors of the seventh galaxy." (p. 167)

3. **Proposition.** The rotational center of our minor sector is situated in Sagittarius, from whose opposite sides emerge two star streams in stupendous stellar coils.

> "The rotational center of your minor sector is situated far away in the enormous and dense star cloud of Sagittarius, around which your local universe and its associated creations all move, and from opposite sides of the vast Sagittarius subgalactic system you may observe two great streams of star clouds emerging in stupendous stellar coils." (p. 168)

4. **Proposition.** Sagittarius and similar groups are in rotation around Uversa. The illusions and distortions of stellar movements are due to numerous influences.

> "The Sagittarius sector and all other sectors and divisions of Orvonton are in rotation around Uversa, and some of the confusion of Urantian star observers arises out of the illusions and relative distortions produced by the following multiple revolutionary movements:
>
> "1. The revolution of Urantia around its sun.
>
> "2. The circuit of your solar system about the nucleus of the former Andronover nebula.
>
> "3. The rotation of the Andronover stellar family and the associated clusters about the composite rotation-gravity center of the star cloud of Nebadon.
>
> "4. The swing of the local star cloud of Nebadon and its associated creations around the Sagittarius center of their minor sector.
>
> "5. The rotation of the one hundred minor sectors, including Sagittarius, about their major sector.
>
> "6. The whirl of the ten major sectors, the so-called star drifts, about the Uversa headquarters of Orvonton.
>
> "7. The movement of Orvonton and six associated superuniverses around Paradise and Havona, the counterclockwise processional of the superuniverse space level." (p. 168)

5. **Proposition.** The Milky Way galaxy is composed of modified spiral and other nebulae as well as enormous aggregations like the Magellanic Cloud.

 > "The Milky Way galaxy is composed of vast numbers of former spiral and other nebulae; and many still retain their original configuration. But as the result of internal catastrophes and external attraction, many have suffered such distortion and rearrangement as to cause these enormous aggregations to appear as gigantic luminous masses of blazing suns, like the Magellanic Cloud. The globular type of star clusters predominates near the outer margins of Orvonton." (p. 170)

6. **Proposition.** Uversa is the headquarters for about one trillion inhabitable worlds.

 > "Uversa is the spiritual and administrative headquarters for approximately one trillion inhabited or inhabitable worlds. The glory, grandeur, and perfection of the Orvonton capital surpass any of the wonders of the time-space creations." (p. 175)

7. **Proposition.** The superuniverse circuits are many and varied.

 > "*The Superuniverse Circuits*:
 > "1. The unifying intelligence circuit of one of the Seven Master Spirits of Paradise. Such a cosmic-mind circuit is limited to a single superuniverse.
 > "2. The reflective-service circuit of the seven Reflective Spirits in each superuniverse.
 > "3. The secret circuits of the Mystery Monitors, in some manner interassociated and routed by Divington to the Universal Father on Paradise.
 > "4. The circuit of the intercommunion of the Eternal Son with his Paradise Sons.
 > "5. The flash presence of the Infinite Spirit.
 > "6. The broadcasts of Paradise, the space reports of Havona.
 > "7. The energy circuits of the power centers and the physical controllers.
 > "*The Local Universe Circuits*:
 > "1. The bestowal spirit of the Paradise Sons, the Comforter of the bestowal worlds. The Spirit of Truth, the spirit of Michael on Urantia.
 > "2. The circuit of the Divine Ministers, the local universe Mother Spirits, the Holy Spirit of your world.
 > "3. The intelligence-ministry circuit of a local universe, including the diversely functioning presence of the adjutant mind-spirits." (p. 177)

8. **Proposition.** The superuniverse government is directed by one of the Seven Master Spirits, through one of the Seven Supreme Executives on the special worlds of the Spirit.

> "The headquarters of the superuniverses are the seats of the high spiritual government of the time-space domains. The executive branch of the supergovernment, taking origin in the Councils of the Trinity, is immediately directed by one of the Seven Master Spirits of supreme supervision, beings who sit upon seats of Paradise authority and administer the superuniverses through the Seven Supreme Executives stationed on the seven special worlds of the Infinite Spirit, the outermost satellites of Paradise." (p. 178)

9. **Proposition.** The endless metamorphoses of making and remaking universes goes on, but the universes do not run down.

> "The superuniverse of Orvonton is apparently now running down; the outer universes seem to be winding up for unparalleled future activities; the central Havona universe is eternally stabilized. Gravity and absence of heat (cold) organize and hold matter together; heat and antigravity disrupt matter and dissipate energy. The living power directors and force organizers are the secret of the special control and intelligent direction of the endless metamorphoses of universe making, unmaking, and remaking. Nebulae may disperse, suns burn out, systems vanish, and planets perish, but the universes do not run down." (p. 176)

10. **Proposition.** The executive branch of a superuniverse government consists of seven groups.

> "Each superuniverse is presided over by three Ancients of Days, the joint chief executives of the supergovernment. In its executive branch the personnel of the superuniverse government consists of seven different groups:
>
> "1. Ancients of Days.
> "2. Perfectors of Wisdom.
> "3. Divine Counselors.
> "4. Universal Censors.
> "5. Mighty Messengers.
> "6. Those High in Authority.
> "7. Those without Name and Number." (p. 178)

11. **Proposition.** The superuniverse co-ordinate council is composed of the seven executive groups.

> "The co-ordinate council of the superuniverse is composed of the seven executive groups previously named and the following sector rulers and other regional overseers:
> "1. Perfections of Days — the rulers of the superuniverse major sectors.
> "2. Recents of Days — the directors of the superuniverse minor sectors.
> "3. Unions of Days — the Paradise advisers to the rulers of the local universes.
> "4. Faithfuls of Days — the Paradise counselors to the Most High rulers of the constellation governments.
> "5. Trinity Teacher Sons who may chance to be on duty at superuniverse headquarters.
> "6. Eternals of Days who may happen to be present at superuniverse headquarters.
> "7. The seven Reflective Image Aids — the spokesmen of the seven Reflective Spirits and through them representatives of the Seven Master Spirits of Paradise." (p. 179)

12. **Proposition.** On Uversa, the autocracy of perfection and the democracy of evolution meet face to face.

> "It is on such worlds as Uversa that the beings representative of the autocracy of perfection and the democracy of evolution meet face to face. The executive branch of the super government originates in the realms of perfection; the legislative branch springs from the flowering of the evolutionary universes." (p. 179)

13. **Proposition.** The executive branch consists in perfection, the legislative in ascending evolutionary creatures.

> "The deliberative assembly of the superuniverse is confined to the headquarters world. This legislative or advisory council consists of seven houses, to each of which every local universe admitted to the superuniverse councils elects a native representative." (p. 179)

14. **Proposition.** The superuniverse government consists of executive, legislative, and judicial divisions which are variously constituted.

> "When we speak of executive and deliberative branches of the Uversa government, you may, from the analogy of certain forms of Urantian civil government, reason that we must have a third or judicial branch, and we do; but it does not have a separate personnel. Our courts are constituted as follows:

There presides, in accordance with the nature and gravity of the case, an Ancient of Days, a Perfector of Wisdom, or a Divine Counselor. The evidence for or against an individual, a planet, system, constellation, or universe is presented and interpreted by the Censors. The defense of the children of time and the evolutionary planets is offered by the Mighty Messengers, the official observers of the superuniverse government to the local universes and systems. The attitude of the higher government is portrayed by Those High in Authority. And ordinarily the verdict is formulated by a varying-sized commission consisting equally of Those without Name and Number and a group of understanding personalities chosen from the deliberative assembly." (p. 180)

15. **PROPOSITION.** Mandates of judgment originate in the local universes, but when extinction of will creatures is involved, they are executed from the headquarters of the superuniverses.

"Mandates of judgment originate in the local universes, but sentences involving the extinction of will creatures are always formulated on, and executed from, the headquarters of the superuniverse. The Sons of the local universes can decree the survival of mortal man, but only the Ancients of Days may sit in executive judgment on the issues of eternal life and death." (p. 180)

16. **PROPOSITION.** Superuniverse capitals are the abiding place of the Reflective Spirits and their Reflective Image Aids.

"The superuniverse headquarters are the abiding places of the Reflective Spirits and the Reflective Image Aids. From this midway position these marvelous beings conduct their tremendous reflectivity operations, thus ministering to the central universe above and to the local universes below." (p. 178)

17. **PROPOSITION.** Orvonton is best known because of its lavish bestowal of merciful ministry.

"Orvonton, the seventh superuniverse, the one to which your local universe belongs, is known chiefly because of its tremendous and lavish bestowal of merciful ministry to the mortals of the realms. It is renowned for the manner in which justice prevails as tempered by mercy and power rules as conditioned by patience, while the sacrifices of time are freely made to secure the stabilization of eternity. Orvonton is a universe demonstration of love and mercy." (p. 182)

X. THE SPHERES OF SPACE

1. **Proposition.** Matter always swings true to the great space circuits. These space paths, separated by the quiescent space zones, prevent the wild dispersion of energy.

   "The successive space levels of the master universe constitute the major divisions of pervaded space — total creation, organized and partially inhabited or yet to be organized and inhabited. If the master universe were not a series of elliptical space levels of lessened resistance to motion, alternating with zones of relative quiescence, we conceive that some of the cosmic energies would be observed to shoot off on an infinite range, off on a straight-line path into trackless space; but we never find force, energy, or matter thus behaving; ever they whirl, always swinging onward in the tracks of the great space circuits." (p. 128)

2. **PROPOSITION.** One-half million light-years beyond the grand universe, in the first outer space level, unbelievable action is taking place — extending for twenty-five millon light-years.

   "*The Outer Space Levels*. Far out in space, at an enormous distance from the seven inhabited superuniverses, there are assembling vast and unbelievably stupendous circuits of force and materializing energies. Between the energy circuits of the seven superuniverses and this gigantic outer belt of force activity, there is a space zone of comparative quiet, which varies in width but averages about four hundred thousand light-years. These space zones are free from star dust — cosmic fog. Our students of these phenomena are in doubt as to the exact status of the space-forces existing in this zone of relative quiet which encircles the seven superuniverses. But about one-half million light-years beyond the periphery of the present grand universe we observe the beginnings of a zone of an unbelievable energy action which increases in volume and intensity for over twenty-five million light-years. These tremendous wheels of energizing forces are situated in the first outer space level, a continuous belt of cosmic activity encircling the whole of the known, organized, and inhabited creation." (p. 129)

3. **Proposition.** The alternate clockwise and counterclockwise movement of the galaxies is a factor of gravity control and acts as a brake on dangerous velocities.

> "This alternate zoning of the master universe, in association with the alternate clockwise and counterclockwise flow of the galaxies, is a factor in the stabilization of physical gravity designed to prevent the accentuation of gravity pressure to the point of disruptive and dispersive activities. Such an arrangement exerts antigravity influence and acts as a brake upon otherwise dangerous velocities." (p. 125)

4. **Proposition.** The fact that all forms of basic energy swing around Paradise suggests that the master universe is circular and delimited.

> "The observable behavior of the material creation constitutes evidence of a physical universe of definite limits. The final proof of both a circular and delimited universe is afforded by the, to us, well-known fact that all forms of basic energy ever swing around the curved path of the space levels of the master universe in obedience to the incessant and absolute pull of Paradise gravity." (p. 128)

XI. ENERGY CONTROL AND REGULATION

1. **Proposition.** All energy is one and comes from nether Paradise. Space is the womb of many modified forms of matter.

> "All physical force, energy, and matter are one. All force-energy originally proceeded from nether Paradise and will eventually return thereto following the completion of its space circuit. But the energies and material organizations of the universe of universes did not all come from nether Paradise in their present phenomenal states; space is the womb of several forms of matter and prematter." (p. 123)

2. **Proposition.** All units of cosmic energy are in primary revolution. Nothing in the master universe is stationary except Paradise.

> "All units of cosmic energy are in primary revolution, are engaged in the execution of their mission, while swinging around the universal orbit. The universes of space and their component systems and worlds are all revolving spheres, moving along the endless circuits of the master universe space levels. Absolutely nothing is stationary in all the master universe except the very center of Havona, the eternal Isle of Paradise, the center of gravity." (p. 133)

3. **Proposition.** The forces of outer space are the concern of the Paradise force organizers.

> "We are informed that the metamorphosis of cosmic force in these outer space levels is a function of the Paradise force organizers. We also know that these forces are ancestral to those physical energies which at present activate the grand universe. The Orvonton power directors, however, have nothing to do with these far-distant realms, neither are the energy movements therein discernibly connected with the power circuits of the organized and inhabited creations." (p. 131)

4. **Proposition.** Paradise force organizers transmute space potency into primordial and secondary energies of physical reality. When responsive to gravity, the superuniverse power directors take over.

> "The Paradise force organizers transmute space potency into primordial force and evolve this prematerial potential into the primary and secondary energy manifestations of physical reality. When this energy attains gravity-responding levels, the power directors and their associates of the superuniverse regime appear upon the scene and begin their never-ending manipulations designed to establish the manifold power circuits and energy channels of the universes of time and space. Thus does physical matter appear in space, and so is the stage set for the inauguration of universe organization." (p. 169)

5. **Proposition.** There is some mystery associated with the force-charge of space. It does not respond to gravity, but ever it swings around Paradise.

> "While creation and universe organization remain forever under the control of the infinite Creators and their associates, the whole phenomenon proceeds in accordance with an ordained technique and in conformity to the gravity laws of force, energy, and matter. But there is something of mystery associated with the universal force-charge of space; we quite understand the organization of the material creations from the ultimatonic stage forward, but we do not fully comprehend the cosmic ancestry of the ultimatons. We are confident that these ancestral forces have a Paradise origin because they forever swing through pervaded space in the exact gigantic outlines of Paradise. Though nonresponsive to Paradise gravity, this force-charge of space, the ancestor of all materialization, does always respond to the presence of nether Paradise, being apparently circuited in and out of the nether Paradise center." (p. 169)

PART VI — *COSMOLOGY*

6. **PROPOSITION.** Superuniverse headquarters spheres function as power-energy regulators for the directionization of energies to the component sectors.

> "The headquarters spheres of the superuniverses are so constructed that they are able to function as efficient power-energy regulators for their various sectors, serving as focal points for the directionization of energy to their component local universes. They exert a powerful influence over the balance and control of the physical energies circulating through organized space." (p. 175)

7. **PROPOSITION.** The superuniverse power directors assume partial control of the thirty energy systems of the gravita domain. Uversa energy circuits require 968 million years to complete the superuniverse circuits.

> "The power centers and physical controllers of the superuniverses assume direction and partial control of the thirty energy systems which comprise the gravita domain. The physical-energy circuits administered by the power centers of Uversa require a little over 968 million years to complete the encirclement of the superuniverse." (p. 175)

8. **PROPOSITION.** Universe equilibrium requires the everlasting making and unmaking of material units. Universe Power Directors can condense and detain, or expand and liberate, energy.

> "The universal plan for the maintenance of equilibrium between matter and energy necessitates the everlasting making and unmaking of the lesser material units. The Universe Power Directors have the ability to condense and detain, or to expand and liberate, varying quantities of energy." (p. 175)

XII. ASTRONOMY

1. **PROPOSITION.** The mysterious stretches of outer space exhibit the amazing evolution of the plans of the Architects of the Master Universe.

> "When Urantia astronomers peer through their increasingly powerful telescopes into the mysterious stretches of outer space and there behold the amazing evolution of almost countless physical universes, they should realize that they are gazing upon the mighty outworking of the unsearchable plans of the Architects of the Master Universe." (p. 130)

2. **Proposition.** As far as known, no material creatures or spirit beings exist in the realms of outer space."

> As far as we know, no material beings on the order of humans, no angels or other spirit creatures, exist in this outer ring of nebulae, suns, and planets. This distant domain is beyond the jurisdiction and administration of the superuniverse governments." (p. 131)

3. **Proposition.** Your world may appear to be taking one long plunge into uncharted space — but it is not. It is following a well-known and perfectly controlled processional around Paradise.

> "Within the limited range of the records, observations, and memories of the generations of a million or a billion of your short years, to all practical intents and purposes, Urantia and the universe to which it belongs are experiencing the adventure of one long and uncharted plunge into new space; but according to the records of Uversa, in accordance with older observations, in harmony with the more extensive experience and calculations of our order, and as a result of conclusions based on these and other findings, we know that the universes are engaged in an orderly, well-understood, and perfectly controlled processional, swinging in majestic grandeur around the First Great Source and Center and his residential universe." (p. 164)

4. **Proposition.** Only the Universal Father knows the name, number, and location of every inhabited world.

> "Only the Universal Father knows the location and actual number of inhabited worlds in space; he calls them all by name and number. I can give only the approximate number of inhabited or inhabitable planets, for some local universes have more worlds suitable for intelligent life than others. Nor have all projected local universes been organized." (p. 165)

5. **Proposition.** There are ten diverse origins of the majority of suns, planets, and other spheres.

> "As to origin, the majority of the suns, planets, and other spheres can be classified in one of the following ten groups:
>   1. Concentric Contraction Rings.
>   2. The Whirled Stars.
>   3. Gravity-explosion Planets.
>   4. Centrifugal Planetary Daughters.
>   5. Gravity-deficiency Spheres.
>   6. Contractural Stars.
>   7. Cumulative Spheres.

       8. Burned-out Suns.
       9. Collisional Spheres.
      10. Architectural Worlds"
See pages 170 and 171.

6. **PROPOSITION.** Paradise force organizers are nebulae originators; their cyclones of force mobilize the ultimatonic units of universe matter.

> "Paradise force organizers are nebulae originators; they are able to initiate about their space presence the tremendous cyclones of force which, when once started, can never be stopped or limited until the all-pervading forces are mobilized for the eventual appearance of the ultimatonic units of universe matter." (p. 169)

7. **PROPOSITION.** Some suns are solitary, some are double stars. Suns exist in a thousand different states. There are also suns that shine without heat.

> "*The Suns.* These are the stars of space in all their various stages of existence. Some are solitary evolving space systems; others are double stars, contracting or disappearing planetary systems. The stars of space exist in no less than a thousand different states and stages. You are familiar with suns that emit light accompanied by heat; but there are also suns which shine without heat." (p. 172)

8. **PROPOSITION.** The superuniverse of Orvonton is illuminated and warmed by more than ten trillion blazing suns. In the master universe there are as many suns as there are glasses of water in the oceans of Urantia.

> "The superuniverse of Orronton is illuminated and warmed by more than ten trillion blazing suns. These suns are the stars of your observable astronomic system. More than two trillion are too distant and too small ever to be seen from Urantia. But in the master universe there are as many suns as there are glasses of water in the oceans of your world." (p. 172)

9. **PROPOSITION.** The dark islands of space are dead suns and other aggregations of cold matter. Sometimes their density is unbelievable.

> "*The Dark Islands of Space.* These are the dead suns and other large aggregations of matter devoid of light and heat. The dark islands are sometimes enormous in mass and exert a powerful influence in universe equilibrium and energy manipulation. The density of

some of these large masses is well-nigh unbelievable. And this great concentration of mass enables these dark islands to function as powerful balance wheels, holding large neighboring systems in effective leash." (p. 173)

10. **Proposition.** Comets are wild offspring, being brought under control of the suns. They have numerous origins.

   "Many comets are unestablished wild offspring of the solar mother wheels, which are being gradually brought under control of the central governing sun. Comets also have numerous other origins. A comet's tail points away from the attracting body or sun because of the electrical reaction of its highly expanded gases and because of the actual pressure of light and other energies emanating from the sun." (p. 173)

11. **Proposition.** Not all adolescent suns pass through pulsating stages. Our sun exhibits a legacy of its former three and one-half day pulsations in its eleven and one-half year sunspot cycles.

   "While all adolescent suns do not pass through a pulsating stage, at least not visibly, when looking out into space you may observe many of these younger stars whose gigantic respiratory heaves require from two to seven days to complete a cycle. Your own sun still carries a diminishing legacy of the mighty upswellings of its younger days, but the period has lengthened from the former three and one-half day pulsations to the present eleven and one-half year sunspot cycles." (p. 459)

12. **Proposition.** The suns are not very dense. Density prevents escape of light and if increased would cause explosions.

   "That the suns of space are not very dense is proved by the steady streams of escaping light-energies. Too great a density would retain light by opacity until the light-energy pressure reached the explosion point. There is a tremendous light or gas pressure within a sun to cause it to shoot forth such a stream of energy as to penetrate space for millions upon millions of miles to energize, light, and heat the distant planets. Fifteen feet of surface of the density of Urantia would effectually prevent the escape of all X rays and light-energies from a sun until the rising internal pressure of accumulating energies resulting from atomic dismemberment overcame gravity with a tremendous outward explosion." (p. 460)

Part VI — Cosmology

13. **Proposition.** Light plus propulsive gases is highly explosive when confined at high temperatures. Light is real. Sunlight would be economical at a million dollars a pound.

    "Light, in the presence of the propulsive gases, is highly explosive when confined at high temperatures by opaque retaining walls. Light is real. As you value energy and power on your world, sunlight would be economical at a million dollars a pound." (p. 460)

14. **Proposition.** Calcium escapes from the sun by literally riding the light beams to liberty.

    "As your physicists have suspected, these mutilated remnants of solar calcium literally ride the light beams for varied distances, and thus their widespread dissemination throughout space is tremendously facilitated. The sodium atom, under certain modifications, is also capable of light and energy locomotion. The calcium feat is all the more remarkable since this element has almost twice the mass of sodium. Local space-permeation by calcium is due to the fact that it escapes from the solar photosphere, in modified form, by literally riding the outgoing sunbeams. Of all the solar elements, calcium, notwithstanding its comparative bulk — containing as it does twenty revolving electrons — is the most successful in escaping from the solar interior to the realms of space. This explains why there is a calcium layer, a gaseous stone surface, on the sun six thousand miles thick; and this despite the fact that nineteen lighter elements, and numerous heavier ones, are underneath." (p. 462)

15. **Proposition.** Planets follow an orbit around the sun. They may be gaseous, liquid, or solid. Sometimes they are built up by assemblage of cold space matter.

    "*The Planets.* These are the larger aggregations of matter which follow an orbit around a sun or some other space body; they range in size from planetesimals to enormous gaseous, liquid, or solid spheres. The cold worlds which have been built up by the assemblage of floating space material, when they happen to be in proper relation to a near-by sun, are the more ideal planets to harbor intelligent inhabitants." (p. 173)

XIII. SUN STABILITY

1. **PROPOSITION.** Solar energy proceeds in direct lines. Its wavy manifestation is due to other energies which cause light to appear to be chopped up into portions of definite length.

   "Solar energy may seem to be propelled in waves, but that is due to the action of coexistent and diverse influences. A given form of organized energy does not proceed in waves but in direct lines. The presence of a second or a third form of force-energy may cause the stream under observation to *appear* to travel in wavy formation, just as, in a blinding rainstorm accompanied by a heavy wind, the water sometimes appears to fall in sheets or to descend in waves. The raindrops are coming down in a direct line of unbroken procession, but the action of the wind is such as to give the visible appearance of sheets of water and waves of raindrops.

   "The action of certain secondary and other undiscovered energies present in the space regions of your local universe is such that solar-light emanations appear to execute certain wavy phenomena as well as to be chopped up into infinitesimal portions of definite length and weight." (p. 461)

2. **PROPOSITION.** Sun stability is maintained by seven diverse factors.

   "All of these phenomena are indicative of enormous energy expenditure, and the sources of solar energy, named in the order of their importance, are:

   "1. Annihilation of atoms and, eventually, of electrons.

   "2. Transmutation of elements, including the radioactive group of energies thus liberated.

   "3. The accumulation and transmission of certain universal space-energies.

   "4. Space matter and meteors which are incessantly diving into the blazing suns.

   "5. Solar contraction; the cooling and consequent contraction of a sun yields energy and heat sometimes greater than that supplied by space matter.

   "6. Gravity action at high temperatures transforms certain circuitized power into radiative energies.

   "7. Receptive light and other matter which are drawn back into the sun after having left it, together with other energies having extrasolar origin." (p. 463)

3. **Proposition.** Only suns functioning in direct channels of universe energy can shine on forever.

> "Only those suns which function in the direct channels of the main streams of universe energy can shine on forever. Such solar furnaces blaze on indefinitely, being able to replenish their material losses by the intake of space-force and analogous circulating energy. But stars far removed from these chief channels of recharging are destined to undergo energy depletion — gradually cool off and eventually burn out." (p. 464)

XIV. UNIVERSE LEVELS OF REALITY

1. **Proposition.** Reality is divided into four grand divisions.

> "From the viewpoint of time and space, reality is further divisible as:
>
> "1. *Actual and Potential.* Realities existing in fullness of expression in contrast to those which carry undisclosed capacity for growth. The Eternal Son is an absolute spiritual actuality; mortal man is very largely an unrealized spiritual potentiality.
>
> "2. *Absolute and Subabsolute.* Absolute realities are eternity existences. Subabsolute realities are projected on two levels: Absonites — realities which are relative with respect to both time and eternity. Finites — realities which are projected in space and are actualized in time.
>
> "3. *Existential and Experiential.* Paradise Deity is existential, but the emerging Supreme and Ultimate are experiential.
>
> "4. *Personal and Impersonal.* Deity expansion, personality expression, and universe evolution are forever conditioned by the Father's freewill act which forever separated the mind-spirit-personal meanings and values of actuality and potentiality centering in the Eternal Son from those things which center and inhere in the eternal Isle of Paradise." (p. 7)

2. **Proposition.** Reality is realizable on seven diverse levels of universe actualization.
    1. Undeified Reality.
    2. Deified Reality.
    3. Interassociated Reality.
        See p. 6
    1. Incomplete finites.
    2. Maximum finites.
    3. Transcendantals.
    4. Ultimates.
    5. Coabsolutes.
    6. Absolutes.
    7. Infinity.
        See pages 1162-3.

PART VII
THE LOCAL UNIVERSE

Part Seven
THE LOCAL UNIVERSE

1. **Proposition.** Local universes are evolutionary and are the handiwork of the Paradise Creator Sons.

   "A local universe is the handiwork of a Creator Son of the Paradise order of Michael. It comprises one hundred constellations, each embracing one hundred systems of inhabited worlds. Each system will eventually contain approximately one thousand inhabited spheres.
   "These universes of time and space are all evolutionary. The creative plan of the Paradise Michaels always proceeds along the path of gradual evolvement and progressive development of the physical, intellectual, and spiritual natures and capacities of the manifold creatures who inhabit the varied orders of spheres comprising such a local universe." (p. 357)

2. **Proposition.** When conditions are ripe, a Creator Son and a Creative Spirit appear upon the scene to begin the architectural worlds which are the foundation for a local universe.

   "When energy-matter has attained a certain stage in mass materialization, a Paradise Creator Son appears upon the scene, accompanied by a Creative Daughter of the Infinite Spirit. Simultaneously with the arrival of the Creator Son, work is begun upon the architectural sphere which is to become the headquarters world of the projected local universe. For long ages such a local creation evolves, suns become stabilized, planets form and swing into their orbits, while the work of creating the architectural worlds which are to serve as constellation headquarters and system capitals continues." (p. 358)

3. **Proposition.** The energy charge of a local universe is about one one-hundred-thousandth of the force endowment of a superuniverse.

   "The energy charge of a local universe is approximately one one-hundred-thousandth of the force endowment of its superuniverse. In the case of Nebadon, your local universe, the mass materialization is a trifle less. Physically speaking, Nebadon possesses all of the physical endowment of energy and matter that may be found in any of the Orvonton local creations. The only physical limitation upon the developmental expansion of the Nebadon universe consists in the quantitative charge of space-energy held captive by the gravity control of the associated powers and personalities of the combined universe mechanism." (p. 358)

4   **Proposition.** The cosmic geography of Urantia.

> "Your local universe of Nebadon belongs to Orvonton, the seventh superuniverse, which swings on between superuniverses one and six, having not long since (as we reckon time) turned the southeastern bend of the superuniverse space level. Today, the solar system to which Urantia belongs is a few billion years past the swing around the southern curvature so that you are just now advancing beyond the southeastern bend and are moving swiftly through the long and comparatively straightaway northern path. For untold ages Orvonton will pursue this almost direct northerly course." (p. 165)

5.   **Proposition.** The cosmology of Urantia.

> "Urantia belongs to a system which is well out towards the borderland of your local universe; and your local universe is at present traversing the periphery of Orvonton. Beyond you there are still others, but you are far removed in space from those physical systems which swing around the great circle in comparative proximity to the Great Source and Center." (p. 164)

6.   **Proposition.** The headquarters worlds from Jerusem to Uversa.

> "*Jerusem*, the headquarters of your local system of Satania, has its seven worlds of transition culture, each of which is encircled by seven satellites, among which are the seven mansion worlds of morontia detention, man's first postmortal residence. As the term heaven has been used on Urantia, it has sometimes meant these seven mansion worlds, the first mansion world being denominated the first heaven, and so on to the seventh.
>
> "*Edentia*, the headquarters of your constellation of Norlatiadek, has its seventy satellites of socializing culture and training, on which ascenders sojourn upon the completion of the Jerusem regime of personality mobilization, unification, and realization.
>
> "*Salvington*, the capital of Nebadon, your local universe, is surrounded by ten university clusters of forty-nine spheres each. Hereon is man spiritualized following his constellation socialization.
>
> "*Uminor the third*, the headquarters of your minor sector, Ensa, is surrounded by the seven spheres of the higher physical studies of the ascendant life.

PART VII — THE LOCAL UNIVERSE

> "*Umajor the fifth*, the headquarters of your major sector, Splandon, is surrounded by the seventy spheres of the advancing intellectual training of the superuniverse.
>
> "*Uversa*, the headquarters of Orvonton, your superuniverse, is immediately surrounded by the seven higher universities of advanced spiritual training for ascending will creatures." (p. 174)

7. PROPOSITION. Minor sector organization.

    > "The *minor sector* governments are presided over by three Recents of Days. Their administration is concerned mainly with the physical control, unification, stabilization, and routine coordination of the administration of the component local universes. Each minor sector embraces as many as one hundred local universes, ten thousand constellations, one million systems, or about one billion inhabitable worlds.
    >
    > "Minor sector headquarters worlds are the grand rendezvous of the Master Physical Controllers. These headquarters worlds are surrounded by the seven instruction spheres which constitute the entrance schools of the superuniverse and are the centers of training for physical and administrative knowledge concerning the universe of universes." (p. 181)

8. PROPOSITION. Identification of Urantia up through the grand universe. See p. 182.

9. PROPOSITION. Local universe headquarters is not legislative, but many advisory bodies are functional, such as the supreme council and the one hundred councils of supreme sanction.

    > "While true legislation is not enacted at the universe headquarters, there do function on Salvington a variety of advisory and research assemblies, variously constituted and conducted in accordance with their scope and purpose. Some are permanent; others disband upon the accomplishment of their objective.
    >
    > "*The supreme council* of the local universe is made up of three members from each system and seven representatives from each constellation. Systems in isolation do not have representation in this assembly, but they are permitted to send observers who attend and study all its deliberations.
    >
    > "*The one hundred councils of supreme sanction* are also situated on Salvington. The presidents of these councils constitute the immediate working cabinet of Gabriel." (p. 373)

10. **Proposition.** In diameter, suns average one million miles — ours is less. The largest star in the universe is four hundred fifty times that of our sun. But the suns have as much room in space as one dozen oranges in the interior of Urantia.

> "The suns of Nebadon are not unlike those of other universes. The material composition of all suns, dark islands, planets, and satellites, even meteors, is quite identical. These suns have an average diameter of about one million miles, that of your own solar orb being slightly less. The largest star in the universe, the stellar cloud Antares, is four hundred and fifty times the diameter of your sun and is sixty million times its volume. But there is abundant space to accommodate all of these enormous suns. They have just as much comparative elbow room in space as one dozen oranges would have if they were circulating about throughout the interior of Urantia, and were the planet a hollow globe." (p. 458)

11. **Proposition.** The mass of your sun is about two octillion tons. Its density is halfway between the most diffuse and the most dense stars — about one and a half times the density of water.

> "The mass of your sun is slightly greater than the estimate of your physicists, who have reckoned it as about two octillion (2×10^{27}) tons. It now exists about halfway between the most dense and the most diffuse stars, having about one and one-half times the density of water. But your sun is neither a liquid nor a solid — it is gaseous — and this is true notwithstanding the difficulty of explaining how gaseous matter can attain this and even much greater densities." (p. 459)

12. **Proposition.** Havona is the educational training ground for the Paradise Michaels before they go forth as Creator Sons.

> "5. *The Co-ordinate Creator Sons.* Havona is the educational training ground where the Paradise Michaels are prepared for their subsequent adventures in universe creation. This divine and perfect creation is a pattern for every Creator Son. He strives to make his own universe eventually attain to these Paradise-Havona levels of perfection." (p. 162)

13. **Proposition.** Our sun radiates almost one hundred billion tons of matter annually. Before becoming stabilized, the larger suns are given to convulsive pulsations.

> "Your own solar center radiates almost one hundred billion tons of actual matter annually, while the giant suns lose matter at a prodigious rate during their earlier growth, the first billion years. A sun's life becomes stable after the maximum of internal temperature is reached, and the subatomic energies begin to be released. And it is just at this critical point that the larger suns are given to convulsive pulsations." (p. 465)

14. **Proposition.** The Universe Mother Spirit is a cocreator in the local universe.

> "*The Co-ordinate Ministering Daughters.* The Universe Mother Spirits, cocreators of the local universes, secure their prepersonal training on the worlds of Havona in close association with the Spirits of the Circuits. In the central universe the Spirit Daughters of the local universes were duly trained in the methods of co-operation with the Sons of Paradise, all the while subject to the will of the Father." (p. 162)

15. **Proposition.** On Edentia, the Faithful of Days dwells on the holy mount of assembly. He is the Trinity counselor of the Most High Fathers.

> "The most holy mount of assembly is the dwelling place of the Faithful of Days, the representative of the Paradise Trinity who functions on Edentia.
>
> "This Faithful of Days is a Trinity Son of Paradise and has been present on Edentia as the personal representative of Immanuel since the creation of the headquarters world. Ever the Faithful of Days stands at the right hand of the Constellation Fathers to counsel them, but never does he proffer advice unless it is asked for. The high Sons of Paradise never participate in the conduct of the affairs of a local universe except upon the petition of the acting rulers of such domains. But all that a Union of Days is to a Creator Son, a Faithful of Days is to the Most Highs of a constellation." (p. 489)

16. **Proposition.** Architectural worlds enjoy ten forms of material life — three vegetable and three animal. The intervening four are difficult of comprehension.

> "The architectural worlds enjoy ten forms of life of the material order. On Urantia there is plant and animal life, but on such a world as Edentia there are ten divisions of the material orders of life. Were you to view these ten divisions of Edentia life, you would quickly classify the first three as vegetable and the last three as animal, but you would be utterly unable to comprehend the nature of the intervening four groups of prolific and fascinating forms of life." (p. 492)

17. **Proposition.** The broadcast receiving station seats over five billion beings, not to mention innumerable spirit personalities.

> "This Jerusem broadcast-receiving station is encircled by an enormous amphitheater, constructed of scintillating materials largely unknown on Urantia and seating over five billion beings — material and morontia — besides accommodating innumerable spirit personalities. It is the favorite diversion for all Jerusem to spend their leisure at the broadcast station, there to learn of the welfare and state of the universe. And this is the only planetary activity which is not slowed down during the recession of light." (p. 522)

18. **Proposition.** Universe-wide messages are received on the sea of glass, not to mention reflectivity with its visualization of messages.

> "At this broadcast-receiving amphitheater the Salvington messages are coming in continuously. Near by, the Edentia word of the Most High Constellation Fathers is received at least once a day. Periodically the regular and special broadcasts of Uversa are relayed through Salvington, and when Paradise messages are in reception, the entire population is assembled around the sea of glass, and the Uversa friends add the reflectivity phenomena to the technique of the Paradise broadcast so that everything heard becomes visible. And it is in this manner that continual foretastes of advancing beauty and grandeur are afforded the mortal survivors as they journey inward on the eternal adventure." (p. 522)

PART VIII
EVOLUTION

Part Eight
EVOLUTION

I. INTRODUCTION

1. **Proposition.** While reason demands monotheistic unity, experience requires diversity of absolutes—even differentials, variables, modifiers, and qualifiers.

   "While reason demands a monotheistic unity of cosmic reality, finite experience requires the postulate of plural Absolutes and of their co-ordination in cosmic relationships. Without co-ordinate existences there is no possibility for the appearance of diversity of absolute relationships, no chance for the operation of differentials, variables, modifiers, attenuators, qualifiers, or diminishers." (p. 1146)

2. **Proposition.** Transcendentals are subinfinite and subabsolute, but superfinite. They are an integrating level for correlating the supervalues of the absonite with the maximum values of the finite.

   "Transcendentals are subinfinite and subabsolute but superfinite and supercreatural. Transcendentals eventuate as an integrating level correlating the supervalues of absolutes with the maximum values of finites. From the creature standpoint, that which is transcendental would appear to have eventuated as a consequence of the finite; from the eternity viewpoint, in anticipation of the finite; and there are those who have considered it as a 'pre-echo' of the finite." (p. 1159)

3. **Proposition.** Man will never find the secrets of life. The analysis of dead protoplasm does not disclose the true nature of living protoplasm.

   "It is impossible accurately to determine, simultaneously, the exact location and the velocity of a moving object; any attempt at measurement of either inevitably involves change in the other. The same sort of a paradox confronts mortal man when he undertakes the chemical analysis of protoplasm. The chemist can elucidate the chemistry of *dead* protoplasm, but he cannot discern either the physical organization or the dynamic performance of *living* protoplasm. Ever will the scientist come nearer and nearer the secrets of life, but never will he find them and for no other reason than that he must kill protoplasm in order to analyze it. Dead protoplasm weighs the same as living protoplasm, but it is not the same." (p. 737)

II. MATERIAL MIND SYSTEMS

1. **Proposition.** The ability to learn from experience marks the beginning function of the adjutant mind spirits.

    "The acquisition of the potential of the ability to *learn* from experience marks the beginning of the functioning of the adjutant spirits, and they function from the lowliest minds of primitive and invisible existences up to the highest types in the evolutionary scale of human beings." (p. 739)

2. **Proposition.** Cosmological levels of thought include:
    A. Curiosity.
    B. Aesthetic appreciation.
    C. Ethic sensitivity.

    "The attainment of cosmologic levels of thought includes:
    "1. *Curiosity*. Hunger for harmony and thirst for beauty. Persistent attempts to discover new levels of harmonious cosmic relationships.
    "2. *Aesthetic appreciation*. Love of the beautiful and ever-advancing appreciation of the artistic touch of all creative manifestations on all levels of reality.
    "3. *Ethic sensitivity*. Through the realization of truth the appreciation of beauty leads to the sense of the eternal fitness of those things which impinge upon the recognition of divine goodness in Deity relations with all beings; and thus even cosmology leads to the pursuit of divine reality values—to God-consciousness." (p. 646)

III. UNIVERSE MECHANISMS

1. **Proposition.** Mechanisms do not dominate the total creation; the universes are mind planned and administered. Mechanism dominance by the infinite mind is too perfect for detection by the finite mind.

    "Mechanisms do not absolutely dominate the total creation; the universe of universes *in toto* is mind planned, mind made, and mind administered. But the divine mechanism of the universe of universes is altogether too perfect for the scientific methods of the finite mind of man to discern even a trace of the dominance of the infinite mind. For this creating, controlling, and upholding mind is neither material mind nor creature mind; it is spirit-mind functioning on and from creator levels of divine reality." (p. 481)

2. **Proposition.** Higher universe mechanisms must appear to be mindless to the lower creatures. But philosophy would imply mindedness in the apparently self-maintaining universe.

> "Extremely complex and highly automatic-appearing cosmic mechanisms always tend to conceal the presence of the originative or creative indwelling mind from any and all intelligences very far below the universe levels of the nature and capacity of the mechanism itself. Therefore is it inevitable that the higher universe mechanisms must appear to be mindless to the lower orders of creatures. The only possible exception to such a conclusion would be the implication of mindedness in the amazing phenomenon of an *apparently self-maintaining universe*—but that is a matter of philosophy rather than one of actual experience." (p. 482)

3. **Proposition.** Ability to discover mindedness in universe mechanisms depends on the ability and capacity of the investigating mind.

> "The ability to discern and discover mind in universe mechanisms depends entirely on the ability, scope, and capacity of the investigating mind engaged in such a task of observation. Time-space minds, organized out of the energies of time and space, are subject to the mechanisms of time and space." (p. 482)

4. **Proposition.** The controlling mind of universe mechanisms is infinite and therefore beyond the full discernment of the finite mind.

> "The higher the universe mind associated with any universe phenomenon, the more difficult it is for the lower types of mind to discover it. And since the mind of the universe mechanism is creative spirit-mind (even the mindedness of the Infinite), it can never be discovered or discerned by the lower-level minds of the universe, much less by the *lowest* mind of all, the human. The evolving animal mind, while naturally God-seeking, is not alone and of itself inherently Godknowing." (p. 482)

5. **Proposition.** Mind is concealed in the evolution of cosmic mechanisms. Mind always reaches out towards definite activities.

> "The evolution of mechanisms implies and indicates the concealed presence and dominance of creative mind. The ability of the mortal intellect to conceive, design, and create automatic mechanisms demonstrates the superior, creative, and

purposive qualities of man's mind as the dominant influence on the planet. Mind always reaches out towards:

"1. Creation of material mechanisms.
"2. Discovery of hidden mysteries.
"3. Exploration of remote situations.
"4. Formulation of mental systems.
"5. Attainment of wisdom goals.
"6. Achievement of spirit levels.
"7. The accomplishment of divine destinies—supreme, ultimate, and absolute." (p. 483)

IV. PATTERN AND FORM—MIND SYSTEMS

1. **Proposition.** Universe energies are associated on four levels of mind activity.

"The universal nonspiritual energies are reassociated in the living systems of non-Creator minds on various levels, certain of which may be depicted as follows:

"1. *Preadjutant-spirit minds.* This level of mind is nonexperiencing and on the inhabited worlds is ministered by the Master Physical Controllers. This is mechanical mind, the nonteachable intellect of the most primitive forms of material life, but the nonteachable mind functions on many levels beside that of primitive planetary life.

"2. *Adjutant-spirt minds.* This is the ministry of a local universe Mother Spirit functioning through her seven adjutant mind-spirits on the teachable (nonmechanical) level of material mind. On this level material mind is experiencing: as subhuman (animal) intellect in the first five adjutant: as human (moral) intellect in the seven adjutants; as superhuman (midwayer) intellect in the last two adjutants.

"3. *Evolving morontia minds*—the expanding consciousness of evolving personalities in the local universe ascending careers. This is the bestowal of the local universe Mother Spirit in liaison with the Creator Son. This mind level connotes the organization of the morontia type of life vehicle, a synthesis of the material and the spiritual which is effected by the Morontia Power Supervisors of a local universe. Morontia mind functions differentially in response to the 570 levels of morontia life, disclosing increasing associative capacity with the cosmic mind on the higher levels of attainment. This is the evolutionary course of mortal creatures, but mind of a nonmorontia order is also bestowed by a Universe Son and a Universe Spirit upon the nonmorontia children of the local creations.

"*The cosmic mind.* This is the sevenfold diversified mind of time and space, one phase of which is ministered by each of the Seven Master Spirits to one of the seven superuniverses. The cosmic mind encompasses all finite-mind levels and co-ordinates experientially with the evolutionary-deity levels of the Supreme Mind and transcendentally with the existential levels of absolute mind—the direct circuits of the Conjoint Actor." (pp. 480-81)

2. **PROPOSITION.** Physics and chemistry alone cannot explain human evolution. Mind only can explain the results of education and training.

"Physics and chemistry alone cannot explain how a human being evolved out of the primeval protoplasm of the early seas. The ability to learn, memory and differential response to environment, is the endowment of mind. The laws of physics are not responsive to training; they are immutable and unchanging. The reactions of chemistry are not modified by education; they are uniform and dependable." (p. 738)

3. **PROPOSITION.** The seven adjutant mind-spirits are bestowed from universe headquarters and are independent of the Life Carriers.

"The seven adjutant mind-spirits are the versatile mind ministers to the lower intelligent existences of a local universe. This order of mind is ministered from the local universe headquarters or from some world connected therewith, but there is influential direction of lower-mind function from the system capitals.

"On an evolutionary world much, very much, depends on the work of these seven adjutants. But they are mind ministers; they are not concerned in physical evolution, the domain of the Life Carriers." (p. 738)

V. EVOLUTION OF HUMAN MIND

1. **PROPOSITION.** The great universe adventure is man's transit of mortal mind from mechanical statics to spiritual dynamics—by constancy of decisions—"not my will but yours be done."

"An automatic universe reaction is stable and, in some form, continuing in the cosmos. A personality who knows God and desires to do his will, who has spirit insight, is divinely stable and eternally existent. Man's great universe adventure consists in the transit of his mortal mind from the stability of mechanical statics to the divinity of spiritual dynamics, and he achieves this transformation by the force and constancy of his own personality decisions, in each of life's situations declaring, 'It is my will that your will be done.'" (p. 1303)

2. **Proposition.** The ghost dream was a potent factor in the evolution of society—it drove men together

"Probably the greatest single factor in the evolution of human society was the ghost dream. Although most dreams greatly perturbed the primitive mind, the ghost dream actually terriorized early men, driving these superstitious dreamers into each other's arms in willing and earnest association for mutual protection against the vague and unseen imaginary dangers of the spirit world. The ghost dream was one of the earliest appearing differences between the animal and human types of mind. Animals do not visualize survival after death." (p. 766)

3. **Proposition.** The appearance of intelligent evolutionary beings is the signal for the assignment of a Planetary Prince.

"The signal for a System Sovereign to act in the matter of assigning a ruler to a given planet is the reception of a request from the Life Carriers for the dispatch of an administrative head to function on this planet whereon they have established life and developed intelligent evolutionary beings. All planets which are inhabited by evolutionary mortal creatures have assigned to them a planetary ruler of this order of sonship." (p. 572)

VI. LIFE CARRIER FUNCTIONS

1. **Proposition.** Life Carriers function on three levels.

"Life Carriers are able to function and do function on the following three levels:
"1. The physical level of electrochemistry.
"2. The usual mid-phase of quasi-morontial existence.
"3. The advanced semispiritual level." (p. 730)

2. **Proposition.** When Life Carriers are ready for life implantation, they are prepared by an archangel commission of transmutation.

"When the Life Carriers make ready to engage in life implantation, and after they have selected the sites for such an undertaking, they summon the archangel commission of Life Carrier transmutation. This group consists of ten orders of diverse personalities, including the physical controllers and their associates, and is presided over by the chief of archangels, who acts in this capacity by the mandate of Gabriel and with the permission of the Ancients of Days. When these beings are properly encircuited, they can effect such modifications in the Life Carriers as will enable them immediately to function on the physical levels of electrochemistry." (p. 731)

3. **Proposition.** Life Carriers are the instigators of the energy circuits of living matter, which differs in each local universe.

"The biologic unit of material life is the protoplasmic cell, the communal association of chemical, electrical, and other basic energies. The chemical formulas differ in each system, and the technique of living cell reproduction is slightly different in each local universe, but the Life Carriers are always the living catallyzers who initiate the primordial reactions of material life; they are the instigators of the energy circuits of living matter." (p. 560)

4. **Proposition.** When Life Carriers choose to remain on a planet after the human type has evolved, they must submit to transformation to their semi-spiritual phase.

"After organic evolution has run a certain course and free will of the human type has appeared in the highest evolving organisms, the Life Carriers must either leave the planet or take renunciation vows; that is, they must pledge themselves to refrain from all attempts further to influence the course of organic evolution. And when such vows are voluntarily taken by those Life Carriers who choose to remain on the planet as future advisers to those who shall be intrusted with the fostering of the newly evolved will creatures, there is summoned a commission of twelve, presided over by the chief of the Evening Stars, acting by authority of the System Sovereign and with permission of Gabriel; and forthwith these Life Carriers are transmuted to the third phase of personality existence—the semispiritual level of being. And I have functioned on Urantia in this third phase of existence since the times of Aridon and Fonta." (p. 731)

5. **Proposition.** Life Carriers may utilize fortuitous circumstances to favor life evolution—but not arbitrary intervention.

"Life Carriers may employ every possible natural resource and may utilize any and all fortuitous circumstances which will enhance the developmental progress of the life experiment, but we are not permitted mechanically to intervene in, or arbitrarily to manipulate the conduct and course of, either plant or animal evolution." (p. 733)

6. **Proposition.** We do not fully understand the mystery of life. We know life flows from the Father through the Son, by the co-operation of the Master Spirits, Ancients of Days, and the Universe Mother Spirits.

> "There are some things connected with the elaboration of life on the evolutionary planets which are not altogether clear to us. We fully comprehend the physical organization of the electrochemical formulas of the Life Carriers, but we do not wholly understand the nature and source of the *life-activation spark*. We know that life flows from the Father through the Son and *by* the Spirit. It is more than possible that the Master Spirits are the sevenfold channel of the river of life which is poured out upon all creation. But we do not comprehend the technique whereby the supervising Master Spirit participates in the initial episode of life bestowal on a new planet. The Ancients of Days, we are confident, also have some part in this inauguration of life on a new world, but we are wholly ignorant of the nature thereof. We do know that the Universe Mother Spirit actually vitalizes the lifeless patterns and imparts to such activated plasm the prerogatives of organismal reproduction." (p. 404)

7. **Proposition.** There exists in human blood the possibility of upward of fifteen million chemical reactions.

> "But many seemingly mysterious adjustments of living organisms are purely chemical, wholly physical. At any moment of time, in the blood stream of any human being there exists the possibility of upward of 15,000,000 chemical reactions between the hormone output of a dozen ductless glands." (p. 737)

VII. FOSTERING EVOLUTION

1. **Proposition.** Outside of Havona, perfection is a progressive attainment—and almost infinite variety characterizes these plans of advancement.

> "Except in the central universe, perfection is a progressive attainment. In the central creation we have a pattern of perfection, but all other realms must attain that perfection by the

methods established for the advancement of those particular worlds or universes. And an almost infinite variety characterizes the plans of the Creator Sons for organizing, evolving, disciplining, and settling their respective local universes." (p. 360)

2. **PROPOSITION.** Evolution is not an accident. Over fifty thousand facts of physics and chemistry prove an intelligent purpose in evolution.

> "And yet some of the less imaginative of your mortal mechanists insist on viewing material creation and human evolution as an accident. The Urantia midwayers have assembled over fifty thousand facts of physics and chemistry which they deem to be incompatible with the laws of accidental chance, and which they contend unmistakably demonstrate the presence of intelligent purpose in the material creation." (p. 665)

3. **PROPOSITION.** More than a hundred thousand facts prove the presence of mind in the planning of the cosmos.

> "And all of this takes no account of their catalogue of more than one hundred thousand findings outside the domain of physics and chemistry which they maintain prove the presence of mind in the planning, creation, and maintenance of the material cosmos." (p. 665)

4. **PROPOSITION.** Evolution can be delayed —but it cannot be stopped. Even the small influence the human race got from Adam greatly advanced civilization.

> "REGARDLESS of the ups and downs of the miscarriage of the plans for world betterment projected in the missions of Caligastia and Adam, the basic organic evolution of the human species continued to carry the races forward in the scale of human progress and racial development. Evolution can be delayed but it cannot be stopped.
>
> "The influence of the violet race, though in numbers smaller than had been planned, produced an advance in civilization which, since the days of Adam, has far exceeded the progress of mankind throughout its entire previous existence of almost a million years." (p. 900)

PART VIII — *Evolution*

VIII. THE URANTIA ADVENTURE

1. **Proposition.** Many bacteria and fungi represent retrograde movement in evolution and this explains their disease-causing proclivities.

   "The bacteria, simple vegetable organisms of a very primitive nature, are very little changed from the early dawn of life; they even exhibit a degree of retrogression in their parasitic behavior. Many of the fungi also represent a retrograde movement in evolution, being plants which have lost their chlorophyll-making ability and have become more or less parasitic. The majority of disease-causing bacteria and their auxiliary virus bodies really belong to this group of renegade parasitic fungi. During the intervening ages all of the vast kingdom of plant life has evolved from ancestors from which the bacteria have also descended." (p. 732)

2. **Proposition.** On Urantia it was the frog that led to the final culmination of man himself.

   "The stage was thus set for the appearance of the first backboned animals, the fishes. From this fish family there sprang two unique modifications, the frog and the salamander. And it was the frog which began that series of progressive differentiations in animal life that finally culminated in man himself." (p. 732)

3. **Proposition.** The frog is the only early ancestor of man now living on the face of the earth.

   "The frog is one of the earliest of surviving human-race ancestors, but it also failed to progress, persisting today much as in those remote times. The frog is the only species ancestor of the early dawn races now living on the face of the earth. The human race has no surviving ancestry between the frog and the Eskimo." (p. 732)

4. **Proposition.** The mammalian species sprang suddenly from a reptilian dinosaur.

   "It was from an agile little reptilian dinosaur of carnivorous habits but having a comparatively large brain that the placental mammals *suddenly* sprang. These mammals developed rapidly and in many different ways, not only giving rise to the common modern varieties but also evolving into marine types, such as whales and seals, and into air navigators like the bat family." (p. 733)

5. **Proposition.** Urantia was a life-experiment world—the sixtieth attempt in Satania. Twenty-eight modifications were successful.

> "Do not overlook the fact that Urantia was assigned to us as a life-experiment world. On this planet we made our sixtieth attempt to modify and, if possible, improve the Satania adaptation of the Nebadon life designs, and it is of record that we achieved numerous beneficial modifications of the standard life patterns. To be specific, on Urantia we worked out and have satisfactorily demonstrated not less that twenty-eight features of life modification which will be of service to all Nebadon throughout all future time." (p. 734)

6. **Proposition.** But life is never experimental in the uncontrolled or accidental sense.

> "But the establishment of life on no world is ever experimental in the sense that something untried and unknown is attempted. The evolution of life is a technique ever progressive, differential, and variable, but never haphazard, uncontrolled, nor wholly experimental, in the accidental sense." (p. 735)

7. **Proposition.** One of the new features of life on Urantia had to do with wound healing. Half a million experiments preceded this attempt.

> "This chemical action and reaction concerned in wound healing and cell reproduction represents the choice of the Life Carriers of a formula embracing over one hundred thousand phases and features of possible chemical reactions and biologic repercussions. More than half a million specific experiments were made by the Life Carriers in their laboratories before they finally settled upon this formula for the Urantia life experiment." (p. 735)

8. **Proposition.** More knowledge of this healing process will assist in treating certain diseases.

> "When Urantia scientists know more of these healing chemicals, they will become more efficient in the treatment of injuries, and indirectly they will know more about controlling certain serious diseases.
>
> "Since life was established on Urantia, the Life Carriers have improved this healing technique as it has been introduced on another Satania world, in that it affords more pain relief and exercises better control over the proliferation capacity of the associated normal cells." (p. 735)

9. **PROPOSITION.** The two unique features of the Urantia life experiment were:
   A. *The Andonic race appearing before the colored races.*
   B. *The simultaneous appearance of the six Sangik colored races.*

   "There were many unique features of the Urantia life experiment, but the two outstanding episodes were the appearance of the Andonic race prior to the evolution of the six colored peoples and the later simultaneous appearance of the Sangik mutants in a single family. Urantia is the first world in Satania where the six colored races sprang from the same human family. They ordinarily arise in diversified strains from independent mutations within the prehuman animal stock and usually appear on earth one at a time and successively over long periods of time, beginning with the red man and passing on down through the colors to indigo." (p. 735)

10. **PROPOSITION.** Evolution of life on Urantia was handicapped by the Caligastia betrayal and the Adamic default.

    "It was a source of regret to the Life Carriers that our special efforts to modify intelligent life on Urantia should have been so handicapped by tragic perversions beyond our control: the Caligastia betrayal and the Adamic default." (p. 736)

11. **PROPOSITION.** Failure to obtain more of the Adamic life plasm predisposed the human race to many diseases.

    "But throughout all of this biologic adventure our greatest disappointment grew out of the reversion of certain primitive plant life to the prechlorophyll levels of parasitic bacteria on such an extensive and unexpected scale. This eventuality in plant-life evolution caused many distressful diseases in the higher mammals, particularly in the more vulnerable human species. When we were confronted with this perplexing situation, we somewhat discounted the difficulties involved because we knew that the subsequent admixture of the Adamic life plasm would so reinforce the resisting powers of the resulting blended race as to make it practically immune to all diseases produced by the vegetable type of organism. But our hopes were doomed to disappointment owing to the misfortune of the Adamic default." (p. 736)

12. **PROPOSITION.** Two important advances in plant evolution were the appearance of the seed and chlorophyll.

    "The most important step in plant evolution was the development of chlorophyll-making ability, and the second greatest advance was the evolution of the spore into the complex seed. The spore is most efficient as a reproductive agent, but it lacks the potentials of variety and versatility inherent in the seed." (p. 737)

13. **PROPOSITION.** In animal evolution, the double role of iron in the blood was an important advance.

    "One of the most serviceable and complex episodes in the evolution of the higher types of animals consisted in the development of the ability of the iron in the circulating blood cells to perform in the double role of oxygen carrier and carbon dioxide remover. And this performance of the red blood cells illustrates how evolving organisms are able to adapt their functions to varying or changing environment. The higher animals, including man, oxygenate their tissues by the action of the iron of the red blood cells, which carries oxygen to the living cells and just as efficiently removes the carbon dioxide. But other metals can be made to serve the same purpose. The cuttlefish employs copper for this function, and the sea squirt utilizes vanadium." (p. 737)

14. **PROPOSITION.** The adjutant mind-spirits are more circuitlike than entitylike. They are somewhat handicapped on all life-experiment planets.

    "The seven adjutant spirits are more circuitlike than entitylike, and on ordinary worlds they are encircuited with other adjutant functionings throughout the local universe. On life-experiment planets, however, they are relatively isolated. And on Urantia, owing to the unique nature of the life patterns, the lower adjutants experienced far more difficulty in contacting with the evolutionary organisms than would have been the case in a more standardized type of life endowment." (p. 738)

15. **PROPOSITION.** Narration of the early life of the primitive twins who were the immediate ancestors of the human family.

    "Going back to the birth of the superior twins, one male and one female, to the two leading members of the mid-mannal tribe: These animal babies were of an unusual order; they had still less hair on their bodies than their parents and, when very young, insisted on walking upright. Their ancestors had always learned to walk on their hind legs, but these Primates twins stood erect from the beginning. They attained a height of over five feet, and their heads grew larger in comparison with others among the tribe. While early learning to communicate with each other by means of signs and sounds, they were never able to make their people understand these new symbols.

"When about fourteen years of age, they fled from the tribe, going west to raise their family and establish the new species of Primates. And these new creatures are very properly denominated *Primates* since they were the direct and immediate animal ancestors of the human family itself.

"Thus it was that the Primates came to occupy a region on the west coast of the Mesopotamian peninsula as it then projected into the southern sea, while the less intelligent and closely related tribes lived around the peninsula point and up the eastern shore line." (p. 706)

16. **PROPOSITION.** From A. D. 1934, the birth of the first two human beings occurred 993,419 years ago. They were physically perfect human beings and had a potential life span of seventy-five years.

"From the year A. D. 1934 back to the birth of the first two human beings is just 993,419 years.

"These two remarkable creatures were true human beings. They possessed perfect human thumbs, as had many of their ancestors, while they had just as perfect feet as the present-day human races. They were walkers and runners, not climbers; the grasping function of the big toe was absent, completely absent. When danger drove them to the treetops, they climbed just like the humans of today would. They would climb up the trunk of a tree like a bear and not as would a chimpanzee or a gorilla, swinging up by the branches.

"These first human beings (and their descendants) reached full maturity at twelve years of age and possessed a potential life span of about seventy-five years." (p. 707)

17. **PROPOSITION.** The spirit of worship contacted the mind of the female twin at ten years of age. One year later, the spirit of wisdom began to function upon their decision to journey north.

"Imagine our joy one day—the twins were about ten years old—when the *spirit of worship* made its first contact with the mind of the female twin and shortly thereafter with the male. We knew that something closely akin to human mind was approaching culmination; and when, about a year later, they finally resolved, as a result of meditative thought and purposeful decision, to flee from home and journey north, then did the *spirit of wisdom* begin to function on Urantia and in these two now recognized human minds." (p. 709)

18. **Proposition.** The disconsolation and tragic end of the father of the ancestral twins.

    "Soon after this young couple forsook their associates to found the human race, their Primates father became disconsolate—he was heartbroken. He refused to eat, even when food was brought to him by his other children. His brilliant offspring having been lost, life did not seem worth living among his ordinary fellows; so he wandered off into the forest, was set upon by hostile gibbons and beaten to death." (p. 709)

19. **Proposition.** From A. D. 1934, it is 993,408 years since Urantia was recognized as a planet of human habitation.

    "It is just 993,408 years ago (from the year A. D. 1934) that Urantia was formally recognized as a planet of human habitation in the universe of Nebadon. Biologic evolution had once again achieved the human levels of will dignity; man had arrived on planet 606 of Satania." (p. 710)

20. **Proposition.** Among colored races, the first three are usually superior to the later races. It is unfortunate that we so largely lost the blue man.

    "The earlier races are somewhat superior to the later; the red man stands far above the indigo—black—race. The life Carriers impart the full bestowal of the living energies to the initial or red race, and each succeeding evolutionary manifestation of a distinct group of mortals represents variation at the expense of the original endowment. Even mortal stature tends to decrease from the red man down to the indigo race, although on Urantia unexpected strains of giantism appeared among the green and orange peoples.

    "On those worlds having all six evolutionary races the superior peoples are the first, third, and fifth races—the red, the yellow, and the blue. The evolutionary races thus alternate in capacity for intellectual growth and spiritual development, the second, fourth, and sixth being somewhat less endowed. These secondary races are the peoples that are missing on certain worlds; they are the ones that have been exterminated on many others. It is a misfortune on Urantia that you so largely lost your superior blue men, except as they persist in your amalgamated 'white race.' The loss of your orange and green stocks is not of such serious concern." (p. 584)

21. **PROPOSITION.** Upon the exhaustion of the biologic potentials of human evolution, the Material Son and Daughter arrive on a planet.

"Long before the Material Son and Daughter, the biologic uplifters, arrive on a planet, the human potentials of the evolving animal species have been exhausted. This biologic status of animal life is disclosed to the Life Carriers by the phenomenon of the third phase of adjutant spirit mobilization, which automatically occurs concomitantly with the exhaustion of the capacity of all animal life to give origin to the mutant potentials of prehuman individuals." (p. 734)

22. **PROPOSITION.** It is the mission of the Adamic regime to evolve man from a hunter to a herder, and on to agriculture and urban civilization.

"It is the prime purpose of the Adamic regime to influence evolving man to complete the transit from the hunter and herder stage of civilization to that of the agriculturist and horticulturist, to be later supplemented by the appearance of the urban and industrial adjuncts to civilization. Ten thousand years of this dispensation of the biologic uplifters is sufficient to effect a marvelous transformation. Twenty-five thousand years of such an administration of the conjoint wisdom of the Planetary Prince and the Material Sons usually ripens the sphere for the advent of a Magisterial Son." (p. 593)

23. **PROPOSITION.** The color of the amalgamated human race is an olive shade of the violet hue—the racial "white" of the spheres.

"By the end of the Adamic dispensation on a normal planet the races are practically blended, so that it can be truly proclaimed that 'God has made of one blood all the nations,' and that his Son 'has made of one color all peoples.' The color of such an amalgamated race is somewhat of an olive shade of the violet hue, the racial 'white' of the spheres." (p. 593)

24. **PROPOSITION.** Skull measurements are most reliable in detecting racial origins.

"Although these skull dimensions are serviceable in deciphering racial origins, the skeleton as a whole is far more dependable. In the early development of the Urantia races there were originally five distinct types of skeletal structure:

> "1. Andonic, Urantia aborigines.
> "2. Primary Sangik, red, yellow, and blue.
> "3. Secondary Sangik, orange, green and indigo.
> "4. Nodites, descendants of the Dalamatians.
> "5. Adamites, the violet race." (p. 904)

25. **Proposition.** Early evolutionary man had little self-restraint—hence the value of hunger and fear. Later on, wisdom functions as an aid to adjustment.

> "The whole principle of biologic evolution makes it impossible for primitive man to appear on the inhabited worlds with any large endowment of self-restraint. Therefore does the same creative design which purposed evolution likewise provide those external restraints of time and space, hunger and fear, which effectively circumscribe the subspiritual choice range of such uncultured creatures. As man's mind successfully overstrides increasingly difficult barriers, this same creative design has also provided for the slow accumulation of the racial heritage of painfully garnered experiential wisdom—in other words, for the maintenance of a balance between the diminishing external restraints and the augmenting internal restraints." (p. 1302)

26. **Proposition.** Understanding a man's motivation makes a great difference. If you really know men you will eventually fall in love with them.

> "In the mind's eye conjure up a picture of one of your primitive ancestors of cave-dwelling times—a short, misshapen, filthy, snarling hulk of a man standing, legs spread, club upraised, breathing hate and animosity as he looks fiercely just ahead. Such a picture hardly depicts the divine dignity of man. But allow us to enlarge the picture. In front of this animated human crouches a saber-toothed tiger. Behind him, a woman and two children. Immediately you recognize that such a picture stands for the beginnings of much that is fine and noble in the human race, but the man is the same in both pictures. Only in the second sketch you are favored with a widened horizon. You therein discern the motivation of this evolving mortal. His attitude becomes praiseworthy because you understand him. If you could only fathom the motives of your associates, how much better you would understand them. If you could only know your fellows, you would eventually fall in love with them." (p. 1098)

PART VIII — *EVOLUTION*

27. **PROPOSITION.** Man's primordial ancestors were the slime of the ocean bed. His ascent from seaweed to lordship of the earth is a romance of biologic struggle and survival.

   "The story of man's ascent from seaweed to the lordship of earthly creation is indeed a romance of biologic struggle and mind survival. Man's primordial ancestors were literally the slime and ooze of the ocean bed in the sluggish and warm-water bays and lagoons of the vast shore lines of the ancient inland seas, those very waters in which the Life Carriers established the three independent life implantations on Urantia." (p. 731)

28. **PROPOSITION.** The Satania local system has 619 inhabited worlds—Urantia is 606.

   "Satania itself is an unfinished system containing only 619 inhabited worlds. Such planets are numbered serially in accordance with their registration as inhabited worlds, as worlds inhabited by will creatures. Thus was Urantia given the number *606 of Satania*, meaning the 606th world in this local system on which the long evolutionary life process culminated in the appearance of human beings. There are thirty-six uninhabited planets nearing the life-endowment stage, and several are now being made ready for the Life Carriers. There are nearly two hundred spheres which are evolving so as to be ready for life implantation within the next few million years." (p. 559)

IX. EVOLUTIONARY VICISSITUDES

1. **PROPOSITION.** Natural law may appear to be indifferent to our ideals and spiritual insight, but this view is modified by our progress in cosmic intelligence and improved spiritual attainment.

   "In the beginnings on an evolutionary world the natural occurrences of the material order and the personal desires of human beings often appear to be antagonistic. Much that takes place on an evolving world is rather hard for mortal man to understand—natural law is so often apparently cruel, heartless, and indifferent to all that is true, beautiful, and good in human comprehension. But as humanity progresses in planetary development, we observe that this viewpoint is modified by the following factors:
   "1. *Man's augmenting vision*—his increased understanding of the world in which he lives; his enlarging capacity for the comprehension of the material facts of time, the meaningful ideas of

thought, and the valuable ideals of spiritual insight. As long as men measure only by the yardstick of the things of a physical nature, they can never hope to find unity in time and space.

"2. *Man's increasing control*—the gradual accumulation of the knowledge of the laws of the material world, the purposes of spiritual existence, and the possibilities of the philosophic co-ordination of these two realities. Man, the savage, was helpless before the onslaughts of natural forces, was slavish before the cruel mastery of his own inner fears.

"3. *Man's universe integration*—the increase of human insight plus the increase of human experiential achievement brings him into closer harmony with the unifying presences of Supremacy—Paradise Trinity and Supreme Being. And this is what establishes the sovereignty of the Supreme on the worlds long settled in light and life." (p. 1306)

2. **PROPOSITION.** Evolutionary creature life is beset by certain inevitabilities.

"The uncertainties of life and the vicissitudes of existence do not in any manner contradict the concept of the universal sovereignty of God. All evolutionary creature life is beset by certain *inevitabilities*. Consider the following:

"1. Is *courage*—strength of character—desirable? Then must man be reared in an environment which necessitates grappling with hardships and reacting to disappointments.

"2. Is *altruism*—service of one's fellows—desirable? Then must life experience provide for encountering situations of social inequality.

"3. Is *hope*—the grandeur of trust—desirable? Then human existence most constantly be confronted with insecurities and recurrent uncertainties.

"4. Is *faith*—the supreme assertion of human thought—desirable? Then must the mind of man find itself in that troublesome predicament where it ever knows less than it can believe."

"5. Is the *love of truth* and the willingness to go wherever it leads, desirable? Then must man grow up in a world where error is present and falsehood always possible.

"6. Is *idealism*—the approaching concept of the divine—desirable? Then must man struggle in an environment of relative goodness and beauty, surroundings stimulative of the irrepressible reach for better things.

"7. Is *loyalty*—devotion to highest duty—desirable? Then must man carry on amid the possibilities of betrayal and desertion. The valor of devotion to duty consists in the implied danger of default.

"8. Is *unselfishness*—the spirit of self-forgetfulness—desirable? Then must mortal man live face to face with the incessant clamoring of an inescapable self for recognition and honor. Man could not dynamically choose the divine life if there were no self-life to forsake. Man could never lay saving hold on righteousness if there were no potential evil to exalt and differentiate the good by contrast.

"9. Is *pleasure*—the satisfaction of happiness—desirable? Then must man live in a world where the alternative of pain and the likelihood of suffering are ever-present experiential possibilities." (p. 51)

X. EVOLUTION IN TIME AND SPACE

1. **PROPOSITION.** Our sun was a pulsating star when the approaching Angona system drew off the solar system.

    "Some of the variable stars, in or near the state of maximum pulsation, are in process of giving origin to subsidiary systems, many of which will eventually be much like your own sun and its revolving planets. Your sun was in just such a state of mighty pulsation when the massive Angona system swung into near approach, and the outer surface of the sun began to erupt veritable streams— continuous sheets—of matter. This kept up with ever-increasing violence until nearest apposition, when the limits of solar cohesion were reached and a vast pinnacle of matter, the ancestor of the solar system, was disgorged. In similar circumstances the closest approach of the attracting body sometimes draws off whole planets, even a quarter or third of a sun. These major extrusions form certain peculiar cloud-bound types of worlds, spheres much like Jupiter and Saturn." (p. 465)

2. **PROPOSITION.** Evolution consists in converting potentials into actuals. This means evolution on the finite level, eventuation on the absonite.

    "The entire scheme of universal creation and evolution on all experiencing levels is apparently a matter of the conversion of potentialities into actualities; and this transmutation has to do equally with the realms of space potency, mind potency, and spirit potency.

> "The apparent method whereby the possibilities of the cosmos are brought into actual existence varies from level to level, being experiential evolution in the finite and experiential eventnation in the absonite. Existential infinity is indeed unqualified in all-inclusiveness, and this very all-inclusiveness must, perforce, encompass even the possibility of evolutionary finite experiencing. And the possibility for such experiential growth becomes a universe actuality through triodity relationships impinging upon and in the Supreme." (p. 1261)

3. **PROPOSITION.** Sudden mental evolutions and spiritual transformations can take place where conditions are favorable.

   > "When physical conditions are ripe, *sudden* mental evolutions may take place; when mind status is propitious, *sudden* spiritual transformations may occur; when spiritual values receive proper recognition, then cosmic meanings become discernible, and increasingly the personality is released from the handicaps of time and delivered from the limitations of space." (p. 740)

4. **PROPOSITION.** Man's yardstick of his temporal life makes evolution appear to be a long-drawn-out process. On Paradise, all things are present in the mind of Infinity and the acts of Eternity.

   > "The individual's yardstick for the time measurement is the length of his life. All creatures are thus time conditioned, and therefore do they regard evolution as being a long-drawn-out process. To those of us whose life span is not limited by a temporal existence, evolution does not seem to be such a protracted transaction. On Paradise, where time is nonexistent, these things are all *present* in the mind of Infinity and the acts of Eternity." (p. 739)

5. **PROPOSITION.** In evolutionary universes, energy-matter is dominant except in personality, where spirit, by the mediation of mind, is striving for the mastery.

   > "In the evolutionary superuniverses energy-matter is dominant except in personality, where spirit through the mediation of mind is struggling for the mastery. The goal of the evolutionary universes is the subjugation of energy-matter by mind, the co-ordination of mind with spirit, and all of this by virtue of the creative and unifying presence of personality. Thus, in relation to personality, do physical systems become subordinate; mind systems, co-ordinate; and spirit systems, directive." (p. 1275)

XI. FACTORS IN SOCIAL PROGRESS

1. **Proposition.** Food hunger and sex love brought primitive humans together. Vanity and fear held them together.

   "Two great influences which contributed to the early association of human beings were food hunger and sex love; these instinctive urges man shares with the animal world. Two other emotions which drove human beings together and *held* them together were vanity and fear, more particularly ghost fear." (p. 765)

2. **Proposition.** Primitive man only thought when he was hungry. Later, other types of craving entered into the picture.

   "History is but the record of man's agelong food struggle. *Primitive man only thought when he was hungry*; food saving was his first self-denial, self-discipline. With the growth of society, food hunger ceased to be the only incentive for mutual association. Numerous other sorts of hunger, the realization of various needs, all led to the closer association of mankind." (p. 765)

3. **Proposition.** Today man suffers as a result of the overgrowth of supposed needs, desires, and longings.

   "But today society is top-heavy with the overgrowth of supposed human needs. Occidental civilization of the twentieth century groans wearily under the tremendous overload of luxury and the inordinate multiplication of human desires and longings. Modern society is enduring the strain of one of its more dangerous phases of far-flung interassociation and highly complicated interdependence." (p. 765)

4. **Proposition.** The mores were man's first social institution. All this was an effort to avoid pain and insure pleasure.

   "It must be borne in mind that the mores originated in an effort to adjust group living to the conditions of mass existence; the mores were man's first social institution. And all of these tribal reactions grew out of the effort to avoid pain and humiliation while at the same time seeking to enjoy pleasure and power. The origin of folkways, like the origin of languages, is always unconscious and unintentional and therefore always shrouded in mystery." (p. 767)

5. **Proposition.** Emotionally, man transcends the animal because he can appreciate humor, art, and religion. Socially, man exhibits his superiority as a toolmaker, communicator, and institution builder.

> "EMOTIONALLY man transcends his animal ancestors in his ability to appreciate humor, art, and religion. Socially, man exhibits his superiority in that he is a toolmaker, a communicator, and an institution builder." (p. 772)

XII. LAND TECHNIQUES

1. **Proposition.** Land is the stage of society; men are the actors. Mores evolution depends on the land-man ratio. Man's land technique, plus his standard of living, equals the sum total of the folkways.

> "Land is the stage of society; men are the actors. And man must ever adjust his performances to conform to the land situation. The evolution of the mores is always dependent on the land-man ratio. This is true notwithstanding the difficulty of its discernment. Man's land technique, or maintenance arts, plus his standards of living, equal the sum total of the folkways, the mores. And the sum of man's adjustment to the life demands equals his cultural civilization." (p. 768)

2. **Proposition.** Social law decrees that population must vary with the land arts and inversely with the standard of living. The law of supply and demand determines the value of both land and men.

> "Human society is controlled by a law which decrees that the population must vary directly in accordance with the land arts and inversely with a given standard of living. Throughout these early ages, even more than at present, the law of supply and demand as concerned men and land determined the estimated value of both. During the times of plentiful land—unoccupied territory—the need for men was great, and therefore the value of human life was much enhanced; hence the loss of life was more horrifying. During periods of land scarcity and associated overpopulation, human life became comparatively cheapened so that war, famine, and pestilence were regarded with less concern." (p. 769)

3. **Proposition.** Evolution may be slow, but it is effective. Climatic changes forced man to give up hunting for herding and farming.

> "Climatic evolution is now about to accomplish what all other efforts had failed to do, that is, to compel Eurasian man to abandon hunting for the more advanced callings of herding and farming. Evolution may be slow, but it is terribly effective." (p. 900)

PART VIII — *EVOLUTION*

XIII. CULTURAL EVOLUTION

1. **PROPOSITION.** There were four major steps in the march of civilization.

> "The earliest human cultures arose along the rivers of the Eastern Hemisphere, and there were four great steps in the forward march of civilization. They were:
> "1. *The collection stage*. Food coercion, hunger, led to the first form of industrial organization, the primitive food-gathering lines. Sometimes such a line of hunger march would be ten miles long as it passed over the land gleaning food. This was the primitive nomadic stage of culture and is the mode of life now followed by the African Bushmen.
> "2. *The hunting stage*. The invention of weapon tools enabled man to become a hunter and thus to gain considerable freedom from food slavery. A thoughtful Andonite who had severely bruised his fist in a serious combat rediscovered the idea of using a long stick for his arm and a piece of hard flint, bound on the end with sinews, for his fist. Many tribes made independent discoveries of this sort, and these various forms of hammers represented one of the great forward steps in human civilization. Today some Australian natives have progressed little beyond this stage.
> "3. *The pastoral stage*. This phase of Civilization was made possible by the domestication of animals. The Arabs and the natives of Africa are among the more recent pastoral peoples.
> "Pastoral living afforded further relief from food slavery; man learned to live on the interest of his capital, the increase in his flocks; and this provided more leisure for culture and progress.
> "4. *The agricultural stage*. This era was brought about by the domestication of plants, and it represents the highest type of material civilization. Both Caligastia and Adam endeavored to teach horticulture and agriculture. Adam and Eve were gardeners, not shepherds, and gardening was an advanced culture in those days. The growing of plants exerts an ennobling influence on all races of mankind." (pp. 768-9)

2. **PROPOSITION.** Evolutionary religion is the mother of science, art, and philosophy.

    "Evolutionary religion is the mother of the science, art, and philosophy which elevated man to the level of receptivity to revealed religion, including the bestowal of Adjusters and the coming of the Spirit of Truth." (p. 68)

3. **PROPOSITION.** It is false altruism to harbor unsalvable abnormal and inferior human strains.

    "It is neither tenderness nor altruism to bestow futile sympathy upon degenerated human beings, unsalvable abnormal and inferior mortals. There exist on even the most normal of the evolutionary worlds sufficient differences between individuals and between numerous social groups to provide for the full exercise of all those noble traits of altruistic sentiment and unselfish mortal ministry without perpetuating the socially unfit and the morally degenerate strains of evolving humanity." (p. 592)

4. **PROPOSITION.** There are plenty of opportunities for unselfish ministry without preserving those who have lost their moral heritage.

    "There is abundant opportunity for the exercise of tolerance and the function of altruism in behalf of those unfortunate and needy individuals who have not irretrievably lost their moral heritage and forever destroyed their spiritual birthright." (p. 592)

5. **PROPOSITION.** Evolutionary peoples commonly pass through seven epochs.

    1. The nutrition epoch.
    2. The security age.
    3. The material-comfort era.
    4. The quest for knowledge and wisdom.
    5. The epoch of philosophy and brotherhood.
    6. The age of spiritual striving.
    7. The era of light and live.

    See pages 576-77

XIV. DAWN OF INDUSTRY

1. **Proposition.** Even a growing industrial evolution must rest upon a sound agricultural basis.

    "And now is industry supplementing agriculture, with consequently increased urbanization and multiplication of nonagricultural groups of citizenship classes. But an industrial era cannot hope to survive if its leaders fail to recognize that even the highest social developments must ever rest upon a sound agricultural basis." (p. 769)

2. **Proposition.** The Planetary Prince, Adam, and the Hebrew God put a premium on labor. The Jews taught: "He who does not work shall not eat."

    "Labor, the efforts of design, distinguishes man from the beast, whose exertions are largely instinctive. The necessity for labor is man's paramount blessing. The Prince's staff all worked; they did much to ennoble physical labor on Urantia. Adam was a gardener; the God of the Hebrews labored—he was the creator and upholder of all things. The Hebrews were the first tribe to put a supreme premium on industry; they were the first people to decree that 'he who does not work shall not eat.' But many of the religions of the world reverted to the early ideal of idleness. Jupiter was a revelor, and Buddha became a reflective devotee of leisure." (p. 773)

3. **Proposition.** Pottery has been a continuing factor in world-wide civilization.

    "While pottery had been first introduced by the staff of the Prince about one-half million years ago, the making of clay vessels had practically ceased for over one hundred and fifty thousand years. Only the gulf coast pre-Sumerian Nodites continued to make clay vessels. The art of pottery making was revived during Adam's time. The dissemination of this art was simultaneous with the extension of the desert areas of Africa, Arabia, and central Asia, and it spread in successive waves of improving technique from Mesopotamia out over the Eastern Hemisphere." (p. 903)

4. **Proposition.** The early cities were always surrounded by zones of agriculture and husbandry.

    "About twelve thousand years ago the era of the independent cities was dawning. And these primitive trading and manufacturing cities were always surrounded by zones of agriculture and cattle raising. While it is true that industry was promoted by the elevation of the standards of living, you should have no misconception regarding the refinements of early urban life." (p. 903)

5. **Proposition.** Primitive villages rose in height one to two feet every twenty-five years as the result of accumulating trash.

> "The early races were not overly neat and clean, and the average primitive community rose from one to two feet every twenty-five years as the result of the mere accumulation of dirt and trash. Certain of these olden cities also rose above the surrounding ground very quickly because their unbaked mud huts were short-lived, and it was the custom to build new dwellings directly on top of the ruins of the old." (p. 903)

6. **Proposition.** Metals were a feature of early industry in an evolving civilization.

> "The widespread use of metals was a feature of this era of the early industrial and trading cities. You have already found a bronze culture in Turkestan dating before 9000 B.C., and the Andites early learned to work in iron, gold, and copper, as well. But conditions were very different away from the more advanced centers of civilization. There were no distinct periods, such as the Stone, Bronze, and Iron Ages; all three existed at the same time in different localities." (p. 903)

7. **Proposition.** There were eight major factors which led to the accumulation of capital.

   1. Hunger—associated with foresight.
   2. Love of family.
   3. Vanity.
   4. Position.
   5. Power.
   6. Fear of the ghosts of the dead.
   7. Sex urge.
   8. Numerous forms of self-gratification.

   See page 776

PART VIII — *EVOLUTION*

8. **PROPOSITION.** The evolution of writing was an important factor in the development of civilization.

   "Modern writing originated in the early trade records; the first literature of man was a trade-promotion document, a salt advertisement. Many of the earlier wars were fought over natural deposits, such as flint, salt, and metals. The first formal tribal treaty concerned the intertribalizing of a salt deposit. These treaty spots afforded opportunity for friendly and peaceful interchange of ideas and the intermingling of various tribes.
   "Writing progressed up through the stages of the 'message stick,' knotted cords, picture writing, hieroglyphics, and wampum belts, to the early symbolic alphabets. Message sending evolved from the primitive smoke signal up through runners, animal riders, railroads, and airplanes, as well as telegraph, telephone, and wireless communication." (p. 775)

XV. FIRE AND ANIMALS

1. **PROPOSITION.** Fire was a basic evolutionary discovery.

   "Fire building, by a single bound, forever separated man from animal; it is the basic human invention, or discovery. Fire enabled man to stay on the ground at night as all animals are afraid of it. Fire encouraged eventide social intercourse; it not only protected against cold and wild beasts but was also employed as security against ghosts. It was at first used more for light than heat; many backward tribes refuse to sleep unless a flame burns all night." (p. 777)

2. **PROPOSITION.** The dog was the first animal to be domesticated. They served as protection against both material and "spirit" disturbers.

   "The dog was the first animal to be domesticated, and the difficult experience of taming it began when a certain dog, after following a hunter around all day, actually went home with him. For ages dogs were used for food, hunting, transportantion, and companionship. At first dogs only howled, but later on they learned to bark. The dog's keen sense of smell led to the notion it could see spirits, and thus arose the dog-fetish cults. The employment of watchdogs made it first possible for the whole clan to sleep at night. It then became the custom to employ watchdogs to protect the home against spirits as well as material enemies. When the dog barked, man or beast approached, but when the dog howled, spirits were near. Even now many still believe that a dog's howling at night betokens death." (p. 778)

XVI. MAINTENANCE OF CIVILIZATION

1. **Proposition.** The evolutionary races are destined to blend with the Adamic uplifters. But before this blending, the inferior strains of the races are eliminated.

    "These six evolutionary races are destined to be blended and exalted by amalgamation with the progeny of the Adamic uplifters. But before these peoples are blended, the inferior and unfit are largely eliminated. The Planetary Prince and the Material Son, with other suitable planetary authorities, pass upon the fitness of the reproducing strains. The difficulty of executing such a radical program on Urantia consists in the absence of competent judges to pass upon the biologic fitness or unfitness of the individuals of your world races. Notwithstanding this obstacle, it seems that you ought to be able to agree upon the biologic disfellowshiping of your more markedly unfit, defective, degenerate, and antisocial stocks." (p. 585)

2. **Proposition.** Civilization is an acquirement. It is not biological—hence each new generation must be educated. Culture is the preservation of social inheritance.

    "Civilization is a racial acquirement; it is not biologically inherent; hence must all children be reared in an environment of culture, while each succeeding generation of youth must receive anew its education. The superior qualities of civilization—scientific, philosophic, and religious—are not transmitted from one generation to another by direct inheritance. These cultural achievements are preserved only by the enlightened conservation of social inheritance." (p. 763)

3. **Proposition.** Society was founded on the reciprocity of necessity and the enhanced safety of association.

    "Primitive society was thus founded on the reciprocity of necessity and on the enhanced safety of association. And human society has evolved in agelong cycles as a result of this isolation fear and by means of reluctant co-operation." (p. 763)

4. **Proposition.** Society is concerned with self-perpetuation, self-maintenance, and self-gratification—not to mention self-realization.

    "Society is concerned with self-perpetuation, self-maintenance, and self-gratification, but human self-realization is worthy of becoming the immediate goal of many cultural groups." (p. 764)

PART VIII — *Evolution*

5. **PROPOSITION.** Vanity was a factor in the birth of society. Self-maintenance builds society; self-gratification destroys civilization.

    "Vanity contributed mightily to the birth of society; but at the time of these revelations the devious strivings of a vainglorious generation threaten to swamp and submerge the whole complicated structure of a highly specialized civilization. Pleasure-want has long since superseded hunger-want; the legitimate social aims of self-maintenance are rapidly translating themselves into base and threatening forms of self-gratification. Self-maintenance builds society; unbridled self-gratification unfailingly destroys civilization." (p. 766)

6. **PROPOSITION.** Hunger and love drove men together; vanity and ghost fear held them together. Revelation overcame the irritations and suspicions of human interassociations.

    "Hunger and love drove men together; vanity and ghost fear held them together. But these emotions alone, without the influence of peace-promoting revelations, are unable to endure the strain of the suspicions and irritations of human interassociations. Without help from superhuman sources the strain of society breaks down upon reaching certain limits, and these very influences of social mobilization— hunger, love, vanity, and fear—conspire to plunge mankind into war and bloodshed." (p. 766)

7. **PROPOSITION.** Traders and explorers did much to advance civilization. Military conquests, colonization, and missionaries were also influential.

    "The traveling trader and the roving explorer did more to advance historic civilization than all other influences combined. Military conquests, colonization, and missionary enterprises fostered by the later religions were also factors in the spread of culture; but these were all secondary to the trading relations, which were ever accelerated by the rapidly developing arts and sciences of industry." (p. 904)

8. **PROPOSITION.** There were four major advancement factors in civilization.

    "The first four great advances in human civilization were:
    "1. The taming of fire.
    "2. The domestication of animals.
    "3. The enslavement of captives.
    "4. Private property."
    (p. 901)

XVII. CONTROL AND OVERCONTROL

1. **Proposition.** Finite evolutionary creatures ascend to Paradise because the unity of Deity controls and integrates the mechanisms of the universe of universes.

   "GOD is unity. Deity is universally co-ordinated. The universe of universes is one vast integrated mechanism which is absolutely controlled by one infinite mind. The physical, intellectual, and spiritual domains of universal creation are divinely correlated. The perfect and imperfect are truly interrelated, and therefore may the finite evolutionary creature ascend to Paradise in obedience to the Universal Father's mandate: 'Be you perfect, even as I am perfect.'" (p. 637)

2. **Proposition.** Evolution is always purposeful—never accidental. It is integrated by Life Carriers, physical controllers, and the spirit adjutants.

   "It is the integrated functioning of the Life Carriers, the physical controllers, and the spirit adjutants that conditions the course of organic evolution on the inhabited worlds. And this is why evolution—on Urantia or elsewhere—is always purposeful and never accidental." (p. 730)

3. **Proposition.** Man is a machine—but he is much more. He is mind endowed and spirit indwelt. The material machine can be subordinated to the wisdom of experience and the spiritual urges of the Thought Adjuster.

   "Mortal man is a machine, a living mechanism; his roots are truly in the physical world of energy. Many human reactions are mechanical in nature; much of life is machinelike. But man, a mechanism, is much more than a machine; he is mind endowed and spirit indwelt; and though he can never throughout his material life escape the chemical and electrical mechanics of his existence, he can increasingly learn how to subordinate this physical-life machine to the directive wisdom of experience by the process of consecrating the human mind to the execution of the spiritual urges of the indwelling Thought Adjuster." (p. 1301)

XVIII. THE UNIVERSAL RULE OF EVOLUTION

1. **PROPOSITION.** Evolution extends from your world of origin up through the local universe to the headquarters—Salvington.

   "ALL mortal-inhabited worlds are evolutionary in origin and nature. These spheres are the spawning ground, the evolutionary cradle, of the mortal races of time and space. Each unit of the ascendant life is a veritable training school for the stage of existence just ahead, and this is true of every stage of man's progressive Paradise ascent; just as true of the initial mortal experience on an evolutionary planet as of the final universe headquarters school of the Melchizedeks, a school which is not attended by ascending mortals until just before their translation to the regime of the superuniverse and the attainment of first-stage spirit existence." (p. 559)

2. **PROPOSITION.** Evolution is the rule of human development, but the Life Carriers have great latitude in life initiation.

   "Evolution is the rule of human development, but the process itself varies greatly on different worlds. Life is sometimes initiated in one center, sometimes in three, as it was on Urantia. On the atmospheric worlds it usually has a marine origin, but not always; much depends on the physical status of a planet. The Life Carriers have great latitude in their function of life initiation." (p. 560)

3. **PROPOSITION.** Superuniverse creatures are finite evolutionary and constantly progressive.

   "Excepting perfect beings of Deity origin, all will creatures in the superuniverses are of evolutionary nature, beginning in lowly estate and climbing ever upward, in reality inward. Even highly spiritual personalities continue to ascend the scale of life by progressive translations from life to life and from sphere to sphere. And in the case of those who entertain the Mystery Monitors, there is indeed no limit to the possible heights of their spiritual ascent and universe attainment." (p. 361)

4. **PROPOSITION.** Never will scientists be able to produce living organisms; life is not inherent in matter. Life is both material and spiritual.

   "Life is both mechanistic and vitalistic—material and spiritual. Ever will Urantia physicists and chemists progress in their understanding of the protoplasmic forms of vegetable and animal, life, but never will they be able to produce living organisms. Life is something different from all energy manifestations; even the material life of physical creatures is not inherent in matter." (p. 403)

5. **Proposition.** Progressive evolutionary capacity of the universe is inexhaustible in the infinity of spontaneity and complexity.

> "Since mind co-ordinates the universe, fixity of mechanisms is nonexistent. The phenomenon of progressive evolution associated with cosmic self-maintenance is universal. The evolutionary capacity of the universe is inexhaustible in the infinity of spontaneity. Progress towards harmonious unity, a growing experiential synthesis superimposed on an ever-increasing complexity of relationships, could be effected only by a purposive and dominant mind. (p. 482)

6. **Proposition.** Perfection of evolutionary creature attainment is a bona fide personality possession—the result of actual reaction to existing environment.

> "The perfection of the creatures of time, when finally achieved, is wholly an acquirement, a bona fide personality possession. While the elements of grace are freely admixed, nevertheless, the creature attainments are the result of individual effort and actual living, personality reaction to the existing environment." (p. 361)

7. **Proposition.** Infinitude must some how be so qualified that its repleteness may be reconciled with the incompleteness of the evolving universes.

> "In some manner the eternal repleteness of infinity must be reconciled with the time-growth of the evolving universes and with the incompleteness of the experiential inhabitants thereof. In some way the conception of total infinitude must be so segmented and qualified that the mortal intellect and the morontia soul can grasp this concept of final value and spiritualizing significance." (p. 1146)

PART IX
THE SUPREME SPIRITS

Part Nine
THE SUPREME SPIRITS

I. INTRODUCTION

1. **Proposition.** The seven Supreme Spirit groups are the co-ordinating directors of the seven superuniverses.

    "The seven Supreme Spirit groups are the universal co-ordinating directors of the seven-segmented administration of the grand universe. Although all are classed among the functional family of the Infinite Spirit, the following three groups are usually classified as children of the Paradise Trinity:
    "1. The Seven Master Spirits.
    "2. The Seven Supreme Executives.
    "3. The Reflective Spirits.
    "The remaining four groups are brought into being by the creative acts of the Infinite Spirit or by his associates of creative status:
    "4. The Reflective Image Aids.
    "5. The Seven Spirits of the Circuits.
    "6. The Local Universe Creative Spirits.
    "7. The Adjutant Mind-Spirits."
    (p. 197)

2. **Proposition.** The Trinitized Executives of the Master Spirits are stationed on the seven Paradise worlds of the Infinite Spirit.

    "The executive headquarters of the Master Spirits occupy the seven Paradise satellites of the Infinite Spirit, which swing around the central Isle between the shining spheres of the Eternal Son and the innermost Havona circuit. These executive spheres are under the direction of the Supreme Executives, a group of seven who were trinitized by the Father, Son, and Spirit in accordance with the specifications of the Seven Master Spirits for beings of a type that could function as their universal representatives." (p. 198)

3. **Proposition.** The Master Spirits maintain force-focal stations on the Paradise periphery and these stations maintain position opposite the superuniverse of supervision.

    "The Master Spirits have many functions, but at the present time their particular domain is the central supervision of the seven superuniverses. Each Master Spirit maintains an enormous force-focal headquarters, which slowly circulates around the periphery of Paradise, always maintaining a position opposite the superuniverse of immediate supervision and at the Paradise focal point of its specialized power control and segmental energy distribution. The radial boundary lines of any one of the superuniverses do actually converge at the Paradise headquarters of the supervising Master Spirit." (p. 184)

4. **PROPOSITION.** The Master Spirits exhibit seven different natures.

"The Seven Master Spirits thus have their origin in, and derive their individual characteristics from, the following seven likenesses:

"1. The Universal Father.
"2. The Eternal Son.
"3. The Infinite Spirit.
"4. The Father and the Son.
"5. The Father and the Spirit.
"6. The Son and the Spirit.
"7. The Father, Son, and Spirit."

(p. 184)

II. RELATION TO TRIUNE DEITY

1. **PROPOSITION.** When the Master Spirits vacate their individual seats of authority and assemble about the Conjoint Actor, they are collectively representative of the Trinity.

"But when the Seven Master Spirits vacate their individual seats of personal power and superuniverse authority and assemble about the Conjoint Actor in the triune presence of Paradise Deity, then and there are they collectively representative of the functional power, wisdom, and authority of undivided Deity—the Trinity—to and in the evolving universes." (p. 185)

2. **PROPOSITION.** Master Spirit Number One is the representative of the Father. He is adviser to Mystery Monitors and Personalized Adjusters.

"*Master Spirit Number One.* In a special manner this Spirit is the direct representation of the Paradise Father. He is a peculiar and efficient manifestation of the power, love, and wisdom of the Universal Father. He is the close associate and supernal adviser of the chief of Mystery Monitors, that being who presides over the College of Personalized Adjusters on Divinington. In all associations of the Seven Master Spirits, it is always Master Spirit Number One who speaks for the Universal Father." (p. 186)

3. **PROPOSITION**. Master Spirit Number Two portrays the Eternal Son and fosters all of the Sons of God.

   "*Master Spirit Number Two*. This Spirit adequately portrays the matchless nature and charming character of the Eternal Son, the first-born of all creation. He is always in close association with all orders of the Sons of God whenever they may happen to be in the residential universe as individuals or in joyous conclave. In all the assemblies of the Seven Master Spirits he always speaks for, and in behalf of, the Eternal Son." (p. 187)

4. **PREPOSITION**. Master Spirit Number Three represents the Infinite Spirit and directs the children of the Spirit.

   "*Master Spirit Number Three*. This Spirit personality especially resembles the Infinite Spirit, and he directs the movements and work of many of the high personalities of the Infinite Spirit. He presides over their assemblies and is closely associated with all personalities who take exclusive origin in the Third Source and Center. When the Seven Master Spirits are in council, it is Master Spirit Number Three who always speaks for the Infinite Spirit." (p. 187)

5. **PROPOSITION**. Master Spirit Number Four represents the Father and the Son, advises their children, and fosters ascenders who have attained the Infinite Spirit.

   "*Master Spirit Number Four*. Partaking of the combined natures of the Father and the Son, this Master Spirit is the determining influence regarding Father-Son policies and procedures in the councils of the Seven Master Spirits. This Spirit is the chief director and adviser of those ascendant beings who have attained the Infinite Spirit and thus have become candidates for seeing the Son and the Father. He fosters that enormous group of personalities taking origin in the Father and the Son. When it becomes necessary to represent the Father and the Son in the association of the Seven Master Spirits, it is always Master Spirit Number Four who speaks." (p. 187)

6. **PROPOSITION**. Master Spirit Number Five represents the Father and the Spirit and fosters all beings with origin in these Deities, and is adviser to the power directors, power centers, and physical controllers

   "*Master Spirit Number Five*. This divine personality who exquisitely blends the character of the Universal Father and the Infinite Spirit is the adviser of that enormous group of beings known as the power directors, power centers, and physical controllers. This Spirit also fosters all personalities taking origin in the Father and the Conjoint Actor. In the councils of the Seven Master Spirits, when the Father-Spirit attitude is in question, it is always Master Spirit Number Five who speaks." (p. 187)

7. **Proposition.** Master Spirit Number Six is adviser to the children of the Son and Spirit.

> "*Master Spirit Number Six.* This divine being seems to portray the combined character of the Eternal Son and the Infinite Spirit. Whenever the creatures jointly created by the Son and the Spirit forgather in the central universe, it is this Master Spirit who is their adviser; and whenever, in the councils of the Seven Master Spirits, it becomes necessary to speak conjointly for the Eternal Son and the Infinite Spirit, it is Master Spirit Number Six who responds." (p. 187)

8. **Proposition.** Master Spirit Number Seven represents the Father, Son, and Spirit and is adviser to all triune-origin beings as well as the ascending pilgrims of Havona.

> "*Master Spirit Number Seven.* The presiding Spirit of the seventh superuniverse is a uniquely equal portrayal of the Universal Father, the Eternal Son, and the Infinite Spirit. The Seventh Spirit, the fostering adviser of all triune-origin beings, is also the adviser and director of all the ascending pilgrims of Havona, those lowly beings who have attained the courts of glory through the combined ministry of the Father, the Son, and the Spirit." (p. 188)

9. **Proposition.** The Seven Master Spirits not only represent the Infinite Spirit, but they also are the personalized physical power, cosmic mind, and spiritual presence of triune Deity.

> "The Seven Master Spirits are the full representation of the Infinite Spirit to the evolutionary universes. They represent the Third Source and Center in the relationships of energy, mind, and spirit. While they function as the co-ordinating heads of the universal administrative control of the Conjoint Actor, do not forget that they have their origin in the creative acts of the Paradise Deities. It is literally true that these Seven Spirits are the personalized physical power, cosmic mind, and spiritual presence of the triune Deity, 'the Seven Spirits of God sent forth to all the universe.'" (p. 189)

10. **Proposition.** No one of the Master Spirits represents the Trinity, but when they unite they equivalate to the level associable with the Trinity. Master Spirit Number Seven is spokesman for the Sevenfold-Spirit-union regarding the attitude of the Threefold-Deity-union—the Trinity.

> "No one of the Seven Spirits is organically representative of the Paradise Trinity, but when they unite as sevenfold Deity, this union in a deity sense—not in a personal sense—equivalates to a functional level associable with Trinity functions. In this sense the 'Sevenfold Spirit' is functionally associable with the Paradise Trinity. It is also in this sense that Master Spirit Number Seven sometimes speaks in confirmation of Trinity attitudes or, rather, acts as spokesman for the attitude of the Sevenfold-Spirit-union regarding the attitude of the Threefold-Deity-union, the attitude of the Paradise Trinity." (p. 188)

III. ATTRIBUTES AND FUNCTIONS

1. **Proposition.** The Master Spirits are indescribable beings—but they are definitely personal. While they are akin, they are diverse.

> "The Seven Master Spirits are indescribable beings, but they are distinctly and definitely personal. They have names, but we elect to introduce them by number. As primary personalizations of the Infinite Spirit, they are akin, but as primary expressions of the seven possible associations of triune Deity, they are essentially diverse in nature, and this diversity of nature determines their differential of superuniverse conduct." (p. 186)

2. **Proposition.** Master Spirit Number Seven is nonfunctional with regard to the Trinity, and that explains how he can act personally for the Supreme Being.

> "The Master Spirits singly and collectively represent any and all possible Deity functions, single and several, but not collective, not the Trinity. Master Spirit Number Seven is personally nonfunctional with regard to the Paradise Trinity, and that is just why he can function *personally* for the Supreme Being." (p. 185)

3. **Proposition.** Outside of Havona, the Infinite Spirit speaks only by the voices of the Seven Master Spirits.

> "To the universe of universes the Paradise Father speaks only through his Son, while he and the Son conjointly act only through the Infinite Spirit. Outside of Paradise and Havona the Infinite Spirit *speaks* only by the voices of the Seven Master Spirits." (p. 186)

4. **PROPOSITION.** Collectively, the Seven Master Spirits are endowed with supreme-ultimate attributes of the Third Source and Center.

> "The Seven Master Spirits are collectively endowed with the supreme-ultimate attributes of the Third Source and Center. While each one individually partakes of this endowment, only collectively do they disclose the attributes of omnipotence, omniscience, and omnipresence." (p. 186)

5. **PROPOSITION.** The Master Spirits create Power Directors and their associates. They assist Creator Sons in universe organization.

> "The Seven Master Spirits are the creators of the Universe Power Directors and their associates, entities who are indispensable to the organization, control, and regulation of the physical energies of the grand universe. And these same Master Spirits very materially assist the Creator Sons in the work of shaping and organizing the local universes." (p. 189)

6. **PROPOSITION.** Since God the Supreme is not yet contactable, the Seventh Master Spirit functions in his place.

> "The inability of the Havona pilgrims fully to find God the Supreme is compensated by the Seventh Master Spirit, whose triune nature in such a peculiar manner is revelatory of the spirit person of the Supreme. During the present universe age of the noncontactability of the person of the Supreme, Master Spirit Number Seven functions in the place of the God of ascendant creatures in the matter of personal relationships. He is the one high spirit being that all ascenders are certain to recognize and somewhat comprehend when they reach the centers of glory." (p. 188)

7. **PROPOSITION.** The Orvonton Master Spirit influences seven spheres of activity.

> "It is highly probable, though we cannot offer definite proof, that the Master Spirit of Orvonton exerts a decided influence in the following spheres of activity:
>
> "1. The life-initiation procedures of the local universe Life Carriers.
>
> "2. The life activations of the adjutant mind-spirits bestowed upon the worlds by a local universe Creative Spirit.
>
> "3. The fluctuations in energy manifestations exhibited by the linear-gravity-responding units of organized matter.
>
> "4. The behavior of emergent energy when fully liberated from the grasp of the Unqualified Absolute, thus becoming responsive to the direct influence of linear gravity and to the manipulations of the Universe Power Directors and their associates.

"5. The bestowal of the ministry spirit of a local universe Creative Spirit, known on Urantia as the Holy Spirit.

"6. The subsequent bestowal of the spirit of the bestowal Sons, on Urantia called the Comforter or the Spirit of Truth.

"7. The reflectivity mechanism of the local universes and the superuniverse. Many features connected with this extraordinary phenomenon can hardly be reasonably explained or rationally understood without postulating the activity of the Master Spirits in association with the Conjoint Actor and the Supreme Being."
(p. 190)

IV. RELATION TO CREATURES

1. PROPOSITION. The physical stamp of a Master Spirit is a part of man's origin and an ascending mortal never fully eradicates this characteristic stamp.

   "The distinctive personality trends exhibited in the life experience of evolutionary mortals, which are characteristic in each superuniverse, and which are directly expressive of the nature of the dominating Master Spirit, are never fully effaced, not even after such ascenders are subjected to the long training and unifying discipline encountered on the one billion educational spheres of Havona. Even the subsequent intense Paradise culture does not suffice to eradicate the earmarks of superuniverse origin. Throughout all eternity an ascendant mortal will exhibit traits indicative of the presiding Spirit of his superuniverse of nativity. Even in the Corps of the Finality, when it is desired to arrive at or to portray a *complete* Trinity relationship to the evolutionary creation, always a group of seven finaliters is assembled, one from each superuniverse." (p. 191)

2. PROPOSITION. There are three inalienables of human nature—moral intuition, scientific curiosity, and spiritual insight.

   "Intelligence alone cannot explain the moral nature. Morality, virtue, is indigenous to human personality. Moral intuition, the realization of duty, is a component of human mind endowment and is associated with the other inalienables of human nature: scientific curiosity and spiritual insight." (p. 192)

3. **Proposition.** The reality of these three endowments is recognized by cosmic self-revelation.

> "Stated otherwise, the recognition of the *reality* of these three manifestations of the Infinite is by a cosmic technique of self-revelation. Matter-energy is recognized by the mathematical logic of the senses; mind-reason intuitively knows its moral duty; spirit-faith (worship) is the religion of the reality of spiritual experience." (p. 192)

4. **Proposition.** It is the purpose of education to sharpen these innate endowments; of civilization to express them; of life experience to realize them; of religion to ennoble them; and of personality to unify them.

> "It is the purpose of education to develop and sharpen these innate endowments of the human mind; of civilization to express them; of life experience to realize them; of religion to ennoble them; and of personality to unify them." (p. 192)

V. THE COSMIC MIND

1. **Proposition.** The Master Spirits are the source of the cosmic mind, which is subabsolute and related to the mind of the Supreme Being.

> "The Master Spirits are the sevenfold source of the cosmic mind, the intellectual potential of the grand universe. This cosmic mind is a subabsolute manifestation of the mind of the Third Source and Center and, in certain ways, is functionally related to the mind of the evolving Supreme Being." (p. 191)

2. **Proposition.** "Reality response" is a quality of the cosmic mind which saves man from becoming a helpless victim of implied a priori assumptions of science, philosophy, and religion.

> "There exists in all personality associations of the cosmic mind a quality which might be denominated the 'reality response.' It is this universal cosmic endowment of will creatures which saves them from becoming helpless victims of the implied a priori assumptions of science, philosophy, and religion. This reality sensitivity of the cosmic mind responds to certain phases of reality just as energy-material responds to gravity. It would be still more correct to say that these supermaterial realities so respond to the mind of the cosmos." (p. 191)

3. **Proposition.** The cosmic mind recognizes response on three levels of reality.

> "The cosmic mind unfailingly responds (recognizes response) on three levels of universe reality. These responses are self-evident to clear-reasoning and deep-thinking minds. These levels of reality are:
> "1. *Causation*—the reality domain of the physical senses, the scientific realms of logical uniformity, the differentiation of the factual and the nonfactual, reflective conclusions based on cosmic response. This is the mathematical form of the cosmic discrimination.
> "2. *Duty*—the reality domain of morals in the philosophic realm, the arena of reason, the recognition of relative right and wrong. This is the judicial form of the cosmic discrimination.
> "3. *Worship*—the spiritual domain of the reality of religious experience, the personal realization of divine fellowship, the recognition of spirit values, the assurance of eternal survival, the ascent from the status of servants of God to the joy and liberty of the sons of God. This is the highest insight of the cosmic mind, the reverential and worshipful form of the cosmic discrimination." (p. 192)

4. **Proposition.** Animal selective response is limited to the physical level. Man has insight prior to exploration.

> "The selective response of an animal is limited to the motor level of behavior. The supposed insight of the higher animals is on a motor level and usually appears only after the experience of motor trial and error. Man is able to exercise scientific, moral, and spiritual insight prior to all exploration or experimentation." (p. 193)

5. **Proposition.** Personality can look before it leaps; therefore it can learn from looking as well as from leaping.

> "Only a personality can know what it is doing before it does it; only personalities possess insight in advance of experience. A personality can look before it leaps and can therefore learn from looking as well as from leaping. A nonpersonal animal ordinarily learns only by leaping." (p. 193)

6. **Proposition.** When man fails to respond to the impulses of the cosmic mind which discriminate the ends of mortal striving, he descends to the level of animal existence.

> "When man fails to discriminate the ends of his mortal striving, he finds himself functioning on the animal level of existence. He has failed to avail himself of the superior advantages of that

material acumen, moral discrimination, and spiritual insight which are an integral part of his cosmic-mind endowment as a personal being." (p. 193)

VI. THE SEVEN SUPREME EXECUTIVES

1. **Proposition.** The Master Spirits act in the persons of their Supreme Executives who act on the headquarters of the superuniverses through the Reflective Spirits.

   "In all matters of an executive nature—rulings, regulations, adjustments, and administrative decisions—the Master Spirits act in the persons of the Seven Supreme Executives. In the central universe the Master Spirits may function through the Seven Spirits of the Havona Circuits; on the headquarters of the seven superuniverses they reveal themselves through the channel of the Reflective Spirits and act through the persons of the Ancients of Days, with whom they are in personal communication through the Reflective Image Aids." (p. 197)

2. **Proposition.** Each Supreme Executive has two advisory cabinets—one consisting of children of the Infinite Spirit and the other composed of ascending pilgrims and the trinitized sons of glorified mortals.

   "Each Supreme Executive has two advisory cabinets: The children of the Infinite Spirit on the headquarters of each superuniverse choose representatives from their ranks to serve for one millennium in the primary advisory cabinet of their Supreme Executive. In all matters affecting the ascending mortals of time, there is a secondary cabinet, consisting of mortals of Paradise attainment and of the trinitized sons of glorified mortals; this body is chosen by the perfecting and ascending beings who transiently dwell on the seven superuniverse headquarters. All other chiefs of affairs are appointed by the Supreme Executives." (p. 199)

VII. MAJESTON—GHIEF OF REFLECTIVITY

1. **Proposition.** Majeston is a true person and the infallible center of reflectivity in the grand universe.

   "Majeston is a true person, the personal and infallible center of reflectivity phenomena in all seven superuniverses of time and space. He maintains permanent Paradise headquarters near the center of all things at the rendezvous of the Seven Master

Spirits. He is concerned solely with the co-ordination and maintenance of the reflectivity service in the far-flung creation; he is not otherwise involved in the administration of universe affairs." (p. 200)

2. **Proposition.** Majeston was the first creative act of the Supreme Being and the reaction in the Deity Absolute was unexpected.

"The creation of Majeston signalized the first supreme creative act of the Supreme Being. This will to action was volitional in the Supreme Being, but the stupendous reaction of the Deity Absolute was not foreknown. Not since the eternity-appearance of Havona had the universe witnessed such a tremendous factualization of such a gigantic and far-flung alignment of power and co-ordination of functional spirit activities. The Deity response to the creative wills of the Supreme Being and his associates was vastly beyond their purposeful intent and greatly in excess of their conceptual forecasts." (p. 200)

3. **Proposition.** The reflectivity mechanism is the news-gathering and decree-disseminating organization of the grand universe.

"The reflectivity organization is also the news-gathering and the decree-disseminating mechanism of all creation. It is in constant operation in contrast with the periodic functioning of the various broadcast services." (p. 201)

VIII. THE REFLECTIVE SPIRITS

1. **Proposition.** By liaison of one of the Master Spirits and the Trinity, seven Reflective Spirits were created per creative episode.

"The Reflective Spirits are of divine Trinity origin. There are fifty of these unique and somewhat mysterious beings. Seven of these extraordinary personalities were created at a time, and each such creative episode was effected by a liaison of the Paradise Trinity and one of the Seven Master Spirits." (p. 199)

2. **Proposition.** When the Reflective Spirit cycle was completed Majeston appeared as the result of a far-reaching reaction in the Deity Absolute.

"This momentous transaction, occurring in the dawn of time, represents the initial effort of the Supreme Creator Personalities, represented by the Master Spirits, to function as cocreators with the Paradise Trinity. This union of the creative power of the Supreme Creators with the creative potentials of the Trinity is the very source of the actuality of the Supreme

Being. Therefore, when the cycle of reflective creation had run its course, when each of the Seven Master Spirits had found perfect creative synchrony with the Paradise Trinity, when the forty-ninth Reflective Spirit had personalized, then a new and far-reaching reaction occurred in the Deity Absolute which imparted new personality prerogatives to the Supreme Being and culminated in the personalization of Majeston, the reflectivity chief and Paradise center of all the work of the forty-nine Reflective Spirits and their associates throughout the universe of universes." (p. 199)

3. **PROPOSITION.** The Reflective Spirits are of Trinity origin, but in type of being they resemble the cocreative Master Spirit concerned. There are, therefore, seven different types of spirits.

"The forty-nine Reflective Spirits are of Trinity origin, but each of the seven creative episodes attendant upon their appearance was productive of a type of being in nature resembling the characteristics of the coancestral Master Spirit. Thus they variously reflect the natures and characters of the seven possible combinations of the association of the divinity characteristics of the Universal Father, the Eternal Son, and the Infinite Spirit. For this reason it is necessary to have seven of these Reflective Spirits on the headquarters of each superuniverse." (p. 200)

4. **PROPOSITION.** Reflective Spirits are retentive personalities as well as transmitting agents. Every spirit value is preserved by secoraphic personalities on their staff.

"The Reflective Spirits are not merely transmitting agents; they are retentive personalities as well. Their offspring, the seconaphim, are also retentive or record personalities. Everything of true spiritual value is registered in duplicate, and one impression is preserved in the personal equipment of some member of one of the numerous orders of secoraphic personalities belonging to the vast staff of the Reflective Spirits." (p. 201)

5. **PROPOSITION.** The forty-nine Reflective Image Aids were created by the Reflective Spirits—seven now residing on the headquarters of each super-universe.

"The forty-nine Reflective Image Aids were created by the Reflective Spirits, and there are just seven Aids on the headquarters of each superuniverse. The first creative act of the seven Reflective Spirits of Uversa was the production of their seven Image Aids, each Reflective Spirit creating his own Aid. The Image Aids are, in certain attributes and characteristics, perfect reproductions of their Reflective Mother Spirits; they are virtual duplications minus the attribute of reflectivity. They are true images and constantly function as the channel of communication between the Reflective Spirits and the superuniverse authorities." (p. 202)

IX. THE SOLITARY MESSENGERS

1. **PROPOSITION.** Solitary Messengers are the early creation of the Infinite Spirit and their number is stationary.

   "Solitary Messengers are the personal and universal corps of the Conjoint Creator; they are the first and senior order of the Higher Personalities of the Infinite Spirit. They represent the initial creative action of the Infinite Spirit in solitary function for the purpose of bringing into existence solitary personality spirits. Neither the Father nor the Son directly participated in this stupendous spiritualization.

   "These spirit messengers were personalized in a single creative episode, and their number is stationary. Although I have one of these extraordinary beings associated with me on this present mission, I do not know how many such personalities exist in the universe of universes. I only know, from time to time, how many are of registry-record as functioning for the time being within the jurisdiction of our superuniverse. From the last Uversa report I observe that there were almost 7,690 trillion Solitary Messengers then operating within the boundaries of Orvonton; and I conjecture that this is considerably less than one seventh of their total number." (p. 256)

2. **PROPOSITION.** There is a technical reason why Solitary Messengers must function alone. They are "short circuited" if two or more are in close proximity. They are automatically alerted by the presence of either Inspired Spirits or Thought Adjusters.

   "There is a technical reason why these Solitary Messengers must travel and work alone. For short periods and when stationary, they can collaborate in a group, but when thus ensembled, they are altogether cut off from the sustenance and direction of their Paradise circuit; they are wholly isolated. When in transit, or when operating in the circuits of space and the currents of time, if two or more of this order are in close proximity, both or all are thrown out of liaison with the higher circulating forces. They are 'short circuited' as you might

Part IX — The Supreme Spirits

describe it in illustrative symbols. Therefore they have inherent within them a power of automatic alarm, a warning signal, which unerringly operates to apprise them of approaching conflicts and unfailingly keeps them sufficiently separated as not to interfere with their proper and effective functioning. They also possess inherent and automatic powers which detect and indicate the proximity of both the Inspired Trinity Spirits and the divine Thought Adjusters." (p. 257)

3. **Proposition.** Since no more Solitary Messengers are being created, interesting questions are raised about their future service.

    "No matter how much the universe may enlarge, no more Solitary Messengers will probably ever be created. As the universes grow, the expanded work of administration must be increasingly borne by other types of spirit ministers and by those beings who take origin in these new creations, such as the creatures of the Sovereign Sons and the local universe Mother Spirits." (p. 262)

4. **Proposition.** Solitary Messengers function in seven groups.

    "Solitary Messengers are assigned by the Infinite Spirit to the following seven divisions of service:

    "1. Messengers of the Paradise Trinity.
    "2. Messengers of the Havona Circuits.
    "3. Messengers of the Superuniverses.
    "4. Messengers of the Local Universes.
    "5. Explorers of Undirected Assignment.
    "6. Ambassadors and Emissaries of Special Assignment.
    "7. Revelators of Truth."

    (p. 258)

5. **Proposition.** Solitary Messengers can function as emergency lines of communication over a distance of about one hundred light-years.

    "The Solitary Messengers are able to function as emergency lines of communication throughout remote space regions, realms not embraced within the established circuits of the grand universe. It develops that one messenger, when so functioning, can transmit a message or send an impulse through space to a fellow messenger about one hundred light-years away as Urantia astronomers estimate stellar distances." (p. 261)

6. **Proposition.** When a Finaliter and a Paradise Citizen trinitize a "child of time and eternity," this unclassified personalilty is dispatched to Vicegerington. Such a being involves the mind potential of the Supreme-Ultimate. A Solitary Messenger accompanies these sons to Vicegerington. Not one of these pairs has ever left Vicegerington.

> "When a finaliter and a Paradise Citizen co-operate in the trinitization of a 'child of time and eternity'—a transaction involving the unrevealed mind potentials of the Supreme-Ultimate—and when such an unclassified personality is dispatched to Vicegerington, a Solitary Messenger (a conjectured personality repercussion of the bestowal of such deity mind) is always assigned as guaradian-companion to such a creature-trinitized son. This messenger accompanies the new son of destiny to the world of his assignment and nevermore leaves Vicegerington. When thus attached to the destinies of a child of time and eternity, a Solitary Messenger is forever transferred to the sole supervision of the Architects of the Master Universe. What the future of such an extraordinary association may be, we do not know. For ages these partnerships of unique personalities have continued to forgather on Vicegerington, but not even a single pair has ever gone forth therefrom." (p. 262)

7. **Proposition.** Many mysteries are associated with these trinitized sons and their Solitary Messenger companions forgathering on Vicegerington under the supervision of the Architects of the Master Universe.

See page 262

X. SERVICE OF SOLITARY MESSENGERS

1. **Proposition.** Solitary Messengers, like Universe Power Directors, are exempt from apprehension by the tribunals of time and space.

   > "The Solitary Messengers, like the Universe Power Directors, are among the very few types of beings operating throughout the realms who are exempt from apprehension or detention by the tribunals of time and space." (p. 257)

2. **Proposition.** Solitary Messengers are the explorers of the unchartered regions of outer space.

   > "These messenger-explorers of undirected assignment patrol the master universe. They are constantly out on exploring expeditions to the uncharted regions of all outer space. Very much of the information which we possess of transactions in the realms of outer space, we owe to the explorations of the Solitary Messengers as they often work and study with the celestial astronomers." (p. 260)

PART IX — THE SUPREME SPIRITS

3. **PROPOSITION.** Solitary Messengers are the only personal service for the transmission of rapid communication when the reflectivity mechanism is not used.

> "The Solitary Messengers are the highest type of perfect and confidential personality available in all realms for the quick transmission of important and urgent messages when it is inexpedient to utilize either the broadcast service or the reflectivity mechanism. They serve in an endless variety of assignments, helping out the spiritual and material beings of the realms, particularly where the element of time is involved. Of all orders assigned to the services of the superuniverse domains, they are the highest and most versatile personalized beings who can come so near to defying time and space." (p. 260)

4. **PROPOSITION.** Solitary Messengers function between the instantaneous velocities of gravity messengers and the slow speeds of seraphim.

> "There are, however, no transit or messenger personalities who function between the instantaneous velocities of the gravity traversers and the comparatively slow speeds of the seraphim, except the Solitary Messengers." (p. 261)

5. **PROPOSITION.** It is difficult to explain how a Solitary Messenger can be a real person and yet traverse space at such velocities.

> "It is wholly beyond my ability to explain to the material type of mind how a spirit can be a real person and at the same time traverse space at such tremendous velocities. But these very Solitary Messengers actually come to, and go from, Urantia at these imcomprehensible speeds; indeed, the whole economy of universal administration would be largely deprived of its personal element were this not a fact." (p. 261)

6. **PROPOSITION.** Solitary Messengers are personalities even though they are without form. They possess the advantages of formless spirits coupled with prerogatives of personality.

> "I am at a loss to explain to Urantia mortals how the Solitary Messengers can be without form and yet possess real and definite personalities. Although they are without that form which would naturally be associated with personality, they do possess a spirit presence which is discernible by all higher types of spirit beings. The Solitary Messengers are the only

- 273 -

class of beings who seem to be possessed of well-nigh all the advantages of a formless spirit coupled with all the prerogatives of a full-fledged personality. They are true persons, yet endowed with nearly all of the attributes of impersonal spirit manifestation." (p. 261)

7. **Proposition.** Solitary Messengers co-ordinate all types of finite creatures. They may possibly be related to the bestowal of Supreme-Ultimate Mind by the Infinite Spirit.

"The Solitary Messengers demonstrate such an amazing ability to co-ordinate all types and orders of finite personality—even to make contact with the absonite regime of the master universe overcontrollers— that some of us postulate that the creation of these messengers by the Infinite Spirit is in some manner related to the Conjoint Actor's bestowal of Supreme-Ultimate Mind." (p. 262)

XI. HIGHER PERSONALITIES OF THE INFINITE SPIRIT

A. *Universe Circuit Supervisors.*

1. **Proposition.** Universe Circuit Supervisors serve the Infinite Spirit and function in four orders.

"Universe Circuit Supervisors are the exclusive creation of the Infinte Spirit, and they function solely as the agents of the Conjoint Actor. They are personalized for service in the following four orders:
1. Supreme Circuit Supervisors.
2. Associate Circuit Supervisors.
3. Secondary Circuit Supervisors.
4. Tertiary Circuit Supervisors.

"The supreme supervisors of Havona and the associate supervisors of the seven superuniverses are of completed numbers; no more of these orders are being created. The supreme supervisors are seven in number and are stationed on the pilot worlds of the seven Havona circuits. The circuits of the seven superuniverses are in the charge of a marvelous group of seven associate supervisors, who maintain headquarters on the seven Paradise spheres of the Infinite Spirit, the worlds of the Seven Supreme Executives. From here they supervise and direct the circuits of the superuniverses of space." (p. 265)

PART IX — THE SUPREME SPIRITS

2. **PROPOSITION.** The Seven Spirits of the Havona Circuits are the joint impersonal representation of the Infinite Spirit and the Seven Master Spirits.

    "The Seven Spirits of the Havona Circuits are the joint impersonal representation of the Infinite Spirit and the Seven Master Spirits to the seven circuits of the central universe. They are the servants of the Master Spirits, whose collective offspring they are." (p. 202)

3. **PROPOSITION.** The Circuit Spirits did not create tertiary supernaphim until the arrival of Grandfanda.

    "While the Circuit Spirits are coexistent with the Seven Master Spirits, their function in the creation of tertiary supernaphim did not attain major importance until the first pilgrims of time arrived on the outer circuit of Havona in the days of Grandfanda." (p. 203)

B. *Census Directors.*

1. **PROPOSITION.** The Census Directors are cognizant of the presence of will anywhere in the master universe. They operate over the reflectivity mechanism and are aware of the birth and death of will creatures.

    "The Census Directors are a special and completed creation of the Infinite Spirit, and they exist in numbers unknown to us. They are so created as to be able to maintain perfect synchrony with the reflectivity technique of the superuniverses, while at the same time they are personally sensitive and responsive to intelligent *will*. These directors, by a not-fully-understood technique, are made immediately aware of the birth of will in any part of the grand universe. They are, therefore, always competent to give us the number, nature, and whereabouts of all will creatures in any part of the central creation and the seven superuniverses. But they do not function on Paradise; there is no need for them there. On Paradise knowledge is inherent; the Deities know all things." (p. 266)

2. **PROPOSITION.** Census Directors are concerned only with recording the fact of will function.

    "The Census Directors are concerned with human beings—as with other will creatures—only to the extent of recording the fact of will function. They are not concerned with the records of your life and its doings; they are not in any sense recording personalities. The Census Director of Nebadon, number

81,412 of Orvonton, now stationed on Salvington, is at this very moment personally conscious and aware of your living presence here on Urantia; and he will afford the records confirmation of your death the moment you cease to function as a will creature." (p. 267)

C. *Personal Aids.*

    1. **Proposition.** The Personal Aids are the personal messengers of the Infinite Spirit. They are not persons and they flash to and fro to the uttermost parts of creation.

"We have no authentic knowledge as to the time or manner of the creation of the Personal Aids. Their number must be legion, but it is not of record on Uversa. From conservative deductions based on our knowledge of their work, I venture to estimate that their number extends high into the trillions. We hold the opinion that the Infinite Spirit is not limited as to numbers in the creation of these Personal Aids.

"The Personal Aids of the Infinite Spirit exist for the exclusive assistance of the Paradise presence of the Third Person of Deity. Although attached directly to the Infinite Spirit and located on Paradise, they flash to and fro to the uttermost parts of creation. Wherever the circuits of the Conjoint Creator extend, there these Personal Aids may appear for the purpose of executing the bidding of the Infinite Spirit. They traverse space much as do the Solitary Messengers but are not persons in the sense that the messengers are." (p. 268)

D. *Associate Inspectors.*

    1. **Proposition.** Associate Inspectors are stationed on local universe headquarters and are the personal embodiment of the authority of the Supreme Executives.

"The Seven Supreme Executives, on the seven Paradise spheres of the Infinite Spirit, collectively function as the administrative board of supermanagers for the seven superuniverses. The Associate Inspectors are the personal embodiment of the authority of the Supreme Executives to the local universes of time and space. These high observers of the affairs of the local creations are the joint offspring of the Infinite Spirit and the Seven Master Spirits of Paradise. In the near times of eternity seven hundred thousand were personalized, and their reserve corps abides on Paradise." (p. 268)

Part IX — *The Supreme Spirits*

E. *Assigned Sentinels.*

    1. **Proposition.** Assigned Sentinels are the co-ordinating personalities of the Seven Supreme Executives stationed on the system capital.

    "The Assigned Sentinels are co-ordinating personalities and liaison representatives of the Seven Supreme Executives. They were personalized on Paradise by the Infinite Spirit and were created for the specific purposes of their assignment. They are of stationary numbers, and there are exactly seven billion in existence.

    "Much as an Associate Inspector represents the Seven Supreme Executives to a whole local universe, so in each of the ten thousand systems of that local creation there is an Assigned Sentinel, who acts as the direct representative of the far-distant and supreme board of supercontrol for the affairs of all seven superuniverses. The sentinels on duty in the local system governments of Orvonton are acting under the direct authority of Supreme Executive Number Seven, the co-ordinator of the seventh superuniverse. But in their administrative organization all sentinels commissioned in a local universe are subordinate to the Associate Inspector stationed at universe headquarters." (p. 268)

F. *Graduate Guides.*

    1. **Proposition.** Graduate Guides conduct the ministry of technical and spiritual instruction for mortal ascenders on their way to Paradise.

    "The Graduate Guides, as a group, sponsor and conduct the high university of technical instruction and spiritual training which is so essential to mortal attainment of the goal of the ages: God, rest, and then eternity of perfected service. These highly personal beings take their name from the nature and purpose of their work. They are exclusively devoted to the tasks of guiding the mortal graduates from the superuniverses of time through the Havona course of instruction and training which serves to prepare the ascending pilgrims for admission to Paradise and the Corps of the Finality." (p. 269)

    2. **Proposition.** Malvorian, the first Graduate Guide, conducted Grandfanda from the outer circuit of Havona to Paradise destiny.

    "On the Paradise records of Havona, in the section denominated 'Graduate Guides,' there appears this initial entry:

"'And Malvorian, the first of this order, did greet and instruct the pilgrim discoverer of Havona and did conduct him from the outer circuits of initial experience, step by step and circuit by circuit, until he stood in the very presence of the Source and Destiny of all personality, subsequently crossing the threshold of eternity to Paradise.'" (p. 270)

3. PROPOSITION. Graduate Guides are evolved Havona Servitals. "Though evolution is not the order of the central universe, we believe that the Graduate Guides are the perfected or more experienced members of another order of central universe creatures, the Havona Servitals." (p. 270)

4. PROPOSITION. Arrival of the first mortal ascender in Havona resulted in sweeping changes in the central universe—the appearance of the Graduate Guides and other modifications. "The Havona now traversed by ascending mortals differs in many respects from the central universe as it was before the times of Grandfanda. The arrival of mortal ascenders on the Havona circuits inaugurated sweeping modifications in the organization of the central and divine creation, modifications undoubtedly initiated by the Supreme Being—the God of evolutionary creatures—in response to the arrival of the first of his experiential children from the seven superuniverses. The appearance of the Graduate Guides, together with the creation of the tertiary supernaphim, is indicative of these performances of God the Supreme." (p. 271)

XII. MESSENGER HOSTS OF SPACE

1. PROPOSITION. Of the Messenger Hosts of Space, only three groups were created as such; the other four groups are recruited by selection.

    "RANKING intermediately in the family of the Infinite Spirit are the Messenger Hosts of Space. These versatile beings function as the connecting links between the higher personalities and the ministering spirits. The messenger hosts include the following orders of celestial beings:
    1. Havona Servitals.
    2. Universal Conciliators.
    3. Technical Advisers.
    4. Custodians of Records on Paradise.
    5. Celestial Recorders.
    6. Morontia Companions.
    7. Paradise Companions

Part IX — The Supreme Spirits

"Of the seven groups enumerated, only three—servitals, conciliators, and Morontia Companions—are created as such; the remaining four represent attainment levels of the angelic orders. In accordance with inherent nature and attained status, the messenger hosts variously serve in the universe of universes but always subject to the direction of those who rule the realms of their assignment." (p. 273)

A. *Havona Servitals.*

1. *Proposition.* About one quarter of Havona Servitals who enter the divine embrace never return—they translate into Graduate Guides.

    "On returning from superuniverse service, a Havona Servital may enjoy numerous divine embraces and emerge therefrom merely an exalted servital. Experiencing the luminous embrace does not necessarily signify that the servital must translate into a Graduate Guide, but almost one quarter of those who achieve the divine embrace never return to the service of the realms." (p. 271)

2. **Proposition**. Servitals are the "midway creatures" of Havona. They are created by the Seven Master Spirits and the Seven Supreme Power Directors.

    "Though denominated servitals, these 'midway creatures' of the central universe are not servants in any menial sense of the word. In the spiritual world there is no such thing as menial work; all service is sacred and exhilarating; neither do the higher orders of beings look down upon the lower orders of existence.

    "The Havona Servitals are the joint creative work of the Seven Master Spirits and their associates, the Seven Supreme Power Directors. This creative collaboration comes the nearest to being the pattern for the long list of reproductions of the dual order in the evolutionary universes, extending from the creation of a Bright and Morning Star by a Creator Son-Creative Spirit liaison down to sex procreation on worlds like Urantia." (p. 273)

3. **Proposition**. One fourth of servitals are semimaterial creatures. The law of spiritual dominance prevails in Havona.

    "The number of servitals is prodigious, and more are being created all the time. They appear in groups of one thousand on the third moment following the assembly of the Master Spirits and the Supreme Power Directors at their joint area in the far northerly sector of Paradise. Every fourth servital is more physical in type than the others; that is, out of each thousand, seven hundred and fifty are apparently true to spirit type, but two hundred and fifty are semiphysical in nature. These *fourth creatures* are somewhat on the order of material beings (material in the Havona sense), resembling the physical power directors more than the Master Spirits.

"In personality relationships the spiritual is dominant over the material, even though it does not now so appear on Urantia; and in the production of Havona Servitals the law of spirit dominance prevails; the established ratio yields three spiritual beings to one semiphysical." (p. 273)

B. *Universal Conciliators.*

1. PROPOSITION. For every Havona Servital created, seven Universal Conciliators are created.

    "For every Havona Servital created, seven Universal Conciliators are brought into being, one in each superuniverse. This creative enactment involves a definite superuniverse technique of reflective response to transactions taking place on Paradise." (p. 275)

2. PROPOSITION. On the superuniverse headquarters, reflexively with the creation of servitals in Havona, the Reflective Spirits produce Conciliators of orders similar to the nature of the Master Spirit concerned.

    "And every time the Master Spirits associate themselves with the power directors for the purpose of creating a group of Havona Servitals, there is a simultaneous focalization upon one of the Reflective Spirits in each of the superuniverse groups, and forthwith and full-fledgedly an equal number of Universal Conciliators appear on the headquarters worlds of the supercreations. If, in the creation of servitals, Master Spirit Number Seven should take the initiative, none but the Reflective Spirits of the seventh order would become pregnant with conciliators; and concurrently with the creation of one thousand Orvontonlike servitals, one thousand of the seventh-order conciliators would appear on each superuniverse capital. Out of these episodes, reflecting the sevenfold nature of the Master Spirits, arise the seven created orders of conciliators serving in each superuniverse." (p. 275)

3. **Proposition.** Conciliators automatically segregate into groups of four—three spirit personalities and a fourth creature—semimaterial.
"In each superuniverse the Universal Conciliators find themselves strangely and innately segregated into groups of four, associations in which they continue to serve. In each group, three are spirit personalities, and one, like the fourth creatures of the servitals, is a semimaterial being. This quartet constitutes a conciliating commission and is made up as follows:

"1. *The Judge-Arbiter.* The one unanimously designated by the other three as the most competent and best qualified to act as judicial head of the group.

"2. *The Spirit-Advocate.* The one appointed by the judge-arbiter to present evidence and to safeguard the rights of all personalities involved in any matter assigned to the adjudication of the conciliating commission.

"3. *The Divine Executioner.* The conciliator qualified by inherent nature to make contact with the material beings of the realms and to execute the decisions of the commission. Divine executioners, being fourth creatures—quasi-material beings—are almost, but not quite, visible to the short-range vision of the mortal races.

"4. *The Recorder.* The remaining member of the commission automatically becomes the recorder, the clerk of the tribunal. He makes certain that all records are properly prepared for the archives of the superuniverse and for the records of the local universe. If the commission is serving on an evolutionary world, a third report, with the assistance of the executioner, is prepared for the physical records of the system government of jurisdiction." (pp. 275-6)

C. *Technical Advisers.*

1. **Proposition.** Technical Advisers were first chosen from supernaphim and omniaphim—one million by the Infinite Spirit.
"These legal and technical minds of the spirit world were not created as such. From the early supernaphim and omniaphim, one million of the most orderly minds were chosen by the Infinite Spirit as the nucleus of this vast and versatile group. And ever since that far-distant time, actual experience in the application of the laws of perfection to the plans of evolutionary creation has been required of all who aspire to become Technical Advisers." (p. 279)

2. **Proposition.** Technical Advisers are recruited from several groups.

    "The Technical Advisers are recruited from the ranks of the following personality orders:
    1. The Supernaphim.
    2. The Seconaphim.
    3. The Tertiaphim.
    4. The Omniaphim.
    5. The Seraphim.
    6. Certain Types of Ascending Mortals.
    7. Certain Types of Ascending Midwayers.

    "At the present time, not counting the mortals and midwayers who are all of transient attachment, the number of Technical Advisers registered on Uversa and operating in Orvonton is slightly in excess of sixty-one trillion." (p. 279)

3. **Proposition.** Ministering spirits above cherubim may become Technical Advisers.

    "After long training and actual experience, any of the ministering spirits above the status of cherubim are permitted to receive permanent appointment as Technical Advisers. All candidates voluntarily enter this order of service; but having once assumed such responsibilities, they may not relinquish them. Only the Ancients of Days can transfer these advisers to other activities." (p. 280)

4. **Proposition.** Technical Advisers are the living law libraries of time and space. They are teachers of creatures concerning the technique of the Creators.

    "These advisers are more than legal experts; they are students and teachers of *applied* law, the laws of the universe applied to the lives and destinies of all who inhabit the vast domains of the far-flung creation. As time passes, they become the living law libraries of time and space, preventing endless trouble and needless delays by instructing the personalities of time regarding the forms and modes of procedure most acceptable to the rulers of eternity. They are able so to counsel the workers of space as to enable them to function in harmony with the requirements of Paradise; they are the teachers of all creatures concerning the technique of the Creators." (p. 280)

PART IX — THE SUPREME SPIRITS

D. Custodians of Records

   1. **PROPOSITION.** The Paradise archives are maintained by the Custodians of Records—tertiary supernaphim.

      "From among the tertiary supernaphim in Havona, certain of the senior chief recorders are chosen as Custodians of Records, as keepers of the formal archives of the Isle of Light, those archives which stand in contrast to the living records of registry in the minds of the custodians of knowledge, sometimes designated the 'living library of Paradise.'" (p. 281)

E. Celestial Recorders

   1. **PROPOSITION.** Celestial Recorders are a recruited group making both spiritual and semimaterial records on superuniverse headquarters.

      "These are the recorders who execute all records in duplicate, making an original spirit recording and a semimaterial counterpart—what might be called a carbon copy. This they can do because of their peculiar ability simultaneously to manipulate both spiritual and material energy. Celestial Recorders are not created as such; they are ascendant seraphim from the local universes. They are received, classified, and assigned to their spheres of work by the councils of the Chiefs of Records on the headquarters of the seven superuniverses. There also are located the schools for training Celestial Recorders. The school on Uversa is conducted by the Perfectors of Wisdom and the Divine Counselors." (p. 281)

F. Morontia Companions.

   1. **PROPOSITION.** Morontia Companions are the gracious hosts and play sponsors of ascending mortals.

      "These children of the local universe Mother Spirits are the friends and associates of all who live the ascending morontia life. They are not indispensable to an ascender's real work of creature progression, neither do they in any sense displace the work of the seraphic guardians who often accompany their mortal associates on the Paradise journey. The Morontia Companions are simply gracious hosts to those who are just beginning the long inward ascent. They are also skillful play sponsors and are ably assisted in this work by the reversion directors." (p. 228)

G. Paradise Companions.

   1. **PROPOSITION.** Paradise Companions are a composite and recruited group assigned to this temporary service.

"The Paradise Companions are a composite or assembled group recruited from the ranks of the seraphim, seconaphim, supernaphim, and omniaphim. Though serving for what you would regard as an extraordinary length of time, they are not of permanent status. When this ministry has been completed, as a rule (but not invariably) they return to those duties they performed when summoned to Paradise service.

"Members of the angelic hosts are nominated for this service by the local universe Mother Spirits, by the superuniverse Reflective Spirits, and by Majeston of Paradise. They are summoned to the central Isle and are commissioned as Paradise Companions by one of the Seven Master Spirits. Aside from permanent status on Paradise, this temporary service of Paradise companionship is the highest honor ever conferred upon the ministering spirits." (p. 283)

PART X
THE PARADISE SONS

Part Ten
THE PARADISE SONS

I. INTRODUCTION

1. **Proposition.** There are three orders of the Paradise Sons of God—depending on parental origin.

    "The Paradise Sons of God are of threefold origin: The primary or Creator Sons are brought into being by the Universal Father and the Eternal Son; the secondary or Magisterial Sons are children of the Eternal Son and the Infinite Spirit; the Trinity Teacher Sons are the offspring of the Father, Son, and Spirit. From the standpoint of service, worship, and supplication the Paradise Sons are as one; their spirit is one, and their work is identical in quality and completeness." (p. 224)

2. **Proposition.** The Paradise Sons are the gifts of Deity to the ascendant creatures—they are devoted to helping the mortals of time attain the spiritual goal of eternity.

    "The Paradise Sons are the divine presentation of the acting natures of the three persons of Deity to the domains of time and space. The Creator, Magisterial, and Teacher Sons are the gifts of the eternal Deities to the children of men and to all other universe creatures of ascension potential. These Sons of God are the divine ministers who are unceasingly devoted to the work of helping the creatures of time attain the high spiritual goal of eternity." (p. 232)

3. **Proposition.** The Paradise Sons follow the divine expansion of the First Source and Center from Paradise to the unknown depths of space.

    "In the harmony of their triune activities these Paradise Sons of God ever function in the vanguard of the personalities of Deity as they follow the never-ending expansion of the divinity of the First Great Source and Center from the everlasting Isle of Paradise into the unknown depths of space." (p. 233)

II. MAGISTERIAL SONS

1. **Proposition.** Magisterial Sons are produced by the Eternal Son and the Infinite Spirit. Through creature incarnation, they earn the right to serve as judges of survival in the time-space creations.

    "Much as the Creator Sons are personalized by the Father and the Son, so are the *Magisterial Sons* personalized by the Son and the Spirit. These are the Sons who, in the experiences of creature incarnation, earn the right to serve as the Judges of survival in the creations of time and space." (p. 88)

2. **PROPOSITION.** Avonal Sons are produced by the absolute concept of the Eternal Son and the divine ideal of the Infinite Spirit.

> "Every time an original and absolute concept of being formulated, by the Eternal Son unites with a new and divine ideal of loving service conceived by the Infinite Spirit, a new and original Son of God, a Paradise Magisterial Son, is produced. These Sons constitute the order of Avonals." (p. 224)

3. **PROPOSITION.** Avonals are planetary ministers and judges. They number about one billion.

> "The Avonals are planetary ministers and judges, the magistrates of the time-space realms—of all races, to all worlds, and in all universes.
> "We have reasons for believing that the total number of Magisterial Sons in the grand universe is about one billion. They are of a selfgoverning order, being directed by their supreme council on Paradise, which is made up of experienced Avonals drawn from the services of all universes." (p. 225)

4. **PROPOSITION.** The Avonals have a threefold function.

   a. Judicial actions.
   b. Magisterial missions.
   c. Bestowal Sons.
   See page 225

5. **PROPOSITION.** Avonals may serve many times on magisterial and bestowal missions. After numerous missions they may join the staffs of the Creator Sons.

> "There is no limit to the number of times the Avonal Sons may serve on magisterial and on bestowal missions, but usually, when the experience has been seven times traversed, there is suspension in favor of those who have had less of such service. These Sons of multiple bestowal experience are then assigned to the high personal council of a Creator Son, thud becoming participants in the administration of universe affairs." (p. 8)

6. **PROPOSITION.** The mission of a Magisterial Son is just as effective as that of a Creator Son.

> "To all intents and purposes their work on the inhabited spheres is just as effective and acceptable as would have been the service of a Creator Son upon such worlds of mortal habitation." (p. 225)

7. **Proposition.** The Avonals are the adjudicators of a planetary dispensation. They preside over the judgment of the living and the resurrection of the dead.

> "The Avonals are known as Magisterial Sons because they are the high magistrates of the realms, the adjudicators of the successive dispensations of the worlds of time. They preside over the awakening of the sleeping survivors, sit in judgment on the realm, bring to an end a dispensation of suspended justice, execute the mandates of an age of probationary mercy, reassign the space creatures of planetary ministry to the tasks of the new dispensation, and return to the headquarters of their local universe upon the completion of their mission." (p. 226)

8. **Proposition.** Magisterial missions sometimes, and bestowal missions always, are incarnations. On other missions they may appear as spiritual beings.

> "The arrival of a Paradise Avonal on an evolutionary world for the purpose of terminating a dispensation and of inaugurating a new era of planetary progression is not necessarily either a magisterial mission or a bestowal mission. Magisterial missions sometimes, and bestowal missions always, are incarnations; that is, on such assignments the Avonals serve on a planet in material form—literally. Their other visits are 'technical,' and in this capacity an Avonal is not incarnated for planetary service. If a Magisterial Son comes solely as a dispensational adjudicator, he arrives on a planet as a spiritual being, invisible to the material creatures of the realm. Such technical visits occur repeatedly in the long history of an inhabited world." (p. 226)

9. **Proposition.** Prior to the mission of a bestowal Son, an incarnated Avonal usually appears on a magisterial mission.

> "Prior to the planetary appearance of a bestowal Son, an inhabited world is usually visited by a Paradise Avonal on a magisterial mission. If it is an initial magisterial visitation, the Avonal is always incarnated as a material being. He appears on the planet of assignment as a full-fledged male of the mortal races, a being fully visible to, and in physical contact with, the mortal creatures of his day and generation. Throughout a magisterial incarnation the connection of the Avonal Son with the local and the universal spiritual forces is complete and unbroken." (p. 226)

10. **Proposition.** Urantia may yet be visited by an incarnated Avonal Son on a magisterial mission.

> "Urantia may yet be visited by an Avonal commissioned to incarnate on a magisterial mission, but regarding the future appearance of Paradise Sons, not even 'the angels in heaven know the time or manner of such visitations,' for a Michael-bestowal world becomes the individual and personal ward of a Master Son and, as such, is wholly subject to his own plans and rulings." (p. 227)

III. BESTOWAL OF THE SONS

1. **Proposition.** Incarnated Paradise Sons have experienced Adjusters which are often personalized after the incarnation.

> "When incarnated on either bestowal or magisterial missions, the Paradise Sons have experienced Adjusters, and these Adjusters are different for each incarnation. The Adjusters that occupy the minds of the incarnated Sons of God can never hope for personality through fusion with the human-divine beings of their indwelling, but they are often personalized by fiat of the Universal Father." (p. 227)

2. **Proposition.** Bestowals of Paradise Sons are essential to the universal bestowal of Thought Adjusters and the coming of the Spirit of Truth.

> "Some order of Paradise Son must be bestowed upon each mortal-inhabited world in order to make it possible for Thought Adjusters to indwell the minds of all normal human beings on that sphere, for the Adjusters do not come to *all* bona fide human beings until the Spirit of Truth has been poured out upon all flesh; and the sending of the Spirit of Truth is dependent upon the return to universe headquarters of a Paradise Son who has successfully executed a mission of mortal bestowal upon an evolving world." (p. 227)

3. **Proposition.** In a bestowal experience, disaster is possible—but it has never occurred.

> "Though the possibility of disaster always attends these Paradise Sons during their bestowal incarnations, I have yet to see the record of the failure or default of either a Magisterial or a Creator Son on a mission of bestowal. Both are of origin too close to absolute perfection to fail." (p. 228)

4. **Proposition.** The technique of the incarnation of a Paradise Son is a universe mystery.

> "The method whereby a Paradise Son becomes ready for mortal incarnation as a bestowal Son, becomes enmothered on the bestowal planet, is a universal mystery; and any effort to detect the working of this Sonarington technique is doomed to meet with certain failure." (p. 228)

5. **Proposition.** A bestowal Son is always born of woman and grows up as a male child of the realm.

> "On a mortal-bestowal mission a Paradise Son is always born of woman and grows up as a male child of the realm, as Jesus did on Urantia. These Sons of supreme service all pass from infancy through youth to manhood just as does a human being. In every respect they become like the mortals of the race into which they are born." (p. 229)

6. **Proposition.** Mortal bestowals of Michaels and Avonals are similar but not identical.

> "The mortal-bestowal careers of the Michaels and the Avonals, while comparable in most respects, are not identical in all: Never does a Magisterial Son proclaim, 'Whosoever has seen the Son has seen the Father,' as did your Creator Son when on Urantia and in the flesh. But a bestowed Avonal does declare, 'Whosoever has seen me has seen the Eternal Son of God.'" (p. 229)

7. **Proposition.** Bestowal Sons die and reappear on the third day. But it is not required that they meet with a tragic death.

> "When the bestowal Sons, Creator or Magisterial, enter the portals of death, they reappear on the third day. But you should not entertain the idea that they always meet with the tragic end encountered by the Creator Son who sojourned on your world nineteen hundred years ago. The extraordinary and unusually cruel experience through which Jesus of Nazareth passed has caused Urantia to become locally known as 'the world of the cross.' It is not necessary that such inhuman treatment be accorded a Son of God, and the vast majority of planets have afforded them a more considerate reception, allowing them to finish their mortal careers, terminate the age, adjudicate the sleeping survivors, and inaugurate a new dispensation, without imposing a violent death." (p. 229)

8. **Proposition.** Bestowal Sons can voluntarily pass through death to resurrection—and all this is a part of the bestowal experience.

> "When bestowal Sons are not put to death by violence, they voluntarily relinquish their lives and pass through the portals of death, not to satisfy the demands of 'stern justice' or 'divine wrath,' but rather to complete the bestowal, 'to drink the cup' of the career of incarnation and personal experience in all that constitutes a creature's life as it is lived on the planets of mortal existence. Bestowal is a planetary and a universe necessity, and physical death is nothing more than a necessary part of a bestowal mission." (p. 229)

9. **Proposition.** The bestowal of a Creator Son modifies the Spirit of Truth previously sent by an Avonal Son.

> "Upon the completion of a Creator Son's final bestowal the Spirit of Truth previously sent into all Avonal-bestowal worlds of that local universe changes in nature, becoming more literally the spirit of the sovereign Michael. This phenomenon takes place concurrently with the liberation of the Spirit of Truth for service on the Michael-mortal-bestowal planet. Thereafter, each world honored by a Magisterial bestowal will receive the same spirit Comforter from the sevenfold Creator Son, in association with that Magisterial Son, which it would have received had the local universe Sovereign personally incarnated as its bestowal Son." (p. 230)

10. **Proposition.** The attribute of bestowal is inherent in the Paradise Sons. The Eternal Son has seven times bestowed himself upon the seven circuits of Havona.

> "The attribute of bestowal is inherent in the Paradise Sons of the Universal Father. In their desire to come close to the life experiences of their subordinate living creatures, the various orders of the Paradise Sons are reflecting the divine nature of their Paradise parents. The Eternal Son of the Paradise Trinity led the way in this practice, having seven times bestowed himself upon the seven circuits of Havona during the times of the ascension of Grandfanda and the first of the pilgrims from time and space. And the Eternal Son continues to bestow himself upon the local universes of space in the persons of his representatives, the Michael and Avonal Sons." (p. 1308)

11. **Proposition.** The bestowal of Sons is not to placate the Heavenly Father. It is a part of their experiential training designed to make them safe and understanding rulers.

> "On Urantia there is a widespread belief that the purpose of a Son's bestowal is, in some manner, to influence the attitude of the Universal Father. But your enlightenment should indicate that this is not true. The bestowals of the Avonal and the Michael Sons are a necessary part of the experiential process designed to make these Sons safe and sympathetic magistrates and rulers of the peoples and planets of time and space." (p. 227)

IV. TRINITY TEACHER SONS

1. **Proposition.** Trinity Teacher Sons are constantly increasing. In Orvonton there are more than twenty-one billion.

> "While the Stationary Sons of the Trinity are of completed numbers, the Teacher Sons are constantly increasing. What the final number of Teacher Sons will be I do not know. I can, however, state that, at the last periodic report to Uversa, the Paradise records indicated 21,001,624,821 of these Sons in service." (p. 214)

2. **Proposition.** Trinity Teacher Sons are the universal educators.

> "They are the universal educators, being dedicated to the spiritual awakening and moral guidance of all realms. Their ministry is intimately interrelated with that of the personalities of the Infinite Spirit and is closely associated with the Paradise ascension of creature beings." (p. 230)

3. **Proposition.** Trinity Teacher Sons go directly to superuniverse headquarters, from which they are sent to varied services in the local universes.

> "Unlike their Paradise brethren, Michaels and Avonals, Trinity Teacher Sons receive no preliminary training in the central universe. They are dispatched directly to the headquarters of the superuniverses and from there are commissioned for service in some local universe. In their ministry to these evolutionary realms they utilize the combined spiritual influence of a Creator Son and the associated Magisterial Sons, for the Daynals do not possess a spiritual drawing power in and of themselves." (p. 230)

PART X — THE PARADISE SONS

4. **PROPOSITION.** The Teacher Sons conduct schools and examinations from the planets up to the College of Wisdom on Salvington.

> "The Teacher Sons compose the faculties who administer all examinations and conduct all tests for the qualification and certification of all subordinate phases of universe service, from the duties of outpost sentinels to those of star students. They conduct an agelong course of training, ranging from the planetary courses up to the high College of Wisdom located on Salvington." (p. 231)

5. **PROPOSITION.** Trinity Teacher Sons will function on Urantia after its inhabitants gain deliverance from the shackles of animalism and the fetters of materialism.

> "When the progress of events on an evolutionary world indicates that the time is ripe to initiate a spiritual age, the Trinity Teacher Sons always volunteer for this service. You are not familiar with this order of sonship because Urantia has never experienced a spiritual age, a millennium of cosmic enlightenment. But the Teacher Sons even now visit your world for the purpose of formulating plans concerning their projected sojourn on your sphere. They will be due to appear on Urantia after its inhabitants have gained comparative deliverance from the shackles of animalism and from the fetters of materialism." (p. 231)

6. **PROPOSITION.** Trinity Teacher Sons have only to do with the initiation of a spiritual age—the era of spiritual realities.

> "Trinity Teacher Sons have nothing to do with terminating planetary dispensations. They neither judge the dead nor translate the living, but on each planetary mission they are accompanied by a Magisterial Son who performs these services. Teacher Sons are wholly concerned with the initiation of a spiritual age, with the dawn of the era of spiritual realities on an evolutionary planet." (p. 231)

7. **PROPOSITION.** Teacher Sons usually remain on a planet for one thousand years. The Evening Stars facilitate their contact with world Inhabitants.

> "The Teacher Sons usually remain on their visitation planets for one thousand years of planetary time. One Teacher Son presides over the planetary millennial reign and is assisted by seventy associates of his order. The Daynals do not incarnate or otherwise so materialize themselves as to be visible to mortal beings; therefore is contact with the world of visitation maintained through the activities of the Brilliant Evening Stars, local universe personalities who are associated with the Trinity Teacher Sons." (p. 232)

8. **Proposition.** In the next universe age, the Teacher Sons may become eternally associated with the Paradise Corps of the Finality.

> "On Uversa it is our belief that, when the superuniverses are finally settled in light and life, these Paradise Teacher Sons, who have become so thoroughly familiar with the problems of evolutionary worlds and have been so long associated with the career of evolutionary mortals, will probably be transferred to eternal association with the Paradise Corps of the Finality." (p. 232)

V. TRINITY-EMBRACED SONS

1. **Proposition.** In addition to the descending and ascending Sons of God, there is a third group called Trinitized or Trinity-embraced sons.

   > "There are three groups of beings who are called Sons of God. In addition to descending and ascending orders of sonship there is a third group known as the Trinitized Sons of God. The trinitized order of sonship is subdivided into three primary divisions in accordance with the origins of its many types of personalities, revealed and unrevealed. These primary divisions are:
   >   1. Deity-trinitized Sons.
   >   2. Trinity-embraced Sons.
   >   3. Creature-trinitized Sons
   >
   > "Irrespective of origin all Trinitized Sons of God have in common the experience of trinitization, either as a part of their origin or as an experience of Trinity embrace subsequently attained. The Deity-trinitized Sons are unrevealed in these narratives; therefore will this presentation be confined to a portrayal of the remaining two groups, more particularly the Trinity-embraced sons of God." (p. 243)

2. **Proposition.** The Trinity-embraced sons consist of seven groups.

   > "All Trinity-embraced sons are originally of dual or single origin, but subsequent to the Trinity embrace they are forever devoted to Trinity service and assignment. This corps, as revealed and as organized for superuniverse service, embraces seven orders of personalities:
   >   1. Mighty Messengers.
   >   2. Those High in Authority.
   >   3. Those without Name and Number.
   >   4. Trinitized Custodians.
   >   5. Trinitized Ambassadors.
   >   6. Celestial Guardians.
   >   7. High Son Assistants."

   (p. 243)

3. **PROPOSITION.** The Trinitized Sons of Attainment are all Adjuster-fused ascendant mortals and after Trinity embrace their names are removed from the finaliter roll.

   "*The Trinitized Sons of Attainment*—the Mighty Messengers, Those High in Authority, and Those without Name and Number—are all Adjuster-fused ascendant mortals who have attained Paradise and the Corps of the Finality. But they are not finaliters; when they have been Trinity embraced, their names are removed from the finaliter roll call." (p. 244)

4. **PROPOSITION.** Trinitized Sons of Selection are recruited from seraphim, midwayers, and Spirit-fused and Son-fused mortals.

   "*The Trinitized Sons of Selection* embrace the Trinitized Custodians and the Trinitized Ambassadors. They are recruited from certain of the evolutionary seraphim and translated midway creatures who have traversed Havona and have attained Paradise, as well as from certain of the Spirit-fused and the Son-fused mortals who have likewise ascended to the central Isle of Light and Life. Subsequent to their embrace by the Paradise Trinity and after a brief training in Havona, the Trinitized Sons of Selection are assigned to the courts of the Ancients of Days." (p. 244)

5. **PROPOSITION.** Trinitized Sons of Perfection are the trinitized sons of Paradise-Havona personalities or perfected finaliters.

   "*The Trinitized Sons of Perfection.* The Celestial Guardians and their co-ordinates, the High Son Assistants, comprise a unique group of twice-trinitized personalities. They are the creature-trinitized sons of Paradise-Havona personalities or of perfected ascendant mortals who have long distinguished themselves in the Corps of the Finality. Some of these creature-trinitized sons, after service with the Supreme Executives of the Seven Master Spirits and after serving under the Trinity Teacher Sons, are retrinitized (embraced) by the Paradise Trinity and then commissioned to the courts of the Ancients of Days as Celestial Guardians and as High Son Assistants. Trinitized Sons of Perfection are assigned directly to the superuniverse service without further training." (p. 244)

6. **PROPOSITION.** For this universe age, the Trinity-embraced sons are assigned to the service of the superuniverses.

> "Apparently the Trinity-embraced sons have been permanently assigned to the service of the seven superuniverses; certainly this assignment is for the duration of the present universe age, but we have never been informed that it is to be eternal." (p. 244)

7. **PROPOSITION.** Not all creature-trinitized sons are Trinity embraced. Some become associates of the Master Spirits, the Reflective Spirits, and local universe Mother Spirits. Others serve on the secret worlds of Paradise.

> "Not all creature-trinitized sons are Trinity embraced; many become the associates and ambassadors of the Seven Master Spirits of Paradise, of the Reflective Spirits of the superuniverses, and of the Mother Spirits of the local creations. Others may accept special assignments on the eternal Isle. Still others may enter the special services on the secret worlds of the Father and on the Paradise spheres of the Spirit. Eventually many find their way into the conjoint corps of the Trinitized Sons on the inner circuit of Havona." (p. 252)

8. **PROPOSITION.** Except those forgathering on Vicegerington, creature-trinitized sons are destined to enter the Corps of Trinitized Finaliters.

> "Excepting the Trinitized Sons of Perfection and those who are forgathering on Vicegerington, the supreme destiny of all creature-trinitized sons appears to be entrance into the Corps of Trinitized Finaliters, one of the seven Paradise Corps of the Finality." (p. 252)

9. **PROPOSITION.** Trinitized Sons of Perfection are deficient in time-space experience. They will gain experience in a future universe age.

> "Trinitized Sons of Perfection are limited in contrast to other Trinity-embraced sons because their experiential capacity is time-space inhibited. They are experience-deficient, despite long training with the Supreme Executives and the Teacher Sons, and if this were not the case, experiential saturation would preclude their being left in reserve for acquiring experience in a future universe age. There is simply nothing in all universal existence which can take the place of actual personal experience, and these creature-trinitized sons are held in reserve for experiential function in some future universe epoch.

"On the mansion worlds I have often seen these dignified officers of the high courts of the superuniverse look so longingly and appealingly at even the recent arrivals from the evolutionary worlds of space that one could not help realizing that these possessors of nonexperiential trinitization really envied their supposedly less fortunate brethren who ascend the universal path by steps of bona fide experience and actual living. Notwithstanding their handicaps and limitations they are a wonderfully useful and ever-willing corps of workers when it comes to the execution of the complex administrative plans of the superuniverse governments." (p. 253)

VI. MIGHTY MESSENGERS

1. **PROPOSITION.** Mighty Messengers belong to the ascendant group of Trinitized Sons. They are rebellion-tested mortals.

    "Mighty Messengers belong to the ascendant group of the Trinitized Sons. They are a class of perfected mortals who have been rebellion tested or otherwise equally proved as to their personal loyalty; all have passed through some definite test of universe allegiance. At some time in their Paradise ascent they stood firm and loyal in the face of the disloyalty of their superiors, and some did actively and loyally function in the places of such unfaithful leaders." (p. 245)

2. **PROPOSITION.** An ascendant creature who prevents or withstands rebellion in a universe crisis is destined to become a Mighty Messenger.

    "Every ascendant mortal of insurrectionary experience who functions loyally in the face of rebellion is eventually destined to become a Mighty Messenger of the superuniverse service. Likewise is any ascendant creature who effectively prevents such upheavals of error, evil, or sin; for action designed to prevent rebellion or to effect higher types of loyalty in a universe crisis is regarded as of even greater value than loyalty in the face of actual rebellion." (p. 245)

3. **PROPOSITION.** Mighty Messengers are embraced in groups of seven hundred thousand. Almost one trillion are commissioned on Uversa.

    "Mighty Messengers are embraced by the Paradise Trinity in classes of seven hundred thousand, one hundred thousand for assignment to each superuniverse. Almost one trillion Mighty

Messengers are commissioned on Uversa, and there is every reason to believe that the number serving in each of the seven superuniverses is exactly the same." (p. 245)

4. **Proposition.** Mighty Messengers are superuniverse observers; they are defenders of individuals and planets. They assist in the direction of the major sectors.

> "In the superuniverse courts, Mighty Messengers act as defenders of both individuals and planets when they come up for adjudication; they also assist the Perfections of Days in the direction of the affairs of the major sectors. As a group, their chief assignment is that of superuniverse observers. They are stationed on the various headquarters worlds and on individual planets of importance as the official observers of the Ancients of Days." (p. 245)

5. **Proposition.** Mighty Messengers are fully conscious of their ascendant careers.

> "Mighty Messengers are fully conscious of their entire ascendant careers, and that is why they are such useful and sympathetic ministers, understanding messengers, for service on any world of space and to any creature of time." (p. 246)

VII. THOSE HIGH IN AUTHORITY

1. **Proposition.** Those High in Authority are ascendant mortals of superior administrative ability. Seventy thousand are trinitized at a time.

> "Those High in Authority, the second group of the Trinitized Sons of Attainment, are all Adjuster-fused beings of mortal origin. These are the perfected mortals who have exhibited superior administrative ability and have shown extraordinary executive genius throughout their long ascending careers. They are the cream of governing ability derived from the surviving mortals of space. "Seventy thousand of Those High in Authority are trinitized at each Trinity liaison." (p. 246)

2. **Proposition.** Those High in Authority are the executives of the Ancients of Days.

> "Those High in Authority are administrators without limitation. They are the everywhere-present and always-efficient executives of the Ancients of Days. They serve on any sphere, on any inhabited world, and in any phase of activity in any of the seven superuniverses." (p. 246)

VIII. THOSE WITHOUT NAME AND NUMBER

1. **Proposition.** Those without Name and Number are the ascendant souls who have learned to worship beyond the skill of evolutionary mortals. Their concept of the eternal purpose of God transcends that of their fellows.

> "Those without Name and Number constitute the third and last group of the Trinitized Sons of Attainment; they are the ascendant souls who have developed the ability to worship beyond the skill of all the sons and daughters of the evolutionary races from the worlds of time and space. They have acquired a spiritual concept of the eternal purpose of the Universal Father which comparatively transcends the comprehension of the evolutionary creatures of name or number; therefore are they denominated Those without Name and Number. More strictly translated, their name would be 'Those above Name and Number.'
> "This order of sons is embraced by the Paradise Trinity in groups of seven thousand. There are of record on Uversa over one hundred million of these sons commissioned in Orvonton." (p. 248)

IX. TRINITIZED CUSTODIANS

1. **Proposition.** Trinitized Custodians are ascendant seraphim and midwayers who have been Trinity embraced.

> "The Trinitized Custodians are Trinitized Sons of Selection. Not only do your races and other mortals of survival value traverse Havona, attain Paradise, and sometimes find themselves destined to superuniverse service with the Stationary Sons of the Trinity, but your faithful seraphic guardians and your equally faithful midway associates may also become candidates for the same Trinity recognition and superb personality destiny.
> "Trinitized Custodians are ascendant seraphim and translated midway creatures who have passed through Havona and have attained Paradise and the Corps of the Finality. Subsequently they were embraced by the Paradise Trinity and were assigned to the service of the Ancients of Days." (p. 247)

X. TRINITIZED AMBASSADORS

1. **Proposition.** Trinitized Ambassadors are ascendant Spirit-fused and Son-fused mortals.

> "Trinitized Ambassadors are the second order of the Trinitized Sons of Selection and like their associates, the Custodians, are

recruited from two types of ascendant creatures. Not all ascending mortals are Adjuster or Father fused; some are Spirit fused, some are Son fused. Certain of these Spirit- and Son-fused mortals reach Havona and attain Paradise. From among these Paradise ascenders, candidates are selected for the Trinity embrace, and from time to time they are trinitized in classes of seven thousand." (p. 248)

XI. HIGH SON ASSISTANTS

1. **PROPOSITION.** High Son Assistants are the superior group of the retrinitized trinitized sons of ascendant mortals.

    "The High Son Assistants are the superior group of the retrinitized trinitized sons of glorified ascendant beings of the Mortal Corps of the Finality and of their eternal associates, the Paradise-Havona personalities. They are assigned to the superuniverse service and function as personal aids to the high sons of the governments of the Ancients of Days. They might fittingly be denominated private secretaries. They act, from time to time, as clerks for special commissions and other group associations of the high sons. They serve Perfectors of Wisdom, Divine Counselors, Universal Censors, Mighty Messengers, Those High in Authority, and Those without Name and Number." (p. 253)

2. **PROPOSITION.** These High Son Assistants are affectionate, loyal, and intelligent beings. They are supremely wise regarding the single idea of their origin.

    "They are touchingly affectionate, superbly loyal, exquisitely intelligent, supremely wise—regarding a single idea—and transcendently humble. While they can impart to you the lore of the universe concerning their one idea or ideal, it is well-nigh pathetic to observe them seeking knowledge and information on hosts of other subjects, even from the ascending mortals." (p. 254)

XII. TECHNIQUE OF TRINITIZATION

1. **PROPOSITION.** The techniques of trinitization are among the secrets of Vicegerington and Solitarington. Aside from Deity, only Paradise-Havona personalities and certain members of the Finality Corps engage in trinitization.

    "I cannot fully unfold to the material mind the experience of the supreme creative performance of perfect and perfected spiritual beings—the act of trinitization. The techniques of

PART X — THE PARADISE SONS

trinitization are among the secrets of Vicergerington and Solitarington and are revealable to, and understandable by, none save those who have passed through these unique experiences. Therefore is it beyond the possibility of any being successfully to portray to the human mind the nature and purport of this extraordinary transaction.

"Aside from the Deities, only Paradise-Havona personalities and certain members of each of the finaliter corps engage in trinitization. Under specialized conditions of Paradise perfection, these superb beings may embark upon the unique adventure of concept-identity, and they are many times successful in the production of a new being, a creature-trinitized son." (p. 249)

2. **PROPOSITION**. Description of the technique of two mortals engaged in trinitization.

"If two mortal finaliters, on going before the Architects of the Master Universe, demonstrate that they have independently chosen an identical concept for trinitization, the Architects are empowered, on their own discretion, to promulgate mandates permitting these glorified mortal ascenders to extend their recess and to remove themselves for a time to the trinitizing sector of the Paradise Citizens. At the end of this assigned retreat, if they report that they have singly and jointly elected to make the paradisiacal effort to spiritualize, idealize, and actualize a selected and original concept which has not theretofore been trinitized, then does Master Spirit Number Seven issue orders authorizing such an extraordinary undertaking." (p. 249)

3. **PROPOSITION**. Trinitization by ascendant creatures eventuates in spiritual union of the parents—they become one on the ultimate functional level.

"Simultaneously with the appearance of a new creature-trinitized son, there occurs this functional spiritual union of the two ancestors; the two trinitizing parents become one on the ultimate functional level." (p. 250)

4. **PROPOSITION**. Mortal or Paradise-Havona trinitizing parents are separated from Paradise, Havona, and finaliter associations. They forgather in a special corps.

"If parental bi-unification involves a mortal (or other) finaliter and a Paradise-Havona personality, the united parental beings function neither with the Paradisers, Havoners, nor finaliters. Such mixed unions forgather in a special corps made up of similar beings. And in all trinitization unions, mixed or otherwise, the parental beings are conscious of, and can communicate with, each other, and they can perform duties that neither could have previously discharged." (p. 250)

5. **PROPOSITION.** The Seven Master Spirits sanction trinitization of finaliters and Paradise-Havona personalities. Their sons become wards of the Master Architects.

   "The Seven Master Spirits have authority to sanction the trinitizing union of finaliters and Paradise-Havona personalities, and such mixed liaisons are always successful. The resultant magnificent creature-trinitized sons are representative of concepts unsuited to the comprehension of either the eternal creatures of Paradise or the time creatures of space; hence they become the wards of the Architects of the Master Universe." (p. 250)

6. **PROPOSITION.** The trinitization adventures of the central universe embrace three groups.

   "In their trinitization adventures the superb creatures of the central universe and Paradise are engaged in a threefold exploration of the Deity of the Supreme which results in the production of three orders of creature-trinitized sons:

   "1. *Ascender-trinitized Sons.* In their creative efforts the finaliters are attempting to trinitize certain conceptual realities of the Almighty Supreme which they have experientially acquired in their ascension through time and space to Paradise.

   "2. *Paradise-Havona-trinitized Sons.* The creative efforts of the Paradise Citizens and the Havoners result in the trinitization of certain high spiritual aspects of the Supreme Being which they have experientially acquired on a supersupreme background bordering on the Ultimate and the Eternal.

   "3. *Trinitized Sons of Destiny.* But when a finaliter and a Paradise-Havoner together trinitize a new creature, this conjoint effort repercusses in certain phases of the Supreme-Ultimate Mind. The resulting creature-trinitized sons are supercreational; they represent actualities of Supreme-Ultimate Deity which have not been otherwise experientially attained, and which, therefore, automatically fall within the province of the Architects of the Master Universe, custodians of those things which transcend the creational limits of the present universe age." (p. 251)

7. **Proposition.** Some trinitized sons are lacking in ascendant experience. They are fully conscious of this deficiency.

> "These twice-trinitized sons are marvelous beings, but they are neither as versatile nor dependable as their ascendant associates; they lack that tremendous and profound personal experience which the rest of the sons belonging to this group have acquired by actually climbing up to glory from the dark domains of space. We of the ascendant career love them and do all in our power to compensate their deficiencies, but they make us ever grateful for our lowly origin and our capacity for experience. Their willingness to recognize and acknowledge their deficiencies in the experiencible realities of universe ascension is transcendently beautiful and sometimes most touchingly pathetic." (p. 252)

8. **Proposition.** Trinitized sons are the very idea which achieved their trinitization.

> "As far as that particular concept is revealable to the universes, these personalities embody all of everything that any creature or Creator intelligence could possibly conceive, express, or exemplify. *They are that idea personified.*" (p. 253)

9. **Proposition.** Creature-trinitized sons live in the present universe age, but they do not grow—they are not a part of the Supreme. They belong to the next universe age.

> "Consider the status of the creature-trinitized sons: They are born and live in the present universe age; they have personalities, together with mind and spirit endowments. They have experiences and the memory thereof, but they do not *grow* as do ascenders. It is our belief and understanding that these creature-trinitized sons, while they are *in* the present universe age, are really *of* the next universe age—the age which will follow the completion of the growth of the Supreme. Hence they are not *in* the Supreme as of his present status of incompleteness and consequent growth. Thus they are nonparticipating in the experiential growth of the present universe age, being held in reserve for the next universe age." (p. 1280)

PART XI
ANGELS

Part Eleven
ANGELS

I. MINISTERING SPIRITS

1. **Proposition.** The ministering spirits of the grand universe.

    "The ministering spirits of the grand universe are classified as follows:
    1. Supernaphim.
    2. Seconaphim.
    3. Tertiaphim.
    4. Omniaphim.
    5. Seraphim.
    6. Cherubim and Sanobim.
    7. Midway Creatures."

    (p. 285)

2. **Proposition.** The differing orders of angels are variously created.

    "Together with their Infinite Mother Spirit, the Supreme Spirit groups are the immediate creators of the vast creature family of the Third Source and Center. All orders of the ministering spirits spring from this association. Primary supernaphim originate in the Infinite Spirit; secondary beings of this order are created by the Master Spirits; tertiary supernaphim by the Seven Spirits of the Circuits. The Reflective Spirits, collectively, are the mothermakers of a marvelous order of the angelic hosts, the mighty seconaphim of the superuniverse services. A Creative Spirit is the mother of the angelic orders of a local creation; such seraphic ministers are original in each local universe, though they are fashioned after the patterns of the central universe. All these creators of ministering spirits are only indirectly assisted by the central lodgment of the Infinite Spirit, the original and eternal mother of all the angelic ministers." (p. 205)

3. **Proposition.** The angelic hosts are sustained by spiritual energy.

    "These brilliant creatures of light are sustained directly by the intake of the spiritual energy of the primary circuits of the universe. Urantia mortals must obtain light-energy through the vegetative incarnation, but the angelic hosts are encircuited; they 'have food that you know not.' They also partake of the circulating teachings of the marvelous Trinity Teacher Sons; they have a reception of knowledge and an intake of wisdom much resembling their technique of assimilating the life energies." (p. 286)

4. **Proposition.** There are three groups of the superuniverse ministering spirits.

> "As presented in these narratives, the ministering spirits of the superuniverses embrace the following three orders:
> 1. The Seconaphim.
> 2. The Tertiaphim.
> 3. The Omniaphim."
>
> (p. 306)

5. **Proposition.** Omniaphim are created by the Infinite Spirit and the Seven Supreme Executives and they are exclusive servants of the Supreme Executives.

> "Omniaphim are created by the Infinite Spirit in liaison with the Seven Supreme Executives, and they are the exclusive servants and messengers of these same Supreme Executives. Omniaphim are of grand universe assignment, and in Orvonton their corps maintains headquarters in the northerly parts of Uversa, where they reside as a special courtesy colony. They are not of registry on Uversa, nor are they attached to our administration. Neither are they directly concerned with the ascendant scheme of mortal progression." (p. 307)

II. PRIMARY SUPERNAPHIM

1. **Proposition.** Supernaphim are the ministering spirits of Paradise; they are the highest order of angels.

> "Supernaphim are the ministering spirits of Paradise and the central universe; they are the highest order of the lowest group of the children of the Infinite Spirit—the angelic hosts. Such ministering spirits are to be encountered from the Isle of Paradise to the worlds of time and space. No major part of the organized and inhabited creation is without their services." (p. 285)

2. **Proposition.** Supernaphim minister to all who live in Havona and on Paradise.

> "The supernaphim are the skilled ministers to all types of beings who sojourn on Paradise and in the central universe. These high angels are created in three major orders: primary, secondary, and tertiary." (p. 286)

3. **Proposition.** Primary supernaphim are children of the Conjoint Actor.

> "*Primary supernaphim* are the exclusive offspring of the Conjoint Creator. They divide their ministry about equally between certain groups of the Paradise Citizens and the ever-enlarging corps

of ascendant pilgrims. These angels of the eternal Isle are highly efficacious in furthering the essential training of both groups of Paradise dwellers." (p. 287)

4. **PROPOSITION.** Primary supernaphim have served on Paradise from eternity in seven groups.

"From eternity the primary supernaphim have served on the Isle of Light and have gone forth on missions of leadership to the worlds of space, but they have functioned as now classified only since the arrival on Paradise of the Havona pilgrims of time. These high angels now minister chiefly in the following seven orders of service:
1. Conductors of Worship.
2. Masters of Philosophy.
3. Custodians of Knowledge.
4. Directors of Conduct.
5. Interpreters of Ethics.
6. Chiefs of Assignment.
7. Instigators of Rest."
(p. 298)

III. SECONDARY SUPERNAPHIM

1. **PROPOSITION.** Secondary supernaphim function on the seven circuits of Havona—serving both ascending and descending pilgrims.

"The secondary supernaphim are ministers to the seven planetary circuits of the central universe. Part are devoted to the service of the pilgrims of time, and one half of the entire order is assigned to the training of the Paradise pilgrims of eternity. These Paradise Citizens, in their pilgrimage through the Havona circuits, are also attended by volunteers from the Mortal Finality Corps, an arrangement that has prevailed since the completion of the first finaliter group.

"According to their periodic assignment to the ministry of the ascending pilgrims, secondary supernaphim work in the following seven groups:
1. Pilgrim Helpers.
2. Supremacy Guides.
3. Trinity Guides.
4. Son Finders.
5. Father Guides.
6. Counselors and Advisers.
7. Complements of Rest."
(p. 289)

2. **PROPOSITION.** Graduate Guides and associated servitals minister to pilgrims on all the Havona circuits.

> "When an ascendant soul actually starts for Paradise, he is accompanied only by the transit trio: the superaphic circle associate, the Graduate Guide, and the ever-present servital associate of the latter. These excursions from the Havona circles to Paradise are trial trips; the ascenders are not yet of Paradise status." (p. 293)

3. **PROPOSITION.** The complements of rest accompany the sleeping pilgrims on their last sleep extending from time to eternity.

> "And now, at the culmination of the Havona career, as you mortals go to sleep on the pilot world of the inner circuit, you go not alone to your rest as you did on the worlds of your origin when you closed your eyes in the natural sleep of mortal death, nor as you did when you entered the long transit trance preparatory for the journey to Havona. Now, as you prepare for the attainment rest, there moves over by your side your long-time associate of the first circle, the majestic complement of rest, who prepares to enter the rest as one with you, as the pledge of Havona that your transition is complete, and that you await only the final touches of perfection." (p. 297)

IV. TERTIARY SUPERNAPHIM

1. **PROPOSITION.** Tertiary supernaphim are produced by the Seven Spirits of the Circuits have been greatly increased in number since the times of Grandfanda.

> "*Tertiary supernaphim* take origin in these Seven Spirits of the Circuits. Each one of them, on the separate Havona circles, is empowered by the Infinite Spirit to create a sufficient number of high superaphic ministers of the tertiary order to meet the needs of the central universe. While the Circuit Spirits produced comparatively few of these angelic ministers prior to the arrival in Havona of the pilgrims of time, the Seven Master Spirits did not even begin the creation of secondary supernaphim until the landing of Grandfanda." (p. 287)

2. **PROPOSITION.** The tertiary supernaphim work in seven divisions.

   1. The Harmony Supervisors.
   2. The Chief Recorders.
   3. The Broadcasters.
   4. The Messengers.
   5. The Intelligence Co-ordinators.
   6. The Transport Personalities.
   7. The Reserve Corps.   *(See pages 288-89)*

V. PRIMARY SECONAPHIM

1. **Proposition.** Seconaphim are produced by the seven Reflective Spirits and reflectivity is their nature.

   "The secoraphic hosts are produced by the seven Reflective Spirits assigned to the headquarters of each superuniverse. There is a definite Paradise-responsive technique associated with the creation of these angels in groups of seven. In each seven there are always one primary, three secondary, and three tertiary seconaphim; they always personalize in this exact proportion. When seven such seconaphim are created, one, the primary, becomes attached to the service of the Ancients of Days. The three secondary angels are associated with three groups of Paradise-origin administrators in the supergovernments: the Divine Counselors, the Perfectors of Wisdom, and the Universal Censors. The three tertiary angels are attached to the ascendant trinitized associates of the superuniverse rulers: the Mighty Messengers, Those High in Authority, and Those without Name and Number.

   "These seconaphim of the superuniverses are the offspring of the Reflective Spirits, and therefore reflectivity is inherent in their nature." (p. 307)

2. **Proposition.** Primary seconaphim are living mirrors. The Ancients of Days can instantly look both ways, hear both ways, and know both ways.

   "The primary secondaphim, of assignment to the Ancients of Days, are living mirrors in the service of these triune rulers. Think what it means in the economy of a superuniverse to be able to turn, as it were, to a living mirror and therein to see and therewith to hear the certain responses of another being a thousand or a hundred thousand light-years distant and to do all this instantly and unerringly. Records are essential to the conduct of the universes, broadcasts are serviceable, the work of the Solitary and other messengers is very helpful, but the Ancients of Days from their position midway between the inhabited worlds and Paradise—between man and God—can instantly look both ways, hear both ways, and know both ways." (p. 307)

PART XI — ANGELS

3. **PROPOSITION.** These angels function in seven grand divisions:

   1. The Voice of the Conjoint Actor.
   2. The Voice of the Seven Master Spirits.
   3. The Voice of the Creator Sons.
   4. The Voice of the Angelic Hosts.
   5. Broadcast Receivers.
   6. Transport Personalities.
   7. The Reserve Corps.

   See pages 308-310

VI. SECONDARY SECONAPHIM

1. **PROPOSITION.** Secondary seconaphim are no less reflective and are assigned to the associates of the Ancients of Days.

   "Seconaphim of the secondary order are no less reflective than their primary fellows. Being classed as primary, secondary, and tertiary does not indicate a differential of status or function in the case of seconaphim; it merely denotes orders of procedure. Identical qualities are exhibited by all three groups in their activities.
   "The seven reflective types of secondary seconaphim are assigned to the services of the co-ordinate Trinity-origin associates of the Ancients of Days as follows:
   "To the Perfectors of Wisdom—the Voices of Wisdom, the Souls of Philosophy, and the Unions of Souls.
   "To the Divine Counselors—The Hearts of Counsel, the Joys of Existence, and the Satisfactions of Service.
   "To the Universal Censors—the Discerners of Spirits.
   "Like the primary order, this group is created serially; that is, the first-born was a Voice of Wisdom, and the seventh thereafter was similar, and so with the six other types of these reflective angels."
   (p. 310)

2. **PROPOSITION.** These seconaphim serve in seven groups.

   1. The Voice of Wisdom.
   2. The Soul of Philosophy.
   3. The Union of Souls.
   4. The Heart of Counsel.
   5. The Joy of Existence.
   6. The Satisfaction of Service.
   7. The Discerner of Spirits.

   (See pages 310-313)

VII. TERTIARY SECONAPHIM

1. **Proposition.** All tertiary seconaphim are assigned to the Trinitized Sons of Attainment. There are seven types:
    1. Significance of Origins.
    2. Memory of Mercy.
    3. Import of Time.
    4. Solemnity of Trust.
    5. Sanctity of Service.
    6 and 7. The Secret of Greatness and the Soul of Goodness.

    "In the same manner as their fellows, these angels are created serially and in seven reflective types, but these types are not assigned individually to the separate services of the superuniverse administrators. All tertiary seconaphim are collectively assigned to the Trinitized Sons of Attainment, and these ascendant sons use them interchangeably; that is, the Mighty Messengers can and do utilize any of the tertiary types, and so do their co-ordinates, Those High in Authority and Those without Name and Number." (p. 313)

    (See pages 314-17)

VIII. MINISTERING SPIRITS OF THE LOCAL UNIVERSE

1. **Proposition.** Angels possess automatic powers of knowing things.

    "While in personal status angels are not so far removed from human beings, in certain functional performances seraphim far transcend them. They possess many powers far beyond human comprehension. For example: You have been told that the 'very hairs of your head are numbered,' and it is true they are, but a seraphim does not spend her time counting them and keeping the number corrected up to date. Angels possess inherent and automatic (that is, automatic as far as you could perceive) powers of knowing such things; you would truly regard a seraphim as a mathematical prodigy. Therefore, numerous duties which would be tremendous tasks for mortals are performed with exceeding ease by seraphim." (p. 419)

2. **Proposition.** Angels are not objects of worship.

    "You do well to love them, but you should not adore them; angels are not objects of worship. The great seraphim, Loyalatia, when your seer 'fell down to worship before the feet of the angel,' said: 'See that you do it not; I am a fellow servant with you and with your races, who are all enjoined to worship God.'" (p. 419)

3. **Proposition.** Strictly speaking, "angels" are limited to the designation of the offspring of the Universe Mother Spirit.

> "Numerous orders of spirit beings function throughout the domains of the local universe that are unrevealed to mortals because they are in no manner connected with the evolutionary plan of Paradise ascension. In this paper the word "angel" is purposely limited to the designation of those seraphic and associated offspring of the Universe Mother Spirit who are so largely concerned with the operation of the plans of mortal survival." (p. 420)

IX. SERAPHIM

1. **Proposition.** The Universe Mother Spirit creates many and diverse orders of seraphim.

> "As far as we are cognizant, the Infinite Spirit, as personalized on the local universe headquarters, intends to produce uniformly perfect seraphim, but for some unknown reason these seraphic offspring are very diverse. This diversity may be a result of the unknown interposition of evolving experiential Deity; if so, we cannot prove it. But we do observe that, when seraphim have been subjected to educational tests and training discipline, they unfailingly and distinctly classify into the following seven groups:
>
>   1. Supreme Seraphim.
>   2. Superior Seraphim.
>   3. Supervisor Seraphim.
>   4. Administrator Seraphim.
>   5. Planetary Helpers.
>   6. Transition Ministers.
>   7. Seraphim of the Future.
>
> "To say that any one seraphim is inferior to an angel of any other group would hardly be true. Nevertheless every angel is at first service-limited to the group of original and inherent classification. My seraphic associate in the preparation of this statement, Manotia, is a supreme seraphim and one time functioned only as a supreme seraphim. By application and devoted service she has, one by one, achieved all seven of the seraphic services, having functioned in well-nigh every avenue of activity open to a seraphim, and now holds the commission of associate chief of seraphim on Urantia." (p. 426)

2. **Proposition.** How the idea that angels have wings may have originated.

   "The erroneous idea that angels possess wings is not wholly due to olden notions that they must have wings to fly through the air. Human beings have sometimes been permitted to observe seraphim that were being prepared for transport service, and the traditions of these experiences have largely determined the Urantian concept of angels. In observing a transport seraphim being made ready to receive a passenger for interplanetary transit, there may be seen what are apparently double sets of wings extending from the head to the foot of the angel. In reality these wings are energy insulators—friction shields." (p. 438)

3. **Proposition.** Seraphim may be elevated to numerous advanced positions.

   "Seraphim are of origin in the local universes, and in these very realms of their nativity some achieve service destiny. With the help and counsel of the senior archangels some seraphim may be elevated to the exalted duties of Brilliant Evening Stars, while others attain the status and service of the unrevealed co-ordinates of the Evening Stars." (p. 440)

4. **Proposition.** Seraphim are the most nearly standardized type of being in the superuniverses.

   "The seraphim are all fairly uniform in design. From universe to universe, throughout all seven of the superuniverses, they show a minimum of variation; they are the most nearly standard of all spirit types of personal beings. Their various orders constitute the corps of the skilled and common ministers of the local creations." (p. 418)

5. **Proposition.** The Universe Mother Spirit creates seraphim—41,472 at a time.

   "Seraphim are created by the Universe Mother Spirit and have been projected in unit formation—41,472 at a time—ever since the creation of the 'pattern angels' and certain angelic archetypes in the early times of Nebadon. The Creator Son and the universe representation of the Infinite Spirit collaborate in the creation of a large number of Sons and other universe personalities." (p. 418)

6. **Proposition.** Seraphim are being periodically created.

> "Seraphim are still being periodically created; the universe of Nebadon is still in the making. The Universe Mother Spirit never ceases creative activity in a growing and perfecting universe." (p. 418)

7. **Proposition.** Angels share our nonsensual emotions. They are affectionate and understand our tribulations.

> "Angels do not have material bodies, but they are definite and discrete beings; they are of spirit nature and origin. Though invisible to mortals, they perceive you as you are in the flesh without the aid of transformers or translators; they intellectually understand the mode of mortal life, and they share all of man's nonsensuous emotions and sentiments. They appreciate and greatly enjoy your efforts in music, art, and real humor. They are fully cognizant of your moral struggles and spiritual difficulties. They love human beings, and only good can result from your efforts to understand and love them.
>
> "Though seraphim are very affectionate and sympathetic beings, they are not sex-emotion creatures. They are much as you will be on the mansion worlds, where you will 'neither marry nor be given in marriage but will be as the angels of heaven.' For all who 'shall be accounted worthy to attain the mansion worlds neither marry nor are given in marriage; neither do they die any more, for they are equal to the angels.'" (p. 419)

8. **Proposition.** The ninth group of primary spheres in Salvington are the worlds of the angels.

> "The ninth group of seven primary spheres in the Salvington circuit are the worlds of the seraphim. Each of these worlds has six tributary satellites, whereon are the special schools devoted to all phases of seraphic training. While the seraphim have access to all forty-nine worlds comprising this group of Salvington spheres, they exclusively occupy only the first cluster of seven. The remaining six clusters are occupied by the six orders of angelic associates unrevealed on Urantia; each such group maintains headquarters on one of these six primary worlds and carries on specialized activities on the six tributary satellites. Each angelic order has free access to all the worlds of these seven diverse groups." (p. 420)

9. **Proposition.** Seraphim are not sex creatures—they are negative and positive.

> "Though not male and female as are the Material Sons and the mortal races, seraphim are negative and positive. In the majority of assignments it requires two angels to accomplish the task." (p. 420)

10. **Proposition.** Seraphim range the universe and superuniverse and minister to a host of spirit and material beings.

> "When once seraphim are commissioned, they may range all Nebadon, even Orvonton, on assignment. Their work in the universe is without bounds and limitations; they are closely associated with material creatures of the worlds and are ever in the service of the lower orders of spiritual personalities, making contact between these beings of the spirit world and the mortals of the material realms." (p. 421)

11. **Proposition.** Seraphim are organized for service in many groups.

> "After the second millennium of sojourn at seraphic headquarters the seraphim are organized under chiefs into groups of twelve (12 pairs, 24 seraphim), and twelve such groups constitute a company (144 pairs, 288 seraphim), which is commanded by a leader. Twelve companies under a commander constitute a battalion (1,728 pairs or 3,456 seraphim), and twelve battalions under a director equal a seraphic unit (20,736 pairs or 41,472 individuals), while twelve units, subject to the command of a supervisor, constitute a legion numbering 248,832 pairs or 497,664 individuals. Jesus alluded to such a group of angels that night in the garden of Gethsemane when he said: 'I can even now ask my Father, and he will presently give me more than twelve legions of angels.'
>
> "Twelve legions of angels comprise a host numbering 2,985,984 pairs or 5,971,968 individuals, and twelve such hosts (35,831,808 pairs or 71,663,616 individuals) make up the largest operating organization of seraphim, an angelic army. A seraphic host is commanded by an archangel or by some other personality of co-ordinate status, while the angelic armies are directed by the Brilliant Evening Stars or by other immediate lieutenants of Gabriel. And Gabriel is the 'supreme commander of the armies of heaven,' the chief executive of the Sovereign of Nebadon, 'the Lord God of hosts.'" (p. 421)

X. CHERUBIM AND SANOBIM

1. **PROPOSITION.** In origin, but not destiny, cherubim are like seraphim. They are efficient and affectionate.

   "In all essential endowments cherubim and sanobim are similar to seraphim. They have the same origin but not always the same destiny. They are wonderfully intelligent, marvelously efficient, touchingly affectionate, and almost human. They are the lowest order of angels, hence all the nearer of kin to the more progressive types of human beings on the evolutionary worlds." (p. 422)

2. **PROPOSITION.** Cherubim and sanobim are inherently associated. Cherubim are positively charged—sanobim negatively.

   "Cherubim and sanobim are inherently associated, functionally united. One is an energy positive personality; the other, energy negative. The right-hand deflector, or positively charged angel, is the cherubim—the senior or controlling personality. The left-hand deflector, or negatively charged angel, is the sanobim—the complement of being." (p. 422)

3. **PROPOSITION.** Cherubim and sanobim are near the morontia level of existence. Every fourth cherubim and sanobim are quasi-material creatures.

   "Cherubim and sanobim are by nature very near the morontia level of existence, and they prove to be most efficient in the borderland work of the physical, morontial, and spiritual domains. These children of the local universe Mother Spirit are characterized by 'fourth creatures' much as are the Havona Servitals and the conciliating commissions. Every fourth cherubim and every fourth sanobim are quasimaterial, very definitely resembling the morontia level of existence.

   "These angelic fourth creatures are of great assistance to the seraphim in the more literal phases of their universe and planetary activities. Such morontia cherubim also perform many indispensable borderline tasks on the morontia training worlds and are assigned to the service of the Morontia Companions in large numbers." (p. 422)

4. **PROPOSITION.** Cherubim and sanobim can advance in status in three ways.

   "Numerous avenues of advancing service are open to cherubim and sanobim leading to an enhancement of status, which may be still further augmented by the embrace of the Divine

Minister. There are three great classes of cherubim and sanobim with regard to evolutionary potential:

"1. *Ascension Candidates.* These beings are by nature candidates for seraphic status. Cherubim and sanobim of this order are brilliant, though not by inherent endowment equal to the seraphim; but by application and experience it is possible for them to attain full seraphic standing.

"2. *Mid-phase Cherubim.* All cherubim and sanobim are not equal in ascension potential, and these are the inherently limited beings of the angelic creations. Most of them will remain cherubim and sanobim, although the more gifted individuals may achieve limited seraphic service.

"3. *Morontia Cherubim.* These 'fourth creatures' of the angelic orders always retain their quasi-material characteristics. They will continue on as cherubim and sanobim, together with a majority of their mid-phase brethren, pending the completed factualization of the Supreme Being." (p. 423)

XI. SUPREME SERAPHIM

1. PROPOSITION. Supreme seraphim are classified as follows:
    1. Son-Spirit Ministers.
    2. Court Advisers.
    3. Universe Orientators.
    4. Teaching Counselors.
    5. Directors of Assignment.
    6. The Recorders.
    7. Unattached Ministers.

    See pages 427-29

XII. SUPERIOR SERAPHIM

1. PROPOSITION. Superior seraphim function in the seven following groups:
    1. The Intelligence Corps.
    2. The Voice of Mercy.
    3. Spirit Co-ordinators.
    4. Assistant Teachers.
    5. The Transporters.
    6. The Recorders.
    7. The Reserves.

    See pages 429-31

XIII. SUPERVISOR SERAPHIM

1. **Proposition.** Supervisor seraphim function in seven groups:
   1. Supervising Assistants.
   2. Law Forecasters.
   3. Social Architects.
   4. Ethical Sensitizers.
   5. The Transporters.
   6. The Recorders.
   7. The Reserves.

   See pages 432-33

XIV. ADMINISTRATOR SERAPHIM

1. **Proposition.** Administrator seraphim function in seven orders:
   1. Administrative Assistants.
   2. Justice Guides.
   3. Interpreters of Cosmic Citizenship.
   4. Quickeners of Morality.
   5. The Transporters.
   6. The Recorders.
   7. The Reserves.

   See pages 434-36

XV. PLANETARY HELPERS

1. **Proposition.** Planetary helpers serve in seven groups.
   1. The Voices of the Garden.
   2. The Spirits of Brotherhood.
   3. The Souls of Peace.
   4. The Spirits of Trust.
   5. The Transporters.
   6. The Recorders.
   7. The Reserves.

   See pages 437-39

XVI. TRANSITION MINISTERS

1. **Proposition.** The transition ministers function in seven groups.

   "As their name might suggest, seraphim of transitional ministry serve wherever they can contribute to creature transition from the material to the spiritual estate. These angels serve from the inhabited worlds to the system capitals, but those in Satania at

present direct their greatest efforts toward the education of the surviving mortals on the seven mansion worlds. This ministry is diversified in accordance with the following seven orders of assignment:
1. Seraphic Evangels.
2. Racial Interpreters.
3. Mind Planners.
4. Morontia Counselors.
5. Technicians.
6. Recorder-Teachers.
7. Ministering Reserves."

See page 439

XVII. GUARDIAN ANGELS

1. PROPOSITION. The teaching about guardian angels is not a myth.

   "The teaching about guardian angels is not a myth; certain groups of human beings do actually have personal angels. It was in recognition of this that Jesus, in speaking of the children of the heavenly kingdom, said: 'Take heed that you despise not one of these little ones, for I say to you, their angels do always behold the presence of the spirit of my Father.'" (p. 1241)

2. PROPOSITION. As regards assignment of guardian angels, mankind is grouped in three classes:
   a. Subnormal minded.
   b. Average minded.
   c. Supernormal minded.

   "Originally, the seraphim were definitely assigned to the separate Urantia races. But since the bestowal of Michael, they are assigned in accordance with human intelligence, spirituality, and destiny. Intellectually, mankind is divided into three classes:
   "1. The subnormal minded—those who do not exercise normal will power; those who do not make average decisions. This class embraces those who cannot comprehend God; they lack capacity for the intelligent worship of Deity. The subnormal beings of Urantia have a corps of seraphim, one company, with one battalion of cherubim, assigned to minister to them and to witness that justice and mercy are extended to them in the life struggles of the sphere.
   "2. The average, normal type of human mind. From the standpoint of seraphic ministry, most men and women are grouped in seven classes in accordance with their status in

- 322 -

making the circles of human progress and spiritual development.
"3. The supernormal minded—those of great decision and undoubted potential of spiritual achievement; men and women who enjoy more or less contact with their indwelling Adjusters; members of the various reserve corps of destiny. No matter in what circle a human happens to be, if such an individual becomes enrolled in any of the several reserve corps of destiny, right then and there, personal seraphim are assigned, and from that time until the earthly career is finished, that mortal will enjoy the continuous ministry and unceasing watchcare of a guardian angel. Also, when any human being makes *the* supreme decision, when there is a real betrothal with the Adjuster, a personal guardian is immediately assigned to that soul." (p. 1241)

3. **PROPOSITION.** Guardian angels are assigned according to the attainment of the psychic circles of mind and spirit achievement.

"In the ministry to so-called normal beings, seraphic assignments are made in accordance with the human attainment of the circles of intellectuality and spirituality. You start out in your mind of mortal investment in the seventh circle and journey inward in the task of self-understanding, self-conquest, and self-mastery; and circle by circle you advance until (if natural death does not terminate your career and transfer your struggles to the mansion worlds) you reach the first or inner circle of relative contact and communion with the indwelling Adjuster." (p. 1242)

4. **PROPOSITION.** Upon attainment of the third psychic circle, mortals are assigned personal guardians for life.

"When a mortal mind breaks through the inertia of animal legacy and attains the third circle of human intellectuality and acquired spirituality, a personal angel (in reality two) will henceforth be wholly and exclusively devoted to this ascending mortal. And thus these human souls, in addition to the ever-present and increasingly efficient indwelling Thought Adjusters, receive the undivided assistance of these personal guardians of destiny in all their efforts to finish the third circle, traverse the second, and attain the first." (p. 1242)

5. **PROPOSITION.** Group guardians are assigned in accordance with psychic circle attainment.

"Human beings in the initial or seventh circle have one guardian angel with one company of assisting cherubim assigned to the watchcare and custody of one thousand mortals. In the sixth circle, a seraphic pair with one company of cherubim is assigned to guide these ascending mortals in groups of five hundred. When the fifth circle is attained, human beings are grouped in companies of approximately one hundred, and a pair of guardian seraphim with a group of cherubim is placed in charged. Upon attainment of the fourth circle, mortal beings are assembled in groups of ten, and again charge is given to a pair of seraphim, assisted by one company of cherubim." (p. 1242)

6. **PROPOSITION.** Guardians work in groups of four—two seraphim, one cherubim, one sanobim.

> "When a seraphic pair accept guardian assignment, they serve for the remainder of the life of that human being. The complement of being (one of the two angels) becomes the recorder of the undertaking. These complemental seraphim are the recording angels of the mortals of the evolutionary worlds. The records are kept by the pair of cherubim (a cherubim and a sanobim) who are always associated with the seraphic guardians, but these records are always sponsored by one of the seraphim." (p. 1243)

7. **PROPOSITION.** Seraphic guardians correlate the manifold influences of:
   a. *The Infinite Spirit.*
   b. *Physical controllers.*
   c. *Adjutant mind-spirits*
   d. *The Holy Spirit.*

   > "More especially can and does this seraphic guardian correlate the manifold agencies and influences of the Infinite Spirit, ranging from the domains of the physical controllers and the adjutant mind-spirits up to the Holy Spirit of the Divine Minister and to the Omnipresent Spirit presence of the Paradise Third Source and Center. Having thus unified and made more personal these vast ministries of the Infinite Spirit, the seraphim then undertakes to correlate this integrated influence of the Conjoint Actor with the spirit presences of the Father and the Son." (p. 1244)

8. **PROPOSITION.** Seraphic guidance will not lead to ease but rather to rugged moral choosing and spirit progress.

   > "Seraphim function as teachers of men by guiding the footsteps of the human personality into paths of new and progressive experiences. To accept the guidance of a seraphim rarely means attaining a life of ease. In following this leading you are sure to encounter, and if you have the courage, to traverse, the rugged hills of moral choosing and spiritual progress." (p. 1245)

9. **Proposition.** Guardians and Adjusters always work in perfect harmony.

> "While there is apparently no communication between the indwelling Adjusters and the encompassing seraphim, they always seem to work in perfect harmony and exquisite accord. The guardians are most active at those times when the Adjusters are least active, but their ministry is in some manner strangely correlated. Such superb co-operation could hardly be either accidental or incidental." (p. 1245)

10. **Proposition.** Guardians, with midwayer help, can minister in material ways—but only rarely.

> "Seraphim are able to function as material ministers to human beings under certain circumstances, but their action in this capacity is very rare. They are able, with the assistance of the midway creatures and the physical controllers, to function in a wide range of activities in behalf of human beings, even to make actual contact with mankind, but such occurrences are very unusual. In most instances the circumstances of the material realm proceed unaltered by seraphic action, although occasions have arisen, involving jeopardy to vital links in the chain of human evolution, in which seraphic guardians have acted, and properly, on their own initiative." (p. 1246)

11. **Proposition.** Failure of survival after receiving a personal guardian entails that the guardian must be absolved by the archangels' tribunal.

> "In case the human soul fails of survival after having received the assignment of a personal angel, the attending seraphim must proceed to the headquarters of the local universe, there to witness to the complete records of her complement as previously reported. Next she goes before the tribunals of the archangels, to be absolved from blame in the matter of the survival failure of her subject; and then she goes back to the worlds, again to be assigned to another mortal of ascending potentiality or to some other division of seraphic ministry." (p. 1247)

12. **Proposition.** The procedure of the guardian upon the death of her human subject.

> "Having told you something of the ministry of seraphim during natural life, I will endeavor to inform you about the conduct of the guardians of destiny at the time of the mortal dissolution of their human associates. Upon your death, your records, identity specifications, and the morontia entity of the human soul—conjointly evolved by the ministry of mortal mind and the divine Adjuster—are faithfully conserved by the destiny guardian together with all other values related to your future existence, everything that constitutes you, the real you, except the identity of continuing existence represented by the departing Adjuster and the actuality of personality.
>
> "The instant the pilot light in the human mind disappears, the spirit luminosity which seraphim associate with the presence of the Adjuster, the attending angel reports in person to the commanding angels, successively, of the group, company, battalion, unit, legion, and host; and after being duly registered for the final adventure of time and space, such an angel receives certification by the planetary chief of seraphim for reporting to the Evening Star (or other lieutenant of Gabriel) in command of the seraphic army of this candidate for universe ascension. And upon being granted permission from the commander of this highest organizational unit, such a guardian of destiny proceeds to the first mansion world and there awaits the consciousizing of her former ward in the flesh." (p. 1246)

13. **Proposition.** The guardian seraphim becomes the custodian of mind patterns, memory formulas, and soul realities of survival value during transition from death to resurrection.

> "And herein is revealed the reason why the seraphic guardian eventually becomes the personal custodian of the mind patterns, memory formulas, and soul realities of the mortal survivor during that interval between physical death and morontia resurrection. None but the ministering children of the Infinite Spirit could thus function in behalf of the human creature during this phase of transition from one level of the universe to another and higher level. Even when you engage in your terminal transition slumber, when you pass from time to eternity, a high supernaphim likewise shares the transit with you as the custodian of creature identity and the surety of personal integrity." (p. 1244)

14. **Proposition.** Guardians are custodians of soul values and Adjusters identify you for repersonalization by the guardian.

> "The guardian seraphim is the custodial trustee of the survival values of mortal man's slumbering soul as the absent Adjuster *is* the identity of such an immortal universe being. When these two collaborate in the resurrection halls of mansonia in conjunction with the newly fabricated morontia form, there occurs the reassembly of the constituent factors of the personality of the mortal ascender.
> "The Adjuster will identify you; the guardian seraphim will repersonalize you and then represent you to the faithful Monitor of your earth days." (p. 1247)

15. **Proposition.** Guardians attend morontia mortals and are open companions.

> "On the morontia spheres the attending seraphim (there are two of them) are your open companions. These angels not only consort with you as you progress through the career of the transition worlds, in every way possible assisting you in the acquirement of morontia and spirit status, but they also avail themselves of the opportunity to advance by study in the extension schools for evolutionary seraphim maintained on the mansion worlds." (p. 1248)

XVIII. SERAPHIC DESTINY

1. **Proposition.** Some destiny guardians follow along with their mortal subjects. Others traverse Seraphington to the Seraphic Corps of Completion.

> "Some of the destiny guardians of attachment during the mortal career follow the course of the ascending pilgrims through Havona. The others bid their long-time mortal associates a temporary farewell, and then, while these mortals traverse the circles of the central universe, these guardians of destiny achieve the circles of Seraphington. And they will be in waiting on the shores of Paradise when their mortal associates awaken from the last transit sleep of time into the new experiences of eternity. Such ascending seraphim subsequently enter upon divergent services in the finaliter corps and in the Seraphic Corps of Completion." (p. 1248)

2. **Proposition.** The surest way of attaining Paradise is for a seraphim to become a destiny guardian.

> "For seraphim, the surest way of achieving the Paradise Deities is by successfully guiding a soul of evolutionary origin to the portals of Paradise. Therefore is the assignment of guardian of destiny the most highly prized seraphic duty." (p. 1249)

3. **Proposition.** Before becoming finaliters, seraphim are fused with a non Adjuster fragment of the Universal Father.

> "Only destiny guardians are mustered into the primary or mortal Corps of the Finality, and such pairs have engaged in the supreme adventure of identity at-oneness; the two beings have achieved spiritual bi-unification on Seraphington prior to their reception into the finaliter corps. In this experience the two angelic natures, so complemental in all universe functions; achieve ultimate spirit two-in-oneness, repercussing in a new capacity for the reception of, and fusion with, a non-Adjuster fragment of the Paradise Father. And so do some of your loving seraphic associates in time also become your finaliter associates in eternity, children of the Supreme and perfected sons of the Paradise Father." (p. 1249)

4. **Proposition.** Seraphington is the destiny sphere for all types of angels.

> "Seraphington is the destiny sphere for angels, and their attainment of this world is quite different from the experiences of the mortal pilgrims on Ascendington. Angels are not absolutely sure of their eternal future until they have attained Seraphington. No angel attaining Seraphington has ever been known to go astray; sin will never find response in the heart of a seraphim of completion." (p. 441)

5. **Proposition.** Angels of the Seraphic Corps of Completion serve hosts of high personalities on all levels of the grand universe.

> "After attainment of the Father of spirits and admission to the seraphic service of completion, angels are sometimes assigned to the ministry of worlds settled in light and life. They gain attachment to the high trinitized beings of the universes and to the exalted services of Paradise and Havona. These seraphim of the local universes have experientially compensated the differential in divinity potential formerly setting them apart from the ministering spirits of the central and superuniverses. Angels of the Seraphic Corps of Completion serve as associates of the superuniverse seconaphim and as assistants to the high

Paradise-Havona orders of supernaphim. For such angels the career of time is finished; henceforth and forever they are the servants of God, the consorts of divine personalities and the peers of the Paradise finaliters." (p. 441)

XIX. SERAPHIM OF PLANETARY SUPERVISION

1. **Proposition.** The angels of planetary supervision have much to do with the kingdoms of men on Urantia. More than half a billion pairs of angels are stationed on Urantia.

   "The Most Highs rule in the kingdoms of men through many celestial forces and agencies but chiefly through the ministry of seraphim.

   "At noon today the roll call of planetary angels, guardians, and others on Urantia was 501,234,619 pairs of seraphim. There were assigned to my command two hundred seraphic hosts—597,196,800 pairs of seraphim, or 1,194,393,600 individual angels. The registry, however, shows 1,002,469,238 individuals; it follows therefore that 191,924,362 angels were absent from this world on transport, messenger, and death duty. (On Urantia there are about the same number of cherubim as seraphim, and they are similarly organized.)

   "Seraphim and their associated cherubim have much to do with the details of the superhuman government of a planet, especially of worlds which have been isolated by rebellion. The angels, ably assisted by the midwayers, function on Urantia as the actual supermaterial ministers who execute the mandates of the resident governor general and all his associates and subordinates. Seraphim as a class are occupied with many assignments other than those of personal and group guardianship." (p. 1250)

2. **Proposition.** The angels of planetary supervision function in twelve categories.
   1. The epochal angels.
   2. The progress angels.
   3. The reglious guardians.
   4. The angels of nation life.
   5. The angels of the races.
   6. The angels of the future.
   7. The angels of enlightenment.
   8. The angels of health.
   9. The home seraphim.
   10. The angels of industry.

11. The angels of diversion.
12. The angels of superhuman ministry.

See pages 1254-56

THE BIBLE

"Do you think that I cannot appeal to my Father, and he will at once send me more than twelve legions of angels?" **Matt. 26:53**

"Truly, truly, I say to you, you will see heaven opened, and the angels of God ascending and descending upon the Son of Man." **John 1:51**

"Are they not all ministering spirits sent forth to serve, for the sake of those who are to obtain salvation?" **Heb. 1:14**

For he will give his angels charge of you to guard you in all your ways." **Ps. 91:11**

"See to it that you do not despise one of these little ones; for I tell you that in heaven their angels always behold the face of my Father who is in heaven." **Matt. 18:10**

"And he will send out his angels with a loud trumpet call, and they will gather his elect from the four winds, from one end of heaven to the other." **Matt. 24:31**

PART XII
THE CREATOR SONS

Part Twelve
THE CREATOR SONS

I. INTRODUCTION

1. **PROPOSITION.** Power directors precede Creator Sons in the work of universe organization. Later, the Michaels establish the inhabited worlds.

   "The Creator Sons are preceded in universe organization by the power directors and other beings originating in the Third Source and Center. From the energies of space, thus previously organized, Michael, your Creator Son, established the inhabited realms of the universe of Nebadon and ever since has been painstakingly devoted to their administration. From pre-existent energy these divine Sons materialize visible matter, project living creatures, and with the co-operation of the universe presence of the Infinite Spirit, create a diverse retinue of spirit personalities." (p. 358)

2. **PROPOSITION.** These Creator Michaels, when settled in supreme authority, are known as Master Michaels.

   "These primary Paradise Sons are personalized as Michaels. As they go forth from Paradise to found their universes, they are known as Creator Michaels. When settled in supreme authority, they are called Master Michaels. Sometimes we refer to the sovereign of your universe of Nebadon as Christ Michael. Always and forever do they reign after the 'order of Michael,' that being the designation of the first Son of their order and nature." (p. 234)

3. **PROPOSITION.** There are more than seven hundred thousand Creator Sons in existence; there are just seven hundred thousand Unions of Days.

   "I do not know the exact number of Creator Sons in existence, but I have good reasons for believing that there are more than seven hundred thousand. Now, we know that there are exactly seven hundred thousand Unions of Days and no more are being created. We also observe that the ordained plans of the present universe age seem to indicate that one Union of Days is to be stationed in each local universe as the counseling ambassador of the Trinity. We note further that the constantly increasing number of Creator Sons already exceeds the stationary number of the Unions of Days. But concerning the destiny of the Michaels beyond seven hundred thousand, we have never been informed." (p. 235)

II. ORIGIN AND NATURE OF CREATOR SONS

1. **PROPOSITION.** The Creator Son of Nebadon is No. 611,121 of the Michael order. He is the "only-begotten Son" of this universal concept of divinity and infinity.

   "Our Creator Son is the personification of the 611,121st original concept of infinite identity of simultaneous origin in the Universal Father and the Eternal Son. The Michael of Nebadon is the 'only-begotten Son' personalizing this 611,121st universal concept of divinity and infinity. His headquarters is in the threefold mansion of light on Salvington. And this dwelling is so ordered because Michael has experienced the living of all three phases of intelligent creature existence: spiritual, morontial, and material. Because of the name associated with his seventh and final bestowal on Urantia, he is sometimes spoken of as Christ Michael." (p. 366)

2. **PROPOSITION.** The Universal Father and the Eternal Son create the Michaels. Each Son is unique both in nature and personality.

   "The Creator Sons are the makers and rulers of the local universes of time and space. These universe creators and sovereigns are of dual origin, embodying the characteristics of God the Father and God the Son. But each Creator Son is different from every other; each is unique in nature as well as in personality; each is the 'onlybegotten Son' of the perfect deity ideal of his origin." (p. 234)

3. **PROPOSITION.** Some Creator Sons are more like the Father—some more like the Son. Michael of Nebadon resembles the Mother Son.

   "Some Creator Sons appear to be more like God the Father; others more like God the Son. For example: The trend of administration in the universe of Nebadon suggests that its Creator and ruling Son is one whose nature and character more resemble that of the Eternal Mother Son." (p. 235)

4. **PROPOSITION.** Creator Sons are unique—the unqualified, finished, and final expression of the concept of their origin.

   "Each Creator Son is the only-begotten and only-begettable offspring of the perfect union of the original concepts of the two infinite and eternal and perfect minds of the ever-existent Creators of the universe of universes. There never can be another such Son because each Creator Son is the unqualified, finished, and final expression and embodiment of all of every phase of every feature of every possibility of every divine reality that could, throughout all eternity, ever be found in, expressed by, or evolved from, those divine creative potentials which united to bring this Michael Son into existence. Each Creator Son is the absolute of the united deity concepts which constitute his divine origin." (p. 235)

5. **Proposition.** When the concept of absolute spiritual ideation in the Eternal Son encounters an absolute personality concept in the Universal Father—an original Creator Son is produced.

"When the fullness of absolute spiritual ideation in the Eternal Son encounters the fullness of absolute personality concept in the Universal Father, when such a creative union is finally and fully attained, when such absolute identity of spirit and such infinite oneness of personality concept occur, then, right then and there, without the loss of anything of personality or prerogative by either of the infinite Deities, there flashes into full-fledged being a new and original Creator Son, the only-begotten Son of the perfect ideal and the powerful idea whose union produces this new creator personality of power and perfection." (p. 234)

6. **Proposition.** Creator Sons are jointly produced by the Father and the Son projecting a new, original, identical, unique, and absolute personal concept.

"Every time the Universal Father and the Eternal Son jointly project a new, original, identical, unique, and absolute personal thought, that very instant this creative idea is perfectly and finally personalized in the being and personality of a new and original *Creator Son*. In spirit nature, divine wisdom, and co-ordinate creative power, these Creator Sons are potentially equal with God the Father and God the Son." (p. 88)

7. **Proposition.** Creator Sons do not encompass all of the unqualified potentials of the universal absoluteness of the infinite nature of the First Source and Center, but the Father is in every way divinely present in these Sons.

"The natures of the Paradise Creator Sons do not encompass all the unqualified potentials of the universal absoluteness of the infinite nature of the First Great Source and Center, but the Universal Father is in every way *divinely* present in the Creator Sons. The Father and his Sons are one. These Paradise Sons of the order of Michael are perfect personalities, even the pattern for all local universe personality from that of the Bright and Morning Star down to the lowest human creature of progressing animal evolution." (p. 28)

8. **Proposition.** The Creator Sons possess spiritual drawing power. They also embody spirit reality which they can bestow upon others—the Spirit of Truth.

> "The Creator Sons seem to possess a spiritual endowment centering in their persons, which they control and which they can bestow, as did your own Creator Son when he poured out his spirit upon all mortal flesh on Urantia. Each Creator Son is endowed with this spiritual drawing power in his own realm; he is personally conscious of every act and emotion of every descending Son of God serving in his domain." (p. 224)

III. CREATORS OF LOCAL UNIVERSES

1. **Proposition.** The Michaels, before entering upon their creator adventures, are subjected to training on Paradise and in Havona.

> "The Paradise Sons of the primary order are the designers, creators, builders, and administrators of their respective domains, the local universes of time and space, the basic creative units of the seven evolutionary superuniverses.......And prior to all this, the Michael Son will have completed his long and unique experience of Paradise observation and Havona training." (p. 235)

2. **Proposition.** Each Creator Son is associated with a Creative Daughter of the Infinite Spirit — the Divine Minister.

> "Therefore is each Creator Son accompanied by a Creative Daughter of the Infinite Spirit, that being who is destined to become the Divine Minister, the Mother Spirit of the new local universe." (p. 236)

3. **Proposition.** The Creator Sons suffer three limitations of power and authority.

> "Among these limitations to the otherwise all-powerful creator prerogatives of a local universe Father are the following:
>
> "1. *Energy-matter* is dominated by the Infinite Spirit. Before any new forms of things, great or small, may be created, before any new transformations of energy-matter may be attempted, a Creator Son must secure the consent and working co-operation of the Infinite Spirit.
>
> "2. *Creature designs and types* are controlled by the Eternal Son. Before a Creator Son may engage in the creation of any new type of being, any new design of creature, he must secure the consent of the Eternal and Original Mother Son.

"3. *Personality* is designed and bestowed by the Universal Father. "The types and patterns of *mind* are determined by the precreature factors of being. After these have been associated to constitute a creature (personal or otherwise), mind is the endowment of the Third Source and Center, the universal source of mind ministry to all beings below the level of Paradise Creators." (p. 236)

4. **Proposition.** The first creative act of Michael in association with the Creative Spirit was the production of Gabriel.

"Presently, the physical plan of a universe is completed, and the Creator Son, in association with the Creative Spirit, projects his plan of life creation; whereupon does this representation of the Infinite Spirit begin her universe function as a distinct creative personality. When this first creative act is formulated and executed, there springs into being the Bright and Morning Star, the personification of this initial creative concept of identity and ideal of divinity. This is the chief executive of the universe, the personal associate of the Creator Son, one like him in all aspects of character, though markedly limited in the attributes of divinity." (p. 359)

5. **Proposition.** The local universe of Nebadon has 3,840,101 inhabited worlds. The local system of Satania has 619 inhabited worlds.

"The organization of planetary abodes is still progressing in Nebadon, for this universe is, indeed, a young cluster in the starry and planetary realms of Orvonton. At the last registry there were 3,840,101 inhabited planets in Nebadon, and Satania, the local system of your world, is fairly typical of other systems. "Satania is not a uniform physical system, a single astronomic unit or organization. Its 619 inhabited worlds are located in over five hundred different physical systems. Only five have more than two inhabited worlds, and of these only one has four peopled planets, while there are forty-six having two inhabited worlds." (p. 359)

6. **Proposition.** In the superuniverse, one half of the nature of its beings are quite alike, being derived from the uniform Creative Mother Spirits. The other half are diverse, being derived from the unique Creator Sons.

"Within any superuniverse, one half of their inherent attributes are quite alike, being derived from the uniform Creative Spirits; the other half vary, being derived from the diversified Creator Sons. But such diversity does not characterize those creatures of sole origin in the Creative Spirit nor those imported beings who are native to the central or superuniverses." (p. 236)

7. **Proposition.** When absent from universe headquarters, the Creator Son invests the Mother Spirit with overcontrol of many activities.

> "During these absences a Creator Son is able to invest the associated Mother Spirit with the overcontrol of his spiritual presence on the inhabited worlds and in the hearts of his mortal children. And the Mother Spirit of a local universe remains always at its headquarters, extending her fostering care and spiritual ministry to the uttermost parts of such an evolutionary domain." (p. 237)

8. **Proposition.** Creator Sons enjoy the co-operation of the creative agencies of the Third Source and Center.

> "The Creator Sons go out from Paradise into the universes of time and, with the co-operation of the controlling and creative agencies of the Third Source and Center, complete the organization of the local universes of progressive evolution." (p. 88)

9. **Proposition.** Creator Sons are transformative creators in the cosmic sense. They effect transmutations of potentials into experiential actuals.

> "*Creation and evolution of universe actuals.* It is upon a cosmos impregnated by the capacity-producing presence of the Ultimacy of Deity that the Supreme Creators operate to effect the time transmutations of matured potentials into experiential actuals. Within the master universe all actualization of potential reality is limited by ultimate capacity for development and is time-space conditioned in the final stages of emergence. The Creator Sons going out from Paradise are, in actuality, *transformative* creators in the cosmic sense. But this in no manner invalidates man's concept of them as creators; from the finite viewpoint they certainly can and do create." (p. 1298)

IV. LOCAL UNIVERSE SOVEREIGNTY

1. **Proposition.** A Creator Son is given the range of his universe by the Paradise Trinity with confirmation by the Master Spirit of supervision.

> "A Creator Son is given the range of a universe by the consent of the Paradise Trinity and with the confirmation of the supervising Master Spirit of the superuniverse concerned. Such action constitutes title of physical possession, a cosmic leasehold. But the elevation of a Michael Son from this initial and self-limited stage of rulership to the experiential supremacy of self-earned sovereignty comes as a result of his own personal experiences in the work of universe creation and incarnated bestowal. Until the achievement of bestowal-earned sovereignty, he rules as vicegerent of the Universal Father." (p. 237)

2. **Proposition.** In accepting vicegerent sovereignty, a Creator Son takes a Trinity oath not to assume complete sovereignty until the completion of his bestowal experience.

   "In accepting the initial vicegerent sovereignty of a projected local universe, a Creator Michael takes an oath to the Trinity not to assume supreme sovereignty until the seven creature bestowals have been completed and certified by the superuniverse rulers. But if a Michael Son could not, at will, assert such unearned sovereignty, there would be no meaning in taking an oath not to do so." (p. 238)

3. **Proposition.** If a Creator Son should assert full sovereignty before the completion of his bestowals, then would the Union of Days withdraw.

   "A Creator Son could assert full sovereignty over his personal creation at any time, but he wisely chooses not to. If, prior to passing through the creature bestowals, he assumed an unearned supreme sovereignty, the Paradise personalities resident in his local universe would withdraw. But this has never happened throughout all the creations of time and space." (p. 237)

4. **Proposition.** All Micheals prefer to earn their sovereignty—no one is known to have asserted it.

   "The fact of creatorship implies the fullness of sovereignty, but the Michaels choose to experientially *earn* it, thereby retaining the full co-operation of all Paradise personalities attached to the local universe administration. We know of no Michael who ever did otherwise; but they all could, they are truly freewill Sons." (p. 237)

5. **Proposition.** Every Creator Son must bestow himself in the likeness of his own creatures as a part of the price of his supreme sovreignty.

   "The technique of obtaining supreme sovereignty over a local universe involves the following seven experiential steps:
   "1. Experientially to penetrate seven creature levels of being through the technique of incarnated bestowal in the very likeness of the creatures on the level concerned.
   "2. To make an experiential consecration to each phase of the sevenfold will of Paradise Deity as it is personified in the Seven Master Spirits.
   "3. To traverse each of the seven experiences on the creature levels simultaneously with the execution of one of the seven consecrations to the will of Paradise Deity.

"4. On each creature level, experientially to portray the acme of creature life to Paradise Deity and to all universe intelligences.

"5. On each creature level, experientially to reveal one phase of the sevenfold will of Deity to the bestowal level and to all the universe.

"6. Experientially to unify the sevenfold creature experience with the sevenfold experience of consecration to the revelation of the nature and will of Deity.

"7. To achieve new and higher relationship with the Supreme Being. The repercussion of the totality of this Creator-creature experience augments the superuniverse reality of God the Supreme and the time-space sovereignty of the Almighty Supreme and factualizes the supreme local universe sovereignty of a Paradise Michael." (pp. 238-39)

7. **Proposition.** The sovereignty of a Creator Son passes through six to seven stages.

"The sovereignty of a Creator Son in a local universe passes through six, perhaps seven, stages of experiential manifestation. These appear in the following order:

"1. Initial vicegerent sovereignty—the solitary provisional authority exercised by a Creator Son before the acquirement of personal qualities by the associated Creative Spirit.

"2. Conjoint vicegerent sovereignty—the joint rule of the Paradise pair subsequent to the personality achievement of the Universe Mother Spirit.

"3. Augmenting vicegerent sovereignty—the advancing authority of a Creator Son during the period of his seven creature bestowals.

"4. Supreme sovereignty—the settled authority following the completion of the seventh bestowal. In Nebadon, supreme sovereignty dates from the completion of Michael's bestowal on Urantia. It has existed just slightly over nineteen hundred years of your planetary time.

"5. Augmenting supreme sovereignty—the advanced relationship growing out of the settling of a majority of the creature domains in light and life. This stage pertains to the unachieved future of your local universe.

"6. Trinitarian sovereignty—exercised subsequent to the settling of the entire local universe in light and life.

"7. Unrevealed sovereignty—the unknown relationships of a future universe age." (p. 238)

8. **Proposition.** Upon attaining supreme sovereignty of the local universe, a Creator Son gives up the right to create any entirely new types of creatures.

> "With the achievement of supreme local universe sovereignty, there passes from a Michael Son the power and opportunity to create entirely new types of creature beings during the present universe age. But a Master Son's loss of power to originate entirely new orders of beings in no way interferes with the work of life elaboration already established and in process of unfoldment; this vast program of universe evolution goes on without interruption or curtailment." (p. 240)

9. **Proposition.** The subordination of the local universe Creative Spirit to the Creator Son constitutes these Master Sons the repository of the manifestable divinity of the Father, Son, and Spirit.

> "This subordination of the Divine Ministers to the Creator Sons of the local universes constitutes these Master Sons the personal repositories of the finitely manifestable divinity of the Father, Son, and Spirit, while the creature-bestowal experiences of the Michaels qualify them to portray the experiential divinity of the Supreme Being. No other beings in the universes have thus personally exhausted the potentials of present finite experience, and no other beings in the universes possess such qualifications for solitary sovereignty." (p. 367)

10. **Proposition.** Completed sovereignty ends agelong uncertainty. That which cannot be co-ordinated with cosmic reality will eventually be destroyed.

> "The elevation of a sevenfold bestowal Son to the unquestioned sovereignty of his universe means the beginning of the end of agelong uncertainty and relative confusion. Subsequent to this event, that which cannot be sometime spiritualized will eventually be disorganized; that which cannot be sometime co-ordinated with cosmic reality will eventually be destroyed." (p. 241)

11. **Proposition.** When mercy is exhausted, justice will prevail. What mercy cannot rehabilitate justice will annihilate.

> "When the provisions of endless mercy and nameless patience have been exhausted in an effort to win the loyalty and devotion of the will creatures of the realms, justice and righteousness will prevail. That which mercy cannot rehabilitate justice will eventually annihilate." (p. 241)

12. **Proposition.** While Michael of Nebadon is not a member of the Paradise Trinity, he possesses all of the attributes that the Eternal Son would wield if functioning on Salvington. Michaels are the most versatile and powerful of all divine beings functioning in the evolutionary universes.

> "Our Creator Son is not the Eternal Son, the existential Paradise associate of the Universal Father and the Infinite Spirit. Michael of Nebadon is not a member of the Paradise Trinity. Nevertheless our Master Son possesses in his realm all of the divine attributes and powers that the Eternal Son himself would manifest were he actually to be present on Salvington and functioning in Nebadon. Michael possesses even additional power and authority, for he not only personifies the Eternal Son but also fully represents and actually embodies the personality presence of the Universal Father to and in this local universe. He even represents the Father-Son. These relationships constitute a Creator Son the most powerful, versatile, and influential of all divine beings who are capable of direct administration of evolutionary universes and of personality contact with immature creature beings." (p. 366)

13. **Proposition.** The Creator Son administers the affairs of a universe just as efficiently as would both the Universal Father and the Eternal Son.

> "In the person of the Creator Son we have a ruler and divine parent who is just as mighty, efficient, and beneficent as would be the Universal Father and the Eternal Son if both were present on Salvington and engaged in the administration of the affairs of the universe of Nebadon." (p. 367)

V. THE MICHAEL BESTOWALS

1. **Proposition.** The original Michael has not experienced incarnation, but has seven times bestowed himself upon the circuits of Havona.

> "The original or first-born Michael has never experienced incarnation as a material being, but seven times he passed through the experience of spiritual creature ascent on the seven circuits of Havona, advancing from the outer spheres to the innermost circuit of the central creation." (p. 234)

2. **Proposition.** Creator Sons are classified in accordance with the number of their bestowals.

> "There are seven groups of bestowal Creator Sons, and they are so classified in accordance with the number of times they have

bestowed themselves upon the creatures of their realms. They range from the initial experience up through five additional spheres of progressive bestowal until they attain the seventh and final episode of creature-Creator experience." (p. 239)

3. **Proposition.** Michael's bestowals have to do with the sevenfold expression of Deity will.

"Avonal bestowals are always in the likeness of mortal flesh, but the seven bestowals of a Creator Son involve his appearing on seven creature levels of being and pertain to the revelation of the seven primary expressions of the will and nature of Deity. Without exception, all Creator Sons pass through this seven times giving of themselves to their created children before they assume settled and supreme jurisdiction over the universes of their own creation." (p. 239)

4. **Proposition.** In each bestowal experience the Creator Son adds to his nature that of the creature.

"When a Creator deigns to effect a bestowal, a real and permanent change is destined to take place. True, the bestowal Son is still and none the less a Creator, but he has added to his nature the experience of a creature, which forever removes him from the divine level of a Creator Son and elevates him to the experiential plane of a Master Son, one who has fully earned the right to rule a universe and administer its worlds." (p. 240)

5. **Proposition.** Only once in the bestowal career does a Michael Son enter the incarnation as a babe born of woman.

"Only once in his sevenfold career as a bestowal Son is a Paradise Michael born of woman as you have the record of the babe of Bethlehem. Only once does he live and die as a member of the lowest order of evolutionary will creatures." (p. 239)

6. **Proposition.** Jesus of Nazareth was on his seventh bestowal when he sojourned on Urantia.

"It is of record that the divine Son of last appearance on your planet was a Paradise Creator Son who had completed six phases of his bestowal career; consequently, when he gave up the conscious grasp of the incarnated life on Urantia, he could, and did, truly say, 'it is finished'—it was literally finished. His death on Urantia completed his bestowal career; it was the last step in fulfilling the sacred oath of a Paradise Creator Son." (p. 240)

VI. DESTINY OF MASTER MICHAELS

1. **Proposition.** Michaels are the absolute of the concept of their origin. They embody phases of infinity not revealed in this finite universe age.

   "No one may with finality of authority presume to discuss either the natures or the destinies of the sevenfold Master Sovereigns of the local universes; nevertheless, we all speculate much regarding these matters. We are taught, and we believe, that each Paradise Michael is the *absolute* of the dual deity concepts of his origin; thus he embodies actual phases of the infinity of the Universal Father and the Eternal Son. The Michaels must be partial in relation to total infinity, but they are probably absolute in relation to that part of infinity concerned in their origin. But as we observe their work in the present universe age, we detect no action that is more than finite; any conjectured superfinite capacities must be self-contained and as yet unrevealed." (p. 241)

2. **Proposition.** The undisclosed powers of a Creator Son may appear in another universe age in outer space when, in liaison with the Creative Spirit, new and transcendental values may be produced.

   "It is highly probably that these undisclosed creator powers will remain self-contained throughout the present universe age. But sometime in the far-distant future, in the now mobilizing universes of outer space, we believe that the liaison between a sevenfold Master Son and a seventh-stage Creative Spirit may attain to absonite levels of service attended by the appearance of new things, meanings, and values on transcendental levels of ultimate universe significance." (p. 242)

3. **Proposition.** In outer space Creator Sons and matured Creative Spirits may unite to create a new type of superadministrator.

   "In the eternity of the past the Father and the Son found union in the unity of the expression of the Infinite Spirit. If, in the eternity of the future, the Creator Sons and the Creative Spirits of the local universes of time and space should attain creative union in the realms of outer space, what would their unity create as the combined expression of their divine natures? It may well be that we are to witness a hitherto unrevealed manifestation of Ultimate Deity, a new type of superadministrator. Such beings would embrace unique prerogatives of personality, being the union of personal Creator, impersonal Creative Spirit, mortal-creature experience, and progressive personalization of the Divine Minister.

> Such beings could be ultimate in that they would embrace personal and impersonal reality, while they would combine the experiences of Creator and creature. Whatever the attributes of such third persons of these postulated functioning trinities of the creations of outer space, they will sustain something of the same relation to their Creator Fathers and their Creative Mothers that the Infinite Spirit does to the Universal Father and the Eternal Son." (p. 1304)

4. **Proposition.** The Creator Son is truly "the way, the truth, and the life," leading from supreme divinity through ultimate absonity to eternal finality.

> "Just as the Deity of the Supreme is actualizing by virtue of experiential service, so are the Creator Sons achieving the personal realization of the Paradise-divinity potentials bound up in their unfathomable natures. When on Urantia, Christ Michael once said, 'I am the way, the truth, and the life.' And we believe that in eternity the Michaels are literally destined to be 'the way, the truth, and the life,' ever blazing the path for all universe personalities as it leads from supreme divinity through ultimate absonity to eternal deity finality." (p. 242)

VII. LOCAL UNIVERSE ORGANIZATION

1. **Proposition.** To a local universe, a Michael Son is, to all practical purposes, God. He is the personification of the Father and the Son.

> "To the children of a local universe a Michael Son is, to all practical intents and purposes, God. He is the local universe personification of the Universal Father and the Eternal Son. The Infinite Spirit maintains personal contact with the children of these realms through the Universe Spirits, the administrative and creative associates of the Paradise Creator Sons." (p. 66)

2. **Proposition.** Certain limitations are imposed upon the local universe courts.

> "As regards jurisdiction, the local universe courts are limited in the following matters:
> "1. The administration of the local universe is concerned with creation, evolution, maintenance, and ministry. The universe tribunals are, therefore, denied the right to pass upon those cases involving the question of eternal life and death. This has no reference to natural death as it obtains on Urantia, but if the

question of the right of continued existence, life eternal, comes up for adjudication, it must be referred to the tribunals of Orvonton, and if decided adversely to the individual, all sentences of extinction are carried out upon the orders, and through the agencies, of the rulers of the supergovernment.

"2. The default or defection of any of the Local Universe Sons of God which jeopardizes their status and authority as Sons is never adjudicated in the tribunals of a Son; such a misunderstanding would be immediately carried to the superuniverse courts.

"3. The question of the readmission of any constituent part of a local universe—such as a local system—to the fellowship of full spiritual status in the local creation subsequent to spiritual isolation must be concurred in by the high assembly of the superuniverse." (p. 372)

3. **Proposition.** Gabriel presides over the judicial mechanism of Nebadon. The seventy branches of the Salvington courts function in seven divisions of ten sections each.

"The entire judicial mechanism of Nebadon is under the supervision of Gabriel. The high courts, located on Salvington, are occupied with problems of general universe import and with the appellate cases coming up from the system tribunals. There are seventy branches of these universe courts, and they function in seven divisions of ten sections each. In all matters of adjudication there presides a dual magistracy consisting of one judge of perfection antecedents and one magistrate of ascendant experience." (p. 372)

VIII. MICHAEL OF NEBADON

1. **Proposition.** A Creator Son may be somewhat limited by space, but he is not limited by time within the bounds of his own universe.

"Though the spirit-gravity circuit of the Eternal Son operates independently of both time and space, all functions of the Creator Sons are not exempt from space limitations. If the transactions of the evolutionary worlds are excepted, these Michael Sons seem to be able to operate relatively independent of time. A Creator Son is not handicapped by time, but he is conditioned by space; he cannot personally be in two places at the same time. Michael of Nebadon acts timelessly within his own universe and by reflectivity practically so in the superuniverse. He communicates timelessly with the Eternal Son directly." (p. 377)

2. **PROPOSITION.** Creator Sons devote themselves to the spiritualization of their creations. They promote the Paradise plan of mortal ascension. When mortals reject the ascension plan the Ancients of Days decree their dissolution.

> "The rule of the Creator Sons in the local universes is one of creation and spiritualization. These Sons devote themselves to the effective execution of the Paradise plan of progressive mortal ascension, to the rehabilitation of rebels and wrong thinkers, but when all such loving efforts are finally and forever rejected, the final decree of dissolution is executed by forces acting under the jurisdiction of the Ancients of Days." (p. 37)

IX. THE SEVEN BESTOWALS OF MICHAEL

1. **PROPOSITION.** About one billion years ago, Michael executed the preliminaries of his first bestowal. *See page 1309.*
    1. First Bestowal: As a Melchizedek.
    2. Second Bestowal: As a Lanonandek Son.
    3. Third Bestowal: As a Material Son.
    4. Fourth Bestowal: As a seraphim.
    5. Fifth Bestowal: As a spirit ascender.
    6. Sixth Bestowal: As a morontia mortal.
    7. Seventh Bestowal: As a Urantia mortal.

    See Paper 119

PART XIII
LOCAL UNIVERSE CREATIVE SPIRIT

PART THIRTEEN
LOCAL UNIVERSE CREATIVE SPIRIT

I. PERSONALIZATION OF THE CREATIVE SPIRIT

1. **PROPOSITION.** Concomitant with the creation of a Creator Son, the Infinite Spirit individualizes a new and unique representation of himself to become the companion of the Creator Son.

    "When a Creator Son is personalized by the Universal Father and the Eternal Son, then does the Infinite Spirit individualize a new and unique representation of himself to accompany this Creator Son to the realms of space, there to be his companion, first, in physical organization and, later, in creation and ministry to the creatures of the newly projected universe." (p. 374)

2. **PROPOSITION.** Upon the completion of physical creation, the Master Spirit of the superuniverse initiates the personalization of the local universe Mother Spirit

    "...when the Deity-embraced Master Spirit emerges to the recognition of his fellows, there occurs what is known as a 'primary eruption.' This is a tremendous spiritual flash, a phenomenon clearly discernible as far away as the headquarters of the superuniverse concerned; and simultaneously with this little-understood Trinity manifestation there occurs a marked change in the nature of the creative spirit presence and power of the Infinite Spirit resident in the local universe concerned. In response to these Paradise phenomena there immediately personalizes, in the very presence of the Creator Son, a new personal representation of the Infinite Spirit. This is the Divine Minister. The individualized Creative Spirit helper of the Creator Son has become his personal creative associate, the local universe Mother Spirit." (p. 374)

3. **PROPOSITION.** During physical creation the Creative Spirit is incompletely differentiated from the Infinite Spirit, but after the divine embrace of the Master Spirit, she changes to the personal likeness of this Master Spirit.

    "The Spirit presence in the local universe during the time of purely physical creation or organization was incompletely differentiated from the spirit of the Paradise Infinite Spirit; whereas, after the reappearance of the supervising Master Spirit from the secret embrace of the Gods and following the flash of spiritual energy, the local universe manifestation of the Infinite

Spirit suddenly and completely changes to the personal likeness of that Master Spirit who was in transmuting liaison with the Infinite Spirit. The local universe Mother Spirit thus acquires a personal nature tinged by that of the Master Spirit of the superuniverse of astronomic jurisdiction." (p. 375)

4. **Proposition.** The Universe Spirit of Nebadon is of the sixth group of Supreme Spirits, No. 611,121.

"The Universe Mother Spirit of Salvington, the associate of Michael in the control and administration of Nebadon, is of the sixth group of Supreme Spirits, being the 611,121st of that order. She volunteered to accompany Michael on the occasion of his liberation from Paradise obligations and has ever since functioned with him in creating and governing his universe." (p. 368)

II. NATURE OF THE DIVINE MINISTER

1. **Proposition.** The Universe Mother Spirit possesses all of the latter, she also has complete control of mind gravity.

"From the earliest association with the Creator Son the Universe Spirit possesses all the physical-control attributes of the Infinite Spirit, including the full endowment of antigravity. Upon the attainment of personal status the Universe Spirit exerts just as full and complete control of mind gravity, in the local universe, as would the Infinite Spirit if personally present." (p. 375)

2. **Proposition.** The Creative Spirit is coresponsible with the Creator Son for the creation and fostering of their universe.

"The Creative Spirit is coresponsible with the Creator Son in producing the creatures of the worlds and never fails the Son in all efforts to uphold and conserve these creations. Life is ministered and maintained through the agency of the Creative Spirit. 'You send forth your Spirit, and they are created. You renew the face of the earth.'" (p. 376)

III. UNIVERSE SON AND CREATIVE SPIRIT

1. **Proposition.** Both the Son and the Spirit react to both physical and spiritual realities.

"A Creative Spirit reacts to both physical and spiritual realities; so does a Creator Son; and thus are they co-ordinate and associate in the administration of a local universe of time and space." (p. 374)

2. **Proposition.** While the Mother Spirit acknowledges the Son as sovereign, the Son accords the Spirit co-ordinate position and equality of authority.

> "The Master Creator Son is the personal sovereign of his universe, but in all the details of its management the Universe Spirit is codirector with the Son. While the Spirit ever acknowledges the Son as sovereign and ruler, the Son always accords the Spirit a co-ordinate position and equality of authority in all the affairs of the realm. In all his work of love and life bestowal the Creator Son is always and ever perfectly sustained and ably assisted by the all-wise and ever-faithful Universe Spirit and by all of her diversified retinue of angelic personalities. Such a Divine Minister is in reality the mother of spirits and spirit personalities, the ever-present and all-wise adviser of the Creator Son, a faithful and true manifestation of the Paradise Infinite Spirit." (p. 368)

3. **Proposition.** The Creative Spirit is limited by time; the Creator Son is not. Working together, they function independently of both time and space.

> "Only as regards the element of time is a Creative Spirit ever limited in her universe ministrations. A Creator Son acts instantaneously throughout his universe; but the Creative Spirit must reckon with time in the ministration of the universal mind except as she consciously and designedly avails herself of the personal prerogatives of the Universe Son." (p. 376)

4. **Proposition.** The Mother Spirit never leaves the universe headquarters. The Creator Son may come and go.

> "The Universe Mother Spirit, however, never leaves the local universe headquarters world. The spirit of the Creator Son may and does function independently of the personal presence of the Son, but not so with her personal spirit. The Holy Spirit of the Divine Minister would become nonfunctional if her personal presence should be removed from Salvington." (p. 378)

IV. THE MINISTRY OF THE SPIRIT

1. **Proposition.** In the universe, the Son functions as a father, the Spirit as a mother.

> "The Son functions as a father in his local universe. The Spirit, as mortal creatures would understand, enacts the role of a mother, always assisting the Son and being everlastingly indispensable to the administration of the universe." (p. 368)

2. **Proposition.** The Creative Spirit is independent of space, but not of time. She is equally and diffusely present throughout her entire local universe.

   "In personal prerogatives a Creative Spirit is wholly and entirely independent of space, but not of time. There is no specialized personal presence of such a Universe Spirit on either the constellation or system headquarters. She is equally and diffusely present throughout her entire local universe and is, therefore, just as literally and personally present on one world as on any other." (p. 376)

3. **Proposition.** The local universe has three spirit circuits.

   "There are three distinct spirit circuits in the local universe of Nebadon:
   "1. The bestowal spirit of the Creator Son, the Comforter, the Spirit of Truth.
   "2. The spirit circuit of the Divine Minister, the Holy Spirit.
   "3. The intelligence-ministry circuit, including the more or less unified activities but diverse functioning of the seven adjutant mind-spirits." (p. 377)

4. **Proposition.** The Creative Spirit functions with the Son in producing a vast array of Sons extending from Gabriel to the Material Sons.

   "In the creation of a universe of intelligent creatures the Creative Mother Spirit functions first in the sphere of universe perfection, collaborating with the Son in the production of the Bright and Morning Star. Subsequently the offspring of the Spirit increasingly approach the order of created beings on the planets, even as the Sons grade downward from the Melchizedeks to the Material Sons, who actually contact with the mortals of the realms." (p. 376)

5. **Proposition.** When Life Carriers fabricate mortal bodies the Creative Spirit contributes the "breath of life."

   "In the later evolution of mortal creatures the Life Carrier Sons provide the physical body, fabricated out of the existing organized material of the realm, while the Universe Spirit contributes the 'breath of life.'" (p. 376)

V. THE SPIRIT AS RELATED TO MAN

1. **PROPOSITION.** It is the purpose of spirit ministry to provide strength for the "inner man." Those "who are led by the spirit of God are the sons of God."

   "The purpose of all this ministration is, 'That you may be strengthened with power through His spirit in the inner man.' And all this represents but the preliminary steps to the final attainment of the perfection of faith and service, that experience wherein you shall be 'filled with all the fullness of God,' 'for all those who are led by the spirit of God are the sons of God.'" (p. 381)

2. **PROPOSITION.** The presence of the divine spirit is the "water of life" which prevents the consuming thirst of mortal discontent.

   "It is the presence of the divine Spirit, the water of life, that prevents the consuming thirst of mortal discontent and that indescribable hunger of the unspiritualized human mind. Spirit-motivated beings 'never thirst, for this spiritual water shall be in them a well of satisfaction springing up into life everlasting.'" (p. 381)

3. **PROPOSITION.** Such divinely refreshed souls are all but independent of mortal environment.

   "Such divinely watered souls are all but independent of material environment as regards the joys of living and the satisfactions of earthly existence. They are spiritually illuminated and refreshed, morally strengthened and endowed." (p. 381)

4. **PROPOSITION.** Man's power and achievement is "according to his mercy, through the renewing of the Spirit." Spiritual effort results in spiritual exhaustion. "The Spirit gives life."

   "The divine Spirit is the source of continual ministry and encouragement to the children of men. Your power and achievement is 'according to his mercy, through the renewing of the Spirit.' Spiritual life, like physical energy, is consumed. Spiritual effort results in relative spiritual exhaustion. The whole ascendant experience is real as well as spiritual; therefore, it is truly written, 'It is the Spirit that quickens.' 'The Spirit gives life.'" (p. 380)

5. **PROPOSITION.** The spirit of the Divine Minister and the Spirit of Truth work with mortals as one presence.

   "The Spirit of Truth works as one with the presence of the spirit of the Divine Minister. This dual spirit liaison hovers over the worlds, seeking to teach truth and to spiritually enlighten the minds of men, to inspire the souls of the creatures of the ascending races, and to lead the peoples dwelling on the evolutionary planets ever towards their Paradise goal of divine destiny." (p. 379)

6. **PROPOSITION.** The Spirit never drives, only leads. The domination of the Spirit is never tainted with coercion nor compromised by compulsion.

   "The Spirit never *drives*, only leads. If you are a willing learner, if you want to attain spirit levels and reach divine heights, if you sincerely desire to reach the eternal goal, then the divine Spirit will gently and lovingly lead you along the pathway of sonship and spiritual progress. Every step you take must be one of willingness, intelligent and cheerful co-operation. The domination of the Spirit is never tainted with coercion nor compromised by compulsion." (p. 381)

7. **PROPOSITION.** Theory cannot transform human character. Theoretical truth is dead unless the Spirit breathes upon the forms and formulas of righteousness.

   "The dead theory of even the highest religious doctrines is powerless to transform human character or to control mortal behavior. What the world of today needs is the truth which your teacher of old declared: 'Not in word only but also in power and in the Holy Spirit.' The seed of theoretical truth is dead, the highest moral concepts without effect, unless and until the divine Spirit breathes upon the forms of truth and quickens the formulas of righteousness." (p. 380)

8. **PROPOSITION.** Spirit domination of a human life yields the fruits of the spirit: Love, joy, peace, long-suffering, gentleness, goodness, faith, meekness, and temperance.

   "The consciousness of the spirit domination of a human life is presently attended by an increasing exhibition of the characteristics of the Spirit in the life reactions of such a spirit-led mortal, 'for the fruits of the spirit are love, joy, peace, long-suffering, gentleness, goodness, faith, meekness, and temperance.' Such spirit-guided and divinely illuminated mortals, while they yet tread the lowly paths of toil and in human faithfulness perform the duties of their earthly assignments, have already begun to discern the lights of eternal life as they glimmer on the faraway shores of another world; already have they begun to comprehend the reality of that inspiring and comforting truth, 'The kingdom of God is not meat and drink but righteousness, peace, and joy in the Holy Spirit.'" (p. 381)

9. **Proposition.** Mind, before capacity to learn from experience, is the domain of the Master Physical Controllers. Before worship and wisdom, mind is the domain of the adjutant spirits. When spiritual response is established, mind becomes encircuited with the universe Mother Spirit.

> "Living mind, prior to the appearance of capacity to learn from experience, is the ministry domain of the Master Physical Controllers. Creature mind, before acquiring the ability to recognize divinity and worship Deity, is the exclusive domain of the adjutant spirits. With the appearance of the spiritual response of the creature intellect, such created minds at once become superminded, being instantly encircuited in the spirit cycles of the local universe Mother Spirit." (p. 403)

VI. SEVEN STAGES OF DEVELOPMENT

1. **Proposition.** There are seven stages to the career of a local universe Mother Spirit:
   1. Initial Paradise Differentiation.
   2. Preliminary Creatorship Training.
   3. The Stage of Physical Creation.
   4. The Life-Creation Era.
   5. The Postbestowal Ages.
   6. The Ages of Light and Life.
   7. The Unrevealed Career.

   See pages 203-4

2. **Proposition.** After the pledge of subordination, the Creator Son constituted the Spirit coruler of the universe.

   > "After this pledge of subordination by the Creative Mother Spirit, Michael of Nebadon nobly acknowledged his eternal dependence on his Spirit companion, constituting the Spirit coruler of his universe domains and requiring all their creatures to pledge themselves in loyalty to the Spirit as they had to the Son; and there issued and went forth the final 'Proclamation of Equality.'" (p. 369)

3. **Proposition.** The postbestowal stage of the Divine Minister becomes settled and secure.

   > "Upon the completion of the Creator Son's seventh and final creature bestowal, the uncertainties of periodic isolation terminate for the Divine Minister, and the Son's universe helper

PART XIII — LOCAL UNIVERSE CREATIVE SPIRIT

becomes forever settled in surety and control. It is at the enthronement of the Creator Son as a Master Son, at the jubilee of jubilees, that the Universe Spirit, before the assembled hosts, first makes public and universal acknowledgment of subordination to the Son, pledging fidelity and obedience. This event occurred in Nebadon at the time of Michael's return to Salvington after the Urantian bestowal." (p. 368)

VII. SEVEN ADJUTANT MIND-SPIRITS

1. **PROPOSITION.** These spirits function in the human mind in accordance with its capacity of receptivity.

   The seven adjutant mind-spirits are called by names which are the equivalents of the following designations: intuition, understanding, courage, knowledge, counsel, worship, and wisdom. These mind-spirits send forth their influence into all the inhabited worlds as a differential urge, each seeking receptivity capacity for manifestation quite apart from the degree to which its fellows may find reception and opportunity for function." (p. 401)

2. **PROPOSITION.** Description of the seven adjutant spirits.

   "We are handicapped for words adequately to designate these seven adjutant mind-spirits. They are ministers of the lower levels of experiential mind, and they may be described, in the order of evolutionary attainment, as follows:

   "1. *The spirit of intuition*—quick perception, the primitive physical and inherent reflex instincts, the directional and other self-preservative endowments of all mind creations; the only one of the adjutants to function so largely in the lower orders of animal life and the only one to make extensive functional contact with the nonteachable levels of mechanical mind.

   "2. *The spirit of understanding*—the impulse of co-ordination, the spontaneous and apparently automatic association of ideas. This is the gift of the co-ordination of acquired knowledge, the phenomenon of quick reasoning, rapid judgment, and prompt decision.

   "3. *The spirit of courage*—the fidelity endowment—in personal beings, the basis of character acquirement and the intellectual root of moral stamina and spiritual bravery. When enlightened by facts and inspired by truth, this becomes the secret of the urge of evolutionary ascension by the channels of intelligent and conscientious self-direction.

"**4.** *The spirit of knowledge*—the curiosity-mother of adventure and discovery, the scientific spirit; the guide and faithful associate of the spirits of courage and counsel; the urge to direct the endowments of courage into useful and progressive paths of growth.

"**5.** *The spirit of counsel*—the social urge, the endowment of species co-operation; the ability of will creatures to harmonize with their fellows; the origin of the gregarious instinct among the more lowly creatures.

"**6.** *The spirit of worship*—the religious impulse, the first differential urge separating mind creatures into the two basic classes of mortal existence. The spirit of worship forever distinguishes the animal of its association from the soulless creatures of mind endowment. Worship is the badge of spiritual-ascension candidacy.

"**7.** *The spirit of wisdom*—the inherent tendency of all moral creatures towards orderly and progressive evolutionary advancement. This is the highest of the adjutants, the spirit co-ordinator and articulator of the work of all the others. This spirit is the secret of that inborn urge of mind creatures which initiates and maintains the practical and effective program of the ascending scale of existence; that gift of living things which accounts for their inexplicable ability to survive and, in survival, to utilize the co-ordination of all their past experience and present opportunities for the acquisition of all of everything that all of the other six mental ministers can mobilize in the mind of the organism concerned. Wisdom is the acme of intellectual performance. Wisdom is the goal of a purely mental and moral existence." (pp. 402-3)

3. **Proposition.** The adjutants operate from the Life Carrier worlds. The Life Carriers observe their function on any world and in any mind.

> "The central lodgments of the adjutant spirits on the Life Carrier headquarters world indicate to the Life Carrier supervisors the extent and quality of the mind function of the adjutants on any world and in any given living organism of intellect status." (p. 401)

PART XIV
THE POWER DIRECTORS

Part Fourteen
THE POWER DIRECTORS

I. INTRODUCTION

1. **Proposition.** In the evolutionary cosmos energy-matter is dominant except in personality, where spirit, through the mediation of mind, strives for the mastery.

   "On Paradise the three energies, physical, mindal, and spiritual, are co-ordinate. In the evolutionary cosmos energy-matter is dominant except in personality, where spirit, through the mediation of mind, is striving for the mastery." (p. 140)

2. **Proposition.** Matter is a philosophic shadow cast by mind in the presence of spirit luminosity. But this does not invalidate the reality of matter.

   "In cosmic evolution matter becomes a philosophic shadow cast by mind in the presence of spirit luminosity of divine enlightenment, but this does not invalidate the reality of matter-energy. Mind, matter, and spirit are equally real, but they are not of equal value to personality in the attainment of divinity. Consciousness of divinity is a progressive spiritual experience." (p. 140)

3. **Proposition.** Mortal mind can grasp only three of the seven levels of reality.

   "Though it is hardly possible for the mortal mind to comprehend the seven levels of relative cosmic reality, the human intellect should be able to grasp much of the meaning of three functioning levels of finite reality:

   "1. *Matter.* Organized energy which is subject to linear gravity except as it is modified by motion and conditioned by mind.
   "2. *Mind.* Organized consciousness which is not wholly subject to material gravity, and which becomes truly liberated when modified by spirit.
   "3. *Spirit.* The highest personal reality. True spirit is not subject to physical gravity but eventually becomes the motivating influence of all evolving energy systems of personality dignity." (p. 140)

4. **Proposition.** Chemical elements exhibit a sevenfold recurrence of similar chemical properties when the elements are arranged according to atomic weight.

> "This sevenfold persistence of creative constitution is exhibited in the chemical domains as a recurrence of similar physical and chemical properties in segregated periods of seven when the basic elements are arranged in the order of their atomic weights. When the Urantia chemical elements are thus arranged in a row, any given quality or property tends to recur by sevens. This periodic change by sevens recurs diminishingly and with variations throughout the entire chemical table, being most markedly observable in the earlier or lighter atomic groupings. Starting from any one element, after noting some one property, such a quality will change for six consecutive elements, but on reaching the eighth, it tends to reappear, that is, the eighth chemically active element resembles the first, the ninth the second, and so on." (p. 480)

5. **Proposition.** This phenomenon points to the sevenfold constitution of ancestral energy and is indicative of the sevenfold diversity of the creations of time and space.

> "Such a fact of the physical world unmistakably points to the sevenfold constitution of ancestral energy and is indicative of the fundamental reality of the sevenfold diversity of the creations of time and space. Man should also note that there are seven colors in the natural spectrum." (p. 480)

II. SEVEN SUPREME POWER DIRECTORS

1. **Proposition.** The Supreme Power Directors create seven groups of associates.

> "The Seven Supreme Power Directors are not able, individually, to reproduce themselves, but collectively, and in association with the Seven Master Spirits, they can and do reproduce—create—other beings like themselves. Such is the origin of the Supreme Power Centers of the grand universe, who function in the following seven groups:
> 1. Supreme Center Supervisors.
> 2. Havona Centers.
> 3. Superuniverse Centers.
> 4. Local Universe Centers.
> 5. Constellation Centers.
> 6. System Centers.
> 7. Unclassified Centers." (p. 320)

2. **Proposition.** The Power Directors have existed from the near times of eternity. With their parents, they created more than ten billion associates.

> "The Supreme Power Directors and Centers have existed from the near times of eternity, and as far as we know, no more beings of these orders have been created. The Seven Supreme Directors were personalized by the Seven Master Spirits, and then they collaborated with their parents in the production of more than ten billion associates. Before the days of the power directors the energy circuits of space outside of the central universe were under the intelligent supervision of the Master Force Organizers of Paradise." (p. 319)

3. **Proposition.** The Supreme Power Directors are the physical energy regulators of the grand universe.

> "The Seven Supreme Power Directors are the physical-energy regulators of the grand universe. Their creation by the Seven Master Spirits is the first recorded instance of the derivation of semimaterial progeny from true spirit ancestry. When the Seven Master Spirits create individually, they bring forth highly spiritual personalities on the angelic order; when they create collectively, they sometimes produce these high types of semimaterial beings. But even these quasi-physical beings would be invisible to the short-range vision of Urantia mortals." (p. 320)

4. **Proposition.** The Supreme Power Directors operate from the periphery of Paradise, their circulating presence indicating the force-focal headquarters of the Master Spirits.

> "The Seven Supreme Power Directors are stationed on peripheral Paradise, where their slowly circulating presences indicate the whereabouts of the force-focal headquarters of the Master Spirits. These power directors function singly in the power-energy regulation of the superuniverses but collectively in the administration of the central creation. They operate from Paradise but maintain themselves as effective power centers in all divisions of the grand universe." (p. 320)

5. **Proposition.** Power directors are energy catalyzers. They can organize and assemble energy.

> "These power directors themselves are energy catalyzers; that is, they cause energy to segment, organize, or assemble in unit formation by their presence. And all this implies that there must be something inherent in energy which causes it thus to function in the presence of these power entities." (p. 471)

III. SUPREME POWER CENTERS

1. **Proposition.** The power centers and controllers exert perfect control over only seven of the ten forms of energy. Both the Universal and the Unqualified Absolute may be involved in energy control.

   "The power centers and controllers exert perfect control over only seven of the ten forms of energy contained in each basic universe current; those forms which are partly or wholly exempt from their control must represent the unpredictable realms of energy manifestation dominated by the Unqualified Absolute. If they exert an influence upon the primordial forces of this Absolute, we are not cognizant of such functions, though there is some slight evidence which would warrant the opinion that certain of the physical controllers are sometimes automatically reactive to certain impulses of the Universal Absolute." (p. 324)

2. **Proposition.** Power centers and physical controllers never play. They are always on duty.

   "Having no ascendant past to revert to in memory, power centers and physical controllers never play; they are thoroughly business-like in all their actions. They are always on duty; there is no provision in the universal scheme for the interruption of the physical lines of energy; never for a fraction of a second can these beings relinquish their direct supervision of the energy circuits of time and space." (p. 323)

3. **Proposition.** Power centers work with three basic currents of ten energies each. They have nothing to do with the force actions of outer space.

   "The power centers and their subordinate controllers are assigned to the working of all of the physical energies of organized space. They work with the three basic currents of ten energies each. That is the energy charge of organized space; and organized space is their domain. The Universe Power Directors have nothing whatever to do with those tremendous actions of force which are now taking place outside the present boundaries of the seven superuniverses." (p. 323)

4. **Proposition.** Power centers can transmute the ultimaton into the circuits of the electron, but they are curtailed when energy swings into the atomic systems.

> "The power centers and their associates are much concerned in the work of transmuting the ultimaton into the circuits and revolutions of the electron. These unique beings control and compound power by their skillful manipulation of the basic units of materialized energy, the ultimatons. They are masters of energy as it circulates in this primitive state. In liaison with the physical controllers they are able to effectively control and direct energy even after it has transmuted to the electrical level, the so-called electronic stage. But their range of action is enormously curtailed when electronically organized energy swings into the whirls of the atomic systems. Upon such materialization, these energies fall under the complete grasp of the drawing power of linear gravity." (p. 473)

5. **Proposition.** The supreme power centers and Directors are intelligent and volitional. They are concerned with both physical and mindal energies.

> "These power centers together with the Supreme Power Directors are beings of high will freedom and action. They are all endowed with Third-Source personality and disclose unquestioned volitional capacity of a high order. These directing centers of the universe power system are the possessors of exquisite intelligence endowment; they are the intellect of the power system of the grand universe and the secret of the technique of the mind control of all the vast network of the far-flung functions of the Master Physical Controllers and the Morontia Power Supervisors." (p. 321)

IV. MASTER PHYSICAL CONTROLLERS

1. **Proposition.** The grand universe is kept in equilibrium by the function of the power control creatures of the God of Action.

   "The universe of universes is permeated by the power-control creatures of the Third Source and Center: physical controllers, power directors, power centers, and other representatives of the God of Action who have to do with the regulation and stabilization of physical energies. These unique creatures of physical function all possess varying attributes of power control, such as antigravity, which they utilize in their efforts to establish the physical equilibrium of the matter and energies of the grand universe." (p. 101)

2. **Proposition.** Physical controllers traverse space at velocities near those of the Solitary Messengers.

   "These beings are the mobile subordinates of the Supreme Power Centers. The physical controllers are endowed with capabilities of individuality metamorphosis of such a nature that they can engage in a remarkable variety of autotransport, being able to traverse local space at velocities approaching the flight of Solitary Messengers. But like all other space traversers they require the assistance of both their fellows and certain other types of beings in overcoming the action of gravity and the resistance of inertia in departing from a material sphere." (p. 324)

3. **Proposition.** Master Physical Controllers function throughout the grand universe; as far as the superuniverses, they are governed by the Supreme Power Directors; from there out they are directed by the Council of Equilibrium composed of Associate Master Force Organizers.

   "The Master Physical Controllers serve throughout the grand universe. They are directly governed from Paradise by the Seven Supreme Power Directors as far as the headquarters of the superuniverses; from here they are directed and distributed by the Council of Equilibrium, the high commissioners of power dispatched by the Seven Master Spirits from the personnel of the Associate Master Force Organizers. These high commissioners are empowered to interpret the readings and registrations of the master frandalanks, those living instruments which indicate the power pressure and the energy charge of an entire superuniverse." (p. 324)

THE THEOLOGY OF *THE URANTIA BOOK*

4. **PROPOSITION**. Mind can think even when deprived of all power of choice, as in lower animals and subordinate physical controllers.

> "Personality is not necessarily a concomitant of mind. Mind can think even when deprived of all power of choice as in numerous of the lower types of animals and in certain of these subordinate physical controllers. Many of these more automatic regulators of physical power are not persons in any sense of the term. They are not endowed with will and independence of decision, being wholly subservient to the mechanical perfection of design for the tasks of their allotment. Nonetheless all of them are highly intelligent beings." (p. 325)

5. **PROPOSITION**. There are seven grand divisions of the Master Physical Controllers.

> "The Master Physical Controllers are the direct offspring of the Supreme Power Centers, and their numbers include the following:
> 1. Associate Power Directors.
> 2. Mechanical Controllers.
> 3. Energy Transformers.
> 4. Energy Transmitters.
> 5. Primary Associators.
> 6. Secondary Dissociators.
> 7. The Frandalanks and Chronoldeks."

See page 324

V. MASTER FORCE ORGANIZERS

1. **PROPOSITION**. Three groups of beings have to do with force control and energy regulation.

> "Even now I am permitted fully to disclose only the last of the following three groups of living beings having to do with force control and energy regulation in the master universe:
> 1. Primary Eventuated Master Force Organizers.
> 2. Associate Transcendental Master Force Organizers.
> 3. Universe Power Directors." (p. 319)

2. **PROPOSITION**. Paradise force organizers function throughout the master universe under the supervision of the Master Architects.

> "The force organizers are resident on Paradise, but they function throughout the master universe, more particularly in the domains of unorganized space. These extraordinary beings are neither creators nor creatures, and they comprise two grand divisions of service:

- 370 -

1. Primary Eventuated Master Force Organizers.
2. Associate Transcendental Master Force Organizers.

"These two mighty orders of primordial-force manipulators work exclusively under the supervision of the Architects of the Master Universe, and at the present time they do not function extensively within the boundaries of the grand universe." (p. 329)

3. **Proposition.** Master Force Organizers can withstand temperature and other physical conditions unbearable to any other type of being.

"The Master Force Organizers withstand temperatures and function under physical conditions which would be intolerable even to the versatile power centers and physical controllers of Orvonton. The only other types of revealed beings capable of functioning in these realms of outer space are the Solitary Messengers and the Inspired Trinity Spirits." (p. 329)

VI. PARADISE FORCES AND ENERGIES

1. **Proposition.** Cosmic force comes from Paradise and circulates throughout the master universe as the force charge of pervaded space.

"The bestowal of cosmic force, the domain of cosmic gravity, is the function of the Isle of Paradise. All original force-energy proceeds from Paradise, and the matter for the making of untold universes now circulates throughout the master universe in the form of a supergravity presence which constitutes the force-charge of pervaded space." (p. 139)

2. **Proposition.** Cosmic force swings on forever around the eternal space paths.

"Whatever the transformations of force in the outlying universes, having gone out from Paradise, it journeys on subject to the never-ending, ever-present, unfailing pull of the eternal Isle, obediently and inherently swinging on forever around the eternal space paths of the universes. Physical energy is the one reality which is true and steadfast in its obedience to universal law." (p. 139)

3. **Proposition.** All energy is derived from Paradise and is inherent in the Universal Father.

"Matter—energy—for they are but diverse manifestations of the same cosmic reality, as a universe phenomenon is inherent in the Universal Father. 'In him all things consist.' Matter may appear to manifest inherent energy and to exhibit self-contained powers, but the lines of gravity involved in the energies concerned in all these physical phenomena are derived from, and are dependent on, Paradise. The ultimaton, the first measurable form of energy, has Paradise as its nucleus." (p. 467)

4. **Proposition.** There are seven grand divisions of universal energy:
   1. Space potency — ABSOLUTA.
   2. Primordial force — SEGREGATA.
   3. Emergent energies — ULTIMATA.
      a. *Puissant energy*
      b. *Gravity energy*
   4. Universe power — GRAVITA.
   5. Havona energy — TRIATA.
   6. Transcendental energy — TRANOSTA.
   7. Monota.

   See pages 469-71

VII. UNIVERSAL NONSPIRITUAL ENERGY SYSTEMS

1. **Proposition.** Pattern may be material, mindal, or spiritual—or any combination of these energies.

    "Pattern can be projected as material, spiritual, or mindal, or any combination of these energies. It can pervade personalities, identities, entities, or nonliving matter. But pattern is pattern and remains pattern; only *copies* are multiplied." (p 10)

2. **Proposition.** As mind is spiritualized, it becomes less subject to physical gravity. Physical gravity measures quantity—spirit gravity quality.

    "As the mind of any personality in the universe becomes more spiritual—Godlike—it becomes less responsive to material gravity. Reality, measured by physical-gravity response, is the antithesis of reality as determined by quality of spirit content. Physical-gravity action, is a quantitative determiner of nonspirit energy; spiritual-gravity action is the qualitative measure of the living energy of divinity." (p. 140)

VIII. CLASSIFICATION OF MATTER

1. **Proposition.** Universe matter is classified in ten divisions.

    "In the varied suns, planets, and space bodies there are ten grand divisions of matter:
    "1. Ultimatonic matter—the prime physical units of material existence, the energy particles which go to make up electrons.

"2. Subelectronic matter—the explosive and repellent stage of the solar supergases.

"3. Electronic matter—the electrical stage of material differentiation—electrons, protons, and various other units entering into the varied constitution of the electronic groups.

"4. Subatomic matter—matter existing extensively in the interior of the hot suns.

"5. Shattered atoms—found in the cooling suns and throughout space.

"6. Ionized matter—individual atoms stripped of their outer (chemically active) electrons by electrical, thermal, or X-ray activities and by solvents.

"7. Atomic matter—the chemical stage of elemental organization, the component units of molecular or visible matter.

"8. The molecular stage of matter—matter as it exists on Urantia in a state of relatively stable materialization under ordinary conditions.

"9. Radioactive matter—the disorganizing tendency and activity of the heavier elements under conditions of moderate heat and diminished gravity pressure.

"10. Collapsed matter—the relatively stationary matter found in the interior of the cold or dead suns. This form of matter is not really stationary; there is still some ultimatonic even electronic activity, but these units are in very close proximity, and their rates of revolution are greatly diminished." (p. 472)

IX. ENERGY AND MATTER TRANSMUTATIONS

1. **PROPOSITION.** Energy can apply to spiritual, mindal, or material realms. Force is also broadly used. Power is limited to the material level.

    "ENERGY we use as an all-inclusive term applied to spiritual, mindal, and material realms. *Force* is also thus broadly used. *Power* is ordinarily limited to the designation of the electronic level of material or linear-gravity-responsive matter in the grand universe. Power is also employed to designate sovereignty. We cannot follow your generally accepted definitions of force, energy, and power. There is such paucity of language that we must assign multiple meanings to these terms." (p. 9)

2. **Proposition.** When mass becomes overaggregated and threatens to unbalance energy, the physical controllers intervene. Eventually, the larger physical systems become stabilized.

> "When mass becomes overaggregated and threatens to unbalance energy, to deplete the physical power circuits, the physical controllers intervene unless gravity's own further tendency to overmaterialize energy is defeated by the occurrence of a collision among the dead giants of space, thus in an instant completely dissipating the cumulative collections of gravity. In these collisional episodes enormous masses of matter are suddenly converted into the rarest form of energy, and the struggle for universal equilibrium is begun anew. Eventually the larger physical systems become stabilized, become physically settled, and are swung into the balanced and established circuits of the superuniverses. Subsequent to this event no more collisions or other devastating catastrophes will occur in such established systems." (p. 176)

3. **Proposition.** Plus energy produces power disturbances and electric manifestations. Minus energy favors aggregation of matter.

> "During the times of plus energy there are power disturbances and heat fluctuations accompanied by electrical manifestations. During times of minus energy there are increased tendencies for matter to aggregate, condense, and to get out of control in the more delicately balanced circuits, with resultant tidal or collisional adjustments which quickly restore the balance between circulating energy and more literally stabilized matter. To forecast and otherwise to understand such likely behavior of the blazing suns and the dark islands of space is one of the tasks of the celestial star observers." (p. 176)

4. **Proposition.** Manipulation of universe energy is always in accordance with the will and mandates of Paradise Deity.

> "The manipulation of universe energy is ever in accordance with the personal will and the all-wise mandates of the Universal Father. This personal control of manifested power and circulating energy is modified by the co-ordinate acts and decisions of the Eternal Son, as well as by the united purposes of the Son and the Father executed by the Conjoint Actor." (p. 467)

5. **PROPOSITION.** The creation of energy and the bestowal of life are Deity prerogatives. The force organizers turn space force into energy and the power directors transmute energy into matter.

> "The creation of energy and the bestowal of life are the prerogatives of the Universal Father and his associate Creator personalities. The river of energy and life is a continuous outpouring from the Deities, the Universal and united stream of Paradise force going forth to all space. This divine energy pervades all creation. The force organizers initiate those changes and institute those modifications of space-force which eventuate in energy; the power directors transmute energy into matter; thus the material worlds are born." (p. 468)

6. **PROPOSITION.** Force-energy is imperishable, indestructible. They may transmute and transform, but they never suffer extinction.

> "Force derived from self-existent Deity is in itself ever existent. Force-energy is imperishable, indestructible; these manifestations of the Infinite may be subject to unlimited transmutation, endless transformation, and eternal metamorphosis; but in no sense or degree, not even to the slightest imaginable extent, could they or ever shall they suffer extinction. But energy, though springing from the Infinite, is not infinitely manifest; there are outer limits to the presently conceived master universe." (p. 468)

7. **PROPOSITION.** Hot suns transform matter into energy and the dark, cold worlds convert energy into matter.

> "The blazing suns can transform matter into various forms of energy, but the dark worlds and all outer space can slow down electronic and ultimatonic activity to the point of converting these energies into the matter of the realms. Certain electronic associations of a close nature, as well as many of the basic associations of nuclear matter, are formed in the exceedingly low temperatures of open space, being later augmented by association with larger accretions of materializing energy." (p. 473)

8. **PROPOSITION.** Increase of mass in matter is equal to the increase of energy divided by the square of the velocity of light. Work which resting matter can perform is equal to the energy expended in bringing its parts from Paradise, minus the resistance overcome in transit and the attraction exerted by the parts on one another.

> "The increase of mass in matter is equal to the increase of energy divided by the square of the velocity of light. In a dynamic sense

the work which resting matter can perform is equal to the energy expended in bringing its parts together from Paradise minus the resistance of the forces overcome in transit and the attraction exerted by the parts of matter on one another." (p. 474)

X. WAVE ENERGY MANIFESTATIONS

1. **Proposition.** Energy taken in or given out when electronic positions are shifted is always a "quantum" or some multiple thereof. "Waves" are 860 times the diameter of the unit involved.

   "The quantity of energy taken in or given out when electronic or other positions are shifted is always a 'quantum' or some multiple thereof, but the vibratory or wavelike behavior of such units of energy is wholly determined by the dimensions of the material structures concerned. Such wavelike energy ripples are 860 times the diameters of the ultimatons, electrons, atoms, or other units thus performing. The never-ending confusion attending the observation of the wave mechanics of quantum behavior is due to the superimposition of energy waves: Two crests can combine to make a double-height crest, while a crest and a trough may combine, thus producing mutual cancellation." (p. 474)

2. **Proposition.** There are ten types of wave energy:

   1. Infraultimatonic rays.
   2. Ultimatonic rays.
   3. The short space rays.
   4. The electronic stage.
   5. Gamma rays.
   6. The X-ray group.
   7. Ultraviolet rays.
   8. White light.
   9. Infrared rays.
   10. Hertzian waves.

   See pages 474-75

XI. ULTIMATONS AND ELECTRONS

1. **Proposition.** In space, cold and other influences are at work organizing ultimatons into electrons. Heat is the measure of electronic activity.

   "Throughout all space, cold and other influences are at work creatively organizing ultimatons into electrons. Heat is the measurement of electronic activity, while cold merely signifies absence of heat—comparative energy rest—the status of the universal force-charge of space provided neither emergent energy nor organized matter were present and responding to gravity." (p. 473)

2. **Proposition.** The ultimaton, having three types of motion, is unknown on Urantia.

"The ultimatons, unknown on Urantia, slow down through many phases of physical activity before they attain the revolutionary-energy prerequisites to electronic organization. Ultimatons have three varieties of motion: mutual resistance to cosmic force, individual revolutions of antigravity potential, and the intraelectronic positions of the one hundred mutually interassociated ultimatons." (p. 476)

XII. ATOMIC MATTER

1. **Proposition.** No matter how much scientists gain control of energy and matter, they will not create one atom or add to matter that which we call life.

"Subsequent to even still greater progress and further discoveries, after Urantia has advanced immeasurably in comparison with present knowledge, though you should gain control of the energy revolutions of the electrical units of matter to the extent of modifying their physical manifestations—even after all such possible progress, forever will scientists be powerless to create one atom of matter or to originate one flash of energy or ever to add to matter that which we call life." (p. 468)

2. **Proposition.** Temperature is secondary only to gravity in energy evolution. Low temperature favors electronic construction. High temperature favors breakup.

"Temperature—heat and cold—is secondary only to gravity in the realms of energy and matter evolution. Ultimatons are humbly obedient to temperature extremes. Low temperatures favor certain forms of electronic construction and atomic assembly, while high temperatures facilitate all sorts of atomic breakup and material disintegration." (p. 473)

3. **Proposition.** A typical electron has one hundred ultimatons. Loss of ultimatons destroys typical electronic identity.

"Mutual attraction holds one hundred ultimatons together in the constitution of the electron; and there are never more nor less than one hundred ultimatons in a typical electron. The loss of one or more ultimatons destroys typical electronic identity, thus bringing into existence one of the ten modified forms of the electron." (p. 476)

4. **Proposition.** Ultimatons do not whirl about in circuits within the electron. They spread or cluster in accordance with their axial revolutionary velocities.

> "Ultimatons do not describe orbits or whirl about in circuits within the electrons, but they do spread or cluster in accordance with their axial revolutionary velocities, thus determining the differential electronic dimensions. This same ultimatonic velocity of axial revolution also determines the negative or positive reactions of the several types of electronic units. The entire segregation and grouping of electronic matter, together with the electric differentiation of negative and positive bodies of energy-matter, result from these various functions of the component ultimatonic interassociation." (p. 476)

5. **Proposition.** If mass of matter should be magnified until an electron equaled one tenth of an ounce, and size were proportionally magnified, then would such an electron become as large as the earth. If the volume of a proton should be magnified to the size of a pinhead, then the pin's head would have a diameter equal to that of the earth's orbit around the sun.

> "If the mass of matter should be magnified until that of an electron equaled one tenth of an ounce, then were size to be proportionately magnified, the volume of such an electron would become as large as that of the earth. If the volume of a proton—eighteen hundred times as heavy as an electron—should be magnified to the size of the head of a pin, then, in comparison, a pin's head would attain a diameter equal to that of the earth's orbit around the sun." (p. 477)

6. **Proposition.** In an atom, the electron revolves about the central proton with the same comparative room that the planets have as they revolve about the sun in the solar system.

> "Within the atom the electrons revolve about the central proton with about the same comparative room the planets have as they revolve about the sun in the space of the solar system. There is the same relative distance, in comparison with actual size, between the atomic nucleus and the inner electronic circuit as exists between the inner planet, Mercury, and your sun." (p. 477)

7. **Proposition.** In Orvonton, only one hundred electrons will naturally assemble in one atom. Introduction of additional electrons will disrupt the proton.

> "In Orvonton it has never been possible naturally to assemble over one hundred orbital electrons in one atomic system. When one hundred and one have been artificially introduced into the orbital field, the result has always been the instantaneous disruption of the central proton with the wild dispersion of the electrons and other liberated energies." (p. 478)

8. **Proposition.** In atoms, only the ten outer electrons of the larger atoms revolve about the nucleus as distinct bodies. The thirty electrons nearest the center are difficult to detect as separate bodies.

> "While atoms may contain from one to one hundred orbital electrons, only the outer ten electrons of the larger atoms revolve about the central nucleus as distinct and discrete bodies, intactly and compactly swinging around on precise and definite orbits. The thirty electrons nearest the center are difficult of observation or detection as separate and organized bodies. This same comparative ratio of electronic behavior in relation to nuclear proximity obtains in all atoms regardless of the number of electrons embraced. The nearer the nucleus, the less there is of electronic individuality. The wavelike energy extension of an electron may so spread out as to occupy the whole of the lesser atomic orbits; especially is this true of the electrons nearest the atomic nucleus." (p. 478)

9. **Proposition.** The thirty innermost electrons of a large atom have individuality, but their energy systems intermingle. The next thirty have increasing individuality. The next thirty have still more control of their systems.

> "The thirty innermost orbital electrons have individuality, but their energy systems tend to intermingle, extending from electron to electron and well-nigh from orbit to orbit. The next thirty electrons constitute the second family, or energy zone, and are of advancing individuality, bodies of matter exerting a more complete control over their attendant energy systems. The next thirty electrons, the third energy zone, are still more individualized and circulate in more distinct and definite orbits." (p. 478)

10. **PROPOSITION.** Only the last ten electrons in the heavier atoms possess independence.

> "The last ten electrons, present in only the ten heaviest elements, are possessed of the dignity of independence and are, therefore, able to escape more or less freely from the control of the mother nucleus. With a minimum variation in temperature and pressure, the members of this fourth and outermost group of electrons will escape from the grasp of the central nucleus, as is illustrated by the spontaneous disruption of uranium and kindred elements." (p. 478)

11. **PROPOSITION.** While gravity contributes to holding atoms together, there is also present a powerful and unknown energy—the secret of their basic constitution.

> "While gravity is one of several factors concerned in holding together a tiny atomic energy system, there is also present in and among these basic physical units a powerful and unknown energy, the secret of their basic constitution and ultimate behavior, a force which remains to be discovered on Urantia. This universal influence permeates all the space embraced within this tiny energy organization." (p. 478)

12. **PROPOSITION.** Interelectronic space is not empty—it is activated by wavelike manifestations which are synchronized with electronic velocity and ultimatonic revolutions.

> "The interelectronic space of an atom is not empty. Throughout an atom this interelectronic space is activated by wavelike manifestations which are perfectly synchronized with electronic velocity and ultimatonic revolutions. This force is not wholly dominated by you recognized laws of positive and negative attraction; its behavior is therefore sometimes unpredictable. This unnamed influence seems to be a space-force reaction of the Unqualified Absolute." (p. 478)

13. **PROPOSITION.** It is the superior force-mass of the mesotron that holds the nucleus of the atom together. It causes electric charges to be tossed back and forth between protons and neutrons.

> "As atoms are constituted, neither electric nor gravitational forces could hold the nucleus together. The integrity of the nucleus is maintained by the reciprocal cohering function of the mesotron, which is able to hold charged and uncharged particles together because of superior force-mass power and by the further function of causing protons and neutrons

constantly to change places. The mesotron causes the electric charge of the nuclear particles to be incessantly tossed back and forth between protons and neutrons. At one infinitesimal part of a second a given nuclear particle is a charged proton and the next an uncharged neutron. And these alternations of energy status are so unbelievably rapid that the electric charge is deprived of all opportunity to function as a disruptive influence. Thus does the mesotron function as an 'energy-carrier' particle which mightily contributes to the nuclear stability of the atom." (p.479)

PART XV
LOCAL UNIVERSE SONS

PART FIFTEEN
LOCAL UNIVERSE SONS

I. INTRODUCTION

1. **PROPOSITION.** Apart from Gabriel, there are four ranking Sons of the local universe.

    "The types of Sons about to be considered are of local universe origin; they are the offspring of a Paradise Creator Son in varied association with the complemental Universe Mother Spirit. The following orders of local universe sonship find mention in these narratives:
    1. Melchizedek Sons.
    2. Vorondadek Sons.
    3. Lanonandek Sons.
    4. Life Carrier Sons." (p. 384)

2. **PROPOSITION.** Immanuel, the Union of Days, is the Trinity ambassador to the universe of Nebadon. He is number 611,121 of the Supreme Trinity Personalities. He is the personal representative of the Father.

    "At the head of this Paradise group in Nebadon is the ambassador of the Paradise Trinity—Immanuel of Salvington—the Union of Days assigned to the local universe of Nebadon. In a certain sense this high Trinity Son is also the personal representative of the Universal Father to the court of the Creator Son; hence his name, Immanuel.

    "Immanuel of Salvington, number 611,121 of the sixth order of Supreme Trinity Personalities, is a being of sublime dignity and of such superb condesension that he refuses the worship and adoration of all living creatures. He bears the distinction of being the only personality in all Nebadon who has never acknowledged subordination to his brother Michael. He functions as adviser to the Sovereign Son but gives counsel only on request." (p. 370)

3. **PROPOSITION.** Spironga, created by Gabriel and the Father Melchizedek, are the spirit helpers of the local universe.

    "The *Spironga* are the spirit offspring of the Bright and Morning Star and the Father Melchizedek. They are exempt from personality termination but are not evolutionary or ascending beings. Neither are they functionally concerned with the evolutionary ascension regime. They are the spirit helpers of the local universe, executing the routine spirit tasks of Nebadon." (p. 416)

- 384 -

4. **Proposition.** Spornagia are devoted to the material care and culture of all headquarters worlds. They are neither spirits nor persons.

> "The *Spornagia*. The architectural headquarters worlds of the local universe are real worlds—physical creations. There is much work connected with their physical upkeep, and herein we have the assistance of a group of physical creatures call spornagia. They are devoted to the care and culture of the material phases of these headquarters worlds, from Jerusem to Salvington. Spornagia are neither spirits nor persons; they are an animal order of existence, but if you could see them, you would agree that they seem to be perfect animals." (p. 416)

II. GABRIEL

1. **Proposition.** Gabriel is the personalization of the first concept of identity and ideal of personality conceived by the Creator Son and the Creative Spirit.

> "The Bright and Morning Star is the personalization of the first concept of identity and ideal of personality conceived by the Creator Son and the local universe manifestation of the Infinite Spirit. Going back to the early days of the local universe, before the union of the Creator Son and the Mother Spirit in the bonds of creative association, back to the times before the beginning of the creation of their versatile family of sons and daughters, the first conjoint act of this early and free association of these two divine persons results in the creation of the highest spirit personality of the Son and the Spirit, the Bright and Morning Star." (p. 369)

2. **Proposition.** Gabriel is the chief executive of the universe of Nebadon.

> "Gabriel of Salvington is the chief executive of the universe of Nebadon and the arbiter of all executive appeals respecting its administration. This universe executive was created fully endowed for his work, but he has gained experience with the growth and evolution of our local creation." (p. 370)

III. THE MELCHIZEDEKS

1. **Proposition.** The Melchizedeks preside over seven headquarters worlds.

> "These Melchizedek worlds are:
>   1. The pilot world—the home world of the Melchizedek Sons.

2. The world of the physical-life schools and the laboratories of living energies.
3. The world of morontia life.
4. The sphere of initial spirit life.
5. The world of mid-spirit life.
6. The sphere of advancing spirit life.
7. The domain of co-ordinate and supreme self-realization." (p. 387)

2. **PROPOSITION.** The Father Melchizedek was created by a special joint act of the Creator Son and the Creative Spirit.

"After bringing into existence the beings of personal aid, such as the Bright and Morning Star and other administrative personalities, in accordance with the divine purpose and creative plans of a given universe, there occurs a new form of creative union between the Creative Son and the Creative Spirit, the local universe Daughter of the Infinite Spirit. The personality offspring resulting from this creative partnership is the original Melchizedek—the Father Melchizedek—that unique being who subsequently collaborates with the Creator Son and the Creative Spirit to bring into existence the entire group of that name." (p. 384)

3. **PROPOSITION.** The Melchizedeks were created by the Creator Son, Creative Spirit, and the original Father Melchizedek.

"The Melchizedeks of our universe were all created within one millennial period of standard time by the Creator Son and the Creative Spirit in liaison with the Father Melchizedek. Being an order of sonship wherein one of their own number functioned as co-ordinate creator, Melchizedeks are in constitution partly of self-origin and therefore candidates for the realization of a supernal type of self-government." (p. 385)

4. **PROPOSITION.** Melchizedeks are efficient ministers to mortals, seeing that they are midway between the highest personalities and the lowest.

"The Melchizedeks are the first order of divine Sons to approach sufficiently near the lower creature life to be able to function directly in the ministry of mortal uplift, to serve the evolutionary races without the necessity of incarnation. These Sons are naturally at the mid-point of the great personality descent, by origin being just about midway between the highest Divinity and the lowest creature life of will endowment. They

PART XV — LOCAL UNIVERSE SONS

5. **PROPOSITION.** The number of Melchizedeks is stationary—over ten million.

> "These Sons are not an increasing order; their number is stationary, although varying in each local universe. The number of Melchizedeks of record on their headquarters planet in Nebadon is upward of ten million." (p. 387)

6. **PROPOSITION.** The Melchizedeks occupy the pilot world of the Salvington circuit of seventy primary spheres. These worlds, with their 420 tributaries, are called the Melchizedek University.

> "The Melchizedeks occupy a world of their own near Salvington, the universe headquarters. This sphere, by name Melchizedek, is the pilot world of the Salvington circuit of seventy primary spheres, each of which is encircled by six tributary spheres devoted to specialized activities. These marvelous spheres— seventy primaries and 420 tributaries—are often spoken of as the Melchizedek University." (p. 387)

7. **PROPOSITION.** Melchizedeks are the "eldest sons," and they patrol the universe.

> "The Melchizedek order of sonship occupies the position, and assumes the responsibility, of the eldest son in a large family. Most of their work is regular and somewhat routine, but much of it is voluntary and altogether self-imposed. A majority of the special assemblies which, from time to time, convene on Salvington are called on motion of the Melchizedeks. On their own initiative these Sons patrol their native universe. They maintain an autonomous organization devoted to universe intelligence, making periodical reports to the Creator Son independent of all information coming up to universe headquarters through the regular agencies concerned with the routine administration of the realm. They are by nature unprejudiced observers; they have the full confidence of all classes of intelligent beings." (p. 386)

8. **PROPOSITION.** While well-nigh perfect, the Melchizedeks are not infallible. They sometimes err in judgment.

> "The Melchizedeks are well-nigh perfect in wisdom, but they are not infallible in judgment. When detached and alone on planetary missions, they have sometimes erred in minor matters,

that is, they have elected to do certain things which their supervisors did not subsequently approve. Such an error of judgment temporarily disqualifies a Melchizedek until he goes to Salvington and, in audience with the Creator Son, receives that instruction which effectually purges him of the disharmony which caused disagreement with his fellows; and then, following the correctional rest, reinstatement to service ensues on the third day. But these minor misadaptations in Melchizedek function have rarely occurred in Nebadon." (p. 386)

9. **Proposition.** The Melchizedeks and the Trinity Teacher Sons supervise the vast educational systems of ascending mortals.

"A highly specialized branch of Melchizedek activities has to do with the supervision of the progressive morontia career of the ascending mortals. Much of this training is conducted by the patient and wise seraphic ministers, assisted by mortals who have ascended to relatively higher levels of universe attainment, but all of this educational work is under the general supervision of the Melchizedeks in association with the Trinity Teacher Sons." (p. 388)

10. **Proposition.** The Melchizedeks are called "emergency Sons." Wherever special help is needed—there you will find them.

"On Edentia, your constellation headquarters, they are known as emergency Sons. They are always ready to serve in all exigencies— physical, intellectual, or spiritual—whether on a planet, in a system, in a constellation, or in the universe. Whenever and wherever special help is needed, there you will find one or more of the Melchizedek Sons." (p. 389)

IV. THE VORONDADEKS

1. **Proposition.** Vorondadeks are the Constellation Fathers—they number one million.

"After the creation of the personal aids and the first group of the versatile Melchizedeks, the Creator Son and the local universe Creative Spirit planned for, and brought into existence, the second great and diverse order of universe sonship, the Vorondadeks. They are more generally known as Constellation Fathers because a Son of this order is uniformly found at the head of each constellation government in every local universe.

"The number of Vorondadeks varies in each local universe, just one million being the recorded number in Nebadon. These Sons, like their co-ordinates, the Melchizedeks, possess no power of reproduction. There exists no known method whereby they can increase their numbers." (p. 389)

2. **Proposition.** Vorondadeks have been cited for administrative errors, but they have never been in rebellion.

"Although the decisions and rulings of this order of Sons are always in accordance with the spirit of divine sonship and in harmony with the policies of the Creator Son, they have been cited for error to the Creator Son, and in details of technique their decisions have sometimes been reversed on appeal to the superior tribunals of the universe. But these Sons rarely fall into error, and they have never gone into rebellion; never in all the history of Nebadon has a Vorondadek been found in contempt of the universe government." (p. 390)

3. **Proposition.** The one hundred Constellation Fathers make up the supreme advisory cabinet of the Creator Son.

"The one hundred Constellation Fathers, the actual presiding heads of the constellation governments, constitute the supreme advisory cabinet of the Creator Son. This council is in frequent session at universe headquarters and is unlimited in the scope and range of its deliberations but is chiefly concerned with the welfare of the constellations and with the unificiation of the administration of the entire local universe." (p. 390)

V. THE LANONANDEKS

1. **Proposition.** Lanonandeks perform many tasks but are best known as System Sovereigns and Planetary Princes. They are trained and classified by the Melchizedeks.

"After the creation of the Vorondadeks, the Creator Son and the Universe Mother Spirit unite for the purpose of bringing into existence the third order of universe sonship, the Lanonandeks. Although occupied with varied tasks connected with the system administrations, they are best known as System Sovereigns, the rulers of the local systems, and as Planetary Princes, the administrative heads of the inhabited worlds."

> "Being a later and lower—as concerns divinity levels—order of sonship creation, these beings were required to pass through certain courses of training on the Melchizedek worlds in preparation for subsequent service. They were the first students in the Melchizedek University and were classified and certified by their Melchizedek teachers and examiners according to ability, personality, and attainment." (p. 392)

2. **PROPOSITION.** Nebadon began with twelve million Lanonandeks certified by the Melchizedeks in three divisions.

> "The universe of Nebadon began its existence with exactly twelve million Lanonandeks, and when they had passed through the Melchizedek sphere, they were divided in the final tests into three classes:
>
> "1. *Primary Lanonandeks.* Of the highest rank there were 709,841. These are the Sons designated as System Sovereigns and assistants to the supreme councils of the constellations and as counselors in the higher administrative work of the universe.
>
> "2. *Secondary Lanonandeks.* Of this order emerging from Melchizedek there were 10,234,601. They are assigned as Planetary Princes and to the reserves of that order.
>
> "3. *Tertiary Lanonandeks.* This group contained 1,055,558. These Sons function as subordinate assistants, messengers, custodians, commissioners, observers, and prosecute the miscellaneous duties of a system and its component worlds." (p. 392)

3. **PROPOSITION.** Planetary Princes usually arrive on a world at the time of the appearance of will creatures.

> "The advent of a Lanonandek Son on an average world signifies that will, the ability to choose the path of eternal survival, has developed in the mind of primitive man. But on Urantia the Planetary Prince arrived almost half a million years after the appearance of human will." (p. 741)

4. **PROPOSITION.** Calagistia, Planetary Prince of Urantia, was a secondary Lanonandek Son, No. 9,344. He was an experienced administrator.

> "Caligastia was a Lanonandek Son, number 9,344 of the secondary order. He was experienced in the administration of the affairs of the local universe in general and, during later ages, with the management of the local system of Satania in particular." (p. 741)

5. **Proposition.** Daligastia was the associate-assistant of Caligastia—No. 319,407 of the secondary order.

> "At the head of this group was Daligastia, the associate-assistant of the Planetary Prince. Daligastia was also a secondary Lanonandek Son, being number 319,407 of that order. He ranked as an assistant at the time of his assignment as Caligastia's associate." (p. 742)

6. **Proposition.** Over seven hundred Lanonandek Sons have been lost in rebellion in Nebadon.

> "Our local universe has been unfortunate in that over seven hundred Sons of the Lanonandek order have rebelled against the universe government, thus precipitating confusion in several systems and on numerous planets. Of this entire number of failures only three were System Sovereigns; practically all of these Sons belonged to the second and third orders, Planetary Princes and tertiary Lanonandeks." (p. 393)

VI. THE LIFE CARRIERS

1. **Proposition.** There are seven worlds in the Life Carrier group.

> "The Melchizedeks have the general oversight of the fourth group of seven primary spheres in the Salvington circuit. These worlds of the Life Carriers are designated as follows:
> 1. The Life Carrier headquarters.
> 2. The life-planning sphere.
> 3. The life-conservation sphere.
> 4. The sphere of life evolution.
> 5. The sphere of life associated with mind.
> 6. The sphere of mind and spirit in living beings.
> 7. The sphere of unrevealed life." (p. 397)

2. **Proposition.** Life Carriers are the only group of universe Sons in whose creation the rulers of the superuniverse participate. There are one hundred million in Nebadon.

> "Though the Life Carriers belong to the family of divine sonship, they are a peculiar and distinct type of universe Sons, being the only group of intelligent life in a local universe in whose creation the rulers of a superuniverse participate. The Life Carriers are the offspring of three pre-existent personalities: the Creator Son, the Universe Mother Spirit, and, by designation, one of the three Ancients of Days presiding over

the destinies of the superuniverse concerned. These Ancients of Days, who alone can decree the extinction of intelligent life, participate in the creation of the Life Carriers, who are intrusted with establishing physical life on the evolving worlds.

"In the universe of Nebadon we have on record the creation of one hundred million Life Carriers." (p. 396)

3. **PROPOSITION.** Life is not spontaneous. Life Carriers must initiate life on the evolutionary worlds.

> "Life does not spontaneously appear in the universes; the Life Carriers must initiate it on the barren planets. They are the carriers, disseminators, and guardians of life as it appears on the evolutionary worlds of space. All life of the order and forms known on Urantia arises with these Sons, though not all forms of planetary life are existent on Urantia," (p. 399)

4. **PROPOSITION.** A considerable staff comes to a world to inaugurate life. They may carry life or they may organize its patterns on the planet.

> "The corps of Life Carriers commissioned to plant life upon a new world usually consists of one hundred senior carriers, one hundred assistants, and one thousand custodians. The Life Carriers often carry actual life plasm to a new world, but not always. They sometimes organize the life patterns after arriving on the planet of assignment in accordance with formulas previously approved for a new adventure in life establishment. Such was the origin of the planetary life of Urantia." (p. 399)

5. **PROPOSITION.** When the formulas of life have been provided, the Life Carriers catalyze the lifeless material—their persons transmit the vital spark.

> "When, in accordance with approved formulas, the physical patterns have been provided, then do the Life Carriers catalyze this lifeless material, imparting through their persons the vital spirit spark; and forthwith do the inert patterns become living matter." (p. 399)

6. **PROPOSITION.** The vital spark is bestowed through the Life Carriers—not by them. The essential factors of life come from the Universe Mother Spirit.

> "The vital spark—the mystery of life—is bestowed through the Life Carriers, not by them. They do indeed supervise such transactions, they formulate the life plasm itself, but it is the Universe Mother Spirit who supplies the essential factor of the living plasm. From the Creative Daughter of the Infinite Spirit comes that energy spark which enlivens the body and presages the mind." (p. 399)

7. **Proposition.** Before the times of moral choice, the Life Carriers are permitted to foster and manipulate the environment so as to favor the course of biologic evolution.

> "During the ages intervening between life establishment and the emergence of human creatures of moral status, the Life Carriers are permitted to manipulate the life environment and otherwise favorably directionize the course of biologic evolution. And this they do for long periods of time.
>
> "When the Life Carriers operating on a new world have once succeeded in producing a being with will, with the power of moral decision and spiritual choice, then and there their work terminates—they are through; they may manipulate the evolving life no further." (p. 400)

8. **Proposition.** Each local system has a midsonite world on which a Melchizedek has functioned as a Life Carrier.

> "In every local system of inhabited worlds throughout Nebadon there is a single sphere whereon the Melchizedeks have functioned as life carriers. These abodes are known as the system *midsonite* worlds, and on each of them a materially modified Melchizedek Son has mated with a selected Daughter of the material order of sonship. The Mother Eves of such midsonite worlds are dispatched from the system headquarters of jurisdiction, having been chosen by the designated Melchizedek life carrier from among the numerous volunteers who respond to the call of the System Sovereign addressed to the Material Daughters of his sphere." (p. 400)

9. **Proposition.** When a world is finally settled in light and life, the Life Carriers are organized into higher deliberative and administrative bodies.

> "When an evolutionary planet is finally settled in light and life, the Life Carriers are organized into the higher deliberative bodies of advisory capacity to assist in the further administration and development of the world and its glorified beings. In the later and settled ages of an evolving universe these Life Carriers are intrusted with many new duties." (p. 396)

VII. BRILLIANT EVENING STARS

1. **Proposition.** Brilliant Evening Stars were planned by the Melchizedeks and are assistants of Gabriel.

   "These brilliant creatures were planned by the Melchizedeks and were then brought into being by the Creator Son and the Creative Spirit. They serve in many capacities but chiefly as liaison officers of Gabriel, the local universe chief executive. One or more of these beings function as his representatives at the capital of every constellation and system in Nebadon.

   "As chief executive of Nebadon, Gabriel is ex officio chairman of, or observer at, most of the Salvington conclaves, and as many as one thousand of these are often in session simultaneously. The Brilliant Evening Stars represent Gabriel on these occasions; he cannot be in two places at the same time, and these superangels compensate for this limitation. They perform an analogous service for the corps of the Trinity Teacher Sons." (p. 407)

2. **Proposition.** There are two orders of Evening Stars. There are 4,832 of created dignity and 8,309 are ascendant seraphim and others unrevealed.

   "The Brilliant Evening Stars are a unique twofold order, embracing some of created dignity and others of attained service. The Nebadon corps of these superangels now numbers 13,641. There are 4,832 of created dignity, while 8,809 are ascendant spirits who have attained this goal of exalted service. Many of these ascendant Evening Stars started their universe careers as seraphim; others have ascended from unrevealed levels of creature life. As an attainment goal this high corps is never closed to ascension candidates so long as a universe is not settled in light and life." (p. 407)

VIII. ARCHANGELS

1. **Proposition.** The archangels, as a rule, do not work under Gabriel's jurisdiction. They are largely dedicated to creature survival. We have almost eight hundred thousand.

   "Archangels are the offspring of the Creator Son and the Universe Mother Spirit. They are the highest type of high spirit being produced in large numbers in a local universe, and at the time of the last registry there were almost eight hundred thousand in Nebadon.

"Archangels are one of the few groups of local universe personalities who are not normally under the jurisdiction of Gabriel. They are not in any manner concerned with the routine administration of the universe, being dedicated to the work of creature survival and to the furtherance of the ascending career of the mortals of time and space. While not ordinarily subject to the direction of the Bright and Morning Star, the archangels do sometimes function by his authority. They also collaborate with others of the Universe Aids, such as the Evening Stars, as is illustrated by certain transactions depicted in the narrative of life transplantation on your world." (p. 408)

2. **PROPOSITION.** In recent times, a division of the archangels was established on Urantia.

"The archangel corps of Nebadon is directed by the first-born of this order, and in more recent times a divisional headquarters of the archangels has been maintained on Urantia. It is this unusual fact that soon arrests the attention of extra-Nebadon student visitors. Among their early observations of intrauniverse transactions is the discovery that many ascendant activities of the Brilliant Evening Stars are directed from the capital of a local system, Satania. On further examination they discover that certain archangel activities are directed from a small and apparently insignificant inhabited world called Urantia. And then ensues the revelation of Michael's bestowal on Urantia and there immediately quickened interest in you and your lowly sphere." (p. 408)

IX. OTHER GROUPS OF SONS

1. **PROPOSITION.** High Son Assistants are a group of volunteer beings of origin outside the local universe.

"The Most High Assistants are a group of volunteering beings, of origin outside the local universe, who are temporarily assigned as central and superuniverse representatives to, or observers of, the local creations. Their number varies constantly but is always far up in the millions.

"From time to time we thus benefit from the ministry and assistance of such Paradise-origin beings as Perfectors of Wisdom, Divine Counselors, Universal Censors, Inspired Trinity Spirits, Trinitized Sons, Solitary Messengers, supernaphim, seconaphim, tertiaphim, and other gracious ministers, who sojourn with us for the purpose of helping our native personalities in the effort to bring all Nebadon into fuller harmony with the ideas of Orvonton and the ideals of Paradise." (p. 409)

2. **PROPOSITION.** High Commissioners are Spirit-fused ascendant mortals.

> "The High Commissioners are Spirit-fused ascendant mortals; they are not Adjuster fused. You quite well understand about the universe-ascension career of a mortal candidate for Adjuster fusion, that being the high destiny in prospect for all Urantia mortals since the bestowal of Christ Michael. But this is not the exclusive destiny of all mortals in the prebestowal ages of worlds like yours, and there is another type of world whose inhabitants are never permanently indwelt by Thought Adjusters. Such mortals are never permanently joined in union with a Mystery Monitor of Paradise bestowal; nevertheless, the Adjusters do transiently indwell them, serving as guides and patterns for the duration of the life in the flesh." (p. 410)

3. **PROPOSITION.** Celestial Overseers are a recruited teaching corps.

> "The Nebadon education system is jointly administered by the Trinity Teacher Sons and the Melchizedek teaching corps, but much of the work designed to effect its maintenance and upbuilding is carried on by the Celestial Overseers. These beings are a recruited corps embracing all types of individuals connected with the scheme of educating and training the ascending mortals. There are upward of three million of them in Nebadon, and they are all volunteers who have qualified by experience to serve as educational advisers to the entire realm." (p. 412)

4. **PROPOSITION.** Mansion World Teachers are recruited glorified cherubim.

> "The Mansion World Teachers are recruited and glorified cherubim. Like most other instructors in Nebadon they are commissioned by the Melchizedeks. They function in most of the educational enterprises of the morontia life, and their number is quite beyond the comprehension of mortal mind." (p. 413)

X. MATERIAL SONS

1. **PROPOSITION.** The material or sex Sons and Daughters are the offspring of the Creator Son. One pair is created in each local system.

> "The material or sex Sons and Daughters are the offspring of the Creator Son; the Universe Mother Spirit does not participate in the production of these beings who are destined to function as physical uplifters on the evolutionary worlds.

Part XV — Local Universe Sons

> "The material order of sonship is not uniform throughout the local universe. The Creator Son produces only one pair of these beings in each local system; these original pairs are diverse in nature, being attuned to the life pattern of their respective systems. This is a necessary provision since otherwise the reproductive potential of the Adams would be nonfunctional with that of the evolving mortal beings of the worlds of any one particular system. The Adam and Eve who came to Urantia were descended from the original Satania pair of Material Sons." (p. 580)

2. **Proposition.** Material Sons emit light—both blood and light circulate in their bodies. They are eight to ten feet tall.

   > "Material Sons vary in height from eight to ten feet, and their bodies glow with the brilliance of radiant light of a violet hue. While material blood circulates through their material bodies, they are also surcharged with divine energy and saturated with celestial light. These Material Sons (the Adams) and Material Daughters (the Eves) are equal to each other, differing only in reproductive nature and in certain chemical endowments. They are equal but differential, male and female—hence complemental—and are designed to serve on almost all assignments in pairs." (p. 580)

3. **Proposition.** Material Sons are the permanent citizens of the local system capitals. They are the link between the spiritual and physical worlds.

   > "While living as permanent citizens on the system capitals, even when functioning on descending missions to the evolutionary planets, the Material Sons do not possess Thought Adjusters, but it is through these very services that they acquire experiential capacity for Adjuster indwellment and the Paradise ascension career. These unique and wonderfully useful beings are the connecting links between the spiritual and physical worlds. They are concentrated on the system headquarters, where they reproduce and carry on as material citizens of the realm, and whence they are dispatched to the evolutionary worlds." (p. 581)

PART XVI
PERMANENT CITIZENS

Part Sixteen
PERMANENT CITIZENS

I. THE PLANETS—MIDWAYERS

1. **PROPOSITION.** The midwayers provide for a continuity of planetary administration in the face of short-lived mortal sojourn and ever-changing celestial ministers.

   "On Urantia the midway ministers are in reality the actual custodians of the planet; they are, practically speaking, the citizens of Urantia. Mortals are indeed the physical and material inhabitants of an evolutionary world, but you are all so short-lived; you tarry on your nativity planet such a short time. You are born, live, die, and pass on to other worlds of evolutionary progression. Even the superhuman beings who serve on the planets as celestial ministers are of transient assignment; few of them are long attached to a given sphere. The midway creatures, however, provide continuity of planetary administration in the face of ever-changing celestial ministries and constantly shifting mortal inhabitants. Throughout all of this never-ceasing changing and shifting, the midway creatures remain on the planet uninterruptedly carrying on their work." (p. 415)

2. **PROPOSITION.** Midwayers have a threefold classification:
   a. *Ascending Sons.*
   b. *Permanent Citizens.*
   c. *Ministering Spirits.*

   "The midway creatures have a threefold classification: They are properly classified with the ascending Sons of God; they are factually grouped with the orders of permanent citizenship, while they are functionally reckoned with the ministering spirits of time because of their intimate and effective association with the angelic hosts in the work of serving mortal man on the individual worlds of space." (p. 424)

3. **PROPOSITION.** Midwayers appear on the majority of worlds—always on decimal planets.

   "These unique creatures appear on the majority of the inhabited worlds and are always found on the decimal or life-experiment planets, such as Urantia. Midwayers are of two types—primary and secondary—and they appear by the following techniques:
   "1. *Primary Midwayers,* the more spiritual group, are a somewhat standardized order of beings who are uniformly derived from the

modified ascendant-mortal staffs of the Planetary Princes. The number of primary midway creatures is always fifty thousand, and no planet enjoying their ministry has a larger group.

"2. *Secondary Midwayers*, the more material group of these creatures, vary greatly in numbers on the different worlds, though the average is around fifty thousand. They are variously derived from the planetary biologic uplifters, the Adams and Eves, or from their immediate progeny. There are no less than twenty-four diverse techniques involved in the production of these secondary midway creatures on the evolutionary worlds of space. The mode of origin for this group on Urantia was unusual and extraordinary." (p. 424)

4. **PROPOSITION.** A couple of the Prince's staff produced the first primary midwayers. The entire staff produced 50,000.

    "In conformity to their instructions the staff did not engage in sexual reproduction, but they did painstakingly study their personal constitutions, and they carefully explored every imaginable phase of intellectual (mind) and morontia (soul) liaison. And it was during the thirty-third year of their sojourn in Dalamatia, long before the wall was completed, that number two and number seven of the Danite group accidentally discovered a phenomenon attendant upon the liaison of their morontia selves (supposedly nonsexual and nonmaterial); and the result of this adventure proved to be the first of the primary midway creatures. This new being was wholly visible to the planetary staff and to their celestial associates but was not visible to the men and women of the various human tribes. Upon authority of the Planetary Prince the entire corporeal staff undertook the production of similar beings, and all were successful, following the instructions of the pioneer Danite pair. Thus did the Prince's staff eventually bring into being the original corps of 50,000 primary midwayers." (p. 744)

5. **PROPOSITION.** The story of Adamson and Ratta—the origin of almost two thousand secondary midwayers.

    "A company of twenty-seven followed Adamson northward in quest of these people of his childhood fantasies. In a little over three years Adamson's party actually found the object of their adventure, and among these people he discovered a wonderful and beautiful woman, twenty years old, who claimed to be the last pure-line descendant of the Prince's staff. This woman, Ratta, said that her ancestors were all descendants of two of the fallen staff of the Prince. She was the last of her race, having no living brothers or sisters. She had about decided not to mate, had about made up her mind to die without issue, but she lost her heart to the majestic Adamson. And when she heard the story of Eden, how the predictions of Van and Amadon had really come to pass, and as she listened to the recital of the Garden default, she was encompassed with but a single thought—to marry this son and heir of Adam. And quickly the idea grew upon Adamson. In a little more than three months they were married.

"Adamson and Ratta had a family of sixty-seven children. They gave origin to a great line of the world's leadership, but they did something more. It should be remembered that both of these beings were really superhuman. Every fourth child born to them was of a unique order. It was often invisible. Never in the world's history had such a thing occurred. Ratta was greatly perturbed—even superstitious—but Adamson well knew of the existence of the primary midwayers, and he concluded that something similar was transpiring before his eyes. When the second strangely behaving offspring arrived, he decided to mate them, since one was male and the other female, and this is the origin of the secondary order of midwayers. Within one hundred years, before this phenomenon ceased, almost two thousand were brought into being." (p. 861)

6. **PROPOSITION.** Adamson and Ratta had sixteen progenitors of the secondary midwayers—equally divided as to sex.

"Among the children of Adamson there were just sixteen of the peculiar progenitors of the secondary midwayers. These unique children were equally divided as regards sex, and each couple was capable of producing a secondary midwayer every seventy days by a combined technique of sex and nonsex liaison. And such a phenomenon was never possible on earth before that time, nor has it ever occurred since." (p. 862)

7. **PROPOSITION.** Each of these electrically energized couples produced 248 midwayers—a total of 1,984.

"These sixteen children lived and died (except for their peculiarities) as mortals of the realm, but their electrically energized offspring live on and on, not being subject to the limitations of mortal flesh.

PART XVI — *PERMANENT CITIZENS*

"Each of the eight couples eventually produced 248 midwayers, and thus did the original secondary corps—1,984 in number—come into existence. There are eight subgroups of secondary midwayers. They are designated as A-B-C the first, second, third, and so on. And then there are D-EF the first, second, and so on." (p. 862)

8. **PROPOSITION.** Of the 50,000 primary midwayers, 40,119 joined the Lucifer rebellion. Of the 1,984 secondary midwayers, 873 went against Michael's rule.

   "The majority of the primary midwayers went into sin at the time of the Lucifer rebellion. When the devastation of the planetary rebellion was reckoned up, among other losses it was discovered that of the original 50,000, 40,119 had joined the Caligastia secession.

   "The original number of secondary midwayers was 1,984, and of these 873 failed to align themselves with the rule of Michael and were duly interned in connection with the planetary adjudication of Urantia on the day of Pentecost. No one can forecast the future of these fallen creatures." (p. 863)

9. **PROPOSITION.** The United Midwayers now number 10,992. They united shortly after Pentecost.

   "At the last adjudication of this world, when Michael removed the slumbering survivors of time, the midway creatures were left behind, left to assist in the spiritual and semispiritual work on the planet. They now function as a single corps, embracing both orders and numbering 10,992. The *United Midwayers of Urantia* are at present governed alternately by the senior member of each order. This regime has obtained since their amalgamation into one group shortly after Pentecost." (p. 864)

10. **PROPOSITION.** The checkered history of the secondary midwayers down to their union with the primary group.

    "After the death of Adamson the remainder of the secondary midwayers became a strange, unorganized, and unattached influence on Urantia. From that time to the days of Machiventa Melchizedek they led an irregular and unorganized existence. They were partially brought under control by this Melchizedek but were still productive of much mischief up to the days of Christ Michael. And during his sojourn on earth they all made final decisions as to their future destiny, the loyal majority then enlisting under the leadership of the primary midwayers." (p. 863)

11. **Proposition.** Secondary midwayers engage in numerous missions—even contact with the material world.

> "The 1,111 loyal secondary midwayers are engaged in important missions on earth. As compared with their primary associates, they are decidedly material. They exist just outside the range of mortal vision and possess sufficient latitude of adaptation to make, at will, physical contact with what humans call 'material things.' These unique creatures have certain definite powers over the things of time and space, not excepting the beasts of the realm." (p. 865)

12. **Proposition.** On Urantia, many phenomena ascribed to angels have been performed by midwayers.

> "Many of the more literal phenomena ascribed to angels have been performed by the secondary midway creatures. When the early teachers of the gospel of Jesus were thrown into prison by the ignorant religious leaders of that day, an actual 'angel of the Lord' 'by night opened the prison doors and brought them forth.' But in the case of Peter's deliverance after the killing of James by Herod's order, it was a secondary midwayer who performed the work ascribed to an angel." (p. 865)

13. **Proposition.** Today midwayers are associated with the reserve corps of destiny and they initiated the Urantia revelation.

> "Their chief work today is that of unperceived personal-liaison associates of those men and women who constitute the planetary reserve corps of destiny. It was the work of this secondary group, ably seconded by certain of the primary corps, that brought about the coordination of personalities and circumstances on Urantia which finally induced the planetary celestial supervisors to initiate those petitions that resulted in the granting of the mandates making possible the series of revelations of which this presentation is a part." (p. 865)

II. THE LOCAL SYSTEMS—MATERIAL SONS

1. **Proposition.** Upon completion of the joint creation, the Creator Son personalizes the Material sex Sons and Daughters—the Adams and Eves of the local systems.

> "*The Material Sons of God.* When a creative liaison between the Creator Son and the universe representative of the Infinite Spirit, the Universe Mother Spirit, has completed its cycle, when nomore offspring of the combined nature are forthcoming,

then does the Creator Son personalize in dual form his last concept of being, thus finally confirming his own and original dual origin. In and of himself he then creates the beautiful and superb Sons and Daughters of the material order of universe sonship. This is the origin of the original Adam and Eve of each local system of Nebadon. They are a reproducing order of sonship, being created male and female. Their progeny function as the relatively permanent citizens of a system capital, though some are commissioned as Planetary Adams." (p. 415)

2. **Proposition.** Material Sons and Daughters are the permanent citizens of the local system capitals.

"At the last millennial registration on Salvington there were of record in Nebadon 161,432,840 Material Sons and Daughters of citizenship status on the local system capitals. The number of Material Sons varies in the different systems, and their number is being constantly increased by natural reproduction. In the exercise of their reproductive functions they are not guided wholly by the personal desires of the contacting personalities but also by the higher governing bodies and advisory councils. "These Material Sons and Daughters are the permanent inhabitants of Jerusem and its associated worlds. They occupy vast estates on Jerusem and participate liberally in the local management of the capital sphere, administering practically all routine affairs with the assistance of the midwayers and the ascenders." (p. 515)

III. THE CONSTELLATIONS—UNIVITATIA

1. **Proposition.** The univitatia, the permanent citizens of the constellation worlds, are midway between the Material Sons and the spirit sustia.

"Univitatia are the permanent citizens of Edentia and its associated worlds, all seven hundred seventy worlds surrounding the constellation headquarters being under their supervision. These children of the Creator Son and the Creative Spirit are projected on a plane of existence in between the material and the spiritual, but they are not morontia creatures. The natives of each of the seventy major spheres of Edentia possess different visible forms, and the morontia mortals have their morontia forms attuned to correspond with the ascending scale of the univitatia each time they change residence from one Edentia sphere to another as they pass successively from world number one to world number seventy."(p. 493)

IV. THE LOCAL UNIVERSE—
SUSATIA AND SPIRIT-FUSED MORTALS

1. **Proposition.** Susatia are the natives of Salvington. They are closely associated with the Spirit-fused mortals.

    "The Susatia. These marvelous beings reside and function as permanent citizens on Salvington, the headquarters of this local universe. They are the brilliant offspring of the Creator Son and Creative Spirit and are closely associated with the ascendant citizens of the local universe, the Spirit-fused mortals of the Nebadon Corps of Perfection." (p. 414)

2. **Proposition.** Spirit-fused mortals also are permanent citizens of the local universes.

    "Spirit-fused mortals are the permanent citizens of the local universes; they may aspire to Paradise destiny, but they cannot be sure of it. In Nebadon their universe home is the eighth group of worlds encircling Salvington,..." (p. 451)

3. **Proposition.** The destiny of permanent citizens—like Spirit-fused mortals—is unknown. They may play a part in manning the superuniverses when the pilgrims of outer space stream through Orvonton on their way to Paradise.

    "What the ultimate destiny of these stationary orders of local and of superuniverse citizenship will be we do not know, but it is quite possible that, when the Paradise finaliters are pioneering the expanding frontiers of divinity in the planetary systems of the first outer space level, their Son- and Spirit-fused brethren of the ascendant evolutionary struggle will be acceptably contributing to the maintenance of the experiential equilibrium of the perfected superuniverses while they stand ready to welcome the incoming stream of Paradise pilgrims who may, at that distant day, pour in through Orvonton and its sister creations as a vast spirit-questing torrent from these now uncharted and uninhabited galaxies of outer space." (p. 453)

V. THE SUPERUNIVERSE—
ABANDONTERS AND SON-FUSED MORTALS

1. **Proposition.** Abandonters are a type of permanent resident of the superuniverses.

    "But the Uversa headquarters spheres are continuously fostered by an amazing group of beings known as the *abandonters*, the creation, of the unrevealed agents of the Ancients of Days and the seven Reflective Spirits resident on the capital of Orvonton." (p. 416)

2. **PROPOSITION.** Son-fused mortals are residents of the superuniverse. There are less than one million in Orvonton.

"They frequently journey to Paradise on superuniverse assignment but seldom permanently reside there, being, as a class, confined to the superuniverse of their nativity." (p. 450)

VI. HAVONA—HAVONA NATIVES

1. **PROPOSITION.** Havona natives are the creatures of the Paradise Trinity. Their endowments are beyond human imagination.

"The Havona natives are the direct creation of the Paradise Trinity, and their number is beyond the concept of your circumscribed minds. Neither is it possible for Urantians to conceive of the inherent endowments of such divinely perfect creatures as these Trinity-origin races of the eternal universe. You can never truly envisage these glorious creatures; you must await your arrival in Havona, when you can greet them as spirit comrades." (p. 221)

2. **PROPOSITION.** Havoners may evolve in status—may have an unrevealed destiny. They fuse with non-Adjuster Father fragments and even enter the Corps of the Finality.

"Havona natives, like all other Trinity-origin personalities, are projected in divine perfection, and as with other Trinity-origin personalities, the passing of time may add to their stores of experiential endowments. But unlike the Stationary Sons of the Trinity, Havoners may evolve in status, may have an unrevealed future eternity-destiny. This is illustrated by those Havoners who service-factualize capacity for fusion with a non-Adjuster Father fragment and so qualify for membership in the Mortal Corps of the Finality. And there are other finaliter corps open to these natives of the central universe." (p. 221)

VII. PARADISE—PARADISE CITIZENS (PROBATIONARY NURSERY CHILDREN)

1. **PROPOSITION.** There are more than three thousand orders of Paradise Citizens.

"There are resident on Paradise numerous groups of superb beings, the Paradise Citizens. They are not directly concerned with the scheme of perfecting ascending will creatures and are not, therefore, fully revealed to Urantia mortals. There are more than three thousand orders of these supernal intelligences, the last group having been personalized simultaneously with the mandate of the Trinity which promulgated the creative plan of the seven superuniverses of time and space.

"Paradise Citizens and Havona natives are sometimes designated collectively as *Paradise-Havona personalities*." (p. 222)

2. **Proposition.** There are on Paradise more than one thousand groups of supercitizens—transcendentalers of absonite attributes.

"Part of the perfected mortal's experience on Paradise as a finalter consists in the effort to achieve comprehension of the nature and function of more than one thousand groups of the transcendental supercitizens of Paradise, eventuated beings of absonite attributes. In their association with these superpersonalities, the ascendant finaliters receive great assistance from the helpful guidance of numerous orders of transcendental ministers who are assigned to the task of introducing the evolved finaliters to their new Paradise brethren. The entire order of the Tranacendentalers live in the west of Paradise in a vast area which they exclusively occupy." (p. 350)

3. **Proposition.** Salvaged probation nursery children who ascend to Paradise become permanent citizens of the eternal Isle.

"But if they choose the Paradise path of perfection, they are immediately made ready for translation to the first mansion world, where many of them arrive in time to join their parents in the Havona ascent. After passing through Havona and attaining the Deities, these salvaged souls of mortal origin constitute the permanent ascendant citizenship of Paradise. These children who have been deprived of the valuable and essential evolutionary experience on the worlds of mortal nativity are not mustered into the Corps of the Finality." (p. 532)

Note: The worlds of the Father's circuit around Paradise harbor "a distinct type of permanent citizenship." *See page 143*

"Each world in the circuit of the Father and the circuit of the Spirit has a distinct type of permanent citizenship." (p. 143)

PART XVII
MAN

Part Seventeen
MAN

I. INTRODUCTION

1. **Proposition.** The evolutionary worlds harbor seven varieties of mortal creatures.

    "There is a standard and basic pattern of vegetable and animal life in each system. But the Life Carriers are oftentimes confronted with the necessity of modifying these basic patterns to conform to the varying physical conditions which confront them on numerous worlds of space. They foster a generalized system type of mortal creature, but there are seven distinct physical types as well as thousands upon thousands of minor variants of these seven outstanding differentiations:
    1. Atmospheric types.
    2. Elemental types.
    3. Gravity types.
    4. Temperature types.
    5. Electric types.
    6. Energizing types.
    7. Unnamed types." (p. 560)

2. **Proposition.** Planetary types of mortals may be viewed from seven different angles.

    "It will be somewhat difficult to make an adequate portrayal of the planetary series of mortals because you know so little about them, and because there are so many variations. Mortal creatures may, however, be studied from numerous viewpoints, among which are the following:
    1. Adjustment to planetary environment.
    2. Brain-type series.
    3. Spirit-reception series.
    4. Planetary-mortal epochs.
    5. Creature-kinship serials.
    6. Adjuster-fusion series.
    7. Techniques of terrestrial escape." (p. 565)

3. **Proposition.** Evolutionary mind is only fully stabilized when functioning on the extremes of cosmic intelligence—the wholly mechanized or the wholly spiritualized.

> "Evolutionary mind is only fully stable and dependable when manifesting itself upon the two extremes of cosmic intellectuality—the wholly mechanized and the entirely spiritualized. Between the intellectual extremes of pure mechanical control and true spirit nature there intervenes that enormous group of evolving and ascending minds whose stability and tranquillity are dependent upon personality choice and spirit identification." (p. 1217)

II. ANDON AND FONTA

1. **Proposition.** Man is not an evolutionary accident.

> "The early stages of life evolution are not altogether in conformity with your present-day views. *Mortal man is not an evolutionary accident.* There is a precise system, a universal law, which determines the unfolding of the planetary life plan on the spheres of space. Time and the production of large numbers of a species are not the controlling influences. Mice reproduce much more rapidly than elephants, yet elephants evolve more rapidly than mice." (p. 560)

2. **Proposition.** In many respects, Andon and Fonta were the most remarkable pair of human beings that have ever lived on Urantia.

> "In many respects, Andon and Fonta were the most remarkable pair of human beings that have every lived on the face of the earth. This wonderful pair, the actual parents of all mankind, were in every way superior to many of their immediate descendants, and they were radically different from all of their ancestors, both immediate and remote." (p. 711)

3. **Proposition.** On discovering fire, they sat up all night and did not leave it for three days.

> "This was one of the most joyous moments in their short but eventful lives. All night long they sat up watching their fire burn, vaguely realizing that they had made a discovery which would make it possible for them to defy climate and thus forever to be independent of their animal relatives of the southern lands. After three days' rest and enjoyment of the fire, they journeyed on." (p. 712)

4. **Proposition.** Andon and Fonta had a sizable family of children, grandchildren, and great-grandchildren.

> "Andon and Fonta had nineteen children in all, and they lived to enjoy the association of almost half a hundred grandchildren and half a dozen great-grandchildren. The family was domiciled in four adjoining rock shelters, or semicaves, three of which were interconnected by hallways which had been excavated in the soft limestone with flint tools devised by Andon's children." (p. 713)

5. **Proposition.** Upon the death of Andon and Fonta, Sontad assumed leadership of the clan.

> "Upon the death of his parents, Sontad, despite a seriously injured foot, immediately assumed the leadership of the clan and was ably assisted by his wife, his eldest sister. Their first task was to roll up stones to effectively entomb their dead parents, brothers, sisters, and children. Undue significance should not attach to this act of burial. Their ideas of survival after death were very vague and indefinite, being largely derived from their fantastic and variegated dream life." (p. 713)

6. **Proposition.** Before the dispersion of the Andonic clans, they had a well-developed language which became the word of Urantia.

> "Before the extensive dispersion of the Andonic clans a well-developed language had evolved from their early efforts to intercommunicate. This language continued to grow, and almost daily additions were made to it because of the new inventions and adaptations to environment which were developed by these active, restless, and curious people. And this language became the word of Urantia, the tongue of the early human family, until the later appearance of the colored races." (p. 714)

7. **Proposition.** The descendants of Andon and Fonta overspread Europe and established more than one thousand settlements along the rivers leading to the North Sea.

> "Before this extensive ice sheet reached France and the British Isles, the descendants of Andon and Fonta had pushed on westward over Europe and had established more than one thousand separate settlements along the great rivers leading to the then warm waters of the North Sea." (p. 715)

8. **Proposition.** Shortly after Andon and Fonta arrived on Jerusem, they received permission to return to the first mansion world to welcome Urantia pilgrims.

> "Andon and Fonta, shortly after their arrival on Jerusem, received permission from the System Sovereign to return to the first mansion world to serve with the morontia personalities who welcome the pilgrims of time from Urantia to the heavenly spheres. And they have been assigned indefinitely to this service. They sought to send greetings to Urantia in connection with these revelations, but this request was wisely denied them." (p. 717)

III. THE PRINCE'S CORPOREAL STAFF

1. **Proposition.** Planetary Princes take with them one hundred volunteer, unfused, ascending mortals.

    > "On going to a young world, a Planetary Prince usually takes with him a group of volunteer ascending beings from the local system headquarters. These ascenders accompany the prince as advisers and helpers in the work of early race improvement. This corps of material helpers constitutes the connecting link between the prince and the world races. The Urantia Prince, Caligastia, had a corps of one hundred such helpers." (p. 574)

2. **Proposition.** The Prince's staff of one hundred functioned in ten divisions:

    1. The council on food and material welfare.
    2. The board of animal domestication and utilization.
    3. The advisers regarding the conquest of predatory animals.
    4. The faculty on dissemination and conservation of knowledge.
    5. The commission on industry and trade.
    6. The college of revealed religion.
    7. The guardians of health and life.
    8. The planetary council on art and science.
    9. The governors of advanced tribal relations.
    10. The supreme court of tribal co-ordination and racial co-operation.

    See pages 745-49

3. **Proposition.** Hap's moral law was the law of Dalamatia for three hundred thousand years.

    > "Hap presented the early races with a moral law. This code was known as 'The Father's Way' and consisted of the following seven commands:

"1. You shall not fear nor serve any God but the Father of all.
"2. You shall not disobey the Father's Son, the world's ruler, nor show disrespect to his superhuman associates.
"3. You shall not speak a lie when called before the judges of the people.
"4. You shall not kill men, women, or children.
"5. You shall not steal your neighbor's goods or cattle.
"6. You shall not touch your friend's wife.
"7. You shall not show disrespect to your parents or to the elders of the tribe.
"This was the law of Dalamatia for almost three hundred thousand years. And many of the stones on which this law was inscribed now lie beneath the waters off the shores of Mesopotamia and Persia. It became the custom to hold one of these commands in mind for each day of the week, using it for salutations and mealtime thanksgiving." (p. 751)

4. **PROPOSITION.** Students of the Prince's school were agriculturists and horticulturists. They divided their time in five ways.

"In the headquarters settlement on your world every human habitation was provided with abundance of land. Although the remote tribes continued in hunting and food foraging, the students and teachers in the Prince's schools were all agriculturists and horticulturists. The time was about equally divided between the following pursuits:
"1. *Physical labor*. Cultivation of the soil, associated with home building and embellishment.
"2. *Social activities*. Play performances and cultural social groupings.
"3. *Educational application*. Individual instruction in connection with family-group teaching, supplemented by specialized class training.
"4. *Vocational training*. Schools of marriage and homemaking, the schools of art and craft training, and the classes for the training of teachers—secular, cultural, and religious.
"5. *Spiritual culture*. The teacher brotherhood, the enlightenment of childhood and youth groups, and the training of adopted native children as missionaries to their people." (p. 575)

5. **PROPOSITION.** When the prince's assistants mate among themselves, two types of beings are produced:
    a. *Primary midwayers.*
    b. *High types of material creatures.*

"These assistants to the Planetary Prince seldom mate with the world races, but they do always mate among themselves. Two classes of beings result from these unions: the primary type of midway creatures and certain high types of material beings who remain attached to the prince's staff after their parents have been removed from the planet at the time of the arrival of Adam and Eve. These children do not mate with the mortal races except in certain emergencies and then only by direction of the Planetary Prince. In such an event, their children—the grandchildren of the corporeal staff—are in status as of the superior races of their day and generation. All of the offspring of these semimaterial assistants of the Planetary Prince are Adjuster indwelt." (p. 574)

IV. THE COLORED RACES

1. **Proposition.** Among the highland Badonites there appeared the Sangik family—the parents of the six colored races.

    "And now, among these highland Badonites there was a new and strange occurrence. A man and woman living in the northeastern part of the then inhabited highland region began *suddenly* to produce a family of unusually intelligent children. This was the *Sangik family*, the ancestors of all of the six colored races of Urantia.

    "These Sangik children, nineteen in number, were not only intelligent above their fellows, but their skins manifested a unique tendency to turn various colors upon exposure to sunlight. Among these nineteen children were five red, two orange, four yellow, two green, four blue, and two indigo. These colors became more pronounced as the children grew older, and when these youths later mated with their fellow tribesmen, all of their offspring tended toward the skin color of the Sangik parent." (p. 722)

2. **Proposition.** There are six basic evolutionary races:
    a. *Three primary—red, yellow, blue.*
    b. *Three secondary—orange, green, indigo.*

    "There are six basic evolutionary races: three primary—red, yellow, and blue; and three secondary—orange, green, and indigo. Most inhabited worlds have all of these races, but many of the three-brained planets harbor only the three primary types. Some local systems also have only these three races." (p. 564)

V. ADAM AND EVE

1. **PROPOSITION.** The second Eden was the cradle of civilization for almost thirty thousand years. The Adamic peoples sent their progeny to the ends of the earth.

   "The second Eden was the cradle of civilization for almost thirty thousand years. Here in Mesopotamia the Adamic peoples held forth, sending out their progeny to the ends of the earth, and latterly, as amalgamated with the Nodite and Sangik tribes, were known as the Andites. From this region went those men and women who initiated the doings of historic times, and who have so enormously accelerated cultural progress on Urantia." (p. 868)

2. **PROPOSITION.** The leadership of the second garden was heroic—an inspiring epic of Urantia's history. The sons and daughters of Adam and Eve went forth as uplifters of all races.

   "The heroism displayed in the leadership of the second garden constitutes one of the amazing and inspiring epics of Urantia's history. These splendid souls never wholly lost sight of the purpose of the Adamic mission, and therefore did they valiantly fight off the influences of the surrounding and inferior tribes while they willingly sent forth their choicest sons and daughters in a steady stream as emissaries to the races of earth. Sometimes this expansion was depleting to the home culture, but always these superior peoples would rehabilitate themselves." (p. 869)

3. **PROPOSITION.** The culture of the Adamites was far above that of the evolutionary races, but it was artificial. Not having been evolved, it was doomed to gravitate down to the evolutionary level.

   "The civilization, society, and cultural status of the Adamites were far above the general level of the evolutionary races of Urantia. Only among the old settlements of Van and Amadon and the Adamsonites was there a civilization in anyway comparable. But the civilization of the second Eden was an artificial structure—*it had not been evolved*—and was therefore doomed to deteriorate until it reached a natural evolutionary level." (p. 870)

VI. THE VIOLET RACE

1. **PROPOSITION.** After the times of Adam the superior races were widely distributed.

   "1. *The voilet race—Adamites and Adamsonites.* The chief center of Adamite culture was in the second garden, located in the triangle of the Tigris and Euphrates rivers; this was indeed the cradle of

Occidental and Indian civilizations. The secondary or northern center of the violet race was the Adamsonite headquarters, situated east of the southern shore of the Caspian Sea near the Kopet mountains. From these two centers there went forth to the surrounding lands the culture and life plasm which so immediately quickened all the races.

"2. *Pre-Sumerians and other Nodites.* There were also present in Mesopotamia, near the mouth of the rivers, remnants of the ancient culture of the days of Dalamatia. With the passing millenniums, this group became thoroughly admixed with the Adamites to the north, but they never entirely lost their Nodite traditions. Various other Nodite groups that had settled in the Levant were, in general absorbed by the later expanding violet race.

"3. *The Andonites* maintained five or six fairly representative settlements to the north and east of the Adamson headquarters. They were also scattered throughout Turkestan, while isolated islands of them persisted throughout Eurasia, especially in mountainous regions. These aborigines still held the northlands of the Eurasian continent, together with Iceland and Greenland, but they had long since been driven from the plains of Europe by the blue man and from the river valleys of farther Asia by the expanding yellow race." (p. 868)

2. **Proposition.** There were seven major invasions of Europe by the Andites, the last coming on horseback in three great waves.

"While the Andites poured into Europe in a steady stream, there were seven major invasions, the last arrivals coming on horseback in three great waves. Some entered Europe by way of the islands of the Aegean and up the Danube valley, but the majority of the earlier and purer strains migrated to northwestern Europe by the northern route across the grazing lands of the Volga and the Don.

"Between the third and fourth invasions a horde of Andonites entered Europe from the north, having come from Siberia by way of the Russian rivers and the Baltic. They were immediately assimilated by the northern Andite tribes." (p. 892)

3. **Proposition.** The Adamites were pacific; the Nodites belligerent. Their union, plus the Sangiks, produced the able, aggressive Andites.

"The earlier expansions of the purer violet race were far more pacific than were those of their later semimilitary and conquest-loving Andite descendants. The Adamites were pacific; the Nodites were belligerent. The union of these stocks, as later mingled with the Sangik races, produced the able, aggressive Andites who made actual military conquests." (p 892)

4. **Proposition.** The horse determined the dominance of the Andites in the Occident. Moving rapidly, they reached Europe as coherent groups—retaining much of their culture.

> "But the horse was the evolutionary factor which determined the dominance of the Andites in the Occident. The horse gave the dispersing Andites the hitherto nonexistent advantage of mobility, enabling the last groups of Andite cavalrymen to progress quickly around the Caspian Sea to overrun all of Europe. All previous waves of Andites had moved so slowly that they tended to disintegrate at any great distance from Mesopotamia. But these later waves moved so rapidly that they reached Europe as coherent groups, still retaining some measure of higher culture." (p. 892)

5. **Proposition.** Around 19,000 B.C., the Adamites were a nation numbering four and a half million.

> "But the Adamites were a real nation around 19,000 B.C., numbering four and a half million, and already they had poured forth millions of their progeny into the surrounding peoples." (p. 870)

6. **Proposition.** The Andites were a blend of violet, Nodite, and Sangik peoples. Their racial inheritance was from one-eighth to one-sixth violet.

> "The Andite races were the primary blends of the pure-line violet race and the Nodites plus the evolutionary peoples. In general, Andites should be thought of as having a far greater percentage of Adamic blood than the modern races. In the main, the term Andite is used to designate those peoples whose racial inheritance was from one-eighth to one-sixth violet. Modern Urantians, even the northern white races, contain much less than this percentage of the blood of Adam." (p. 871)

7. **Proposition.** The Aryan race was formed in the highlands of Turkestan. The dialect was a mixture of the language of the Adamsonites and the Andites.

> "The civilization of Turkestan was constantly being revived and refreshed by the newcomers from Mesopotamia, especially by the later Andite cavalrymen. The so-called Aryan mother tongue was in process of formation in the highlands of Turkestan; it was a blend of the Andonic dialect of that region with the language of

the Adamsonites and later Andites. Many modern languages are derived from this early speech of these central Asian tribes who conquered Europe, India, and the upper stretches of the Mesopotamian plains. This ancient language gave the Occidental tongues all of that similarity which is called Aryan." (p. 872)

8. **PROPOSITION.** The last three waves of Andites left Mesopotamia between 8000 and 6000 B.C. They conquered and blended with the newly appearing white race.

> "The last three waves of Andites poured out of Mesopotamia between 8000 and 6000 B.C. These three great waves of culture were forced out of Mesopotamia by the pressure of the hill tribes to the east and the harassment of the plainsmen of the west. The inhabitants of the Euphrates valley and adjacent territory went forth in their final exodus in several directions:
> "Sixty-five per cent entered Europe by the Caspian Sea route to conquer and amalgamate with the newly appearing white races—the blend of the blue men and the earlier Andites." (p. 873)

VII. THE SUMERIANS AND ARYANS

1. **PROPOSITION.** After the last Andite dispersion from Mesopotamia, there remained near the mouths of the rivers the Sumerians with their largely Nodite culture.

> "When the last Andite dispersion broke the biologic backbone of Mesopotamian civilization, a small minority of this superior race remained in their homeland near the mouths of the rivers. These were the Sumerians, and by 6000 B.C. they had become largely Andite in extraction, though their culture was more exclusively Nodite in character, and they clung to the ancient traditions of Dalamatia. Nonetheless, these Sumerians of the coastal regions were the last of the Andites in Mesopotamia. But the races of Mesopotamia were already thoroughly blended by this late date, as is evidenced by the skull types found in the graves of this era." (p. 875)

2. **PROPOSITION.** The last exodus of the Andites from Turkestan was the Aryan invasion of India.

> "The second Andite penetration of India was the Aryan invasion during a period of almost five hundred years in the middle of the third millennium before Christ. This migration marked the terminal exodus of the Andites from their homelands in Turkestan.

"The early Aryan centers were scattered over the northern half of India, notably in the northwest. These invaders never completed the conquest of the country and subsequently met their undoing in this neglect since their lesser numbers made them vulnerable to absorption by the Dravidians of the south, who subsequently overran the entire peninsula except the Himalayan provinces." (p. 882)

VIII. RACIAL TYPES

1. **PROPOSITION.** Human remains of the last twenty thousand years do not disclose the original five types, but they do reveal the three modern groups.

   "In general, therefore, as the human remains of the last twenty thousand years are unearthed, it will be impossible clearly to distinguish the five original types. Study of such skeletal structures will disclose that mankind is now divided into approximately three classes:

   "1. *The Caucasoid*—the Andite blend of the Nodite and Adamic stocks, further modified by primary and (some) secondary Sangik admixture and by considerable Andonic crossing. The Occidental white races, together with some Indian and Turanian peoples, are included in this group. The unifying factor in this division is the greater or lesser proportion of Andite inheritance.

   "2. *The Mongoloid*—the primary Sangik type, including the original red, yellow, and blue races. The Chinese and Amerinds belong to this group. In Europe the Mongoloid type has been modified by secondary Sangik and Andonic mixture; still more by Andite infusion. The Malayan and other Indonesian peoples are included in this classification, though they contain a high percentage of secondary Sangik blood.

   "3. *The Negroid*—the secondary Sangik type, which originally included the orange, green, and indigo races. This is the type best illustrated by the Negro, and it will be found through Africa, India, and Indonesia wherever the secondary Sangik races located." (p. 905)

Part XVII — Man

2. **Proposition.** At the end of the Andite migrations, there existed in Europe three white races.

> "The racial blends in Europe toward the close of the Andite migrations became generalized into the three white races as follows:
>
> "1. *The northern white race.* This so-called Nordic race consisted primarily of the blue man plus the Andite but also contained a considerable amount of Andonite blood, together with smaller amounts of the red and yellow Sangik. The northern white race thus encompassed these four most desirable human stocks. But the largest inheritance was from the blue man. The typical early Nordic was long-headed, tall, and blond. But long ago this race became thoroughly mixed with all of the branches of the white peoples.
>
> "The primitive culture of Europe, which was encountered by the invading Nordics, was that of the retrograding Danubians blended with the blue man. The Nordic-Danish and the Danubian-Andonite cultures met and mingled on the Rhine as is witnessed by the existence of two racial groups in Germany today.
>
> "The Nordics continued the trade in amber from the Baltic coast, building up a great commerce with the broadheads of the Danube valley via the Brenner Pass. This extended contact with the Danubians led these northerners into mother worship, and for several thousands of years cremation of the dead was almost universal throughout Scandinavia. This explains why remains of the earlier white races, although buried all over Europe, are not to be found—only their ashes in stone and clay urns. These white men also built dwellings; they never lived in caves. And again this explains why there are so few evidences of the white man's early culture, although the preceding Cro-Magnon type is well preserved where it has been securely sealed up in caves and grottoes. As it were, one day in northern Europe there is a primitive culture of the retrogressing Danubians and the blue man and the next that of a suddenly appearing and vastly superior white man.
>
> "2. *The central white race.* While this group includes strains of blue, yellow, and Andite, it is predominantly Andonite. These people are broad-headed, swarthy, and stocky. They are driven like a wedge between the Nordic and Mediterranean races, with the broad base resting in Asia and the apex penetrating eastern France.
>
> "3. *The southern white race.* This brunet Mediterranean race consisted of a blend of the Andite and the blue man, with a smaller Andonite strain than in the north. This group also absorbed a considerable amount of secondary Sangik blood

through the Saharans. In later times this southern division of the white race was infused by strong Andite elements from the eastern Mediterranean." (pp. 897-98)

IX. THE BLUE MAN

1. **PROPOSITION.** The blue man did not achieve a great culture, but he was the foundation of the most potent and aggressive civilization since the times of Adam.

   "Although the European blue man did not of himself achieve a great cultural civilization, he did supply the biologic foundation which, when its Adamized strains were blended with the later Andite invaders, produced one of the most potent stocks for the attainment of aggressive civilization ever to appear on Urantia since the times of the violet race and their Andite successors." (p. 889)

2. **PROPOSITION.** Modern white peoples are derived from the Adamic stock admixed with Sangik strains—mostly the blue man.

   "The modern white peoples incorporate the surviving strains of the Adamic stock which became admixed with the Sangik races, some red and yellow but more especially the blue. There is a considerable percentage of the original Andonite stock in all the white races and still more of the early Nodite strains." (p. 889)

3. **PROPOSITION.** Adam's blood was shared by many peoples, but all races were not equally attractive to the Adamites.

   "Adam's blood has been shared with most of the human races, but some secured more than others. The mixed races of India and the darker peoples of Africa were not attractive to the Adamites. They would have mixed freely with the red man had he not been far removed in the Americas, and they were kindly disposed toward the yellow man, but he was likewise difficult of access in faraway Asia. Therefore, when actuated by either adventure or altruism, or when driven out of the Euphrates valley, they very naturally chose union with the blue races of Europe." (p. 890)

4. **PROPOSITION.** There was great sex attraction between the blue man and the Adamites and their religions were not antagonistic.

   "The blue men, then dominant in Europe, had no religious practices which were repulsive to the earlier migrating Adamites, and there was great sex attraction between the violet and the blue races. The best of the blue men deemed it a high

Part XVII — Man

honor to be permitted to mate with the Adamites. Every blue man entertained the ambition of becoming so skillful and artistic as to win the affection of some Adamite woman, and it was the highest aspiration of a superior blue woman to receive the attentions of an Adamite." (p. 890)

5. **Proposition.** The Europeans were a blend of the art and vigor of the blue man and the creative imagination of the Adamites. The Cro-Magnoids resisted the religion of the Adamites because of the dishonesty and immorality of the mixed Adamites.

> "The European civilization of this early post-Adamic period was a unique blend of the vigor and art of the blue men with the creative imagination of the Adamites. The blue men were a race of great vigor, but they greatly deteriorated the cultural and spiritual status of the Adamites. It was very difficult for the latter to impress their religion upon the Cro-Magnoids because of the tendency of so many to cheat and to debauch the maidens. For ten thousand years religion in Europe was at a low ebb as compared with the developments in India and Egypt.
>
> "The blue men were perfectly honest in all their dealings and were wholly free from the sexual vices of the mixed Adamites. They respected maidenhood, only practicing polygamy when war produced a shortage of males." (p. 891)

6. **Proposition.** The Cro-Magnons were brave and farseeing. They were efficient in child culture and industry.

> "These Cro-Magnon peoples were a brave and farseeing race. They maintained an efficient system of child culture. Both parents participated in these labors, and the services of the older children were fully utilized. Each child was carefully trained in the care of the caves, in art, and in flint making. At an early age the women were well versed in the domestic arts and in crude agriculture, while the men were skilled hunters and courageous warriors." (p. 891)

7. **Proposition.** For three thousand years the military headquarters of the Andites was in Denmark.

> "For three thousand years the military headquarters of the northern Andites was in Denmark. From this central point there went forth the successive waves of conquest, which grew decreasingly Andite and increasingly white as the passing centuries witnessed the final blending of the Mesopotamian conquerors with the conquered peoples." (p. 893)

8. **Proposition.** The white cavalry raiders absorbed the blue man and were resisted by the Cro-Magnons but finally wiped out the older peoples.

> "While the blue man had been absorbed in the north and eventually succumbed to the white cavalry raiders who penetrated the south, the advancing tribes of the mixed white race met with stubborn and protracted resistance from the Cro-Magnons, but superior intelligence and ever-augmenting biologic reserves enabled them to wipe the older race out of existence." (p. 893)

X. THE RED AND YELLOW RACES

1. **Proposition.** Eighty-five thousand years ago, the last of the red men left Asia coming over the Bering isthmus to North America.

> "One hundred thousand years ago the decimated tribes of the red race were fighting with their backs to the retreating ice of the last glacier, and when the land passage to the west, over the Bering isthmus, became passable, these tribes were not slow in forsaking the inhospitable shores of the Asiatic continent. It is eighty-five thousand years since the last of the pure red men departed from Asia, but the long struggle left its genetic imprint upon the victorious yellow race. The northern Chinese peoples, together with the Andonite Siberians, assimilated much of the red stock and were in considerable measure benefited thereby." (p. 883)

2. **Proposition.** The red man never contacted the Andites. American Indians were hunters who practiced agriculture on the side.

> "The North American Indians never came in contact with even the Andite offspring of Adam and Eve, having been dispossessed of their Asiatic homelands some fifty thousand years before the coming of Adam. During the age of Andite migrations the pure red strains were spreading out over North America as nomadic tribes, hunters who practiced agriculture to a small extent. These races and cultural groups remained almost completely isolated from the remainder of the world from their arrival in the Americas down to the end of the first millennium of the Christian era, when they were discovered by the white races of Europe. Up to that time the Eskimos were the nearest to white men the northern tribes of red men had ever seen." (p. 884)

3. **Proposition.** After driving the red man to North America, the Chinese drove the Andites to Siberia and Turkestan.

> "Sometime after driving the red man across to North America, the expanding Chinese cleared the Andonites from the river valleys of eastern Asia, pushing them north into Siberia and west into Turkestan, where they were soon to come in contact with the superior culture of the Andites." (p. 884)

4. **Proposition.** In Burma and Indo-China the cultures of India and China blended.

> "In Burma and the peninsula of Indo-China the cultures of India and China mixed and blended to produce the successive civilizations of those regions. Here the vanished green race has persisted in larger proportion than anywhere else in the world." (p. 884)

5. **Proposition.** The superiority of the yellow race was derived from four factors.

> "The superiority of the ancient yellow race was due to four great factors:
>
> "1. *Genetic.* Unlike their blue cousins in Europe, both the red and yellow races had largely escaped mixture with debased human stocks. The northern Chinese, already strengthened by small amounts of the superior red and Andonic strains, were soon to benefit by a considerable influx of Andite blood. The southern Chinese did not fare so well in this regard, and they had long suffered from absorption of the green race, while later on they were to be further weakened by the infiltration of the swarms of inferior peoples crowded out of India by the Dravidian-Andite invasion. And today in China there is a definite difference between the northern and southern races.
>
> "2. *Social.* The yellow race early learned the value of peace among themselves. Their internal peaceableness so contributed to population increase as to insure the spread of their civilization among many millions. From 25,000 to 5000 B.C. the highest mass civilization on Urantia was in central and northern China. The yellow man was first to achieve a racial solidarity—the first to attain a large-scale cultural, social, and political civilization.
>
> "3. *Spiritual.* During the age of Andite migrations the Chinese were among the more spiritual peoples of earth. Long adherence to the worship of the One Truth proclaimed by Singlangton kept them ahead of most of the other races. The stimulus of a progressive and advanced religion is often a decisive factor

in cultural development; as India languished, so China forged ahead under the invigorating stimulus of a religion in which truth was enshrined as the supreme Deity.

"4. *Geographic*. China is protected by the mountains to the west and the Pacific to the east. Only in the north is the way open to attack, and from the days of the red man to the coming of the later descendants of the Andites, the north was not occupied by any aggressive race." (p. 885)

XI. CIVILIZATION

1. PROPOSITION. There are three general classes of human institutions.

    "All human institutions minister to some social need, past or present, notwithstanding that their overdevelopment unfailingly detracts from the worthwhileness of the individual in that personality is overshadowed and initiative is diminished. Man should control his institutions rather than permit himself to be dominated by these creations of advancing civilization.
    "Human institutions are of three general classes:
    "1. *The institutions of self-maintenance*. These institutions embrace those practices growing out of food hunger and its associated instincts of self-preservation. They include industry, property, war for gain, and all the regulative machinery of society. Sooner or later the fear instinct fosters the establishment of these institutions of survival by means of taboo, convention, and religious sanction. But fear, ignorance, and superstition have played a prominent part in the early origin and subsequent development of all human institutions.
    "2. *The institutions of self-perpetuation*. These are the establishments of society growing out of sex hunger, maternal instinct, and the higher tender emotions of the races. They embrace the social safeguards of the home and the school, of family life, education, ethics, and religion. They include marriage customs, war for defense, and home building.
    "3. *The institutions of self-gratification*. These are the practices growing out of vanity proclivities and pride emotions; and they embrace customs in dress and personal adornment, social usages, war for glory, dancing, amusement, games, and other phases of sensual gratification. But civilization has never evolved distinctive institutions of self-gratification." (p. 772)

2. **Proposition.** After the last Andite migration, culture declined in the Euphrates valley—the center of civilization shifted to the Nile.

> "From the times of the terminal Andite migrations, culture declined in the Euphrates valley, and the immediate center of civilization shifted to the valley of the Nile. Egypt became the successor of Mesopotamia as the headquarters of the most advanced group on earth." (p. 894)

3. **Proposition.** About 12,000 B.C. a brilliant tribe of Andites—Vanite-Nodites—settled on Crete. They were skillful workers.

> "About 12,000 B.C. a brilliant tribe of Andites migrated to Crete. This was the only island settled so early by such a superior group, and it was almost two thousand years before the descendants of these mariners spread to the neighboring isles. This group were the narrow-headed, smaller-statured Andites who had intermarried with the Vanite division of the northern Nodites. They were all under six feet in height and had been literally driven off the mainland by their larger and inferior fellows. These emigrants to Crete were highly skilled in textiles, metals, pottery, plumbing, and the use of stone for building material. They engaged in writing and carried on as herders and agriculturists." (p. 895)

4. **Proposition.** Two thousand years after the settlement of Crete, a group of tall Adamsonites settled in Greece. This group of 375 was led by Sato.

> "Almost two thousand years after the settlement of Crete a group of the tall descendants of Adamson made their way over the northern islands to Greece, coming almost directly from their highland home north of Mesopotamia. These progenitors of the Greeks were led westward by Sato, a direct descendant of Adamson and Ratta.
>
> "The group which finally settled in Greece consisted of three hundred and seventy-five of the selected and superior people comprising the end of the second civilization of the Adamsonites. These later sons of Adamson carried the then most valuable strains of the emerging white races. They were of a high intellectual order and, physically regarded, the most beautiful of men since the days of the first Eden." (p. 895)

5. **Proposition.** The civilization of Urantia is predicated on fifteen factors:
   1. Natural circumstances.
   2. Capital goods.
   3. Scientific knowledge.
   4. Human resources.
   5. Effectiveness of material resources.
   6. Effectiveness of language.
   7. Effectiveness of mechanical devices.
   8. Character of torchbearers.
   9. The racial ideals.
   10. Co-ordination of specialists.
   11. Place-finding devices.
   12. The willingness to co-operate.
   13. Effectiveness of wise leadership.
   14. Social changes.
   15. The prevention of transitional breakdowns.

   See pages 906-11.

6. **Proposition.** The economics of a world settled in light and life is conducted on a definite plan.

   "Human government in the conduct of material affairs continues to function throughout this age of relative progress and perfection. The public activities of a world in the first stage of light and life which I recently visited were financed by the tithing technique. Every adult worker—and all able-bodied citizens worked at something—paid ten per cent of his income or increase to the public treasury, and it was disbursed as follows:

   "1. Three per cent was expended in the promotion of truth—science, education, and philosophy.

   "2. Three per cent was devoted to beauty—play, social leisure, and art.

   "3. Three per cent was dedicated to goodness—social service, altruism, and religion.

   "4. One per cent was assigned to the insurance reserves against the risk of incapacity for labor resultant from accident, disease, old age, or unpreventable disasters." (p. 625)

XII. HUMAN FREE WILL

1. **Proposition.** In the matter of the choice of eternal survival, the human will is absolutely sovereign.

   "No other being, force, creator, or agency in all the wide universe of universes can interfere to any degree with the absolute sovereignty of the mortal free will, as it operates within the realms of choice, regarding the eternal destiny of the personality of the choosing mortal. As pertains to eternal survival, God has decreed the sovereignty of the material and mortal will, and that decree is absolute." (p. 71)

2. **Proposition.** Morality is never advanced by law or force. It depends on personal free will and is spread by the contagion of personal contact with morally fragrant persons.

   "Morality can never be advanced by law or by force. It is a personal and freewill matter and must be disseminated by the contagion of the contact of morally fragrant persons with those who are less morally responsive, but who are also in some measure desirous of doing the Father's will." (p. 193)

XIII. THE DIVINE MONITOR

1. **Proposition.** Many of man's troubles grow out of the fact that he is a part of nature—yet he transcends nature, since a spark of infinity resides within him.

   "Many of the temporal troubles of mortal man grow out of his twofold relation to the cosmos. Man is a part of nature—he exists in nature—and yet he is able to transcend nature. Man is finite, but he is indwelt by a spark of infinity. Such a dual situation not only provides the potential for evil but also engenders many social and moral situations fraught with much uncertainty and not a little anxiety." (p. 1221)

2. **Proposition.** Man's spiritual endowment is uniform and unique—no matter how much persons may differ intellectually, socially, economically, and even morally.

   "However Urantia mortals may differ in their intellectual, social, economic, and even moral opportunities and endowments, forget not that their spiritual endowment is uniform and unique. They all enjoy the same divine presence of the gift from the Father, and they are all equally privileged to seek intimate personal communion with this indwelling spirit of divine origin, while they may all equally choose to accept the uniform spiritual leading of these Mystery Monitors." (p. 63)

3. **Proposition.** Man's mind-energy system surrounds a spirit nucleus, and such a relationship constitutes the potential of eternal personality.

> "Mortal man has a spirit nucleus. The mind is a personal-energy system existing around a divine spirit nucleus and functioning in a material environment. Such a living relationship of personal mind and spirit constitutes the universe potential of eternal personality. Real trouble, lasting disappointment, serious defeat, or inescapable death can come only after self-concepts presume fully to displace the governing power of the central spirit nucleus, thereby disrupting the cosmic scheme of personality identity." (p. 142)

4. **Proposition.** Evolutionary mortals can realize the faith-fact of sonship with God because of:
    a. *The Holy Spirit of the local universe.*
    b. *The Spirit of Truth.*
    c. *The Adjuster presence.*

> "The presence of the Holy Spirit of the Universe Daughter of the Infinite Spirit, of the Spirit of Truth of the Universe Son of the Eternal Son, and of the Adjuster-spirit of the Paradise Father in or with an evolutionary mortal, denotes symmetry of spiritual endowment and ministry and qualifies such a mortal consciously to realize the faith-fact of sonship with God." (p. 380)

5. **Proposition.** After your morontia resurrection, the Thought Adjuster will recall all of your memories of spiritual value.

> "The Thought Adjuster will recall and rehearse for you only those memories and experiences which are a part of, and essential to, your universe career. If the Adjuster has been a partner in the evolution of aught in the human mind, then will these worthwhile experiences survive in the eternal consciousness of the Adjuster. But much of your past life and its memories, having neither spiritual meaning nor morontia value, will perish with the material brain; much of material experience will pass away as one time scaffolding which, having bridged you over to the morontia level, no longer serves a purpose in the universe." (p. 1235)

6. **Proposition.** Personality relationships have cosmic value and will always persist. On the mansion worlds you will know and be known.

> "But personality and the relationships between personalities are never scaffolding; mortal memory of personality relationships has cosmic value and will persist. On the mansion worlds you will know and be known, and more, you will remember, and be remembered by, your onetime associates in the short but intriguing life on Urantia." (p. 1235)

XIV. GOD-CONSCIOUSNESS

1. **Proposition.** The relative free will of human self-consciousness is manifested in seven directions.

    "The relative free will which characterizes the self-consciousness of human personality is involved in:
    1. Moral decision, highest wisdom.
    2. Spiritual choice, truth discernment.
    3. Unselfish love, brotherhood service.
    4. Purposeful co-operation, group loyalty.
    5. Cosmic insight, the grasp of universe meanings.
    6. Personality dedication, wholehearted devotion to doing the Father's will.
    7. Worship, the sincere pursuit of divine values and the wholehearted love of the divine Value-Giver." (p. 194)

2. **Proposition.** The cosmic-minded, Adjuster-indwelt mortal possesses innate realization of physical, mental, and spiritual reality. Will creatures are thus equipped to discern the fact, the law, and the love of God.

    "The cosmic-mind-endowed, Adjuster-indwelt, personal creature possesses innate recognition-realization of energy reality, mind reality, and spirit reality. The will creature is thus equipped to discern the fact, the law, and the love of God. Aside from these three inalienables of human consciousness, all human experience is really subjective except that intuitive realization of validity attaches to the *unification* of these three universe reality responses of cosmic recognition." (p. 195)

3. **Proposition.** Self-consciousness is in reality a communal experience— God and man. In the human mind four realities are inherent.

    "Self-consciousness is in essence a communal consciousness: God and man, Father and Son, Creator and creature. In human self-consciousness four universe-reality realizations are latent and inherent:
    "1. The quest for knowledge, the logic of science.
    "2. The quest for moral values, the sense of duty.
    "3. The quest for spiritual values, the religious experience.
    "4. The quest for personality values, the ability to recognize the reality of God as a personality and the concurrent realization of our fraternal relationship with fellow personalities." (p. 196)

4. **Proposition.** When the human mind attempts to approach the higher from the lower—whether in biology or theology—it encounters four dangers.

> "When the human mind undertakes to follow the philosophic technique of starting from the lower to approach the higher, whether in biology or theology, it is always in danger of committing four errors of reasoning:
>
> "1. It may utterly fail to perceive the final and completed evolutionary goal of either personal attainment or cosmic destiny.
>
> "2. It may commit the supreme philosophical blunder by oversimplifying cosmic evolutionary (experiential) reality, thus leading to the distortion of facts, to the perversion of truth, and to the misconception of destinies.
>
> "3. The study of causation is the perusal of history. But the knowledge of *how* a being becomes does not necessarily provide an intelligent understanding of the present status and true character of such a being.
>
> "4. History alone fails adequately to reveal future development—destiny. Finite origins are helpful, but only divine causes reveal final effects. Eternal ends are not shown in time beginnings. The present can be truly interpreted only in the light of the correlated past and future." (p. 215)

5. **Proposition.** We employ the method of approaching man by starting with the Paradise source and center of all personality and cosmic reality.

> "Therefore, because of these and for still other reasons, do we employ the technique of approaching man and his planetary problems by embarkation on the time-space journey from the infinite, eternal, and divine Paradise Source and Center of all personality reality and all cosmic existence." (p. 215)

XV. URANTIA PERSONALITY

1. **Proposition.** We know many things about personality, but they do not provide a definition.

> "While it would be presumptuous to attempt the definition of personality, it may prove helpful to recount some of the things which are known about personality:

"1. Personality is that quality in reality which is bestowed by the Universal Father himself or by the Conjoint Actor, acting for the Father.

"2. It may be bestowed upon any living energy system which includes mind or spirit.

"3. It is not wholly subject to the fetters of antecedent causation. It is relatively creative or cocreative.

"4. When bestowed upon evolutionary material creatures, it causes spirit to strive for the mastery of energy-matter through the mediation of mind.

"5. Personality, while devoid of identity, can unify the identity of any living energy system.

"6. It discloses only qualitative response to the personality circuit in contradistinction to the three energies which show both qualitative and quantitative response to gravity.

"7. Personality is changeless in the presence of change.

"8. It can make a gift to God—dedication of the free will to the doing of the will of God.

"9. It is characterized by morality—awareness of relativity of relationship with other persons. It discerns conduct levels and choosingly discriminates between them.

"10. Personality is unique, absolutely unique: It is unique in time and space; it is unique in eternity and on Paradise; it is unique when bestowed—there are no duplicates; it is unique during every moment of existence; it is unique in relation to God—he is no respector of persons, but neither does he add them together, for they are nonaddable—they are associable but nontotalable.

"11. Personality responds directly to other-personality presence.

"12. It is one thing which can be added to spirit, thus illustrating the primacy of the Father in relation to the Son. (Mind does not have to be added to spirit.)

"13. Personality may survive mortal death with identity in the surviving soul. The Adjuster and the personality are changeless; the relationship between them (in the soul) is nothing but change, continuing evolution; and if this change (growth) ceased, the soul would cease.

"14. Personality is uniquely conscious of time, and this is something other than the time perception of mind or spirit."
(p. 1225-26)

2. **Proposition.** All phases of personality are potentially cocreational. Identity can be associated with pattern, but personality is associated with living energy systems.

   "All subinfinite orders and phases of personality are associative attainables and are potentially cocreational. The prepersonal, the personal, and the superpersonal are all linked together by mutual potential or co-ordinate attainment, progressive achievement, and cooreational capacity. But never does the impersonal directly transmute to the personal. Personality is never spontaneous; it is the gift of the Paradise Father. Personality is superimposed upon energy, and it is associated only with living energy systems; identity can be associated with nonliving energy patterns." (p. 8)

3. **Proposition.** Personality is not body, mind, spirit, or soul. It is the changeless reality of an otherwise ever-changing creature experience.

   "*Personality*. The personality of mortal man is neither body, mind, nor spirit; neither is it the soul. Personality is the one changeless reality in an otherwise ever-changing creature experience; and it unifies all other associated factors of individuality. The personality is the unique bestowal which the Universal Father makes upon the living and associated energies of matter, mind, and spirit, and which survives with the survival of the morontial soul." (p. 9)

4. **Proposition.** Human personality is the time-space image-shadow cast by the Creator personality and should be interpreted in terms of the substance.

   "Human personality is the time-space image-shadow cast by the divine Creator personality. And no actuality can ever be adequately comprehended by an examination of its shadow. Shadows should be interpreted in terms of the true substance." (p. 29)

5. **Proposition.** Urantia mortals are endowed with personality of the finite-mortal type, functioning on the level of the ascending sons of God.

   "The Universal Father bestows personality upon numerous orders of beings as they function on diverse levels of universe actuality. Urantia human beings are endowed with personality of the finite-mortal type, functioning on the level of the ascending sons of God." (p. 194)

6. **Proposition.** The bestowal of personality is antecedent to the bestowal of Thought Adjusters.

   "Personality is a unique endowment of original nature whose existence is independent of, and antecedent to, the bestowal of the Thought Adjuster. Nevertheless, the presence of the Adjuster does augment the qualitative manifestation of personality." (p. 194)

7. **Proposition.** Personality is that feature of an individual which we know.

   "Personality is that feature of an individual which we *know*, and which enables us to identify such a being at some future time regardless of the nature and extent of changes in form, mind, or spirit status. Personality is that part of any individual which enables us to recognize and positively identify that person as the one we have previously known, no matter how much he may have changed because of the modification of the vehicle of expression and manifestation of his personality." (p. 194)

8. **Proposition.** Creature personality is distinguished by self-consciousness and relative free will.

   "Creature personality is distinguished by two self-manifesting and characteristic phenomena of mortal reactive behavior: self-consciousness and associated relative free will." (p. 194)

9. **Proposition.** Self-consciousness is intellectual awareness of personality actuality and includes ability to recognize other personalities.

   "Self-consciousness consists in intellectual awareness of personality actuality; it includes the ability to recognize the reality of other personalities. It indicates capacity for individualized experience in and with cosmic realities, equivalating to the attainment of identity status in the personality relationships of the universe." (p. 194)

10. **Proposition.** Personality confers cosmic citizenship and ability to react to cosmic realities.

    "The bestowal of the divine gift of personality upon such a mind-endowed mortal mechanism confers the dignity of cosmic citizenship and enables such a mortal creature forthwith to become reactive to the constitutive recognition of the three basic mind realities of the cosmos:

"1. The mathematical or logical recognition of the uniformity of physical causation.

"2. The reasoned recognition of the obligation of moral conduct.

"3. The faith-grasp of the fellowship worship of Deity, associated with the loving service of humanity." (p. 195)

11. **PROPOSITION.** The full recognition of personality endowment is realization of Deity kinship—sonship with God.

    "The full function of such a personality endowment is the beginning realization of Deity kinship. Such a selfhood, indwelt by a prepersonal fragment of God the Father, is in truth and in fact a spiritual son of God." (p. 195)

12. **PROPOSITION.** Throughout all your evolutionary ascension, there is one part of you which remains unchanged—your personality.

    "And throughout all of these successive ages and stages of evolutionary growth, there is one part of you that remains absolutely unaltered, and that is personality—permanence in the presence of change." (p. 1225)

13. **PROPOSITION.** Personality functions on three cosmic planes—universe phases.

    "Personality is bestowed by the Universal Father upon his creatures as a potentially eternal endowment. Such a divine gift is designed to function on numerous levels and in successive universe situations ranging from the lowly finite to the highest absonite, even to the borders of the absolute. Personality thus performs on three cosmic planes or in three universe phases:
    "1. *Position status.* Personality functions equally efficiently in the local universe, in the superuniverse, and in the central universe.
    "2. *Meaning status.* Personality performs effectively on the levels of the finite, the absonite, and even as impinging upon the absolute.
    "3. *Value status.* Personality can be experientially realized in the progressive realms of the material, the morontial, and the spiritual." (p. 1226)

14. **PROPOSITION.** Only three of the seven dimensions of personality are realizable on the finite level.

    "The type of personality bestowed upon Urantia mortals has a potentiality of seven dimensions of self-expression or person-realization. These dimensional phenomena are realizable as three on the finite level, three on the absonite level, and one on the absolute level. On subabsolute levels this seventh or totality dimension is experiencible as the *fact* of personality. This supreme dimension is an associable absolute and, while not infinite, is dimensionally potential for subinfinite penetration of the absolute." (p. 1226)

15. **Proposition.** Man is a social creature. Personality craves belongingness.

> "Personality cannot very well perform in isolation. Man is innately a social creature; he is dominated by the craving of belongingness. It is literally true, 'No man lives unto himself.'" (p. 1227)

16. **Proposition.** Personality signifies the unification of all factors of reality.

> "But the concept of the personality as the meaning of the whole of the living and functioning creature means much more than the integration of relationships; it signifies the *unification* of all factors of reality as well as co-ordination of relationships. Relationships exist between two objects, but three or more objects eventuate a *system*, and such a system is much more than just an enlarged or complex relationship. This distinction is vital, for in a cosmic system the individual members are not connected with each other except in relation to the whole and through the individuality of the whole." (p. 1227)

17. **Proposition.** Coming from God, man's personality is eternal, but as regards identity, it is conditioned on man's choosing to survive.

> "That which comes from the Father is like the Father eternal, and this is just as true of personality, which God gives by his own freewill choice, as it is of the divine Thought Adjuster, an actual fragment of God. Man's personality is eternal but with regard to identity a conditioned eternal reality. Having appeared in response to the Father's will, personality will attain Deity destiny, but man must choose whether or not he will be present at the attainment of such destiny. In default of such choice, personality attains experiential Deity directly, becoming a part of the Supreme Being. The cycle is foreordained, but man's participation therein is optional, personal, and experiential." (p. 1232)

XVI. FAITH SONS OF GOD

1. **Proposition.** Faith sons live and work on levels far above the conflicts of unrestrained physical impulses.

    "Those God-knowing men and women who have been born of the Spirit experience no more conflict with their mortal natures than do the inhabitants of the most normal of worlds, planets which have never been tainted with sin nor touched by rebellion. Faith sons work on intellectual levels and live on spiritual planes far above the conflicts produced by unrestrained or unnatural physical desires." (p. 383)

2. **Proposition.** Normal urges of animal beings are not in serious conflict with high spiritual attainment.

    "The normal urges of animal beings and the natural appetites and impulses of the physical nature are not in conflict with even the highest spiritual attainment except in the minds of ignorant, mistaught, or unfortunately overconscientious persons." (p. 383)

3. **Proposition.** Man's feelings of insecurity grow out of the differences between his physical and spiritual natures. Only faith can sustain him in these perplexities.

    "It is only natural that mortal man should be harassed by feelings of insecurity as he views himself inextricably bound to nature while he possesses spiritual powers wholly transcendent to all things temporal and finite. Only religious confidence—living faith—can sustain man amid such difficult and perplexing problems." (p. 1222)

XVII. THE SEVEN STAGES OF LIGHT AND LIFE

1. **Proposition.** As worlds pass from the first to the seventh stage of light and life, they successively grasp the realization of the reality of God the Sevenfold.

    "As the worlds settled in life and light progress from the initial stage to the seventh epoch, they successively grasp for the realization of the reality of God the Sevenfold, ranging from the adoration of the Creator Son to the worship of his Paradise Father. Throughout the continuing seventh stage of such a world's history the ever-progressing mortals grow in the knowledge of God the Supreme, while they vaguely discern the reality of the overshadowing ministry of God the Ultimate." (p. 646)

2. **PROPOSITION.** All of this attainment is achieved before mortals even enter upon the morontia career.

> "This is the story of the magnificent goal of mortal striving on the evolutionary worlds; and it all takes place even before human beings enter upon their morontia careers; all of this splendid development is attainable by material mortals on the inhabited worlds, the very first stage of that endless and incomprehensible career of Paradise ascension and divinity attainment." (p. 631)

3. **PROPOSITION.** The chief pursuit of these mortals is the realization of truth, beauty, and goodness, and the study of philosophy, cosmology, and divinity.

> "Throughout this glorious age the chief pursuit of the ever-advancing mortals is the quest for a better understanding and a fuller realization of the comprehensible elements of Deity—truth, beauty and goodness. This represents man's effort to discern God in mind, matter, and spirit. And as the mortal pursues this quest, he finds himself increasingly absorbed in the experiential study of philosophy, cosmology, and divinity." (p. 646)

4. **PROPOSITION.** The era of light and life is inaugurated by the Trinity Teacher Sons.

> "This era of light and life, inaugurated by the Teacher Sons at the conclusion of their final planetary mission, continues indefinitely on the inhabited worlds. Each advancing stage of settled status may be segregated by the judicial actions of the Magisterial Sons into a succession of dispensations; but all such judicial actions are purely technical, in no way modifying the course of planetary events." (p. 621)

5. **PROPOSITION.** When finally settled in light and life, a world receives the morontia temple and the Planetary Prince is elevated to Planetary Sovereign.

> "The presence of a morontia temple at the capital of an inhabited world is the certificate of the admission of such a sphere to the settled ages of light and life. Before the Teacher Sons leave a world at the conclusion of their terminal mission, they inaugurate this final epoch of evolutionary attainment; they preside on that day when the 'holy temple comes down upon earth.' This event, signalizing the dawn of the era of light and life, is always honored by the personal presence of the Paradise bestowal Son of that planet, who comes to witness this great day. There in this temple of unparalleled beauty, this

bestowal Son of Paradise proclaims the long-time Planetary Prince as the new Planetary Sovereign and invests such a faithful Lanonandek Son with new powers and extended authority over planetary affairs. The System Sovereign is also present and speaks in confirmation of these pronouncements." (p. 622)

6. **PROPOSITION.** The translation of living mortals is by the consuming fire of Adjuster fusion.

> "Such a morontia temple also serves as the place of assembly for witnessing the translation of living mortals to the morontia existence. It is because the translation temple is composed of morontia material that it is not destroyed by the blazing glory of the consuming fire which so completely obliterates the physical bodies of those mortals who therein experience final fusion with their divine Adjusters. On a large world these departure flares are almost continuous, and as the number of translations increases, subsidiary morontia life shrines are provided in different areas of the planet. Not long since I sojourned on a world in the far north whereon twenty-five morontia shrines were functioning." (p. 622)

7. **PROPOSITION.** Frequency of translation from the mortal to the morontia state increases as the evolutionary status of a world progresses.

> "This experience of translation from the material life to the morontia state—fusion of the immortal soul with the indwelling Adjuster—increases in frequency commensurate with the evolutionary progress of the planet." (p. 623)

8. **PROPOSITION.** The family and friends of a fusion candidate assemble in the morontia temple to await the "life flash" delivering the ascender from the bonds of the flesh.

> "When the family, friends, and working group of such a fusion candidate have forgathered in the morontia temple, they are distributed around the central stage whereon the fusion candidates are resting, meantime freely conversing with their assembled friends. A circle of intervening celestial personalities is arranged to protect the material mortals from the action of the energies manifest at the instant of the 'life flash' which delivers the ascension candidate from the bonds of material flesh, thereby doing for such an evolutionary mortal everything that natural death does for those who are thereby delivered from the flesh." (p. 623)

PART XVII — *MAN*

9. **PROPOSITION.** Advanced notice of Adjuster fusion may be given so that the candidate may prepare for planetary departure.

> "Farther along in the era of light and life the midway creatures or their associates sense the approaching status of probable soul-Adjuster union and signify this to the destiny guardians, who in turn communicate these matters to the finaliter group under whose jurisdiction this mortal may be functioning; then there is issued the summons of the Planetary Sovereign for such a mortal to resign all planetary duties, bid farewell to the world of his origin, and repair to the inner temple of the Planetary Sovereign, there to await morontia transit, the translation flash, from the material domain of evolution to the morontia level of prespirit progression." (p. 623)

10. **PROPOSITION.** The translated mortal proceeds by Adjuster transit to the proper morontia world.

> "Mortal observers can see nothing of their translated associates subsequent to the fusion flash. Such translated souls proceed by Adjuster transit direct to the resurrection hall of the appropriate morontia-training world. These transactions concerned with the translation of living human beings to the morontia world are supervised by an archangel who was assigned to such a world on the day when it was first settled in light and life." (p. 624)

11. **PROPOSITION.** From the worlds in the flowering ages of light and life, the Son-seized mortals bypass most of the morontia life, beginning their semispirit ascension on the worlds of the universe headquarters.

> "The translated souls of the flowering ages of the settled spheres do not pass through the mansion worlds. Neither do they sojourn, as students, on the morontia worlds of the system or constellation. They do not pass through any of the earlier phases of morontia life. They are the only ascending mortals who so nearly escape the morontia transition from material existence to semispirit status. The initial experience of such *Son-seized* mortals in the ascension career is in the services of the progression worlds of the universe headquarters. And from these study worlds of Salvington they go back as teachers to the very worlds they passed by, subsequently going on inward to Paradise by the established route of mortal ascension." (p. 624)

THE THEOLOGY OF *THE URANTIA BOOK*

12. **PROPOSITION.** The handicaps of Urantia in attaining the status of light and life are many and varied.

    "The great handicap confronting Urantia in the matter of attaining the high planetary destiny of light and life is embraced in the problems of disease, degeneracy, war, multicolored races, and multilingualism." (p. 626)

13. **PROPOSITION.** To progress beyond the first stage of light and life a world must have one language, one philosophy, and one religion.

    "No evolutionary world can hope to progress beyond the first stage of settledness in light until it has achieved one language, one religion, and one philosophy. Being of one race greatly facilitates such achievement, but the many peoples of Urantia do not preclude the attainment of higher stages." (p. 626)

14. **PROPOSITION.** There are seven stages of the unfoldment of the era of light and life.

    "There are seven stages in the unfoldment of the era of light and life on an evolutionary world, and in this connection it should be noted that the worlds of the Spirit-fused mortals evolve along lines identical with those of the Adjuster-fusion series. These seven stages of light and life are:

    1. The first or planetary stage.
    2. The second or system stage.
    3. The third or constellation stage.
    4. The fourth or local universe stage.
    5. The fifth or minor sector stage.
    6. The sixth or major sector stage.
    7. The seventh or superuniverse stage." (p. 621)

15. **PROPOSITION.** A brief description of the seven stages of light and life.

    See pages 627-28

XVIII. PERSONALITY SURVIVAL

1. **PROPOSITION.** Mortal choosing determines the survival potential of the human soul. When the mind believes God, and with the Adjuster desires God, survival is assured.

    "Eternal survival of personality is wholly dependent on the choosing of the mortal mind, whose decisions determine the survival potential of the immortal soul. When the mind believes God and the soul knows God, and when, with the fostering Adjuster, they all *desire* God, then is survival assured." (p. 69)

- 444 -

2. **Proposition.** Survival of the God-choosing soul cannot be prevented by any and all of the limitations of human nature.

   "Limitations of intellect, curtailment of education, deprivation of culture, impoverishment of social status, even inferiority of the human standards of morality resulting from the unfortunate lack of educational, cultural, and social advantages, cannot invalidate the presence of the divine spirit in such unfortunate and humanly handicapped but believing individuals." (p. 69)

3. **Proposition.** Evolutionary mortals from the worlds of space ascend to Paradise to await mustering into the Corps of the Finality.

   "Evolutionary mortals are born on the planets of space, pass through the morontia worlds, ascend the spirit universes, traverse the Havona spheres, find God, attain Paradise, and are mustered into the primary Corps of the Finality, therein to await the next assignment of universe service. There are six other assembling finality corps, but Grandfanda, the first mortal ascender, presides as Paradise chief of all orders of finaliters. And as we view this sublime spectacle we all exclaim: What a glorious destiny for the animal-origin children of time, the material sons of space!" (p. 354)

4. **Proposition.** Mortal survival depends on the spiritualizing ministry of the Adjuster in evolving the immortal soul.

   "But mortal mind without immortal spirit cannot survive. The mind of man is mortal; only the bestowed spirit is immortal. Survival is dependent on spiritualization by the ministry of the Adjuster—on the birth and evolution of the immortal soul; at least, there must not have developed an antagonism towards the Adjuster's mission of effecting the spiritual transformation of the material mind." (p. 565)

5. **Proposition.** Special resurrections are conducted from time to time and always every one thousand years.

   "From time to time, on motion of the planetary authorities or the system rulers, special resurrections of the sleeping survivors are conducted. Such resurrections occur at least every millennium of planetary time, when not all but 'many of those who sleep in the dust awake.' These special resurrections are the occasion for mobilizing special groups of ascenders for specific service in the local universe plan of mortal ascension. There are both practical reasons and sentimental associations connected with these special resurrections." (p. 568)

6. **Proposition.** The evolving soul—the child of mortal mind and the Divine Adjuster—survives death as the morontia self.

> "There is something real, something of human evolution, something additional to the Mystery Monitor, which survives death. This newly appearing entity is the soul, and it survives the death of both your physical body and your material mind. This entity is the conjoint child of the combined life and efforts of the human you in liaison with the divine you, the Adjuster. This child of human and divine parentage constitutes the surviving element of terrestrial origin; it is the morontia self, the immortal soul." (p. 1234)

7. **Proposition.** During death, the soul is unconscious and is in the keeping of the destiny guardian.

> "This child of persisting meaning and surviving value is wholly unconscious during the period from death to repersonalization and is in the keeping of the seraphic destiny guardian throughout this season of waiting. You will not function as a conscious being, following death, until you attain the new consciousness of morontia on the mansion worlds of Satania." (p. 1234)

8. **Proposition.** If there is doubt about an individual's having had opportunity to choose survival, if the accidents and handicaps of material existence prevent sufficient progress, then such souls will be granted transitional status—they will have a chance to choose survival.

> "Though the cosmic circles of personality growth must eventually be attained, if, through no fault of your own, the accidents of time and the handicaps of material existence prevent your mastering these levels on your native planet, if your intentions and desires are of survival value, there are issued the decrees of probation extension. You will be afforded additional time in which to prove yourself.
>
> "If ever there is doubt as to the advisability of advancing a human identity to the mansion worlds, the universe governments invariably rule in the personal interests of that individual; they unhesitatingly advance such a soul to the status of a transitional being, while they continue their observations of the emerging morontia intent and spiritual purpose. Thus divine justice is certain of achievement, and divine mercy is accorded further opportunity for extending its ministry." (p. 1233)

Part XVII — Man

9. **Proposition.** The reassembly of the constituent parts of a onetime material personality involves a number of transactions.

> "The situation which makes repersonalization possible is brought about in the resurrection halls of the morontia receiving planets of a local universe. Here in these life-assembly chambers the supervising authorities provide that relationship of universe energy—morontial, mindal, and spiritual—which makes possible the reconsciousizing of the sleeping survivor. The reassembly of the constituent parts of a onetime material personality involves:
>
> "1. The fabrication of a suitable form, a morontia energy pattern, in which the new survivor can make contact with nonspiritual reality, and within which the morontia variant of the cosmic mind can be encircuited.
>
> "2. The return of the Adjuster to the waiting morontia creature. The Adjuster is the eternal custodian of your ascending identity; your Monitor is the absolute assurance that you yourself and not another will occupy the morontia form created for your personality awakening. And the Adjuster will be present at your personality reassembly to take up once more the role of Paradise guide to your surviving self.
>
> "3. When these prerequisites of repersonalization have been assembled, the seraphic custodian of the potentialities of the slumbering immortal soul, with the assistance of numerous cosmic personalities, bestows this morontia entity upon and in the awaiting morontia mind-body form while committing this evolutionary child of the Supreme to eternal association with the waiting Adjuster. And this completes the repersonalization, reassembly of memory, insight, and consciousness—identity." (pp. 1234-35)

10. **Proposition.** Children dying before getting Thought Adjusters are repersonalized on the finaliter worlds concomitant with the arrival of either parent on the mansion world.

> "Children who die when too young to have Thought Adjusters are repersonalized on the finaliter world of the local systems concomitant with the arrival of either parent on the mansion worlds. A child acquires physical entity at mortal birth, but in the matter of survival all Adjusterless children are reckoned as still attached to their parents." (p. 570)

11. **Proposition.** And then Thought Adjusters come to indwell these little ones, together with seraphic ministry.

> "In due course Thought Adjusters come to indwell these little ones, while the seraphic ministry to both groups of the probationary-dependent orders of survival is in general similar to that of the more advanced parent or is equivalent to that of the parent in case only one survives. Those attaining the third circle, regardless of the status of their parents, are accorded personal guardians." (p. 570)

12. **Proposition.** Probation nurseries are maintained on finaliter worlds of the constellation and at universe headquarters for the Adjusterless children of those who skip the lower mansion worlds.

> "Similar probation nurseries are maintained on the finaliter spheres of the constellation and the universe headquarters for the Adjusterless children of the primary and secondary modified orders of ascenders." (p. 570)

13. **Proposition.** When mortal man fails to survive, spiritual values of human experience survive in the Thought Adjuster—personality values persist in the Supreme Being.

> "If mortal man fails to survive natural death, the real spiritual values of his human experience survive as a part of the continuing experience of the Thought Adjuster. The personality values of such a nonsurvivor persist as a factor in the personality of the actualizing Supreme Being. Such persisting qualities of personality are deprived of identity but not of experiential values accumulated during the mortal life in the flesh. The survival of identity is dependent on the survival of the immortal soul of morontia status and increasingly divine value. Personality identity survives in and by the survival of the soul." (p. 195)

14. **Proposition.** These merciful provisions do not mean that humans are to have a second probation, but they do mean that every mortal will have one undoubted opportunity to make a true and final choice.

> "This does not mean that human beings are to enjoy a second opportunity in the face of the rejection of a first, not at all. But it does signify that all will creatures are to experience one true opportunity to make one undoubted, self-conscious, and final choice. The sovereign Judges of the universes will not deprive any being of personality status who has not finally and fully made the eternal choice; the soul of man must and will be given full and ample opportunity to reveal its true intent and real purpose." (p. 1233)

PART XVIII
EDUCATION

PART EIGHTEEN
EDUCATION

1. **PROPOSITION.** Civilizations are unstable because they are not cosmic. They must be nurtured by the constitutive factors of science, morality, and religion.

   "Civilizations are unstable because they are not cosmic; they are not innate in the individuals of the races. They must be nurtured by the combined contributions of the constitutive factors of man—science, morality, and religion. Civilizations come and go, but science, morality, and religion always survive the crash." (p. 196)

2. **PROPOSITION.** The Nebadon educational system consists in teaching you how to perform the things they command you to do.

   "Fundamentally, the Nebadon educational system provides for your assignment to a task and then affords you opportunity to receive instruction as to the ideal and divine method of best performing that task. You are given a definite task to perform, and at the same time you are provided with teachers who are qualified to instruct you in the best method of executing your assignment. The divine plan of education provides for the intimate association of work and instruction. We teach you how best to execute the things we command you to do." (p. 412)

3. **PROPOSITION.** The schools of the Planetary Prince and the Garden of Eden were concerned with a wide range of subjects.

   "The schools of the Planetary Prince are primarily concerned with philosophy, religion, morals, and the higher intellectual and artistic achievements. The garden schools of Adam and Eve are usually devoted to practical arts, fundamental intellectual training, social culture, economic development, trade relations, physical efficiency, and civil government. Eventually these world centers amalgamate, but this actual affiliation sometimes does not occur until the times of the first Magisterial Son." (p. 587)

4. **PROPOSITION.** The true state is founded on culture, dominated by ideals, and motivated by service.

   "The enduring state is founded on culture, dominated by ideals, and motivated by service. The purpose of education should be acquirement of skill, pursuit of wisdom, realization of selfhood, and attainment of spiritual values." (p. 806)

Part XVIII — Education

5. **Proposition.** Education has five major goals.

   "In the ideal state, education continues throughout life, and philosophy sometimes becomes the chief pursuit of its citizens. The citizens of such a commonwealth pursue wisdom as an enhancement of insight into the significance of human relations, the meanings of reality, the nobility of values, the goals of living, and the glories of cosmic destiny." (p. 806)

6. **Proposition.** Education is the business of living.

   "Education is the business of living; it must continue throughout a lifetime so that mankind may gradually experience the ascending levels of mortal wisdom, which are:
   1. The knowledge of things.
   2. The realization of meanings.
   3. The appreciation of values.
   4. The nobility of work—duty.
   5. The motivation of goals—morality.
   6. The love of service—character.
   7. Cosmic insight—spiritual discernment." (p. 806)

7. **Proposition.** When man studies the universe from the outside, he produces the physical sciences; when he approaches the universe from the inside, he originates metaphysics and theology—religion.

   "When man approaches the study and examination of his universe from the *outside*, he brings into being the various physical sciences; when he approaches the research of himself and the universe from the *inside*, he gives origin to theology and metaphysics. The later art of philosophy develops in an effort to harmonize the many discrepancies which are destined at first to appear between the findings and teachings of these two diametrically opposite avenues of approaching the universe of things and beings." (p. 1135)

8. **Proposition.** The inner and outer worlds have a different set of values. Civilization is in jeopardy because so many youth enter the materialistic professions.

   "The inner and the outer worlds have a different set of values. Any civilization is in jeopardy when three quarters of its youth enter materialistic professions and devote themselves to the pursuit of the sensory activities of the outer world. Civilization is in danger when youth neglect to interest themselves in ethics, sociology, eugenics, philosophy, the fine arts, religion, and cosmology." (p. 1220)

9. **Proposition.** Ideas may take origin in stimuli of the outer world; ideals are born in the creative realms of the inner world.

> "Ideas may take origin in the stimuli of the outer world, but ideals are born only in the creative realms of the inner world. Today the nations of the world are directed by men who have a superabundance of ideas, but they are poverty-stricken in ideals. That is the explanation of poverty, divorce, war, and racial hatreds." (p. 1220)

10. **Proposition.** Even secular education should contribute to life planning, character development, enhanced personality, and moral discipline.

> "Even secular education could help in this great spiritual renaissance if it would pay more attention to the work of teaching youth how to engage in life planning and character progression. The purpose of all education should be to foster and further the supreme purpose of life, the development of a majestic and well-balanced personality. There is great need for the teaching of moral discipline in the place of so much self-gratification. Upon such a foundation religion may contribute its spiritual incentive to the enlargement and enrichment of mortal life, even to the security and enhancement of life eternal." (p. 2086)

PART XIX
MARRIAGE AND THE HOME

Part Nineteen
MARRIAGE AND THE HOME

I. INTRODUCTION

1. **Proposition.** Marriage is the ancestor of civilization's most sublime and useful institution—the home.

    "Material necessity founded marriage, sex hunger embellished it, religion sanctioned and exalted it, the state demanded and regulated it, while in later times evolving love is beginning to justify and glorify marriage as the ancestor and creator of civilization's most useful and sublime institution, the home. And home building should be the center and essence of all educational effort." (p. 931)

2. **Proposition.** Among the ancients, the large family was not always due to affection. They desired many children for various reasons.

    "The large families among ancient peoples were not necessarily affectional. Many children were desired because:
    1. They were valuable as laborers.
    2. They were old-age insurance.
    3. Daughters were salable.
    4. Family pride required extension of name.
    5. Sons afforded protection and defense.
    6. Ghost fear produced a dread of being alone.
    7. Certain religions required offspring." (p. 940)

3. **Proposition.** The function of marriage is to insure race survival, not merely the realization of personal happiness.

    "The function of marriage in evolution is the insurance of race survival, not merely the realization of personal happiness; self-maintenance and self-perpetuation are the real objects of the home. Self-gratification is incidental and not essential except as an incentive insuring sex assocation. Nature demands survival, but the arts of civilization continue to increase the pleasures of marriage and the satisfactions of family life." (p. 765)

II. THE MATING INSTINCT

1. **Proposition.** Notwithstanding the differences between men and women, the sex urge is sufficient to bring them together for the reproduction of the species.

    "Notwithstanding the personality gulf between men and women, the sex urge is sufficient to insure their coming together for the reproduction of the species. This instinct operated effectively long before humans experienced much of what was later called love, devotion, and marital loyalty. Mating is an innate propensity, and marriage is its evolutionary social repercussion." (p. 913)

2. **PROPOSITION.** The Sangik and other primitive peoples had a mating instinct but were largely devoid of what is modernly known as "sex appeal."

"The Sangik races had normal animal passion, but they displayed little imagination or appreciation of the beauty and physical attractiveness of the opposite sex. What is called sex appeal is virtually absent even in present-day primitive races; these unmixed peoples have a definite mating instinct but insufficient sex attraction to create serious problems requiring social control." (P. 914)

III. EARLY MARRIAGE MORES

1. **PROPOSITION.** The evolution of marriage is the story of sex control through the pressure of social, religious, and civil restrictions.

"The story of the evolution of marriage is simply the history of sex control through the pressure of social, religious, and civil restrictions. Nature hardly recognizes individuals; it takes no cognizance of so-called morals; it is only and exclusively interested in the reproduction of the species." (p. 914)

2. **PROPOSITION.** Woman's low status during Old Testament times reflects the mores of the herdsmen.

"The scant courtesy paid womankind during the Old Testament era is a true reflection of the mores of the herdsmen. The Hebrew patriarchs were all herdsmen, as is witnessed by the saying, 'The Lord is my Shepherd.'" (p. 934)

3. **PROPOSITION.** In primitive times marriage was the price of social standing — a wife was a badge of distinction.

"In primitive times marriage was the price of social standing; the possession of a wife was a badge of distinction. The savage looked upon his wedding day as marking his entrance upon responsibility and manhood. In one age, marriage has been looked upon as a social duty; in another, as a religious obligation; and in still another, as a political requirement to provide citizens for the state." (p. 915)

4. **Proposition.** Child marriages originated in the idea that it was a disgrace —even a sin—not to be married. Unmarried persons could not enter spiritland.

> "The fact that ancient peoples regarded it as a disgrace, or even a sin, not to be married, explains the origin of child marriages; since one must be married, the earlier the better. It was also a general belief that unmarried persons could not enter spiritland, and this was a further incentive to child marriages even at birth and sometimes before birth, contingent upon sex." (p. 916)

5. **Proposition.** Primitive marriages were arranged by parents; later a marriage broker functioned. At first, marriage was a group affair.

> "Primitive marriages were always planned by the parents of the boy and girl. The transition stage between this custom and the times of free choosing was occupied by the marriage broker or professional matchmaker. These matchmakers were at first the barbers; later, the priests. Marriage was originally a group affair; then a family matter; only recently has it become an individual adventure." (p. 923)

6. **Proposition.** The ancients mistrusted love and promises. They wanted marriage guaranteed by property. The purchase price of a wife was a forfeit in case of desertion.

> "The ancients mistrusted love and promises; they thought that abiding unions must be guaranteed by some tangible security, property. For this reason, the purchase price of a wife was regarded as a forfeit or deposit which the husband was doomed to lose in case of divorce or desertion. Once the purchase price of a bride had been paid, many tribes permitted the husband's brand to be burned upon her. Africans still buy their wives. A love wife, or a white man's wife, they compare to a cat because she costs nothing." (p. 923)

IV. RACIAL MIXTURES

1. **Proposition.** The bad results of some inbreeding led to the formulation of taboos against marriage among near relatives.

> "While the inbreeding of good stock sometimes resulted in the upbuilding of strong tribes, the spectacular cases of the bad results of the inbreeding of hereditary defectives more forcibly impressed the mind of man, with the result that the advancing mores increasingly formulated taboos against all marriages among near relatives." (p. 918)

PART XIX — *MARRIAGE AND THE HOME*

2. **PROPOSITION.** Outmarriage dominated because it favored the man— he got away from in-laws. Familiarity breeds contempt.

> "Outmarriage finally dominated because it was favored by the man; to get a wife from the outside insured greater freedom from in-laws. Familiarity breeds contempt; so, as the element of individual choice began to dominate mating, it became the custom to choose partners from outside the tribe." (p. 919)

3. **PROPOSITION.** The real danger to the human species rests on the unrestrained multiplication of inferior strains rather than in racial interbreeding.

> "After all, the real jeopardy of the human species is to be found in the unrestrained multiplication of the inferior and degenerate strains of the various civilized peoples rather than in any supposed danger of their racial interbreeding." (p. 921)

4. **PROPOSITION.** If present-day races could get rid of their deteriorated specimens, there would be less objection to limited race amalgamation.

> "If the present-day races of Urantia could be freed from the curse of their lowest strata of deteriorated, antisocial, feeble-minded, and outcast specimens, there would be little objection to a limited race amalgamation. And if such racial mixtures could take place between the highest types of the several races, still less objection could be offered." (p. 920)

5. **PROPOSITION.** Aside from inferior strains, most of the prejudice against race mixture rests on social and cultural grounds.

> "As long as present-day races are so overloaded with inferior and degenerate strains, race intermingling on a large scale would be most detrimental, but most of the objections to such experiments rest on social and cultural prejudices rather than on biological considerations." (p. 920)

V. MARRIAGE AS A SOCIAL INSTITUTION

1. **PROPOSITION.** Turning from hunting to agriculture favored the development of family life, together with domestication of animals and improvement of home arts.

> "During this age agriculture makes its appearance. The growth of the family idea is incompatible with the roving and unsettled life of the hunter. Gradually the practices of settled habitations and the cultivation of the soil become established. The domestication of animals and the development of home arts proceed apace.

Upon reaching the apex of biologic evolution, a high level of civilization has been attained, but there is little development of a mechanical order; invention is the characteristic of the succeeding age." (p. 592)

2. **Proposition.** The family is the master civilizer—the home is indispensable.

   "While religious, social, and educational institutions are all essential to the survival of cultural civilization, *the family is the master civilizer*. A child learns most of the essentials of life from his family and the neighbors." (p. 913)

3. **Proposition.** Marriage has always been closely linked to both property and religion.

   "Marriage has always been closely linked with both property and religion. Property has been the stabilizer of marriage; religion, the moralizer." (p. 917)

4. **Proposition.** Marriages are not made in heaven—marriage is a human institution.

   "But while marriages may be approved or disapproved on high, they are hardly made in heaven. The human family is a distinctly human institution, an evolutionary development. Marriage is an institution of society, not a department of the church. True, religion should mightily influence it but should not undertake exclusively to control and regulate it." (p. 922)

5. **Proposition.** Primitive marriage was largely industrial; modern marriage is becoming multimotivated.

   "Primitive marriage was primarily industrial; and even in modern times it is often a social or business affair. Through the influence of the mixture of the Andite stock and as a result of the mores of advancing civilization, marriage is slowly becoming mutual, romantic, parental, poetical, affectionate, ethical, and even idealistic." (p. 922)

6. **Proposition.** Marriage is man's most exalted institution, but it should not be called a sacrament.

   "Marriage which culminates in the home is indeed man's most exalted institution, but it is essentially human; it should never have been called a sacrament. The Sethite priests made marriage a religious ritual; but for thousands of years after Eden, mating continued as a purely social and civil institution." (p. 929)

PART XIX — *Marriage and the Home*

7. **Proposition.** Marriage is a social institution growing out of co-operation in self-maintenance and partnership in self-perpetuation. Self-gratification was incidental.

   "The home is basically a sociologic institution. Marriage grew out of co-operation in self-maintenance and partnership in self-perpetuation, the element of self-gratification being largely incidental. Nevertheless, the home does embrace all three of the essential functions of human existence, while life propagation makes it the fundamental human institution, and sex sets it off from all other social activities." (p. 931)

8. **Proposition.** Woman's status is a fair criterion of the evolutionary progress of marriage, and marriage registers the advances of civilization.

   "Generally speaking, during any age woman's status is a fair criterion of the evolutionary progress of marriage as a social institution, while the progress of marriage itself is a reasonably accurate gauge registering the advances of human civilization." (p. 935)

9. **Proposition.** Science, not religion, really emancipated modern woman—it was the factory. Man power is no longer so superior to woman power.

   "Science, not religion, really emancipated woman; it was the modern factory which largely set her free from the confines of the home. Man's physical abilities became no longer a vital essential in the new maintenance mechanism; science so changed the conditions of living that man power was no longer so superior to woman power." (p. 937)

10. **Proposition.** Marriage embraces antagonisms—it is a program of antagonistic co-operation. Marriage is sociologic—not biologic.

    "Every successful human institution embraces antagonisms of personal interest which have been adjusted to practical working harmony, and homemaking is no exception. Marriage, the basis of home building, is the highest manifestation of that antagonistic co-operation which so often characterizes the contacts of nature and society. The conflict is inevitable. Mating is inherent; it is natural. But marriage is not biologic; it is sociologic. Passion insures that man and woman will come together, but the weaker parental instinct and the social mores hold them together." (p. 938)

11. **Proposition.** Women have more intuition than men but are somewhat less logical. Woman has always been the moral standard-bearer—the spiritual leader.

> "Women seem to have more intuition than men, but they also appear to be somewhat less logical. Woman, however, has always been the moral standard-bearer and the spiritual leader of mankind. The hand that rocks the cradle still fraternizes with destiny." (p. 938)

12. **Proposition.** Family life is becoming more expensive—children are no longer an asset. Shifting responsibility to state or church will prove suicidal.

> "In the present industrial and urban era the marriage institution is evolving along new economic lines. Family life has become more and more costly, while children, who used to be an asset, have become economic liabilities. But the security of civilization itself still rests on the growing willingness of one generation to invest in the welfare of the next and future generations. And any attempt to shift parental responsibility to state or church will prove suicidal to the welfare and advancement of civilization." (p. 941)

13. **Proposition.** The wedding ceremony grew out of the fact that marriage was originally a community affair.

> "The wedding ceremony grew out of the fact that marriage was originally a community affair, not just the culmination of a decision of two individuals. Mating was a group concern as well as a personal function." (p. 924)

14. **Proposition.** The change from the mother-family to the father-family was one of the most radical social adjustments ever made by the human race.

> "The stupendous change from the mother-family to the father-family is one of the most radical and complete right-about-face adjustments ever executed by the human race. This change led at once to greater social expression and increased family adventure." (p. 933)

VI. PLURAL MARRIAGES

1. **Proposition.** Polygamy recognized four sorts of wives.

> "The institution of polygyny recognized, at various times, four sorts of wives:
> 1. The ceremonial or legal wives.
> 2. Wives of affection and permission.
> 3. Concubines, contractual wives.
> 4. Slave wives." (p. 926)

2. **Proposition.** In polygamy, the number of wives was limited by the man's ability to support them. The infant mortality was high.

> "The number of wives was only limited by the ability of the man to provide for them. Wealthy and able men wanted large numbers of children, and since the infant mortality was very high, it required an assembly of wives to recruit a large family. Many of these plural wives were mere laborers, slave wives." (p. 926)

VII. TRUE MONOGAMY

1. **Proposition.** Monogamy has always been the idealistic goal of sex evolution. Ideal marriage entails self-denial and self-control.

> "Monogamy always has been, now is, and forever will be the idealistic goal of human sex evolution. This ideal of true pair marriage entails self-denial, and therefore does it so often fail just because one or both of the contracting parties are deficient in that acme of all human virtues, rugged self-control." (p. 927)

2. **Proposition.** Monogamy is the yardstick measuring the advance of social civilization.

> "Monogamy is the yardstick which measures the advance of social civilization as distinguished from purely biologic evolution. Monogamy is not necessarily biologic or natural, but it is indispensable to the immediate maintenance and further development of social civilization. It contributes to a delicacy of sentiment, a refinement of moral character, and a spiritual growth which are utterly impossible in polygamy. A woman never can become an ideal mother when she is all the while compelled to engage in rivalry for her husband's affections." (p. 927)

3. **Proposition.** Young people should be prepared for marriage. Youthful idealization should be tempered with some degree of disillusionment.

> "But young men and women should be taught something of the realities of marriage before they are plunged into the exacting demands of the interassociations of family life; youthful idealization should be tempered with some degree of premarital disillusionment." (p. 930)

VIII. WOMAN'S EARLY STATUS

1. **PROPOSITION.** Love of children constrained primitive women to submit to many hardships. Mother love has always been a handicapping emotion.

    "The mother and child relation is natural, strong, and instinctive, and one which, therefore, constrained primitive women to submit to many strange conditions and to endure untold hardships. This compelling mother love is the handicapping emotion which has always placed woman at such a tremendous disadvantage in all her struggles with man. Even at that, maternal instinct in the human species is not overpowering; it may be thwarted by ambition, selfishness, and religious conviction." (p. 932)

2. **PROPOSITION.** Marriage enhanced survival, hence it persisted in spite of its antagonisms.

    "Regardless of the antagonisms of these early pairs, notwithstanding the looseness of the association, the chances for survival were greatly improved by these male-female partnerships. A man and a woman, co-operating, even aside from family and offspring, are vastly superior in most ways to either two men or two women. This pairing of the sexes enhanced survival and was the very beginning of human society. The sex division of labor also made for comfort and increased happiness." (p. 932)

3. **PROPOSITION.** Early woman was not to man a friend and lover, but rather a piece of property—a servant and childbearer.

    "Early woman was not to man a friend, sweetheart, lover, and partner but rather a piece of property, a servant or slave and, later on, an economic partner, plaything, and childbearer. Nonetheless, proper and satisfactory sex relations have always involved the element of choice and co-operation by woman, and this has always given intelligent women considerable influence over their immediate and personal standing, regardless of their social position as a sex. But man's distrust and suspicion were not helped by the fact that women were all along compelled to resort to shrewdness in the effort to alleviate their bondage." (p. 935)

4. **PROPOSITION.** Man has regarded woman with mistrust and fascination, if not with suspicion and contempt. Women were regarded as bringing evil upon the race.

    "The sexes have had great difficulty in understanding each other. Man found it hard to understand woman, regarding her with a strange mixture of ignorant mistrust and fearful fascination, if not with suspicion and contempt. Many tribal and racial traditions relegate trouble to Eve, Pandora, or some other representative of womankind. These narratives were always distorted so as to make it appear that the woman brought evil upon man; and all this indicates the onetime universal distrust of woman. Among the reasons cited in support of a celibate priesthood, the chief was the baseness of woman. The fact that most supposed witches were women did not improve the olden reputation of the sex." (p. 935)

5. **PROPOSITION.** It was a great advance when man was denied the right to kill his wife and when she could own property.

"A great advance was made when a man was denied the right to kill his wife at will. Likewise, it was a forward step when a woman could own the wedding gifts. Later, she gained the legal right to own, control, and even dispose of property, but she was long deprived of the right to hold office in either church or state. Woman has always been treated more or less as property, right up to and in the twentieth century after Christ. She has not yet gained world-wide freedom from seclusion under man's control. Even among advanced peoples, man's attempt to protect woman has always been a tacit assertion of superiority." (p. 936)

6. **PROPOSITION.** Primitive women did not pity themselves.

"But primitive women did not pity themselves as their more recently liberated sisters are wont to do. They were, after all, fairly happy and contented; they did not dare to envision a better or different mode of existence." (p. 936)

IX. IDEALS OF FAMILY LIFE

1. **PROPOSITION.** Ideal marriage is found on the system capitals among the Material Sons and Daughters.

"Nevertheless, there is an ideal of marriage on the spheres on high. On the capital of each local system the Material Sons and Daughters of God do portray the height of the ideals of the union of man and woman in the bonds of marriage and for the purpose of procreating and rearing offspring. After all, the ideal mortal marriage is *humanly* sacred." (p. 930)

2. **Proposition.** The ideal of sex equality is not found in nature. When might is right, man lords it over woman. Her social position varies inversely with militarism.

> "The modern idea of sex equality is beautiful and worthy of an expanding civilization, but it is not found in nature. When might is right, man lords it over woman; when more justice, peace, and fairness prevail, she gradually emerges from slavery and obscurity. Woman's social position has generally varied inversely with the degree of militarism in any nation or age." (p. 936)

3. **Proposition.** Man did not intentionally seize woman's rights and grudgingly restore them—it was all an unconscious process.

> "But man did not consciously nor intentionally seize woman's rights and then gradually and grudgingly give them back to her; all this was an unconscious and unplanned episode of social evolution. When the time really came for woman to enjoy added rights, she got them, and all quite regardless of man's conscious attitude. Slowly but surely the mores change so as to provide for those social adjustments which are a part of the persistent evolution of civilization. The advancing mores slowly provided increasingly better treatment for females; those tribes which persisted in cruelty to them did not survive." (p. 937)

4. **Proposition.** In modern times woman has won dignity, equality, and education—will she be worthy of her social liberation?

> "In the ideals of pair marriage, woman has finally won recognition, dignity, independence, equality, and education; but will she prove worthy of all this new and unprecedented accomplishment? Will modern woman respond to this great achievement of social liberation with idleness, indifference, barrenness, and infidelity? Today, in the twentieth century, woman is undergoing the crucial test of her long world existence!" (p. 937)

5. **Proposition.** Men and women eternally need each other. Their differences in viewpoint persist throughout the ascendant career—even in the Corps of the Finality.

> "Men and women need each other in their morontial and spiritual as well as in their mortal careers. The differences in viewpoint between male and female persist even beyond the first life and throughout the local and superuniverse ascensions. And even in Havona, the pilgrims who were once men and women will still be aiding each other in the Paradise ascent. Never, even in the Corps of the Finality, will the creature metamorphose so far as to

obliterate the personality trends that humans call male and female; always will these two basic variations of humankind continue to intrigue, stimulate, encourage, and assist each other; always will they be mutually dependent on co-operation in the solution of perplexing universe problems and in the overcoming of manifold cosmic difficulties." (p. 939)

6. **PROPOSITION.** The new mores of marriage will more fully stabilize the home.

> "1. The new role of religion—the teaching that parental experience is essential, the idea of procreating cosmic citizens, the enlarged understanding of the privilege of procreation—giving sons to the Father.
> "2. The new role of science—procreation is becoming more and more voluntary, subject to man's control. In ancient times lack of understanding insured the appearance of children in the absence of all desire therefor.
> "3. The new function of pleasure lures—this introduces a new factor into racial survival; ancient man exposed undesired children to die; moderns refuse to bear them.
> "4. The enhancement of parental instinct. Each generation now tends to eliminate from the reproductive stream of the race those individuals in whom parental instinct is insufficiently strong to insure the procreation of children, the prospective parents of the next generation." (pp. 939-40)

X. DANGERS OE SELF-GRATIFICATION

1. **PROPOSITION.** Man has well earned some of his joys and pleasures, but pleasure is suicidal if it brings about decadence of the home—man's supreme evolutionary achievement and civilization's hope of survival.

> "Let man enjoy himself; let the human race find pleasure in a thousand and one ways; let evolutionary mankind explore all forms of legitimate self-gratification, the fruits of the long upward biologic struggle. Man has well earned some of his present-day joys and pleasures. But look you well to the goal of destiny! Pleasures are indeed suicidal if they succeed in destroying property, which has become the institution of self-maintenance; and self-gratifications have indeed cost a fatal price if they bring about the collapse of marriage, the decadence of family life, and the destruction of the home—man's supreme evolutional acquirement and civilization's only hope of survival." (p. 943)

2. **PROPOSITION.** Marriage was founded on self-maintenance, led to self-perpetuation, and concomitantly provided a form of self-gratification.

> "The great threat against family life is the menacing rising tide of self-gratification, the modern pleasure mania. The prime incentive to marriage used to be economic; sex attraction was secondary. Marriage, founded on self-maintenance, led to self-perpetuation and concomitantly provided one of the most desirable forms of self-gratification. It is the only institution of human society which embraces all three of the great incentives for living." (p. 942)

XI. CHILD CULTURE

1. **PROPOSITION.** Divorce will remain prevalent as long as youths are not properly educated for marriage—just as long as youthful idealism is the determiner of fitness for marriage.

> "But just so long as society fails to properly educate children and youths, so long as the social order fails to provide adequate premarital training, and so long as unwise and immature youthful idealism is to be the arbiter of the entrance upon marriage, just so long will divorce remain prevalent. And in so far as the social group falls short of providing marriage preparation for youths, to that extent must divorce function as the social safety valve which prevents still worse situations during the ages of the rapid growth of the evolving mores." (p. 929)

2. **PROPOSITION.** Child culture has been rendered more difficult by a number of factors.

> "Modern problems of child culture are rendered increasingly difficult by:
> 1. The large degree of race mixture.
> 2. Artificial and superficial education.
> 3. Inability of the child to gain culture by imitating parents—the parents are absent from the family picture so much of the time." (p. 941)

3. **PROPOSITION.** The family-council practice of the Anditin would be helpful to modern society.

> "Human society would be greatly improved if the civilized races would more generally return to the family-council practices of the Anditin. They did not maintain the patriarchal or autocratic form of family government. They were very brotherly and

associative, freely and frankly discussing every proposal and regulation of a family nature. They were ideally fraternal in all their family government. In an ideal family filial and parental affection are both augmented by fraternal devotion." (p. 941)

4. **PROPOSITION.** Jesus discusses right and wrong methods of child culture with John Mark. *See page 1921-1923.*

PART XX
THE STATE

Part Twenty
THE STATE

I. WAR

1. **Proposition.** War is the natural heritage of evolving man; peace is the social yardstick measuring the advance of civilization.

   "War is the natural state and heritage of evolving man; peace is the social yardstick measuring civilization's advancement. Before the partial socialization of the advancing races man was exceedingly individualistic, extremely suspicious, and unbelievably quarrelsome. Violence is the law of nature, hostility the automatic reaction of the children of nature, while war is but these same activities carried on collectively. And wherever and whenever the fabric of civilization becomes stressed by the complications of society's advancement, there is always an immediate and ruinous reversion to these early methods of violent adjustment of the irritations of human interassociations." (p. 783)

2. **Proposition.** When early chiefs prevented war they had to provide annual stone fights.

   "When the early chiefs would try to iron out misunderstandings, they often found it necessary, at least once a year, to permit the tribal stone fights. The clan would divide up into two groups and engage in an all-day battle. And this for no other reason than just the fun of it; they really enjoyed fighting." (p. 784)

3. **Proposition.** Early wars involved whole tribes—but sometimes they would stake all on a duel—like David and Goliath.

   "Early wars were fought between tribes as a whole, but in later times, when two individuals in different tribes had a dispute, instead of both tribes fighting, the two disputants engaged in a duel. It also became a custom for two armies to stake all on the outcome of a contest between a representative chosen from each side, as in the instance of David and Goliath." (p. 785)

4. **Proposition.** War persists because man is evolved from bellicose animals. There were many causes of early wars.

   See page 784

Part XX — *The State*

5. **Proposition.** The first refinement of war was the taking of prisoners. Next, women were exempted and noncombatants were recognized.

> "The first refinement of war was the taking of prisoners. Next, women were exempted from hostilities, and then came the recognition of noncombatants. Military castes and standing armies soon developed to keep pace with the increasing complexity of combat. Such warriors were early prohibited from associating with women, and women long ago ceased to fight, though they have always fed and nursed the soldiers and urged them on to battle." (p. 785)

6. **Proposition.** These early wars had certain social values.

> "War has had a social value to past civilizations because it:
> 1. Imposed discipline, enforced co-operation.
> 2. Put a premium on fortitude and courage.
> 3. Fostered and solidified nationalism.
> 4. Destroyed weak and unfit peoples.
> 5. Dissolved the illusion of primitive equality and selectively stratified society." (p. 785)

7. **Proposition.** Ancient wars decimated inferior peoples; modern war destroys the best human stocks.

> "Ancient warfare resulted in the decimation of inferior peoples; the net result of modern conflict is the selective destruction of the best human stocks. Early wars promoted organization and efficiency, but these have now become the aims of modern industry." (p. 786)

8. **Proposition.** Man does not give up war until he learns that peace is best for his material welfare.

> "Man will never accept peace as a normal mode of living until he has been thoroughly and repeatedly convinced that peace is best for his material welfare, and until society has wisely provided peaceful substitutes for the gratification of that inherent tendency periodically to let loose a collective drive designed to liberate those ever-accumulating emotions and energies belonging to the self-preservation reactions of the human species." (p. 786)

9. **Proposition.** War selected great men for leaders and taught a race of arrogant individualists to submit to authority.

> "But even in passing, war should be honored as the school of experience which compelled a race of arrogant individualists to submit themselves to highly concentrated authority—a chief executive. Old-fashioned war did select the innately great men

for leadership, but modern war no longer does this. To discover leaders society must now turn to the conquests of peace: industry, science, and social achievement." (p. 786)

II. EARLY HUMAN ASSOCIATIONS

1. **PROPOSITION.** Primitive society was a horde—children were common property. Later, the clan emerged and the family took over children.

   "In the most primitive society the *horde* is everything; even children are its common property. The evolving family displaced the horde in child rearing, while the emerging clans and tribes took its place as the social unit." (p. 787)

2. **PROPOSITION.** Families grew into clans. The first government was the council of the elders.

   "With the gradual emergence of the family units the foundations of government were established in the clan organization, the grouping of consanguineous families. The first real governmental body was the *council of the elders*. This regulative group was composed of old men who had distinguished themselves in some efficient manner." (p. 788)

3. **PROPOSITION.** The clans were held together by a group of common interests.

   "The clans were blood-tie groups within the tribe, and they owed their existence to certain common interests, such as:
   1. Tracing origin back to a common ancestor.
   2. Allegiance to a common religious totem.
   3. Speaking the same dialect.
   4. Sharing a common dwelling place.
   5. Fearing the same enemies.
   6. Having had a common military experience." (p. 788)

III. CLUBS AND SECRET SOCIETIES

1. **PROPOSITION.** Natural inequalities insure that social classes will appear. The only worlds without social classes are the very primitive and the most advanced.

   "The mental and physical inequality of human beings insures that social classes will appear. The only worlds without social strata are the most primitive and the most advanced. A dawning civilization has not yet begun the differentiation of social levels, while a world settled in light and life has largely effaced these divisions of mankind, which are so characteristic of all intermediate evolutionary stages." (p. 792)

2. **Proposition.** Ten groupings appear in an evolving society.

   See page 792.

3. **Proposition.** Secret societies performed numerous functions for primitive society.

   "All secret associations imposed an oath, enjoined confidence, and taught the keeping of secrets. These orders awed and controlled the mobs; they also acted as vigilance societies, thus practicing lynch law. They were the first spies when the tribes were at war and the first secret police during times of peace. Best of all they kept unscrupulous kings on the anxious seat. To offset them, the kings fostered their own secret police.
   "These societies gave rise to the first political parties. The first party government was 'the strong' *vs.* 'the weak.' In ancient times a change of administration only followed civil war, abundant proof that the weak had become strong." (p. 792)

IV. MONARCHIAL GOVERNMENT

1. **Proposition.** Kings were sometimes chosen for special abilities other than military.

   "In later times some chiefs were chosen for other than military service, being selected because of unusual physique or outstanding personal abilities. The red men often had two sets of chiefs—the sachems, or peace chiefs, and the hereditary war chiefs. The peace rulers were also judges and teachers." (p. 789)

2. **Proposition.** Effective state government only came with a chief executive— conferring power on a person—not endowing an idea.

   "Effective state rule only came with the arrival of a chief with full executive authority. Man found that effective government could be had only by conferring power on a personality, not by endowing an idea." (p. 789)

3. **Proposition.** Rulership grew out of family authority and wealth. Kings came from heroes—they had a divine origin.

   "Rulership grew out of the idea of family authority or wealth. When a patriarchal kinglet became a real king, he was sometimes called 'father of his people.' Later on, kings were thought to have sprung from heroes. And still further on, rulership became hereditary, due to belief in the divine origin of kings." (p. 789)

4. PROPOSITION. Early kings were fetish persons—kept in seclusion. They were represented by a prime minister.

> "The early fetish king was often kept in seclusion; he was regarded as too sacred to be viewed except on feast days and holy days. Ordinarily a representative was chosen to impersonate him, and this is the origin of prime ministers." (p. 790)

5. PROPOSITION. Group power produced the myth of the absolute obligation of the citizen to live and die for the state. The state is not divine in origin—it is evolutionary.

> "The modern state is the institution which survived in the long struggle for group power. Superior power eventually prevailed, and it produced a creature of fact—the state—together with the moral myth of the absolute obligation of the citizen to live and die for the state. But the state is not of divine genesis; it was not even produced by volitionally intelligent human action; it is purely an evolutionary institution and was wholly automatic in origin." (p. 800)

V. HUMAN RIGHTS

1. PROPOSITION. Nature confers no rights on man, only a life and a world in which to live it. Nature does not even confer the right to live.

> "Nature confers no rights on man, only life and a world in which to live it. Nature does not even confer the right to live, as might be deduced by considering what would likely happen if an unarmed man met a hungry tiger face to face in the primitive forest. Society's prime gift to man is security." (p. 793)

2. PROPOSITION. Gradually society asserted its rights.

> "Gradually society asserted its rights and, at the present time, they are:
> 1. Assurance of food supply.
> 2. Military defense—security through preparedness.
> 3. Internal peace preservation—prevention of personal violence and social disorder.
> 4. Sex control—marriage, the family institution.
> 5. Property—the right to own.
> 6. Fostering of individual and group competition.
> 7. Provision for educating and training youth.
> 8. Promotion of trade and commerce—industrial development.

PART XX — *The State*

   9. Improvement of labor conditions and rewards.

   10. The guarantee of the freedom of religious practices to the end that all of these other social activities may be exalted by becoming spiritually motivated." (p. 793)

3. **Proposition.** Equality is the child of civilization, it is not found in nature. Culture demonstrates inherent inequality of men by their unequal capacity therefor. Society can administer varying rights with fairness.

> "But this equality ideal is the child of civilization; it is not found in nature. Even culture itself demonstrates conclusively the inherent inequality of men by their very unequal capacity therefor. The sudden and nonevolutionary realization of supposed natural equality would quickly throw civilized man back to the crude usages of primitive ages. Society cannot offer equal rights to all, but it can promise to administer the varying rights of each with fairness and equity. It is the business and duty of society to provide the child of nature with a fair and peaceful opportunity to pursue selfmaintenance, participate in self-perpetuation, while at the same time enjoying some measure of self-gratification, the sum of all three constituting human happiness." (p. 794)

VI. EVOLUTION OF JUSTICE

1. **Proposition.** Government evolved by trial and error—an unconscious development. It became traditional because it had survival value.

> "Government is an unconscious development; it evolves by trial and error. It does have survival value; therefore it becomes traditional. Anarchy augmented misery; therefore government, comparative law and order, slowly emerged or is emerging. The coercive demands of the struggle for existence literally drove the human race along the progressive road to civilization." (p. 783)

2. **Proposition.** The idea of natural justice is a man-made theory—it is not a reality—it is a fiction.

> "Natural justice is a man-made theory; it is not a reality. In nature, justice is purely theoretic, wholly a fiction. Nature provides but one kind of justice—inevitable conformity of results to causes." (p. 794)

3. **PROPOSITION.** In primitive society public opinion operated directly—law officers were not needed.

> "In the earliest primitive society public opinion operated directly; officers of law were not needed. There was no privacy in primitive life. A man's neighbors were responsible for his conduct; therefore their right to pry into his personal affairs. Society was regulated on the theory that the group membership should have an interest in, and some degree of control over, the behavior of each individual." (p. 795)

4. **PROPOSITION.** The evolution of justice is well illustrated by an Old Testament ordeal pertaining to a wife suspected of infidelity.

> "The Old Testament records one of these ordeals, a marital guilt test: If a man suspected his wife of being untrue to him, he took her to the priest and stated his suspicions, after which the priest would prepare a concoction consisting of holy water and sweepings from the temple floor. After due ceremony, including threatening curses, the accused wife was made to drink the nasty potion. If she was guilty, 'the water that causes the curse shall enter into her and become bitter, and her belly shall swell, and her thighs shall rot, and the woman shall be accursed among her people.' If, by any chance, any woman could quaff this filthy draught and not show symptoms of physical illness, she was acquitted of the charges made by her jealous husband." (p. 795)

5. **PROPOSITION.** The imposition of fines for taboo violations was an advance in regulative function—they were the first public revenue.

> "Another advance was the imposition of fines for taboo violations, the provision of penalties. These fines constituted the first public revenue. The practice of paying 'blood money' also came into vogue as a substitute for blood vengeance. Such damages were usually paid in women or cattle; it was a long time before actual fines, monetary compensation, were assessed as punishment for crime. And since the idea of punishment was essentially compensation, everything, including human life, eventually came to have a price which could be paid as damages. The Hebrews were the first to abolish the practice of paying blood money. Moses taught that they should 'take no satisfaction for the life of a murderer, who is guilty of death; he shall surely be put to death.'" (p. 796)

Part XX — The State

6. **Proposition.** Law is a codified record of human experience—public opinion crystallized and legalized.

> "Law is a codified record of long human experience, public opinion crystallized and legalized. The mores were the raw material of accumulated experience out of which later ruling minds formulated the written laws. The ancient judge had no laws. When he handed down a decision, he simply said, 'It is the custom.'" (p. 797)

7. **Proposition.** The first courts were fistic encounters—judges were umpires. Might was right—later on verbal arguments took the place of physical combat.

> "The first courts were regulated fistic encounters; the judges were merely umpires or referees. They saw to it that the fight was carried on according to approved rules. On entering a court combat, each party made a deposit with the judge to pay the costs and fine after one had been defeated by the other. 'Might was still right.' Later on, verbal arguments were substituted for physical blows." (p. 797)

VII. REPRESENTATIVE GOVERNMENT

1. **Proposition.** Public opinion has always delayed society, but it does preserve civilization.

> "Public opinion, common opinion, has always delayed society; nevertheless, it is valuable, for, while retarding social evolution, it does preserve civilization. Education of public opinion is the only safe and true method of accelerating civilization; force is only a temporary expedient, and cultural growth will increasingly accelerate as bullets give way to ballots. Public opinion, the mores, is the basic and elemental energy in social evolution and state development, but to be of state value it must be nonviolent in expression." (p. 802)

2. **Proposition.** Democracy is an ideal, but it is beset by certain dangers.

> "Democracy, while an ideal, is a product of civilization, not of evolution. Go slowly! select carefully! for the dangers of democracy are:
> 1. Glorification of mediocrity.
> 2. Choice of base and ignorant rulers.
> 3. Failure to recognize the basic facts of social evolution.
> 4. Danger of universal suffrage in the hands of uneducated and indolent majorities.
> 5. Slavery to public opinion; the majority is not always right." (p. 801)

3. **Proposition.** There are ten stages in evolution of representative government.
   See page 802.

VIII. IDEALS OF STATEHOOD

1. **Proposition.** Ideals of statehood are attained by evolution. The level of any civilization is indicated by the caliber of its citizens who volunteer for public service.

   "The ideals of statehood must be attained by evolution, by the slow growth of civic consciousness, the recognition of the obligation and privilege of social service. At first men assume the burdens of government as a duty, following the end of the administration of political spoilsmen, but later on they seek such ministry as a privilege, as the greatest honor. The status of any level of civilization is faithfully portrayed by the caliber of its citizens who volunteer to accept the responsibilities of statehood." (p. 803)

2. **Proposition.** To remain free, after choosing a charter of liberty, men must maintain certain safeguards.

   "If men would maintain their freedom, they must, after having chosen their charter of liberty, provide for its wise, intelligent, and fearless interpretation to the end that there may be prevented:
   1. Usurpation of unwarranted power by either the executive or legislative branches.
   2. Machinations of ignorant and superstitious agitators.
   3. Retardation of scientific progress.
   4. Stalemate of the dominance of mediocrity.
   5. Domination by vicious minorities.
   6. Control by ambitious and clever would-be dictators.
   7. Disastrous disruption of panics.
   8. Exploitation by the unscrupulous.
   9. Taxation enslavement of the citizenry by the state.
   10. Failure of social and economic fairness.
   11. Union of church and state.
   12. Loss of personal liberty." (p. 798)

3. **Proposition.** Cities should be governed just like any business should be conducted.

   "In a real commonwealth the business of governing cities and provinces is conducted by experts and is managed just as are all other forms of economic and commercial associations of people." (p. 803)

4. **Proposition.** Idealists should avoid extinction. The great test of idealism is to maintain effective military preparedness and refrain from offensive acts of military aggrandizement.

> "Idealism can never survive on an evolving planet if the idealists in each generation permit themselves to be exterminated by the baser orders of humanity. And here is the great test of idealism: Can an advanced society maintain that military preparedness which renders it secure from all attack by its war-loving neighbors without yielding to the temptation to employ this military strength in offensive operations against other peoples for purposes of selfish gain or national aggrandizement? National survival demands preparedness, and religious idealism alone can prevent the prostitution of preparedness into aggression. Only love, brotherhood, can prevent the strong from oppressing the weak." (p. 804)

5. **Proposition.** The great problem of statehood is to regulate society without becoming parasitical or tyrannical.

> "The ideal state undertakes to regulate social conduct only enough to take violence out of individual competition and to prevent unfairness in personal initiative. Here is a great problem in statehood: How can you guarantee peace and quiet in industry, pay the taxes to support state power, and at the same time prevent taxation from handicapping industry and keep the state from becoming parasitical or tyrannical?" (p. 805)

6. **Proposition.** Statehood evolves from level to level through a dozen stages.

See pages 806-7

IX. PROGRESSIVE CIVILIZATION

1. **Proposition.** Society has not progressed very far when it permits idleness and tolerates poverty.

> "No society has progressed very far when it permits idleness or tolerates poverty. But poverty and dependence can never be eliminated if the defective and degenerate stocks are freely supported and permitted to reproduce without restraint." (p. 803)

2. **Proposition.** The progressive program of advancing civilization embraces many factors.

> "The progressive program of an expanding civilization embraces:
> 1. Preservation of individual liberties.
> 2. Protection of the home.
> 3. Promotion of economic security.
> 4. Prevention of disease.
> 5. Compulsory education.
> 6. Compulsory employment.
> 7. Profitable utilization of leisure.
> 8. Care of the unfortunate.
> 9. Race improvement.
> 10. Promotion of science and art.
> 11. Promotion of philosophy—wisdom.
> 12. Augmentation of cosmic insight—spirituality."

(p. 804)

3. **Proposition.** The nations of Urantia are engaged in the gigantic struggle between nationalistic militarism and the perils of industrialism.

> "The nations of Urantia have already entered upon the gigantic struggle between nationalistic militarism and industrialism, and in many ways this conflict is analogous to the agelong struggle between the herder-hunter and the farmer. But if industrialism is to triumph over militarism, it must avoid the dangers which beset it. The perils of budding industry on Urantia are:
> 1. The strong drift toward materialism, spiritual blindness.
> 2. The worship of wealth-power, value distortion.
> 3. The vices of luxury, cultural immaturity.
> 4. The increasing dangers of indolence, service insensitivity.
> 5. The growth of undesirable racial softness, biologic deterioration.
> 6. The threat of standardized industrial slavery, personality stagnation. Labor is ennobling but drudgery is benumbing."

(p. 786)

4. **Proposition.** Unless profit motivation can be augmented by service motives, it is doomed. Ruthless competition is destructive of even those things it seeks to uphold.

> "Present-day profit-motivated economics is doomed unless profit motives can be augmented by service motives. Ruthless competition based on narrow-minded self-interest is ultimately destructive

of even those things which it seeks to maintain. Exclusive and self-serving profit motivation is incompatible with Christian ideals— much more incompatible with the teachings of Jesus." (p. 805)

5. **Proposition.** Profit motivation should not be taken away from men until they are in possession of superior nonprofit motives.

"Profit motivation must not be taken away from men until they have firmly possessed themselves of superior types of nonprofit motives for economic striving and social serving—the transcendent urges of superlative wisdom, intriguing brotherhood, and excellency of spiritual attainment." (p. 805)

X. PRIVATE PROPERTY AND SLAVERY

1. **Proposition.** The development of industry demanded law, and private property necessitated government.

"No sooner had man partially solved the problem of making a living than he was confronted with the task of regulating human contacts. The development of industry demanded law, order, and social adjustment; private property necessitated government." (p. 783)

2. **Proposition.** Primitive communism did not level men down, but it did put a premium on idleness. It failed because it was contrary to four basic human urges.

See page 780.

3. **Proposition.** Private ownership increased liberty and enhanced stability. Improved machinery is setting men free from slavish toil.

"Private ownership brought increased liberty and enhanced stability; but private ownership of land was given social sanction only after communal control and direction had failed, and it was soon followed by a succession of slaves, serfs, and landless classes. But improved machinery is gradually setting men free from slavish toil." (p. 782)

4. **Proposition.** Property rights are purely social. But all of the blessings of civilization have grown up around private ownership of property.

"The right to property is not absolute; it is purely social. But all government, law, order, civil rights, social liberties, conventions, peace, and happiness, as they are enjoyed by modern peoples, have grown up around the private ownership of property." (p. 782)

5. **Proposition.** Present social orders are not necessarily right—much less sacred. But we should move slowly in making changes. What we have is better than anything known to our ancestors.

> "The present social order is not necessarily right—not divine or sacred—but mankind will do well to move slowly in making changes. That which you have is vastly better than any system known to your ancestors. Make certain that when you change the social order you change for the better. Do not be persuaded to experiment with the discarded formulas of your forefathers. Go forward, not backward! Let evolution proceed! Do not take a backward step." (p. 782)

6. **Proposition.** Enslavement was a merciful forward step in the treatment of war prisoners. Even the Hebrews "utterly destroyed" their enemies.

> "Enslavement was a forward step in the merciful treatment of war captives. The ambush of Ai, with the wholesale slaughter of men, women, and children, only the king being saved to gratify the conqueror's vanity, is a faithful picture of the barbaric slaughter practiced by even supposedly civilized peoples. The raid upon Og, the king of Bashan, was equally brutal and effective. The Hebrews 'utterly destroyed' their enemies, taking all their property as spoils. They put all cities under tribute on pain of the 'destruction of all males.' But many of the contemporary tribes, those having less tribal egotism, had long since begun to practice the adoption of superior captives." (p. 779)

7. **Proposition.** Slavery was indispensable in the development of civilization —it compelled backward and lazy people to work and thus provide wealth and leisure for the advancement of superior peoples.

> "Slavery was an indispensable link in the chain of human civilization. It was the bridge over which society passed from chaos and indolence to order and civilized activities; it compelled backward and lazy peoples to work and thus provide wealth and leisure for the social advancement of their superiors." (p. 779)

XI. SUPERHUMAN GOVERNMENT

1. **Proposition.** Every one hundred years the 24 Jerusem supervisors send one of their number to act as governor general of Urantia.

> "Every one hundred years of Urantia time, the Jerusem corps of twenty-four planetary supervisors designate one of their number

to sojourn on your world to act as their executive representative, as resident governor general. During the times of the preparation of these narratives this executive officer was changed, the nineteenth so to serve being succeeded by the twentieth. The name of the current planetary supervisor is withheld from you only because mortal man is so prone to venerate, even to deify, his extraordinary compatriots and superhuman superiors." (p. 1252)

2. **PROPOSITION.** The governor general has no personal authority—acts for the twenty-four counselors.

> "The resident governor general has no actual personal authority in the management of world affairs except as the representative of the twenty-four Jerusem counselors. He acts as the co-ordinator of superhuman administration and is the respected head and universally recognized leader of the celestial beings functioning on Urantia. All orders of angelic hosts regard him as their co-ordinating director, while the united midwayers, since the departure of 1-2-3 the first to become one of the twenty-four counselors, really look upon the successive governors general as their planetary fathers." (p. 1252)

3. **PROPOSITION.** The Most High observer is empowered to seize authority in times of crisis and has done so thirty-three times.

> "A Most High observer is empowered, at his discretion, to seize the planetary government in times of grave planetary crises, and it is of record that this has happened thirty-three times in the history of Urantia. At such times the Most High observer functions as the Most High regent, exercising unquestioned authority over all ministers and administrators resident on the planet excepting only the divisional organization of the archangels." (p. 1253)

4. **PROPOSITION.** The cabinet of the governor general consists of twelve seraphim, the chiefs of the special angelic groups.

> "The direct administrative cabinet of the governor general consists of twelve seraphim, the acting chiefs of the twelve groups of special angels functioning as the immediate superhuman directors of planetary progress and stability." (p. 1254)

5. **Proposition.** The reserve corps of destiny consists of persons selected by the superhuman administrators to assist in the conduct of world affairs.

> "The reserve corps of destiny consists of living men and women who have been admitted to the special service of the superhuman administration of world affairs. This corps is made up of the men and women of each generation who are chosen by the spirit directors of the realm to assist in the conduct of the ministry of mercy and wisdom to the children of time on the evolutionary worlds. It is the general practice in the conduct of the affairs of the ascension plans to begin this liaison utilization of mortal will creatures immediately they are competent and trustworthy to assume such responsibilities. Accordingly, as soon as men and women appear on the stage of temporal action with sufficient mental capacity, adequate moral status, and requisite spirituality, they are quickly assigned to the appropriate celestial group of planetary personalities as human liaisons, mortal assistants." (p. 1257)

6. **Proposition.** The reservists unconsciously act as conservators of essential planetary information.

> "The reservists unconsciously act as conservators of essential planetary information. Many times, upon the death of a reservist, a transfer of certain vital data from the mind of the dying reservist to a younger successor is made by a liaison of the two Thought Adjusters. The Adjusters undoubtedly function in many other ways unknown to us, in connection with these reserve corps." (p. 1258)

PART XXI
ASCENDING SONS OF GOD

Part Twenty-one
ASCENDING SONS OF GOD

I. INTRODUCTION

1. **Proposition.** There are seven groups of the Ascending Sons of God.

   "As in many of the major groups of universe beings, seven general classes of the Ascending Sons of God have been revealed:
   1. Father-fused Mortals.
   2. Son-fused Mortals.
   3. Spirit-fused Mortals.
   4. Evolutionary Seraphim.
   5. Ascending Material Sons.
   6. Translated Midwayers.
   7. Personalized Adjusters." (p. 443)

2. **Proposition.** Curiosity, love of adventure, and dread of monotony are inherent traits which will be fully gratified in an endless career of everlasting adventure and eternal discovery.

   "Love of adventure, curiosity, and dread of monotony—these traits inherent in evolving human nature—were not put there just to aggravate and annoy you during your short sojourn on earth, but rather to suggest to you that death is only the beginning of an endless career of adventure, an everlasting life of anticipation, an eternal voyage of discovery.
   "Curiosity—the spirit of investigation, the urge of discovery, the drive of exploration—is a part of the inborn and divine endowment of evolutionary space creatures. These natural impulses were not given you merely to be frustrated and repressed. True, these ambitious urges must frequently be restrained during your short life on earth, disappointment must be often experienced, but they are to be fully realized and gloriously gratified during the long ages to come." (pp. 159-60)

II. ASCENDING MORTALS—FATHER-FUSED

1. **Proposition.** Mortals are the lowest group of beings called sons of God.

   "Mortals represent the last link in the chain of those beings who are called sons of God. The personal touch of the Original and Eternal Son passes on down through a series of decreasingly divine and increasingly human personalizations until there arrives a being much like yourselves, one you can see, hear, and touch.

- 492 -

And then you are made spiritually aware of the great truth which your faith may grasp—sonship with the eternal God!" (p. 445)

2. **PROPOSITION.** It is a solemn fact that lowly mortals are sons of God.

> "It is a solemn and supernal fact that such lowly and material creatures as Urantia human beings are the sons of God, faith children of the Highest. 'Behold, what manner of love the Father has bestowed upon us that we should be called the sons of God.' 'As many as received him, to them gave he the power to recognize that they are the sons of God.' While 'it does not yet appear what you shall be,' even now 'you are the faith sons of God'; 'for you have not received the spirit of bondage again to fear, but you have received the spirit of sonship, whereby you cry, "our Father."' Spoke the prophet of old in the name of the eternal God: 'Even to them will I give in my house a place and a name better than sons; I will give them an everlasting name, one that shall not be cut off.' 'And because you are sons, God has sent forth the spirit of his Son into your hearts.'" (p. 448)

3. **PROPOSITION.** Mortals cannot be perfect in the infinite sense, but as concerns self-realization, they can achieve creature perfection.

> "Urantia mortals can hardly hope to be perfect in the infinite sense, but it is entirely possible for human beings, starting out as they do on this planet, to attain the supernal and divine goal which the infinite God has set for mortal man; and when they do achieve this destiny, they will, in all that pertains to self-realization and mind attainment, be just as replete in their sphere of divine perfection as God himself is in his sphere of infinity and eternity." (p. 22)

4. **PROPOSITION.** Mortals do attain finite perfection of divinity of will and personality motivation.

> "Such perfection may not be universal in the material sense, unlimited in intellectual grasp, or final in spiritual experience, but it is final and complete in all finite aspects of divinity of will, perfection of personality motivation, and God-consciousness." (p. 22)

5. **PROPOSITION.** Will creatures can obey the injunction: "Be you perfect, even as I am perfect." This is the supreme ambition of those who crave to be like God.

> "The will creatures of universe upon universe have embarked upon the long, long Paradise journey, the fascinating struggle of the eternal adventure of attaining God the Father. The transcendent

goal of the children of time is to find the eternal God, to comprehend the divine nature, to recognize the Paradise perfection of personality and in his universal sphere of righteous supremacy. From the Universal Father who inhabits eternity there has gone forth the supreme mandate, 'Be you perfect, even as I am perfect.' In love and mercy the messengers of Paradise have carried this divine exhortation down through the ages and out through the universes, even to such lowly animal-origin creatures as the human races of Urantia." (p. 21)

6. PROPOSITION. Vast time is involved in attaining God—ever you swing inward toward Paradise, and someday will see him face to face.

"The fact that vast time is involved in the attainment of God makes the presence and personality of the Infinite none the less real. Your ascension is a part of the circuit of the seven superuniverses, and though you swing around it countless times, you may expect, in spirit and in status, to be ever swinging inward. You can depend upon being translated from sphere to sphere, from the outer circuits ever nearer the inner center, and some day, doubt not, you shall stand in the divine and central presence and see him, figuratively speaking, face to face." (p. 63)

7. PROPOSITION. The pilgrim discoverer of Havona was Grandfanda from superuniverse number one. This event inaugurated the broadcast service of the universe of universes.

"The name of this pilgrim discoverer of Havona is Grandfanda, and he hailed from planet 341 of system 84 in constellation 62 of local universe 1,131 situated in superuniverse number one. His arrival was the signal for the establishment of the broadcast service of the universe of universes. Theretofore only the broadcasts of the superuniverses and the local universes had been in operation, but the announcement of the arrival of Grandfanda at the portals of Havona signalized the inauguration of the 'space reports of glory,' so named because the initial universe broadcast reported the Havona arrival of the first of the evolutionary beings to attain entrance upon the goal of ascendant existence." (p. 270)

8. PROPOSITION. Adjuster-fused mortals attain Paradise by seven stages. *See pages 340-43.*

9. **Proposition.** As related to Adjusters, there are three classes of mortals.

> "Spirit identification constitutes the secret of personal survival and determines the destiny of spiritual ascension. And since the Thought Adjusters are the only spirits of fusion potential to be identified with man during the life in the flesh, the mortals of time and space are primarily classified in accordance with their relation to these divine gifts, the indwelling Mystery Monitors. This classification is as follows:
> 1. Mortals of the transient or experiential Adjuster sojourn.
> 2. Mortals of the non-Adjuster-fusion types.
> 3. Mortals of Adjuster-fusion potential." (p. 445)

10. **Proposition.** When man and his Adjuster fuse, then in fact he becomes a son of God.

> "When you and your Adjuster are finally and forever fused, when you two are made one, even as in Christ Michael the Son of God and the Son of Man are one, then in fact have you become the ascending sons of God." (p. 449)

11. **Proposition.** At death, when the material body returns to dust, two nonmaterial factors survive—the Thought Adjuster and the morontia soul.

> "After death the material body returns to the elemental world from which it was derived, but two nonmaterial factors of surviving personality persist: The pre-existent Thought Adjuster, with the memory transcription of the mortal career, proceeds to Divinington; and there also remains, in the custody of the destiny guardian, the immortal morontia soul of the deceased human. These phases and forms of soul, these once kinetic but now static formulas of identity, are essential to repersonalization on the morontia worlds; and it is the reunion of the Adjuster and the soul that reassembles the surviving personality, that reconsciousizes you at the time of the morontia awakening." (p. 1230)

12. **Proposition.** It should be noted that there are three kinds of death.

See pages 1229-30.

13. **Proposition.** When mortals fail to survive, their Adjusters return to Divinington.

> "When the mortals of time fail to achieve the eternal survival of their souls in planetary association with the spirit gifts of the

Universal Father, such failure is never in any way due to neglect of duty, ministry, service, or devotion on the part of the Adjuster. At mortal death, such deserted Monitors return to Divinington, and subsequently, following the adjudication of the nonsurvivor, they may be reassigned to the worlds of time and space. Sometimes, after repeated services of this sort or following some unusual experience, such as functioning as the indwelling Adjuster of an incarnated bestowal Son, these efficient Adjusters are personalized by the Universal Father." (p. 444)

III. SON-FUSED MORTALS

1. **Proposition.** When an ascending mortal fails of Adjuster fusion, through no fault of his own, he is immediately fused with an individualized gift of the spirit of the Creator Son.

    "When it becomes apparent that some synchronizing difficulty is inhibiting Father fusion, the survival referees of the Creator Son are convened. And when this court of inquiry, sanctioned by a personal representative of the Ancients of Days, finally determines that the ascending mortal is not guilty of any discoverable cause for failure to attain fusion, they so certify on the records of the local universe and duly transmit this finding to the Ancients of Days. Thereupon does the indwelling Adjuster return forthwith to Divinington for confirmation by the Personalized Monitors, and upon this leave-taking the morontia mortal is immediately fused with an individualized gift of the spirit of the Creator Son." (p. 449)

2. **Proposition.** Some Son-fused mortals, like some Spirit-fused creatures, attain Havona and even reach Paradise.

    "Like their Spirit-fused brethren, the Son fusers neither traverse Havona nor attain Paradise unless they have undergone certain modifying transformations. For good and sufficient reasons, such changes have been wrought in certain Son-fused survivors, and these beings are to be encountered ever and anon on the seven circuits of the central universe. Thus it is that certain numbers of both the Son-and the Spirit-fused mortals do actually ascend to Paradise, do attain a goal in many ways equal to that which awaits the Father-fused mortals. (p. 453)

IV. SPIRIT-FUSED MORTALS

1. **Proposition.** Experiential Adjusters live with their subjects throughout a lifetime and contribute much to their personality advancement.

   "An experiential Adjuster remains with a primitive human being throughout his entire lifetime in the flesh. The Adjusters contribute much to the advancement of primitive men but are unable to form eternal unions with such mortals." (p. 446)

2. **Proposition.** Spirit-fused mortals are fused with individualizations of the premind spirit of the Third Source and Center.

   "Ascending Spirit-fused mortals are not Third Source personalities; they are included in the Father's personality circuit, but they have fused with individualizations of the premind spirit of the Third Source and Center. Such Spirit fusion never occurs during the span of natural life; it takes place only at the time of mortal reawakening in the morontia existence on the mansion worlds. In the fusion experience there is no overlapping; the will creature is either Spirit fused, Son fused, or Father fused. Those who are Adjuster or Father fused are never Spirit or Son fused." (p. 450)

3. **Proposition.** Spirit-fused mortals receive this spirit of the Divine Minister at repersonalization on the mansion world.

   "When such sleeping survivors are repersonalized on the mansion worlds, the place of the departed Adjuster is filled by an individualization of the spirit of the Divine Minister, the representative of the Infinite Spirit in the local universe concerned. This spirit infusion constitutes these surviving creatures Spirit-fused mortals. Such beings are in every way your equals in mind and spirit; and they are indeed your contemporaries, sharing the mansion and morontia spheres in common with your order of fusion candidates and with those who are to be Son fused." (p. 450)

4. **Proposition.** Spirit-fused mortals regain much of their world memory by having things told them by their guardian seraphim.

   "Such children of the local universe are enabled to repossess themselves of much of their former human memory experience through having it retold by the associated seraphim and cherubim and by consulting the records of the mortal career filed by the recording angels." (p. 451)

5. **PROPOSITION.** When Spirit-fused mortals are told unremembered events, the soul invests the narration with emotional tinge and the intellectual quality of fact.

   "When a Spirit-fused mortal is told about the events of the unremembered past experience, there is an immediate response of experiential recognition within the soul (identity) of such a survivor which instantly invests the narrated event with the emotional tinge of reality and with the intellectual quality of fact; and this dual response constitutes the reconstruction, recognition, and validation of an unremembered facet of mortal experience." (p. 451)

6. **PROPOSITION.** Spirit-fused survivors also learn much about their lives in the flesh by visiting their nativity worlds in a subsequent planetary age.

   "A Spirit-fused survivor is also able to learn much about the life he lived in the flesh by revisiting his nativity world subsequent to the planetary dispensation in which he lived. Such children of Spirit fusion are enabled to enjoy these opportunities for investigating their human careers since they are in general confined to the service of the local universe." (p. 451)

7. **PROPOSITION.** In general, Spirit-fused mortals are confined to the local universe, Son-fused to the superuniverse.

   "Spirit-fused mortals are, generally speaking, confined to a local universe; Son-fused survivors are restricted to a superuniverse; Adjuster-fused mortals are destined to penetrate the universe of universes. The spirits of mortal fusion always ascend to the level of origin; such spirit entities unfailingly return to the sphere of primal source." (p. 452)

8. **PROPOSITION.** To consign all ascendant mortals to Paradise destiny would be unfair. Both local universes and superuniverses need a permanent citizenship of ascendant beings.

   "We have analyzed this problem and have reached the undoubted conclusion that the consignment of all mortals to an ultimate Paradise destiny would be unfair to the time-space universes inasmuch as the courts of the Creator Sons and of the Ancients of Days would then be wholly dependent on the services of those who were in transit to higher realms. And it does seem to be no more than fitting that the local and the superuniverse governments should each be provided with a permanent group of ascendant citizenship; that the functions of these administrations should be enriched by the efforts of certain groups of glorified mortals who are of permanent status, evolutionary complements of the abandonters and of the susatia." (p. 452)

V. EVOLUTIONARY SERAPHIM

1. **Proposition.** The angelic hosts share with mortals the status of ascending Sons of God. All guardian seraphim attain Paradise and many are mustered into the Corps of Mortal Finality,

   "Mortal creatures of animal origin are not the only beings privileged to enjoy sonship; the angelic hosts also share the supernal opportunity to attain Paradise. Guardian seraphim, through experience and service with the ascending mortals of time, also achieve the status of ascendant sonship. Such angels attain Paradise through Seraphington, and many are even mustered into the Corps of Mortal Finality." (p. 443)

VI. MATERIAL SONS

1. **Proposition.** A certain number of the Material Sons ascend to Paradise and join the Corps of Mortal Finality.

   "After these formalities such liberated Adams and Eves are accredited as ascending Sons of God and may immediately begin the long journey to Havona and Paradise, starting at the exact point of their then present status and spiritual attainment. And they make this journey in company with the mortal and other ascending Sons, continuing until they have found God and have achieved the Corps of Mortal Finality in the eternal service of the Paradise Deities." (p. 444)

VII. TRANSLATED MIDWAYERS

1. **Proposition.** Even though long deferred, the midwayers, if not before, are liberated at some stage of settlement in light and life to begin the Paradise ascent by the same routes ordained for mortal progression.

   "Although deprived of the immediate benefits of the planetary bestowals of the descending Sons of God, though the Paradise ascent is long deferred, nevertheless, soon after an evolutionary planet has attained the intermediate epochs of light and life (if not before), both groups of midway creatures are released from planetary duty. Sometimes the majority of them are translated, along with their human cousins, on the day of the descent of the temple of light and the elevation of the Planetary Prince to the dignity of Planetary Sovereign. Upon being relieved of planetary service, both orders are registered in the local universe of ascending Sons of God and immediately begin the long Paradise ascent by the very routes ordained for the progression of the mortal races of the material worlds." (p. 444)

VIII. PERSONALIZED ADJUSTERS

1. **PROPOSITION.** Some Personalized Adjusters become classified as ascending Sons of God.

   See page 444.

IX. MIDSONITERS

1. **PROPOSITION.** In the ascending scheme of mortals, midsoniters are a puzzle. After one thousand years on their native worlds, they go to universe headquarters. They are hardly mortal or immortal—human or divine.

   > "The midsonite creatures live and function as reproducing beings on their magnificent worlds until they are one thousand standard years of age; whereupon they are translated by seraphic transport. Midsoniters are nonreproducing beings thereafter because the technique of dematerialization which they pass through in preparation for enseraphiming forever deprives them of reproductive prerogatives.
   > "The present status of these beings can hardly be reckoned as either mortal or immortal, neither can they be definitely classified as human or divine. These creatures are not Adjuster indwelt, hence hardly immortal. But neither do they seem to be mortal; no midsoniter has experienced death. All midsoniters ever born in Nebadon are alive today, functioning on their native worlds, on some intervening sphere, or on the Salvington midsonite sphere in the finaliter's group of worlds." (p. 400)

2. **PROPOSITION.** The destiny of midsoniters is unknown—probably they belong to a future universe age. The Melchizedeks think they will sometime be endowed with the transcendental spirit of absonity.

   > "The purpose of the midsonite creatures is not at present known, but it would appear that these personalities are forgathering on the seventh finaliter world in preparation for some future eventuality in universe evolution. Our inquiries concerning the midsonite races are always referred to the finaliters, and always do the finaliters decline to discuss the destiny of their wards. Regardless of our uncertainty as to the future of the midsoniters, we do know that every local universe in Orvonton harbors

such an accumulating corps of these mysterious beings. It is the belief of the Melchizedek life carriers that their midsonite children will some day be endowed with the transcendental and eternal spirit of absonity by God the Ultimate." (p. 401)

X. THE MANSION WORLDS

1. **Proposition.** The Temple of New Life has seven wings of one hundred thousand resurrection chambers. These wings terminate in class assembly halls accommodating one million souls.

   "From the Temple of New Life there extend seven radial wings, the resurrection halls of the mortal races. Each of these structures is devoted to the assembly of one of the seven races of time. There are one hundred thousand personal resurrection chambers in each of these seven wings terminating in the circular class assembly halls, which serve as the awakening chambers for as many as one million individuals. These halls are surrounded by the personality assembly chambers of the blended races of the normal post-Adamic worlds. Regardless of the technique which may be employed on the individual worlds of time in connection with special or dispensational resurrections, the real and conscious reassembly of actual and complete personality takes place in the resurrection halls of mansonia number one. Throughout all eternity you will recall the profound memory impressions of your first witnessing of these resurrection mornings." (p. 533)

2. **Proposition.** After resurrection you are assigned permanent residence. Then come the ten days of liberty.

   "From the resurrection halls you proceed to the Melchizedek sector, where you are assigned permanent residence. Then you enter upon ten days of personal liberty. You are free to explore the immediate vicinity of your new home and to familiarize yourself with the program which lies immediately ahead. You also have time to gratify your desire to consult the registry and call upon your loved ones and other earth friends who may have preceded you to these worlds. At the end of your ten-day period of leisure you begin the second step in the Paradise journey, for the mansion worlds are actual training spheres, not merely detention planets." (p. 533)

3. **PROPOSITION.** Mansion world number one attains to the status of the post-Adamic dispensation on a normal world.

   "The sojourn on mansion world number one is designed to develop mortal survivors at least up to the status of the post-Adamic dispensation on the normal evolutionary worlds. Spiritually, of course, the mansion world students are far in advance of such a state of mere human development." (p. 534)

4. **PROPOSITION.** At the end of ten days, if you are not to be detained, you advance.

   "If you are not to be detained on mansion world number one, at the end of ten days you will enter the translation sleep and proceed to world number two, and every ten days thereafter you will thus advance until you arrive on the world of your assignment." (p. 534)

5. **PROPOSITION.** On the second mansion world you get rid of conflict and mental disharmony and learn morontia mota. The culture is that of a post-Magisterial Son dispensation.

   "Mansonia number two more specifically provides for the removal of all phases of intellectual conflict and for the cure of all varieties of mental disharmony. The effort to master the significance of morontia mota, begun on the first mansion world, is here more earnestly continued. The development on mansonia number two compares with the intellectual status of the post-Magisterial Son culture of the ideal evolutionary worlds." (p. 535)

6. **PROPOSITION.** On the third world you really begin your morontia culture. The first two worlds were largely deficiency spheres. You begin to correlate morontia mota and human philosophy. The culture resembles that of a postbestowal Son dispensation.

   "Mansonia the third is a world of great personal and social achievement for all who have not made the equivalent of these circles of culture prior to release from the flesh on the mortal nativity worlds. On this sphere more positive educational work is begun. The training of the first two mansion worlds is mostly of a deficiency nature—negative—in that it has to do with supplementing the experience of the life in the flesh. On this third mansion world the survivors really begin their progressive morontia culture. The chief purpose of this training is to enhance the understanding of the correlation of morontia mota and mortal logic, the co-ordination of morontia mota and human philosophy. Surviving mortals now gain practical insight into true metaphysics. This is the real introduction to the intelligent comprehension of cosmic meanings and universe interrelationships. The culture of the third mansion world partakes of the nature of the postbestowal Son age of a normal inhabited planet." (p. 536)

7. **Proposition.** On the fourth world ascenders continue to advance in morontia culture and enter upon real morontia social life. Ascenders are becoming God-knowing, God-revealing, God-seeking, and God-finding.

"On the fourth mansonia the individual ascender more fittingly finds his place in the group working and class functions of the morontia life. Ascenders here develop increased appreciation of the broadcasts and other phases of local universe culture and progress.
"It is during the period of training on world number four that the ascending mortals are really first introduced to the demands and delights of the true social life of morontia creatures. And it is indeed a new experience for evolutionary creatures to participate in social activities which are predicated neither on personal aggrandizement nor on self-seeking conquest. A new social order is being introduced, one based on the understanding sympathy of mutual appreciation, the unselfish love of mutual service, and the overmastering motivation of the realization of a common and supreme destiny—the Paradise goal of worshipful and divine perfection. Ascenders are all becoming self-conscious of God-knowing, God-revealing, God-seeking, and God-finding." (p. 536)

8. **Proposition.** On world number five the birth of cosmic consciousness takes place—real enthusiasm for the Havona ascent appears. Morontia character is budding and a real morontia creature is evolving.

"A real birth of cosmic consciousness takes place on mansonia number five. You are becoming universe minded. This is indeed a time of expanding horizons. It is beginning to dawn upon the enlarging minds of the ascending mortals that some stupendous and magnificent, some supernal and divine, destiny awaits all who complete the progressive Paradise ascension, which has been so laboriously but so joyfully and auspiciously begun. At about this point the average mortal ascender begins to manifest bona fide experiential enthusiasm for the Havona ascent. Study is becoming voluntary, unselfish service natural, and worship spontaneous. A real morontia character is budding; a real morontia creature is evolving." (p. 537)

9. **PROPOSITION.** On world number six ascending mortals attain an approximation of the initial stage of light and life and are divested of the coarse vestiges of planetary animal origin.

> "During the sojourn on world number six the mansion world students achieve a status which is comparable with the exalted development characterizing those evolutionary worlds which have normally progressed beyond the initial stage of light and life. The organization of society on this mansonia is of a high order. The shadow of the mortal nature grows less and less as these worlds are ascended one by one. You are becoming more and more adorable as you leave behind the coarse vestiges of planetary animal origin. 'Coming up through great tribulation' serves to make glorified mortals very kind and understanding, very sympathetic and tolerant." (p. 538)

10. **PROPOSITION.** On the seventh world differences between ascenders from the isolated worlds and those from the more advanced spheres are disappearing. The last remnants of the "mark of the beast" are eradicated.

> "The experience on this sphere is the crowning achievement of the immediate postmortal career. During your sojourn here you will receive the instruction of many teachers, all of whom will co-operate in the task of preparing you for residence on Jerusem. Any discernible differences between those mortals hailing from the isolated and retarded worlds and those survivors from the more advanced and enlightened spheres are virtually obliterated during the sojourn on the seventh mansion world. Here you will be purged of all the remnants of unfortunate heredity, unwholesome environment, and unspiritual planetary tendencies. The last remnants of the 'mark of the beast' are here eradicated." (p. 538)

11. **PROPOSITION.** All mortals, midwayers, and seraphim must experience parental relationship to an evolving child. This experience is indispensable to all ascenders.

> "No surviving mortal, midwayer, or seraphim may ascend to Paradise, attain the Father, and be mustered into the Corps of the Finality without having passed through that sublime experience of achieving parental relationship to an evolving child of the worlds or some other experience analogous and equivalent thereto. The relationship of child and parent is fundamental to the essential concept of the Universal Father and his universe children. Therefore does such an experience become indispensable to the experiential training of all ascenders." (p. 516)

Part XXI — Ascending Sons of God

12. **Proposition.** The probation nursery is maintained by morontia personalities on the finaliters' world. Here are assembled the offspring of the evolving worlds who died before acquiring spiritual status. The survival of either parent insures the repersonalization of these children.

> "This probation nursery of Satania is maintained by certain morontia personalities on the finaliters' world, one half of the planet being devoted to this work of child rearing. Here are received and reassembled certain children of surviving mortals, such as those offspring who perished on the evolutionary worlds before acquiring spiritual status as individuals. The ascension of either of its natural parents insures that such a mortal child of the realms will be accorded repersonalization on the system finaliter planet and there be permitted to demonstrate by subsequent freewill choice whether or not it elects to follow the parental path of mortal ascension. Children here appear as on the nativity world except for the absence of sex differentiation. There is no reproduction of mortal kind after the life experience on the inhabited worlds." (p. 516)

XI. THE SYSTEM SOJOURN

1. **Proposition.** John saw a company of ascenders arriving on Jerusem. The harps of God are broadcast receiving mechanisms.

> "John the Revelator saw a vision of the arrival of a class of advancing mortals from the seventh mansion world to their first heaven, the glories of Jerusem. He recorded: 'And I saw as it were a sea of glass mingled with fire; and those who had gained the victory over the beast that was originally in them and over the image that persisted through the mansion worlds and finally over the last mark and trace, standing on the sea of glass, having the harps of God, and singing the song of deliverance from mortal fear and death.' (Perfected space communication is to be had on all these worlds; and your anywhere reception of such communications is made possible by carrying the 'harp of God,' a morontia contrivance compensating for the inability to directly adjust the immature morontia sensory mechanism to the reception of space communications.)" (p. 539)

2. **Proposition.** The apostle Paul had a view of these Jerusem ascenders.

> "Paul also had a view of the ascendant-citizen corps of perfecting mortals on Jerusem, for he wrote: 'But you have come to Mount Zion and to the city of the living God, the heavenly Jerusalem, and to an innumerable company of angels, to the grand assembly of Michael, and to the spirits of just men being made perfect.'" (p. 539)

3. **Proposition.** On Jerusem, ascenders from the isolated worlds live together and are known as agondonters.

> "On Jerusem the ascenders from these isolated worlds occupy a residential sector by themselves and are known as the *agondonters*, meaning evolutionary will creatures who can believe without seeing, persevere when isolated, and triumph over insuperable difficulties even when alone. This functional grouping of the agondonters persists throughout the ascension of the local universe and the traversal of the superuniverse; it disappears during the sojourn in Havona but promptly reappears upon the attainment of Paradise and definitely persists in the Corps of the Mortal Finality. Tabamantia is an *agondonter* of finalter status, having survived from one of the quarantined spheres involved in the first rebellion ever to take place in the universes of time and space." (p. 579)

XII. IN HAVONA

1. **Proposition.** Pilgrims land on the pilot world of Havona with just one endowment of perfection—perfection of purpose.

> "The pilgrim lands on the receiving planet of Havona, the pilot world of the seventh circuit, with only one endowment of perfection, perfection of purpose. The Universal Father has decreed: 'Be you perfect, even as I am perfect.' That is the astounding invitation-command broadcast to the finite children of the worlds of space. The promulgation of that injunction has set all creation astir in the co-operative effort of the celestial beings to assist in bringing about the fulfillment and realization of that tremendous command of the First Great Source and Center." (p. 290)

2. **Proposition.** Perfection of purpose embraces:
    1. *Your purpose has been fully proved.*
    2. *Your faith has been tested.*
    3. *You are disappointment proof.*
    4. *Not even failure to discern Deity will matter.*
    5. *Your sincerity is sublime.*

> "When, through and by the ministry of all the helper hosts of the universal scheme of survival, you are finally deposited on the receiving world of Havona, you arrive with only one sort of perfection—*perfection of purpose*. Your purpose has been thoroughly proved; your faith has been tested. You are known to be disappointment proof. Not even the failure to discern the

Universal Father can shake the faith or seriously disturb the trust of an ascendant mortal who has passed through the experience that all must traverse in order to attain the perfect spheres of Havona. By the time you reach Havona, your sincerity has become sublime. Perfection of purpose and divinity of desire, with steadfastness of faith, have secured your entrance to the settled abodes of eternity; your deliverance from the uncertainties of time is full and complete; and now must you come face to face with the problems of Havona and the immensities of Paradise, to meet which you have so long been in training in the experiential epochs of time on the world schools of space." (p. 290)

3. **Proposition.** Faith has won for the ascending pilgrim that perfection of purpose which admits the children of time to the portals of eternity. Next begins the development of the perfection of understanding and the technique of comprehension essential to the perfection of Paradise status.

"Faith has won for the ascendant pilgrim a perfection of purpose which admits the children of time to the portals of eternity. Now must the pilgrim helpers begin the work of developing that perfection of understanding and that technique of comprehension which are so indispensable to Paradise perfection of personality." (p. 290)

4. **Proposition.** Ability to comprehend is the passport to Paradise. Believing was the key to Havona. Acceptance of sonship was the price of evolutionary survival.

"*Ability to comprehend is the mortal passport to Paradise.* Willingness to believe is the key to Havona. The acceptance of sonship, cooperation with the indwelling Adjuster, is the price of evolutionary survival." (p. 290)

XIII. ON PARADISE

1. **Proposition.** Not many pilgrims fail to attain Deity on reaching Paradise. Those who do, after additional trainings, never fail the second time.

   "Not many pilgrims experience the delay of seeming failure in the Deity adventure. Nearly all attain the Infinite Spirit, though occasionally a pilgrim from superuniverse number one does not succeed on the first attempt. The pilgrims who attain the Spirit seldom fail in finding the Son; of those who do fail on the first adventure, almost all hail from superuniverses three and five. The great majority of those who fail on the first adventure to attain the Father, after finding both the Spirit and the Son, hail from superuniverse number six, though a few from numbers two and three are likewise unsuccessful. And all this seems clearly to indicate that there is some good and sufficient reason for these apparent failures; in reality, simply unescapable delays." (p. 294)

2. **Proposition.** The ascendant career has been mastered; the goal of Deity has been attained. Survival is complete in the supremacy of divinity. Time is lost in eternity.

   "Step by step, life by life, world by world, the ascendant career has been mastered, and the goal of Deity has been attained. Survival is complete in perfection, and perfection is replete in the supremacy of divinity. Time is lost in eternity; space is swallowed up in worshipful identity and harmony with the Universal Father." (p. 295)

3. **Proposition.** The broadcasts proclaim that the animal origin creature has become in reality the perfected son of God.

   "The broadcasts of Havona flash forth the space reports of glory, the good news that in very truth the conscientious creatures of animal nature and material origin have, through evolutionary ascension, become in reality and eternally the perfected sons of God." (p. 295)

4. **Proposition.** On Paradise, the ascender has obeyed the Father's mandate: "Be you perfect, even as I am perfect." Also:
   1. *The test of time is almost over.*
   2. *The race for eternity is all but over.*
   3. *The days of uncertainty are ending.*
   4. *Temptation to doubt is vanishing.*

   "The test of time is almost over; the race for eternity has been all but run. The days of uncertainty are ending; the temptation to doubt is vanishing; the injunction to be *perfect* has been obeyed.

From the very bottom of intelligent existence the creature of time and material personality has ascended the evolutionary spheres of space, thus proving the feasibility of the ascension plan while forever demonstrating the justice and righteousness of the command of the Universal Father to his lowly creatures of the worlds: 'Be you perfect, even as I am perfect.'" (p. 295)

5. **PROPOSITION.** The last sleep on entering Paradise differs from all previous ones. The instigators and companions of sleep are essential to this last metamorphic sleep

"But the last metamorphic sleep is something more than those previous transition slumbers which have marked the successive status attainments of the ascendant career; thereby do the creatures of time and space traverse the innermost margins of the temporal and the spatial to attain residential status in the timeless and spaceless abodes of Paradise. The instigators and the complements of rest are just as essential to this transcending metamorphosis as are the seraphim and associated beings to the mortal creature's survival of death." (p. 299)

6. **PROPOSITION.** You go to sleep on the last Havona circuit and are eternally resurrected on Paradise. This is the last grand stretch of faith.

"You enter the rest on the final Havona circuit and are eternally resurrected on Paradise. And as you there spiritually repersonalize, you will immediately recognize the instigator of rest who welcomes you to the eternal shores as the very primary supernaphim who produced the final sleep on the innermost circuit of Havona; and you will recall the last grand stretch of faith as you once again made ready to commend the keeping of your identity into the hands of the Universal Father." (p. 299)

7. **PROPOSITION.** The last rest of time—the last transition sleep is over. You now awake on the everlasting shores of the eternal abode.

"The last rest of time has been enjoyed; the last transition sleep has been experienced; now you awake to life everlasting on the shores of the eternal abode. 'And there shall be no more sleep. The presence of God and his Son are before you and you are eternally his servants; you have seen his face, and his name is your spirit. There shall be no night there; and they need no light of the sun for the Great Source and Center gives them light; they shall live forever and ever. And God shall wipe away all tears from their eyes; there shall be no more death, neither sorrow nor crying, neither shall there be any more pain, for the former things have passed away.'" (p. 299)

PART XXII
THE MORONTIA LIFE

Part Twenty-Two
THE MORONTIA LIFE

I. INTRODUCTION

1. **Proposition.** You do not survive just to enjoy endless bliss and eternal ease. There is a transcendent goal beyond this universe age of training.

    "The mortal-survival plan has a practical and serviceable objective; you are not the recipients of all this divine labor and painstaking training only that you may survive just to enjoy endless bliss and eternal ease. There is a goal of transcendent service concealed beyond the horizon of the present universe age. If the Gods designed merely to take you on one long and eternal joy excursion, they certainly would not so largely turn the whole universe into one vast and intricate practical training school, requisition a substantial part of the celestial creation as teachers and instructors, and then spend ages upon ages piloting you, one by one, through this gigantic universe school of experiential training." (p. 558)

2. **Proposition.** Execution of the mortal perfection plan enlists much of the activity of the celestial intelligences of the present organized universe.

    "The furtherance of the scheme of mortal progression seems to be one of the chief businesses of the present organized universe, and the majority of innumerable orders of created intelligences are either directly or indirectly engaged in advancing some phase of this progressive perfection plan." (p. 558)

3. **Proposition.** Mortal death is the technique of escape from life in the flesh. The morontia life intervenes between the material existence and the higher spirit attainment.

    "Mortal death is a technique of escape from the material life in the flesh; and the mansonia experience of progressive life through seven worlds of corrective training and cultural education represents the introduction of mortal survivors to the morontia career, the transition life which intervenes between the evolutionary material existence and the higher spirit attainment of the ascenders of time who are destined to achieve the portals of eternity." (p. 540)

4. PROPOSITION. The Gods do not transform an animal creature into a perfected spirit by some sort of creative magic.

> "The Gods cannot—at least they do not—transform a creature of gross animal nature into a perfected spirit by some mysterious act of creative magic. When the Creators desire to produce perfect beings, they do so by direct and original creation, but they never undertake to convert animal-origin and material creatures into beings of perfection in a single step." (p. 541)

5. PROPOSITION. Always does this intermediate or transition morontia state intervene between the mortal state and the spirit status of surviving human beings.

> "Always this morontia transition intervenes between the mortal estate and the subsequent spirit status of surviving human beings. This intermediate state of universe progress differs markedly in the various local creations, but in intent and purpose they are all quite similar. The arrangement of the mansion and higher morontia worlds in Nebadon is fairly typical of the morontia transition regimes in this part of Orvonton." (p. 541)

6. PROPOSITION. Resurrected mortals have the same type of body that Jesus had when he arose from the tomb.

> "The mortals of the realms will arise in the morning of the resurrection with the same type of transition or morontia body that Jesus had when he arose from the tomb on this Sunday morning. These bodies do not have circulating blood, and such beings do not partake of ordinary material food; nevertheless, these morontia forms are *real*. When the various believers saw Jesus after his resurrection, they really saw him; they were not the self-deceived victims of visions or hallucinations." (p. 2029)

II. MORONTIA COMPANIONS

1. PROPOSITION. Morontia Companions are the children of the universe Mother Spirit who creates them in groups of one hundred thousand.

> "These hosts of the mansion and morontia worlds are the offspring of a local universe Mother Spirit. They are created from age to age in groups of one hundred thousand, and in Nebadon there are at present over seventy billion of these unique beings." (p. 545)

2. **PROPOSITION.** Morontia Companions maintain headquarters on the first mansion worlds of the local systems. Thousands were lost in the Lucifer rebellion.

> "The Morontia Companions maintain ten thousand headquarters in a local universe—on each of the first mansion worlds of the local systems. They are almost wholly a self-governing order and are, in general, an intelligent and loyal group of beings; but every now and then, in connection with certain unfortunate celestial upheavals, they have been known to go astray. Thousands of these useful creatures were lost during the times of the Lucifer rebellion in Satania. Your local system now has its full quota of these beings, the loss of the Lucifer rebellion having only recently been made up." (p. 545)

3. **PROPOSITION.** These Companions are the interpreters and translators of the morontia worlds—the linguists of the realms. You do not acquire new languages automatically.

> "*Interpreters and Translators.* During the early mansonia career you will have frequent recourse to the interpreters and the translators. They know and speak all the tongues of a local universe; they are the linguists of the realms.
>
> "You will not acquire new languages automatically; you will learn a language over there much as you do down here, and these brilliant beings will be your language teachers. The first study on the mansion worlds will be the tongue of Satania and then the language of Nebadon. And while you are mastering these new tongues, the Morontia Companions will be your efficient interpreters and patient translators. You will never encounter a visitor on any of these worlds but that some one of the Morontia Companions will be able to officiate as interpreter." (p. 546)

III. REVERSION DIRECTORS

1. **PROPOSITION.** Joyful mirth and the smile-equivalent are as universal as music and are the morontia equivalent of laughter. The ascendant life is about equally divided between work and play.

> "Joyful mirth and the smile-equivalent are as universal as music. There is a morontial and a spiritual equivalent of mirth and laughter. The ascendant life is about equally divided between work and play— freedom from assignment." (p. 547)

PART XXII — *The Morontia Life*

2. **Proposition.** Morontia Companions are skillful play sponsors, and are ably supported by the reversion directors in fostering celestial relaxation.

    "Celestial relaxation and superhuman humor are quite different from their human analogues, but we all actually indulge in a form of both; and they really accomplish for us, in our state, just about what ideal humor is able to do for you on Urantia. The Morontia Companions are skillful play sponsors, and they are most ably supported by the reversion directors." (p. 547)

3. **Proposition.** Reversion directors may be likened to the higher types of Urantia humorists—though this would be a crude comparison.

    "You would probably best understand the work of the reversion directors if they were likened to the higher types of humorists on Urantia, though that would be an exceedingly crude and somewhat unfortunate way in which to try to convey an idea of the function of these directors of change and relaxation, these ministers of the exalted humor of the morontia and spirit realms." (p. 547)

4. **Proposition.** Reversion directors are a recruited group ranging from Havona natives to morontia progressors. They are devoted to facilitating thought change and mind rest.

    "The reversion directors themselves are not a created group; they are a recruited corps embracing beings ranging from the Havona natives down through the messenger hosts of space and the ministering spirits of time to the morontia progressors from the evolutionary worlds. All are volunteers, giving themselves to the work of assisting their fellows in the achievement of thought change and mind rest, for such attitudes are most helpful in recuperating depleted energies." (p. 548)

5. **Proposition.** In magnifying our self-importance, if we stop to think of our Makers, our self-glorification becomes ridiculous. Humor is the divine antidote for exaltation of ego.

    "When we are tempted to magnify our self-importance, if we stop to contemplate the infinity of the greatness and grandeur of our Makers, our own self-glorification becomes sublimely ridiculous, even verging on the humorous. One of the functions of humor is to help all of us take ourselves less seriously. *Humor is the divine antidote for exaltation of ego.*" (p. 549)

6. **Proposition.** Humor is a safety valve preventing pressure from monotony, self-contemplation, and intense effort. Humor lessens the shock of any sudden impact of truth, fact, or other reality situation.

> "Humor should function as an automatic safety valve to prevent the building up of excessive pressures due to the monotony of sustained and serious self-contemplation in association with the intense struggle for developmental progress and noble achievement. Humor also functions to lessen the shock of the unexpected impact of fact or of truth, rigid unyielding fact and flexible ever-living truth. The mortal personality, never sure as to which will next be encountered, through humor swiftly grasps— sees the point and achieves insight— the unexpected nature of the situation be it fact or be it truth." (p. 549)

IV. MANSION WORLD TEACHERS

1. **Proposition.** Mansion World Teachers are deserted and glorified cherubim. When mortals enter the morontia life, attending seraphim have no need of their formerly associated cherubim and sanobim.

> "The Mansion World Teachers are a corps of deserted but glorified cherubim and sanobim. When a pilgrim of time advances from a trial world of space to the mansion and associated worlds of morontia training, he is accompanied by his personal or group seraphim, the guardian of destiny. In the worlds of mortal existence the seraphim is ably assisted by cherubim and sanobim; but when her mortal ward is delivered from the bonds of the flesh and starts out on the ascendant career, when the postmaterial or morontia life begins, the attending seraphim has no further need of the ministrations of her former lieutenants, the cherubim and sanobim." (p. 550)

V. MORONTIA WORLD SERAPHIM

1. **Proposition.** While many angels minister on the morontia worlds, the transition ministers work exclusively on these spheres.

> "While all orders of angels, from the planetary helpers to the supreme seraphim, minister on the morontia worlds, the transition ministers are more exclusively assigned to these activities. These angels are of the sixth order of seraphim servers, and their ministry is devoted to facilitating the transit of material and mortal creatures from the temporal life in the flesh on into the early stages of morontia existence on the seven mansion worlds." (p. 551)

2. **Proposition.** The mind planners are the psychologists of the morontia worlds. The majority have had previous experience as guardian angels.

> "*Mind Planners.* These seraphim are devoted to the effective grouping of morontia beings and to organizing their teamwork on the mansion worlds. They are the psychologists of the first heaven. The majority of this particular division of seraphic ministers have had previous experience as guardian angels to the children of time, but their wards, for some reason, failed to personalize on the mansion worlds or else survived by the technique of Spirit fusion." (p. 553)

VI. MORONTIA MOTA

1. **Proposition.** The lower planes of mota join directly with the higher planes of human philosophy. On the first mansion world they teach the less advanced students by the parallel technique.

> "The lower planes of morontia mota join directly with the higher levels of human philosophy. On the first mansion world it is the practice to teach the less advanced students by the parallel technique; that is, in one column are presented the more simple concepts of mota meanings, and in the opposite column citation is made of analogous statements of mortal philosophy." (p. 556)

2. **Proposition.** Metaphysics is man's unavailing attempt to span the chasm between science and religion—to compensate for the absence of morontia mota.

> "But many mortals have recognized the desirability of having some method of reconciling the interplay between the widely separated domains of science and religion; and metaphysics is the result of man's unavailing attempt to span this well-recognized chasm. But human metaphysics has proved more confusing than illuminating. Metaphysics stands for man's well-meant but futile effort to compensate for the absence of the mota of morontia." (p. 1136)

3. **Proposition.** Metaphysics is a failure; mota, man cannot perceive. Revelation is the only technique to take the place of mota.

> "Metaphysics has proved a failure; mota, man cannot perceive. Revelation is the only technique which can compensate for the absence of the truth sensitivity of mota in a material world. Revelation authoritatively clarifies the muddle of reason-developed metaphysics on an evolutionary sphere." (p. 1136)

4. **PROPOSITION.** Revelation is man's only hope of bridging the morontia gulf. Without mota insight, man cannot discern truth, love, and goodness in the material world.

> "Revelation is evolutionary man's only hope of bridging the morontia gulf. Faith and reason, unaided by mota, cannot conceive and construct a logical universe. Without the insight of mota, mortal man cannot discern goodness, love, and truth in the phenomena of the material world." (p. 1137)

5. **PROPOSITION.** The highest philosophy of man must be based on the reason of science, the faith of religion, and the truth insight of revelation.

> "The highest attainable philosophy of mortal man must be logically based on the reason of science, the faith of religion, and the truth insight afforded by revelation. By this union man can compensate somewhat for his failure to develop an adequate metaphysics and for his inability to comprehend the mota of the morontia." (p. 1137)

6. **PROPOSITION.** Mota is more than a superior philosophy. It is to philosophy as two eyes are to one. Material man sees with one eye—morontians with two.

> "Mota is more than a superior philosophy; it is to philosophy as two eyes are to one; it has a stereoscopic effect on meanings and values. Material man sees the universe, as it were, with but one eye—flat. Mansion world students achieve cosmic perspective—depth—by superimposing the perceptions of the morontia life upon the perceptions of the physical life. And they are enabled to bring these material and morontial viewpoints into true focus largely through the untiring ministry of their seraphic counselors, who so patiently teach the mansion world students and the morontia progressors." (p. 554)

VII. MORONTIA PROGRESSORS

1. **PROPOSITION.** Before morontians leave the local universe to begin the spirit career, they will be satiated respecting every intellectual, artistic, and social longing. They have achieved the satisfaction of self-realization.

> "Before ascending mortals leave the local universe to embark upon their spirit careers, they will be satiated respecting every intellectual, artistic, and social longing or true ambition which ever characterized their mortal or morontia planes of existence. This is the achievement of equality of the satisfaction of self-expression and self-realization but not the attainment of identical experiential status nor the complete obliteration of characteristic individuality in skill, technique, and expression." (p. 508)

2. **Proposition.** The differential of personal attainment will not be equalized until you finish the last circle of Havona.

> "But the new spirit differential of personal experiential attainment will not become thus leveled off and equalized until after you have finished the last circle of the Havona career. And then will the Paradise residents be confronted with the necessity of adjusting to that absonite differential of personal experience which can be leveled off only by the group attainment of the ultimate of creature status—the seventh-stage-spirit destiny of the mortal finaliters." (p. 508)

VIII. CELESTIAL ARTISANS

1. **Proposition.** Celestial artisans are a composite group of morontia and lower spirit beings. They engage in morontia embellishment and spiritual beautification.

> "Among the courtesy colonies of the various divisional and universe headquarters worlds may be found the unique order of composite personalities denominated the celestial artisans. These beings are the master artists and artisans of the morontia and lower spirit realms. They are the spirits and semispirits who are engaged in morontia embellishment and in spiritual beautification. Such artisans are distributed throughout the grand universe—on the headquarters worlds of the superuniverses, the local universes, the constellations, and systems, as well as on all spheres settled in light and life; but their chief realm of activity is in the constellations and especially on the seven hundred seventy worlds surrounding each headquarters sphere." (p. 497)

2. **Proposition.** Celestial artisans serve in seven groups.

> "All celestial artisans are registered on the superuniverse headquarters but are directed by morontia supervisors on the local universe capitals. They are commissioned in the following seven major divisions of activity by the central corps of morontia supervisors functioning on the headquarters world of each local universe:
> 1. Celestial Musicians.
> 2. Heavenly Reproducers.
> 3. Divine Builders.
> 4. Thought Recorders.
> 5. Energy Manipulators.
> 6. Designers and Embellishers.
> 7. Harmony Workers." (p. 497)

IX. THE PROBATION NURSERY

1. PROPOSITION. Children who die before achieving survival status are received into the probation nursery schools of the finaliters, in the event of the survival of one or both parents.

   "The infant-receiving schools of Satania are situated on the finaliter world, the first of the Jerusem transition-culture spheres. These infant-receiving schools are enterprises devoted to the nurture and training of the children of time, including those who have died on the evolutionary worlds of space before the acquirement of individual status on the universe records. In the event of the survival of either or both of such a child's parents, the guardian of destiny deputizes her associated cherubim as the custodian of the child's potential identity, charging the cherubim with the responsibility of delivering this undeveloped soul into the hands of the Mansion World Teachers in the probationary nurseries of the morontia worlds." (p. 531)

2. PROPOSITION. Children having Thought Adjusters, but who die before choosing concerning the Paradise career, are repersonalized on the finaliter world along with those without Adjusters.

   "All children on the evolving worlds who have Thought Adjusters, but who before death had not made a choice concerning the Paradise career, are also repersonalized on the finaliter world of the system, where they likewise grow up in the families of the Material Sons and their associates as do those little ones who arrived without Adjusters, but who will subsequently receive the Mystery Monitors after attaining the requisite age of moral choice." (p. 532)

X. THE MORONTIA SELF

1. PROPOSITION. Upon the union of an immortal soul with the divine Adjuster, the seraphim summons the archangel who proclaimss: "This is a beloved son in whom I am well pleased."

   "The union of the evolving immortal soul with the eternal and divine Adjuster is signalized by the seraphic summoning of the supervising superangel for resurrected survivors and of the archangel of record for those going to judgment on the third day; and then, in the presence of such a survivor's morontia associates, these messengers of confirmation speak: 'This is a beloved son in whom I am well pleased.' This simple ceremony marks the entrance of an ascending mortal upon the eternal career of Paradise service." (p. 538)

2. **Proposition.** Upon confirmation of Adjuster fusion the new name is conferred upon the morontia being who is still more or less material—they are far from being true spirits.

> "Immediately upon the confirmation of Adjuster fusion the new morontia being is introduced to his fellows for the first time by his new name and is granted the forty days of spiritual retirement from an routine activities wherein to commune with himself and to choose some one of the optional routes to Havana and to select from the differential techniques of Paradise attainment.
>
> "But still are these brilliant beings more or less material; they are far from being true spirits; they are more like supermortals, spiritually speaking, still a little lower than the angels. But they are truly becoming marvelous creatures." (p. 538)

3. **Proposition.** The adjutant mind is left behind on the native world. The morontian is dependent on the morontia intellect.

> "When a creature leaves his native planet, he leaves the adjutant ministry behind and becomes solely dependent on morontia intellect. When an ascender leaves the local universe, he has attained the spiritual level of existence, having passed beyond the morontia level. This newly appearing spirit entity then becomes attuned to the direct ministry of the cosmic mind of Orvonton." (p. 1237)

4. **Proposition.** Morontians are endowed with the Nebadon modification of the cosmic mind. Certain phases of mortal mind persist in the surviving soul, while other values are held by the Adjuster.

> "In the morontia estate the ascending mortal is endowed with the Nebadon modification of the cosmic-mind endowment of the Master Spirit of Orvonton. The mortal intellect, as such, has perished, has ceased to exist as a focalized universe entity apart from the undifferentiated mind circuits of the Creative Spirit. But the meanings and values of the mortal mind have not perished. Certain phases of mind are continued in the surviving soul; certain experiential values of the former human mind are held by the Adjuster; and there persist in the local universe the records of the human life as it was lived in the flesh, together with certain living registrations in the numerous beings who are concerned with the final evaluation of the ascending mortal, beings extending in range from seraphim to Universal Censors and probably on beyond to the Supreme." (p. 1236)

5. **Proposition.** The morontia mind evolves by direct contact with the cosmic mind, as modified by the Creative Mother Spirit of the local universe.

   "There are no influences in the local universe career comparable to the seven adjutant mind-spirits of human existence. The morontia mind must evolve by direct contact with cosmic mind, as this cosmic mind has been modified and translated by the creative source of local universe intellect—the Divine Minister." (p. 1236)

XI. THE MORONTIA WORLDS

1. **Proposition.** On the mansion worlds resurrected mortals resume their lives just where they left off when overtaken by death.

   "On the mansion worlds the resurrected mortal survivors resume their lives just where they left off when overtaken by death. When you go from Urantia to the first mansion world, you will notice considerable change, but if you had come from a more normal and progressive sphere of time, you would hardly notice the difference except for the fact that you were in possession of a different body; the tabernacle of flesh and blood has been left behind on the world of nativity." (p. 532)

2. **Proposition.** On the first mansion world the center of activities is the resurrection hall. The destiny guardians, Thought Adjusters, archangels, and Life Carriers are all concerned with resurrection.

   "The very center of all activities on the first mansion world is the resurrection hall, the enormous temple of personality assembly. This gigantic structure consists of the central rendezvous of the seraphic destiny guardians, the Thought Adjusters, and the archangels of the resurrection. The Life Carriers also function with these celestial beings in the resurrection of the dead." (p. 532)

3. **Proposition.** All morontia worlds are architectural spheres. Such worlds have one hundred elements and one hundred forms of unique energy—morontia material.

   "All of these worlds are architectural spheres, and they have just double the number of elements of the evolved planets. Such made-to-order worlds not only abound in the heavy metals and crystals, having one hundred physical elements, but likewise have exactly one hundred forms of a unique energy organization called *morontia material*. The Master Physical Controllers and the Morontia Power Supervisors are able so to modify the revolutions of the primary units of matter and at the same time so to transform these associations of energy as to create this new substance." (p. 541)

4. **Proposition.** Paul knew about the morontia worlds and morontia materials. "They have in heaven a better and more enduring substance."

> "Paul learned of the existence of the morontia worlds and of the reality of morontia materials, for he wrote, 'They have in heaven a better and more enduring substance.' And these morontia materials are real, literal, even as in 'the city which has foundations, whose builder and maker is God.' And each of these marvelous spheres is 'a better country, that is, a heavenly one.'" (p. 542)

5. **Proposition.** Morontia worlds are accessible alike to material and spirit beings. Morontia beings remain in contact with material beings while they also fraternize with spirit persons.

> "All morontia transition realms are accessible alike to material and spirit beings. As morontia progressors you will remain in full contact with the material world and with material personalities, while you will increasingly discern and fraternize with spirit beings; and by the time of departure from the morontia regime, you will have seen all orders of spirits with the exception of a few of the higher types, such as Solitary Messengers." (p. 545)

6. **Proposition.** As systems are settled in light and life, the mansion worlds cease to function as transition spheres, and the finaliters institute their training in cosmic consciousness.

> "As systems and universes are settled in light and life, the mansion worlds increasingly cease to function as transition spheres of morontia training. More and more the finaliters institute their new training regime, which appears to be designed to translate the cosmic consciousness from the present level of the grand universe to that of the future outer universes. The Morontia Companions are destined to function increasingly in association with the finaliters and in numerous other realms not at present revealed on Urantia." (p. 547)

XII. THE SPORNAGIA

1. **Proposition.** On Jerusem, the agricultural achievements of the spornagia are amazing. Land is cultivated largely for aesthetic and ornamental effects. Spornagia are the landscape gardeners.

> "On Jerusem you will be amazed by the agricultural achievements of the wonderful spornagia. There the land is cultivated largely for aesthetic and ornamental effects. The spornagia are the landscape gardeners of the headquarters worlds, and they are

both original and artistic in their treatment of the open spaces of Jerusem. They utilize both animals and numerous mechanical contrivances in the culture of the soil. They are intelligently expert in the employment of the power agencies of their realms as well as in the utilization of numerous orders of their lesser brethren of the lower animal creations, many of which are provided them on these special worlds. This order of animal life is now largely directed by the ascending midway creatures from the evolutionary spheres." (p. 527)

2. **PROPOSITION**. Spornagia are not Adjuster indwelt—they do not have survival souls. But they have long lives—fifty thousand standard years.

   "Spornagia are not Adjuster indwelt. They do not possess survival souls, but they do enjoy long lives, sometimes to the extent of forty to fifty thousand standard years. Their number is legion, and they afford physical ministry to all orders of universe personalities requiring material service." (p. 528)

3. **PROPOSITION**. Spornagia do not have personality, but they evolve an individuality which can experience reincarnation. With the aid of Life Carriers, new bodies are fabricated.

   "Although spornagia neither possess nor evolve survival souls, though they do not have personality, nevertheless, they do evolve an individuality which can experience reincarnation. When, with the passing of time, the physical bodies of these unique creatures deteriorate from usage and age, their creators, in collaboration with the Life Carriers, fabricate new bodies in which the old spornagia reestablish their residences." (p. 528)

4. **PROPOSITION**. Spornagia are the only creatures in all the universe who experience reincarnation. They are reactive to the first five adjutant mind-spirits which produce a sixth persisting totality reality of experiential identity.

   "Spornagia are the only creatures in all the universe of Nebadon who experience this or any other sort of reincarnation. They are only reactive to the first five of the adjutant mind-spirits; they are not responsive to the spirits of worship and wisdom. But the five-adjutant mind equivalates to a totality or sixth reality level, and it is this factor which persists as an experiential identity." (p. 528)

PART XXII — *The Morontia Life*

XIII. MORONTIA POWER SUPERVISORS

1. **Proposition.** The Morontia Power Supervisors function in seven groups.

    "The creation of the first Morontia Power Supervisors is simultaneous with the arrival of the first mortal survivor on the shores of some one of the first mansion worlds in a local universe. They are created in groups of one thousand, classified as follows:
    1. Circuit Regulators   400
    2. System Co-ordinators   200
    3. Planetary Custodians   100
    4. Combined Controllers   100
    5. Liaison Stabilizers   100
    6. Selective Assorters   50
    7. Associate Registrars   50" (p. 542)

2. **Proposition.** Morontia Power Supervisors are able to unite material and spiritual energies—morontia material. As you traverse the morontia life of Nebadon, they provide you with 570 morontia bodies.

    "The Morontia Power Supervisors are able to effect a union of material and of spiritual energies, thereby organizing a morontia form of materialization which is receptive to the superimposition of a controlling spirit. When you traverse the morontia life of Nebadon, these same patient and skillful Morontia Power Supervisors will successively provide you with 570 morontia bodies, each one a phase of your progressive transformation. From the time of leaving the material worlds until you are constituted a first-stage spirit on Salvington, you will undergo just 570 separate and ascending morontia changes. Eight of these occur in the system, seventy-one in the constellation, and 491 during the sojourn on the spheres of Salvington." (p. 542)

PART XXIII
THE CORPS OF THE FINALITY

Part Twenty-Three
THE CORPS OF THE FINALITY

I. INTRODUCTION

1. **Proposition.** There are seven Corps of the Finality, and they are controlled by the senior Master Architect.

    "The senior Master Architect has the oversight of the seven Corps of the Finality, and they are:
    1. The Corps of Mortal Finaliters.
    2. The Corps of Paradise Finaliters.
    3. The Corps of Trinitized Finaliters.
    4. The Corps of Conjoint Trinitized Finaliters.
    5. The Corps of Havona Finaliters.
    6. The Corps of Transcendental Finaliters.
    7. The Corps of Unrevealed Sons of Destiny." (p. 352)

2. **Proposition.** Finaliters may partially attain the Deity Absolute, but the Universal Absolute will continue to mystify and baffle you, since it will grow proportionately with the material universe.

    "It may be possible that the finaliters will partially attain the Deity Absolute, but even if they should, still in the eternity of eternities the problem of the Universal Absolute will continue to intrigue, mystify, baffle, and challenge the ascending and progressing finaliters, for we perceive that the unfathomability of the cosmic relationships of the Universal Absolute will tend to grow in proportions as the material universes and their spiritual administration continue to expand.

    "Only infinity can disclose the Father-Infinite." (p. 117)

3. **Proposition.** In Orvonton we believe that the finaliters are destined to serve in the universes of outer space. The future may hold for you the same enthralling spectacles the past held for us.

    "Throughout Orvonton it is believed that a new type of creation is in process, an order of universes destined to become the scene of the future activities of the assembling Corps of the Finality; and if our conjectures are correct, then the endless future may hold for all of you the same enthralling spectacles that the endless past has held for your seniors and predecessors." (p. 131)

4. **Proposition.** The Corps of Mortal Finaliters is composed of six groups.

> "The Corps of Mortal Finaliters represents the present known destination of the ascending Adjuster-fused mortals of time. But there are other groups who are also assigned to this corps. The primary finaliter corps is composed of the following:
> 1. Havona Natives.
> 2. Gravity Messengers.
> 3. Glorified Mortals.
> 4. Adopted Seraphim.
> 5. Glorified Material Sons.
> 6. Glorified Midway Creatures." (p. 345)

II. HAVONA NATIVES

1. **Proposition.** After requisite experience with evolutionary beings, Havona natives can receive a fragment of the Universal Father and elect to enter the Corps of Mortal Finaliters.

> "Havona natives must achieve certain experiential developments in liaison with evolutionary beings which will create reception capacity for the bestowal of a fragment of the spirit of the Universal Father. The Mortal Finaliter Corps has as permanent members only such beings as have been fused with the spirit of the First Source and Center, or who, like the Gravity Messengers, innately embody this spirit of God the Father." (p. 346)

2. **Proposition.** Havoners are received into the Finality Corps in the ratio of one in a thousand. Ascendant creatures number 997 to one Havoner and one Gravity Messenger.

> "The inhabitants of the central universe are received into the corps in the ratio of one in a thousand—a finaliter company. The corps is organized for temporary service in companies of one thousand, the ascendant creatures numbering 997 to one Havona native and one Gravity Messenger." (p. 346)

3. **Proposition.** The oath of a finaliter is of sweeping implications and eternal import.

> "Finaliters are thus mobilized in companies, but the finality oath is administered individually. It is an oath of sweeping implications and eternal import. The Havona native takes the same oath and becomes forever attached to the corps." (p. 346)

III. GRAVITY MESSENGERS

1. **Proposition.** Gravity Messengers are under the jurisdiction of Grandfanda. Wherever Gravity Messengers are functioning the finaliters are in command.

   "Wherever and whenever Gravity Messengers are functioning, the finaliters are in command. All Gravity Messengers are under the exclusive jurisdiction of Grandfanda, and they are assigned only to the primary Corps of the Finality." (p. 346)

2. **Proposition.** Gravity Messengers hail from Divinington; they are modified and personalized Adjusters. They are personal, but no one understands their timeless technique of traversing space.

   "Gravity Messengers hail from Divinington, and they are modified and personalized Adjusters, but no one of our Uversa group will undertake to explain the nature of one of these messengers. We know they are highly personal beings, divine, intelligent, and touchingly understanding, but we do not comprehend their timeless technique of traversing space." (p. 347)

3. **Proposition.** Gravity Messengers may be attached to a finaliter company in unlimited numbers, but only one messenger is a member of the corps and he has assigned to him 999 fellow messengers.

   "Gravity Messengers may be attached to a finaliter company in unlimited numbers, but only one messenger, the chief of his fellows, is mustered into the Mortal Corps of the Finality. This chief however has assigned to him a permanent staff of 999 fellow messengers, and as occasion may require, he may call upon the reserves of the order for assistants in unlimited numbers." (p. 347)

4. **Proposition.** Gravity Messengers and glorified mortals achieve a profound affection for one another—they have much in common.

   "Gravity Messengers and glorified mortal finaliters achieve a touching and profound affection for one another; they have much in common: One is a direct personalization of a fragment of the Universal Father, the other a creature personality existent in the surviving immortal soul fused with a fragment of the same Universal Father, the spirit Thought Adjuster." (p. 347)

IV. GLORIFIED MORTALS

1. **Proposition.** Finaliters are domiciled on Paradise, but Ascendington is their home.

   "As finaliters you will be domiciled on Paradise, but Ascendington will be your home address at all times, even when you enter service in outer space. Through all eternity you will regard Ascendington as your home of sentimental memories and reminiscent recollections. When you become seventh-stage spirit beings, possibly you will give up your residential status on Paradise." (p. 148)

2. **Proposition.** Together with seraphim, mortals constitute 990 of each finaliter company of one thousand. Havona natives, Material Sons, midwayers, Gravity Messengers, and the unknown member make up one per cent of the corps.

   "Ascendant Adjuster-fused mortals compose the bulk of the primary Corps of the Finality. Together with the adopted and glorified seraphim they usually constitute 990 in each finaliter company. The proportion of mortals and angels in any one group varies, though the mortals far outnumber the seraphim. The Havona natives, glorified Material Sons, glorified midway creatures, the Gravity Messengers, and the unknown and missing member make up only one per cent of the corps; each company of one thousand finaliters has places for just ten of these nonmortal and nonseraphic personalities." (p. 347)

3. **Proposition.** Notwithstanding all the training and experience of the finaliters, they are only sixth-stage spirits. They have gained a stage by each advance in the Paradise ascent. They are destined to future service of ultimate finality status. They have been trained to the limit of their capacity in universe administration.

   "Notwithstanding that these ascendant mortals have attained Paradise, have been mustered into the Corps of the Finality, and have been sent back in large numbers to participate in the conduct of local universes and to assist in the administration of superuniverse affairs—in the face of even this apparent destiny, there remains the significant fact that they are of record as only sixth-stage spirits. There undoubtedly remains one more step in the career of the Mortal Corps of the Finality. We do not know the nature of that step, but we have taken cognizance of, and here call attention to, three facts:

"1. We know from the records that mortals are spirits of the first order during their sojourn in the minor sectors, and that they advance to the second order when translated to the major sectors, and to the third when they go forward to the central training worlds of the superuniverse. Mortals become quartan or graduate spirits after reaching the sixth circle of Havona and become spirits of the fifth order when they find the Universal Father. They subsequently attain the sixth stage of spirit existence upon taking the oath that musters them forever into the eternity assignment of the Corps of the Mortal Finality.

"2. The mortal finaliters have fully complied with the injunction of the ages, 'Be you perfect'; they have ascended the universal path of mortal attainment; they have found God, and they have been duly inducted into the Corps of the Finality. Such beings have attained the present limit of spirit progression but not *finality of ultimate spirit status*. They have achieved the present limit of creature perfection but not *finality of creature service*. They have experienced the fullness of Deity worship but not *finality of experiential Deity attainment*.

"3. The glorified mortals of the Paradise Corps of Finality are ascendant beings in possession of experiential knowledge of every step of the actuality and philosophy of the fullest possible life of intelligent existence, while during the ages of this ascent from the lowest material worlds to the spiritual heights of Paradise, these surviving creatures have been trained to the limits of their capacity respecting every detail of every divine principle of the just and efficient, as well as merciful and patient, administration of all the universal creation of time and space." (pp. 347-8)

4. **PROPOSITION**. Finaliters take an oath to the Paradise Trinity, pledging fidelity to God the Supreme—the Trinity as comprehended by finite creatures.

"When mortal ascenders are admitted to the finaliter corps of Paradise, they take an oath to the Paradise Trinity, and in taking this oath of allegiance, they are thereby pledging eternal fidelity to God the Supreme, who *is* the Trinity as comprehended by all finite creature personalities. Subsequently, as the finaliter companies function throughout the evolving universes, they are solely amenable to the mandates of Paradise origin until the eventful times of the settling of local universes in light and life. As the new governmental organizations of these perfected creations begin to be reflective of the emerging sovereignty of the Supreme, we observe that the outlying finaliter companies then acknowledge the jurisdictional authority of such new governments. It appears that God the Supreme is evolving unifier of the evolutionary Corps of the Finality, but it is highly probable that the eternal destiny of these seven corps will be directed by the Supreme as a member of the Ultimate Trinity." (p. 1292)

5. **Proposition.** During this age, finaliters do postgraduate work in all of the superuniverses.

"During the present universe age the finaliters return to serve in the universes of time. They are assigned to labor successively in the different superuniverses and never in their native superuniverses until after they have served in all the other six supercreations. Thus may they acquire the sevenfold concept of the Supreme Being." (p. 345)

V. ADOPTED SERAPHIM

1. **Proposition.** Many guardian seraphim go through the ascendant career with their human subjects, become Father fused, and join their subjects in taking the finaliter oath.

"Many of the faithful seraphic guardians of mortals are permitted to go through the ascendant career with their human wards, and many of these guardian angels, after becoming Father fused, join their subjects in taking the finaliter oath of eternity and forever accept the destiny of their mortal associates." (p. 348)

VI. GLORIFIED MATERIAL SONS

1. **Proposition.** The Adamic citizens of the local systems may seek release for the purpose of joining the ascending mortals on their journey to Paradise and the Corps of the Finality.

"There is provision in the universes of time and space whereby the Adamic citizens of the local systems, when long delayed in receiving planetary assignment, may initiate a petition for release from permanent-citizenship status. And if granted, they join the ascending pilgrims on the universe capitals and thence proceed onward to Paradise and the Corps of the Finality." (p. 349)

VII. GLORIFIED MIDWAYERS

1. **Proposition.** When midwayers are released from planetary duty, they follow the ascension career in company with their mortal cousins.

   "On many planets the midway creatures are produced in large numbers, but they seldom tarry on their native world subsequent to its being settled in light and life. Then, or soon thereafter, they are released from permanent-citizenship status and start on the ascension to Paradise, passing through the morontia worlds, the superuniverse, and Havona in company with the mortals of time and space." (p. 349)

VIII. EVANGELS OF LIGHT

1. **Proposition.** The vacant place in finaliter companies is occupied by the chief of the Evangels as assigned on single missions, but these beings are transient members.

   "At the present time every finaliter company numbers 999 personalities of oath status, permanent members. The vacant place is occupied by the chief of attached Evangels of Light assigned on any single mission. But these beings are only transient members of the corps." (p. 349)

2. **Proposition.** We conjecture as to the identity of the seventh group of mortal finaliters, but we really do not know.

   "We of Uversa often conjecture respecting the identity of the seventh group of finaliters. We entertain many ideas, embracing possible assignment of some of the accumulating corps of the numerous trinitized groups on Paradise, Vicegerington, and the inner Havona circuit. It is even conjectured that the Corps of the Finality nay be permitted to trinitize many of their assistants in the work of universe administration in the event they are destined to the service of universes now in the making.
   "One of us holds the opinion that this vacant place in the corps will be filled by some type of being of origin in the new universe of their future service; the other inclines to the belief that this place will be occupied by some type of Paradise personality not yet created, eventuated, or trinitized. But we will most likely await the entrance of the finaliters upon their seventh stage of spirit attainment before we really know." (p. 350)

PART XXIV
YAHWEH

Part Twenty-Four
YAHWEH

I. INTRODUCTION

1. **Proposition.** Men first have many gods, then a tribal deity, and finally, the one and only God. The Jews, Hindus, and the Mesopotamians passed through just such an evolution of Deity.

   "In conceiving of Deity, man first includes all gods, then subordinates all foreign gods to his tribal deity, and finally excludes all but the one God of final and supreme value. The Jews synthesized all gods into their more sublime concept of the Lord God of Israel. The Hindus likewise combined their multifarious deities into the 'one spirituality of the gods' portrayed in the Rig-Veda, while the Mesopotamians reduced their gods to the more centralized concept of Bel-Marduk. These ideas of monotheism matured all over the world not long after the appearance of Machiventa Melchizedek at Salem in Palestine." (p. 1052)

2. **Proposition.** Melchizedek's concept of Deity was different—he taught a God based on creative attributes.

   "But the Melchizedek concept of Deity was unlike that of the evolutionary philosophy of inclusion, subordination, and exclusion; it was based exclusively on *creative power* and very soon influenced the highest deity concepts of Mesopotamia, India, and Egypt." (p. 1052)

II. DEITY AMONG THE SEMITES

1. **Proposition.** The Salem religion, based on Melchizedek's covenant with Abraham, persisted among the Kenites and was later adopted by the Hebrews as modified by many influences.

   "The Salem religion persisted among the Kenites in Palestine as their creed, and this religion as it was later adopted by the Hebrews was influenced, first, by Egyptian moral teachings; later, by Babylonian theologic thought; and lastly, by Iranian conceptions of good and evil. Factually the Hebrew religion is predicated upon the covenant between Abraham and Machiventa Melchizedek, evolutionally it is the outgrowth of many unique situational circumstances, but culturally it has borrowed freely from the religion, morality, and philosophy of the entire Levant. It is through the Hebrew religion that much of the morality and religious thought of Egypt, Mesopotamia, and Iran was transmitted to the Occidental peoples." (p. 1052)

Part XXIV — Yahweh

2. **Proposition.** The evolution of Hebrew theology embraced five concepts of Deity.

   See page 1053

3. **Proposition.** At the time the Hebrews were at Sinai the volcano was active and they were greatly impressed by the phenomenon.

   > "Up to about 2000 B.C., Mount Sinai was intermittently active as a volcano, occasional eruptions occurring as late as the time of the sojourn of the Israelites in this region. The fire and smoke, together with the thunderous detonations associated with the eruptions of this volcanic mountain, all impressed and awed the Bedouins of the surrounding regions and caused them greatly to fear Yahweh. This spirit of Mount Horeb later became the god of the Hebrew Semites, and they eventually believed him to be supreme over all other gods." (p. 1054)

4. **Proposition.** Many Canaanites believed in El Elyon, but the majority worshiped Yahweh.

   > "The Canaanites had long revered Yahweh, and although many of the Kenites believed more or less in El Elyon, the supergod of the Salem religion, a majority of the Canaanites held loosely to the worship of the old tribal deities." (p. 1054)

5. **Proposition.** The amazing feature of religious history is the continuous evolution of the God concept from the primitive Yahweh up to the high level of the Isaiahs.

   > "The most unique and amazing feature of the religious history of the Hebrews concerns this continuous evolution of the concept of Deity from the primitive god of Mount Horeb up through the teachings of their successive spiritual leaders to the high level of development depicted in the Deity doctrines of the Isaiahs, who proclaimed that magnificent concept of the loving and merciful Creator Father." (p. 1057)

6. **Proposition.** The Hebrews deanthropomorphized God without making him an abstraction of philosophy.

   > "The spiritual leaders of the Hebrews did what no others before them had ever succeeded in doing—they deanthropomorphized their God concept without converting it into an abstraction of Deity comprehensible only to philosophers. Even common people were able to regard the matured concept of Yahweh as a Father, if not of the individual, at least of the race." (p. 1062)

III. MOSES

1. **PROPOSITION.** Moses gave the Hebrews the concept and ideal of a Supreme Creator.

   "The beginning of the evolution of the Hebraic concepts and ideals of a Supreme Creator dates from the departure of the Semites from Egypt under that great leader, teacher, and organizer, Moses. His mother was of the royal family of Egypt; his father was a Semitic liaison officer between the government and the Bedouin captives. Moses thus possessed qualities derived from superior racial sources; his ancestry was so highly blended that it is impossible to classify him in any one racial group. Had he not been of this mixed type, he would never have displayed that unusual versatility and adaptability which enabled him to manage the diversified horde which eventually became associated with those Bedouin Semites who fled from Egypt to the Arabian desert under his leadership." (p. 1055)

2. **PROPOSITION.** The fact that the Hebrews believed in Yahweh explains why they tarried so long at Sinai—perfecting their religious ceremonials.

   "The fact that Yahweh was the god of the fleeing Hebrews explains why they tarried so long before the holy mountain of Sinai, and why they there received the ten commandments which Moses promulgated in the name of Yahweh, the god of Horeb. During this lengthy sojourn before Sinai the religious ceremonials of the newly evolving Hebrew worship were further perfected." (p. 1056)

3. **PROPOSITION.** Moses taught his people that Yahweh was a "jealous God." He was building a national consciousness. But he also taught that "The eternal God is your refuge, and underneath are the everlasting arms."

   "Moses proclaimed that Yahweh was the Lord God of Israel, who had singled out the Hebrews as his chosen people; he was building a new nation, and he wisely nationalized his religious teachings, telling his followers that Yahweh was a hard taskmaster, a 'jealous God.' But none the less he sought to enlarge their concept of divinity when he taught them that Yahweh was the 'God of the spirits of all flesh,' and when he said, 'The eternal God is your refuge, and underneath are the everlasting arms.'" (p. 1057)

4. **PROPOSITION.** Moses feared to proclaim mercy, preferring to awe his people with the fear of the justice of God.

> "Moses feared to proclaim the mercy of Yahweh, preferring to awe his people with the fear of the justice of God, saying: 'The Lord your God is God of Gods, and Lord of Lords, a great God, a mighty and terrible God, who regards not man.' Again he sought to control the turbulent clans when he declared that 'your God kills when you disobey him; he heals and gives life when you obey him.' But Moses taught these tribes that they would become the chosen people of God only on condition that they 'kept all his commandments and obeyed all his statutes.'" (p. 1058)

5. **PROPOSITION.** Little of God's mercy was taught the early Hebrews. God was the Almighty, a God of battles, glorious in power.

> "Little of the mercy of God was taught the Hebrews during these early times. They learned of God as 'the Almighty; the Lord is a man of war, God of battles, glorious in power, who dashes in pieces his enemies.' 'The Lord your God walks in the midst of the camp to deliver you.' The Israelites thought of their God as one who loved them, but who also 'hardened Pharaoh's heart' and 'cursed their enemies.'" (p. 1058)

IV. YAHWEH AFTER MOSES

1. **PROPOSITION.** After the death of Moses the concept of God rapidly deteriorated. Joshua did his best, but the people went back to the older ideas of Yahweh.

> "Upon the death of Moses his lofty concept of Yahweh rapidly deteriorated. Joshua and the leaders of Israel continued to harbor the Mosaic traditions of the all-wise, beneficent, and almighty God, but the common people rapidly reverted to the older desert idea of Yahweh. And this backward drift of the concept of Deity continued increasingly under the successive rule of the various tribal sheiks, the so-called Judges." (p. 1059)

2. **PROPOSITION.** But even in these dark times, a prophet would arise to proclaim Moses' concept of Yahweh.

> "But even in this dark age, every now and then a solitary teacher would arise proclaiming the Mosaic concept of divinity: 'You children of wickedness cannot serve the Lord, for he is a holy God.' 'Shall mortal man be more just than God? shall a man be more pure than his Maker?' 'Can you by searching find

out God? Can you find out the Almighty to perfection? Behold, God is great and we know him not. Touching the Almighty, we cannot find him out.'" (p. 1059)

V. SAMUEL

1. **Proposition.** Samuel was a resolute teacher and sought to turn all Israel back to the worship of the Yahweh of Mosaic times.

    "Samuel sprang from a long line of the Salem teachers who had persisted in maintaining the truths of Melchizedek as a part of their worship forms. This teacher was a virile and resolute man. Only his great devotion, coupled with his extraordinary determination, enabled him to withstand the almost universal opposition which he encountered when he started out to turn all Israel back to the worship of the supreme Yahweh of Mosaic times." (p. 1062)

2. **Proposition.** Samuel proclaimed that God was changeless—not a God of fitful whims. "...he is not a man, that he should repent."

    "But the great contribution which Samuel made to the development of the concept of Deity was his ringing pronouncement that Yahweh was *changeless*, forever the same embodiment of unerring perfection and divinity. In these times Yahweh was conceived to be a fitful God of jealous whims, always regretting that he had done thus and so; but now, for the first time since the Hebrews sallied forth from Egypt, they heard these startling words, 'The Strength of Israel will not lie nor repent, for he is not a man, that he should repent.'" (p. 1063)

3. **Proposition.** Samuel preached a God of sincerity—a covenant-keeping God. "You are great, O Lord God, for there is none like you…"

    "And he preached anew the story of God's sincerity, his covenant-keeping reliability. Said Samuel: 'The Lord will not forsake his people.' 'He has made with us an everlasting covenant, ordered in all things and sure.' And so, throughout all Palestine there sounded the call back to the worship of the supreme Yahweh. Ever this energetic teacher proclaimed, 'You are great, O Lord God, for there is none like you, neither is there any God beside you.'" (p. 1063)

4. **Proposition.** Samuel continued to grow in Deity concept. "Let us fall now into the hands of the Lord, for his mercies are great."

> "As the years passed, the grizzled old leader progressed in the understanding of God, for he declared: 'The Lord is a God of knowledge, and actions are weighed by him. The Lord will judge the ends of the earth, showing mercy to the merciful, and with the upright man he will also be upright.' Even here is the dawn of mercy, albeit it is limited to those who are merciful. Later he went one step further when, in their adversity, he exhorted his people: 'Let us fall now into the hands of the Lord, for his mercies are great.' 'There is no restraint upon the Lord to save many or few.'" (p. 1063)

VI. ELIJAH

1. **Proposition.** Elijah restored the God concept of Samuel. He carried forward his reforms in spite of opposition by an idolatrous monarch.

> "Elijah restored to the northern kingdom a concept of God comparable with that held in the days of Samuel. Elijah had little opportunity to present an advanced concept of God; he was kept busy, as Samuel had been before him, overthrowing the altars of Baal and demolishing the idols of false gods. And he carried forward his reforms in the face of the opposition of an idolatrous monarch; his task was even more gigantic and difficult than that which Samuel had faced." (p. 1064)

2. **Proposition.** The controversy between the followers of Yahweh and Baal was a socioeconomic clash of ideologies rather than a religious difference.

> "The long-drawn-out controversy between the believers in Yahweh and the followers of Baal was a socioeconomic clash of ideologies rather than a difference in religious beliefs." (p. 1064)

3. **Proposition.** The peoples of Palestine differed in their attitude toward private ownership of land. The Yahwehites regarded land as belonging to the clan.

> "The inhabitants of Palestine differed in their attitude toward private ownership of land. The southern or wandering Arabian tribes (the Yahwehites) looked upon land as an inalienable—as a gift of Deity to the clan. They held that land could not be sold or mortgaged. 'Yahweh spoke, saying, "The land shall not be sold, for the land is mine."'" (p. 1064)

4. **Proposition.** The Baalites freely bought and sold land. The cult was concerned with land—its ownership and fertility.

> "The northern and more settled Canaanites (the Baalites) freely bought, sold, and mortgaged their lands. The word Baal means owner. The Baal cult was founded on two major doctrines: First, the validation of property exchange, contracts, and covenants—the right to buy and sell land. Second, Baal was supposed to send rain—he was a god of fertility of the soil. Good crops depended on the favor of Baal. The cult was largely concerned with *land*, its ownership and fertility." (p. 1064)

VII. AMOS AND HOSEA

1. **Proposition.** It was a great step in the transition of a tribal god demanding sacrifices to a God who would punish crime among his own followers—and such was the God proclaimed by Amos.

> "A great step in the transition of the tribal god—the god who had so long been served with sacrifices and ceremonies, the Yahweh of the earlier Hebrews—to a God who would punish crime and immorality among even his own people, was taken by Amos, who appeared from among the southern hills to denounce the criminality, drunkenness, oppression, and immorality of the northern tribes. Not since the times of Moses had such ringing truths been proclaimed in Palestine." (p. 1065)

2. **Proposition.** Amos proclaimed the inexorable justice of Yahweh—"Surely I will never forget any of your works."

> "Said Amos: 'He who formed the mountains and created the wind, seek him who formed the seven stars and Orion, who turns the shadow of death into the morning and makes the day dark as night.' And in denouncing his half-religious, timeserving, and sometimes immoral fellows, he sought to portray the inexorable justice of an unchanging Yahweh when he said of the evildoers: 'Though they dig into hell, thence shall I take them; though they climb up to heaven, thence will I bring them down.' 'And though they go into captivity before their enemies, thence will I direct the sword of justice, and it shall slay them.' Amos further startled his hearers when, pointing a reproving and accusing finger at them, he declared in the name of Yahweh: 'Surely I will never forget any of your works.' 'And I will sift the house of Israel among all nations as wheat is sifted in a sieve.'" (p. 1065)

3. **Proposition.** Hosea followed Amos with the doctrine of a universal God of love—forgiveness through repentance, not by sacrifice—a gospel of loving-kindness and tender mercy.

> "Hosea followed Amos and his doctrine of a universal God of justice by the resurrection of the Mosaic concept of a God of love. Hosea preached forgiveness through repentance, not by sacrifice. He proclaimed a gospel of loving-kindness and divine mercy, saying: 'I will betroth you to me forever; yes, I will betroth you to me in righteousness and judgment and in loving-kindness and in mercies. I will even betroth you to me in faithfulness.' 'I will love them freely, for my anger is turned away.'" (p. 1066)

VIII. THE FIRST ISAIAH

1. **Proposition.** In these times, some threatened punishment for personal sins and for national crime.

> "These were the times when some were proclaiming threatenings of punishment against personal sins and national crime among the northern clans while others predicted calamity in retribution for the transgressions of the southern kingdom. It was in the wake of this arousal of conscience and consciousness in the Hebrew nations that the first Isaiah made his appearance." (p. 1066)

2. **Proposition.** This Isaiah said: "Arise and shine, for your light has come..." "In all their afflictions he was afflicted, and the angel of his presence saved them."

> "Speaking to the fear-ridden and soul-hungry Hebrews, this prophet said: 'Arise and shine, for your light has come, and the glory of the Lord has risen upon you.' 'The spirit of the Lord is upon me because he has anointed me to preach good tidings to the meek; he has sent me to bind up the brokenhearted, to proclaim liberty to the captives and the opening of the prison to those who are bound.' 'I will greatly rejoice in the Lord, my soul shall be joyful in my God, for he has clothed me with the garments of salvation and has covered me with his robe of righteousness.' 'In all their afflictions he was afflicted, and the angel of his presence saved them. In his love and in his pity he redeemed them.'" (p. 1066)

IX. JEREMIAH

1. **Proposition.** While teachers continued to expound the gospel of Isaiah, Jeremiah took the bold step of proclaiming the internationalization of Yahweh.

   "While several teachers continued to expound the gospel of Isaiah, it remained for Jeremiah to take the next bold step in the internationalization of Yahweh, God of the Hebrews." (p. 1067)

2. **Proposition.** Jeremiah proclaimed the just and loving God of Isaiah. "Yes, I have loved you with an everlasting love…" "For he does not afflict willingly the children of men."

   "Jeremiah also preached of the just and loving God described by Isaiah, declaring: 'Yes, I have loved you with an everlasting love; therefore with loving-kindness have I drawn you.' 'For he does not afflict willingly the children of men.'" (p. 1067)

X. THE SECOND ISAIAH

1. **Proposition.** No prophet from Machiventa to Jesus attained a higher concept of God than Isaiah the second presented to the Hebrews.

   "No prophet or religious teacher from Machiventa to the time of Jesus attained the high concept of God that Isaiah the second proclaimed during these days of the captivity. It was no small, anthropomorphic, man-made God that this spiritual leader proclaimed. 'Behold he takes up the isles as a very little thing.' 'And as the heavens are higher than the earth, so are my ways higher than your ways and my thoughts higher than your thoughts.'" (p. 1068)

2. **Proposition.** Isaiah proclaimed a Universal Creator and no more beautiful pronouncements about the heavenly Father have ever been made.

   "This Isaiah conducted a far-flung propaganda of the gospel of the enlarging concept of a supreme Yahweh. He vied with Moses in the eloquence with which he portrayed the Lord God of Israel as the Universal Creator. He was poetic in his portrayal of the infinite attributes of the Universal Father. No more beautiful pronouncements about the heavenly Father have ever been made." (p. 1069)

3. **Proposition.** This daring teacher taught that man was closely related to God. "Every one who is called by name I have created for my glory …" "I…am he who blots out their transgressions for my own sake…"

> "This daring teacher proclaimed that man was very closely related to God, saying: 'Every one who is called by my name I have created for my glory, and they shall show forth my praise. I, even I, am he who blots out their transgressions for my own sake, and I will not remember their sins.'" (p. 1069)

PART XXV
SIN

Part Twenty-Five
SIN

I. THE CONCEPT OF SIN

1. **Proposition.** Philosophically speaking, God loves the sinner but hates the sin. Persons can only love and hate other persons. Toward sin, God has no personal attitude—sin is not a spiritual reality. The love of God saves the sinners; the law of God destroys the sin.

    "God loves the sinner and *hates* the sin: such a statement is true philosophically, but God is a transcendent personality, and persons can only love and hate other persons. Sin is not a person. God loves the sinner because he is a personality reality (potentially eternal), while towards sin God strikes no personal attitude, for sin is not a spiritual reality; it is not personal; therefore does only the justice of God take cognizance of its existence. The love of God saves the sinner; the law of God destroys the sin." (p. 41)

2. **Proposition.** Mistaken judgment (evil) becomes sin only when the human will consciously endorses and knowingly embraces a deliberate immoral judgment.

    "The possibility of mistaken judgment (evil) becomes sin only when the human will consciously endorses and knowingly embraces a deliberate immoral judgment" (p. 52)

3. **Proposition.** The Gods neither create evil nor permit sin. Potential evil is existent in finite differential levels of perfection. Sin is potential when imperfect beings are endowed with free will.

    "The Gods neither create evil nor permit sin and rebellion. Potential evil is time-existent in a universe embracing differential levels of perfection meanings and values. Sin is potential in all realms where imperfect beings are endowed with the ability to choose between good and evil." (p. 613)

4. **Proposition.** The conflicting presence of the true and the false constitutes the potentiality of error. The deliberate choice of evil is sin; the persistent pursuit of sin is iniquity.

    "The very conflicting presence of truth and untruth, fact and falsehood, constitutes the potentiality of error. The deliberate choice of evil constitutes sin; the willful rejection of truth is error; the persistent pursuit of sin and error is iniquity." (p. 613)

- 550 -

Part XXV — Sin

5. **Proposition.** Free will constitutes the potential of sin. Free will is not a symbolic ideal or a mere philosophic concept—it is a universe reality.

   "The moral will creatures of the evolutionary worlds are always bothered with the unthinking question as to why the all-wise Creators permit evil and sin. They fail to comprehend that both are inevitable if the creature is to be truly free. The free will of evolving man or exquisite angel is not a mere philosophic concept, a symbolic ideal. Man's ability to choose good or evil is a universe reality. This liberty to choose for oneself is an endowment of the Supreme Rulers, and they will not permit any being or group of beings to deprive a single personality in the wide universe of this divinely bestowed liberty—not even to satisfy such misguided and ignorant beings in the enjoyment of this misnamed personal liberty." (p. 615)

6. **Proposition.** If you suffer as a result of the wrongdoing of others, rest assured that none of these things can ever jeopardize your eternal prospects.

   "But one thing should be made clear: If you are made to suffer the evil consequences of the sin of some member of your family, some fellow citizen or fellow mortal, even rebellion in the system or elsewhere—no matter what you may have to endure because of the wrongdoing of your associates, fellows, or superiors—you may rest secure in the eternal assurance that such tribulations are transient afflictions. None of these fraternal consequences of misbehavior in the group can ever jeopardize your eternal prospects or in the least degree deprive you of your divine right of Paradise ascension and God attainment." (p. 619)

7. **Proposition.** Sin may be regarded as the attitude of a personality who is knowingly resisting cosmic reality. Error would be misconception or distortion of reality. Evil is a partial realization of, or a maladjustment to, universe reality.

   "There are many ways of looking at sin, but from the universe philosophic viewpoint sin is the attitude of a personality who is knowingly resisting cosmic reality. Error might be regarded as a misconception or distortion of reality. Evil is a partial realization of, or maladjustment to, universe realities." (p. 754)

8. **PROPOSITION.** Sin is a purposeful resistance to reality—iniquity, open defiance.

> "But sin is a purposeful resistance to divine reality—a conscious choosing to oppose spiritual progress—while iniquity consists in an open and persistent defiance of recognized reality and signifies such a degree of personality disintegration as to border on cosmic insanity." (p. 754)

9. **PROPOSITION.** When sin becomes habitual it easily becomes iniquitous. All manner of sin may be forgiven, but the iniquiter experiences no sorrow for wrongdoing and does not accept forgiveness.

> "And when sin has so many times been chosen and so often been repeated, it may become habitual. Habitual sinners can easily become iniquitous, become wholehearted rebels against the universe and all of its divine realities. While all manner of sins may be forgiven, we doubt whether the established iniquiter would ever sincerely experience sorrow for his misdeeds or accept forgiveness for his sins." (p. 755)

10. **PROPOSITION.** Primitive man considered that he was in debt to the spirits—that he needed redemption. This concept developed into the doctrine of sin and salvation.

> "Primitive man regarded himself as being in debt to the spirits, as standing in need of redemption. As the savages looked at it, in justice the spirits might have visited much more bad luck upon them. As time passed, this concept developed into the doctrine of sin and salvation. The soul was looked upon as coming into the world under forfeit—original sin." (p. 974)

11. **PROPOSITION.** The savage thought the spirits derived satisfaction from human suffering. Man became concerned over sins of both commission and omission. The sacrificial system grew up around these ideas.

> "The savage was early possessed with the notion that spirits derive supreme satisfaction from the sight of human misery, suffering, and humiliation. At first, man was only concerned with sins of commission, but later he became exercised over sins of omission. And the whole subsequent sacrificial system grew up around these two ideas. This new ritual had to do with the observance of the propitiation ceremonies of sacrifice." (p. 974)

Part XXV — Sin

12. **Proposition.** The savage envisioned both good and bad spirits, and when taboos received the sanction of religion, the stage was set for the conception of sin. Such a concept made material death seem logical.

    "As the savage mind evolved to that point where it envisaged both good and bad spirits, and when the taboo received the solemn sanction of evolving religion, the stage was all set for the appearance of the new conception of *sin*. The idea of sin was universally established in the world before revealed religion ever made its entry. It was only by the concept of sin that natural death became logical to the primitive mind. Sin was the transgression of taboo, and death was the penalty of sin." (p. 975)

13. **Proposition.** At first sin was ritual, not rational; an act, not a thought. Traditions of Adam fostered the idea of a onetime "golden age"—and that sin brought man down to his later sorry plight.

    "Sin was ritual, not rational; an act, not a thought. And this entire concept of sin was fostered by the lingering traditions of Dilmun and the days of a little paradise on earth. The tradition of Adam and the Garden of Eden also lent substance to the dream of a onetime 'golden age' of the dawn of the races. And all this confirmed the ideas later expressed in the belief that man had his origin in a special creation, that he started his career in perfection, and that transgression of the taboos—sin—brought him down to his later sorry plight." (p. 975)

14. **Proposition.** The habitual violation of a taboo became a vice. Primitive law made vice a crime—religion made it a sin.

    "The habitual violation of a taboo became a vice; primitive law made vice a crime; religion made it a sin. Among the early tribes the violation of a taboo was a combined crime and sin." (p. 976)

15. **Proposition.** Sin is deliberate disloyalty to Deity. There are degrees of disloyalty.

    "*Sin must be redefined as deliberate disloyalty to Deity.* There are degrees of disloyalty: the partial loyalty of indecision; the divided loyalty of confliction; the dying loyalty of indifference; and the death of loyalty exhibited in devotion to godless ideals." (p. 984)

16. **Proposition.** The feeling of guilt is the consciousness of the violation of the mores—it is not necessarily sin.

    "The sense or feeling of guilt is the consciousness of the violation of the mores; it is not necessarily sin. There is no real sin in the absence of conscious disloyalty to Deity." (p. 984)

17. **Proposition.** Even in recent times, sickness was regarded as punishment for sin. It has been attributed to demons and to the stars.

> "In comparatively recent times it has been believed that sickness is a punishment for sin, personal or racial. Among peoples traversing this level of evolution the prevailing theory is that one cannot be afflicted unless one has violated a taboo. To regard sickness and suffering as 'arrows of the Almighty within them' is typical of such beliefs. The Chinese and Mesopotamians long regarded disease as the result of the action of evil demons, although the Chaldeans also looked upon the stars as the cause of suffering. This theory of disease as a consequence of divine wrath is still prevalent among many reputedly civilized groups of Urantians." (p. 990)

18. **Proposition.** The sense of guilt may come from interrupted spiritual communion. Man may fall short of his ideals but he can be true to the purpose of finding God.

> "The sense of guilt (not the consciousness of sin) comes either from interrupted spiritual communion or from the lowering of one's moral ideals. Deliverance from such a predicament can only come through the realization that one's highest moral ideals are not necessarily synonymous with the will of God. Man cannot hope to live up to his highest ideals, but he can be true to his purpose of finding God and becoming more and more like him." (p. 1133)

19. **Proposition.** The fact of finiteness is not evil or sinful. The finite world is good; it is the distortion or perversion of the finite that gives origin to evil and sin.

> "The problem of sin is not self-existent in the finite world. The fact of finiteness is not evil or sinful. The finite world was made by an infinite Creator—it is the handiwork of his divine Sons—and therefore it must be *good*. It is the misuse, distortion, and perversion of the finite that gives origin to evil and sin." (p. 1222)

20. **Proposition.** The existence of sin proves the reality of finite free will. Sin depicts immaturity dazzled by freedom of will which fails to perceive the supreme obligations of cosmic citizenship.

> "Sin in time-conditioned space clearly proves the temporal liberty— even license—of the finite will. Sin depicts immaturity dazzled by the freedom of the relatively sovereign will of personality while failing to perceive the supreme obligations and duties of cosmic citizenship." (p. 1301)

Part XXV — Sin

21. **Proposition.** Iniquity reveals the transient reality of that which is not God identified.

    "Iniquity in the finite domains reveals the transient reality of all God-unidentified selfhood. Only as a creature becomes God identified, does he become truly real in the universes. Finite personality is not self-created, but in the superuniverse arena of choice it does self-determine destiny." (p. 1301)

22. **Proposition.** Jesus, by the power of his personal love of men, could break the hold of sin. The beauty of divine love destroys the charm of evil and sin. Forgiveness provides salvation.

    "Jesus, by the power of his personal love for men, could break the hold of sin and evil. He thereby set men free to choose better ways of living. Jesus portrayed a deliverance from the past which in itself promised a triumph for the future. Forgiveness thus provided salvation. The beauty of divine love, once fully admitted to the human heart, forever destroys the charm of sin and the power of evil." (p. 2018)

II. THE LUCIFER REBELLION

A. *Leader of Rebellion*

1. **Proposition.** Lucifer was a brilliant administrator. Through evil and error he embraced sin. He surrendered to the urge of self and the sophistry of spurious personal liberty.

    "Lucifer was a brilliant primary Lanonandek Son of Nebadon. He had experienced service in many systems, had been a high counselor of his group, and was distinguished for wisdom, sagacity, and efficiency. Lucifer was number 37 of his order, and when commissioned by the Melchizedeks, he was designated as one of the one hundred most able and brilliant personalities in more than seven hundred thousand of his kind. From such a magnificent beginning, through evil and error, he embraced sin and now is numbered as one of three System Sovereigns in Nebadon who have succumbed to the urge of self and surrendered to the sophistry of spurious personal liberty—rejection of universe allegiance and disregard of fraternal obligations, blindness to cosmic relationships." (p. 601)

2. **PROPOSITION.** Lucifer was a created Son of the local universe. He was System Sovereign of Satania—607 inhabited worlds.

   "Lucifer was not an ascendant being; he was a created Son of the local universe, and of him it was said: 'You were perfect in all your ways from the day you were created till unrighteousness was found in you.' Many times had he been in counsel with the Most Highs of Edentia. And Lucifer reigned 'upon the holy mountain of God,' the administrative mount of Jerusem, for he was the chief executive of a great system of 607 inhabited worlds." (p. 601)

3. **PROPOSITION.** Notwithstanding Lucifer's sin, subordinates refrained from showing him disrespect prior to Michael's bestowal on Urantia.

   "Lucifer was a magnificent being, a brilliant personality; he stood next to the Most High Fathers of the constellations in the direct line of universe authority. Notwithstanding Lucifer's transgression, subordinate intelligences refrained from showing him disrespect and disdain prior to Michael's bestowal on Urantia. Even the archangel of Michael, at the time of Moses' resurrection, 'did not bring against him an accusing judgment but simply said, "the Judge rebuke you."' Judgment in such matters belongs to the Ancients of Days, the rulers of the superuniverse." (p. 601)

4. **PROPOSITION.** Self-contemplation is disastrous—pride, fatal.

   "Lucifer is now the fallen and deposed Sovereign of Satania. Self-contemplation is most disastrous, even to the exalted personalities of the celestial world. Of Lucifer it was said: 'Your heart was lifted up because of your beauty; you corrupted your wisdom because of your brightness.' Your olden prophet saw his sad estate when he wrote: 'How are you fallen from heaven, O Lucifer, son of the morning! How are you cast down, you who dared to confuse the worlds!'" (p. 601)

5. **PROPOSITION.** Lucifer became critical of universe administration. Gabriel detected disloyalty in Lucifer before the outbreak of rebellion.

   "Throughout this period Lucifer became increasingly critical of the entire plan of universe administration but always professed wholehearted loyalty to the Supreme Rulers. His first outspoken disloyalty was manifested on the occasion of a visit of Gabriel to Jerusem just a few days before the open proclamation of the

Part XXV — Sin

Lucifer Declaration of Liberty. Gabriel was profoundly impressed with the certainty of the impending outbreak that he went direct to Edentia to confer with the Constellation Fathers regarding the measures to be employed in case of open rebellion." (p. 602)

6. **Proposition**. Lucifer first became insincere—thus evil evolved into deliberate and willful sin. He rejected all offers of salvation.

   "At some point in this experience he became insincere, and evil evolved into deliberate and willful sin. That this happened is proved by the subsequent conduct of this brilliant executive. He was long offered opportunity for repentance, but only some of his subordinates ever accepted the proffered mercy. The Faithful of Days of Edentia, on the request of the Constellation Fathers, in person presented the plan of Michael for the saving of these flagrant rebels, but always was the mercy of the Creator Son rejected and rejected with increasing contempt and disdain." (p. 603)

B. *Outbreak of Rebellion*

1. **Proposition**. Lucifer was permitted to establish his rebel government. The Constellation Fathers quarantined the system.

   "Lucifer was permitted fully to establish and thoroughly to organize his rebel government before Gabriel made any effort to contest the right of secession or to counterwork the rebel propaganda. But the Constellation Fathers immediately confined the action of these disloyal personalities to the system of Satania. Nevertheless, this period of delay was a time of great trial and testing to the loyal beings of all Satania. All was chaotic for a few years, and there was great confusion on the mansion worlds." (p. 605)

2. **Proposition**. Gabriel assumed command of the loyal forces, proceeded to Jerusem, took up headquarters on the Father's world, and displayed the banner of Michael.

   "Since Michael elected to remain aloof from the actual warfare of the Lucifer rebellion, Gabriel called his personal staff together on Edentia and, in counsel with the Most Highs, elected to assume command of the loyal hosts of Satania. Michael remained on Salvington while Gabriel proceeded to Jerusem, establishing himself on the sphere dedicated to the Father—the same Universal Father whose personality Lucifer and Satan had questioned—in the presence of the forgathered hosts of loyal personalities, he displayed the banner of Michael, the material emblem of the Trinity government of all creation, the three azure blue concentric circles on a white background.

"The Lucifer emblem was a banner of white with one red circle, in the center of which a black solid circle appeared." (p. 605)

3. **Proposition.** "There was war in heaven." Lucifer and Gabriel contested for the support of all personalities.

"'There was war in heaven; Michael's commander and his angels fought against the dragon (Lucifer, Satan, and the apostate princes); and the dragon and his rebellious angels fought but prevailed not.' This 'war in heaven' was not a physical battle as such a conflict might be conceived on Urantia. In the early days of the struggle Lucifer held forth continuously in the planetary amphitheater. Gabriel conducted an unceasing exposure of the rebel sophistries from his headquarters taken up near at hand. The various personalities present on the sphere who were in doubt as to their attitude would journey back and forth between these discussions until they arrived at a final decision." (p. 606)

4. **Proposition.** The rebellion was system wide—37 Planetary Princes Joined. On Panoptia, the mortals refused to follow their Prince—they responded to the appeal of Ellanora.

"The Lucifer rebellion was system wide. Thirty-seven seceding Planetary Princes swung their world administrations largely to the side of the archrebel. Only on Panoptia did the Planetary Prince fail to carry his people with him. On this world, under the guidance of the Melchizedeks, the people rallied to the support of Michael. Ellanora, a young woman of that mortal realm, grasped the leadership of the human races, and not a single soul on that strife-torn world enlisted under the Lucifer banner." (p. 607)

C. *Nature of the Conflict*

1. **Proposition.** The final outbreak was launched by the Lucifer threefold Declaration of Liberty.

"Whatever the early origins of trouble in the hearts of Lucifer and Satan, the final outbreak took form as the Lucifer Declaration of Liberty. The cause of the rebels was stated under three heads:

"1. *The reality of the Universal Father*. Lucifer charged that the Universal Father did not really exist, that physical gravity and space-energy were inherent in the universe, and that the Father was a myth invented by the Paradise Sons to enable them to maintain the rule of the universes in the Father's name. He denied that personality was a gift of the Universal Father. ...

Part XXV — Sin

"2. *The universe government of the Creator Son—Michael.* Lucifer contended that the local systems should be autonomous. He protested against the right of Michael, the Creator Son, to assume sovereignty of Nebadon in the name of a hypothetical Paradise Father and require all personalities to acknowledge allegiance to this unseen Father. ...

"3. *The attack upon the universal plan of ascendant mortal training.* Lucifer maintained that far too much time and energy were expended upon the scheme of so thoroughly training ascending mortals in the principles of universe administrations, principles which he alleged were unethical and unsound. He protested against the agelong program for preparing the mortals of space for some unknown destiny and pointed to the presence of the finaliter corps on Jerusem as proof that these mortals had spent ages of preparation for some destiny of pure fiction. ... (pp. 603-04)

2. **PROPOSITION.** Self-assertion was the battle cry of the Lucifer rebellion —"equality of mind,""the brotherhood of intelligence."

"Self-assertion was the battle cry of the Lucifer rebellion. One of his chief arguments was that, if self-government was good and right for the Melchizedeks and other groups, it was equally good for all orders of intelligence. He was bold and persistent in the advocacy of the 'equality of mind' and 'the brotherhood of intelligence.'" (p. 604)

3. **PROPOSITION.** The greatest losses occurred among the angelic ranks, the Material Sons, and the midwayers.

"The greatest loss occurred in the angelic ranks, but most of the lower orders of intelligence were involved in disloyalty. Of the 681,217 Material Sons lost in Satania, ninety-five per cent were casualties of the Lucifer rebellion. Large numbers of midway creatures were lost on those individual planets whose Planetary Princes Joined the Lucifer cause." (p. 608)

4. **PROPOSITION.** Lucifer's folly was the attempt to do the nondoable—to short-circuit time. His crime consisted in the attempted abridgment of the creature's participation in the evolutionary struggle to attain finite perfection.

"Lucifer's folly was the attempt to do the nondoable, to short-circuit time in an experiential universe. Lucifer's crime was the attempted creative disenfranchisement of every personality in Satania, the unrecognized abridgment of the creature's personal participation—freewill participation—in the long evolutionary

- 559 -

struggle to attain the status of light and life both individually and collectively. In so doing this onetime Sovereign of your system set the temporal purpose of his own will directly athwart the eternal purpose of God's will as it is revealed in the bestowal of free will upon all personal creatures." (p. 614)

D. *A Loyal Seraphic Commander*

1. **PROPOSITION.** The story of Manotia—a loyal seraphic commander who acted in place of a defaulting superior.
   See page 606.

E. *Son of Man on Urantia*

1. **PROPOSITION.** Lucifer and Satan roamed the Satania system until the bestowal of Michael.

   "Lucifer and Satan freely roamed the Satania system until the completion of the bestowal mission of Michael on Urantia. They were last on your world together during the time of their combined assault upon the Son of Man.

   "Formerly, when the Planetary Princes, the 'Sons of God,' were periodically assembled, 'Satan came also,' claiming that he represented all of the isolated worlds of the fallen Planetary Princes. But he has not been accorded such liberty on Jerusem since Michael's terminal bestowal. Subsequent to their effort to corrupt Michael when in the bestowal flesh, all sympathy for Lucifer and Satan has perished throughout all Satania, that is, outside the isolated worlds of sin." (p. 609)

2. **PROPOSITION.** Since Michael's triumph on Urantia, all Norlatiadek has been cleansed of rebels.

   "Since the triumph of Christ, all Norlatiadek is being cleansed of sin and rebels. Sometime before Michael's death in the flesh the fallen Lucifer's associate, Satan, sought to attend such an Edentia conclave, but the solidification of sentiment against the archrebels had reached the point where the doors of sympathy were so well-nigh universally closed that there could be found no standing ground for the Satania adversaries. When there exists no open door for the reception of evil, there exists no opportunity for the entertainment of sin. The doors of the hearts of all Edentia closed against Satan; he was unanimously rejected by the assembled System Sovereigns, and it was at this time that the Son of Man 'beheld Satan fall as lightning from heaven.'" (p. 490)

3. **Proposition.** The bestowal of Michael terminated the Lucifer rebellion in Satania aside from the planets of the apostate Planetary Princes.

   "The bestowal of Michael terminated the Lucifer rebellion in all Satania aside from the planets of the apostate Planetary Princes. And this was the significance of Jesus' personal experience, just before his death in the flesh, when he one day exclaimed to his disciples, 'And I beheld Satan fall as lightning from heaven.' He had come with Lucifer to Urantia for the last crucial struggle." (p. 609)

4. **Proposition.** The last act of Michael before leaving Urantia was to offer mercy to Caligastia and Daligastia—they spurned the mercy.

   "The last act of Michael before leaving Urantia was to offer mercy to Caligastia and Daligastia, but they spurned his tender proffer. Caligastia, your apostate Planetary Prince, is still free on Urantia to prosecute his nefarious designs, but he has absolutely no power to enter the minds of men, neither can he draw near to their souls to tempt or corrupt them unless they really desire to be cursed with his wicked presence." (p. 610)

5. **Proposition.** The case of Gabriel vs. Lucifer is now pending. The archrebels are now detained on the Jerusem prison worlds.

   "Satan could come to Urantia because you had no Son of standing in residence—neither Planetary Prince nor Material Son. Machiventa Melchizedek has since been proclaimed vicegerent Planetary Prince of Urantia, and the opening of the case of Gabriel vs. Lucifer has signalized the inauguration of temporary planetary regimes on all the isolated worlds. It is true that Satan did periodically visit Caligastia and others of the fallen princes right up to the time of the presentation of these revelations, when there occurred the first hearing of Gabriel's plea for the annihilation of the archrebels. Satan is now unqualifiedly detained on the Jerusem prison worlds." (p. 611)

6. **Proposition.** Urantia is just as lovingly cherished and watched over as if the sphere had never been betrayed by a faithless Planetary Prince.

   "Your isolated world is not forgotten in the counsels of the universe. Urantia is not a cosmic orphan stigmatized by sin and shut away from divine watchcare by rebellion. From Uversa to Salvington and on down to Jerusem, even in Havona and on

Paradise, they all know we are here; and you mortals now dwelling on Urantia are just as lovingly cherished and just as faithfully watched over as if the sphere had never been betrayed by a faithless Planetary Prince, even more so. It is eternally true, 'the Father himself loves you.'" (p. 1259)

F. *True and False Liberty*

1. **PROPOSITION.** Liberty is self-destroying when unconditioned and uncontrolled. True liberty is regardful of social equity, cosmic fairness, universe fraternity, and divine obligations.

    "Liberty is a self-destroying technique of cosmic existence when its motivation is unintelligent, unconditioned, and uncontrolled. True liberty is progressively related to reality and is ever regardful of social equity, cosmic fairness, universe fraternity, and divine obligations." (p. 613)

2. **PROPOSITION.** Liberty is suicidal when divorced from its reality obligations.

    "Liberty is suicidal when divorced from material justice, intellectual fairness, social forbearance, moral duty, and spiritual values. Liberty is nonexistent apart from cosmic reality, and all personality reality is proportional to its divinity relationships." (p. 613)

3. **PROPOSITION.** True liberty is the associate of self-respect; false liberty is the consort of self-admiration. True liberty is the fruit of self-control; false liberty, the assumption of self-assertion.

    "True liberty is the associate of genuine self-respect; false liberty is the consort of self-admiration. True liberty is the fruit of self-control; false liberty, the assumption of self-assertion Self-control leads to altruistic service; self-admiration tends towards the exploitation of others for the selfish aggrandizement of such a mistaken individual as is willing to sacrifice righteous attainment for the sake of possessing unjust power over his fellow beings." (p. 614)

4. **PROPOSITION.** The Lucifer manifesto, masquerading as a charter of freedom, was a monumental theft of personal liberty.

    "Thus does the Lucifer manifesto, masquerading in the habiliments of liberty, stand forth in the clear light of reason as a monumental threat to consummate the theft of personal liberty and to do it on a scale that has been approached only twice in all the history of Nebadon." (p. 615)

Part XXV — Sin

5. **Proposition.** Most of the liberties Lucifer sought he already had; others he would have received in the future. The desire to possess one's future liberties *now* was the sin of Lucifer.

   "Most of the liberties which Lucifer sought he already had; others he was to receive in the future. All these precious endowments were lost by giving way to impatience and yielding to a desire to possess what one craves now and to possess it in defiance of all obligation to respect the rights and liberties of all other beings composing the universe of universes. Ethical obligations are innate, divine, and universal." (p. 616)

6. **Proposition.** Man should learn how to enjoy liberty without license and pleasure without debauchery.

   "Someday man should learn how to enjoy liberty without license, nourishment without gluttony, and pleasure without debauchery. Self-control is a better human policy of behavior regulation than is extreme self-denial. Nor did Jesus ever teach these unreasonable views to his followers." (p. 977)

7. **Proposition.** Lucifer sought to disrupt the time governor acting to restrain the premature attainment of certain liberties.

   "Lucifer similarly sought to disrupt the time governor operating in restraint of the premature attainment of certain liberties in the local system. A local system settled in light and life has experientially achieved those viewpoints and insights which make feasible the operation of many techniques that would be disruptive and destructive in the presettled eras of that very realm." (p. 1302)

G. *Mercy Time Lag*

1. **Proposition.** Lucifer pointed to the merciful delays of justice as proof that the universe government was powerless to stop the rebellion.

   "All the merciful delays of justice Lucifer pointed to as evidence of the inability of the government of the Paradise Sons to stop the rebellion. He would openly defy and arrogantly challenge Michael, Immanuel, and the Ancients of Days and then point to the fact that no action ensued as postive evidence of the impotency of the universe and the superuniverse governments." (p. 605)

2. **Proposition.** Salvation was offered the rebels, but none of the leaders accepted. Thousands of the angels and others did and were later granted rehabilitation.

   "Early in the days of the Lucifer rebellion, salvation was offered all rebels by Michael. To all who would show proof of sincere repentance, he offered, upon his attainment of complete universe sovereignty, forgiveness and reinstatement in some form of universe service. None of the leaders accepted this merciful proffer. But thousands of the angels and the lower orders of celestial beings, including hundreds of the Material Sons and Daughters, accepted the mercy proclaimed by the Panoptians and were given rehabilitation at the time of Jesus' resurrection nineteen hundred years ago. These beings have since been transferred to the Father's world of Jerusem, where they must be held, technically, until the Uversa courts hand down a decision in the matter of Gabriel *vs.* Lucifer. But no one doubts that, when the annihilation verdict is issued, these repentant and salvaged personalities will be exempted from the decree of extinction. These probationary souls now labor with the Panoptians in the work of caring for the Father's world." (p. 610)

3. **Proposition.** Justice can act instantly when not restrained by mercy. But mercy always provides a time lag—the saving interval between seedtime and harvest.

   "Supreme justice can act instantly when not restrained by divine mercy. But the ministry of mercy to the children of time and space always provides for this time lag, this saving interval between seedtime and harvest. If the seed sowing is good, this interval provides for the testing and upbuilding of character; if the seed sowing is evil, this merciful delay provides time for repentance and rectification. This time delay in the adjudication and execution of evildoers is inherent in the mercy ministry of the seven superuniverses. This restraint of justice by mercy proves that God is love, and that such a God of love dominates the universes and in mercy controls the fate and judgment of all his creatures." (p. 616)

4. **Proposition.** A Mighty Messenger recounts twelve reasons why Lucifer and his associates were not sooner interned or adjudicated.

   See pages 617-18.

Part XXV — Sin

H. *Planetary Prince's Rebellion*

1. **Proposition.** Caligastia resisted authority and resented supervision. He was inclined to join any party of protest.
   "In looking back over the long career of Caligastia, we find only one outstanding feature of his conduct that might have challenged attention; he was ultraindividualistic. He was inclined to take sides with almost every party of protest, and he was usually sympathetic with those who gave mild expression to implied criticism. We detect the early appearance of this tendency to be restless under authority, to mildly resent all forms of supervision. While slightly resentful of senior counsel and somewhat restive under superior authority, nonetheless, whenever a test had come, he had always proved loyal to the universe rulers and obedient to the mandates of the Constellation Fathers. No real fault was ever found in him up to the time of his shameful betrayal of Urantia." (p. 752)

2. **Proposition.** When Satan informed Caligastia of Lucifer's "Declaration of Liberty," the Prince agreed to betray the planet.
   "In the course of this inspection Satan informed Caligastia of Lucifer's then proposed 'Declaration of Liberty,' and as we now know, the Prince agreed to betray the planet upon the announcement of the rebellion. The loyal universe personalities look with peculiar disdain upon Prince Caligastia because of this premeditated betrayal of trust. The Creator Son voiced this contempt when he said: 'You are like your leader, Lucifer, and you have sinfully perpetuated his iniquity. He was a falsifier from the beginning of his self-exaltation because he abode not in the truth.'" (p. 754)

3. **Proposition.** Caligastia was proclaimed "God of Urantia and supreme over all." All intelligent beings on the planet were compelled to choose between sin and righteousness.
   "Daligastia formally proclaimed Caligastia 'God of Urantia and supreme over all.' With this proclamation before them, the issues were clearly drawn; and each group drew off by itself and began deliberations, discussions destined eventually to determine the fate of every superhuman personality on the planet.
   "Seraphim and cherubim and other celestial beings were involved in the decisions of this bitter struggle, this long and sinful conflict. Many superhuman groups that chanced to be on Urantia at the time of its isolation were detained here and, like the seraphim and their associates, were compelled to choose between sin and righteousness— between the ways of Lucifer and the will of the unseen Father." (p. 755)

4. **PROPOSITION.** Under the Caligastia delusions of quick human improvement, society rapidly reverted to its old biologic level.
   "The Caligastia scheme for the immediate reconstruction of human society in accordance with his ideas of individual freedom and group liberties, proved a swift and more or less complete failure. Society quickly sank back to its old biologic level, and the forward struggle began all over, starting not very far in advance of where it was at the beginning of the Caligastia regime, this upheaval having left the world in confusion worse confounded.
   "One hundred and sixty-two years after the rebellion a tidal wave swept up over Dalamatia, and the planetary headquarters sank beneath the waters of the sea, and this land did not again emerge until almost every vestige of the noble culture of those splendid ages had been obliterated." (p. 759)

5. **PROPOSITION.** The most shocking of all Caligastia's callous perfidy was his perversion of the teaching in the Urantia schools.
   "It was one of the most profoundly shocking episodes of this rebellion for me to learn of the callous perfidy of one of my own order of sonship, Caligastia, who, in deliberation and with malice aforethought, systematically perverted the instruction and poisoned the teaching provided in all the Urantia planetary schools in operation at that time. The wreck of these schools was speedy and complete." (p. 576)

6. **PROPOSITION.** The Adjusters of the rebel members of the Prince's staff still tarry on Jerusem—probably will so continue until the Lucifer rebellion is finally adjudicated.
   "When the staff of one hundred came to Urantia, they were temporarily detached from their Thought Adjusters. Immediately upon the arrival of the Melchizedek receivers the loyal personalities (except Van) were returned to Jerusem and were reunited with their waiting Adjusters. We know not the fate of the sixty staff rebels; their Adjusters still tarry on Jerusem. Matters will undoubtedly rest as they now are until the entire Lucifer rebellion is finally adjudicated and the fate of all participants decreed." (p. 758)

7. **Proposition.** The Melchizedek receivers, with the aid of Van, performed heroic work for Urantia. In a thousand years they had 350 outposts of civilization.

"The twelve Melchizedek receivers of Urantia did heroic work. They preserved the remnants of civilization, and their planetary policies were faithfully executed by Van. Within one thousand years after the rebellion he had more than three hundred and fifty advanced groups scattered abroad in the world. These outposts of civilization consisted largely of the descendants of the loyal Andonites slightly admixed with the Sangik races, particularly the blue men, and with the Nodites." (p. 760)

8. **Proposition.** Every person born on Urantia has been time-penalized by the Caligastia rebellion and the Adamic default. But no person has suffered in his personal religious experience because of these blunders.

"Caligastia rebelled, Adam and Eve did default, but no mortal subsequently born on Urantia has suffered in his personal spiritual experience because of these blunders. Every mortal born on Urantia since Caligastia's rebellion has been in some manner time-penalized, but the future welfare of such souls has never been in the least eternity-jeopardized. No person is ever made to suffer vital spiritual deprivation because of the sin of another. Sin is wholly personal as to moral guilt or spiritual consequences, notwithstanding its far-flung repercussions in administrative, intellectual, and social domains." (p. 761)

I. *Van — The Steadfast*

1. **Proposition.** Van and his associates retired to the highlands west of India. They placed human affairs in the hands of ten commissions of four members each.

"The followers of Van early withdrew to the highlands west of India, where they were exempt from attacks by the confused races of the lowlands, and from which place of retirement they planned for the rehabilitation of the world as their early Badonite predecessors had once all unwittingly worked for the welfare of mankind just before the days of the birth of the Sangik tribes.

"Before the arrival of the Melchizedek receivers, Van placed the administration of human affairs in the hands of ten commissions of four each, groups identical with those of the Prince's regime. The senior resident Life Carriers assumed temporary leadership of this council of forty, which functioned throughout the seven years of waiting. Similar groups of Amadonites assumed these responsibilities when the thirty-nine loyal staff members returned to Jerusem." (p759)

2. **PROPOSITION.** Van was left on Urantia until the time of Adam. He and Amadon were sustained by the tree of life and the Melchizedek ministry for over one hundred and fifty thousand years.

"Van was left on Urantia until the time of Adam, remaining as titular head of all superhuman personalities functioning on the planet. He and Amadon were sustained by the technique of the tree of life in conjunction with the specialized life ministry of the Melchizedeks for over one hundred and fifty thousand years." (p. 759)

J. *The Mortal Heroes*

1. **PROPOSITION.** While ascending mortals were vulnerable, not a single member of the ascender group on Jerusem participated in the Lucifer rebellion.

"The ascending mortals were vulnerable, but they withstood the sophistries of rebellion better than the lower spirits. While many on the lower mansion worlds, those who had not attained final fusion with their Adjusters, fell, it is recorded to the glory of the wisdom of the ascension scheme that not a single member of the ascendant citizenship resident on Jerusem participated in the Lucifer rebellion." (p. 608)

2. **PROPOSITION.** Evolutionary survival experience is the greatest security against rebellion. This Jerusem band of faithful ascenders numbered 187,432,811.

"And on to Salvington, Uversa, and Paradise went this message of assurance that the survival experience of mortal ascension is the greatest security against rebellion and the surest safeguard against sin. This noble Jerusem band of faithful mortals numbered just 187,432,811." (p. 609)

3. **PROPOSITION.** Forty members of the Prince's staff on Urantia remained loyal. There was a terrible loss of angels and midwayers.

"On Urantia forty members of the corporeal staff of one hundred (including Van) refused to join the insurrection. Many of the staff's human assistants (modified and otherwise) were also brave and noble defenders of Michael and his universe government. There was a terrible loss of personalities among seraphim

Part XXV — Sin

and cherubim. Almost one half of the administrator and transition seraphim assigned to the planet joined their leader and Daligastia in support of the cause of Lucifer. Forty thousand one hundred and nineteen of the primary midway creatures joined hands with Caligastia, but the remainder of these beings regained true to their trust." (p. 756)

4. **Proposition.** Amadon is the outstanding hero of the Lucifer rebellion. This descendant of Andon and Fonta was associated with Van of the Prince's staff.

"Amadon is the outstanding human hero of the Lucifer rebellion. This male descendant of Andon and Fonta was one of the one hundred who contributed life plasm to the Prince's staff, and ever since that event he had been attached to Van as his associate and human assistant. Amadon elected to stand with his chief throughout the long and trying struggle. And it was an inspiring sight to behold this child of the evolutionary races standing unmoved by the sophistries of Daligastia while throughout the seven-year struggle he and his loyal associates resisted with unyielding fortitude all of the deceptive teachings of the brilliant Caligastia." (p. 757)

5. **Proposition.** Amadon was outstanding in his rejection of the flood tides of sedition. With Van, he was immovable in his loyalty to Michael.

"The Lucifer rebellion was withstood by many courageous beings on the various worlds of Satania; but the records of Salvington portray Amadon as the outstanding character of the entire system in his glorious rejection of the flood tides of sedition and in his unswerving devotion to Van—they stood together unmoved in their loyalty to the supremacy of the invisible Father and his Son Michael." (p. 761)

6. **Proposition.** The steadfastness of Amadon in the seven years of testing was of universe concern. The loyalty of Amadon and his 143 comrades has done more good than can be outweighed by the evil of the rebellion.

"At the time of these momentous transactions I was stationed on Edentia, and I am still conscious of the exhilaration I experienced as I perused the Salvington broadcasts which told from day to day of the unbelievable steadfastness, the transcendent devotion, and the exquisite loyalty of this onetime semisavage springing from the experimental and original stock of the Andonic race.

"From Edentia up through Salvington and even on to Uversa, for seven long years the first inquiry of all subordinate celestial life regarding the Satania rebellion, ever and always, was: 'What of Amadon of Urantia, does he still stand unmoved?'

"If the Lucifer rebellion has handicapped the local system and its fallen worlds, if the loss of this Son and his misled associates has temporarily hampered the progress of the constellation of Norlatiadek, then weigh the effect of the far-flung presentation of the inspiring performance of this one child of nature and his determined band of 143 comrades in standing steadfast for the higher concepts of universe management and administration in the face of such tremendous and adverse pressure exerted by his disloyal superiors. And let me assure you, this has already done more good in the universe of Nebadon and the superuniverse of Orvonton than can ever be outweighed by the sum total of all the evil and sorrow of the Lucifer rebellion." (p. 762)

III. REPERCUSSIONS OF SIN

1. **Proposition.** Urantia peoples are suffering the consequences of a double deprivation—the Caligastia rebellion and the Adamic default.

    "The Urantia peoples are suffering the consequences of a double deprivation of help in this task of progressive planetary spiritual attainment. The Caligastia upheaval precipitated world-wide confusion and robbed all subsequent generations of the moral assistance which a well-ordered society would have provided. But even more disastrous was the Adamic default in that it deprived the races of that superior type of physical nature which would have been more consonant with spiritual aspirations." (p. 382)

2. **Proposition.** Ever since the Lucifer rebellion the Edentia Fathers have exercised a special care over Urantia and the other isolated worlds.

    "Ever since the Lucifer rebellion the Edentia Fathers have exercised a special care over Urantia and the other isolated worlds of Satania. Long ago the prophet recognized the controlling hand of the Constellation Fathers in the affairs of nations. 'When the Most High divided to the nations their inheritance, when he separated the sons of Adam, he set the bounds of the people.'" (p. 491)

PART XXV — *Sin*

3. **PROPOSITION.** At first the Lucifer upheaval appeared as an unmitigated calamity. After twenty-five thousand years the good had come to equal the evil. Now the good resulting from the rebellion is more than a thousand times the sum of the evil.

> "At first the Lucifer upheaval appeared to be an unmitigated calamity to the system and to the universe. Gradually benefits began to accrue. With the passing of twenty-five thousand years of system time (twenty thousand years of Urantia time), the Melchizedeks began to teach that the good resulting from Lucifer's folly had come to equal the evil incurred. The sum of evil had by that time become almost stationary, continuing to increase only on certain isolated worlds, while the beneficial repercussions continued to multiply and extend out through the universe and superuniverse, even to Havona. The Melchizedeks now teach that the good resulting from the Satania rebellion is more than a thousand times the sum of all the evil." (p. 619)

4. **PROPOSITION.** Sin is fraught with fatal consequences to personality survival only when it is the attitude of the whole being—the choice of mind and the will of the soul.

> "But the full consequences of erroneous thinking, evil-doing, or sinful planning are experienced only on the level of actual performance. The transgression of universe law may be fatal in the physical realm without seriously involving the mind or impairing the spiritual experience. Sin is fraught with fatal consequences to personality survival only when it is the attitude of the whole being, when it stands for the choosing of the mind and the willing of the soul." (p. 761)

IV. SACRIFICES—ATONEMENT

1. **PROPOSITION.** Primitive man was so surrounded by grasping gods—creditor deities—that it required priests, rituals, and sacrifices to get him out of debt. Original sin started every person out in debt to spirit powers.

> "Surrounded by so many sensitive spirits and grasping gods, primitive man was face to face with such a host of creditor deities that it required all the priests, ritual, and sacrifices throughout an entire lifetime to get him out of spiritual debt. The doctrine of original sin, or racial guilt, started every person out in serious debt to the spirit powers." (p. 978)

2. **Proposition.** Moses undertook to end human sacrifice by offering a ransom as a substitute. Many backward tribes were greatly weakened by the loss of their first-born sons.

> "Moses attempted to end human sacrifices by inaugurating the ransom as a substitute. He established a systematic schedule which enabled his people to escape the worst results of their rash and foolish vows. Lands, properties, and children could be redeemed according to the established fees, which were payable to the priests. Those groups which ceased to sacrifice their first-born soon possessed great advantages over less advanced neighbors who continued these atrocious acts. Many such backward tribes were not only greatly weakened by this loss of sons, but even the succession of leadership was often broken." (p. 981)

3. **Proposition.** Sacrifice became associated with the idea of a covenant. This was a major step in the stabilization of religion. A covenant takes the place of luck, fear, and superstition.

> "The custom of sacrifice eventually became associated, as a result of advancing teachings, with the idea of the covenant. At last, the gods were conceived of as entering into real agreements with man; and this was a major step in the stabilization of religion. Law, a covenant, takes the place of luck, fear, and superstition." (p. 983)

4. **Proposition.** Evolutionary man eventually acquired such moral dignity that he dared to bargain with his gods—to enter into covenant relations with Deity.

> "But the idea of making a covenant with the gods did finally arrive. *Evolutionary man eventually acquired such moral dignity that he dared to bargain with his gods.* And so the business of offering sacrifices gradually developed into the game of man's philosophic bargaining with God." (p. 983)

V. FORGIVENESS OF SIN

1. **Proposition.** Primitive man would ask forgiveness for sins he intended to commit the following week. Sin was largely ritual.

> "The idea of confession and forgiveness early appeared in primitive religion. Men would ask forgiveness at a public meeting for sins they intended to commit the following week. Confession was merely a rite of remission, also a public notification of defilement, a ritual of crying 'unclean, unclean!' Then followed all the ritualistic schemes of purification. All ancient

peoples practiced these meaningless ceremonies. Many apparently hygienic customs of the early tribes were largely ceremonial." (p. 976)

2. **PROPOSITION.** The majority of the victims of the Lucifer rebellion have long since repented of their folly. All such penitents will be restored to some phase of universe service following the final adjudication of the rebellion.

> "The vast majority of all human and superhuman beings who were victims of the Lucifer rebellion on Jerusem and the various misled planets have long since heartily repented of their folly; and we truly believe that all such sincere penitents will in some manner be rehabilitated and restored to some phase of universe service when the Ancients of Days finally complete the adjudication of the affairs of the Satania rebellion, which they have so recently begun." (p. 758)

3. **PROPOSITION.** While confession of sin is a manful repudiation of disloyalty, it in no wise mitigates the time-space consequences of such disloyalty.

> "The confession of sin is a manful repudiation of disloyalty, but it in no wise mitigates the time-space consequences of such disloyalty. But confession—sincere recognition of the nature of sin—is essential to religious growth and spiritual progress." (p. 984)

4. **PROPOSITION.** The forgiveness of sin marks the resumption of loyalty relations with Deity following a period of the human consciousness of the lapse of such relations. Forgiveness does not have to be sought—only received.

> "The forgiveness of sin by Deity is the renewal of loyalty relations following a period of the human consciousness of the lapse of such relations as the consequence of conscious rebellion. The forgiveness does not have to be sought, only received as the consciousness of re-establishment of loyalty relations between the creature and the Creator. And all the loyal sons of God are happy, service-loving, and ever-progressive in the Paradise ascent." (p. 985)

VI. NATURAL URGES

1. **Proposition.** On normal worlds, mortals do not experience constant warfare between their physical and spiritual natures. Their upward climb is more like educational training than an intense conflict.

   "The mortals of a normal world do not experience constant warfare between their physical and spiritual natures. They are confronted with the necessity of climbing up from the animal levels of existence to the higher planes of spiritual living, but this ascent is more like undergoing an educational training when compared with the intense conflicts of Urantia mortals in this realm of the divergent material and spiritual natures." (p. 382)

2. **Proposition.** Poverty was a part of the ritual of mortification which became incorporated into the teachings of many religions. Penance was the negative form of this ritual.

   "Poverty was just a part of the ritual of the mortification of the flesh which, unfortunately, became incorporated into the writings and teachings of many religions, notably Christianity. Penance is the negative form of this ofttimes foolish ritual of renunciation. But all this taught the savage *self-control*, and that was a worthwhile advancement in social evolution." (p. 976)

3. **Proposition.** Many of these early rituals were worthwhile because they taught self-control and self-denial.

   "Self-denial and self-control were two of the greatest social gains from early evolutionary religion. Self-control gave man a new philosophy of life; it taught him the art of augmenting life's fraction by lowering the denominator of personal demands instead of always attempting to increase the numerator of selfish gratification." (p. 976)

4. **Proposition.** The animal nature may be hereditary, but sin is not transmitted from parent to child. Sin is a conscious rebellion against the Father's will.

   "The animal nature—the tendency toward evildoing—may be hereditary, but sin is not transmitted from parent to child. Sin is the act of conscious and deliberate rebellion against the Father's will and the Sons' laws by an individual will creature." (p. 2016)

5. **Proposition.** Judas met defeat in the battle of life because of many factors.

   See page 2056.

PART XXV — *SIN*

VII. PENALTY FOR SIN

1. **PROPOSITION.** Wholehearted identification with sin is the equivalent of nonexistence—annihilation. Between the cause and the penalty there is always a delay to allow for repentance or adjudication.

   "Although conscious and wholehearted identification with evil (sin) is the equivalent of nonexistence (annihilation), there must always intervene between the time of such personal identification with sin and the execution of the penalty—the automatic result of such a willful embrace of evil—a period of time of sufficient length to allow for such an adjudication of such an individual's universe status as will prove entirely satisfactory to all related universe personalities, and which will be so fair and just as to win the approval of the sinner himself." (p. 615)

2. **PROPOSITION.** The system circuits of Satania will not be restored as long as Lucifer lives.

   "We do not look for a removal of the present Satania restrictions until the Ancients of Days make final disposition of the archrebels. The system circuits will not be reinstated so long as Lucifer lives. Meantime, he is wholly inactive." (p. 611)

VIII. THE DEVIL

1. **PROPOSITION.** The doctrine of a personal devil—notwithstanding it had some foundation in the presence of Caligastia—was wholly fictitious. The freewill of man is supreme in all moral affairs.

   "The doctrine of a personal devil on Urantia, though it had some foundation in the planetary presence of the traitorous and iniquitous Caligastia, was nevertheless wholly fictitious in its teachings that such a 'devil' could influence the normal human mind against its free and natural choosing. Even before Michael's bestowal on Urantia, neither Caligastia nor Daligastia was ever able to oppress mortals or to coerce any normal individual into doing anything against the human will. The free will of man is supreme in moral affairs; even the indwelling Thought Adjuster refuses to compel man to think a single thought or to perform a single act against the choosing of man's own will." (p. 753)

PART XXVI
THE PLAN OF SALVATION

Part Twenty-Six
THE PLAN OF SALVATION

I. INTRODUCTION

1. **Proposition.** God's will may not prevail in the part, but it always does with the whole.

   "The will of God does not necessarily prevail in the part—the heart of any one personality—but his will does actually rule the whole, the universe of universes." (p. 137)

II. THE LOVE OF GOD

1. **Proposition.** God loves every creature but uniquely individualizes his love for every person.

   "God loves *each* individual as an individual child in the heavenly family. Yet God thus loves *every* individual; he is no respecter of persons, and the universality of his love brings into being a relationship of the whole, the universal brotherhood.
   "The love of the Father absolutely individualizes each personality as a unique child of the Universal Father, a child without duplicate in infinity, a will creature irreplaceable in all eternity." (p. 138)

2. **Proposition.** Love, not pressure, stimulates growth.

   "But man is not saved or ennobled by pressure. Spirit growth springs from within the evolving soul. Pressure may deform the personality, but it never stimulates growth. Even educational pressure is only negatively helpful in that it may aid in the prevention of disastrous experiences. Spiritual growth is greatest where all external pressures are at a minimum. 'Where the spirit of the Lord is, there is freedom.' Man develops best when the pressures of home, community, church, and state are least. But this must not be construed as meaning that there is no place in a progressive society for home, social institutions, church, and state." (p. 1135)

BIBLE TEXTS

"And Peter opened his mouth and said: 'Truly I perceive that God shows no partiality, but in every nation any one who fears him and does what is right is acceptable to him.'" **Acts 10:34,35**

"Now the Lord is the Spirit, and where the Spirit of the Lord is, there is freedom." **2 Cor. 3:17**

"He who does not love does not know God, for God is love." **I John 4:8**

III. THE ETERNAL AND DIVINE PURPOSE

1. **PROPOSITION.** We are all a part of a vast and eternal universe purpose.

   "There is a great and glorious purpose in the march of the universes through space. All of your mortal struggling is not in vain. We are all part of an immense plan, a gigantic enterprise, and it is the vastness of the undertaking that renders it impossible to see very much of it at any one time and during any one life. We are all a part of an eternal project which the Gods are supervising and outworking. The whole marvelous and universal mechanism moves on majestically through space to the music of the meter of the infinite thought and the eternal purpose of the First Great Source and Center." (p. 364)

2. **PROPOSITION.** The far-flung and boundless plan of God embraces all of his creatures.

   "There is in the mind of God a plan which embraces every creature of all his vast domains, and this plan is an eternal purpose of boundless opportunity, unlimited progress, and endless life. And the infinite treasures of such a matchless career are yours for the striving!" (p. 365)

3. **PROPOSITION.** Mortal existence is but a link in God's high spiritual plan.

   "The eternal purpose of the eternal God is a high spiritual ideal. The events of time and the struggles of material existence are but the transient scaffolding which bridges over to the other side, to the promised land of spiritual reality and supernal existence. Of course, you mortals find it difficult to grasp the idea of an eternal purpose; you are virtually unable to comprehend the thought of eternity, something never beginning and never ending. Everything familiar to you has an end." (p. 364)

4. **PROPOSITION.** Victory is assured for all who enter the race for eternal perfection.

   "The goal of eternity is ahead! The adventure of divinity attainment lies before you! The race for perfection is on! whosoever will may enter, and certain victory will crown the efforts of every human being who will run the race of faith and trust, depending every step of the way on the leading of the indwelling Adjuster and on the guidance of that good spirit of the Universe Son, which so freely has been poured out upon all flesh." (p. 365)

5. **Proposition.** In surviving the trials of time we strike spiritual step with eternity.

> "To me it seems more fitting, for purposes of explanation to the mortal mind, to conceive of eternity as a cycle and the eternal purpose as an endless circle, a cycle of eternity in some way synchronized with the transient material cycles of time. As regards the sectors of time connected with, and forming a part of, the cycle of eternity, we are forced to recognize that such temporary epochs are born, live, and die just as the temporary beings of time are born, live, and die. Most human beings die because, having failed to achieve the spirit level of Adjuster fusion, the metamorphosis of death constitutes the only possible procedure whereby they may escape the fetters of time and the bonds of material creation, thereby being enabled to strike spiritual step with the progressive procession of eternity. Having survived the trial life of time and material existence, it becomes possible for you to continue on in touch with, even as a part of, eternity, swinging on forever with the worlds of space around the circle of the eternal ages." (p. 364)

Note: *See page 365.*

BIBLE TEXTS

"This was according to the eternal purpose which he has realized in Christ Jesus our Lord." **Eph. 3:11**

"We know that in everything God works for good with those who love him, who are called according to his purpose." **Rom. 8:28**

IV. THE PLAN OF PERFECTION ATTAINMENT

1. **Proposition.** The Father's plan of evolutionary mortal ascension was concurred in by the Eternal Son.

> "*The Plan of Progressive Attainment.* This is the Universal Father's plan of evolutionary ascension, a program unreservedly accepted by the Eternal Son when he concurred in the Father's proposal, 'Let us make mortal creatures in our own image.' This provision for upstepping the creatures of time involves the Father's bestowal of the Thought Adjusters and the endowing of material creatures with the prerogatives of personality." (p. 85)

2. **Proposition**. Intelligent creatures can love God and elect to attain Paradise and find God.

> "The ceaseless and expanding march of the Paradise creative forces through space seems to presage the ever-extending domain of the gravity grasp of the Universal Father and the never-ending multiplication of varied types of intelligent creatures who are able to love God and be loved by him, and who, by thus becoming God-knowing, may choose to be like him, may elect to attain Paradise and find God." (p. 645)

3. **Proposition**. The plan of perfection attainment is at present one of the chief concerns of the superuniverses.

> "The amazing plan for perfecting evolutionary mortals and, after their attainment of Paradise and the Corps of the Finality, providing further training for some undisclosed future work, does seem to be, at present, one of the chief concerns of the seven superuniverses and their many subdivisions; but this ascension scheme for spiritualizing and training the mortals of time and space is by no means the exclusive occupation of the universe intelligences." (p. 54)

4. **Proposition**. Uncertainty with security is the essence of the Paradise adventure.

> "Uncertainty with security is the essence of the Paradise adventure— uncertainty in time and in mind, uncertainty as to the events of the unfolding Paradise ascent; security in spirit and in eternity, security in the unqualified trust of the creature son in the divine compassion and infinite love of the Universal Father; uncertainty as an inexperienced citizen of the universe; security as an ascending son in the universe mansions of an all-powerful, all-wise, and all loving Father." (p. 1223)

BIBLE TEXTS

"Then God said: Let us make man in our image, after our likeness; and let them have dominion over..." **Gen. 1:26**

"You, therefore, must be perfect, as your heavenly Father is perfect." **Matt. 5:43**

V. THE BESTOWAL PLAN

1. Proposition. The incarnate bestowal of the Paradise Sons upon the mortal races is the project of the Eternal Son.

   "*The Bestowal Plan.* The next universal plan is the great Father revelation enterprise of the Eternal Son and his co-ordinate Sons. This is the proposal of the Eternal Son and consists of his bestowal of the Sons of God upon the evolutionary creations, there to personalize and factualize, to incarnate and make real, the love of the Father and the mercy of the Son to the creatures of all universes. Inherent in the bestowal plan, and as a provisional feature of this ministration of love, the Paradise Sons act as rehabilitators of that which misguided creature will has placed in spiritual jeopardy." (p. 85)

2. Proposition. Attainment of the Paradise goal of perfection was enhanced by Michael's bestowal.

   "As mortals you can now recognize your place in the family of divine sonship and begin to sense the obligation to avail yourselves of the advantages so freely provided in and by the Paradise plan for mortal survival, which plan has been so enhanced and illuminated by the life experience of a bestowal Son. Every facility and all power have been provided for insuring your ultimate attainment of the Paradise goal of divine perfection." (p. 454)

BIBLE TEXT

"For the Son of Man came to seek and to save the lost." **Luke 19:10**

VI. THE PLAN OF MERCY MINISTRY

1. Proposition. When the attainment and the bestowal plans were proclaimed, the Infinite Spirit promulgated his plan of mercy ministry.

   "*The Plan of Mercy Ministry.* When the attainment plan and the bestowal plan had been formulated and proclaimed, alone and of himself, the Infinite Spirit projected and put in operation the tremendous and universal enterprise of mercy ministry. This is the service so essential to the practical and effective operation of both the attainment and the bestowal undertakings, and the spiritual personalities of the Third Source and Center all partake of the spirit of mercy ministry which is so much a part of the nature of the Third Person of Deity. Not only in creation but also in administration, the Infinite Spirit functions truly and literally as the conjoint executive of the Father and the Son." (p. 85)

Part XXVI — The Plan of Salvation

2. **Proposition.** The Infinite Spirit ministers for the Father and the Son and also in his own behalf.

> "The Spirit's ministry is not, however, restricted solely to the representation of the Eternal Son and the Universal Father. The Infinite Spirit also possesses the power to minister to the creatures of the realm in his own name and right; the Third Person is of divine dignity and also bestows the universal ministry of mercy in his own behalf." (p. 95)

BIBLE TEXT

"Likewise the Spirit helps us in our weakness; for we do not know how to pray as we ought, but the Spirit himself intercedes for us with sighs too deep for words." **Rom. 8:26**

VII. THE SALVAGE PLAN

1. **Proposition.** In case of rebellion or delay in the attainment plan, the Paradise Sons act as retrievers.

> "Whenever and wherever there occurs a delay in the functioning of the attainment plan, if rebellion, perchance, should mar or complicate this enterprise, then do the emergency provisions of the bestowal plan become active forthwith. The Paradise Sons stand pledged and ready to function as retrievers, to go into the very realms of rebellion and there restore the spiritual status of the spheres. And such a heroic service a co-ordinate Creator Son did perform on Urantia in connection with his experiential bestowal career of sovereignty acquirement." (p. 85)

2. **Proposition.** The Creators are the first to attempt to save man from the results of transgression.

> "The Creators are the very first to attempt to save man from the disastrous results of his foolish transgression of the divine laws. God's love is by nature a fatherly affection; therefore does he sometimes 'chasten us for our own profit, that we may be partakers of his holiness.' Even during your fiery trials remember that 'in all our afflictions he is afflicted with us.'" (p. 39)

BIBLE TEXTS

"For they disciplined us for a short time at their pleasure, but he disciplines us for our good, that we may share his holiness." **Heb. 12:10**

"Who by God's power are guarded through faith for a salvation ready to be revealed in the last time." **1 Peter 1:5**

VIII. THE FAITH SONS OF GOD

1. **Proposition.** Sonship with God is inherent in the divine love; it is not dependent on the bestowals of the Paradise Sons.

   "All that the Son of Man said or did on earth greatly embellished the doctrines of sonship with God and of the brotherhood of men, but these essential relationships of God and men are inherent in the universe facts of God's love for his creatures and the innate mercy of the divine Sons. These touching and divinely beautiful relations between man and his Maker on this world and on all others throughout the universe of universes have existed from eternity; and they are not in any sense dependent on these periodic bestowal enactments of the Creator Sons of God, who thus assume the nature and likeness of their created intelligences as a part of the price which they must pay for the final acquirement of unlimited sovereignty over their respective local universes." (p. 2002)

2. **Proposition.** There are five fundamental reasons why Urantia mortals are entitled to regard themselves as being sons of God.

   "1. You are sons of spiritual promise, faith sons; you have accepted the status of sonship. You believe in the reality of your sonship, and thus does your sonship with God become eternally real.

   "2. A Creator Son of God became one of you; he is your elder brother in fact; and if in spirit you become truly related brothers of Christ, the victorious Michael, then in spirit must you also be sons of that Father which you have in common—even the Universal Father of all.

   "3. You are sons because the spirit of a Son has been poured out upon you, has been freely and certainly bestowed upon all Urantia races. This spirit ever draws you toward the divine Son, who is its source, and toward the Paradise Father, who is the source of that divine Son.

   "4. Of his divine free-willness, the Universal Father has given you your creature personalities. You have been endowed with a measure of that divine spontaneity of freewill action which God shares with all who may become his sons.

   "5. There dwells within you a fragment of the Universal Father, and you are thus directly related to the divine Father of all the Sons of God." (p. 448)

Part XXVI — *The Plan of Salvation*

BIBLE TEXTS

"For all who are led by the Spirit of God are the sons of God." **Rom. 8:14**

"Truly, truly, I say to you, unless one is born anew, he cannot see the kingdom of God." **John 3:3**

"Therefore, if anyone is in Christ, he is a new creation." **2 Cor. 5:17**

"For whatever is born of God overcomes the world and this is the victory that overcomes the world, our faith." **1 John 5:4**

IX. PROVIDENCE

1. **Proposition.** Foreordination of limits or foreknowledge of choice of will in no way abrogates finite volition.

    "The function of Creator will and creature will, in the grand universe, operates within the limits, and in accordance with the possibilities, established by the Master Architects. This foreordination of these maximum limits does not, however, in the least abridge the sovereignty of creature will within these boundaries. Neither does ultimate foreknowledge—full allowance for all finite choice—constitute an abrogation of finite volition. A mature and farseeing human being might be able to forecast the decision of some younger associate most accurately, but this foreknowledge takes nothing away from the freedom and genuineness of the decision itself. The Gods have wisely limited the range of the action of immature will, but it is true will, nonetheless, within these defined limits." (p. 1300)

2. **Proposition.** Providence is the function of the Trinity motivating the cosmic march through time toward the goals of eternity.

    "Providence is the sure and certain march of the galaxies of space and the personalities of time toward the goals of eternity, first in the Supreme, then in the Ultimate, and perhaps in the Absolute. And in infinity we believe there is the same providence, and this is the will, the actions, the purpose of the Paradise Trinity thus motivating the cosmic panorama of universes upon universes." (p. 1307)

3. **Proposition.** Some of the fortuitous circumstances of life may be due to the emerging presence of the Supreme Being.

    "Some of the amazingly fortuitous conditions occasionally prevailing on the evolutionary worlds may be due to the gradually emerging presence of the Supreme, the foretasting of his future universe activities. Most of what a mortal would call providential is not; his judgment of such matters is very handicapped by lack of farsighted vision into the true meanings of the circumstances of life." (p. 1305)

4. **PROPOSITION.** An apparently cruel fate may be the tempering fire that transmutes the soft iron of an immature personality into the tempered steel of a strong character.

> "Much of what a mortal would call good luck might really be bad luck; the smile of fortune that bestows unearned leisure and undeserved wealth may be the greatest of human afflictions; the apparent cruelty of a perverse fate that heaps tribulation upon some suffering mortal may in reality be the tempering fire that is transmuting the soft iron of immature personality into the tempered steel of real character." (p. 1305)

5. **PROPOSITION.** The providence of the overcontrol of Supremacy becomes increasingly apparent as the universe progresses in the attainment of finite destinies.

> "The love of the Father operates directly in the heart of the individual, independent of the actions or reactions of all other individuals; the relationship is personal—man and God. The impersonal presence of Deity (Almighty Supreme and Paradise Trinity) manifests regard for the whole, not for the part. The providence of the overcontrol of Supremacy becomes increasingly apparent as the successive parts of the universe progress in the attainment of finite destinies. As the systems, constellations, universes, and superuniverses become settled in light and life, the Supreme increasingly emerges as the meaningful correlator of all that is transpiring, while the Ultimate gradually emerges as the transcendental unifier of all things." (p. 1305)

6. **PROPOSITION.** God loves the individual; providence functions with regard to the whole.

> "God loves each creature as a child, and that love overshadows each creature throughout all time and eternity. Providence functions with regard to the total and deals with the function of any creature as such function is related to the total. Providential intervention with regard to any being is indicative of the importance of the *function* of that being as concerns the evolutionary growth of some total; such total may be the total race, the total nation, the total planet, or even a higher total. It is the importance of the function of the creature that occasions providential intervention, not the importance of the creature as a person." (p. 1304)

Part XXVI — The Plan of Salvation

7. **Proposition.** God may at any time interpose a fatherly hand in the stream of cosmic events.

   "Nevertheless, the Father as a person may at any time interpose a fatherly hand in the stream of cosmic events all in accordance with the will of God and in consonance with the wisdom of God and as motivated by the love of God." (p. 1305)

8. **Proposition.** Providence is not childish, arbitrary, and material. In accordance with cosmic law, providence labors for the honor of God and the welfare of his children.

   "There is a providence of divine outworking on your world, but it is not the childish, arbitrary, and material ministry many mortals have conceived it to be. The providence of God consists in the interlocking activities of the celestial beings and the divine spirits who, in accordance with cosmic law, unceasingly labor for the honor of God and for the spiritual advancement of his universe children." (p. 54)

9. **Proposition.** Providence is always consistent with the unchanging nature of the supreme Lawmaker.

   "Providence is always consistent with the unchanging and perfect nature of the supreme Lawmaker." (p. 54)

10. **Proposition.** Providence is the partial overcontrol of the incomplete Supreme and must therefore always be partial and unpredictable.

    "Providence is in part the overcontrol of the incomplete Supreme manifested in the incomplete universes, and it must therefore ever be:

    "1. *Partial*—due to the incompleteness of the actualization of the Supreme Being, and

    "2. *Unpredictable*—due to the fluctuations in creature attitude, which ever varies from level to level, thus causing apparently variable reciprocal response in the Supreme." (p. 1307)

11. **Proposition.** The Gods have attributes but the Trinity has functions. Providence is a function of the other-than-personal overcontrol of the universe of universes.

    "The Gods have attributes but the Trinity has functions, and like the Trinity, providence *is* a function, the composite of the other-than-personal overcontrol of the universe of universes, extending from the evolutionary levels of the Sevenfold synthesizing in the power of the Almighty on up through the transcendental realms of the Ultimacy of Deity." (p. 1304)

X. JESUS' LIFE ON EARTH

1. **Proposition.** Believers should trust God as Jesus trusted God and believe in men as he believed in men.

   "It should not be the aim of kingdom believers literally to imitate the outward life of Jesus in the flesh but rather to share his faith; to trust God as he trusted God and to believe in men as he believed in men. Jesus never argued about either the fatherhood of God or the brotherhood of men; he was a living illustration of the one and a profound demonstration of the other." (p. 2091)

2. **Proposition.** Jesus wants you to believe *with* him—rather than *in* him; not only to believe *what* he believed, but also *as* he believed.

   "Jesus does not require his disciples to believe in him but rather to believe *with* him, believe in the reality of the love of God and in full confidence accept the security of the assurance of sonship with the heavenly Father. The Master desires that all his followers should fully share his transcendent faith. Jesus most touchingly challenged his followers, not only to believe *what* he believed, but also to believe *as* he believed. This is the full significance of his one supreme requirement, 'Follow me.'" (p. 2089)

3. **Proposition.** The dispensational resurrection of Urantia sleeping mortals was associated with the morontia resurrection of Jesus.

   "The circuit of the archangels then operated for the first time from Urantia. Gabriel and the archangel hosts moved to the place of the spiritual polarity of the planet; and when Gabriel gave the signal, there flashed to the first of the system mansion worlds the voice of Gabriel, saying: 'By the mandate of Michael, let the dead of a Urantia dispensation rise!' Then all the survivors of the human races of Urantia who had fallen asleep since the days of Adam, and who had not already gone on to judgment, appeared in the resurrection halls of mansonia in readiness for morontia investiture. And in an instant of time the seraphim and their associates made ready to depart for the mansion worlds. Ordinarily these seraphic guardians, onetime assigned to the group custody of these surviving mortals, would have been present at the moment of their awaking in the resurrection halls of mansonia, but they were on this world itself at this time because of the necessity of Gabriel's presence here in connection with the morontia resurrection of Jesus." (p. 2024)

Part XXVI — *The Plan of Salvation*

XI. THE ATONEMENT IDEA

1. **Proposition.** Urantians continue to believe in gods of wrath and anger— the gods of primitive religions.

   "The people of Urantia continue to suffer from the influence of primitive concepts of God. The gods who go on a rampage in the storm; who shake the earth in their wrath and strike down men in their anger; who inflict their judgments of displeasure in times of famine and flood —these are the gods of primitive religion; they are not the Gods who live and rule the universes." (p. 60)

2. **Proposition.** The barbarous idea of appeasing an angry God by the shedding of blood represents a puerile and primitive religion.

   "The barbarous idea of appeasing an angry God, of propitiating an offended Lord, of winning the favor of Deity through sacrifices and penance and even by the shedding of blood, represents a religion wholly puerile and primitive, a philosophy unworthy of an enlightened age of science and truth. Such beliefs are utterly repulsive to the celestial beings and the divine rulers who serve and reign in the universes. It is an affront to God to believe, hold, or teach that innocent blood must be shed in order to win his favor or to divert the fictitious divine wrath." (p. 60)

3. **Proposition.** The atonement concept is rooted in selfishness. Jesus taught service, not sacrifice.

   "All this concept of atonement and sacrificial salvation is rooted and grounded in selfishness. Jesus taught that *service* to one's fellows is the highest concept of the brotherhood of spirit believers. Salvation should be taken for granted by those who believe in the fatherhood of God. The believer's chief concern should not be the selfish desire for personal salvation but rather the unselfish urge to love and, therefore, serve one's fellows even as Jesus loved and served mortal men." (p. 2017)

4. **Proposition.** The idea of ransom and atonement is purely philosophic— human salvation is *real*.

   "This entire idea of the ransom of the atonement places salvation upon a plane of unreality; such a concept is purely philosophic. Human salvation is *real*; it is based on two realities which may be grasped by the creature's faith and thereby become incorporated into individual human experience: the fact of the fatherhood of God and its correlated truth, the brotherhood of man. It is true, after all, that you are to be 'forgiven your debts, even as you forgive your debtors.'" (p. 2017)

5. **Proposition.** According to Paul, Christ is the all-sufficient sacrifice; the divine Judge is now fully and forever satisfied.

> "Paul started out to build a new Christian cult on 'the blood of the everlasting covenant.' And while he may have unnecessarily encumbered Christianity with teachings about blood and sacrifice, he did once and for all make an end of the doctrines of redemption through human or animal sacrifices. His theologic compromises indicate that even revelation must submit to the graduated control of evolution. According to Paul, Christ became the last and all-sufficient human sacrifice; the divine Judge is now fully and forever satisfied." (p. 984)

6. **Proposition.** The atonement doctrine is a philosophic assault upon both the unity and the volition of God.

> "The erroneous supposition that the righteousness of God was irreconcilable with the selfless love of the heavenly Father, presupposed absence of unity in the nature of Deity and led directly to the elaboration of the atonement doctrine, which is a philosophic assault upon both the unity and the free-willness of God." (p. 41)

7. **Proposition.** God is not a divided personality—one of justice and one of mercy. God as a father transcends God as a judge.

> "The affectionate heavenly Father, whose spirit indwells his children on earth, is not a divided personality—one of justice and one of mercy—neither does it require a mediator to secure the Father's favor or forgiveness. Divine righteousness is not dominated by strict retributive justice; God as a father transcends God as a judge." (p. 41)

8. **Proposition.** A Creator Son did not bestow himself upon mankind to reconcile an angry God. He came to reveal the love of God and exalt sonship with God.

> "A Creator Son did not incarnate in the likeness of mortal flesh and bestow himself upon the humanity of Urantia to reconcile an angry God but rather to win all mankind to the recognition of the Father's love and to the realization of their sonship with God. After all, even the great advocate of the atonement doctrine realized something of this truth, for he declared that 'God was in Christ reconciling the world to himself.'" (p. 1083)

PART XXVI — *THE PLAN OF SALVATION*

9. **PROPOSITION.** Jesus did not die as a sacrifice for sin—to atone for the inborn guilt of the race. Guilt is a matter of personal sin.

> "Jesus is not about to die as a sacrifice for sin. He is not going to atone for the inborn moral guilt of the human race. Mankind has no such racial guilt before God. Guilt is purely a matter of personal sin and knowing, deliberate rebellion against the will of the Father and the administration of his Sons." (p. 2003)

10. **PROPOSITION.** The salvation of Urantia mortals would have been just as certain if Jesus had not been put to death by the cruel hands of ignorant mortals. Sonship with God would have in no wise been affected.

> "The salvation of God for the mortals of Urantia would have been just as effective and unerringly certain if Jesus had not been put to death by the cruel hands of ignorant mortals. If the Master had been favorably received by the mortals of earth and had departed from Urantia by the voluntary relinquishment of his life in the flesh, the fact of the love of God and the mercy of the Son—the fact of sonship with God—would have in no wise been affected. You mortals are the sons of God, and only one thing is required to make such a truth factual in your personal experience, and that is your spirit-born faith." (p. 2003)

11. **PROPOSITION.** Jesus swept away all the ceremonials of sacrifice and atonement. God becomes a loving Father to his mortal sons and daughters.

> "Jesus swept away all of the ceremonials of sacrifice and atonement. He destroyed the basis of all this fictitious guilt and sense of isolation in the universe by declaring that man is a child of God; the creature-Creator relationship was placed on a child-parent basis. God becomes a loving Father to his mortal sons and daughters. All ceremonials not a legitimate part of such an intimate family relationship are forever abrogated." (p. 1133)

12. **PROPOSITION.** Christ is not engaged in the ignoble task of persuading his gracious Father to love his lowly creatures. The Father's love is just as real as the Son's mercy.

> "This divine Son is not engaged in the ignoble task of trying to persuade his gracious Father to love his lowly creatures and to show mercy to the wrongdoers of time. How wrong to envisage the Eternal Son as appealing to the Universal Father to show

mercy to his lowly creatures on the material worlds of space! Such concepts of God are crude and grotesque. Rather should you realize that all the merciful ministrations of the Sons of God are a direct revelation of the Father's heart of universal love and infinite compassion. The Father's love is the real and eternal source of the Son's mercy." (p. 75)

13. **PROPOSITION.** The atonement doctrine was designed to make the gospel more acceptable to the Jews—it failed. But it made the gospel less acceptable to all other religions.

> "The effort to connect the gospel teaching directly onto the Jewish theology, as illustrated by the Christian doctrines of the atonement— the teaching that Jesus was the sacrificed Son who would satisfy the Father's stern justice and appease the divine wrath. These teachings originated in a praiseworthy effort to make the gospel of the kingdom more acceptable to disbelieving Jews. Though these efforts failed as far as winning the Jews was concerned, they did not fail to confuse and alienate many honest souls in all subsequent generations." (p. 1670)

BIBLE TEXT

"God was in Christ reconciling the world to himself." **2 Cor. 5:19**

XII. THE RELIGION OF SURVIVAL

1. **PROPOSITION.** Science seeks to identify. Religion grasps at the whole. Philosophy attempts unification. Revelation affirms that the Infinite is the God of human salvation.

> "Science seeks to identify, analyze, and classify the segmented parts of the limitless cosmos. Religion grasps the idea-of-the-whole, the entire cosmos. Philosophy attempts the identification of the material segments of science with the spiritual-insight concept of the whole. Wherein philosophy fails in this attempt, revelation succeeds, affirming that the cosmic circle is universal, eternal, absolute, and infinite. This cosmos of the Infinite I AM is therefore endless, limitless, and all-inclusive—timeless, spaceless, and unqualified. And we bear testimony that the Infinite I AM is also the Father of Michael of Nebadon and the God of human salvation." (p. 1122)

2. **PROPOSITION.** Having embarked on the way of life everlasting, do not fear the doubts and limitations of human nature. At every crossroad, the Spirit of Truth will speak—"This is the way."

> "Having started out on the way of life everlasting, having accepted the assignment and received your orders to advance, do not fear the dangers of human forgetfulness and mortal inconstancy, do not be troubled with doubts of failure or by perplexing confusion, do not falter and question your status and standing, for in every dark hour, at every crossroad in the forward struggle, the Spirit of Truth will always speak, saying, 'This is the way.'" (p. 383)

3. **PROPOSITION.** We have begun an endless unfolding of an almost infinite panorama of ever-widening opportunity for matchless adventure and boundless attainment.

> "You humans have begun an endless unfolding of an almost infinite panorama, a limitless expanding of never-ending, ever-widening spheres of opportunity for exhilarating service, matchless adventure, sublime uncertainty, and boundless attainment." (p. 1194)

4. **PROPOSITION.** When the clouds gather overhead, by faith you should look beyond the mists of mortal uncertainty into the clear shining of the sun of eternal righteousness on the beckoning heights of the mansion worlds of Satania.

> "When the clouds gather overhead, your faith should accept the fact of the presence of the indwelling Adjuster, and thus you should be able to look beyond the mists of mortal uncertainty into the clear shining of the sun of eternal righteousness on the beckoning heights of the mansion worlds of Satania." (p. 1194)

5. **PROPOSITION.** The victorious mortal dares to challenge each recurring episode of human weakness with the unfailing declaration: "Even if I cannot do this, there lives in me one who can and will do it." This is "the victory which overcomes the world, even your faith."

> "The consciousness of a victorious human life on earth is born of that creature faith which dares to challenge each recurring episode of existence when confronted with the awful spectacle of human limitations, by the unfailing declaration: Even if I cannot do this, there lives in me one who can and will do it, a part of the Father-Absolute of the universe of universes. And that is 'the victory which overcomes the world, even your faith.'" (p. 59)

6. **Proposition.** The present destiny of surviving mortals is the Paradise Corps of the Finality. Even more supernal tasks await their future.

> "The present known destiny of surviving mortals is the Paradise Corps of the Finality; this is also the goal of destiny for all Thought Adjusters who become joined in eternal union with their mortal companions. At present the Paradise finaliters are working throughout the grand universe in many undertakings, but we all conjecture that they will have other and even more supernal tasks to perform in the distant future after the seven superuniverses have become settled in light and life, and when the finite God has finally emerged from the mystery which now surrounds this Supreme Deity." (p. 1239)

BIBLE TEXT

"For whatever is born of God overcomes the world; and this is the victory that overcomes the world, our faith." **1 John 5:4**

XIII. PROGRESS THROUGH HAVONA

1. **Proposition.** Starting out on the seventh circuit of Havona, ascenders progress from circuit to circuit until they attain the first, from which they pass inward to Paradise residence and admission to the Corps of the Finality.

> "When intelligent beings first attain the central universe, they are received and domiciled on the pilot world of the seventh Havona circuit. As the new arrivals progress spiritually, attain identity comprehension of their superuniverse Master Spirit, they are transferred to the sixth circle. (It is from these arrangements in the central universe that the circles of progress in the human mind have been designated.) After ascenders have attained a realization of Supremacy and are thereby prepared for the Deity adventure, they are taken to the fifth circuit; and after attaining the Infinite Spirit, they are transferred to the fourth. Following the attainment of the Eternal Son, they are removed to the third; and when they have recognized the Universal Father, they go to sojourn on the second circuit of worlds, where they become more familiar with the Paradise hosts. Arrival on the first circuit of Havona signifies the acceptance of the candidates of time into the service of Paradise. Indefinitely, according to the length and

nature of the creature ascension, they will tarry on the inner circuit of progressive spiritual attainment. From this inner circuit the ascending pilgrims pass inward to Paradise residence and admission to the Corps of the Finality." (p. 158)

2. **Proposition.** On the seven circuits of Havona, your attainment is intellectual, spiritual, and experiential. There is a definite task for each world.

> "On the seven circuits of Havona your attainment is intellectual, spiritual, and experiential. And there is a definite task to be achieved on each of the worlds of each of these circuits." (p. 158)

3. **Proposition.** There are experiential and contrastive differences between the Havona natives and ascendant mortals.

> "The creatures of Havona are naturally brave, but they are not courageous in the human sense. They are innately kind and considerate, but hardly altruistic in the human way. They are expectant of a pleasant future, but not hopeful in the exquisite manner of the trusting mortal of the uncertain evolutionary spheres. They have faith in the stability of the universe, but they are utter strangers to that saving faith whereby mortal man climbs from the status of an animal up to the portals of Paradise. They love the truth, but they know nothing of its soul-saving qualities. They are idealists, but they were born that way; they are wholly ignorant of the ecstasy of becoming such by exhilarating choice. They are loyal, but they have never experienced the thrill of wholehearted and intelligent devotion to duty in the face of temptation to default. They are unselfish, but they never gained such levels of experience by the magnificent conquest of a belligerent self. They enjoy pleasure, but they do not comprehend the sweetness of the pleasure escape from the pain potential." (p. 52)

PART XXVII
ADAM AND EVE

Part Twenty-Seven
ADAM AND EVE

I. INTRODUCTION

1. **Proposition.** The Adams and Eves are biologic uplifters—they go to worlds at the peak of evolutionary development.

   "During the dispensation of a Planetary Prince, primitive man reaches the limit of natural evolutionary development, and this biologic attainment signals the System Sovereign to dispatch to such a world the second order of sonship, the biologic uplifters. These Sons, for there are two of them—the Material Son and Daughter—are usually known on a planet as Adam and Eve." (p. 580)

2. **Proposition.** Adam is one of seven fathers mortal man may acknowledge.

   "With the passing of centuries, through the amalgamation of their progeny with the races of men, this same Material Son and Daughter become accepted as the common ancestors of mankind, the common parents of the now blended descendants of the evolutionary races. It is intended that mortals who start out from an inhabited world have the experience of recognizing seven fathers:
   1. The biologic father—the father in the flesh.
   2. The father of the realm—the Planetary Adam.
   3. The father of the spheres—the System Sovereign.
   4. The Most High Father—the Constellation Father.
   5. The universe Father—the Creator Son and supreme ruler of the local creations.
   6. The super-Fathers—the Ancients of Days who govern the superuniverse.
   7. The spirit or Havona Father—the Universal Father, who dwells on Paradise and bestows his spirit to live and work in the minds of the lowly creatures who inhabit the universe of universes." (p. 587)

3. **Proposition.** Forty thousand years ago, Urantia, at the apex of physical development, was ready for the biologic uplifters.

   "The cultural decadence and spiritual poverty resulting from the Caligastia downfall and consequent social confusion had little effect on the physical or biologic status of the Urantia peoples. Organic evolution proceeded apace, quite regardless of the cultural and moral setback which so swiftly followed the disaffection of Caligastia and Daligastia. And there came a time in the planetary history, almost forty thousand years ago, when the Life Carriers on duty took note that, from a purely biologic standpoint, the developmental progress of the Urantia races was nearing its apex. The Melchizedek receivers, concurring in this opinion, readily agreed to join the Life Carriers in a petition to the Host Highs of Edentia asking that Urantia be inspected with a view to authorizing the dispatch of biologic uplifters, a Material Son and Daughter." (p. 821)

4. **Proposition.** As a result of Tabamantia's inspection, Adam and Eve arrived on this confused and isolated planet.

"Tabamantia, sovereign supervisor of the series of decimal or experimental worlds, came to inspect the planet and, after his survey of racial progress, duly recommended that Urantia be granted Material Sons. In a little less than one hundred years from the time of this inspection, Adam and Eve, a Material Son and Daughter of the local system, arrived and began the difficult task of attempting to untangle the confused affairs of a planet retarded by rebellion and resting under the ban of spiritual isolation." (p. 821)

5. **Proposition.** Van had long proclaimed the advent of a Son of God—a racial uplifter and a teacher of truth.

"For almost one hundred years prior to Tabamantia's inspection, Van and his associates, from their highland headquarters of world ethics and culture, had been preaching the advent of a promised Son of God, a racial uplifter, a teacher of truth, and the worthy successor of the traitorous Caligastia. Though the majority of the world's inhabitants of those days exhibited little or no interest in such a prediction, those who were in immediate contact with Van and Amadon took such teaching seriously and began to plan for the actual reception of the promised Son." (p. 822)

6. **Proposition.** Van and Amadon recruited three thousand volunteers to prepare a home for the expected Adam.

"From their highland headquarters and from sixty-one far-scattered settlements, Van and Amadon recruited a corps of over three thousand willing and enthusiastic workers who, in solemn assembly, dedicated themselves to this mission of preparing for the promised—at least expected—Son." (p. 822)

II. THE EDENIC REGIME

1. **PROPOSITION.** Adam was confronted with confusion, degeneracy, and isolation —he had no one to advise him.

    "The Adamic mission on experimental, rebellion-seared, and isolated Urantia was a formidable undertaking. And the Material Son and Daughter early became aware of the difficulty and complexity of their planetary assignment. Nevertheless, they courageously set about the task of solving their manifold problems. But when they addressed themselves to the all-important work of eliminating the defectives and degenerates from among the human strains, they were quite dismayed. They could see no way out of the dilemma, and they could not take counsel with their superiors on either Jerusem or Edentia. Have they were, isolated and day by day confronted with some new and complicated tangle, some problem that seemed to be unsolvable." (p. 839)

2. **PROPOSITION.** Adam came to set up representative government, but he had to content himself with the establishment of outlying trading posts.

    "Adam and Eve had come to institute representative government in the place of monarchial, but they found no government worthy of the name on the face of the whole earth. For the time being Adam abandoned all effort to establish representative government, and before the collapse of the Edenic regime he succeeded in establishing almost one hundred outlying trade and social centers where strong individuals ruled in his name. Most of these centers had been organized aforetime by Van and Amadon." (p. 834)

3. **PROPOSITION.** Secondary midwayers are indigenous to the Adamic missions.

    "The secondary midway creatures are indigenous to the Adamic missions. As with the corporeal staff of the Planetary Prince, the descendants of the Material Sons and Daughters are of two orders: their physical children and the secondary order of midway creatures. These material but ordinarily invisible planetary ministers contribute much to the advancement of civilization and even to the subjection of insubordinate minorities who may seek to subvert social development and spiritual progress." (p. 583)

Part XXVII — *Adam and Eve*

III. THE GARDEN OF EDEN

1. **Proposition.** From three selected sites for the Garden, the Mediterranean peninsula was chosen.

   > "The committee on location was absent for almost three years. It reported favorably concerning three possible locations: The first was an island in the Persian Gulf; the second, the river location subsequently occupied as the second garden; the third, a long narrow peninsula—almost an island—projecting westward from the eastern shores of the Mediterranean Sea.
   > "The committee almost unanimously favored the third selection. This site was chosen, and two years were occupied in transferring the world's cultural headquarters, including the tree of life, to this Mediterranean peninsula. All but a single group of the peninsula dwellers peaceably vacated when Van and his company arrived." (p. 823)

2. **Proposition.** The home of the biologic uplifters is called the Garden of Eden—suggestive of its floral beauty and botanic grandeur.

   > "When Material Sons, the biologic uplifters, begin their sojourn on an evolutionary world, their place of abode is often called the Garden of Eden because it is characterized by the floral beauty and the botanic grandeur of Edentia, the constellation capital. Van well knew of these customs and accordingly provided that the entire peninsula be given over to the Garden." (p. 823)

3. **Proposition.** The Garden provided land and homes for one million, with the Father's temple at the center.

   > "At the center of the Edenic peninsula was the exquisite stone temple of the Universal Father, the sacred shrine of the Garden. To the north the administrative headquarters was established; to the south were built the homes for the workers and their families; to the west was provided the allotment of ground for the proposed schools of the educational system of the expected Son, while in the 'east of Eden' were built the domiciles intended for the promised Son and his immediate offspring. The architectural plans for Eden provided homes and abundant land for one million human beings." (p. 824)

4. **Proposition.** Although not finished at the time of Adam's arrival, the Garden was a gem of botanic beauty.

   > "Although the work of embellishment was hardly finished at the time of Adam's arrival, the place was already a gem of botanic beauty; and during the early days of his sojourn in Eden

the whole Garden took on new form and assumed new proportions of beauty and grandeur. Never before this time nor after has Urantia harbored such a beautiful and replete exhibition of horticulture and agriculture." (p. 825)

5. **PROPOSITION.** On normal worlds, the Garden, jointly with the Prince's headquarters, becomes the center of world culture.

> "On normal worlds the garden headquarters of the violet race becomes the second center of world culture and, jointly with the headquarters city of the Planetary Prince, sets the pace for the development of civilization. For centuries the city headquarters schools of the Planetary Prince and the garden schools of Adam and Eve are contemporary. They are usually not very far apart, and they work together in harmonious co-operation." (p. 586)

6. **PROPOSITION.** Both public and private worship were encouraged and Adam vainly attempted to establish offerings of the fruit of the land in place of blood sacrifices.

> "The public worship hour of Eden was noon; sunset was the hour of family worship. Adam did his best to discourage the use of set prayers, teaching that effective prayer must be wholly individual, that it must be the 'desire of the soul'; but the Edenites continued to use the prayers and forms handed down from the times of Dalamatia. Adam also endeavored to substitute the offerings of the fruit of the land for the blood sacrifices in the religious ceremonies but had made little progress before the disruption of the Garden." (p. 836)

7. **PROPOSITION.** The laws of the Garden consisted of the seven commandments of Dalamatia.

> "The laws of the Garden were based on the older codes of Dalamatia and were promulgated under seven heads:
> 1. The laws of health and sanitation.
> 2. The social regulations of the Garden.
> 3. The code of trade and commerce.
> 4. The laws of fair play and competition.
> 5. The laws of home life.
> 6. The civil codes of the golden rule.
> 7. The seven commands of supreme moral rule." (p. 836)

8. **Proposition.** Adam attempted to teach the races sex equality.

> "Adam endeavored to teach the races sex equality. The way Eve worked by the side of her husband made a profound impression upon all dwellers in the Garden. Adam definitely taught them that the woman, equally with the man, contributes those life factors which unite to form a new being. Theretofore, mankind had presumed that all procreation resided in the 'loins of the father.' They had looked upon the mother as being merely a provision for nurturing the unborn and nursing the newborn." (p. 836)

9. **Proposition.** The "golden age" is a myth, but Eden was a fact.

> "The 'golden age' is a myth, but Eden was a fact, and the Garden civilization was actually overthrown. Adam and Eve carried on in the Garden for one hundred and seventeen years when, through the impatience of Eve and the errors of judgment of Adam, they presumed to turn aside from the ordained way, speedily bringing disaster upon themselves and ruinous retardation upon the developmental progression of all Urantia." (p. 838)

IV. THE TREE OF LIFE

1. **Proposition.** The "tree of the knowledge of good and evil" may be a figure of speech, but the "tree of life," sent from Edentia, was real.

> "The 'tree of the knowledge of good and evil' may be a figure of speech, a symbolic designation covering a multitude of human experiences, but the 'tree of life' was not a myth; it was real and for a long time was present on Urantia. When the Most Highs of Edentia approved the commission of Caligastia as Planetary Prince of Urantia and those of the one hundred Jerusem citizens as his administrative staff, they sent to the planet, by the Melchizedeks, a shrub of Edentia, and this plant grew to be the tree of life on Urantia. This form of nonintelligent life is native to the constellation headquarters spheres, being also found on the headquarters worlds of the local and superuniverses as well as on the Havona spheres, but not on the system capitals." (p. 825)

2. **Proposition.** After the rebellion, the tree of life was taken by Van to his headquarters, and it served him and Amadon for one hundred and fifty thousand years.

> "During the days of the Prince's rule the tree was growing from the earth in the central and circular courtyard of the Father's temple. Upon the outbreak of the rebellion it was regrown from the central core by Van and his associates in their

temporary camp. This Edentia shrub was subsequently taken to their highland retreat, where it served both Van and Amadon for more than one hundred and fifty thousand years." (p. 826)

3. **Proposition.** After making ready the Garden for Adam and Eve, Van transplanted the tree of life to the courtyard of the Father's temple.

"When Van and his associates made ready the Garden for Adam and Eve, they transplanted the Edentia tree to the Garden of Eden, where, once again, it grew in a central, circular courtyard of another temple to the Father. And Adam and Eve periodically partook of its fruit for the maintenance of their dual form of physical life." (p. 826)

V. ARRIVAL OF ADAM AND EVE

1. **Proposition.** Adam and Eve arrived on Urantia, from A. D. 1934, 37,848 years ago. Ten days were required for rematerialization.

"Adam and Eve arrived on Urantia, from the year A. D. 1934, 37,848 years ago. It was in midseason when the Garden was in the height of bloom that they arrived. At high noon and unannounced, the two seraphic transports, accompanied by the Jerusem personnel intrusted with the transportation of the biologic uplifters to Urantia, settled slowly to the surface of the revolving planet in the vicinity of the temple of the Universal Father. All the work of rematerializing the bodies of Adam and Eve was carried on within the precincts of this newly created shrine. And from the time of their arrival ten days passed before they were re-created in dual human form for presentation as the world's new rulers. They regained consciousness simultaneously. The Material Sons And Daughters always serve together. It is the essence of their service at all times and in all places never to be separated. They are designed to work in pairs; seldom do they function alone." (p. 828)

2. **Proposition.** Adam and Eve, jointly number 14,311, were members of the senior corps of Material Sons on Jerusem.

"The Planetary Adam and Eve of Urantia were members of the senior corps of Material Sons on Jerusem, being jointly number 14,311. They belonged to the third physical series and were a little more than eight feet in height." (p. 828)

Part XXVII — Adam and Eve

3. **Proposition.** Rematerialization restored Adam and Eve to their Jerusem status.

   "Upon arrival at their planetary destination the Material Son and Daughter are rematerialized under the direction of the Life Carriers. This entire process takes ten to twenty-eight days of Urantia time. The unconsciousness of the seraphic slumber continues throughout this entire period of reconstruction. When the reassembly of the physical organism is completed, these Material Sons and Daughters stand in their new homes and on their new worlds to all intents and purposes just as they were before submitting to the dematerializing process on Jerusem." (p. 582)

4. **Proposition.** The bodies of Adam and Eve gave forth a shimmering light— the origin of the traditional halo encircling the hoods of holy men.

   "The bodies of Adam and Eve gave forth a shimmer of light, but they always wore clothing in conformity with the custom of their associates. Though wearing very little during the day, at eventide they donned night wraps. The origin of the traditional halo encircling the heads of supposed pious and holy men dates back to the days of Adam and Eve. Since the light emanations of their bodies were so largely obscured by clothing, only the radiating glow from their heads was discernible. The descendants of Adamson always thus portrayed their concept of individuals believed to be extraordinary in spiritual development." (p. 834)

5. **Proposition.** When Adam and Eve awakened on Urantia, they were welcomed by Van and Amadon.

   "Adam and Eve fell asleep on Jerusem, and when they awakened in the Father's temple on Urantia in the presence of the mighty throng assembled to welcome them, they were face to face with two beings of whom they had heard much, Van and his faithful associate Amadon. These two heroes of the Caligastia secession were the first to welcome them in their new garden home." (p. 829)

6. **Proposition.** The runners hastened to the carrier pigeons' rendezvous, shouting: "Let loose the birds...the promised Son has come."

   "And on that day there was great excitement and joy throughout Eden as the runners went in great haste to the rendezvous of the carrier pigeons assembled from near and far, shouting: 'Let loose the birds; let them carry the word that the promised Son has come.' Hundreds of believer settlements had faithfully, year after year, kept up the supply of these home-reared pigeons for just such an occasion." (p. 829)

7. **PROPOSITION.** After the Melchizedek charge, Van proclaimed Adam and Eve rulers of Urantia. They took oaths of allegiance to the Most Highs and to Michael of Nebadon.

> "The next act was the delivery of the charge of planetary custody to Adam and Eve by the senior Melchizedek, chief of the council of receivership on Urantia. The Material Son and Daughter took the oath of allegiance to the Most Highs of Norlatiadek and to Michael of Nebadon and were proclaimed rulers of Urantia by Van, who thereby relinquished the titular authority which for over one hundred and fifty thousand years he had held by virtue of the action of the Melchizedek receivers." (p. 830)

8. **PROPOSITION.** Gabriel proclaimed the second judgment roll call and the resurrection of the sleeping survivors of the second dispensation on Urantia.

> "Then was heard the archangels' proclamation, and the broadcast voice of Gabriel decreed the second judgment roll call of Urantia and the resurrection of the sleeping survivors of the second dispensation of grace and mercy on 606 of Satania. The dispensation of the Prince has passed, the age of Adam, the third planetary epoch, opens amidst scenes of simple grandeur; and the new rulers of Urantia start their reign under seemingly favorable conditions, notwithstanding the world-wide confusion occasioned by lack of the co-operation of their predecessor in authority on the planet." (p. 830)

9. **PROPOSITION.** The heads of the Edenites were turned; over Van's protest, they wanted to bring Adam and Eve to the temple that they might worship them.

> "The amazing events of the first six days of Adam and Eve on earth were entirely too much for the unprepared minds of even the world's best men; their heads were in a whirl; they were swept along with the proposal to bring the noble pair up to the Father's temple at high noon in order that everyone might bow down in respectful worship and prostrate themselves in humble submission. And the Garden dwellers were really sincere in all of this.
> "Van protested. Amadon was absent, being in charge of the guard of honor which had remained behind with Adam and Eve overnight. But Van's protest was swept aside. He was told that he

Part XXVII — *Adam and Eve*

was likewise too modest, too unassuming; that he was not far from a god himself, else how had he lived so long on earth, and how had he brought about such a great event as the advent of Adam? And as the excited Edenites were about to seize him and carry him up to the mount for adoration, Van made his way out through the throng and, being able to communicate with the midwayers, sent their leader in great haste to Adam." (p. 832)

10. **Proposition.** Transported by midwayers, Adam and Eve appeared on the inaugural mount and, after solemn discourse, explained that they would accept all respect, but worship never.

"It was near the dawn of their seventh day on earth that Adam and Eve heard the startling news of the proposal of these well-meaning but misguided mortals; and then, even while the passenger birds were swiftly winging to bring them to the temple, the midwayers, being able to do such things, transported Adam and Eve to the Father's temple. It was early on the morning of this seventh day and from the mount of their so recent reception that Adam held forth in explanation of the orders of divine sonship and made clear to these earth minds that only the Father and those whom he designates may be worshiped. Adam made it plain that he would accept any honor and receive all respect, but worship never!" (p. 832)

11. **Proposition.** And this was the origin of the Sabbath-day tradition.

"And this was the origin of the Sabbath-day tradition. Always in Eden the seventh day was devoted to the noontide assembly at the temple; long it was the custom to devote this day to self-culture. The forenoon was devoted to physical improvement, the noontime to spiritual worship, the afternoon to mind culture, while the evening was spent in social rejoicing. This was never the law in Eden, but it was the custom as long as the Adamic administration held sway on earth." (p. 832)

12. **Proposition.** On normal worlds, the arrival of Adam would herald an age of invention, progress, and intellectual enlightenment.

"On a normal planet the arrival of the Material Son would ordinarily herald the approach of a great age of invention, material progress, and intellectual enlightenment. The post-Adamic era is the great scientific age of most worlds, but not so on Urantia. Though the planet was peopled by races physically fit, the tribes languished in the depths of savagery and moral stagnation." (p. 821)

VI. TEMPTATION OF EVE

1. **PROPOSITION.** Caligastia frequently visited Eden but was unable to seduce Adam and Eve by direct appeal. He was still titular Planetary Prince—not being deposed until the times of Michael on Urantia.

   > "Caligastia paid frequent visits to the Garden and held many conferences with Adam and Eve, but they were adamant to all his suggestions of compromise and short-cut adventures. They had before them enough of the results of rebellion to produce effective immunity against all such insinuating proposals. Even the young offspring of Adam were uninfluenced by the overtures of Daligastia. And of course neither Caligastia nor his associate had power to influence any individual against his will, much less to persuade the children of Adam to do wrong.
   >
   > "It must be remembered that Caligastia was still the titular Planetary Prince of Urantia, a misguided but nevertheless high Son of the local universe. He was not finally deposed until the times of Christ Michael on Urantia." (p. 840)

2. **PROPOSITION.** After Adam's first one hundred years, Serapatatia became head of the Syrian Nodites. He was from Dalamatia and blue race ancestors.

   > "Adam had just finished his first one hundred years on earth when Serapatatia, upon the death of his father, came to the leadership of the western or Syrian confederation of the Nodite tribes. Serapatatia was a brown-tinted man, a brilliant descendant of the one time chief of the Dalamatia commission on health mated with one of the master female minds of the blue race of those distant days. All down through the ages this line had held authority and wielded a great influence among the western Nodite tribes." (p. 841)

3. **PROPOSITION.** Serapatatia became chairman of the Edenic commission on tribal relations and proposed to Eve plans for immediate racial advancement.

   > "Presently, Serapatatia became the associate chairman of the Edenic commission on tribal relations, and many plans were laid for the more vigorous prosecution of the work of winning the remote tribes to the cause of the Garden.
   >
   > "He held many conferences with Adam and Eve—especially with Eve— and they talked over many plans for improving their

Part XXVII — Adam and Eve

methods. One day, during a talk with Eve, it occurred to Serapatatia that it would be very helpful if, while awaiting the recruiting of large numbers of the violet race, something could be done in the meantime immediately to advance the needy waiting tribes." (p. 841)

4. **Proposition.** Serapatatia was honest—wholly sincere. He had no intention of playing into the hands of Caligastia.

    "It should again be emphasized that Serapatatia was altogether honest and wholly sincere in all that he proposed. He never once suspected that he was playing into the hands of Caligastia and Daligastia." (p. 841)

5. **Proposition.** Eve had no intention of wrongdoing in connection with her increasingly confidential visits with Serapatatia.

    "It was farthest from Eve's intention ever to do anything which would militate against Adam's plans or jeopardize their planetary trust. Knowing the tendency of woman to look upon immediate results rather than to plan farsightedly for more remote effects, the Melchizedeks, before departing, had especially enjoined Eve as to the peculiar dangers besetting their isolated position on the planet and had in particular warned her never to stray from the side of her mate, that is, to attempt no personal or secret methods of furthering their mutual undertakings. Eve had most scrupulously carried out these instructions for more than one hundred years, and it did not occur to her that any danger would attach to the increasingly private and confidential visits she was enjoying with a certain Nodite leader named Serapatatia. The whole affair developed so gradually and naturally that she was taken unawares." (p. 840)

6. **Proposition.** Cano was a leader of friendly Nodites. Eve consented to a secret conference with him, at the suggestion of Serapatatia.

    "For more than five years these plans were secretly matured. At last they had developed to the point where Eve consented to have a secret conference with Cano, the most brilliant mind and active leader of the near-by colony of friendly Nodites. Cano was very sympathetic with the Adamic regime; in fact, he was the sincere spiritual leader of those neighboring Nodites who favored friendly relations with the Garden." (p. 841)

7. **Proposition.** The fateful meeting occurred at twilight of an autumn evening, near the home of Adam. Cano thoroughly believed in the Serapatatia project.

> "The fateful meeting occurred during the twilight hours of the autumn evening, not far from the home of Adam. Eve had never before met the beautiful and enthusiastic Cano—and he was a magnificent specimen of the survival of the superior physique and outstanding intellect of his remote progenitors of the Princess staff. And Cano also thoroughly believed in the righteousness of the Serapatatia project. (Outside of the Garden, multiple mating was a common practice.)" (p. 842)

8. **Proposition.** By flattery and personal persuasion, Eve was unthinkingly led to take the fatal step.

> "Influenced by flattery, enthusiasm, and great personal persuasion, Eve then and there consented to embark upon the much-discussed enterprise, to add her own little scheme of world saving to the larger and more far-reaching divine plan. Before she quite realized what was transpiring, the fatal step had been taken. It was done." (p. 842)

9. **Proposition.** Eve had consented to participate in the practice of good and evil.

> "Eve had consented to participate in the practice of good and evil. Good is the carrying out of the divine plans; sin is a deliberate transgression of the divine will; evil is the misadaptation of plans and the maladjustment of techniques resulting in universe disharmony and planetary confusion." (p. 842)

10. **Proposition.** The celestial life on the planet was astir. Adam now learned of the Serapatatia plan for accelerating world improvement.

> "The celestial life on the planet was astir. Adam recognized that something was wrong, and he asked Eve to come aside with him in the Garden. And now, for the first time, Adam heard the entire story of the long-nourished plan for accelerating world improvement by operating simultaneously in two directions: the prosecution of the divine plan concomitantly with the execution of the Serapatatia enterprise." (p. 842)

11. **Proposition.** As Adam and Eve communed in the moonlit Garden, they were informed that they had transgressed the Garden covenant and defaulted in a sacred trust.

> "And as the Material Son and Daughter thus communed in the moonlit Garden, 'the voice in the Garden' reproved them for disobedience. And that voice was none other than my own announcement to the Edenic pair that they had transgressed the Garden covenant; that they had disobeyed the instructions of the Melchizedeks; that they had defaulted in the execution of their oaths of trust to the sovereign of the universe." (p. 842)

VII. REALIZATION OF DEFAULT

1. **Proposition.** It was Solonia, the seraphim, who called to Adam and Eve in the Garden, asking "Where are you?"

> I talked to the father and mother of the violet race that night in the Garden as became my duty under the sorrowful circumstances. I listened fully to the recital of all that led up to the default of Mother Eve and gave both of them advice and counsel concerning the immediate situation. Some of this advice they followed; some they disregarded. This conference appears in your records as 'the Lord God calling to Adam and Eve in the Garden and asking, "Where are you?"' It was the practice of later generations to attribute everything unusual and extraordinary, whether natural or spiritual, directly to the personal intervention of the Gods." (p. 843)

2. **Proposition.** Eve's disillusionment was pathetic. but brokenhearted Adam was truly sympathetic with his erring mate.

> "Eve's disillusionment was truly pathetic, Adam discerned the whole predicament and, while heartbroken and dejected, entertained only pity and sympathy for his erring mate." (p. 843)

3. **Proposition.** In fear that he might be separated from his mate, Adam sought out Laotta and deliberately committed the folly of Eve.

> "It was in the despair of the realization of failure that Adam, the day after Eve's misstep, sought out Laotta, the brilliant Nodite woman who was head of the western schools of the Garden, and with premeditation committed the folly of Eve. But do not misunderstand; Adam was not beguiled; he knew exactly what he was about; he deliberately chose to share the fate of Eve. He loved his mate with a supermortal affection, and the thought of the possibility of a lonely vigil on Urantia without her was more than he could endure." (p. 843)

4. **PROPOSITION.** After thirty days of wandering, Adam returned home and began planning for the future.

   "The children of Adam sought to comfort their distracted mother while their father wandered in solitude for thirty days. At the end of that time judgment asserted itself, and Adam returned to his home and began to plan for their future course of action." (p. 843)

5. **PROPOSITION.** Seventy days after the default, the Melchizedek receivers returned to Urantia and Adam and Eve knew they had failed.

   "Time passed, but Adam was not certain of the nature of their offense until seventy days after the default of Eve, when the Melchizedek receivers returned to Urantia and assumed jurisdiction over world affairs. And then he knew they had failed." (p. 844)

6. **PROPOSITION.** Never will you gain anything by attempting to circumvent the divine plan by short cuts or other human devices.

   "Never, in all your ascent to Paradise, will you gain anything by impatiently attempting to circumvent the established and divine plan by short cuts, personal inventions, or other devices for improving on the way of perfection, to perfection, and for eternal perfection." (p. 846)

VIII. LEAVING THE GARDEN

1. **PROPOSITION.** Adam and twelve hundred loyal followers went forth from the Garden in quest of a new home.

   "Adam knew that he and Eve had failed; the presence of the Melchizedek receivers told him that, though he still knew nothing of their personal status or future fate. He held an all-night conference with some twelve hundred loyal followers who pledged themselves to follow their leader, and the next day at noon these pilgrims went forth from Eden in quest of new homes. Adam had no liking for war and accordingly elected to leave the first garden to the Nodites unopposed." (p. 844)

2. **PROPOSITION.** All of Adam's younger children and two thirds of the older were taken to Edentia as wards of the Most Highs.

   "The Edenic caravan was halted on the third day out from the Garden by the arrival of the seraphic transports from Jerusem. And for the first time Adam and Eve were informed of what was to become of their children. While the transports stood by, those children who had arrived at the age of choice (twenty years) were given the option of remaining on Urantia with their parents or of becoming wards of the Most Highs on Norlatiadek. Two thirds chose to go to Edentia; about one third elected to remain with their parents. All children of prechoice age were taken to Edentia. No one could have beheld the sorrowful parting of this Material Son and Daughter and their children without realizing that the way of the transgressor is hard. These offspring of Adam and Eve are now on Edentia; we do not know what disposition is to be made of them." (p. 844)

3. PROPOSITION. Gabriel informed Adam and Eve that they were "adjudged in default," that they had "violated the covenant of their trusteeship." They were cheered to learn that they had not been guilty of rebellion.

> "It was while the Edenic caravan was halted that Adam and Eve were informed of the nature of their transgressions and advised concerning their fate. Gabriel appeared to pronounce judgment. And this was the verdict: The Planetary Adam and Eve of Urantia are adjudged in default; they have violated the covenant of their trusteeship as the rulers of this inhabited world.
> "While downcast by the sense of guilt, Adam and Eve were greatly cheered by the announcement that their judges on Salvington had absolved them from all charges of standing in 'contempt of the universe government.' They had not been held guilty of rebellion." (p. 845)

4. PROPOSITION. The Edenic pair learned that they had degraded themselves to the status of mortals of the realm.

> "The Edenic pair were informed that they had degraded themselves to the status of the mortals of the realm; that they must henceforth conduct themselves as man and woman of Urantia, looking to the future of the world races for their future." (p. 845)

5. PROPOSITION. Adam and Eve did fall from their high estate to mortal status, but that was not the fall of man.

> "Adam and Eve did fall from their high estate of material sonship down to the lowly status of mortal man. But that was not the fall of man. The human race has been uplifted despite the immediate consequences of the Adamic default. Although the divine plan of giving the violet race to the Urantia peoples miscarried, the mortal races have profited enormously from the limited contribution which Adam and his descendants made to the Urantia races." (p. 845)

6. **Proposition.** The vacated Garden was later occupied by the northern Nodites for four thousand years, when it sank beneath the waters.

> "After the first garden was vacated by Adam, it was occupied variously by the Nodites, Cutites, and the Suntites. It later became the dwelling place of the northern Nodites who opposed cooperation with the Adamites. The peninsula had been overrun by these lower-grade Nodites for almost four thousand years after Adam left the Garden when, in connection with the violent activity of the surrounding volcanoes and the submergence of the Sicilian land bridge to Africa, the eastern floor of the Mediterranean Sea sank, carrying down beneath the waters the whole of the Edenic peninsula. Concomitant with this vast submergence the coast line of the eastern Mediterranean was greatly elevated." (p. 826)

IX. THE SECOND GARDEN

1. **Proposition.** Hearing that Adam approached, the dwellers in the second garden fled in haste. Adam found it vacated.

> "When word had reached the dwellers in the land of the second garden that the king and high priest of the Garden of Eden was marching on them, they had fled in haste to the eastern mountains. Adam found all of the desired territory vacated when he arrived. And here in this new location Adam and his helpers set themselves to work to build new homes and establish a new center of culture and religion." (p. 847)

2. **Proposition.** With the aid of a defense wall to the north, the two rivers formed a good natural defense.

> "This site was known to Adam as one of the three original selections of the committee assigned to choose possible locations for the Garden proposed by Van and Amadon. The two rivers themselves were a good natural defense in those days, and a short way north of the second garden the Euphrates and Tigris came close together so that a defense wall extending fifty-six miles could be built for the protection of the territory to the south and between the rivers." (p. 847)

3. **Proposition.** The Melchizedeks informed Adam and Eve that their repentance was acceptable and that they would be admitted to the ranks of sleeping survivors.

> "Not long after the establishment of the second Eden, Adam and Eve were duly informed that their repentance was acceptable, and that, while they were doomed to suffer the fate of the

mortals of their world, they should certainly become eligible for admission to the ranks of the sleeping survivors of Urantia. They fully believed this gospel of resurrection and rehabilitation which the Melchizedeks so touchingly proclaimed to them. Their transgression had been an error of judgment and not the sin of conscious and deliberate rebellion." (p. 851)

X. CAIN AND ABEL

1. **Proposition.** Cain and Sansa were born en route to the second garden. Laotta died. Eve adopted Sansa.

    "Cain and Sansa were both born before the Adamic caravan had reached its destination between the rivers in Mesopotamia. Laotta, the mother of Sansa, perished at the birth of her daughter; Eve suffered much but survived, owing to superior strength. Eve took Sansa, the child of Laotta, to her bosom, and she was reared along with Cain. Sansa grew up to be a woman of great ability. She became the wife of Sargan, the chief of the northern blue races, and contributed to the advancement of the blue men of those times." (p. 847)

2. **Proposition.** Abel was born two years after Cain. Abel became a herder—Cain a farmer.

    "Less than two years after Cain's birth, Abel was born, the first child of Adam and Eve to be born in the second garden. When Abel grew up to the age of twelve years, he elected to be a herder; Cain had chosen to follow agriculture." (p. 848)

3. **Proposition.** Abel made animal offerings, Cain the fruits of the field. Abel's offerings were more favored, and therewith he taunted Cain.

    "Now, in those days it was customary to make offerings to the priesthood of the things at hand. Herders would bring of their flocks, farmers of the fruits of the fields; and in accordance with this custom, Cain and Abel likewise made periodic offerings to the priests. The two boys had many times argued about the relative merits of their vocations, and Abel was not slow to note that preference was shown for his animal sacrifices. In vain did Cain appeal to the traditions of the first Eden, to the former preference for the fruits of the field. But this Abel would not allow, and he taunted his older brother in his discomfiture." (p. 848)

4. **PROPOSITION.** Abel never failed to remind Cain that Adam was not his father. Cain nourished an increasing hatred for his brother.

> "The two boys never got along well, and this matter of sacrifices further contributed to the growing hatred between them. Abel knew he was the son of both Adam and Eve and never failed to impress upon Cain that Adam was not his father. Cain was not pure violet as his father was of the Nodite race later admixed with the blue and the red man and with the aboriginal Andonic stock. And all of this, with Cain's natural bellicose inheritance, caused him to nourish an ever-increasing hatred for his younger brother." (p. 848)

5. **PROPOSITION.** At ages eighteen and twenty, Abel's taunts so infuriated Cain that he killed his brother.

> "The boys were respectively eighteen and twenty years of age when the tension between them was finally resolved, one day, when Abel's taunts so infuriated his bellicose brother that Cain turned upon him in wrath and slew him." (p. 848)

6. **PROPOSITION.** Cain fled to the land of Nod and married Remona. He became a Nodite leader and lived peaceably with the Adamites.

> "And so Cain departed for the land of Nod, east of the second Eden. He became a great leader among one group of his father's people and did, to a certain degree, fulfill the predictions of Serapatatia, for he did promote peace between this division of the Nodites and the Adamites throughout his lifetime. Cain married Remona, his distant cousin, and their first son, Enoch, became the head of the Elamite Nodites. And for hundreds of years the Elamites and the Adamites continued to be at peace." (p. 849)

XI. THE VIOLET RACE

1. **PROPOSITION.** Adam and Eve were founders of the violet peoples—the ninth human race. Neither Eve nor the unmixed evolutionary races suffered pain in childbirth.

> "Adam and Eve were the founders of the violet race of men, the ninth human race to appear on Urantia. Adam and his offspring had blue eyes, and the violet peoples were characterized by fair complexions and light hair color—yellow, red, and brown.
> "Eve did not suffer pain in childbirth; neither did the early evolutionary races. Only the mixed races produced by the union of evolutionary man with the Nodites and later with the Adamites suffered the severe pangs of childbirth." (p. 850)

Part XXVII — *Adam and Eve*

2. **Proposition.** Adam's progeny were far more resistant to disease than the Urantia races.

> "The body cells of the Material Sons and their progeny are far more resistant to disease than are those of the evolutionary beings indigenous to the planet. The body cells of the native races are akin to the living disease-producing microscopic and ultramicroscopic organisms of the realm. These facts explain why the Urantia peoples must do so much by way of scientific effort to withstand so many physical disorders. You would be far more disease resistant if your races carried more of the Adamic life." (p. 851)

3. **Proposition.** Adamson, Adam's first son, founded a center of the violet race north of the second garden. The second son, Eveson, became a masterly leader and administrator.

> "The civil rulers of the Adamites were derived hereditarily from the sons of the first garden. Adam's first son, Adamson (Adam ben Adam), founded a secondary center of the violet race to the north of the second Eden. Adam's second son, Eveson, became a masterly leader and administrator; he was the great helper of his father. Eveson lived not quite so long as Adam, and his eldest son, Jansad, became the successor of Adam as the head of the Adamite tribes." (p. 849)

4. **Proposition.** The Adamites excelled in culture—art, literature, and manufacture. They produced the third alphabet and improved architecture.

> "The Adamites greatly excelled the surrounding peoples in cultural achievement and intellectual development. They produced the third alphabet and otherwise laid the foundations for much that was the forerunner of modern art, science, and literature. Here in the lands between the Tigris and Euphrates they maintained the arts of writing, metalworking, pottery making, and weaving and produced a type of architecture that was not excelled in thousands of years." (p. 850)

5. **Proposition.** Adam elected to leave on Urantia as much of his life plasm as possible. The highest type of evolutionary women bore 1,570 superior children, who founded the mighty Andite race.

> "After becoming established in the second garden on the Euphrates, Adam elected to leave behind as much of his life plasm as possible to benefit the world after his death. Accordingly, Eve was made the head of a commission of twelve on race

improvement, and before Adam died this commission had selected 1,682 of the highest type of women on Urantia, and these women were impregnated with the Adamic life plasm. Their children all grew up to maturity except 112, so that the world, in this way, was benefited by the addition of 1,570 superior men and women. Though these candidate mothers were selected from all the surrounding tribes and represented most of the races on earth, the majority were chosen from the highest strains of the Nodites, and they constituted the early beginnings of the mighty Andite race. These children were born and reared in the tribal surroundings of their respective mothers." (p. 851)

XII. DEATH OF ADAM AND EVE

1. **Proposition.** Adam and Eve died natural deaths and were buried in the temple.

   "Adam lived for 530 years; he died of what might be termed old age. His physical mechanism simply wore out; the process of disintegration gradually gained on the process of repair, and the inevitable end came. Eve had died nineteen years previously of a weakened heart. They were both buried in the center of the temple of divine service which had been built in accordance with their plans soon after the wall of the colony had been completed. And this was the origin of the practice of burying noted and pious men and women under the floors of the places of worship." (p. 852)

XIII. SURVIVAL OF ADAM AND EVE

1. **Proposition.** Adam anticipated a dispensational resurrection, but Michael's promise implied that it might be sooner.

   "Adam knew about the dispensational resurrection which occurred simultaneously with his arrival on the planet, and he believed that he and his companion would probably be repersonalized in connection with the advent of the next order of sonship. He did not know that Michael, the sovereign of this universe, was so soon to appear on Urantia; he expected that the next Son to arrive would be of the Avonal order. Even so, it was always a comfort to Adam and Eve, as well as something difficult for them to understand, to ponder the only personal message they ever received from Michael. This message, among other expressions of friendship and comfort, said: 'I have given

Part XXVII — Adam and Eve

consideration to the circumstances of your default, I have remembered the desire of your hearts ever to be loyal to my Father's will, and you will be called from the embrace of mortal slumber when I come to Urantia if the subordinate Sons of my realm do not send for you before that tine.'" (p. 852)

2. **Proposition.** Adam and Eve had strong faith in the Melchizedek promises of survival.

   "Adam and Eve went to their mortal rest with strong faith in the promises made to them by the Melchizedeks that they would sometime awake from the sleep of death to resume life on the mansion worlds, worlds all so familiar to them in the days preceding their mission in the material flesh of the violet race on Urantia." (p. 853)

3. **Proposition.** On the third day after death, Adam and Eve repersonalized with 1,316 of their associates, in the special resurrection number twenty-six.

   "They did not long rest in the oblivion of the unconscious sleep of the mortals of the realm. On the third day after Adam's death, the second following his reverent burial, the orders of Lanaforge, sustained by the acting Most High of Edentia and concurred in by the Union of Days on Salvington, acting for Michael, were placed in Gabriel's hands, directing the special roll call of the distinguished survivors of the Adamic default on Urantia. And in accordance with this mandate of special resurrection, number twenty-six of the Urantia series, Adam and Eve were repersonalized and reassembled in the resurrection halls of the mansion worlds of Satania together with 1,316 of their associates in the experience of the first garden. Many other loyal souls had already been translated at the time of Adam's arrival, which was attended by a dispensational adjudication of both the sleeping survivors and of the living qualified ascenders." (p. 853)

4. **Proposition.** Thus ends the planetary story of Adam and Eve—a story of trial, tragedy, and triumph.

   "And thus ends the story of the Planetary Adam and Eve of Urantia, a story of trial, tragedy, and triumph, at least personal triumph for your well-meaning but deluded Material Son and Daughter and undoubtedly, in the end, a story of ultimate triumph for their world and its rebellion-tossed and evil-harassed inhabitants." (p. 854)

5. **Proposition.** Adam and Eve accelerated biologic progress, but their superb culture was soon submerged. It is the people who make a civilization; civilization does not make the people.

> "When all is summed up, Adam and Eve made a mighty contribution to the speedy civilization and accelerated biologic progress of the human race. They left a great culture on earth, but it was not possible for such an advanced civilization to survive in the face of the early dilution and the eventual submergence of the Adamic inheritance. It is the people who make a civilization; civilization does not make the people." (p. 854)

PART XXVIII
MACHIVENTA MELCHIZEDEK

Part Twenty-Eight
MACHIVENTA MELCHIZEDEK

I. INTRODUCTION

1. **Proposition.** Three times a corps of Melchizedeks has functioned on Urantia.

   "The Melchizedek order of universe sonship has been exceedingly active on Urantia. A corps of twelve served in conjunction with the Life Carriers. A later corps of twelve became receivers for your world shortly after the Caligastia secession and continued in authority until the time of Adam and Eve. These twelve Melchizedeks returned to Urantia upon the default of Adam and Eve, and they continued thereafter as planetary receivers on down to the day when Jesus of Nazareth, as the Son of Man, became the titular Planetary Prince of Urantia." (p. 1014)

2. **Proposition.** Less than a thousand years ago, Machiventa Melchizedek was governor general of Urantia.

   "Less than a thousand years ago this same Machiventa Melchizedek, the onetime sage of Salem, was invisibly present on Urantia for a period of one hundred years, acting as resident governor general of the planet; and if the present system of directing planetary affairs should continue, he will be due to return in the same capacity in a little over one thousand years." (p. 1025)

II. THE MACHIVENTA INCARNATION

1. **Proposition.** The Melchizedek receivers appealed to the universe authorities for help, but none was forthcoming.

   "The twelve Melchizedek receivers knew of Michael's impending bestowal on their planet, but they did not know how soon it would occur; therefore they convened in solemn council and petitioned the Most Highs of Edentia that some provision be made for maintaining the light of truth on Urantia. This plea was dismissed with the mandate that 'the conduct of affairs on 606 of Satania is fully in the hands of the Melchizedek custodians.' The receivers then appealed to the Father Melchizedek for help but only received word that they should continue to uphold truth in the manner of their own election 'until the arrival of a bestowal Son,' who 'would rescue the planetary titles from forfeiture and uncertainty.'" (p. 1014)

2. **Proposition.** Failing to get help, Machiventa Melchizedek volunteered to bestow himself as an incarnated emergency Son.

> "And it was in consequence of having been thrown so completely on their own resources that Machiventa Melchizedek, one of the twelve planetary receivers, volunteered to do that which had been done only six times in all the history of Nebadon: to personalize on earth as a temporary man of the realm, to bestow himself as an emergency Son of world ministry. Permission was granted for this adventure by the Salvington authorities, and the actual incarnation of Machiventa Melchizedek was consummated near what was to become the city of Salem, in Palestine. The entire transaction of the materialization of this Melchizedek Son was completed by the planetary receivers with the co-operation of the Life Carriers, certain of the Master Physical Controllers, and other celestial personalities resident on Urantia." (p. 1014)

3. **Proposition.** 1,973 years before the birth of Jesus, Machiventa appeared at the tent of Amdon, saying: "I am Melchizedek, priest of El Elyon, the Most High..."

> "It was 1,973 years before the birth of Jesus that Machiventa was bestowed upon the human races of Urantia. His coming was unspectacular; his materialization was not witnessed by human eyes. He was first observed by mortal man on that eventful day when he entered the tent of Amdon, a Chaldean herder of Sumerian extraction. And the proclamation of his mission was embodied in the simple statement which he made to this shepherd, 'I am Melchizedek, priest of El Elyon, the Most High, the one and only God.'" (p. 1015)

4. **Proposition.** Machiventa spoke several languages, and wore a breastplate of three concentric circles.

> "In personal appearance, Melchizedek resembled the then blended Nodite and Sumerian peoples, being almost six feet in height and possessing a commanding presence. He spoke Chaldean and a half dozen other languages. He dressed much as did the Canaanite priests except that on his breast he wore an emblem of three concentric circles, the Satania symbol of the Paradise Trinity. In the course of his ministry this insignia of three concentric circles became regarded as so sacred by his followers that they never dared to use it, and it was soon forgotten with the passing of a few generations." (p. 1015)

5. **Proposition.** Machiventa had a special body. He never married.

> "Though Machiventa lived after the manner of the men of the realm, he never married, nor could he have left offspring on earth. His physical body, while resembling that of the human male, was in reality on the order of those especially constructed bodies used by the one hundred materialized members of Prince Caligastia's staff except that it did not carry the life plasm of any human race. Nor was there available on Urantia the tree of life. Had Machiventa remained for any long period on earth, his physical mechanism would have gradually deteriorated; as it was, he terminated his bestowal mission in ninety-four years long before his material body had begun to disintegrate." (p. 1015)

6. **Proposition.** Machiventa received a Thought Adjuster—the one who subsequently indwelt Jesus.

> "This incarnated Melchizedek received a Thought Adjuster, who indwelt his superhuman personality as the monitor of time and the mentor of the flesh, thus gaining that experience and practical introduction to Urantian problems and to the technique of indwelling an incarnated Son which enabled this spirit of the Father to function so valiantly in the human mind of the later Son of God, Michael, when he appeared on earth in the likeness of mortal flesh. And this is the only Thought Adjuster who ever functioned in two minds on Urantia, but both minds were divine as well as human." (p. 1016)

III. MELCHIZEDEK'S TEACHINGS

1. **Proposition.** The three symbolic circles representing the Trinity were little understood by Machiventa's associates.

> "The symbol of the three concentric circles, which Melchizedek adopted as the insignia of his bestowal, a majority of the people interpreted as standing for the three kingdoms of men, angels, and God. And they were allowed to continue in that belief; very few of his followers ever knew that these three circles were emblematic of the infinity, eternity, and universality of the Paradise Trinity of divine maintenance and direction; even Abraham rather regarded this symbol as standing for the three Most Highs of Edentia, as he had been instructed that the three Most Highs functioned as one. To the extent that Melchizedek taught the Trinity concept symbolized in his insignia, he usually associated it with the three Vorondadek rulers of the constellation of Norlatiadek." (p. 1016)

2. **Proposition.** Machiventa taught that God accepted man on terms of personal faith.

> "And thus did Melchizedek prepare the way and set the monotheistic stage of world tendency for the bestowal of an actual Paradise Son of the one God, whom he so vividly portrayed as the Father of all, and whom he represented to Abraham as a God who would accept man on the simple terms of personal faith. And Michael, when he appeared on earth, confirmed all that Melchizedek had taught concerning the Paradise Father." (p. 1017)

3. **Proposition.** Every member of the Salem cult subscribed to three simple beliefs.

> "The ceremonies of the Salem worship were very simple. Every person who signed or marked the clay-tablet rolls of the Melchizedek church committed to memory, and subscribed to, the following belief:
>
> "1. I believe in El Elyon, the Most High God, the only Universal Father and Creator of all things.
>
> "2. I accept the Melchizedek covenant with the Most High, which bestows the favor of God on my faith, not on sacrifices and burnt offerings."
>
> "3. I promise to obey the seven commandments of Melchizedek and to tell the good news of this covenant with the Most High to all men." (p. 1017)

4. **Proposition.** Melchizedek's seven commandments were similar to the law of Dalamatia.

> "The seven commandments promulgated by Melchizedek were patterned along the lines of the ancient Dalamatian supreme law and very much resembled the seven commands taught in the first and second Edens. These commands of the Salem religion were:
>
> "1. You shall not serve any God but the Most High Creator of heaven and earth.
>
> "2. You shall not doubt that faith is the only requirement for eternal salvation.
>
> "3. You shall not bear false witness.
>
> "4. You shall not kill.
>
> "5. You shall not steal.
>
> "6. You shall not commit adultery.
>
> "7. You shall not show disrespect for your parents and elders."
> (p. 1017)

5. **Proposition.** Machiventa tried to substitute the sacrament of bread and wine for the sacrifices of flesh and blood. But Abraham reverted to sacrifices after his military victory.

> "While no sacrifices were permitted within the colony, Melchizedek well knew how difficult it is to suddenly uproot long-established customs and accordingly had wisely offered these people the substitute of a sacrament of bread and wine for the older sacrifice of flesh and blood. It is of record, 'Melchizedek, king of Salem, brought forth bread and wine.' But even this cautious innovation was not altogether successful; the various tribes all maintained auxiliary centers on the outskirts of Salem where they offered sacrifices and burnt offerings. Even Abraham resorted to this barbarous practice after his victory over Chedorlaomer; he simply did not feel quite at ease until he had offered a conventional sacrifice. And Melchizedek never did succeed in fully eradicating this proclivity to sacrifice from the religious practices of his followers, even of Abraham." (p. 1018)

IV. THE SELECTION OF ABRAHAM

1. **Proposition.** It may be wrong to speak of the "chosen people," but Abraham was a chosen individual.

> "Although it may be an error to speak of 'chosen people,' it is not a mistake to refer to Abraham as a chosen individual. Melchizedek did lay upon Abraham the responsibility of keeping alive the truth of one God as distinguished from the prevailing belief in plural deities." (p. 1018)

2. **Proposition.** It was because of the superior stock of Abraham's family that Machiventa appeared at Salem.

> "For some time the Melchizedek receivers had been observing the ancestors of Abraham, and they confidently expected offspring in a certain generation who would be characterized by intelligence, initiative, sagacity, and sincerity. The children of Terah, the father of Abraham, in every way met these expectations. It was this possibility of contact with these versatile children of Terah that had considerable to do with the appearance of Machiventa at Salem, rather than in Egypt, China, India, or among the northern tribes." (p. 1018)

3. **Proposition.** Abraham, along with his nephew, Lot, responded to the invitation to visit Salem.

   "A few weeks after the death of Abraham's father, Terah, Melchizedek sent one of his students, Jaram the Hittite, to extend this invitation to both Abraham and Nahor: 'Come to Salem, where you shall hear our teachings of the truth of the eternal Creator, and in the enlightened offspring of you two brothers shall all the world be blessed.' Now Nahor had not wholly accepted the Melchizedek gospel; he remained behind and built up a strong city-state which bore his name; but Lot, Abraham's nephew, decided to go with his uncle to Salem." (p. 1019)

4. **Proposition.** Abraham, going to Egypt for food, found a relative on the throne and led two military expeditions for him.

   "Not long after they had established themselves near Salem, Abraham and Lot journeyed to the valley of the Nile to obtain food supplies as there was then a drought in Palestine. During his brief sojourn in Egypt Abraham found a distant relative on the Egyptian throne, and he served as the commander of two very successful military expeditions for this king. During the latter part of his sojourn on the Nile he and his wife, Sarah, lived at court, and when leaving Egypt, he was given a share of the spoils of his military campaigns." (p. 1019)

5. **Proposition.** It required courage for Abraham to leave Egyptian honors and return to Melchizedek.

   "It required great determination for Abraham to forego the honors of the Egyptian court and return to the more spiritual work sponsored by Machiventa. But Melchizedek was revered even in Egypt, and when the full story was laid before Pharaoh, he strongly urged Abraham to return to the execution of his vows to the cause of Salem." (p. 1019)

6. **Proposition.** Abraham had kingly ambitions, so Lot left him—turning to business.

   "Abraham had kingly ambitions, and on the way back from Egypt he laid before Lot his plan to subdue all Canaan and bring its people under the rule of Salem. Lot was more bent on business; so, after a later disagreement, he went to Sodom to engage in trade and animal husbandry. Lot liked neither a military nor a herder's life." (p. 1019)

V. THE COVENANT WITH ABRAHAM

1. Proposition. Abraham believed that God had given him victory over his enemies, so he paid a tithe of his spoils.

   "When Melchizedek heard of Abraham's declaration of war, he went forth to dissuade him but only caught up with his former disciple as he returned victorious from the battle. Abraham insisted that the God of Salem had given him victory over his enemies and persisted in giving a tenth of his spoils to the Salem treasury. The other ninety per cent he removed to his capital at Hebron." (p. 1020)

2. PROPOSITION. Abraham became head of the Hebron confederation of eleven tribes.

   "After this battle of Siddim, Abraham became leader of a second confederation of eleven tribes and not only paid tithes to Melchizedek but saw to it that all others in that vicinity did the same. His diplomatic dealings with the king of Sodom, together with the fear in which he was so generally held, resulted in the king of Sodom and others joining the Hebron military confederation; Abraham was really well on the way to establishing a powerful state in Palestine." (p. 1020)

3. PROPOSITION. Melchizedek made a formal covenant with Abraham—who believed "and it was counted to him for righeousness."

   "And Melchizedek made a formal covenant with Abraham at Salem. Said he to Abraham: 'Look now up to the heavens and number the stars if you are able; so numerous shall your seed be.' And Abraham believed Melchizedek, 'and it was counted to him for rightousness.' And then Melchizedek told Abraham the story of the future occupation of Canaan by his offspring after their sojourn in Egypt." (p. 1020)

4. PROPOSITION. The covenant of Abraham provides that God does everything—man only agrees to believe. Faith alone gains God's favor.

   "This covenant of Melchizedek with Abraham represents the great Urantian agreement between divinity and humanity whereby God agrees to do *everything*; man only agrees to *believe* God's promises and follow his instructions. Heretofore it had been believed that salvation could be secured only by works—sacrifices and offerings; now, Melchizedek again brought to Urantia the good news that salvation, favor with God, is to be had by *faith*. But this gospel of simple faith in God was too advanced; the Semitic tribesmen subsequently preferred to go back to the older sacrifices and atonement for sin by the shedding of blood." (p. 1020)

5. **Proposition.** In the Bible, this agreement between Melchizedek and Abraham is represented as a covenant between Abraham and God.

> "What the Old Testament records describe as conversations between Abraham and God were in reality conferences between Abraham and Melchizedek. Later scribes regarded the term Melchizedek as synonymous with God. The record of so many contacts of Abraham and Sarah with 'the angel of the Lord' refers to their numerous visits with Melchizedek." (p. 1023)

6. **Proposition.** Abraham becomes civil and military leader of the Salem colony, and he brought about a host of improvements.

> "Upon the consummation of the solemn covenant, the reconciliation between Abraham and Melchizedek was complete. Abraham again assumed the civil and military leadership of the Salem colony, which at its height carried over one hundred thousand regular tithe payers on the rolls of the Melchizedek brotherhood. Abraham greatly improved the Salem temple and provided new tents for the entire school. He not only extended the tithing system but also instituted many improved methods of conducting the business of the school, besides contributing greatly to the better handling of the department of missionary propaganda. He also did much to effect improvement of the herds and the reorganization of the Salem dairying projects. Abraham was a shrewd and efficient business man, a wealthy man for his day; he was not overly pious, but he was thoroughly sincere, and he did believe in Machiventa Melchizedek." (p. 1021)

7. **Proposition.** In an effort to exalt the Jewish ego, the Old Testament editors removed all of the references to Melchizedek except his meeting Abraham on the battlefield.

> "The national ego of the Jews was tremendously depressed by the Babylonian captivity. In their reaction against national inferiority they swung to the other extreme of national and racial egotism, in which they distorted and perverted their traditions with the view of exalting themselves above all races as the chosen people of God; and hence they carefully edited all their records for the purpose of raising Abraham and their other national leaders high up above all other persons, not excepting Melchizedek himself. The Hebrew scribes therefore destroyed

every record of these momentous times which they could find, preserving only the narrative of the meeting of Abraham and Melchizedek after the battle of Siddim, which they deemed reflected great honor upon Abraham." (p. 1023)

VI. MELCHIZEDEK MISSIONARIES

1. **Proposition.** The Melchizedek gospel of salvation by faith was carried over the entire hemisphere by devoted missionaries—mostly trained natives.

   "The early teachers of the Salem religion penetrated to the remotest tribes of Africa and Eurasia, ever preaching Machiventa's gospel of man's faith and trust in the one universal God as the only price of obtaining divine favor. Melchizedek's covenant with Abraham was the pattern for all the early propaganda that went out from Salem and other centers. Urantia has never had more enthusiastic and aggressive missionaries of any religion than these noble men and women who carried the teachings of Melchizedek over the entire Eastern Hemisphere. These missionaries were recruited from many peoples and races, and they largely spread their teachings through the medium of native converts. They established training centers in different parts of the world where they taught the natives the Salem religion and then commissioned these pupils to function as teachers among their own people." (p. 1027)

VII. DEPARTURE OF MELCHIZEDEK

1. **Proposition.** For many reasons Melchizedek decided to end his mission. He retired one night, but in the morning he had gone.

   "It was shortly after the destruction of Sodom and Gomorrah that Machiventa decided to end his emergency bestowal on Urantia. Melchizedek's decision to terminate his sojourn in the flesh was influenced by numerous conditions, chief of which was the growing tendency of the surrounding tribes, and even of his immediate associates, to regard him as a demigod, to look upon him as a supernatural being, which indeed he was; but they were beginning to reverence him unduly and with a highly superstitious fear. In addition to these reasons, Melchizedek wanted to leave the scene of his earthly activities a sufficient length of time before Abraham's death to insure that the truth of the one and only God would become strongly established in the minds of his followers. Accordingly Machiventa retired one night to his tent at Salem, having said good night to his human companions, and when they went to call him in the morning, he was not there, for his fellows had taken him." (p. 1022)

2. **Proposition.** On the third day after his disappearance he appeared among his fellows and resumed his interrupted career as a planetary receiver.

> "During the years of Machiventa's incarnation the Urantia Melchizedek receivers functioned as eleven. When Machiventa considered that his mission as an emergency Son was finished, he signalized this fact to his eleven associates, and they immediately made ready the technique whereby he was to be released from the flesh and safely restored to his original Melchizedek status. And on the third day after his disappearance from Salem he appeared among his eleven fellows of the Urantia assignment and resumed his interrupted career as one of the planetary receivers of 606 of Satania." (p. 1024)

VIII. PRESENT STATUS OF MELCHIZEDEK

1. **Proposition.** Machiventa became one of the four and twenty directors on Jerusem and recently was elevated to Vicegerent Planetary Prince of Urantia.

> "Machiventa continued as a planetary receiver up to the times of the triumph of Michael on Urantia. Subsequently, he was attached to the Urantia service on Jerusem as one of the four and twenty directors, only just recently having been elevated to the position of personal ambassador on Jerusem of the Creator Son, bearing the title Vicegerent Planetary Prince of Urantia. It is our belief that, as long as Urantia remains an inhabited planet, Machiventa Melchizedek will not be fully returned to the duties of his order of sonship but will remain, speaking in the terms of time, forever a planetary minister representing Christ Michael." (p. 1025)

2. **Proposition.** As Vicegerent Planetary Prince, Machiventa may again appear on earth as the actual ruler of the planet.

> "As his was an emergency bestowal on Urantia, it does not appear from the records what Machiventa's future may be. It may develop that the Melchizedek corps of Nebadon have sustained the permanent loss of one of their number. Recent rulings handed down from the Most Highs of Edentia, and later confirmed by the Ancient of Days of Uversa, strongly suggest

that this bestowal Melchizedek is destined to take the place of the fallen Planetary Prince, Caligastia. If our conjectures in this respect are correct, it is altogether possible that Machiventa Melchizedek may again appear in person on Urantia and in some modified manner resume the role of the dethroned Planetary Prince, or else appear on earth to function as vicegerent Planetary Prince representing Christ Michael, who now actually holds the title of Planetary Prince of Urantia. While it is far from clear to us as to what Machiventa's destiny may be, nevertheless, events which have so recently taken place strongly suggest that the foregoing conjectures are probably not far from the truth." (p. 1025)

3. **PROPOSITION.** It is possible that at some future time we may have Machiventa and numerous other Sons on Urantia at the same time.

> "And all these speculations associated with the certainty of future appearances of both Magisterial and Trinity Teacher Sons, in conjunction with the explicit promise of the Creator Son to return sometime, make Urantia a planet of future uncertainty and render it one of the most interesting and intriguing spheres in all the universe of Nebadon. It is altogether possible that, in some future age when Urantia is approaching the era of light and life, after the affairs of the Lucifer rebellion and the Caligastia secession have been finally adjudicated, we may witness the presence on Urantia, simultaneously, of Machiventa, Adam, Eve, and Christ Michael, as well as either a Magisterial Son or even Trinity Teacher Sons." (p. 1025)

IX. TEACHINGS OF MELCHIZEDEK IN THE ORIENT

1. **PROPOSITION.** Machiventa's teachers spread out all over southwestern Asia, Egypt, Iran, and Arabia.

> "As India gave rise to many of the religions and philosophies of eastern Asia, so the Levant was the homeland of the faiths of the Occidental world. The Salem missionaries spread out all over southwestern Asia, through Palestine, Mesopotamia, Egypt, Iran, and Arabia, everywhere proclaiming the good news of the gospel of Machiventa Melchizedek. In some of these lands their teachings bore fruit; in others they met with varying success. Sometimes their failures were due to lack of wisdom, sometimes to circumstances beyond their control." (p. 1042)

X. TEACHINGS IN THE LEVANT

1. **Proposition.** Moses received much of the Melchizedek teaching through the Katro family.

   "The members of the family of Katro, with whom Melchizedek lived for more than thirty years, knew many of these higher truths and long perpetuated them in their family, even to the days of their illustrious descendant Moses, who thus had a compelling tradition of the days of Melchizedek handed down to him on this, his father's side, as well as through other sources on his mother's side." (p. 1016)

2. **Proposition.** Soon Melchizedek was regarded as a myth, but Joseph and others maintained their faith.

   "It was hard for the next generation to comprehend the story of Melchizedek; within five hundred years many regarded the whole narrative as a myth. Isaac held fairly well to the teachings of his father and nourished the gospel of the Salem colony, but it was harder for Jacob to grasp the significance of these traditions. Joseph was a firm believer in Melchizedek and was, largely because of this, regarded by his brothers as a dreamer. Joseph's honor in Egypt was chiefly due to the memory of his great-grandfather Abraham. Joseph was offered military command of the Egyptian armies, but being such a firm believer in the traditions of Melchizedek and the later teachings of Abraham and Isaac, he elected to serve as a civil administrator, believing that he could thus better labor for the advancement of the kingdom of heaven." (p. 1023)

3. **Proposition.** The Salem religion was revered by the Kenites and other Canaanite tribes.

   "The Salem religion was revered as a tradition by the Kenites and several other Canaanite tribes. And this was one of the purposes of Melchizedek's incarnation: That a religion of one God should be so fostered as to prepare the way for the earth bestowal of a Son of that one God. Michael could hardly come to Urantia until there existed a people believing in the Universal Father among whom he could appear." (p. 1052)

XI. TEACHINGS IN THE OCCIDENT

1. **PROPOSITION.** The Salem teachers largely failed among the Greeks because of lack of organization.

   "The Salem missionaries might have built up a great religious structure among the Greeks had it not been for their strict interpretation of their oath of ordination, a pledge imposed by Machiventa which forbade the organization of exclusive congregations for worship, and which exacted the promise of each teacher never to function as a priest, never to receive fees for religious service, only food, clothing, and shelter." (p. 1077)

2. **PROPOSITION.** The Salem teachings lasted the longest among the Roman Cynics.

   "For a long time in Europe the Salem missionaries carried on their activities, becoming gradually absorbed into many of the cults and ritual groups which periodically arose. Among those who maintained the Salem teachings in the purest form must be mentioned the Cynics. These preachers of faith and trust in God were still functioning in Roman Europe in the first century after Christ, being later incorporated into the newly forming Christian religion." (p. 1077)

3. **PROPOSITION.** The rituals of the mystery religions prevailed over the teachings of the Cynics.

   "The last stand of the dwindling band of Salem believers was made by an earnest group of preachers, the Cynics, who exhorted the Romans to abandon their wild and senseless religious rituals and return to a form of worship embodying Melchizedek's gospel as it had been modified and contaminated through contact with the philosophy of the Greeks. But the people at large rejected the Cynics; they preferred to plunge into the rituals of the mysteries, which not only offered hopes of personal salvation but also gratified the desire for diversion, excitement, and entertainment." (p. 1081)

4. **PROPOSITION.** Much of the Salem doctrine was spread to Europe by Jewish mercenary soldiers.

   "Much of the Salem doctrine was spread in Europe by the Jewish mercenary soldiers who fought in so many of the Occidental military struggles. In ancient times the Jews were famed as much for military valor as for theologic peculiarities.

   "The basic doctrines of Greek philosophy, Jewish theology, and Christian ethics were fundamentally repercussions of the earlier Melchizedek teachings." (p. 1077)

www.ingramcontent.com/pod-product-compliance
Lightning Source LLC
Chambersburg PA
CBHW030102010526
44116CB00005B/55